READER'S DIGEST GUIDE TO
CREATIVE COOKING AND ENTERTAINING

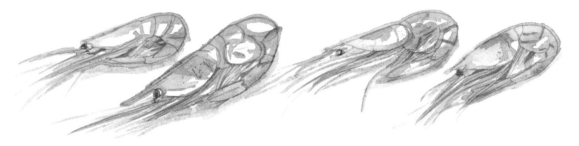

READER'S DIGEST GUIDE TO

CREATIVE COOKING
AND ENTERTAINING

PUBLISHED BY THE READER'S DIGEST ASSOCIATION LIMITED
LONDON NEW YORK

READER'S DIGEST GUIDE TO CREATIVE COOKING AND ENTERTAINING
Edited and designed by The Reader's Digest Association Limited, London
First Edition Copyright © 1986
The Reader's Digest Association Limited, Berkeley Square House, Berkeley Square, London W1X 6AB

Reprinted with amendments 1989

Copyright © 1986, Reader's Digest Association Far East Limited
Philippines Copyright © 1986, Reader's Digest Association Far East Ltd

Printed in Belgium
ISBN 0 276 39825 4

ACKNOWLEDGMENTS

CONSULTANT EDITOR Anne Ager

CONTRIBUTORS
AND ADVISERS
Pat Alburey
Sandy Carr
Ann Cotterell
Liz Downing
Christine France
Jill Goolden
Geraldene Holt
Helen O'Leary
Clare Payne

Jennie Reekie
Pete Smith
Rosemary Wadey
Jeni Wright

PHOTOGRAPHERS
Jan Baldwin
Philip Dowell
Laurie Evans
Ian O'Leary

HOME ECONOMISTS
FOR PHOTOGRAPHY
Anne Ager
Pat Alburey
Jacki Baxter
Allyson Birch
Mary Cadogan
Lisa Collard
Liz and Pete
Dinah Morrison

Jane Suthering
Michelle Thomson

STYLISTS FOR
PHOTOGRAPHY
Gina Carminati
Marie O'Hara
Lesley Richardson
Carolyn Russell

ILLUSTRATORS
Glynn Boyd Harte
Linda Smith

CALLIGRAPHER
George Hoy

*Many people helped to
test the recipes that
appear in this book. The
publishers thank them all.*

*The publishers are also grateful for the help given by
the following people and organisations:*
Anthony Blake Photo Library
Valerie Barrett
Brown Brothers, Australia
Bulgarian Vintners Co Ltd
I. Camisa and Son, Old Compton Street, London
Cantina Sociale di Soave, Italy
Michèle Clark
David Mellor, London and Manchester
Divertimenti, Marylebone Lane, London
Elizabeth David Kitchen Supplies, Covent Garden,
    London

Greater London Council (Kenwood)
Lyn Kite
Laurent-Perrier Champagne
Leon Jaeggi, Tottenham Court Road, London
Diana Lewis
London Cheese Company
Carol and Stuart Malloy
Gerald Mann
Neville Martin
Melita Ltd, Dunstable, Bedfordshire
Montana Wines Ltd, New Zealand
Neal Street East, Covent Garden, London
Ostlers, Clerkenwell Road, London

Frances Pratt
Real Flame, New Kings Road and Balham
    High Road, London
S.A. Fermiers Reunis
Michael Schuster
Grania Sherriff
John Sims
Slater and Cooke, Bisney and Jones Ltd,
    Brewer Street, London
Teltscher Brothers Ltd
Wedgwood Gered, Regent Street, London
Wine and Spirit Education Trust Ltd
Wine Institute of California

EGGS

Late in 1988, the Government warned that in some recent outbreaks of salmonella food poisoning, eggs were the source of infection. Most infections caused only a mild stomach upset, but the effects could be more serious in the very young or old, in those already weakened by poor health, and among pregnant women. They were advised to eat only eggs cooked until hard. To others there was very little risk in cooked eggs; though everyone was advised to avoid raw egg and recipes containing it. Commercial products made with pasteurised egg were not implicated.

CONTENTS

Recipes for every occasion

Special features

Breakfast & Brunch

BREAKFAST TIME, according to professional wit A.P. Herbert, is 'the critical period of matrimony'. On a wider scale, it is also the hour of least understanding between nations. Few Britons, however cosmopolitan their tastes at the dinner table, would share the French enthusiasm for bread and apricot jam in the morning, or the Italian fondness for tomatoes, garlic, olive oil and bread. On the other hand, there is a good chance that the British sausage, let alone black pudding, would fill the other nations with equal dismay.

If the few brave spirits now experimenting with foreign breakfasts are the outriders of a revolution, it would not be the first. Down the ages there have been several changes in breakfast ideals. About 1500, an English gentleman might begin his day with beer and salted fish, while in the 18th century, people of fashion breakfasted upon sweet cakes and coffee or chocolate in assembly rooms. A hundred years or so later, the pendulum had swung dizzily in the opposite direction. Mrs Beeton suggests that for 'the comfortable meal called breakfast' her readers should supply 'cold joints, collared or potted meats, cold game, veal and ham pies, broiled fish, mutton chops and rump steaks, kidneys, sausages, bacon and poached eggs, muffins, toast, marmalade, butter'. Then she adds, 'etcetera, etcetera'.

Brunch, when it was invented in the 1890s, must have come as a light relief. Although it is usually regarded as very much an American meal, it was probably created at Oxford in the 'Charley's Aunt' era to suit late risers. 'Hardened night-birds fondly cherish, All the subtle charms of brunch' sang the 'Westminster Gazette' in 1900.

Planning & Preparation

A special breakfast or brunch has a particular appeal that neither lunch nor dinner quite manages – probably because few people are used to being offered stylish and imaginative food at such an early hour.

Breakfast

Over the last few decades breakfast has lost much of its status. Far from being regarded as one of the most important meals of the day, it has become one that many people miss altogether. And yet, breakfast is essential as the source of energy for the morning ahead. If it is missed, it may mean going for as long as 18 hours without food.

Everyday breakfast will be appreciated more if there is variety. There are many alternatives to a piece of toast and a cup of coffee, or the traditional 'cooked breakfast' of fried food.

Provide food that is light and easy to digest, and quick to prepare, because it is usually eaten in a hurry. Try keeping a supply of homemade rolls, muffins or croissants in the freezer. They can be heated through in the oven while you are getting dressed. Fruit breads such as *Pear and lemon bread* (page 28) keep well and can be eaten as a change from toast. Once made, homemade jams, jellies and marmalades, yoghurt and muesli require no more thought first thing in the morning than bought varieties, and yet they taste much better. Keep a good supply of fresh fruit in season. Fruit juices can be squeezed the night before and kept in the refrigerator.

There are some occasions when a more elaborate breakfast is appropriate: when there are people staying, for example, or at Christmas or before a family day out. Many dishes can largely be prepared the night before such as *Fresh raspberry porridge* (page 12), *Orange and cranberry brunch bowl* (page 11) and *Rhubarb, fig and grapefruit compôte* (page 14). Others require little preparation at all such as *Egg and salmon cocottes* (page 16) and *Smoked halibut and lumpfish roe scramble* (page 19).

A family breakfast is usually very informal, but when there are guests or it is a celebration, the sense of occasion is increased if breakfast is served as a sit-down meal with a pretty tablecloth and napkins. Breakfast dishes look more attractive brought to the table in large serving dishes rather than being served up in the kitchen.

Breakfast in bed is the ultimate treat for many people. Make sure that the tray is large enough to make eating comfortable. Spread the tray with a pretty cloth. Some people will also appreciate a flower. Choose food that is easy to eat and does not require much cutting.

Brunch

A brunch is by its very nature leisurely: ideally suited to a Sunday or a holiday in summer.

Brunch does not usually start before 11.30, often later. This makes it possible to serve more elaborate and substantial dishes than is possible for an earlier breakfast. It is an organised occasion requiring as much planning as a lunch. The menu is usually broken into courses and served like a buffet – even when there is only a small number of guests. People can then help themselves either from a selection of hot dishes or from a Scandinavian-style cold table. Arrange the food in the order in which it is to be eaten, starting with fruit compôtes and juices, followed by meat, fish or egg dishes, and finishing with rolls, bread and preserves.

If the main course is hot, choose something that will keep warm successfully such as *Creamed chipped beef* (page 24) or *Sautéed kidneys with croutons* (page 22). Boiled eggs, poached eggs and fried eggs tend to become rubbery if they are not served immediately. Keep the dishes warm on a table warmer or a portable hot plate. For dishes that dry out very quickly when kept warm, such as scrambled eggs, stand the dish inside a slightly larger dish containing hot water. Bread and rolls can be brought straight from the oven wrapped in foil. This will keep them warm for 10-15 minutes. A portable toaster can be put on the table for people to make their own toast. Provide plenty of butter and marmalade. In the summer you might serve a selection of cold meats, sausages and salamis, or different cheeses. If you have a barbecue, give a brunch barbecue with plenty of sizzling sausages.

Beverages

Tea and coffee are usually served at breakfast or brunch. With a typical continental breakfast of croissants and preserves, coffee is served with the food, but otherwise many people prefer to drink their tea or coffee afterwards. An automatic coffee machine with a warming plate is convenient for a brunch.

A fairly mellow coffee is generally preferred in the morning (see *Coffee*, page 50). Most people like their breakfast tea to be one of the stronger Indian varieties (see *Tea*, page 140).

Fruit juice is a refreshing addition to breakfast. Freshly squeezed juice is the best, but many different juices can now be bought in addition to the familiar orange. Try mixing your own combinations – grapefruit and pineapple, for example.

Other drinks include hot chocolate, cold milk and on very special occasions champagne or the classic breakfast cocktail *Buck's fizz* (page 176).

FRUIT & CEREALS

ORANGE AND CRANBERRY BRUNCH BOWL

Although familiar in this country chiefly in the form of cranberry sauce served with turkey, in the United States cranberries are also served with breakfast dishes such as waffles. They make a refreshing start to the day combined with oranges and then chilled. Fresh cranberries are imported from America in November, December and January, but frozen cranberries can be used when they are out of season.

PREPARATION AND COOKING
TIME: *35 minutes*
CHILLING TIME: *3-4 hours or overnight*

INGREDIENTS – *serves 6:*
6 large oranges
½ pint (285 ml) water
3 oz (75 g) granulated sugar
1 lb (450 g) cranberries

Finely grate the rind from one of the oranges. Thinly pare the rind from another of the oranges, and cut it into thin strips. Blanch the strips in boiling water for 1 minute. Drain, rinse in cold water and set the strips aside. Cut the peel and pith from all 6 oranges. Carefully cut out the segments of flesh, discarding the membrane (page 398).

Put the grated orange rind, water and sugar into a pan and stir over gentle heat until the sugar has dissolved. Simmer for 5 minutes. Add the cranberries, and simmer for a further 5 minutes. Remove from the heat and allow to cool. Stir in the orange segments and chill for 3-4 hours, or overnight.

Serve in small glass bowls, sprinkled with the reserved strips of orange peel. This dish is included in a menu on page 24.

CHILLED CHERRY SOUP

The fresh flavour of cherry soup is prized throughout much of Europe, from the Norwegian version laced with sherry to the Hungarian combination of sour cherries and red wine. In Scandinavia, cherry soup is frequently served as part of a breakfast or light lunch.

It is possible to use tinned black cherries instead of fresh ones, but they should be thoroughly drained, then rinsed. It may be necessary to use less sugar, or even omit it completely, if tinned cherries are used. A liquidiser or food processor is essential to give this soup a smooth texture. It is possible to sieve the cherries, but the texture will then be grainy.

PREPARATION AND COOKING
TIME: *25 minutes*
CHILLING TIME: *4 hours*

INGREDIENTS — *serves 4:*
12 oz (350 g) fresh black cherries
OR 2 × 15 oz (425 g) tins black cherries, well drained
½ pint (285 ml) red table wine
¼ pint (150 ml) fresh orange juice
1-2 level tablespoons caster sugar
2 tablespoons brandy

Stalk and pit the cherries. If you do not have a cherry pitter, cut each cherry in half and scoop out the stone with a knife.

Put the prepared cherries into a pan with the red wine, orange juice and sugar. (If using tinned cherries, omit the sugar and add, to taste, after simmering the soup.) Bring just to the boil and simmer for 5 minutes.

Remove 2 tablespoons of the cherries, and set aside. Blend the remaining cherries with the cooking liquid in a liquidiser or food processor until smooth. Pour into a bowl and stir in the brandy. Cover the soup and chill for at least 4 hours, or preferably overnight.

Serve in small bowls, topped with the reserved cherries, and accompanied by homemade *Yoghurt* (page 12) and slices of *Black rye bread* (page 30). A sprig of fresh cherries can be used as an alternative garnish.

This dish is included in a menu on page 15.

CHERRY RIPE Fresh black cherries make a rich purple soup, as dark as the rye bread accompanying it.

FRESH RASPBERRY PORRIDGE

The word porridge usually conjures up a picture of bowls of very thick, steaming cereal, eaten to keep the cold winter days at bay. This raspberry porridge is very different – it is much lighter and eaten cold, in summer. It has a fresh, natural flavour, but can be sweetened with sugar if you wish. Greek yoghurt – which has a thick texture a little like clotted cream – produces a particularly rich, creamy porridge.

Prepare the porridge and the raspberry purée the night before and keep covered in a cool place or in the refrigerator. The dish can then be assembled first thing in the morning.

PREPARATION TIME: *15 minutes plus chilling time*
COOKING TIME: *3 minutes*

INGREDIENTS – *serves 4:*
8 oz (225 g) raspberries, fresh or frozen and thawed
Juice of 1 orange
1 tablespoon clear honey
1½ oz (40 g) porridge oats
¾ pint (450 ml) milk
¼ pint (150 ml) single cream
4 tablespoons thick Greek yoghurt
GARNISH
A few whole raspberries

Put the raspberries, orange juice and honey into a liquidiser and blend to a smooth purée. (The purée can be made by sieving the fruit, but the seeds will be lost.) Chill the purée.

Put the porridge oats into a pan, preferably a non-stick one, or one with a solid base. Add the milk and bring to the boil, stirring. Simmer for 3 minutes. Remove from the heat and leave to cool slightly.

Transfer the porridge to a bowl and stir in the cream. Once the porridge is quite cold, stir in the yoghurt.

Serve the porridge in small glass bowls, topped with the raspberry purée and decorated with a few whole raspberries.

SUMMER PORRIDGE *The fresh flavour of puréed raspberries contrasts with the cool, richness of porridge made with cream and thick yoghurt – a far cry from Scotland's basic breakfast dish.*

YOGHURT

For thousands of years yoghurt has been one of the staples of Middle-Eastern cooking. It is made by adding special bacteria – lactobacilli – to milk. They curdle the milk, kill any harmful bacteria in it, and make it easier to digest. Yoghurt made at home tastes much fresher and less acid than commercially made varieties. Only 'live' plain yoghurt – in which the lactobacilli are still active – can be used as a starter. In many yoghurts the lactobacilli have been destroyed by added preservatives and emulsifiers, check the label before buying.

Special yoghurt makers can be used, but yoghurt is made just as successfully in a large vacuum flask – one that will take more than 1 pint (570 ml) of milk – or a dish, so long as it can be left to ferment in a warm place. Once ready, the yoghurt can be eaten just as it is, sweetened, or flavoured. It can be poured over fruit or breakfast cereals, or used for cooking.

Skimmed or low-fat milk can be substituted for full fat milk, but it will make a much thinner, less creamy yoghurt.

PREPARATION AND COOKING TIME: *30 minutes*
FERMENTING TIME: *at least 12 hours*

INGREDIENTS – *makes about 1 pint (570 ml) of yoghurt:*
1 pint (570 ml) milk
1 tablespoon live, plain yoghurt

Put the milk in a clean saucepan and bring to the boil. Cool to blood heat – 37°C (98.6°F), or until you can just hold a finger in the milk for a count of ten.

Add the yoghurt to the milk and mix thoroughly. Pour the mixture into a clean vacuum flask, and screw the top down securely. Leave the flask to stand for at least 12 hours.

Alternatively, pour the mixture into a clean shallow dish. Cover the dish with a warmed plate, and wrap in a towel or thick cloth. Leave to stand in a warm place, such as an airing cupboard, for at least 12 hours. The yoghurt can also be made in individual dishes.

The yoghurt can be kept in the refrigerator for up to 6 days. Use a tablespoon of this yoghurt as a starter for the next batch. For a thicker-textured yoghurt, add 1 level tablespoon of powdered skimmed milk to the milk when you add the plain yoghurt.
FLAVOURINGS Add flavouring to homemade yoghurt after fermenting, not before. To each ¼ pint (150ml) of homemade yoghurt, add 1 tablespoon of lightly sweetened fruit such as raspberries, blackberries, strawberries, chopped peach, apricot, banana, pear or apple, or lightly cooked rhubarb. Alternatively add 1 level teaspoon of instant coffee powder, 1 level tablespoon of finely grated chocolate, or 1 level tablespoon of chopped nuts and a few raisins.

This dish is included in a menu on page 15.

HAZELNUT AND BANANA MUESLI

Muesli is a traditional Swiss peasant dish which originally consisted of raw rolled oats, dried fruit, nuts and milk. There are now many commercial varieties, but the advantage of making your own muesli is that you can choose your ingredients and regulate the sweetness. This hazelnut and banana muesli has a particularly crunchy texture. The mixture can be varied by replacing some of the cereal ingredients with rye flakes or wheat germ. Store the muesli in an airtight container so that it keeps fresh and crisp.

PREPARATION TIME: *5 minutes*

INGREDIENTS — *serves 4-6:*
2 oz (50 g) wheat flakes
1 oz (25 g) toasted bran
1 oz (25 g) medium porridge oats
1½ oz (40 g) dried banana
  flakes
1 oz (25 g) ground, chopped or
  flaked hazelnuts

Mix all the ingredients together.
  Serve in small bowls with milk, natural yoghurt (opposite page) or fruit juice, and a little chopped fresh fruit.
  This dish is included in a menu on page 20.

GOLDEN TORTILLAS *Honey, orange juice and the yellow cornmeal from which they are made, all combine to give the tortillas their glorious colour. The effect can be enhanced by thin strips of orange zest.*

TORTILLAS WITH CHEESE AND RAISIN FILLING

Tortillas are large, thin pancakes made with cornmeal. They have been a staple food in Mexico since Aztec times, and Mexicans eat them at almost every meal. For breakfast, for example, tortillas are served with honey and fruit, for lunch they are filled with meat and called *enchiladas*, and for supper they are cut into pieces, fried and added to soup. In this recipe, suitable for a brunch party, the tortillas are rolled around a sweet curd cheese and raisin filling and baked in the oven.
  The tortillas can be served straight from the dish in which they are cooked. Alternatively, pile them up on a warmed serving plate and pour over any honey and orange syrup remaining in the baking dish.
  Tortillas can be bought ready-made, in some supermarkets or delicatessens.

PREPARATION TIME: *35 minutes*
COOKING TIME: *12-15 minutes*
OVEN TEMPERATURE: *preheat to 200°C (400°F, gas mark 6)*

INGREDIENTS — *serves 4:*
8 oz (225 g) curd cheese
2 oz (50 g) raisins
1 level tablespoon chopped
  walnuts
1 level teaspoon ground cinnamon
Generous pinch of ground nutmeg
2 oz (50 g) demerara sugar
Finely grated rind and juice of
  ½ orange
4 tablespoons cooking oil
8 tortillas
2 tablespoons clear honey
Yoghurt (opposite page)

Mix the curd cheese, raisins and chopped walnuts together. In a separate bowl, mix the cinnamon, nutmeg, sugar and orange rind. Stir half the spiced sugar mixture into the curd cheese, raisin and walnut mixture.
  Heat the oil gently in a frying pan and then remove from the heat. Dip the tortillas, one at a time, into the hot oil, allowing about 3 seconds on each side. (This softens the tortillas and makes them easier to roll.) Lay them out flat on a clean work surface.
  Place a little of the curd cheese filling on each tortilla and roll up loosely. Place the tortillas, seam down, in a lightly greased ovenproof dish.
  Warm the honey in a small pan, mix with the orange juice and brush over the rolled tortillas. Sprinkle with the remaining spiced sugar mixture.
  Bake in the preheated oven for 12-15 minutes, until golden and slightly crisp. Serve hot, with plain yoghurt.

RHUBARB, FIG AND GRAPEFRUIT COMPÔTE

Spring, when rhubarb is plentiful, is the ideal time of year to make this compôte. Tinned rhubarb can be used at other times, but it is much squashier than fresh. Use fresh figs, when they are available, for an even better flavour. Chill the compôte overnight so that the flavours mingle. Orange segments can be used as a sweeter alternative to grapefruit.

PREPARATION AND COOKING TIME: *25 minutes plus cooling and chilling time*

INGREDIENTS – *serves 4:*
1 lb (450 g) young, pink rhubarb
½ pint (285 ml) dry cider
2 level tablespoons granulated sugar
2 in (50 mm) piece vanilla pod
4 plump dried figs, soaked overnight (or 4 fresh figs)
2 grapefruit

Wash the rhubarb and cut into 2in (50mm) lengths. Put the cider and sugar into a pan and stir over a gentle heat until the sugar has dissolved. Add the vanilla pod and the rhubarb, cover, and simmer gently for just 3 minutes – no longer. Remove from the heat. Lift the lid off the pan, and leave the rhubarb to cool in its juices. Do not stir or it will break up.

Remove the short stalk from each fig, and cut the figs into halves or quarters. With a sharp knife, cut all the peel and pith from the two grapefruit and divide into neat segments (page 398). Transfer the rhubarb and its juices to a glass bowl, with the vanilla pod. Lightly stir in the figs and grapefruit segments.

Cover and chill for at least 3 hours or overnight. Remove the vanilla pod before serving.

For a special occasion, or for a dessert, serve topped with whipped cream.

ROSY RHUBARB The pink of the young rhubarb in this chilled fruit compôte is echoed in pretty, individual glass bowls.

EGGS, FISH & MEAT

CREAMY TOMATO AND CORIANDER OMELETTE

Omelettes must be served immediately they are made – so this is a breakfast dish for a few special guests. To save time the tomato filling can be prepared the night before. Warm it through when needed.

PREPARATION TIME: *15 minutes*
COOKING TIME: *25-35 minutes*

INGREDIENTS – *serves 4:*
1 small onion, finely chopped
3 oz (75 g) unsalted butter
1 lb (450 g) tomatoes, skinned (page 389), seeded and chopped
1 level tablespoon chopped fresh coriander or continental (flat-leaf) parsley
Salt and freshly ground black pepper
8 oz (225 g) full-fat, soft cream cheese
12 eggs
3 tablespoons water
GARNISH
Sprigs of fresh coriander or continental (flat-leaf) parsley

Gently fry the chopped onion in 1oz (25g) of the butter for 3 minutes. Add the chopped tomatoes, chopped coriander or parsley, and salt and pepper to taste. Simmer steadily for 10-12 minutes, until the mixture is thick and pulpy. Keep warm over a very low heat.

Divide the cheese into small cubes or knobs. Beat the eggs in a measuring jug with the water, and add salt and pepper to taste.

To make each omelette, heat a quarter of the remaining butter in an omelette pan, or a medium non-stick pan. Once the butter is bubbling, add a quarter of the beaten egg mixture. Cook over a moderate heat, shaking the mixture backwards and forwards as the omelette starts to set on the underside. The omelette needs to be just set on the base, but still creamy and slightly liquid on the top.

Remove the pan from the heat and top the omelette with a quarter of the tomato filling and 2oz (50g) of the cream cheese. Tilt the omelette pan carefully over a warm plate, and roll the omelette neatly onto the plate, folding it with a spatula.

Garnish with sprigs of coriander or parsley and serve immediately. Make the remaining three omelettes in the same way.

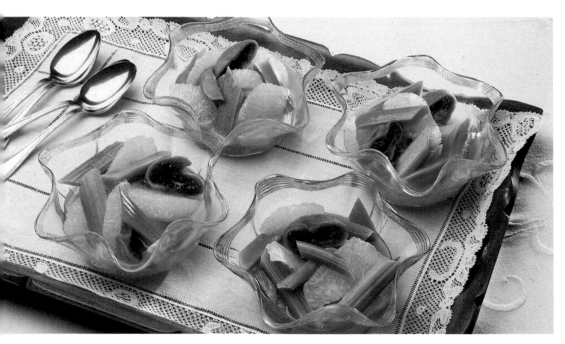

*Scandinavian
Cold Table
Breakfast
for Eight*

YOGHURT *page 12*
with FRUIT

CHILLED CHERRY SOUP
page 11

EGG AND HERRING
DANWICH *this page*

BLACK RYE BREAD
page 30 with
GREENGAGE JELLY
page 32

Make twice the quantity of yoghurt, soup and egg and herring danwich given in the recipes. The rye bread can be used for making the danwiches as well as for serving with the jelly.

IN ADVANCE The rye bread can be made well in advance. The yoghurt should be made 1-2 days in advance. The cherry soup can be made the night before.

ON THE DAY Allow about 30 minutes to make the egg and herring danwiches.

TO DRINK Coffee.

EGG AND HERRING DANWICH

No Danish meal is complete without its open sandwich, or *Smørrebrød* – translated here as danwich in deference to its origins, but meaning literally 'butter on bread'. There are hundreds of different toppings for open sandwiches, but the Danes often start their day with this combination of scrambled egg and pickled herring.

Homemade black rye bread makes a good base for an open sandwich. It does not absorb as much moisture from the topping as other breads do.

PREPARATION AND COOKING
TIME: *20 minutes.*

INGREDIENTS – *serves 4:*
*4 slices black rye bread
(page 30)
Unsalted butter
4 eggs
1 tablespoon single cream and
1 tablespoon double cream OR
2 tablespoons single cream or
top of the milk
Salt and freshly ground black
pepper
4 pickled herring fillets, flat or
rolled
A few thin onion rings
4 small wedges of lemon
Sprigs of dillweed or fennel*

Spread each slice of black rye bread with a generous layer of butter, making sure that the butter goes right to the edges. Beat the eggs with the single

cream, adding salt and pepper to taste. Heat 1oz (25g) of butter in a pan, add the egg mixture and cook over a gentle heat, stirring continuously until the egg forms soft, creamy flakes. Remove from the heat and stir in the double cream. Allow to

cool, but not to become cold.

Spoon the scrambled egg onto the slices of buttered bread. Top with a herring fillet, an onion ring or two, a wedge of lemon and a sprig of dillweed or fennel.

This dish is included in a menu on this page.

OPEN SANDWICH Sprigs of fresh dillweed, wafer-thin slices of onion and wedges of lemon garnish rolled fillets of pickled herring and creamy scrambled egg on circles of black rye bread. Sparkling mineral water is a refreshing, and suitably Scandinavian, accompaniment.

EGG AND SALMON COCOTTES

Eggs baked with cream in small, ovenproof dishes called cocottes are classically French, and they make an excellent light breakfast. In this variation on the traditional recipe, the dishes are lined with smoked salmon. Ramekins or ovenproof teacups can be used in place of cocottes if necessary.

PREPARATION TIME: *10 minutes*
COOKING TIME: *12 minutes*
OVEN TEMPERATURE: *preheat to 180°C (350°F, gas mark 4)*

INGREDIENTS — *serves 4:*
4 slices smoked salmon
4 eggs
Salt and freshly ground black pepper
4 tablespoons single cream
GARNISH
Smoked salmon trimmings, finely shredded

Line the inside of four small cocotte dishes with the smoked salmon. Cut or fold the salmon so that it fits neatly.

Carefully crack an egg into each dish. Season with salt and pepper, and spoon a tablespoon of cream over each egg.

Stand the cocottes on a baking tray, and bake in the preheated oven for about 12 minutes, until the egg whites are just set. This will result in eggs with crusty tops. For moist eggs, stand the cocottes in a roasting tin and fill it to within ½in (15mm) of the rims of the cocottes with hot water. Cover the tin with kitchen foil and then bake as before.

Garnish with smoked salmon trimmings and serve hot with fingers of toast or buttered brown bread.

EGGS SOUBISE

Gently sautéed onions are the main ingredient of one of the classic French sauces – Soubise. Here they bring an echo of French sophistication to the more conventional breakfast fare of poached eggs and slices of smoked ham.

The pieces of crisp fried bread, or croûtes, that are the base of this dish can be prepared in advance and frozen. Drain the fried croûtes on absorbent paper and then pack them, interleaved with greaseproof or waxed paper, in a double layer of freezer wrap. Warm them through in a moderately hot oven when needed. It is worth keeping a supply of croûtes in the freezer, as they can also be used as a base for fillet steaks, small cutlets of fish, or vegetables in a cream sauce.

Use the freshest eggs possible when poaching eggs. The whites will cling to the yolks rather than dispersing in threads. An egg poacher can be used as an alternative to poaching the eggs in water, but the appearance of the dish will not be as good.

PREPARATION AND COOKING TIME: *40 minutes*

INGREDIENTS — *serves 4:*
2 medium onions, finely chopped
About 5 oz (150 g) butter
2 level tablespoons chopped parsley
Salt and freshly ground black pepper
4 large slices bread
1-2 teaspoons white wine vinegar
4 eggs
8 small slices smoked ham

In a covered pan, cook the onions gently in 2oz (50g) of the butter until they are really soft and pale golden in colour. This will take about 20 minutes. Add half the chopped parsley, and salt and pepper to taste.

While the onions are cooking, make the croûtes. Using a large pastry cutter or a small saucer as a guide, cut a circle from each slice of bread. Heat enough butter in a frying pan to give a

SECRET SOUBISE *A layer of onions sautéed as for Sauce Soubise, makes all the difference to the ham and eggs that cover it. The eggs are garnished with a sprig of continental (flat-leaf) parsley.*

depth of about ¼in (5mm). Add the circles of bread and fry gently until evenly golden on both sides. Drain on absorbent kitchen paper.

Half fill a deep frying pan with water. Add the vinegar and bring the water to a rolling boil. One at a time, crack each egg carefully into a cup, and slide the egg into the bubbling water. Work quickly so that there is not much difference in the eggs cooking time. Poach the eggs for about 3 minutes. Using two spoons, gather in the whites as they start to set to give each egg a neat shape. Remove the eggs from the water with a slotted spoon and drain on absorbent kitchen paper.

Place the croûtes on individual plates. Top each one with some of the warm onion mixture, then two folded slices of ham and finally a poached egg. Sprinkle with the remaining chopped parsley and then serve immediately while the eggs are still warm. A sprig of parsley makes an attractive garnish in addition to the chopped parsley.

DEVILLED EGGS

Hot, spicy sauces – devils – were popular in Britain throughout the 19th century. They were used to give flavour to pieces of meat and poultry and to revive leftovers. Devilled kidneys is one of the best known breakfast dishes. This devil sauce is served with poached eggs, but it goes equally well with fried eggs. The sauce can be made the night before and kept covered in the refrigerator. Warm the sauce through just before serving.

An egg poacher can be used, but the appearance of the dish will not be as good.

PREPARATION TIME: *10 minutes*
COOKING TIME: *30 minutes*

INGREDIENTS – *serves 4:*
1 small onion, finely chopped
1 oz (25 g) butter
1 lb (450 g) tomatoes, skinned (page 389), seeded and chopped OR 2 × 14 oz (400 g) tins tomatoes, well-drained and chopped
Juice of ½ lemon
1 tablespoon white wine vinegar
2 level tablespoons tomato purée
1 tablespoon Worcestershire sauce
2 level teaspoons soft brown sugar
½ pint (285 ml) chicken stock (page 367)
2 level tablespoons chopped parsley
Salt and freshly ground black pepper
4 crumpets or muffins
Butter
4 eggs

Fry the chopped onion gently in the butter for 3 minutes. Add the chopped tomatoes, lemon juice, half the vinegar, the tomato purée, Worcestershire sauce, brown sugar, stock, chopped parsley, and salt and pepper to taste. Bring to the boil and simmer gently for 20 minutes until fairly thick. The sauce can then either be left as it is, or sieved to produce a finer texture. Keep the sauce warm.

Lightly toast and butter the crumpets or muffins, and keep them warm.

Half fill a deep frying pan with water. Add the remaining vinegar, and bring the water to a gentle, rolling boil. One at a time, crack each egg carefully into a cup, and slide the egg into the bubbling water. Work fairly quickly so that there is not much difference in the eggs cooking time. Poach the eggs for about 3 minutes. Using two spoons, gather in the whites as they start to set, to give each egg a neat shape. The whites should be set, but the yolks still runny. Lift out each cooked egg with a slotted spoon, allowing all the excess water to drain off. Drain the poached eggs on absorbent kitchen paper.

Put each crumpet or muffin on a plate, and top with a freshly poached egg. Spoon over the hot sauce, and serve immediately.

FISH CAKES WITH EGG SAUCE

Fish cakes are usually regarded as a convenient, if unexciting, way to use up leftover cooked fish. But made with smoked mackerel they have such a good flavour that it is worth buying the fish specially.

The fish cakes can be prepared the night before, ready for cooking in the morning.

PREPARATION TIME: *50 minutes*
CHILLING TIME: *30 minutes or overnight*
COOKING TIME: *10-12 minutes*

INGREDIENTS – *serves 4:*
12 oz (350 g) smoked mackerel fillet
1 level tablespoon chopped chives, or chopped green spring onion
Finely grated rind of 1 lemon
3 hard-boiled eggs, chopped
¼ pint (150 ml) thick Béchamel sauce (page 368)
2 tablespoons double cream (optional)
Salt and freshly ground black pepper
2 oz (50 g) melted butter
COATING
Flour
1 egg, beaten
Fine fresh white breadcrumbs
SAUCE
6 tablespoons thick mayonnaise, homemade (page 369) or ready-made
Finely grated rind of 1 lemon
2 hard-boiled eggs
1 level tablespoon finely chopped parsley

GARNISH
Twists of lemon (page 286)
Spring onion tassels (page 287)

Flake the smoked mackerel fillet. Mix with the chopped chives or spring onion, lemon rind, chopped hard-boiled eggs, white sauce, cream (if used) and salt and pepper to taste. With floured hands, shape the mixture into 8 cakes. Dust each fish cake lightly with flour, dip into beaten egg, and then coat evenly with breadcrumbs. Chill in the refrigerator for at least 30 minutes, or overnight.

To make the sauce, put the mayonnaise and lemon rind into a basin, and add salt and pepper to taste. Crumble the yolks of the hard-boiled eggs and finely chop the whites. Add to the mayonnaise together with the chopped parsley.

Heat the butter in a large frying pan. Add the fish cakes, and fry for about 5-6 minutes on each side. While the fish cakes are cooking, stand the basin of sauce over a pan of simmering water and heat gently.

Arrange the cooked fish cakes on a plate and garnish with twists of lemon and spring onion tassels, then serve hot with the warmed sauce.

LUXURY FISH CAKES It is worth buying the fish specially to make these rich and succulent fish cakes, served with a sauce of mayonnaise, eggs and lemon.

MENU

Anniversary Champagne Breakfast for Two

CHAMPAGNE PUNCH
page 33

SMOKED HALIBUT AND
LUMPFISH ROE SCRAMBLE
opposite page

PEAR AND LEMON BREAD
page 28 with
DRIED APRICOT JAM
page 32

Make half the quantity of smoked halibut scramble given in the recipe.
IN ADVANCE The bread can be made 2-3 days in advance. Put the champagne in the refrigerator and prepare the maraschino cherry ice cubes the night before.
ON THE DAY Allow 15-20 minutes to cook the smoked halibut scramble and mix the champagne punch.
TO DRINK Coffee.

CHAMPAGNE BREAKFAST The perfect treat on a special morning is smoked halibut scramble, with pear and lemon bread and apricot jam, washed down with bubbling champagne punch.

18

SMOKED HALIBUT AND LUMPFISH ROE SCRAMBLE

For a celebration breakfast, this is a luxurious version of scrambled egg. Smoked halibut can be bought from some specialist fishmongers. It is creamy-white with a more delicate flavour than smoked salmon, but, if the halibut is unobtainable, salmon is a good alternative. It is important to use orange lumpfish roe rather than black, otherwise the attractive appearance of the dish will be spoilt.

PREPARATION AND COOKING
   TIME: 15 minutes

INGREDIENTS — serves 4:
4 eggs
1 tablespoon water
2 level teaspoons chopped fresh
   dillweed OR 1/2 teaspoon dried
   dillweed
Salt and freshly ground black
   pepper
8 oz (225 g) smoked halibut,
   thinly sliced
1 1/2 oz (40 g) butter
1 tablespoon orange lumpfish roe
GARNISH
Orange lumpfish roe
Sprigs of fresh dillweed

Beat the eggs with the water. Add the chopped dillweed, and salt and pepper to taste.

Arrange the slices of smoked halibut on four small plates.

Melt the butter in a pan, add the beaten egg mixture and cook over low heat, stirring continuously until the mixture forms soft, creamy flakes. Stir in the lumpfish roe.

Spoon the hot scrambled egg into the centre of each plate, and garnish each portion with a little extra lumpfish roe and a sprig of fresh dillweed. This dish is included in a menu on the opposite page.

BUCKWHEAT BLINIS WITH CREAMED KIPPER

In northern Europe, Russia and Asia, buckwheat has been a staple food for centuries. It looks like a cereal grain but is actually the seed of a flowering plant related to rhubarb. It is available in health food shops and delicatessens, but if you cannot obtain buckwheat, use wheatmeal flour instead.

Buckwheat blinis are a Russian pancake, made with yeast. They are traditionally served with soured cream, and pickled herring, smoked salmon or caviar. These are served with kippers and soured cream. As an alternative, the blinis can be topped with scrambled eggs.

The yeast batter needs to rise for at least 6 hours, but it can be left to rise in the refrigerator overnight.

If soured cream is unavailable, add 1 teaspoon of lemon juice to 1/4 pint (150ml) double cream and leave for 30 minutes.

PREPARATION AND COOKING
   TIME: 50 minutes
RISING TIME: 6 hours or overnight

INGREDIENTS — serves 4:
BATTER
4 tablespoons warm water
2/3 oz (18 g) fresh yeast OR 1/3 oz
   (9 g) dried yeast OR 2/3 sachet
   easy-blend dried yeast
Generous pinch caster sugar
2 oz (50 g) buckwheat flour
5 1/4 oz (155 g) plain flour
1/2 pint (285 ml) milk, warmed
1/4 teaspoon salt
1 oz (25 g) butter
2 eggs, separated
2 tablespoons soured cream
3 oz (75 g) melted butter for
   frying
FILLING
6 oz (175 g) kipper fillets, boned,
   cooked and flaked
4 tablespoons soured cream
1 level tablespoon chopped chives
1/2 teaspoon finely grated lemon
   rind
Freshly ground black pepper
GARNISH
Orange or black lumpfish roe

Put the warm water into a small bowl. Crumble the fresh yeast into the water, or sprinkle in the dried yeast. Add the sugar. Leave to stand in a warm place for about 10 minutes, until a thick froth forms on top of the yeast liquid. If using easy-blend yeast, follow the instructions on the packet. You will not need the sugar.

Put the flours into a large mixing bowl and make a well in the centre. Pour in the yeast liquid, warm milk and salt and beat until smooth. Cover the batter with an oiled plastic bag and leave in the refrigerator, or in a cool place away from draughts, for at least 6 hours or overnight.

Melt the butter in a small saucepan. Allow to cool slightly and then beat it into the yeast batter, together with the egg yolks and soured cream. Whisk the egg whites until stiff but not dry and fold lightly, but thoroughly, into the batter. Leave to stand at room temperature for 30 minutes.

While the blini mixture is standing, make the filling. Mix the kipper with the soured cream, chives, lemon rind, and salt and pepper to taste.

To cook the blinis, brush the bottom of a large heavy-based frying pan, or griddle, with melted butter, and place over moderate heat. Add about 2 tablespoons of batter for each pancake. (The batter makes 12-14 pancakes.) A large pan should be able to take three pancakes at a time, but initially cook them one at a time until you are practised. Cook for 2 minutes only, until the surface has bubbled and begun to dry out, then brush the top of the pancakes with melted butter and flip them over. Cook for a further 2 minutes. Transfer the cooked pancakes to an ovenproof dish, cover and keep warm.

Top each warm blini with kipper mixture and serve flat, garnished with lumpfish roe.

POTTED TROUT

Potted meat and potted fish were familiar Victorian breakfast dishes. This potted trout will keep for 24 hours in the refrigerator. If the surface is covered with a thin layer of melted butter it will keep for 3-4 days. This recipe can also be made with smoked mackerel.

PREPARATION TIME: *25 minutes*

INGREDIENTS — *serves 4-6:*
1 large smoked trout, about
  10 oz (275 g) in weight
Finely grated rind and juice of
  ½ lemon
3 oz (75 g) butter, softened
3 tablespoons double cream
1 level tablespoon chopped chives
Salt and freshly ground black
  pepper
Generous pinch of ground nutmeg

Skin the smoked trout. Carefully flake the flesh, discarding all the bones. Mix the fish with the lemon juice and rind, butter, cream and chives so that they are well combined. Season to taste with salt, pepper and nutmeg. Spoon into a small pot, cover and chill. Spread on bread or hot Melba toast.

To make Melba toast, cut thin slices of white bread and remove the crusts. Toast the slices, then cut them in half horizontally and either toast the uncooked surfaces under a hot grill, or bake them in a moderately hot oven.

This dish is included in a menu on this page.

20

M E N U

Al Fresco
Brunch
for Four

HAZELNUT AND
BANANA MUESLI
page 13

POTTED TROUT
this page
with MELBA TOAST

STRAWBERRY SHRUB
page 34

FRESH FRUIT

IN ADVANCE The muesli and shrub syrup can both be prepared several weeks in advance. The trout can be prepared at least a day ahead. The bread for the Melba toast can be cut ready the night before.
ON THE DAY Allow about 20 minutes to make the Melba toast, keep it warm in a very low oven while you are eating the muesli.
TO DRINK Coffee.

GREEN KEDGEREE Avocado and
plenty of fresh parsley colour this rice
dish pale green. Continental
(flat-leaf) parsley can be used as an
alternative to the more common
curly variety.

BACON AND AVOCADO KEDGEREE

In India, where it originated, *khichri* (kedgeree) traditionally consisted of fish, rice, lentils, onion, butter, spices and fresh limes. A lighter version – made with smoked haddock, eggs and cream – was adopted by the Victorians as a breakfast dish. See also *Khichri* (page 96).

This bacon and avocado kedgeree is a further variation on the traditional recipe. It makes an easily prepared brunch dish. The rice can be prepared the night before, and kept covered in the refrigerator until needed. To prevent the grains of rice from sticking together, stir in 2 tablespoons of olive oil while the rice is still hot.

PREPARATION AND COOKING TIME: *45 minutes*

INGREDIENTS — *serves 4:*
6 oz (175 g) long grain rice
¾ pint (450 ml) chicken stock
  (page 367)
Salt
1 ripe but firm avocado
1½ oz (40 g) butter
4 rashers lean smoked bacon,
  roughly chopped
3 spring onions, chopped
2 hard-boiled eggs, chopped
4 tablespoons single cream
1-2 level tablespoons chopped
  parsley
Freshly ground black pepper
GARNISH
Triangles of toast

Put the rice into a pan with the stock. Add salt to taste. If the stock is very salty, it may not be necessary to add any. Bring to the boil. Stir once, cover the pan and simmer gently for 15 minutes, until the rice is just tender and the stock has been absorbed.

Meanwhile, halve and stone the avocado, scoop out the flesh and chop roughly.

Heat the butter in a large frying pan over a moderate heat. Add the chopped bacon and spring onions and fry for 3-5 minutes to allow all the fat to run from the bacon. Turn the heat down slightly, then add the avocado and fry for 1 minute.

Add the rice to the pan, together with the hard-boiled eggs, cream, parsley, and salt and pepper to taste. Stir gently over a low heat, until the kedgeree is piping hot. Serve immediately, garnished with triangles of toast.

SAGE SAUSAGES WITH MUSTARD SAUCE

The simple pork sausage found on most supermarket shelves is very plain when compared with the rich variety of sausages made in the different regions of Britain. The sausages vary in texture and flavouring. Some are spicy, others – such as these sage sausages – are delicately flavoured with herbs.

Sausages are not difficult to make, although it may take some practice before you are adept at filling the skins. Homemade sausages have the advantage of flavour, freshness and good-quality ingredients.

It is sometimes difficult to obtain sausage skins, but many butchers will order them. You are most likely to be able to get them from a butcher who makes his own sausages. Synthetic skins tend to be easier to handle than natural ones, as long as your hands are free of grease. Natural casings should be rinsed before use. Skins for chipolata sausages are narrower than those for full-size sausages. As an alternative, these sausages can be made without skins. Shape the mixture into sausages, roll them in flour, and then fry them lightly.

The sausages will keep for 2-3 days in the refrigerator. Do not roll skinless sausages in flour until just before frying them.

PREPARATION TIME: *1 hour*
CHILLING TIME: *1-2 hours*
COOKING TIME: *12-15 minutes*

INGREDIENTS – *makes about 20 full-size sausages, or 40 chipolata sausages:*
1½ lb (700 g) very lean pork, finely minced
8 oz (225 g) very lean veal, finely minced
12 oz (350 g) suet, finely shredded
8 oz (225 g) fine fresh wholemeal breadcrumbs
½ teaspoon ground mace
2 level tablespoons finely chopped fresh sage OR 2 level teaspoons dried sage
1 level teaspoon salt
½ teaspoon freshly ground black pepper
1 clove garlic, crushed
Sausage skins, 7-8 ft (2-2.5 m) for large sausages, about 15 ft (5 m) for chipolatas

SAUCE
1 small onion, finely chopped
1 oz (25 g) butter
1½ level tablespoons plain flour
¼ pint (150 ml) chicken stock (page 367)
¼ pint (150 ml) single cream
1 tablespoon coarse grain mustard
Salt and freshly ground black pepper

Mix the minced meats, suet and breadcrumbs together. Add the mace, sage, salt and pepper, and garlic. Mix thoroughly to distribute the seasonings evenly.

Fit a plain nozzle, about ¾-1in (20-25mm) wide, into a large piping bag. Fill the bag

with some of the sausage mixture. Tie a knot in one end of a length of sausage skin about 3ft (900mm) long. Pull the open end of the skin up over the nozzle. Ease the rest of the skin over the nozzle until the knot at the end of the skin is almost touching it.

Squeeze the piping bag so that sausage mixture is forced into the skin – ease the skin out as it fills. Do not fill the skin too

tightly, otherwise the sausages are likely to burst when cooked as the filling expands.

Once the complete length of skin has been stuffed, knot the open end. Twist at 3-4in (80-100mm) intervals. Chill for 1-2 hours, to firm the sausages.

To make the mustard sauce, fry the chopped onion gently in the butter until it starts to soften. Stir in the flour and cook for 1 minute. Gradually add the

SIZZLING SAUSAGES Plump, juicy, sage sausages, browning in a frying pan, are a delicious reward for the time taken to make them.

chicken stock, stirring, and bring to the boil. Stir in the cream, mustard, and salt and pepper to taste. Heat through.

To serve, grill or fry three sausages per person. Serve with the hot mustard sauce.

WHITE HERB SAUSAGES

Recipes for white sausages are found all over Europe. In France they are called *boudin blanc*, in Germany, *weisswurst* and in Ireland, white pudding. Pale meat, such as chicken and veal, is usually the main ingredient. White sausages have a creamy texture and a much more delicate flavour than the usual pork and beef sausages.

These sausages must be encased in skins, see *Sage sausages* on page 21. They will keep for 4-5 days in the refrigerator after their initial boiling.

PREPARATION TIME: *1 hour*
CHILLING TIME: *8 hours*
COOKING TIME: *30 minutes*

INGREDIENTS – *makes 16:*
8 oz (225 g) cooked, boned chicken
8 oz (225 g) lean pork
8 oz (225 g) lean veal
12 oz (350 g) pork fat, free of any skin
2 medium onions, roughly chopped
5 tablespoons single cream
2 oz (50 g) fresh breadcrumbs
3 eggs, beaten
1 level tablespoon chopped fresh tarragon
2 level teaspoons salt
1 level teaspoon freshly ground white pepper
1 level teaspoon ground mace
Sausage skins, about 9 ft (2.7 m)
Strong thread
Juice of 1/2 lemon

Mince the meats and pork fat quite finely. A food processor or a mincing attachment to an electric mixer will make the task much easier. Mince once again, this time together with the chopped onions.

Heat the cream in a small pan until just about to boil, then remove from the heat. Add the breadcrumbs and leave to stand for 5 minutes. Mix the breadcrumbs into the minced meats and onions, together with the eggs, tarragon, salt and pepper, and mace.

Fit a plain nozzle, about ¾-1in (20-25mm) wide, into a large piping bag. Fill the bag with some of the sausage mixture. Tie a knot in one end of the length of sausage skin. Pull the open end of the skin up over the nozzle and ease the rest of the skin over the nozzle until the knot at the end of the skin is almost touching it.

Squeeze the piping bag so that sausage mixture fills the skin to about 6in (150mm). Ease the mixture down the skins as you fill them to disperse pockets of air. Tie with strong thread to secure the filling. (Twisting is not strong enough for this type of sausage.) Draw a short length of skin away from the nozzle and tie again, ready for the next sausage. Cut through the skin between the ties to detach each sausage. Repeat with the remaining filling and sausage skins.

Put the sausages into a chip basket or strainer, and lower into a large pan of simmering water. The juice of half a lemon added to the water will help to reduce the smell as the sausages are cooking. Simmer gently for 20 minutes. The liquid must not boil, otherwise the sausages will burst. As the sausages rise to the surface, pierce them once with a fine skewer. Drain the sausages thoroughly. Allow them to cool, then place them in a covered container and chill in the refrigerator for 8 hours.

To grill the sausages, brush them with melted butter and grill for about 4-5 minutes on each side. They can also be boiled or baked.

A good, grainy mustard goes very well with these sausages. Serve them with mashed potato or with *Hash browns* (page 25).

SAUTÉED KIDNEYS WITH CROUTONS

The silver chafing dish on the sideboard of large Victorian and Edwardian country houses was seldom empty at breakfast of kidneys, whether devilled, lightly grilled or, as in this recipe, sautéed in a rich sauce.

The chopped anchovy in this recipe contributes to a very distinctive flavour, but it may be omitted if preferred. It is essential that the kidneys are prepared just before cooking, but the croutons can be made in advance and then warmed through in the oven for 4–5 minutes before serving.

PREPARATION TIME: *15 minutes*
COOKING TIME: *10-15 minutes*

INGREDIENTS — *serves 4:*
8 lamb's kidneys
2 level tablespoons flour
2 oz (50 g) butter
2 rashers lean bacon, finely chopped
7 fl oz (200 ml) chicken stock (page 367)
2 tablespoons whisky
3 anchovy fillets, finely chopped
Salt and freshly ground black pepper
3 oz (75 g) button mushrooms, thinly sliced
2 tablespoons double cream
GARNISH
Chopped parsley
Triangular croutons of fried bread (page 286)

Skin the kidneys. Cut them in half and remove the cores. Dust the halved kidneys in flour.

Heat the butter in a large frying pan, add the chopped bacon and fry briskly for 3 minutes. Add the kidneys, and fry until sealed on the outside. Add the stock, whisky, anchovy fillets, and salt and pepper to taste. (The anchovies and bacon are quite salty, so it may not be necessary to add salt.) Simmer for 3 minutes. Add the mushrooms and simmer for a further 4 minutes. Add the cream and heat through.

Spoon onto a serving dish, and garnish with the parsley and croutons. Serve with bread or toast to soak up the sauce.

This dish is included in a menu on this page.

M E N U

Christmas Morning Breakfast for Six

BUCK'S FIZZ
page 176

SAUTÉED KIDNEYS WITH CROUTONS
this page

HOT MINCEMEAT LOAF
page 30

Increase the quantity of sautéed kidneys given in the recipe by half as much again. IN ADVANCE The evening before, assemble the loaf, make the croutons, and skin and core the kidneys. ON THE DAY Allow about 20 minutes. Put the loaf into the oven to warm through. Cook the kidneys. While they are cooking, warm through the croutons in the oven. Make the Buck's fizz just before serving. TO DRINK Coffee or tea.

FESTIVE START Piping hot mincemeat loaf and rich sautéed kidneys make a sustaining overture to the exertions of Christmas Day. Glasses of sparkling Buck's fizz will rouse even the sleepiest of revellers.

BLACK PUDDING WITH APPLE SAUCE

Traditionally horseshoe-shaped, the best black puddings have genuine sausage skins, rather than the plastic casings of the small straight variety. Black pudding baked with cider and brown sugar combines well with the mildly tart flavour of apple sauce. The sauce can be made the night before and kept in the refrigerator. It takes little time to warm it through next morning while the black pudding is baking in the oven.

PREPARATION TIME: *20 minutes*
COOKING TIME: *20-25 minutes*
OVEN TEMPERATURE: *preheat to 190°C (375°F, gas mark 5)*

INGREDIENTS – *serves 4:*
1 lb (450 g) cooking apples, peeled, cored and sliced
Grated rind and juice of ½ lemon
2 tablespoons water
4 cloves
1 oz (25 g) butter
1 egg yolk
12 oz (350 g) black pudding
4 tablespoons dry cider
2 level tablespoons demerara sugar

To make the apple sauce, put the sliced apple into a pan with the lemon juice and rind, water and cloves. Cover the pan and cook gently until the apple is just soft. Remove from the heat and allow the apple to cool slightly before beating in the butter and egg yolk.

While the apple is cooking, cut the black pudding into rings about ½in (15mm) thick. Lay them overlapping in a shallow ovenproof dish. Sprinkle the cider and sugar over the pudding. Bake in the preheated oven, uncovered, for 10-12 minutes.

Serve the black pudding with the warm apple sauce.

BAKED PUDDING A tart, fluffy apple sauce is the perfect partner for black pudding cooked with a sprinkling of cider and demerara sugar.

MENU

American Brunch for Four

ORANGE AND CRANBERRY BRUNCH BOWL
page 11

CREAMED CHIPPED BEEF
this page

HASH BROWNS
opposite page

PECAN WAFFLES
page 31
with MAPLE SYRUP

IN ADVANCE Allow about an hour the night before. Make the brunch bowl, chop the beef, and cook the potatoes for the hash browns in their skins (to prevent discoloration) until they are just tender when pierced.
ON THE DAY Allow about 45 minutes. Skin and dice the potatoes and start cooking the hash browns. Serve the brunch bowl, then make the waffle batter and cook the beef. Make the waffles after you have finished eating the beef – serving each one as it is made.
TO DRINK Coffee.

CREAMED CHIPPED BEEF

'Chipped' or chopped beef, in a hot cream sauce, is a popular breakfast or brunch dish in the United States. However, it is rich enough also to be served as a main meal, with baked potatoes, rice or noodles, and a simple green salad.

PREPARATION TIME: *10 minutes*
COOKING TIME: *6-7 minutes*

INGREDIENTS – *serves 4:*
1 lb (450 g) rump steak
1½ oz (40 g) butter
3 spring onions, finely chopped
¼ pint (150 ml) soured cream
1 level teaspoon freshly grated horseradish OR 1½ level teaspoons creamed horseradish
Salt and freshly ground black pepper

Chop the steak very finely. Heat the butter in a large, shallow pan and fry the steak over moderate heat so that the surface of the meat browns very quickly. Increase the heat, add the chopped spring onions to the pan and stir for 1 minute.

Stir in the soured cream, horseradish, and salt and pepper to taste. Stir over the heat for 1 minute.

Serve the beef with chunks of *Snipdoodle* (page 30), or on slices of toast. This dish is included in a menu on this page.

HASH BROWNS

The exact method of cooking the favourite American potato dish varies very much from state to state. The potatoes for hash browns can be sliced, cubed or cut into strips, but they should always be golden-brown and crusty when served.

PREPARATION TIME: *15 minutes*
COOKING TIME: *35-40 minutes*

INGREDIENTS — *serves 4-6:*
6 rashers smoked streaky bacon,
   chopped
2 lb (900 g) potatoes, peeled and
   cut into ¾ in (20 mm) cubes
1½ oz (40 g) butter
Salt and freshly ground black
   pepper

Cook the potatoes in a large pan of boiling water for about 5 minutes, until they just give when pierced with a knife. It is important that they should not be overcooked. Drain thoroughly in a colander and then spread out on a clean towel to dry. Cut the potatoes into slices, smaller cubes or strips.

Fry the bacon in a large frying pan over a high heat, until the fat runs free and the bacon is crisp. Remove the bacon pieces with a slotted spoon. Add the butter to the bacon fat and heat until the butter bubbles. Add the prepared potatoes and half the chopped bacon to the fat, and season with salt and pepper. Press the potatoes down firmly with a slice. The cubes will stick together to form a large, flat potato cake.

Reduce the heat slightly and cook, shaking the pan from time to time to prevent the potatoes from sticking. Continue cooking until a crisp golden crust forms on the underside of the potatoes – this will take about 15-20 minutes. Check whether the crust has formed by lifting the potatoes with a slice. If the underside is still too pale and soft, continue cooking for a few more minutes.

Invert a plate over the frying pan and carefully turn out the hash browns. Sprinkle with the remaining fried bacon pieces and serve immediately, cut into generous wedges.

Hash browns are delicious eaten on their own, but traditional toppings include melted cheese, a fried egg, fried onions or tomato sauce. They can also be served as an accompanying vegetable as part of a lunch or supper menu. This dish is included in a menu on the opposite page.

MUSHROOM, SAUSAGE AND BACON FONDUE

When there is plenty of time for a leisurely breakfast, fondue is the dish to serve. It is quick to prepare, but dipping sausages, pieces of bacon or mushrooms into the melted cheese sauce is not for those who have to rush for a train. It is not essential to use a special fondue set. A casserole dish set over a table warmer will do equally well.

Gouda cheese is substituted for the traditional, but more costly, Gruyère. Cheddar cheese is not suitable for a fondue because it curdles too easily.

PREPARATION AND COOKING
   TIME: *30 minutes*

INGREDIENTS — *serves 4-6:*
½ pint (285 ml) milk
14 oz (400 g) Gouda cheese,
   grated
2 level teaspoons cornflour
1 tablespoon water
1 tablespoon medium sherry
1 level teaspoon dry mustard
2 teaspoons Worcestershire sauce
Salt and freshly ground black
   pepper
DUNKS
10 oz (275 g) streaky bacon
   rashers
8 oz (225 g) button mushrooms
1 lb (450 g) cocktail sausages
Cubes of bread (optional)

First prepare the dunks. Remove the rind and stretch the bacon rashers. Cut each into half widthwise, roll up and thread onto a skewer. Wipe the mushrooms with a damp cloth and prick the sausages with a fork. Grill sausages, bacon rolls and mushrooms. Take care not to overcook the mushrooms. Set aside while making the fondue.

Put the milk into a fondue pot or flameproof casserole over a moderate heat and bring just to the boil. Reduce the heat and stir in the grated cheese.

Blend the cornflour to a smooth paste with the water and sherry, and add to the ingredients in the fondue pot. Stir in the mustard and Worcestershire sauce. Continue stirring over a very gentle heat until the fondue is thoroughly blended and smooth. Season to taste with salt and pepper.

Stand the hot fondue over the

BREAKFAST FONDUE Sausages, mushrooms, bacon and bread, all familiar sights at the breakfast table, take on a new morning role as dunks for a cheese fondue.

fondue burner, or table warmer, and serve immediately. Spike the dunks on fondue sticks, wooden skewers or forks for dipping into the sauce.

BREADS

CROISSANTS

Bakeries in France open early, not just for the sale of bread but to sell hot, flaky croissants ready for dunking in bowls of coffee or chocolate.

Croissants must be eaten warm, either freshly baked or freshened up in a moderately hot oven. The rising time is quite lengthy, but the dough can be prepared the night before and then left to rise in the refrigerator, ready to be shaped into croissants and baked for breakfast. Croissants can also be cooked in a large batch and frozen. They can be warmed through from frozen. This will take 10-12 minutes in an oven heated to about 180°C (350°F, gas mark 4).

The dough for croissants is very rich in butter. Work fast when folding and rolling the dough and try to keep it cool, otherwise it becomes difficult to manage. The technique is similar to that for *Puff pastry* (page 394).

PREPARATION TIME: *1 hour*
RISING AND CHILLING TIME: *about 13 hours*
COOKING TIME: *15-20 minutes*
OVEN TEMPERATURE: *preheat to 220°C (425°F, gas mark 7)*

INGREDIENTS – *makes 12:*
12 oz (350 g) plain flour
¼ teaspoon salt
2½ fl oz (75 ml) warm milk
½ oz (15 g) fresh yeast and a generous pinch of caster sugar OR 2 level teaspoons dried yeast and a generous pinch of caster sugar OR ½ sachet easy-blend dried yeast
2½ fl oz (75 ml) warm water
6 oz (175 g) unsalted butter
1 egg, beaten
Flaked almonds or poppy seeds (optional)

Sieve the flour and salt into a mixing bowl, and make a well in the centre. Leave to stand in a warm place.

Put the warm milk into a small bowl. Crumble the fresh yeast into the milk and then stir in the sugar. If using dried yeast, dissolve the sugar in the warm milk, then sprinkle the dried yeast on top. Leave the yeast mixture to stand in a warm place for about 10 minutes, until a thick froth forms on top of the liquid. If using easy-blend dried yeast, follow the instructions on the packet.

Pour the yeast liquid and the warm water into the well in the flour. Mix to a fairly firm dough, drawing the flour in from the sides of the bowl. Turn the dough onto a floured surface and knead well for 5 minutes.

Put the dough into a floured bowl, and place the bowl in a large, oiled plastic bag. Leave to rise in the refrigerator for 12 hours.

Soften the block of butter slightly; it should be fairly firm but not rock hard. On a lightly floured surface, roll out the chilled dough to a rectangle about 12in × 6in (300mm × 150mm). With one short side of the dough facing you, place the block of softened butter in the centre. Fold the bottom third of the dough up and over the butter, and then bring the top third of dough down over the two. Press the open sides of the parcel together to seal in the butter. Give the dough a half turn, clockwise. Roll the dough out to a rectangle once more, and repeat the folding process. Roll out and fold the dough once more. Wrap and chill for 30 minutes. Repeat the rolling and folding process twice more, and chill covered for a further 30 minutes.

Dampen two or three baking sheets. Roll the chilled dough out very thinly to a large oblong, approximately 18in × 12in (455mm × 300mm). Cut into 6 even-sized squares, and then cut each square in half diagonally. Starting at the base of each triangle, roll up loosely, and secure the point with a little beaten egg. Curl the roll round into a crescent shape. Place on the dampened baking sheets and brush each croissant lightly with beaten egg. They may also be sprinkled with flaked almonds or poppy seeds at this stage. Bake in the preheated oven for about 15-20 minutes, until risen and golden.

As a variation, the hot croissants may be sprinkled with grated Parmesan cheese. Alternatively, make a split along one side of frozen baked croissants and spread a flavoured butter such as brandy butter, or any jam, inside before heating them through. The flavour will permeate the croissants.

BUTTERY CROISSANTS A cool work surface, such as marble, helps when shaping the croissant dough.

CHOCOLATE MUFFINS

These muffins are at their best served still warm from the oven. The first bite reveals a hidden centre of dark, melting chocolate. They can be frozen, or kept for up to a week in an airtight tin. Warm them through in a moderate oven – 180°C (350°F), gas mark 4 – when needed.

Muffin tins are deeper than ordinary patty tins, with straight sides. These muffins can instead be made in deep patty tins 2½in (65mm) across and 1½in (40mm) deep. If shallower tins are used the mixture will make more muffins.

If soured cream is unavailable, add 1 teaspoon of lemon juice to ¼ pint (150ml) double cream and leave to stand for about 30 minutes.

PREPARATION TIME: *15 minutes*
COOKING TIME: *20 minutes*
OVEN TEMPERATURE: *preheat to 200°C (400°F, gas mark 6)*

INGREDIENTS – *makes 12:*
5 oz (150 g) fine cornmeal
2 oz (50 g) self-raising flour
¾ oz (20 g) cocoa powder
1 level tablespoon baking powder
Generous pinch of salt
2 oz (50 g) dark, soft brown sugar
2 oz (50 g) butter
¼ pint (150 ml) soured cream
1 egg
2 tablespoons strong black coffee
2 oz (50 g) plain dark chocolate, broken into 12 equal pieces
Cocoa powder for dusting

Grease 12 muffin tins or deep patty tins.

Sieve the cornmeal, flour, cocoa powder, baking powder and salt into a bowl, and add the sugar. Melt the butter over a gentle heat, then stir into the dry ingredients, together with the soured cream, egg and coffee. Mix until smooth.

Divide half the mixture amongst the prepared tins. Place a piece of chocolate in each tin, then cover the chocolate with the remaining mixture.

Bake in the preheated oven for 20 minutes, until risen and just firm to the touch.

Carefully ease the cooked muffins out of their tins and cool on a rack. Dust the muffins with cocoa powder or, for a sweeter tooth, drinking chocolate, and serve warm.

Chocolate muffins can be served with a bowl of natural *Yoghurt* (page 12).

FRUIT MUFFINS

In North America, muffins are a traditional breakfast dish. Unlike English muffins, made with yeast, American ones are raised with baking powder.

These muffins can be eaten cold, but they are best served still warm from the oven.

PREPARATION TIME: *15 minutes*
COOKING TIME: *15-20 minutes*
OVEN TEMPERATURE: *preheat to 200°C (400°F, gas mark 6)*

INGREDIENTS – *makes 12:*
5 oz (150 g) fine cornmeal
3 oz (75 g) self-raising flour
1 level tablespoon baking powder
Pinch of salt
2 oz (50 g) caster sugar
2 oz (50 g) butter
¼ pint (150 ml) milk
1 large egg
Grated rind and juice of 1 orange
2 oz (50 g) raisins

Grease 12 muffin tins or deep patty tins.

Sieve the cornmeal, flour, baking powder, salt and sugar together in a large bowl. Melt the butter in a pan with the milk over low heat. Beat the egg with the orange rind and juice, and mix with the milk and butter.

Make a well in the centre of the flour and cornmeal and pour

AMERICAN MUFFINS Orange zest and raisins flavour this breakfast favourite from the USA.

in the liquid. Sprinkle the raisins into the well and quickly fold in.

Spoon the mixture into the tins and bake for about 20 minutes in the preheated oven until golden-brown.

PEAR AND LEMON BREAD

In central Europe and Scandinavia fruit breads are a familiar sight at the breakfast table. In Great Britain they are gaining popularity, although the only variety which has so far become widespread is the malt loaf. This pear and lemon loaf is firm and moist, with a tangy lemon flavour. Pear bread (*birnenbrot*) is a Swiss speciality. If millet flakes are unavailable, bran flakes can be used instead.

PREPARATION TIME: *25 minutes*
COOKING TIME: *50 minutes*
OVEN TEMPERATURE: *preheat to 190°C (375°F, gas mark 5)*

INGREDIENTS – *makes one 2 lb (900 g) loaf:*
5 oz (150 g) wholewheat flour
3 oz (75 g) millet flakes
1 oz (25 g) sunflower seeds
4 oz (115 g) butter, softened
12 oz (350 g) lemon curd (see Lime curd, page 138)
3 tablespoons thick natural yoghurt
6 oz (175 g) dried pears, chopped
Extra millet flakes for dusting tin

Put the wholewheat flour, millet flakes, sunflower seeds, softened butter, lemon curd and natural yoghurt into a bowl. Beat until well mixed. The mixture will be quite stiff. Mix in the chopped dried pears.

Lightly grease a ridged loaf tin, about 2lb (900g) in size, or a standard 2lb (900g) loaf tin. Dust the inside lightly with millet flakes. Spoon the mixture into the tin, pressing it down so that it fills the ridges of the tin. Spread the surface flat.

Bake in the preheated oven for 50 minutes. Allow to cool in the tin for about 5 minutes, before turning the loaf onto a cooling rack. Once cool, keep the loaf in an airtight tin, or wrapped in foil, so that it remains moist.

While the loaf is still very fresh, it is delicious spread with unsalted butter and jam as well, if you wish. Once it gets to three or four days old, it is very good toasted.

This dish is included in a menu on page 18.

COLOURFUL PEARS Dried pears, lemon curd, yoghurt, millet flakes, sunflower seeds and flour are ready to be transformed into pear and lemon bread. Millet flakes also line the ridged tin, but an ordinary loaf tin without ridges can be used instead.

DATE AND WALNUT LOAF

Moist, fruit loaves tempt the appetite first thing in the morning. This loaf can be served either warm or cold. If you make it a day ahead, allow the loaf to cool then wrap it tightly in kitchen foil so that it does not dry out.

Use fresh or dried whole dates, as long as they are quite moist. Block dates are too hard and dry to be used in this recipe.

PREPARATION TIME: *15 minutes*
COOKING TIME: *50-60 minutes*
OVEN TEMPERATURE: *preheat to 180°C (350°F, gas mark 4)*

INGREDIENTS – *makes one 2 lb (900 g) loaf:*
2 oz (50 g) butter
2 oz (50 g) light brown sugar
1 large egg
Grated rind and juice of ½ lemon
6 oz (175 g) plain flour
Pinch of salt
1 level tablespoon baking powder
4 fl oz (115 ml) milk
3 oz (75 g) dates, stoned and chopped
3 oz (75 g) walnuts, chopped

Grease a 2lb (900g) loaf tin.

Cream the butter and sugar together until light. Beat in the egg and the rind and juice of the lemon. Sieve the flour, salt and baking powder together. Beat the sieved flour and milk alternately into the mixture in several additions. Fold in the dates and walnuts. Put the mixture into the tin. Bake in the preheated oven for 50-60 minutes. Leave in the tin for a minute and turn out.

This moist loaf is very good eaten without any accompaniment, or spread with butter and honey, or with cream cheese.

MOLASSES OATCAKES

Scotland is usually considered the home of the oatcake, but it is found in slightly different forms throughout the British Isles. Molasses is a thick, dark syrup – a product of raw sugar cane, with a distinctive bitter flavour. The name is ultimately derived from the Latin word for honey, *mel*, and molasses makes a naturally sweeter and richer oatcake than the traditional one. Black treacle can be substituted for molasses if necessary.

Oatcakes are very good served hot, straight from the oven, but they can also be cooled and kept in an airtight tin for up to 2 weeks.

PREPARATION TIME: *15 minutes*
COOKING TIME: *12 minutes*
OVEN TEMPERATURE: *preheat to 190°C (375°F, gas mark 5)*

INGREDIENTS – *makes 12:*
6 oz (175 g) medium oatmeal
2 oz (50 g) plain flour
Generous pinch of salt
¼ teaspoon bicarbonate of soda
2 oz (50 g) butter
3 fl oz (90 ml) molasses, or black treacle

Grease two baking sheets.

Mix the oatmeal, flour, salt and bicarbonate of soda in a bowl. Melt the butter and treacle in a saucepan over a gentle heat, add to the dry ingredients and mix well together.

Spoon the mixture onto the baking sheets in 12 even-sized mounds. Flatten the mounds slightly with the back of a dampened spoon.

Bake in the preheated oven for 12 minutes. Serve hot, spread with butter and homemade jam, or eat with grilled bacon or curd cheese.

If not serving the oatcakes immediately, allow them to cool on the sheets for 1-2 minutes and then transfer carefully onto cooling racks.

CHEESE AND HERB SHORTBREAD

Savoury shortbread can turn a simple breakfast dish such as scrambled eggs into a brunch or even a light supper. This recipe is flavoured with rosemary, but any other fresh herb can be used as an alternative. Sage, for example, is good if the shortbread is to be served with sausages or bacon.

Serve the shortbread while still warm from the oven.

PREPARATION TIME: *15 minutes*
COOKING TIME: *40 minutes*
OVEN TEMPERATURE: *preheat to 150°C (300°F, gas mark 2)*

INGREDIENTS – *serves 6-8:*
7 oz (200 g) plain flour
Generous pinch of salt
Generous pinch of dry mustard
1 oz (25 g) cornflour
5 oz (150 g) butter (at room temperature)
2 oz (50 g) strong cheese (a good mature Cheddar, or Parmesan), grated
2 tablespoons double cream or single cream
1 level tablespoon chopped fresh rosemary

Sieve the flour, salt, mustard and cornflour together into a bowl. Add the butter, grated cheese and cream, and work together with the fingertips until the ingredients form a smooth dough. Knead the chopped rosemary lightly into the dough.

Lightly grease an 8in (200mm) plain flan ring and a baking sheet. Place the flan ring on the baking sheet. Press the prepared shortbread dough evenly inside the ring. Prick the surface of the dough with a fork and score with a sharp knife into 6 or 8 sections.

Bake in the preheated oven for 40 minutes, until straw-coloured. Cut along the divisions while the shortcake is still hot, to divide it into wedges.

SAVOURY SHORTBREAD Rich, crumbly shortbread is more often associated with afternoon tea than with the first meal of the day, but the savoury version tastes delicious with scrambled eggs.

SNIPDOODLE

The excellence of this light, sweet breakfast bread is proclaimed in its name. Both 'snippy' and 'doodle' are old American slang expressions for something of high quality. Quick and easy to make, snipdoodle can be baked for a late breakfast or brunch and served at its best – warm and fresh from the oven. It is a good accompaniment to cooked breakfast dishes.

PREPARATION TIME: *20 minutes*
COOKING TIME: *40-45 minutes*
OVEN TEMPERATURE: *preheat to 180°C (350°F, gas mark 4)*

INGREDIENTS – *makes one loaf:*
8 oz (225 g) soft margarine
10 oz (275 g) soft brown sugar
2 eggs
12 oz (350 g) plain flour
4 level teaspoons baking powder
Generous pinch of salt
¼ pint (150 ml) milk
¼ pint (150 ml) soured cream
1 level tablespoon poppy seeds

TOPPING
2 level tablespoons caster sugar
1 level tablespoon ground cinnamon
½-1 level tablespoon poppy seeds (optional)

Grease and line a shallow cake tin, about 8in × 12in × 1½in (200mm × 300mm × 40mm). Dust the inside lightly with a little flour.

Beat the margarine and sugar until light and fluffy. Gradually beat in the eggs.

Sieve the flour, baking powder and salt together. Beat the flour gradually into the mixture, alternating with the milk and soured cream. Mix in the poppy seeds.

Spoon into the prepared tin and smooth the surface level. Bake in the preheated oven for 40-45 minutes, until the loaf is firm to the touch, and a fine skewer inserted into the centre comes out clean.

Sprinkle the snipdoodle with a mixture of sugar, cinnamon and poppy seeds (if used), and serve warm in the tin. Snipdoodle is traditionally eaten in chunks rather than slices, so cut it into squares or break it into pieces. For an American breakfast serve it with *Creamed chipped beef (page 24).*

WARM FROM THE OVEN American snipdoodle is a good accompaniment to traditional British cooked breakfast dishes such as grilled sausages and bacon.

HOT MINCEMEAT LOAF

This loaf is a sweet version of the more familiar garlic bread. It is specially appropriate for a Christmas breakfast. Assemble the loaf the night before, but do not glaze it with the beaten egg or it will not be crisp. Wrap it loosely in foil. The next morning, open the foil and finish preparing the loaf, then re-seal, ready to put into the oven.

PREPARATION TIME: *15 minutes*
COOKING TIME: *20-25 minutes*
OVEN TEMPERATURE: *preheat to 190°C (375°F, gas mark 5)*

INGREDIENTS – *serves 6:*
1 stubby French loaf, about 14 in (355 mm) long
3 oz (75 g) brandy butter or rum butter
4 generous tablespoons mincemeat (page 138)
1 egg, beaten
1-2 tablespoons chopped nuts
Kitchen foil

Make vertical cuts across the loaf, at 1in (25mm) intervals, taking care not to cut right through the bottom crust.

Ease each cut section open gently, and spread the cut surfaces first with brandy butter or rum butter and then with mincemeat. Ease the sections back together again.

Brush the loaf with beaten egg and then sprinkle with nuts. Enclose the assembled loaf loosely in a parcel of foil, and seal the parcel along the top.

Bake in the preheated oven for 12 minutes. Fold back the foil and return to the oven for a further 8-10 minutes, until the loaf has a rich golden crust.

Serve hot, broken into pieces. This dish is included in a menu on page 22.

BLACK RYE BREAD

There are many types of black bread eaten throughout Europe, all with the same dark colour and slightly coarse texture. Black bread is made with rye flour. Because rye flour is low in gluten – the elastic substance which traps air in the dough – it is often mixed with wheat flour. In Scandinavia, rye bread is traditionally steamed in round tins. Empty fruit or vegetable tins are ideal for providing the round shape, and they can be collected in advance before baking. Otherwise, use any round cake tins or loaf tins.

Rye bread is traditionally baked with a yeast dough, but this loaf made with baking powder has the advantage of being particularly quick and easy to make. It has a tight, dense texture rather like German pumpernickel. If you cannot get rye flour, use wholewheat flour. Soured milk can be simulated by adding a little lemon juice to ordinary milk. Alternatively, use cultured (not sweet) buttermilk.

PREPARATION TIME: *30 minutes*
COOKING TIME: *2 hours*

INGREDIENTS — *makes 4 loaves:*
4 × 15 oz (425 g) fruit or vegetable tins, with one end completely removed
A little oil
3 oz (75 g) plain flour
1½ level teaspoons baking powder
1 level teaspoon salt
½ teaspoon ground cinnamon
½ teaspoon ground nutmeg
4 oz (115 g) rye flour
4 oz (115 g) cornmeal, or fine semolina
2 oz (50 g) blanched almonds, finely chopped
2 level tablespoons dark, soft brown sugar
8 tablespoons black treacle
14 fl oz (400 ml) soured milk or cultured buttermilk

Clean the tins thoroughly and dry them. Brush the insides of the tins with oil.

Sieve the plain flour, baking powder, salt, cinnamon and nutmeg into a mixing bowl. Add the rye flour, cornmeal, chopped nuts and brown sugar. Stir in the black treacle and the soured milk or buttermilk.

Divide the mixture between the oiled tins. Cover each tin tightly with a double layer of greased foil, pinching it around the rims of the tins so that they are well sealed. Cook in a steamer for 2 hours, *without* lifting the lid. If you do not have a steamer, use a large, deep, saucepan with a trivet placed in

the base. Fill the saucepan with water halfway up the tins. You will have to lift the lid of the saucepan to check that it does not boil dry, but do not do so more often than is necessary.

Remove each loaf carefully, and leave to cool. Wrapped well in foil, the bread will keep fresh for about two weeks.

Black rye bread tastes particularly good served with pickled herring or cured fish. See also *Egg and herring danwich*, page 15. This bread is included in a menu on page 15.

PECAN WAFFLES

The Americans adopt an adventurous attitude towards their breakfast waffles. Served as a savoury with sausage and bacon, or sweet with maple syrup and soured cream, waffles are versatile enough for any breakfast or brunch. They should be served and eaten as they are made. If stacked they go soggy.

Pecan nuts are native to North America. They look like long, thin walnuts and have a similar, rich, musty taste.

The batter is cooked in a special waffle iron. These can be bought from department stores or kitchen shops. The waffles are usually rectangular, but round, heart-shaped and fan-shaped irons can also be bought. Some are designed to be used on top of the cooker, while others are self-heated electrically.

PREPARATION TIME: *20 minutes*
COOKING TIME: *about 3-4 minutes per waffle*

INGREDIENTS – *serves 6-8:*
8 oz (225 g) plain flour
1 level teaspoon baking powder
1 level teaspoon bicarbonate of soda
½ teaspoon salt
1½ oz (40 g) caster sugar
3 eggs, separated
1½ tablespoons lemon juice
12 fl oz (340 ml) milk
3 tablespoons oil
4 oz (115 g) pecans, chopped

Sieve the flour, baking powder, bicarbonate of soda and salt into a bowl. Mix in the sugar. Beat the egg yolks with the lemon juice, milk and oil and add to the dry ingredients. Beat until smooth. Whisk the egg whites until stiff but not dry. Fold into the waffle batter with the chopped pecans.

Heat the waffle iron. (Most do not require greasing, but if in doubt check the manufacturer's instructions.) Pour in enough batter to fill the waffle iron. Close the lid and cook until the

WAFFLE HEARTS Standard waffle irons are rectangular in shape, but heart-shaped, circular and fan-shaped irons are also available. Although waffles are conventionally served with syrup, butter and jam are just as good.

steaming stops – this will take about 3-4 minutes.

Serve immediately with butter and maple syrup, golden syrup, honey or with jam. This dish is included in a menu on page 24.

STRAWBERRY SHRUB

A shrub is a traditional Arab cordial, based on a fruit syrup.

Use clear, small screw-top bottles – the kind in which soft drinks are bottled. Select bottles that are shorter than the depth of the pan in which the bottles filled with syrup are to be sterilised. Any fruit with a high juice content may be used instead of strawberries, such as raspberries, blackberries and redcurrants.

PREPARATION AND COOKING
TIME: *1½ hours*

INGREDIENTS – *makes about 1½ pints (850 ml) of syrup:*
3 lb (1.4 kg) strawberries
Granulated sugar (see method)
Citric acid (see method)

Sterilise the bottle tops by boiling them in water for 15 minutes.

Make sure that the strawberries are scrupulously clean, then hull them and put them into a pan. Heat gently, stirring continuously, and bring slowly to the boil. Boil for 1 minute, crushing large pieces of fruit with a wooden spoon.

Strain the fruit through clean muslin or a jelly bag. Press on the fruit left in the muslin to extract the last drop of juice.

Measure the juice into a large, clean jug. Add 12oz (350g) sugar to each pint (570ml) of juice. Stir to dissolve the sugar. (If necessary, heat the juice and sugar gently until the sugar dissolves.) Add 1 level teaspoon of citric acid for each pint (570ml) of juice that was measured.

Pour the syrup into the screw-top glass bottles. Leave ¾in (20mm) of headspace on each bottle to allow room for expansion. Screw the sterilised tops on *loosely*. This allows the air to escape.

Put a folded newspaper into the bottom of a preserving pan or a large, deep saucepan, and stand the filled bottles on top of the paper. Pour cold water into the pan until it comes just above the level of the syrup in the bottles. Simmer for 20 minutes – the temperature of the water should be about 88°C (190°F).

Using heatproof gloves, remove the bottles and stand them on a wooden board. Screw the tops down tightly, immediately. Leave to cool. Wipe the outside of the bottles, and label.

Stored in a cool dark place, homemade fruit syrups will keep for up to a year. Once opened, however, the syrup must be kept refrigerated and used within 10 days.

To serve the shrub, put a good tablespoon of the syrup into a tall glass and dilute with hot or cold water, or soda water, to taste. For a summer party, dilute each measure of strawberry syrup with well-chilled dry white wine instead of water. The shrub is included in a menu on page 20.

FIZZING SHRUB When mixed with soda water, strawberry shrub froths up, then subsides leaving a sparkling summer drink.

Morning Coffee

*C*OFFEE DRINKING IN ENGLAND was mentioned first by the diarist John Evelyn in 1637. The setting was Oxford, and it was in that city that the country's first coffee-house — The Angel — was opened 13 years later. London embraced the notion, and coffee-houses proliferated — cosy, club-like places in which men could meet, read the news-sheets and exchange the gossip of the day. One of them evolved into the great insurance house of Lloyd's, others into true clubs for gentlemen; the remainder have long vanished.

These male preserves, however, had little bearing on the present morning coffee ceremony, which had its beginnings in the Central European capitals — Vienna, Budapest, Berlin and the rest — in the glittering decades before the First World War. Then it was customary for ladies to meet in the mornings or afternoons and discuss the waltzes, fashions and dashing hussars of the parties the evening before.

Such meetings often took place at home, at the 'Kaffeevisite', when the hostess presided from behind silver coffee pots and surveyed acres of canapés, moulded honey cakes, cream cakes and pastries, 'Torten' and 'Strudeln', crystal bowls of 'Vanillecreme' and delicate Meissen china. Equally, a rendezvous might have been arranged at one of the 'Konditorien', the café-pastry shops, all ormolu, gilt mirrors and twisted marble columns.

The influence of these splendid establishments has long crossed the former Imperial frontiers, and versions of their creations can now be found at coffee parties in faraway Britain. Perhaps, though, they are a little more restrained; to be 'vollschlank' — pleasingly plump — is not so fashionable as it once was in Old Vienna.

Planning & Preparation

There are generally two sorts of coffee party: small ones, rarely for more than 6-8 people, which may be given for purely social reasons, or as part of an informal committee meeting for example; and fund-raising parties which can frequently involve 20 guests or more.

Making the coffee

Because coffee is central to the party, this is the time to serve ground coffee rather than instant (see *Coffee*, page 50). It is wise not to serve a very bitter coffee unless you are sure all the guests will like it.

Most coffee makers will hold enough coffee for at least eight cups, and so are ideal for small parties. Those automatic coffee machines which incorporate a warming plate are very useful.

The simplest means of making coffee for large numbers is the jug method (page 50), using large earthenware jugs. Let the coffee infuse and then pour it through a strainer.

Offer cold milk, hot milk and cream if you can – people have distinct preferences – and brown sugar in the form of granules, crystals or cubes.

Planning the menu

A coffee party is an excuse for making a variety of cakes, pastries and biscuits. Savouries, such as sandwiches and toast, are not usually served in the morning. Coffee itself has a more robust flavour than tea, and the cakes, pastries and biscuits served with it tend to have stronger, more intense flavours than those served with tea. In addition, since morning coffee as an occasion has its origin on the Continent, many continental cakes and pastries are served, particularly Austrian recipes like *Kugelhopf* (page 44) and *Cherry strudel* (page 45).

A small party is an opportunity to bake indulgent cakes which would not be practical for large numbers, such as *Chocolate cream torte* (page 42). The guests will probably be sitting down so the food can also be fairly soft and creamy. There is no need to provide more than two or three different items.

For a larger party, plan food that can be baked in batches in advance. Since most parties start around 11 o'clock there will not be much time to do more than add a few decorations to the food before the party. Individual cakes and biscuits that are easy to eat and do not need cutting up, such as *Florentines* (page 40), *Butterscotch cookies with date filling* (page 47) and *Chocolate-coated gingernuts* (page 40), are suitable; cream cakes are not.

Take into account the time of year: serve heavier cakes such as *Hot cinnamon ring* (page 48) or *Apple sauce cake* (page 41) in winter. Something lighter is a better choice in spring and summer, such as *Fresh fruit tartlets* (page 37).

At all parties, balance any very rich cakes with something fairly plain and simple.

Arranging the seating

It is not necessary for every guest to have a seat at a party for more than 6-8. The food at a coffee party is usually quite easy to eat, and so long as there are plenty of surfaces – small tables, shelves or sideboards – where people can put down their coffee cups, they can cope quite adequately standing. However, place some groups of seats in strategic positions for elderly guests or others who are unable to stand for long periods. (See also *Drinks parties*, page 156.)

China and cutlery

Use large coffee cups for morning coffee – demitasse coffee cups (very small ones) are usually kept for after-dinner coffee. For large parties you will have to borrow sets of coffee cups – tea cups can be used as well if necessary – or, alternatively, hire them (look under Catering Hire in *Yellow Pages*).

Provide small plates for the food. For cream gâteaux and sticky cakes, knives or pastry forks (small forks with two prongs, one of which is broad and flat) are helpful. Provide plenty of napkins – the small cocktail ones are best – enough for two each at least.

Allow plenty of time – at least an hour – before the party for setting out cups, saucers and plates. Lay out in advance all the food apart from cream gâteaux and the cream for the coffee. A trolley is an attractive and also useful means of passing food among the guests.

PASTRIES, CAKES & BISCUITS

FRESH FRUIT TARTLETS

Small round or oval tartlets are filled with summer fruit – strawberries, raspberries, blackberries, redcurrants, peaches, nectarines or apricots.

Glaze red fruits, such as raspberries and strawberries, with redcurrant jelly. Use apple jelly or apricot jam to glaze yellow and green fruits. The pastry cases can be frozen, but once filled, the tartlets should be eaten as soon as possible or the pastry will lose its crispness.

PREPARATION TIME: *30 minutes*
CHILLING TIME: *30 minutes*
COOKING TIME: *12-15 minutes*
OVEN TEMPERATURE: *preheat to 200°C (400°F, gas mark 6)*

INGREDIENTS – *makes 8-12:*
3 egg yolks
A few drops vanilla essence
6 oz (175 g) plain flour
Pinch of salt
3 oz (75 g) caster sugar
3 oz (75 g) unsalted butter, slightly softened
1 lb (450 g) fresh fruits

GLAZE
4 level tablespoons apple or redcurrant jelly, or sieved apricot jam

Grease eight 4in (100mm) round, fluted tartlet tins, or 12 oval, 'barquette' tins, or a combination of the two.

Mix the egg yolks with the vanilla essence. Sieve the flour and salt onto a marble slab or cool surface. Make a well in the centre and add the sugar, butter, and the egg yolk mixture. Using fingertips only, first mix the sugar, butter and egg together, then gradually draw in the flour until the mixture is crumbly. Using the heel of your hand, push some of the mixture along the surface to bind it together. Repeat until the mixture forms a ball. Try to handle the pastry as little as possible. Wrap and chill for 30 minutes.

Roll out the pastry on a floured surface and use it to line the prepared tins. Prick the pastry bases with a fork, and chill for 20 minutes.

Place the tins on a baking sheet and bake blind (page 393) in the centre of the preheated oven for 12-15 minutes or until golden. Cool in the tins, then transfer the pastry cases to a wire rack.

Wash the fruit. Pick over and hull strawberries, raspberries and blackberries. With a fork, strip redcurrants carefully from

FLOURISHES OF RED A trio of summer fruits – strawberries, redcurrants and thinly sliced nectarines – are easily arranged to make tartlets fit to grace the window of any French pastry shop.

their stalks. Stone and slice peaches, nectarines and apricots.

Brush glaze over the insides of the pastry cases. Arrange the fruit in each case, and brush with the rest of the glaze.

37

*Morning
Coffee
for Six*

FLORENTINES *page 40*

ICED PETITS FOURS
this page

COFFEE
SPONGE ROLL
WITH
MARSALA CREAM
opposite page

IN ADVANCE Although all the cakes and biscuits can be made 2-3 days in advance, the iced petits fours are best made the day before and the coffee sponge roll is best made and filled on the morning of the party.
ON THE DAY Allow about 2 hours to make the coffee sponge roll. Leave it chilling in the refrigerator until just before serving.
TO DRINK Coffee.

PASTEL ELEGANCE A veil of icing — cool white or tinted the palest rose pink — covers petits fours made from layers of featherlight Genoese sponge sandwiched with apricot jam and covered with marzipan. The decoration should be simple: a spiral of icing, a single pale green pistachio nut, or a sugared rose petal.

ICED PETITS FOURS

A tray of pastel-coloured iced petits fours is an elegant addition to a coffee party or a tea party. The petits fours can be made up to 3 days in advance if kept in a plastic box in the refrigerator.

PREPARATION TIME: *60 minutes plus 4-6 hours for pressing sponge*
COOKING TIME: *20 minutes*
OVEN TEMPERATURE: *preheat to 190°C (375°F, gas mark 5)*

INGREDIENTS – *makes 18-24:*
4 oz (115 g) plain flour
4 eggs
4 oz (115 g) caster sugar
2½ oz (65 g) butter, melted
4 oz (115 g) apricot jam, warmed and sieved
4 oz (115 g) marzipan (page 400)
12 oz (350 g) icing sugar
Hot water to mix
A little white rum, or a dash of any fruit liqueur
Pink food colouring
DECORATION
Crystallised violets, mimosa balls, rose petals (page 290), or a few pistachio nuts

Grease a swiss roll tin 13in × 9in (330mm × 230mm) and line the base with non-stick paper or buttered greaseproof paper. Sieve the flour and leave in a warm place.

Whisk the eggs and the sugar together using an electric beater, or in a mixing bowl set over hot water, until the mixture is pale and foamy and the beater leaves a trail across the surface.

Carefully fold in the sieved flour alternately with the melted butter. Turn the mixture into the prepared tin and spread evenly. Bake in the centre of the preheated oven for 20 minutes until golden and just starting to shrink from the sides of the tin. Cool in the tin for 2 minutes, then turn out onto a sheet of greaseproof paper sprinkled with caster sugar.

Using a long, sharp knife, cut the cake widthwise into 3 equal pieces. Brush the upper side of each piece with the apricot jam. Sandwich the 3 pieces together (there will be a layer of jam on top). Roll out the marzipan into a rectangle the same size as the cake and place it on top.

Cover the cake with greaseproof paper and place a heavy wooden board, such as a bread board or chopping board, on top to press down the cake evenly. Leave for 4-6 hours.

Cut the cake into 1½in (40mm) squares or triangles.

Mix the sieved icing sugar with a little hot water and the white rum, or liqueur, until smooth and thick enough to coat the back of a spoon. Place the cakes on a wire rack over a plate, and spoon icing over half the cakes. Let it run down the sides. Colour the remainder of the icing with a drop or two of food colouring to give a very delicate shade of pink, and ice the rest of the cakes. Allow the

icing to dry for a few minutes.

Mix a little more icing, and pipe a decoration on top of the cakes. Place a crystallised violet or mimosa ball, a sugared rose petal or a pistachio nut on the cakes, and set them aside in a warm place to dry.

The cakes may be placed in paper cases for serving. These cakes are included in a menu on the opposite page.

COFFEE SPONGE ROLL WITH MARSALA CREAM

Jam and a rich cream fill this coffee-flavoured swiss roll. It is best to start from the inside when making a swiss roll; make the fillings first. The roll will keep 2-3 days in a plastic box in the refrigerator.

PREPARATION TIME: *45 minutes*
COOKING TIME: *12-15 minutes*
COOLING TIME: *30 minutes*
OVEN TEMPERATURE: *preheat to 200°C (400°F, gas mark 6)*

INGREDIENTS—*serves 8:*
MARSALA CREAM
4 oz (115 g) caster sugar
2 tablespoons cold water
2 egg yolks
5 oz (150 g) unsalted butter, softened
1 tablespoon Marsala or sweet sherry
JAM FILLING
3-4 tablespoons gooseberry jam or redcurrant jelly

CAKE
2 oz (50 g) plain flour
Pinch of baking powder
2 eggs
2 oz (50 g) caster sugar
1 tablespoon liquid coffee essence
A little extra caster sugar

Dissolve the sugar in the water over low heat, stirring all the time. When the sugar has dissolved, increase the heat and boil the syrup until it reaches 105°C (220°F) or the short-thread stage – when a little of the syrup (cooled in a teaspoon first) forms a short thread when pulled between finger and thumb. This will take 2-3 minutes. Remove from the heat.

Pour the syrup onto the egg yolks in a thin stream, whisking all the time until the mixture turns pale and thickens. This may take 5-10 minutes.

Gradually whisk in the softened butter, adding it in small pieces. Continue to whisk the cream until it is smooth and fluffy, then gradually whisk in the Marsala. Set the cream aside in a cool place (not the refrigerator).

Line the base and ends of a 12in × 8in (300mm × 200mm) swiss roll tin with buttered greaseproof paper or non-stick baking paper.

Sieve the flour and baking powder together and leave in a warm place. Whisk the eggs and sugar with an electric beater, or in a bowl over hot water, until the mixture is pale and foamy and the beater leaves a trail over

the surface. Whisk in the coffee essence and then carefully fold in the flour with a metal spoon.

Turn the mixture into the prepared tin and spread evenly. Bake in the preheated oven for 12-15 minutes until springy to the touch. When the sponge is cooked, turn it out onto a teacloth that has been dusted with caster sugar. Peel off the greaseproof paper and let the cake cool for 2-3 minutes. Trim the edges of the cake with a sharp knife. Carefully roll up the cake with the sugared teacloth so that the teacloth fills the place where the filling will eventually be.

Leave for 30 minutes on a wire rack.

Sieve the jam if you prefer it without pips. Unroll the cake and spread first with the jam and then with the Marsala cream. Re-roll and place the cake on a serving plate with the join at the base. Dust with caster sugar and chill in the refrigerator until ready to serve. This cake is included in a menu on the opposite page.

COFFEE AND CREAM Swirls of lightly whipped double cream are the finishing touch to a swiss roll flavoured with coffee.

FLORENTINES

Despite their Italian-sounding name, Florentines are a speciality of Austria and Germany. These golden discs of caramel, studded with candied fruit and chopped almonds and backed with chocolate, can be stored in an airtight tin for 1–2 weeks.

PREPARATION TIME: *45 minutes plus cooling time*
COOKING TIME: *10-15 minutes*
OVEN TEMPERATURE: *preheat to 180°C (350°F, gas mark 4)*

INGREDIENTS – *makes 18:*
2 oz (50 g) candied orange peel or mixed peel
2 oz (50 g) blanched almonds
1½ oz (40 g) glacé cherries
1 oz (25 g) sultanas
½ oz (15 g) candied angelica
1½ oz (40 g) unsalted butter
2 oz (50 g) caster sugar
1 level tablespoon plain flour, sieved
1 tablespoon double cream
1 teaspoon lemon juice
6 oz (175 g) plain dessert chocolate
Non-stick baking paper

Line three or four baking sheets with non-stick baking paper.

Dice the orange peel or mixed peel finely, cut the almonds into narrow slivers, halve and finely slice the cherries, and chop the sultanas and angelica. Mix all these ingredients in a bowl.

Heat the butter with the sugar in a pan over a medium heat, stirring gently until the butter has melted. Remove from the heat and beat in the sieved flour, cream and lemon juice. Stir in the fruit and nuts.

Place rounded teaspoons of the mixture, spaced at least 2in (50mm) apart, on the lined baking sheets. Bake in the centre of the preheated oven for 10-15 minutes until golden-brown. Take care not to overcook. Leave on the baking paper until quite cold, then carefully peel it away and place the Florentines upside down on a wire tray.

Break the chocolate into small pieces and melt them in a bowl over hot water. With a small palette knife or a dessert knife, spread a thin layer of melted chocolate on the smooth side of the biscuits. When half set, drag a fork across the chocolate in a zigzag pattern to give a combed effect. Leave to cool and set completely.

These biscuits are included in the menu on page 38.

CHOCOLATE CRUNCH

Crisp, and a little like flapjacks, these chocolate-coated squares are quickly mixed in a saucepan, and simple enough for children to make. The crunch will keep 2-3 days in an airtight tin.

PREPARATION TIME: *20 minutes*
COOKING TIME: *25-30 minutes*
OVEN TEMPERATURE: *preheat to 190°C (375°F, gas mark 5)*

INGREDIENTS – *makes 36:*
6 oz (175 g) butter
8 oz (225 g) golden granulated sugar or granulated sugar
5 oz (150 g) self-raising flour, sieved
1 oz (25 g) cocoa powder, sieved
4 oz (115 g) rolled oats
4 oz (115 g) unsweetened desiccated coconut
1 egg, beaten
5 oz (150 g) plain chocolate
1 tablespoon black coffee, or water

Grease a swiss roll tin 12in × 8in (300mm × 200mm).

Melt the butter in a large pan. Remove from the heat and mix in the sugar, sieved flour and cocoa, rolled oats, coconut and egg. Turn the mixture into the tin, and level.

Bake in the centre of the preheated oven for 25-30 minutes, until slightly springy at the centre. Cool in the tin.

When the crunch is almost cold, break the chocolate into pieces and melt with the coffee or water in a bowl over hot water. Pour it over the crunch. When half set, draw the prongs of a fork diagonally across it to make a pattern. When the crunch is cold, cut it into 36 squares.

CHOCOLATE TRIO Gingernuts coated with chocolate, and squares of chocolate crunch share a plate with glistening Florentines.

CHOCOLATE-COATED GINGERNUTS

Crunchy gingernuts are dipped in a chocolate and cream icing. As a variation they can be eaten plain, sandwiched with the icing, or dipped in melted chocolate. The gingernuts will keep for 3-4 days in an airtight tin without icing or filling.

PREPARATION TIME: *25 minutes*
COOKING TIME: *15-20 minutes*
OVEN TEMPERATURE: *preheat to 160°C (325°F, gas mark 3)*

INGREDIENTS – *makes 36:*
3 oz (75 g) butter or margarine
2 oz (50 g) golden syrup
2 oz (50 g) black treacle
1 egg, beaten
8 oz (225 g) self-raising flour
1 level teaspoon bicarbonate of soda
2 level teaspoons ground ginger
¼ teaspoon ground cinnamon
4 oz (115 g) muscovado sugar
4 oz (115 g) plain chocolate
2 tablespoons double cream

Grease two or three baking sheets.

Gently heat the butter with the golden syrup and treacle. Remove from the heat when the butter has melted. Stir in the beaten egg.

Sieve the flour, bicarbonate of soda, ground ginger and ground cinnamon into a bowl. Sieve the muscovado sugar through a coarse sieve or press out the lumps with a wooden spoon. Mix into the flour. Pour in the butter mixture and beat well for 1 minute.

Form rounded teaspoons of the mixture into balls, and flatten onto the baking sheets. Space them out well; they will spread to 2-3in (50-80mm) in diameter. The mixture should make about 36 biscuits.

Bake in the centre of the preheated oven for 15-20 minutes. Do not overcook, or the flavour will be lost. Cool on the baking sheet for a few minutes then transfer to a wire rack.

Break the chocolate into pieces and melt with the cream over hot water. Mix well, then spread the chocolate over the tops of the biscuits. Draw the prongs of a fork across the chocolate when half set, to make a pattern. Cool on the wire rack until set.

APPLE SAUCE CAKE

Streaks of sugar and spice run through this moist ring cake, which is made with cooked apple purée instead of the chopped raw apple usual in apple cakes. For special occasions, serve with cream. It is best served warm from the oven, but it will keep for 1-2 days in an airtight tin or in a plastic box in the refrigerator.

PREPARATION TIME: *25 minutes*
COOKING TIME: *45 minutes*
OVEN TEMPERATURE: *preheat to 200°C (400°F, gas mark 6)*

INGREDIENTS – *serves 6-8:*
4 oz (115 g) granulated sugar
1½ level teaspoons ground cinnamon
½ teaspoon ground mixed spice
6 oz (175 g) unsalted butter
12 oz (350 g) self-raising flour
1 egg
2 tablespoons milk
6 tablespoons apple purée (see method)

To make the apple purée, wash, peel and core about 8oz (225g) of apples. Cook over a gentle heat with a piece of lemon peel and 1-2 tablespoons of water until soft. Liquidise the apple pulp, or push it through a sieve. Sweeten to taste with sugar.

Grease an 8in (200mm) ring mould. In a small bowl, mix the sugar with the cinnamon and mixed spice.

Melt 2oz (50g) of the butter in a pan and keep warm, over a very low heat. Rub the remaining 4oz (115g) of butter into the flour until the mixture resembles breadcrumbs. Beat the egg with the milk and apple purée and add to the flour. Mix to a dough.

Take a dessertspoon of the dough, form into a ball, dip first in the melted butter and then in the spiced sugar mixture. Place in the base of the prepared mould and add nine more to complete the ring. Place a second row of ten balls of dough in the gaps in the first row.

Bake in the centre of the preheated oven for 45 minutes, until the cake is springy to the touch. Cool in the mould for 5 minutes then turn out onto a wooden board or flat plate to serve warm, or onto a wire rack to cool. Serve cut into slices.

PALMIERS

Feather-light palmiers, made with crisp and curving folds of puff pastry that open out during cooking to resemble a palm leaf, are a Parisian speciality. Without the cream filling suggested here, they are very good with ice creams and sorbets.

Vanilla sugar can easily be made by burying a vanilla pod in a sealed jar of caster sugar. The sugar will be flavoured after about a week. Keep topping up the jar as the sugar is used.

PREPARATION TIME: *20 minutes*
RESTING TIME: *10 minutes*
COOKING TIME: *15-20 minutes*
OVEN TEMPERATURE: *preheat to 230°C (450°F, gas mark 8)*

INGREDIENTS – *makes 10 sandwiched palmiers:*
13 oz (375 g) prepared weight puff pastry (page 394)
2 oz (50 g) vanilla sugar or caster sugar
Cold water
¼ pint (150 ml) whipping cream

Grease two or three baking sheets.

Dust a work surface or pastry board with some of the sugar. Roll out the pastry to make a rectangle 13in × 7in (330mm ×

180mm). Sprinkle a thin layer of sugar over the pastry.

Fold the shorter sides of the pastry to the centre, and press down gently with the rolling pin. Sprinkle with more sugar and fold the folded edges to the centre. Dust on a little more sugar and fold the two halves together to make eight layers of pastry.

Use a very sharp knife to cut the folded pastry across into 20 even slices. Brush both sides of each slice with cold water, and dust with sugar. Lay the pastry slices on the baking sheets, cut side down. They will double in

PARISIAN PALMIERS For all their simplicity, palmiers sandwiched with whipped cream make a luxurious coffee-time treat.

size during cooking. Rest them in the refrigerator for 10 minutes.

Bake the pastries in the centre of the preheated oven for 15-20 minutes. Cool on the baking sheets for 2 minutes, then transfer carefully to a wire rack using a spatula.

Whip the cream until stiff. Sandwich pairs of palmiers with the cream.

HUNGARIAN RAISIN CHEESECAKE

Old English recipes and those from central Europe show that, originally, cheesecake was always baked, rather than set with gelatine. This baked cheesecake from Hungary, with a pastry base, is best made a day ahead and then stored in a cool place to allow the flavour to develop. It will keep 4-5 days stored in an airtight plastic box in the refrigerator.

A springform cake tin, with a removable base and opening side, makes it easier to remove the cheesecake without it break-ing, but an ordinary loose-based tin can be used instead.

PREPARATION TIME: *30 minutes*
COOKING TIME: *1 1/2-2 hours*
OVEN TEMPERATURE: *preheat to 200°C (400°F, gas mark 6)*

INGREDIENTS – *serves 8:*
FILLING
4 oz (115 g) seedless raisins
4 tablespoons dark rum
1 lb (450 g) curd cheese
1/4 pint (150 ml) double cream
4 oz (115 g) caster sugar
1/2 teaspoon vanilla essence
1 1/2 oz (40 g) cornflour
2 oz (50 g) candied peel, chopped
3 eggs, separated
PASTRY
2 oz (50 g) plain white flour
2 oz (50 g) wholemeal flour
2 oz (50 g) unsalted butter
1/4 teaspoon ground cinnamon
1 oz (25 g) demerara sugar
Cold water to mix

Mix the raisins with the rum and leave to soften.

Grease an 8in (200mm) springform cake tin, or a loose-based tin, and line the base.

To make the pastry, mix to-gether the white flour and wholemeal flour in a bowl. Rub in the butter until the mixture resembles fine breadcrumbs, then stir in the cinnamon and sugar. Mix to a dough with cold water. If you have time, wrap the pastry in greaseproof paper or kitchen foil and chill for 30 minutes.

Roll out the pastry to fit the base of the prepared tin. Prick lightly with a fork, and bake in the preheated oven for 15-20 minutes until starting to colour. Remove from the oven and leave to cool. Lower the oven tem-perature to 150°C (300°F, gas mark 2).

Mix the curd cheese with the cream, sugar, vanilla essence, cornflour, candied peel, raisins, rum and egg yolks.

Whisk the egg whites until soft and fold them into the cheese mixture. Turn into the cake tin on top of the pastry base and bake in the preheated oven for 1 1/4-1 1/2 hours or until the filling is set. Test with a needle, or by prodding with your finger. The cheesecake will rise during cooking and fall again during cooling, this is normal.

Allow the cake to cool in the tin. Run a knife around the fill-ing, unclip the tin and slide the cheesecake onto a flat wooden board or plate for serving.

M E N U

Austrian Coffee Party for Eight to Ten

CHOCOLATE CREAM TORTE
this page

KUGELHOPF *page 44*

CHERRY STRUDEL
page 45

VIENNESE BISCUITS
page 44

IN ADVANCE Make the bis-cuits 2-3 days in advance. Make the torte the day before. The evening before, prepare the kugelhopf dough and leave it in the refrigerator to rise. Halve and stone the cherries for the strudel filling.
ON THE DAY Allow about 3 hours. Put the kugelhopf dough in its tin to rise, and prepare the strudel. Cook the kugelhopf, then lower the oven temperature and cook the strudel.
TO DRINK Coffee. The Vien-nese drink their coffee strong and black, or serve it with whipped cream.

CHOCOLATE CREAM TORTE

A torte is a layer cake, usually with a rich filling. There are many varieties made all over central and eastern Europe. This chocolate torte is Austrian.

The chocolate cake is very delicate. It is best made in a springform cake tin, but a loose-based tin can be used instead.

The torte can be made the day before the coffee party and kept in the refrigerator.

PREPARATION TIME: *1-1 1/2 hours*
COOKING TIME: *2-2 1/2 hours*
CHILLING TIME: *1 hour*
OVEN TEMPERATURE: *preheat to 180°C (350°F, gas mark 4)*

INGREDIENTS – *serves 12:*
CAKE
2 oz (50 g) plain chocolate
4 eggs
4 oz (115 g) caster sugar
2 oz (50 g) plain flour
1 1/2 oz (40 g) cocoa powder
MERINGUE
3 egg whites
5 oz (150 g) caster sugar
1 level tablespoon cocoa powder
3 oz (75 g) hazelnuts, finely ground
Non-stick baking paper
CHOCOLATE CREAM
8 oz (225 g) plain dessert chocolate
5 tablespoons water
1 pint (570 ml) double cream
12 chocolate leaves OR 6 plain chocolate thins, each cut in half diagonally OR chocolate caraque (page 289)

Grease an 8in (200mm) spring-form cake tin, line the base and then lightly flour the tin.

To make the cake, break the chocolate into small pieces and melt them in a bowl over hot water.

Whisk the eggs and sugar until light and foamy and the whisk leaves a trail across the surface of the mixture. Fold in the melted chocolate with a metal spoon.

Sieve the flour and cocoa together and fold gently into the egg and chocolate mixture. Turn the mixture into the prepared cake tin. Bake in the centre of the preheated oven for 25-30 minutes until it is springy to the touch. Cool the cake in the tin for 2 minutes then turn it out onto a wire rack. Lower the oven temperature to 110°C (225°F, gas mark 1/4).

Draw two circles, 8in (200mm) across, on non-stick baking paper using the base of the cake tin as a guide. Place each piece of marked paper on a baking sheet.

Whisk the egg whites until stiff but not dry. Add half the sugar and continue whisking until the meringue stands in soft peaks. Sieve the cocoa, mix it with the remaining sugar and the ground hazelnuts, then fold into the egg white.

Spoon the mixture into a large piping bag fitted with a 1/2in (15mm) plain nozzle. Pipe a ring of meringue just inside each of the drawn circles. Fill in the circles with a spiral of piped meringue. Alternatively, spoon meringue onto the circles.

Bake in the centre of the preheated oven for 1¾ hours. Cool on the baking sheet, then peel off the baking papers.

Cut the cooled chocolate cake into two layers.

To make the icing, break the chocolate into pieces and melt, with the water, in a bowl set over simmering water. Stir gently if necessary. Remove from the heat and cool a little.

Whisk the cream until it will just stand in peaks. Gradually mix in the melted chocolate.

Place a layer of meringue on a flat cake plate and cover with some of the chocolate cream. Place one layer of cake on top, and cover with cream. Repeat with the other layers of cake and meringue. Spread the remaining cream over the top and sides of the cake.

Arrange the chocolate leaves or chocolate triangles evenly around the top of the cake or cover the top of the cake with chocolate caraque and dust lightly with icing sugar. Chill the torte for 1 hour before serving. This cake is included in the menu on the opposite page.

AUSTRIAN MORNING A ladies' coffee party is a main element in the Austrian social round. For this party the chocolate torte, decorated with simply made chocolate caraque, is served with kugelhopf made in its traditional tin, cherry strudel, and buttery little Viennese biscuits.

VIENNESE BISCUITS

Coffee has been used to flavour these small, piped melting biscuits. To make plain biscuits, simply leave out the coffee essence. Alternatively, for orange-flavoured biscuits, replace the coffee essence with the finely grated rind of half an orange. It is important to use unsalted butter or the subtle flavour will be lost. The biscuits will keep for 5-7 days in an airtight tin.

PREPARATION TIME: *20 minutes*
CHILLING TIME: *1 hour*
COOKING TIME: *10-12 minutes*
OVEN TEMPERATURE: *preheat to 180°C (350°F, gas mark 4)*

INGREDIENTS – *makes 32:*
4 oz (115 g) unsalted butter, softened
1 oz (25 g) icing sugar, sieved
1½ teaspoons coffee essence
3 oz (75 g) plain flour
1 oz (25 g) cornflour
Flaked almonds or walnut pieces
A little icing sugar (optional)

Grease two baking sheets well.

Cream the butter with the sieved icing sugar and the coffee essence until light and fluffy.

Sieve the flour and the cornflour together. Work into the butter mixture and beat until very soft and smooth.

Spoon the mixture into a piping bag fitted with a ½in (15mm) star nozzle. Pipe 32 round biscuits, about 1-1½in (25-40mm) across, onto the prepared baking sheets. Allow room for them to spread a little.

Place a flaked almond or small piece of walnut in the centre of each biscuit. Chill the biscuits for an hour.

Bake in the centre of the preheated oven for 10-12 minutes.

Cool for 2 minutes, then transfer to a wire rack. When cool, the biscuits can be dusted lightly with icing sugar. These biscuits are included in a menu on page 42.

BUTTERY MORSELS These little biscuits, flavoured with coffee, melt in the mouth.

KUGELHOPF

This light, moulded yeast cake originated in Austria, but it is said to have been popularised in France by Marie Antoinette who was very fond of kugelhopf. It is normally baked in a special, fluted, kugelhopf mould, but other deep ring moulds will do almost as well (see method). Kugelhopf is best served warm, to give the full effect of its yeasty aroma.

PREPARATION TIME: *35 minutes*
RISING TIME: *2-3 hours*
COOKING TIME: *30-40 minutes*
OVEN TEMPERATURE: *preheat to 200°C (400°F, gas mark 6)*

INGREDIENTS – *serves 6-8:*
½ oz (15 g) fresh yeast OR
2 level teaspoons dried yeast
OR ½ sachet easy-blend dried yeast
2 fl oz (50 ml) warm water
4 oz (115 g) butter
1 oz (25 g) caster sugar
8 oz (225 g) plain flour
½ teaspoon salt
3 eggs, beaten
A few drops vanilla essence
2 oz (50 g) currants
Finely grated rind of ½ lemon
Butter, for greasing tin
1 oz (25 g) almonds, blanched and cut into slivers
A little icing sugar

Cream the fresh yeast with a little of the caster sugar and mix with the warm water. If using dried yeast, dissolve the sugar in the water then sprinkle the yeast on top. Set aside in a warm place for 10 minutes until frothy. If using easy-blend yeast, follow the instructions on the packet.

Melt the butter in a pan with the sugar over a medium heat, until the sugar has dissolved. Sieve the flour and salt into a bowl. Add the yeast mixture, butter and sugar, eggs, vanilla essence, currants and lemon rind and mix them well together for 2 minutes.

Place the bowl in a large plastic bag and leave in a warm place for 1-2 hours until the mixture has doubled in volume.

Generously butter the inside of an 8in (200mm) kugelhopf mould, or a deep ring mould of similar volume. An 8½-9in (215-230mm) ring mould needs to be about 3in (80mm) deep. Sprinkle two-thirds of the almonds over the butter.

Stir the mixture once, then turn it into the mould. Sprinkle the remaining almonds on top. Place inside a large plastic bag and leave in a warm place for the mixture to rise until almost level with the rim of the mould. This should take about 40 minutes in a warm kitchen.

Bake in the centre of the preheated oven for 30-40 minutes until golden-brown and just starting to shrink from the mould. Turn out onto a wire rack to cool.

Just before serving, warm the kugelhopf in a low oven, and dust it lightly with sieved icing sugar. This cake is included in a menu on page 42.

CHERRY STRUDEL

Austrian cherry strudel is made from paper-thin strudel pastry, which is not complicated but takes some practice to make perfectly. To make an apple strudel, simply replace the cherries with diced cooking apple. If using tinned cherries for this recipe rather than fresh, use 2oz (50g) demerara sugar rather than 3oz (75g).

Strudel is best served warm from the oven, but it can be made a few hours in advance and served cold or reheated for serving.

PREPARATION TIME: *50 minutes*
COOKING TIME: *35-40 minutes*
OVEN TEMPERATURE: *preheat to 180°C (350°F, gas mark 4)*

INGREDIENTS — *serves 6-8:*
STRUDEL PASTRY
8 oz (225 g) strong white flour
Pinch of salt
1 egg, beaten
4 fl oz (115 ml) warm water
1 oz (25 g) butter, melted
FILLING
1 lb (450 g) fresh cherries OR
   2 × 15 oz (425 g) tins cherries, well drained
2 oz (50 g) breadcrumbs
4 oz (115 g) butter
2 oz (50 g) toasted hazelnuts, chopped
2 oz (50 g) sultanas
3 oz (75 g) demerara sugar
1 level tablespoon ground cinnamon
1-2 level tablespoons icing sugar
Non-stick baking paper

To make the pastry, sieve the flour and salt into a bowl. Add the egg, almost all the water, and the melted butter. Mix well to make a soft dough. Add more water if the dough seems too stiff. Shape into a ball.

Knead the dough on a well-floured board for 2 minutes. Cover the dough with an up-turned, warmed bowl and leave to rest for about 30 minutes.

Meanwhile, prepare the filling. Halve the cherries and remove the stones. Put the cherry halves in a bowl. Fry the breadcrumbs in half the butter until crisp, then add them to the cherries. Mix in the hazelnuts, sultanas, demerara sugar and cinnamon. Melt the remaining butter and set it aside.

Cover a table with a clean cloth – the dough will roll out to 2 rectangles, each measuring at least 12in × 15in (300mm × 380mm). Sprinkle the cloth evenly with flour. Cut the dough in half, and roll out each piece to make a rectangle as large and as thin as you can. Keep the cloth well floured. Do not worry if some holes appear in the dough. They can be patched later.

Trim the edges with scissors or a sharp knife, and use the trimmings to repair any holes.

Brush both pieces of rolled-out dough with some of the melted butter. Divide the cherry mixture between them. Spoon it down the centre of each rectangle then spread it all over the dough leaving a margin of 1-2in (25-50mm) on all sides. Carefully fold over the two long edges and one of the short edges. Then lift the edge of the cloth and roll up the dough like a swiss roll, enclosing the filling as you do so. Seal the edge with a little water. Roll each sausage onto a sheet of non-stick baking paper and transfer, still on the paper, to a baking sheet.

Brush the strudel with the remaining melted butter. Bake

TRANSPARENT STRUDEL By tradition, strudel dough should be thin enough to read a love letter through, but a strongly patterned cloth works just as well.

in the centre of the preheated oven for 35-40 minutes until the pastry is golden-brown.

Cool on the baking sheet for 5 minutes, then dust generously with sieved icing sugar and cut each strudel into three or four pieces. Transfer to a hot plate and serve. Whipped cream is a traditional accompaniment. The strudel is included in a menu on page 42.

LEBKUCHEN

Lebkuchen means literally, in German, 'cake of life'. It is a speciality of Nuremberg in West Germany, where the gingerbread house of Hansel and Gretel is known as a Lebkuchen house. Lebkuchen is traditionally baked in Germany at Christmas.

Lebkuchen will keep for 6-8 weeks in an airtight tin.

PREPARATION TIME: *30 minutes*
COOKING TIME: *15-20 minutes*
OVEN TEMPERATURE: *preheat to 180°C (350°F, gas mark 4)*

INGREDIENTS – *makes 24:*
2 in (50 mm) piece of cinnamon
    stick
6 whole cloves
4 cardamom pods
1 finger of mace
4 oz (115 g) blanched almonds,
    finely chopped
2 oz (50 g) candied lemon peel,
    finely diced, or chopped mixed
    peel
Grated rind of ½ lemon
2 large eggs
4 oz (115 g) caster sugar
A few drops vanilla essence
5 oz (150 g) plain flour
½ teaspoon baking powder
Rice paper
ICING
½ egg white
3 oz (75 g) icing sugar, sieved
A few drops white rum, or fruit
    liqueur

Using a pestle and mortar, or an electric coffee grinder, grind the cinnamon, cloves, the black seeds from the cardamom pods, and the mace until fine. Turn the powder into a bowl and stir in the almonds, candied peel and lemon rind.

Whisk the eggs with the sugar until foamy and the whisk leaves a trail across the surface of the mixture.

Sieve the flour with the baking powder, and fold it into the egg mixture with the vanilla essence and the spice mixture.

Place a sheet of rice paper on each of three baking trays. Space level dessertspoons of the mixture, eight to a tray, on the rice paper. Bake in the centre of the preheated oven for 15-20 minutes until golden.

Leave to cool for a few minutes. Remove the lebkuchen to a wire rack and break away the surplus rice paper, leaving a disc under each biscuit.

Lightly whisk the egg white. Mix in the sieved icing sugar, stirring until smooth, and flavour with the rum or liqueur. Brush the icing over the lebkuchen. Leave in a warm place to dry. As a variation, some of the lebkuchen can be coated with melted chocolate.

'CAKE OF LIFE' Sweet and spicy German lebkuchen appear in many different shapes and sizes, but most often as small iced cakes.

MENU

Fund-Raising
Coffee
Morning for
12 to 16

HOT CINNAMON RING
page 48

PASSION CAKE
page 48

BAKLAVA *this page*

BUTTERSCOTCH COOKIES
WITH DATE FILLING
opposite page

Make two rings and twice the quantity of baklava.

IN ADVANCE Make the baklava, the dough for the cinnamon ring, and the cookie dough the day before. Make the cake the day before, but do not ice it.

ON THE DAY Allow at least 2 hours to complete the preparations. Bake the cookies, then ice the cake while they are cooling. Put the rings into the oven about 45 minutes before the guests are due to arrive. Once cooked, cover them with kitchen foil and leave them in a very low oven until needed.

TO DRINK Coffee.

BAKLAVA

Baklava is made from phyllo pastry, a fine, paper-thin dough that can be bought ready-made from delicatessens. Rose water or orange-flower water can be bought from chemists.

Baklava will keep 2-3 days in a plastic box in the refrigerator.

PREPARATION TIME: *25 minutes*
COOKING TIME: *25-30 minutes*
OVEN TEMPERATURE: *preheat to 180°C (350°F, gas mark 4)*

INGREDIENTS – *makes 16:*
2 oz (50 g) hazelnuts, blanched
    and chopped
3 oz (75 g) almonds, blanched
    and chopped
3 oz (75 g) golden granulated
    sugar or granulated sugar
1 level teaspoon ground cinnamon
4 oz (115 g) phyllo pastry
2½ oz (65 g) unsalted butter,
    melted
SYRUP
5 oz (150 g) golden granulated
    sugar or granulated sugar
1 tablespoon lemon juice
1 tablespoon water
Strip of lemon peel
2 in (50 mm) piece of cinnamon
    stick
1 teaspoon rose water or orange-
    flower water

Mix the hazelnuts, almonds, sugar and ground cinnamon.

Cut the pastry to fit a baking tray about 11in × 8in (280mm × 200mm). You will have about 10 sheets. Keep the pastry covered with a damp cloth.

Brush the baking tray with melted butter. Lay a sheet of pastry over the buttered tray, brush its top with more melted butter and repeat with 3 more sheets. Spread half the nut mixture over the pastry.

Brush 2 more sheets of pastry with melted butter, and place on top of the nut mixture. Spread the remainder of the nut mixture over the pastry. Brush the remaining sheets of pastry with butter and place on top of the nut mixture.

Press down the edges all round to seal. With a sharp knife, mark the top layer of pastry into about 16 diamonds.

Bake in the centre of a pre-heated oven for about 25-30 minutes until golden-brown.

Dissolve the sugar in the lemon juice and water, over low heat. Bring to the boil, add the lemon peel and cinnamon and simmer for 2 minutes. Remove from the heat. Reheat just before using.

As soon as the baklava is cooked, remove the lemon peel and cinnamon from the lemon syrup, and pour the hot syrup over the pastry. Leave to cool.

Sprinkle the baklava with the rose water or orange-flower water and cut into diamond-shaped pastries. Baklava is included in the menu on the opposite page.

MIDDLE-EASTERN BAKLAVA These layers of pastry and nuts soaked in syrup originated in Turkey.

BUTTERSCOTCH COOKIES WITH DATE FILLING

The dough for these cookies will store, wrapped, in the refrigerator for up to a fortnight, so that cookies can be cut off and baked when needed. Eat them on the day they are cooked.

PREPARATION TIME: *30 minutes plus cooling time*
CHILLING TIME: *1-2 hours*
COOKING TIME: *15 minutes*
OVEN TEMPERATURE: *preheat to 180°C (350°F, gas mark 4)*

INGREDIENTS – *makes 24-30 large cookies or about 100 small cookies:*
6 oz (175 g) butter
1 tablespoon golden syrup
5 oz (150 g) dark muscovado sugar
1 egg, beaten
A few drops vanilla essence
10 oz (275 g) plain flour
1 level teaspoon baking powder
DATE FILLING
8 oz (225 g) stoned dates
Finely grated rind of ¹/₂ lemon
Juice of 1 lemon, strained
4-6 tablespoons water
1 level teaspoon cornflour
A little muscovado sugar

Cream the butter with the golden syrup in a warmed bowl until soft. Push the sugar through a coarse sieve, or break up the lumps with a wooden spoon. Gradually beat it into the mixture, followed by the beaten egg and the vanilla essence. Sieve the flour with the baking powder. Stir the flour into the mixture working it in until a soft dough results.

Turn the mixture onto a floured work surface or pastry board. For large cookies, divide the mixture in two. Roll each half into a sausage shape about 2in (50mm) across. For small cookies, divide the mixture into 4 pieces and roll each piece into a sausage about 1in (25mm) across. Wrap in greaseproof paper and chill for 1-2 hours or until needed. In hot weather it is often a good idea to half freeze the dough (for 30-60 minutes) so that it cuts evenly.

Grease three large baking sheets. Use a sharp knife to cut the dough into slices ¹/₈-¹/₄in (3-5mm) thick. Place them on the greased baking sheets, with room to spread by about half as much again. Bake in the pre-heated oven for 15 minutes for large cookies or 10-12 minutes for small cookies, or until just changing colour at the edge. Cool on the baking sheet for 2 minutes then transfer to a wire rack using a spatula.

Chop the dates, and heat gently in a pan with the lemon rind, lemon juice, water and cornflour. Cook, stirring, over very low heat until soft and spreadable. Sweeten to taste with muscovado sugar, then leave to cool. Sandwich the cookies with the date filling.

These biscuits are included in the menu on the opposite page.

INSIDE AND OUT Walnuts decorate the top of passion cake and run in a spiced spiral through the centre of hot cinnamon ring.

PASSION CAKE

The sweetness of carrots has been used in cakes since Roman times. Passion cake is one of the best carrot cakes: deliciously moist and gently spiced, filled and frosted with a tangy cream-cheese mixture. The cake will keep in the refrigerator for 2-3 days, but it is best to ice it on the day it is to be served.

PREPARATION TIME: *40 minutes*
SETTING TIME: *1 hour*
COOKING TIME: *1 hour*
OVEN TEMPERATURE: *preheat to 180°C (350°F, gas mark 4)*

INGREDIENTS – *makes one 8 in (200 mm) cake:*
5 oz (150 g) butter
7 oz (200 g) soft brown sugar
8 oz (225 g) finely grated carrots
2 eggs
7 oz (200 g) self-raising flour
3 level teaspoons baking powder
1 level teaspoon ground cinnamon
1/2 teaspoon ground nutmeg
1/2 teaspoon salt
4 oz (115 g) seedless raisins
2 oz (50 g) chopped walnuts
3 tablespoons milk
FROSTING
8 oz (225 g) cream cheese
4 teaspoons lemon juice
1 1/2 oz (40 g) icing sugar
1/4 teaspoon vanilla essence
Walnut halves to decorate

Grease an 8in (200mm) round cake tin, and line the base.

Melt the butter in a bowl over a pan of hot water and beat in the soft brown sugar, grated carrot and eggs. Sieve together the flour, baking powder, cinnamon, nutmeg and salt. Fold evenly into the mixture with the raisins, walnuts and milk.

Turn the mixture into the prepared tin, and level.

Bake in the centre of the oven for about an hour until the cake is springy to the touch and a fine skewer inserted into the centre comes out clean.

Cool in the tin for 5 minutes then turn out onto a wire rack. When cold, cut into two layers.

Beat the cream cheese with the lemon juice, sieved icing sugar and vanilla essence.

Sandwich the two layers of the cake with half the frosting and spread the rest over the top. Use a knife to make a swirled pattern in the frosting, and decorate with a few walnut halves. Leave in a warm room for an hour to set. This cake is included in the menu on page 46.

HOT CINNAMON RING

Rich, yeast breads such as this cinnamon ring are traditionally served with coffee on the Continent. The loaf glistens with honey and chopped nuts, and each slice has a spiral of spiced nuts running through it. The dough can be prepared a day ahead and kept, covered, in the refrigerator. Bring it up to room temperature before baking. A cinnamon ring tastes best served warm, fresh from the oven.

PREPARATION TIME: *25 minutes*
RISING TIME: *2-3 hours*
COOKING TIME: *25-30 minutes*
OVEN TEMPERATURE: *preheat to 200°C (400°F, gas mark 6)*

INGREDIENTS – *serves 6-8:*
2 level teaspoons dried yeast OR 1/2 oz (15 g) fresh yeast OR 1/2 sachet easy-blend dried yeast
2 1/2 fl oz (75 ml) warm water
2 oz (50 g) butter
2 oz (50 g) caster sugar
8 oz (225 g) plain flour
Pinch of salt
1 egg, beaten
FILLING
3 oz (75 g) walnuts, roughly chopped
3 oz (75 g) dark, soft brown sugar
1 1/2 level teaspoons ground cinnamon
2 oz (50 g) butter, melted
TOPPING
2 tablespoons honey, warmed
1/2 teaspoon ground cinnamon
1 oz (25 g) walnuts, roughly chopped

Sprinkle the dried yeast into the water, or if using fresh yeast, cream it with the water. Set aside in a warm place for 10 minutes until frothy. If using easy-blend dried yeast, follow the instructions on the packet.

Melt the butter with the caster sugar over low heat until the sugar has dissolved. Sieve the flour and salt together into a large mixing bowl.

Mix the yeast and butter mixtures and the egg into the flour. Beat the dough for 2 minutes with a wooden spoon.

Cover the bowl with a large plastic bag and leave in a warm place for 1-2 hours until the dough has doubled in volume. Push down the surface of the dough, cover again and leave for a further 30 minutes.

Meanwhile, mix the walnuts, sugar, cinnamon and melted butter together. Butter an 8in (200mm) ring tin generously.

Turn the dough onto a floured work surface or pastry board and knead lightly for 1 minute. Roll out to a rectangle 12in × 8in (300mm × 200mm). Spread the filling evenly over the dough, leaving a small margin on one long side. Roll up the dough like a sausage, starting from the other long side. Place in the prepared tin, and pinch the ends of the roll together firmly.

Leave the tin in a warm place for about 30 minutes or until the dough reaches two-thirds of the way up the tin.

Bake in the centre of the preheated oven for 25-30 minutes when the mixture will be shrinking slightly from the sides of the tin.

Turn out onto a wire rack. Mix the honey with the cinnamon and brush over the hot cake. Sprinkle the chopped walnuts on top and serve, while still hot, cut into slices. This ring is included in the menu on page 46.

PANFORTE DI SIENA

This rich, spicy cake, full of nuts and candied fruit, has a chewy consistency similar to nougat. It is a speciality of Siena in Italy, where it is traditionally baked at Christmas. Pieces of candied orange peel, which have a better flavour than chopped mixed peel, can be found in some delicatessens. Candied papaya (papaw) is sold in some health food shops and Chinese supermarkets. Alternatively, use other crystallised fruit.

Panforte will keep in an airtight tin for up to 3 weeks.

PREPARATION TIME: *40 minutes*
COOKING TIME: *35 minutes*
OVEN TEMPERATURE: *preheat to 160°C (325°F, gas mark 3)*

INGREDIENTS – *makes one 8 in (200 mm) cake:*
4 oz (115 g) whole unblanched almonds
2 oz (50 g) walnuts, roughly chopped
4 oz (115 g) candied orange peel, finely diced, or mixed peel
3 oz (75 g) candied papaya (papaw), finely chopped
3 oz (75 g) candied pineapple, finely chopped
1½ oz (40 g) plain flour
1 level teaspoon ground cinnamon
¼ teaspoon ground cloves
¼ teaspoon ground nutmeg
¼ teaspoon ground coriander
6 oz (175 g) caster sugar
4 tablespoons cold water
Rice paper
1-2 oz (25-50 g) icing sugar

Grease an 8in (200mm) loose-based metal flan tin. Cut the rice paper to fit the base of the tin.

In a mixing bowl combine the almonds, walnuts, orange peel, papaya, pineapple, flour and spices.

Dissolve the sugar in the water over low heat. Raise the heat and boil the syrup for about 3 minutes until it reaches 105°C (220°F) or the short-thread stage – when a little of the syrup (cooled in a teaspoon first) forms a short thread when it is pressed between finger and thumb then pulled out.

Pour the syrup onto the other ingredients and stir well. Turn the mixture into the prepared tin and press down level.

Bake in the centre of the preheated oven for 35 minutes (the cake is not meant to brown). Remove the cake from the oven. It will still be quite soft at this stage, but it firms as it cools. Leave the cake in the tin for a couple of minutes then loosen the edge with a knife and remove the ring. Leave to cool on the base.

When quite cold, remove the cake from the tin base and place on a flat serving dish. Dredge the top of the cake with sieved icing sugar.

SIENESE SPECIALITY A mix of cinnamon, cloves, nutmeg and coriander gives panforte its distinctive flavour. Nuts and candied fruit make the cake rich and sweet, so serve it in small portions.

COFFEE

The coffee plant is native to Africa, but coffee is now cultivated in about 40 countries. The finest quality coffee beans are produced by the species *Coffea arabica*. The other main species, *Coffea robusta*, is less aromatic and is used primarily for commercially blended and instant brands of coffee.

Listed below are some of the main varieties of coffee.

BRAZILIAN The variety *Bourbon Santos* has a smooth, mild, slightly sweet flavour.

COLOMBIAN Rich with a heady aroma and vaguely nutty flavour.

COSTA RICAN A fine, mild flavour, popular for breakfast.

CUBAN Sweet and mellow with a good 'round' flavour.

JAMAICAN The variety *Blue Mountain* has a mellow, sweet flavour, popular for breakfast.

JAVANESE The best Java coffee is rich with a fine acidity.

KENYAN Tart and aromatic with a relatively mild flavour.

MOCHA A coffee from Yemen. Distinctly acid and 'winy'.

PUERTO RICAN Rich and sweet.

Roasting develops the flavour of coffee. Pale roast coffee is good with milk; medium roast is an all-purpose, stronger richer coffee and dark (continental) roast is most often drunk black.

The best way to determine which coffee or blend of coffees you like best is to experiment with small amounts of different types. A shop specialising in coffee will be able to advise you.

Buying and storing coffee

The best results are obtained by buying coffee beans and grinding them yourself just before brewing the coffee. Ground coffee loses its flavour very quickly.

The accuracy of the grind is important; if coffee is ground too coarsely, the water filters through too quickly to pick up enough flavour; if coffee is too fine, water filters through too slowly and retains small particles that form a sediment in the cup. Take account of the way the coffee is to be made when grinding coffee or buying it ready-ground – see below.

Coffee beans can be kept in the freezer for up to four months. The beans can be ground and made into coffee while still frozen. Alternatively, keep the beans in an airtight glass jar. Store ground coffee in an airtight glass jar in the refrigerator and use within a week for the best flavour.

Making coffee

Coffee-making methods vary, but two rules apply regardless of the method. Always use freshly drawn water. Make strong coffee rather than weak. It can always be diluted to taste with milk or boiling water. For coffee of average-strength, allow 2 rounded teaspoons of coffee for every 6fl oz (175ml) of water.

One of the simplest and most successful ways of brewing coffee is to use a china jug. Warm it with boiling water. Tip out the water then put in medium ground coffee. Pour on boiling water and stir once. Cover and leave to infuse for 5 minutes. Pour into the cups through a tea strainer.

COFFEE MAKERS There are many different special coffee makers.

The plunge filter coffee maker (cafetière) is essentially a jug with a plunger to hold back the coffee grounds. With filter coffee makers water is poured through coffee contained in a paper filter – electric machines do this automatically. Vacuum (cona) coffee makers, the non-electric espresso coffee makers and electric percolators operate by forcing water up through the ground coffee. With the vacuum coffee maker and the percolator, however, the coffee can recirculate. This can make it too strong for some tastes. Electric espresso machines make the strong Italian espresso coffee automatically.

Some of the electric coffee machines include hot plates.

Use fine ground coffee for paper filter coffee makers; medium-fine ground coffee for automatic filter machines, the vacuum coffee maker and the espresso makers; and medium ground coffee for the plunge filter coffee maker and the electric percolator.

ICED COFFEE Brew a jug of double-strength coffee and chill. Fill tall glasses with ice cubes. Pour the chilled coffee over the ice. The iced coffee can be mixed with cream, sugar or vanilla ice cream to taste.

CHINA COFFEE JUG

PLUNGE FILTER COFFEE MAKER

FILTER COFFEE MAKER

FILTER COFFEE MACHINE

VACUUM COFFEE MAKER

ESPRESSO COFFEE MAKER

ELECTRIC PERCOLATOR

ESPRESSO COFFEE MACHINE

Lunch, Dinner & Supper

OF ALL OCCASIONS, lunches and suppers are the most difficult to define. It was not always so. About the time that the Spanish Armada set sail, the English day was divided by breakfast — more or less at dawn — dinner, the main meal of the day, in the early afternoon, and supper. In between times, the peckish would indulge in 'a lumpe, a gobbet, a luncheon', most likely of bread and cheese, which might be consumed at any hour.

Not until much later, probably when the breadwinner was prevented by time and distance from attending dinner, was luncheon fixed at midday. In the 1860s, 'in families where there is a nursery', Mrs Beeton thought this was a good opportunity for mothers and children to get together over 'remains of cold joints, nicely garnished, poultry, game, a few sweets', while the hard-working fathers were no doubt 'lunching' at chop houses or City taverns. She suggests a similar modest menu for suppers, except in the case of a ball supper for 70 or 80 persons, a staggering board of hot and cold dishes and puddings that would be equally suitable, she says, for a wedding or christening breakfast.

On the whole, lunches and suppers remain informal, easy-going affairs, 'working lunches' and 'after-theatre suppers', for example. But what about such formal occasions as Literary Lunches, and the fashion for calling even the most elaborate evening meal 'supper', or the many people who, historically correct, still refer to the midday meal as dinner? Definition in either case is difficult, though Lord Curzon (1859-1925), Viceroy of India and arbiter of taste, did his best. 'No gentleman,' he said firmly, 'has soup at luncheon.'

Planning & Preparation

Everyday meals are in many ways more challenging than the formal dinner parties which people often find daunting. Catering every day for the same people, the cook needs to provide interesting, well-balanced and nutritious meals, often on a limited budget and usually with a restriction on time. A dinner party may be extravagant and time-consuming, but it is a one-off occasion.

Planning ahead

Plan a whole week's menus in one go, rather than thinking just a day or two ahead.

You will be able to save time and money by making one major shopping trip a week and may be able to buy in bulk, taking advantage of economy packs. Only small amounts of fresh fruit and vegetables and other perishable foods will have to be bought during the week.

Reviewing your list of menus you will be able to check that you have included plenty of fresh fruit and vegetables and nutritious foods, such as fish, liver, pulses, eggs and cheese, which need not be eaten every day as long as some are taken each week.

Take account of any likely leftovers in your menus to avoid unnecessary waste and expense. As long as leftover foods are combined with ingredients that are fresh, they will not be lacking in nutritional value. Make sure that leftovers look and taste different when served again and that they have been thoroughly reheated.

Cooking in advance

Many dishes can be prepared or cooked completely at least a day in advance. Casseroles often improve in flavour with standing. Allow dishes to cool completely then store them, covered, in the refrigerator. An average-sized casserole at room temperature will take about 40 minutes at 180°C (350°F, gas mark 4) to become piping hot. A dish that has come straight out of the refrigerator or one that is more solid – lasagne, for example – will take 10-20 minutes longer to reheat. The more dishes in the oven the longer they will take to reheat.

Using the freezer

If you can, it is a good idea occasionally to devote a day or part of a day to cooking in bulk for the freezer. This is the most economical way to use the cooker and will also save you having to cook meals on busy days. Alternatively, make a double quantity of a dish you are serving and freeze half of it. Freeze some dishes in single portions for members of the family who occasionally have to eat at odd times. Most frozen dishes take an hour or less to reheat from frozen; in a microwave oven they can be reheated in minutes. The *Menu planner* (pages 407-417) indicates which dishes are suitable for freezing.

Healthy eating

Everyday meals should comprise a healthy balance of nutrients. Aim to include plenty of fibre in your diet (which speeds up the digestive process and reduces the likelihood of bowel disease) and reduce the amount of salt, sugar and fat.

● Use as many fresh ingredients as possible.

● Follow the seasons, especially with fish, fruit and vegetables. This is one of the simplest ways to make sure that there is enough variety in your diet.

● Make it a habit to serve raw salads as well as, or instead of, hot vegetable dishes, and fresh fruit instead of cooked puddings. Raw food provides more nutrients than cooked food.

● Keep tins, packets and convenience foods to a minimum to avoid artificial preservatives, additives and colourings which have been shown to cause some allergies.

● Raw fruits and vegetables, whole grains, cereals, wholemeal bread, pulses, nuts and seeds are the best sources of fibre.

● Use salt sparingly. Cook vegetables with very little salt or none at all. It is better to season after cooking. Herbs and spices will add any extra flavour. Taste carefully before adding salt to casseroles or sauces.

● Keep fat to a minimum. All fats contain different proportions of saturated fat and unsaturated fat. Saturated fats raise the levels of cholesterol in the blood, increasing the likelihood of heart disease. They mostly come from animals – meat, cream, eggs and cheese. As a general rule, it is best to use vegetable oils such as corn oil, sunflower oil and olive oil, which are low in saturated fats, and polyunsaturated margarine rather than butter.

Reduce the amount of dairy products in your diet. Use more low-fat cheeses such as curd, Quark, cottage and Ricotta and skimmed or semi-skimmed milk.

Trim fat off meat before cooking and skim fat or grease off food before serving. In the case of casseroles, chill them overnight, then lift off surface fat before reheating. Buy leaner cuts of red meat and eat more poultry, game and fish which are lower in fat.

● Use as little sugar as possible. Beware of hidden sugar in products such as baked beans and breakfast cereals. Fresh and dried fruits or fruit juices can be used to provide natural sweetness in place of sugar.

● Concentrate on those cooking methods such as steaming, poaching, grilling, stir-frying and baking which tend to preserve nutrients and do not involve large amounts of extra fat.

RECIPES FROM OTHER CHAPTERS

Many recipes from other chapters are suitable for lunch, dinner or supper. The following are some suggestions:

SOUPS, SNACKS & STARTERS

SINGAPORE LAKSA

In this oriental soup, pork is combined with noodles, vegetables, coconut milk and several spices, including ginger, to make a dish that is a meal in itself.

Strictly speaking, the soup should be made with thin rice sticks or noodles called *bun*, which can be bought at oriental food shops, but any thin Chinese egg noodles can be used instead. Other ingredients can be varied, too. Strips of cucumber can be substituted for green pepper, shredded Chinese leaves for the bean sprouts, and chicken breast for the pork. You can also include tinned water chestnuts or bamboo shoots, or slices of plain or deep-fried *tofu* (soya bean curd). Alternatively, 4-6oz (115-175g) of peeled prawns can be added just before serving.

The soup can be prepared up to 24 hours in advance, to the stage before the vegetables are added. Store, covered, in a cold larder or the refrigerator. Add the vegetables just before serving because they must be crisp.

PREPARATION AND COOKING TIME: *1 hour*

INGREDIENTS – *serves 4-6:*
8 oz (225 g) pork fillet (tenderloin)
3 pints (1.7 litres) well-flavoured chicken stock (page 367)
2 tablespoons soya sauce
2 tablespoons dry sherry
1 tablespoon vegetable oil
1 tablespoon sesame oil
2 in (50 mm) piece of fresh root ginger peeled and cut into thin matchstick strips
1-2 cloves garlic, peeled and crushed
1 level teaspoon ground coriander
1 level teaspoon turmeric
¼-½ teaspoon chilli powder, to taste
4 oz (115 g) Chinese egg noodles
4 oz (115 g) creamed coconut, dissolved in ½ pint (285 ml) boiling water
1 green pepper, cored, seeded and cut into thick matchstick strips
4 large spring onions, trimmed and sliced into rings
8 oz (225 g) french beans, topped and tailed and cut in half
2 medium carrots, peeled and cut into thick matchstick strips
4 oz (115 g) bean sprouts
Salt and freshly ground black pepper

Put the pork into a large saucepan and pour in 2½ pints (1.4 litres) of the stock. Add the soya sauce and sherry, bring to the boil and skim off any scum that rises to the surface. Lower the heat, cover and simmer for about 20 minutes, or until the pork is just tender.

Meanwhile, heat the vegetable oil and sesame oil in a separate large saucepan, add the ginger, garlic and spices and fry gently for 5 minutes until softened. Remove from the heat.

Remove the pork from its cooking liquid and set aside. Add the noodles to the liquid and bring back to the boil, stirring. Once it boils, cover tightly and remove from the heat immediately. Leave to stand for 5 minutes. Meanwhile, slice the pork into strips, about ¼in (5mm) wide.

Drain the liquid from the noodles and pour it into the ginger and spice mixture. Stir in the creamed coconut and bring to the boil. Lower the heat, add the green pepper, spring onions, french beans and carrots and simmer for 5 minutes only.

Cut the noodles into short lengths with kitchen scissors, then add to the soup with the remaining stock, the strips of pork, bean sprouts and salt and pepper to taste. Bring to the boil and simmer for 1-2 minutes.

Serve immediately with deep-fried prawn crackers.

SINGAPORE SOUP The cool elegance of Chinese porcelain bowls provides just the right setting for this exotic oriental soup – a mixture of sliced pork, egg noodles, vegetables, coconut, spices and chicken stock. Singapore laksa is substantial enough to be served as a main course.

PRAWN GUMBO

African slaves, brought to the American Deep South in the 18th century, are the source of this soup's name. It comes from *ochin-gambo* or *kingumbo* – African names for okra, the long green tapering vegetable that is the main ingredient. Today, gumbo is traditional to the Louisiana coast of the USA, and is made with all kinds of seafood, or chicken, as well as prawns. Okra is also called 'bhindi' and 'lady's finger'.

The soup can be made up to 24 hours in advance and kept covered in the refrigerator.

PREPARATION TIME: *20 minutes*
COOKING TIME: *25 minutes*

INGREDIENTS – *serves 4-6:*
1-1 1/2 oz (25-40 g) long grain rice
12 oz (350 g) okra
1 medium onion
1 red pepper
4 ripe tomatoes
2 oz (50 g) butter or margarine
2 cloves garlic, peeled and crushed
1/4-1/2 teaspoon cayenne pepper
2 pints (1.1 litres) well-flavoured fish stock (page 367)
Salt and freshly ground black pepper
12 oz (350 g) peeled prawns, defrosted and dried if frozen
Juice of 1/2 lime

Cook the rice in a large pan of salted boiling water for 8-10 minutes or until it is tender, then drain.

Trim and slice the okra. Peel and roughly chop the onion. Core and seed the red pepper and chop it very finely. Skin the tomatoes (page 389) and chop them very finely.

Melt the butter or margarine in a large, heavy-based saucepan or flameproof casserole. Add the chopped onion and fry gently for about 5 minutes until soft and lightly coloured. Add the garlic and red pepper, increase the heat and fry for a further 5 minutes, stirring constantly.

Add cayenne to taste and the

TASTE OF THE DEEP SOUTH Slices of okra, the chief ingredient in gumbo, are mixed with prawns, onion, red pepper and tomatoes.

tomatoes. Stir well to mix, then pour in the fish stock and bring to the boil. Lower the heat and add the okra, and salt and pepper to taste. Cover the pan and simmer for 20 minutes, stirring occasionally.

Add the prawns and rice to the soup with the lime juice. Cover and simmer for a further 5 minutes, then taste and add salt and pepper or cayenne if necessary. Serve hot as a main course soup, with French bread.

COURGETTE SOUP WITH GARLIC AND BLUE CHEESE

Dolcelatte cheese, or as an alternative Gorgonzola, gives this soup an Italian air, but it may equally well be made with Brie, German blue Brie, Stilton or Danish Blue.

A blender or food processor is necessary for this recipe. The soup can be made up to 2 days in advance, and will improve in flavour with keeping. Store it in a covered container in the refrigerator. This soup is also excellent served chilled in the summertime.

PREPARATION AND COOKING
TIME: *1 1/4 hours*

INGREDIENTS – *serves 6:*
1 lb (450 g) courgettes, trimmed and sliced
1 1/2 oz (40 g) butter or margarine
1 medium onion, peeled and roughly chopped
2 cloves garlic, skinned and crushed
2 pints (1.1 litres) vegetable stock (page 368)
2 heaped teaspoons chopped fresh basil OR 1 level teaspoon dried basil
Salt and freshly ground black pepper
6 oz (175 g) Dolcelatte cheese
1/4 pint (150 ml) single cream
GARNISH
Chopped fresh basil or whole sprigs of basil

Melt the butter or margarine in a large, heavy-based saucepan. Add the onion and garlic and fry gently for about 5 minutes until soft and lightly coloured.

Add the courgettes and cook gently for 10 minutes, shaking the pan and stirring frequently. Pour in the stock and bring slowly to the boil, then lower the heat and add the basil, with salt and pepper to taste. Cover and simmer gently for 20 minutes, stirring occasionally.

Meanwhile, remove any rind from the cheese and then dice it. Place in a liquidiser or food processor with all but 4 tablespoons of the cream. Blend to a smooth purée.

Add the hot soup to the machine, a ladleful at a time, and blend to incorporate with the cheese and cream. Blend again until the purée is really smooth. (It may be necessary to do this in batches, depending on the size of the machine.)

Return the soup to the rinsed-out pan and reheat gently. Taste and adjust the seasoning. Pour into a soup tureen or individual bowls and swirl the reserved cream on the top. Garnish with basil.

For a starter, serve with crisp Melba toast (see *Potted trout*, page 20). For a family or informal lunch, the soup is good with crusty rolls or hot garlic or herb bread (page 333).

This dish is included in a menu on page 71.

SPLIT PEA AND SAUSAGE SOUP

Yellow split peas give this soup a warming golden colour. Green split peas can be used instead, but although the taste is the same the soup does not look as attractive. Split peas are like lentils in that they do not need lengthy soaking before cooking. Simply rinse them in cold running water to remove any dust, and pick out and discard any particles of grit that you find.

Although the split peas will be tender after as little as an hour, the lengthy cooking time suggested here gives a much more concentrated flavour. The soup can be made in a shorter time, but remember that the result will not be quite as good.

This soup is garnished with croutons of smoked sausage. The kind of smoked sausage used is really a matter of personal taste. Polish *kabanos* is one that is widely available.

PREPARATION TIME: *30 minutes*
COOKING TIME: *2 hours*

INGREDIENTS – *serves 6:*
2 tablespoons vegetable oil
1 large onion, finely chopped
3 celery sticks, trimmed and finely chopped
3 level teaspoons ground ginger
8 oz (225 g) yellow split peas
3 pints (1.7 litres) well-flavoured chicken stock (page 367)
Salt and freshly ground black pepper
8 oz (225 g) smoked sausage

Heat the oil in a very large, heavy-based saucepan or a flameproof casserole. Add the onion and celery and fry gently for about 10 minutes until softened. Sprinkle in the ginger and continue frying for 5 minutes, stirring all the time.

Add the split peas to the pan and stir to coat in the onion mixture. Pour in 2 pints (1.1 litres) of the stock and bring to the boil, stirring. Lower the heat, cover the pan and simmer very gently for 2 hours. Stir frequently during this time, adding more stock as the peas become a thick purée. Add salt and pepper to taste.

About 15 minutes before the end of the cooking time, slice the sausage into neat rounds or stamp into fancy shapes using aspic or other small cutters. Fry in a heavy-based or non-stick pan until the fat runs and the sausage pieces are crisp. Drain on absorbent kitchen paper.

Dilute the soup with more stock or water to get the consistency you prefer. Adjust the seasoning, but remember that the sausage is highly spiced. Ladle into warmed soup bowls. Float the sausage croutons on top and serve immediately.

For a family weekend lunch serve with crusty French or garlic bread (page 333), cheeses and cooked meats.

STARRY SAUSAGE Crisp star and heart-shaped croutons of smoked sausage garnish yellow split pea soup.

CHUNKY CHOWDER

A chowder is a very thick, substantial American soup – the name comes from the French *chaudière*, meaning 'stew pot'. The ingredients can be varied. Unsmoked fish such as cod or haddock, or cubes of boned chicken, can be used instead of the smoked fish, and onions can be substituted for the leeks.

The flavour of the chowder improves if it is made a day in advance. Reheat very gently, to prevent the delicate flesh of the fish disintegrating.

PREPARATION TIME: *40 minutes*
COOKING TIME: *30 minutes*

INGREDIENTS – *serves 6-8:*
1 lb (450 g) thick fillets smoked fish (haddock or cod), skinned
3 medium leeks, total weight about 1 lb (450 g), trimmed
1 lb (450 g) old potatoes, peeled
8 oz (225 g) tin tomatoes
2 oz (50 g) salt pork or smoked streaky bacon, rind removed
2 pints (1.1 litres) well-flavoured fish stock (page 367)
2 heaped teaspoons chopped fresh marjoram OR 1 heaped teaspoon dried marjoram
Salt and freshly ground black pepper
1 pint (570 ml) milk
4 oz (115 g) frozen or tinned sweetcorn kernels
1 oz (25 g) butter or margarine
6-8 oz (175-225 g) Double Gloucester or Red Leicester cheese
About ¼ teaspoon paprika

Cut the fish into large chunks. Cut the leeks into ½in (15mm) slices, and the potatoes into bite-sized chunks. Purée the tomatoes and their juice in a liquidiser or food processor, or push them through a sieve.

Dice the salt pork or bacon and put it into a large, heavy-based saucepan or flameproof casserole. Heat gently until the fat runs, then fry until the pieces of meat are crisp. Remove from the pan with a slotted spoon and set aside to drain on absorbent kitchen paper.

Add the leeks to the pan and fry gently for about 5 minutes until softened. Add the chunks of potato and toss to mix them with the leeks.

Pour in the puréed tomatoes and fish stock and sprinkle in the marjoram. Bring slowly to the boil, stirring. Add salt sparingly (because of the saltiness of the fish and pork or bacon), but use plenty of pepper. Lower the heat, cover and simmer for 15 minutes or until the potatoes are just tender.

Add the pieces of fish, the

SMOKED FISH CHOWDER A bubbling layer of grilled cheese tops an ample American soup of smoked fish, leeks, potatoes, tomatoes and sweetcorn.

milk and sweetcorn and bring back to the boil, stirring gently to mix. Cover and continue simmering for about 10 minutes, until the fish and potatoes are quite tender. Stir in the butter and pork or bacon. Taste and add more salt and pepper if necessary, then remove the pan from the heat.

Heat the grill to moderate. Spoon the chowder into individual flameproof soup bowls or gratin dishes. Grate the cheese thickly over the top, then sprinkle with paprika. Cook under the preheated grill for about 3 minutes until golden and bubbling. Serve hot as a main course soup with fresh bread or rolls and butter.

MEATY MINESTRONE

No two minestrones are alike, as far as Italians are concerned. Not only does every cook have her own recipe, but each time it is prepared it will have different ingredients – depending on what is to hand.

Pancetta is salted raw belly of pork, available from Italian delicatessens. It gives an authentic flavour to minestrone, but smoked streaky bacon will give a similar, if less strong, flavour.

The cooking time may seem short for minestrone, but this is to ensure that the vegetables retain their crispness. The soup can be made in advance, but do not add the pasta until just

before serving. If the pasta is left to cool in the soup, it will absorb the liquid and swell and become oversoft. It may be necessary to add more stock or water on reheating.

PREPARATION TIME: *40 minutes*
COOKING TIME: *45 minutes*

INGREDIENTS – *serves 4-6:*
3 tablespoons olive oil
4 rashers of pancetta or smoked streaky bacon, cut into thin strips
2 large onions, peeled and chopped
2 cloves garlic, peeled and chopped
2 medium potatoes, peeled and diced
4 medium carrots, peeled and chopped
6 celery sticks, trimmed and chopped
4 tablespoons red or white wine (optional)
2½ pints (1.4 litres) well-flavoured chicken stock (page 367)
1 lb (450 g) tomatoes, skinned OR 14 oz (400 g) tin tomatoes
1 level teaspoon dried oregano
1 level teaspoon dried mixed herbs
Salt and freshly ground black pepper
3 oz (75 g) short-cut pasta or pasta shapes (such as macaroni, spirali, penne, fusilli)
About 8 oz (225 g) boned cooked chicken, skinned and cut into bite-sized pieces
10 oz (275 g) tin red kidney beans, rinsed and drained
GARNISH
Freshly grated Parmesan cheese

Heat 1 tablespoon of the oil in a large, heavy-based saucepan or flameproof casserole. Add the strips of pancetta or bacon and fry over moderate heat until crisp. Remove with a slotted spoon and set aside.

Heat the remaining oil in the pan, add the onions and garlic and fry gently until soft. Add the potatoes, carrots and celery and continue frying for a further 10 minutes until softened, tossing the ingredients constantly. Add the wine, if using, and toss again over high heat.

Return the pancetta to the pan, then pour in the stock. Add the tomatoes, herbs and salt and pepper to taste. Bring to the boil, then lower the heat, cover and simmer for 25 minutes or until the vegetables are just tender.

Add the pasta and cook for a further 10-15 minutes until the pasta is *al dente* (tender but firm to the bite). Then add the chicken and kidney beans and heat through for about 5 minutes. Taste and add extra salt and pepper if necessary.

Serve in individual bowls as a main course soup, with plenty of freshly grated Parmesan handed separately, crusty French bread or rolls and butter. A green salad tossed in vinaigrette (page 371) is a refreshing sequel.

BELGIAN WATERZOOTJE

The word *waterzootje* is Flemish for 'fisherman's soup' – a soup originally made with mixed white fish. Today, Belgians also make it with chicken, as here.

The soup can be made up to 24 hours in advance. Keep it in a covered container in the refrigerator.

PREPARATION TIME: *45 minutes*
COOKING TIME: *1½ hours*

INGREDIENTS – *serves 4-6:*
2-2½ lb (900 g-1.1 kg)
   chicken, with giblets
2 oz (50 g) butter or margarine
3 leeks, trimmed and thickly sliced
3 medium carrots, peeled and
   thinly sliced
1 lemon
2 cloves garlic, peeled and halved
½ pint (285 ml) dry white wine
1 small onion, peeled and stuck
   with a few cloves
2 large sprigs of parsley
2 bay leaves
1 sprig each of thyme and sage
*Salt and freshly ground black
   pepper*
16-20 prunes, soaked and pitted
GARNISH
Chopped fresh parsley

WATERZOOTJE Chicken is often the main ingredient of this Flemish 'fisherman's soup', once made only with fish. Wine, lemon, garlic, vegetables and prunes add to the flavour, which is enhanced by herb and garlic bread.

Melt the butter or margarine in a large, heavy-based saucepan. Add the leeks and carrots. Stir well and cover the pan. Fry gently for about 10 minutes, shaking the pan occasionally.

Meanwhile, remove the giblets from the chicken and wash the chicken well inside and out. Pierce the lemon all over with a skewer, then place it inside the body cavity of the chicken, with the cloves of garlic.

Put the chicken in the pan, on top of the vegetables. Pour in the wine, and enough water just to cover the chicken. Add the giblets (all except the liver), the onion and herbs, and salt and pepper to taste.

Bring to the boil, then lower the heat, half cover with a lid and simmer for 1½ hours, or until the chicken is tender enough to come away easily from the bones. Add the prunes for the last 30 minutes of the cooking time.

Remove the chicken from the pan and discard the lemon, cloves of garlic, giblets, herbs and the cloves from the onion. Stir the liquid and vegetables, to break up the onion.

Take the chicken flesh off the bones and cut it into bite-sized pieces, discarding all skin. Return to the pan and heat through. Taste and add salt and pepper if necessary. Pour into individual bowls, and sprinkle with parsley. Serve as a main meal with chunks of hot fresh bread, or with garlic or herb bread (page 333).

SESAME PRAWN TOASTS

The paste for this Chinese snack can be made very quickly in a liquidiser or food processor. It can also be made by chopping the ingredients finely with a sharp knife, but this takes much longer, and the paste does not spread so evenly – or go so far.

Be sure to use bread that is at least one day old and quite dry – the paste will not stick to fresh bread. If you are worried that the bread is not stale enough, leave the slices exposed to the air for an hour or two, turning them occasionally.

The toasts can be prepared as far as the chilling stage up to 24 hours in advance. Store them, covered, in the refrigerator.

PREPARATION TIME: *30 minutes*
CHILLING TIME: *30 minutes*
COOKING TIME: *25 minutes*

INGREDIENTS – *makes 36:*
8 oz (225 g) peeled prawns, defrosted and thoroughly dried if frozen
1 in (25 mm) piece fresh root ginger, peeled and crushed
2 spring onions, trimmed and roughly chopped
2 level tablespoons cornflour
1 tablespoon soya sauce
Salt and freshly ground black pepper
1 small egg, beaten
12 thin slices stale white bread, from a large loaf
2-3 oz (50-75 g) sesame seeds
Vegetable oil for deep-frying

Put the prawns in a liquidiser or food processor with the ginger, spring onions, cornflour and soya sauce. Blend to a paste, then add salt and pepper to taste and bind with the beaten egg.

Cut the crusts off the bread, then cut each slice into three rectangles. Spread the prawn paste on one side of each rectangle, mounding it up slightly in the centre. Sprinkle sesame seeds evenly over the prawn paste, then chill in the refrigerator for about 30 minutes.

CHINESE TOAST Deep-fried fingers of toast are spread with a paste of prawns and ginger, and sesame seeds. They can be served with chilli sauce.

Pour enough oil for deep-frying (page 372) into a wok or deep-fat fryer. Heat to a temperature of 190°C (375°F), then lower a few of the toasts, coated side downwards, into the hot oil. Deep-fry for 2-3 minutes until golden-brown underneath, then turn them over and deep-fry for 1 minute more. Drain on absorbent kitchen paper while frying the remainder.

Serve hot as a snack or as a starter, with wedges of lemon and chilli sauce to add extra piquancy to the flavour. The toasts may also be served hot with pre-dinner drinks or cocktails, in which case cut the toasts into thinner fingers – say four to each slice of bread.

HOT CORIANDER MUSHROOMS

Button mushrooms have the best appearance for this aromatic variation on mushrooms on toast, but they do not have as much flavour as the dark open or flat mushrooms. These, on the other hand, tend to discolour the soured cream sauce. Which variety you decide to use may depend on the occasion and on the season. In the autumn field mushrooms can be used.

The mushrooms can be served as a snack at any time of day. Alternatively, halve the quantities of the mushroom mixture and serve as an after-dinner savoury, on small toasted rounds of bread. For a special occasion use the wild mushrooms, such as chanterelles, which occasionally appear in shops in the autumn. The mushroom mixture on its own makes an excellent first course served in ramekins, with fingers of hot buttered toast.

PREPARATION AND COOKING TIME: *30 minutes*

INGREDIENTS – *serves 4:*
8 oz (225 g) mushrooms, wiped and neatly sliced
1½ oz (40 g) butter
1 medium onion, peeled and finely chopped
1 clove garlic, peeled and crushed
4 level teaspoons coriander seeds
Salt and freshly ground black pepper
4 slices granary or wholemeal bread
Extra butter, for spreading (optional)
8 level tablespoons soured cream
GARNISH
Chopped fresh coriander leaves

Melt the 1½oz (40g) butter in a heavy-based frying pan, add the onion and crushed garlic and fry gently for 5 minutes or until soft and lightly coloured.

Meanwhile, crush the coriander seeds finely with a pestle and mortar. Add to the onion and garlic and fry, stirring, for 1-2 minutes. Add the mushrooms, increase the heat, add salt and pepper to taste and toss to coat in the onion mixture for 3 minutes or so.

Toast the bread. (The toast can be spread with butter if you wish.) Stir the soured cream into the mushrooms and heat through gently.

Place a piece of toast on each of four plates and spoon the mushrooms on top. Sprinkle with chopped fresh coriander leaves and serve immediately.

PIZZA ALLA CASALINGA

The ingredients in this 'pizza made in the home' can be varied. Different kinds of cheese, anchovies, tuna fish, mushrooms, tinned artichokes, mussels, cooked ham and spicy peperami sausage are other possible toppings.

PREPARATION TIME: *1¼ hours*
RISING TIME: *2¼ hours*
COOKING TIME: *25 minutes*
OVEN TEMPERATURE: *preheat to 220°C (425°F, gas mark 7)*

INGREDIENTS – *serves 4-6:*
DOUGH
1 oz (25 g) fresh yeast and
 1 level teaspoon caster sugar
 OR *½ oz (15 g) dried yeast and*
 1 level teaspoon caster sugar OR
 1 sachet easy-blend dried yeast
4 tablespoons tepid milk
14 oz (400 g) strong white flour
2 level teaspoons salt
3 tablespoons olive oil
About 9 tablespoons tepid water
TOPPING
2 tablespoons olive oil
2 cloves garlic, peeled and finely
 chopped
14 oz (400 g) tin tomatoes,
 drained and chopped
1 heaped teaspoon chopped fresh
 basil OR *½ teaspoon dried basil*
Salt and freshly ground black
 pepper
12 oz (350 g) Mozzarella cheese
6 oz (175 g) Gorgonzola cheese
6 oz (175 g) Italian salami
10 black olives, stoned
1 heaped teaspoon dried oregano

First prepare the dough. Crumble the yeast into a warmed bowl, then blend in the sugar, milk and 4 tablespoons of the flour. Leave in a warm place for about 30 minutes until frothy. If you are using dried yeast, mix together the sugar and the milk. Sprinkle the yeast over the liquid and whisk in with a fork. Leave in a warm place for about 10 minutes until frothy. If using easy-blend yeast follow the instructions on the packet.

Sieve the remaining flour and the salt into a large warmed bowl. Make a well in the centre, add the yeast batter and mix in with a fork. Add the oil and enough water to draw the mixture together.

Turn the dough onto a floured surface and knead for about 10 minutes until smooth and elastic. Place in a floured bowl, cover with a clean tea towel and leave in a warm place for about an hour until doubled in bulk.

While the dough is rising, make the topping. Heat the olive oil in a saucepan, add the garlic and fry gently until lightly coloured. Add the tomatoes, basil, and salt and pepper to taste and bring to the boil, stirring. Lower the heat, cover and simmer for 15-20 minutes.

Cut the Mozzarella into 24 even-sized slices. Chop the Gorgonzola finely, removing any rind. Cut the salami into thin strips, removing the skin. Cut each olive into 3 pieces.

Brush a large baking sheet with oil. Turn the risen dough onto a floured surface and roll out to a rectangle 15in × 13in (380mm × 330mm). Place on the prepared baking sheet and pull the dough up at the edges to make a shallow lip all round. Spread the tomato sauce evenly over the dough, right to the edges.

Place the slices of Mozzarella on top of the tomato sauce, arranging them lengthways in 4 rows of 6 pieces. Put the pieces of Gorgonzola on top of the Mozzarella, then the salami and slices of olive, to make 24 portions of topping. Sprinkle oregano over the top. Leave to rise for about 30 minutes.

Bake in the preheated oven for 25 minutes or until the topping is bubbling and the dough risen. Leave to stand at room temperature for 10 minutes before cutting. Serve either hot, warm or cold.

For a family lunch or supper, serve the pizza cut into large squares or rectangles, with a green salad tossed in an oil and vinegar dressing (page 371). Smaller squares of pizza are excellent for picnics, or as cocktail party snacks.

PIZZA PARTY PIECE Cheese, salami and olives are evenly spread through the pizza topping so that there is a fair share for everyone when the pizza is cut up.

CRISPY BAKED POTATO SKINS WITH AVOCADO AND BLUE CHEESE DIP

For many people the skins are the best part of baked potatoes. This is an American idea for preparing them which can be served as a light main course, or as a first course for an informal supper party. There is no need to waste the potato flesh. It can be mashed and used in another dish such as *Potato and chive galette* (page 226).

The potato skins can be prepared as far as the grilling stage, up to 1 hour in advance. The dip can be made up to 4 hours in advance if covered closely, and kept in the refrigerator. After this length of time, the avocado will begin to discolour, although if you bury the avocado stone in the dip, the discoloration will be slower.

PREPARATION TIME: *30 minutes*
COOKING TIME: *1½ hours*
OVEN TEMPERATURE: *preheat to 200°C (400°F, gas mark 6)*

INGREDIENTS – *serves 4:*
4 large baking potatoes
10 rashers unsmoked streaky bacon
4 oz (115 g) Stilton cheese, grated
Vegetable oil, for brushing the potato skins
Salt and freshly ground black pepper
DIP
4 oz (115 g) Stilton cheese, grated
¼ pint (150 ml) soured cream
1 small ripe avocado
2 teaspoons lemon juice
A dash of Tabasco sauce
Salt and freshly ground black pepper

Scrub the potatoes thoroughly with a stiff vegetable brush under cold running water. Pat dry, then put a metal skewer through each. Place directly on the oven shelf and bake in the preheated oven for 1¼ hours or until soft when pressed gently with the fingers.

While the potatoes are cooking, make the dip. Put the Stilton and soured cream in a bowl and beat together until evenly mixed. Halve and stone the avocado, then scoop out the flesh and mash it with the lemon juice. Add to the cheese mixture with Tabasco and salt and pepper to taste. Beat until smooth and creamy, then turn into a serving bowl. Cover and chill in the refrigerator until ready to serve.

Grill the bacon rashers until crisp, then cut off the rinds and discard. Crumble or chop the bacon into tiny pieces.

When the potatoes are cooked, cut each one in half. Scoop out the flesh with a sharp-edged teaspoon, leaving a thin layer next to the skin. Cut each potato half in two lengthways, to make 16 'boats'.

Mix together the Stilton and two-thirds of the crumbled bacon. Brush the potato skins inside and out with a little oil, then place them in the grill pan. Divide the Stilton and bacon mixture evenly between the boats, then sprinkle with salt and pepper to taste. Put under a preheated grill for 5-10 minutes until crisp and sizzling.

Sprinkle the remaining crumbled bacon over the dip. Serve the potato skins hot on a large flat dish, with a bowl of dip in the centre for dunking.

This recipe is included in a menu on page 67.

POTATO SKIN BOATS Crisp quartered baked potatoes, carrying a mixture of Stilton and bacon, are ready to be dunked in avocado and Stilton dip.

FISH & SHELLFISH

SPANISH FISH CASSEROLE

The flavour and texture of monkfish – called *rape* in Spain, where it is very popular – is often compared with that of scampi or lobster. It is just as firm and meaty, but much less expensive. Unlike softer white fish, such as cod and haddock, it does not disintegrate when cooked. In this country it is also called angler fish and usually the tails only are displayed in fishmongers because of the immensely ugly appearance of its head. Spanish cooks are less squeamish.

In Spain, casseroles like this are usually cooked and served in traditional brown earthenware dishes. If you do not have one of these, a casserole will work just as well; if you use a flameproof one, the fish can be cooked on top of the stove rather than in the oven.

PREPARATION TIME: *45 minutes*
COOKING TIME: *50 minutes*
OVEN TEMPERATURE: *preheat to 180°C (350°F, gas mark 4)*

INGREDIENTS – *serves 4:*

*About 2 lb (900 g) monkfish
  fillets, skinned and cut into
  bite-sized pieces*
4 level tablespoons plain flour
*Salt and freshly ground black
  pepper*
7 tablespoons olive oil
*1 onion, peeled and finely
  chopped*
6 cloves garlic, peeled and crushed
*3 medium potatoes, peeled and
  cut into 1 in (25 mm) cubes*
*6½ oz (185 g) tin red pimentos
  drained and cut into strips*
*4 ripe tomatoes, skinned (page
  389) and roughly chopped*
2 tablespoons wine vinegar
¼ pint (150 ml) dry white wine
*¼ pint (150 ml) fish stock (page
  367) or water*
3 bay leaves
GARNISH
*2 hard-boiled eggs, shelled, and
  quartered or sliced*

Season the flour with salt and pepper and coat the monkfish in it. Heat 4 tablespoons of the olive oil in a large, heavy-based frying pan, add the monkfish and fry for 10 minutes, turning frequently, until the flesh turns white. Remove with a fish slice and set aside on a plate.

Heat the remaining 3 tablespoons of oil in the pan, add the onion and garlic and fry gently for about 5 minutes until softened. Increase the heat, add the cubes of potato and about two-thirds of the pimento strips and fry for a further 5 minutes, tossing the potatoes until they are lightly coloured on all sides.

Transfer the contents of the pan to an earthenware baking dish or a casserole.

Add the tomatoes to the frying pan and stir well, then add the vinegar, wine, stock, bay leaves and salt and pepper to taste. Bring slowly to the boil, stirring, then pour the mixture over the potatoes. Cover and cook in the preheated oven for 30 minutes or until the potatoes are just tender.

Remove the casserole from the oven and add the monkfish, stirring it in gently. Cover again and cook for a further 20 minutes until the fish is tender and the potatoes are really soft. Taste and adjust the seasoning of the sauce before serving, garnished with the remaining pimento strips, and the quartered or sliced hard-boiled eggs.

Serve in shallow soup plates with a typical Spanish salad of lettuce and sliced raw onion tossed in an olive oil and wine vinegar dressing (page 371).

This dish is included in a menu on this page.

COASTAL CASSEROLE Firm, white monkfish is used much more by Spanish cooks than it is in Britain. There it is fried, grilled, poached, baked, or as here, casseroled with wine, potatoes, garlic, pimentos and tomatoes, and garnished with sliced hard-boiled eggs. It needs no other accompaniment than a green salad and a bottle of Spanish dry white wine, which can also be used in the casserole itself.

M E N U

*Informal
Supper
for Eight*

SPANISH
FISH CASSEROLE
opposite page

LETTUCE
AND ONION SALAD

MOCHA CHOCOLATE
CHEESECAKE
page 106

Make twice the quantity of fish casserole given in the recipe, but use only 1½ times the amount of stock, because the larger quantity of liquid will not evaporate so quickly.

IN ADVANCE The cheesecake must be made at least the night before. It can, if you wish, be made 2-3 days in advance.

ON THE DAY Allow about 2 hours. Make the casserole. While it is cooking, decorate the cheesecake, and prepare a salad of crisp lettuce and sliced or chopped raw onion with an oil and vinegar dressing (page 371).

TO DRINK Dry white wine, preferably a Spanish wine such as Rioja.

CRESPELLINI

On a special occasion, the sauce for these pancakes may be made with dry white wine instead of milk; and prawns, mussels or scallops can replace the smoked fish. The dish can be prepared up to the baking stage 24 hours in advance. Keep covered in the refrigerator.

PREPARATION TIME: *1¼ hours*
COOKING TIME: *20 minutes*
OVEN TEMPERATURE: *preheat to 190°C (375°F, gas mark 5)*

INGREDIENTS – *serves 4:*
FILLING
1½-2 lb (700-900 g) smoked
 haddock fillets
1 bay leaf
1 medium onion, peeled and sliced
A few black peppercorns
1 pint (570 ml) milk
1 lb (450 g) fresh spinach,
 cooked, drained and chopped
 OR *8 oz (225 g) frozen*
 spinach, thawed and drained
PANCAKE BATTER
4 oz (115 g) plain flour
Pinch of salt
1 egg, beaten
½ pint (285 ml) milk
Vegetable oil for frying
SAUCE
About ½ pint (285 ml) milk
3 oz (75 g) butter or margarine
3 oz (75 g) plain flour
6 oz (175 g) Gruyère cheese,
 grated
½-1 level teaspoon grated
 nutmeg
Salt and freshly ground black
 pepper

Put the fish in a saucepan with the bay leaf, onion slices and peppercorns. Pour in the milk so that it just covers the fish, adding a little water if there is not enough milk. Bring slowly to the boil and simmer for 5 minutes. Remove from the heat, cover and leave until cold.

To make the pancakes, sieve the flour and salt into a bowl and make a well in the centre.

SAVOURY PANCAKES *Little crêpes, filled with haddock and spinach, are baked in a Gruyère sauce.*

Put the egg into the well and gradually beat in the milk to form a smooth batter. Beat in 1 teaspoon of vegetable oil.

Make the pancakes (page 390) using a lightly oiled 6in (150mm) pan. Stack them as they are made, interleaving them with sheets of greaseproof paper or non-stick baking paper. Continue until there are 12 pancakes altogether.

To make the cheese sauce, drain the milk from the fish into a measuring jug and make up to 1½ pints (850ml) with fresh milk. Melt the butter or margarine in a saucepan over low heat, add the flour and cook, stirring, for 1-2 minutes. Remove from the heat and gradually blend in the milk, then return to the heat and bring to the boil, stirring constantly. Simmer until thickened and smooth, then add the cheese, with nutmeg and salt and pepper to taste. Stir until the cheese has melted, then remove from the heat.

To finish the filling, put the spinach into a bowl. Flake the fish, discarding all skin and any bones, then fold it into the spinach with about one-third of the cheese sauce. Adjust the seasoning.

Divide the filling equally between the 12 pancakes (about a heaped tablespoon of filling each) and roll them up into cigar shapes around the filling. Place three pancakes, with the joins underneath, in each of four buttered individual gratin dishes, or lay all the pancakes in one layer in a large, shallow ovenproof dish. Pour over the remaining cheese sauce. Bake in the preheated oven for 20 minutes or until bubbling. Serve with crusty bread, or a green salad.

WATERCRESS STUFFED TROUT WITH LEMON BUTTER SAUCE

Pink rainbow trout tend to be larger and fleshier than ordinary rainbow trout, most of them weighing 12oz-1lb (350-450g). When you (or the fishmonger) clean and bone them, leave the heads and tails on.

PREPARATION TIME: *45 minutes*
COOKING TIME: *25-30 minutes*
OVEN TEMPERATURE: *preheat to 190°C (375°F, gas mark 5)*

INGREDIENTS – *serves 4:*
4 pink rainbow trout, each
 weighing about 12 oz (350 g),
 cleaned and boned (page 373)
Salt and freshly ground black
 pepper
¾ pint (450 ml) fish stock (page
 367) OR *½ pint (285 ml) fish*
 stock and ¼ pint (150 ml) dry
 white wine or dry cider
Juice of 1 lemon
1 oz (25 g) butter
4 tablespoons single or double
 cream (optional)
STUFFING
2 bunches watercress, total weight
 about 6 oz (175 g)
1 oz (25 g) butter
1 small onion, peeled and finely
 chopped
Finely grated rind of 2 lemons
2 teaspoons lemon juice
¼ teaspoon mustard powder
2 oz (50 g) fresh breadcrumbs
GARNISH
Lemon slices

First make the stuffing. Trim the ends off the watercress stalks and discard any yellow or damaged leaves. Chop the watercress finely, reserving a few whole sprigs for the garnish. Melt the butter in a pan, add the onion and fry gently for about 5 minutes until soft and lightly coloured. Add the watercress and stir to mix with the onion, then turn into a bowl and add the remaining stuffing ingredients, with salt and pepper to taste. Set aside.

Wash and dry the trout. Sprinkle the insides with salt and pepper, then spoon in the stuffing. Close the trout as firmly as possible, to enclose the stuffing tightly.

Butter a baking dish into which the trout just fit comfortably. Arrange the trout in the dish in a single layer. Sprinkle with more salt and pepper. Mix the stock (or stock and wine or cider) with the lemon juice and pour slowly around the trout. The liquid should just cover the fish – if not, add a little more stock or water.

Cover the dish with buttered kitchen foil and bake in the preheated oven for 25-30 minutes until the flesh is opaque.

Drain the cooking liquid carefully from the baking dish into a heavy-based saucepan. Cover the fish with the foil again and return to the oven turned to its lowest setting to keep warm.

To make the sauce, boil the cooking liquid rapidly to reduce its volume by about two-thirds.

Whisk in the butter a little at a time, then taste and adjust the seasoning (the flavour should be fairly sharp and lemony). Remove from the heat and stir in the cream, if it is being used, then pour into a sauceboat. Uncover the trout, and garnish with the reserved watercress sprigs and lemon slices.

Serve hot with the sauce handed separately, accompanied by new potatoes cooked in their skins and tossed in melted butter and chopped fresh mint. Follow with a green, tomato or cucumber salad.

CHINESE STEAMED FISH

Steaming is the lightest way to cook a fish. The method is favoured by the Chinese because it retains most of the moistness, texture and flavour of the fresh fish. However, if you do not have a steamer or fish kettle large enough to hold a whole bass, place the fish in a lightly oiled baking dish and cover it with foil. Bake in an oven, preheated to 180°C (350°F, gas mark 4), for 20-25 minutes.

Sea bass, in French *loup de mer* (literally 'sea wolf'), are available from good fishmongers for most of the year, although the fish may have to be ordered in advance. Grey mullet, large trout or sea bream can be used instead of bass, and may sometimes be more economical.

PREPARATION TIME: *30 minutes*
COOKING TIME: *15-20 minutes*

INGREDIENTS – *serves 4:*
1¹/₂-2 lb (700-900 g) whole sea bass, gutted and cleaned, with head and tail on (page 373)
Salt and freshly ground black pepper
¹/₂ teaspoon sugar
1 bunch spring onions, trimmed and finely sliced
1 in (25 mm) piece root ginger, peeled and cut into thin slivers
4 young carrots, peeled and cut into thin matchstick strips
2 tablespoons vegetable oil
1 green pepper, cored, seeded and cut into thin rings
2 tablespoons soya sauce
2 tablespoons dry sherry
1 tablespoon sesame oil

Wash the fish carefully inside and out, then pat dry with absorbent kitchen paper. With a sharp knife, make diagonal slashes in each side of the fish. Mix 1½ teaspoons salt with pepper to taste and the sugar. Rub the fish inside and out with the salt mixture, then place about one-third of the spring onions and root ginger inside it.

Place the fish in a steamer or fish kettle, cover and steam for 15-20 minutes.

While the fish is cooking, blanch the strips of carrot in boiling water for 2 minutes only. Drain thoroughly. Heat the vegetable oil in a wok or heavy-based frying pan. Add the remaining spring onions and root ginger, the green pepper and the

ORIENTAL FISH Strips of ginger, and vegetables stir-fried in soya sauce and sherry, enhance the delicate flavour of steamed sea bass.

carrot strips. Stir-fry (page 372) for a few minutes, then pour in the soya sauce and sherry and stir-fry until heated through.

Remove the fish from the steamer and pour off any liquid from inside the fish. Arrange the vegetables on a flat serving dish and place the fish on top. Sprinkle the sesame oil over the fish, together with any liquid remaining from stir-frying the vegetables. Serve immediately. Do not cut through the bone – instead lift the fish off the bone in fillets to serve it.

ORIENTAL FISH CURRY

Fresh fish can be used for this curry instead of frozen, but it tends to disintegrate more quickly during cooking. The curry is best if made 24 hours in advance. Store in the refrigerator. Reheat very gently until bubbling.

PREPARATION AND COOKING TIME: *1¼ hours*

INGREDIENTS – serves 4-6:
2 lb (900 g) frozen haddock fillets
4 oz (115 g) peeled prawns (optional)
2 tablespoons vegetable oil
1 medium onion, peeled and finely chopped
2 cloves garlic, peeled and crushed
1 in (25 mm) piece of root ginger, peeled and finely chopped
2 dried red chillies, crushed
2 level teaspoons ground cumin
2 level teaspoons turmeric
4 tomatoes, skinned and finely chopped
4 oz (115 g) creamed coconut, dissolved in ¾ pint (450 ml) boiling water
Juice of 2 limes
1 level teaspoon salt
GARNISH
Lime twists and deep-fried prawn crackers OR toasted shredded coconut

Heat the oil in a large, heavy-based saucepan or flameproof casserole. Add the onion, garlic,

ginger, chillies and cumin and fry very gently, stirring frequently, for about 10 minutes.

Push the onion mixture to one side of the casserole. Add two haddock fillets to the casserole and fry for 4-5 minutes until just defrosted, turning once. With a fish slice, transfer the fillets to a board.

Add two more haddock fillets and fry as before. Meanwhile, remove the skin from the fried fillets, which will separate into two pieces. Fry and skin all the haddock in this way. If using prawns, add them to the casserole and fry for 1-2 minutes until lightly coloured. Remove with a slotted spoon and set aside with the haddock.

Add the turmeric to the casserole and fry gently for about a minute, then add the tomatoes and stir to combine with the onion mixture. Add the coconut milk, half of the lime juice and the salt. Bring to the boil, stirring, then simmer for 15 minutes until thickened.

Add the haddock pieces to the sauce one at a time. When all the pieces are coated in the sauce, add the prawns, if they are being used. Simmer gently for 5 minutes. Do not stir or the fish will break up. Sprinkle with the remaining lime juice and garnish with the lime twists and prawn crackers or coconut.

Serve straight from the casserole with boiled rice and stir-fried green vegetables such as okra, french beans, mangetout or broccoli florets.

MEDITERRANEAN FISH SALAD

Fish salads are served in summer all along the Mediterranean coasts of Spain, France and Italy. The ingredients vary from one country or region to another. If fresh squid and mussels are not available, it is possible to use frozen squid and mussels. A firm-fleshed white fish such as monkfish, hake, halibut or turbot can also be included in the salad. The aïoli can be made with a bowl and wooden spoon or in a liquidiser (see *Mayonnaise,* page 369) instead of a pestle and mortar.

PREPARATION TIME: *2 hours plus cooling time*
COOKING TIME: *1½ hours*
OVEN TEMPERATURE: *preheat to 180°C (350°F, gas mark 4)*

INGREDIENTS – serves 4-6:
2 lb (900 g) squid, cleaned (page 375)
¼ pint (150 ml) dry white wine
¼ pint (150 ml) water
1 clove garlic, peeled and roughly chopped
1 large red pepper
1 large green pepper
2 pints (1.1 litres) mussels, cooked (page 377)
1 medium Spanish onion, peeled and thinly sliced
4-6 oz (115-175 g) peeled prawns (optional)
4 oz (115 g) black olives, halved and stoned
1 level tablespoon capers
1 lettuce, endive or radicchio

AÏOLI SAUCE
3 cloves garlic, peeled and roughly chopped
1 egg yolk
Salt and freshly ground black pepper
¼ pint (150 ml) olive oil
About 4 teaspoons lemon juice

Cut the body of the squid into thin rings, and the tentacles into small pieces. Place in an earthenware baking dish with the wine, water and garlic. Cover and cook in the preheated oven for 1½ hours until tender. Remove from the oven and leave to cool in the cooking liquid.

Meanwhile, make the aïoli sauce. Crush the garlic with a pestle and mortar, then add the egg yolk, ½ teaspoon salt and pepper to taste. Stir with the pestle until well combined, then add the oil a drop at a time, stirring with the pestle after each addition so that the oil is completely absorbed. As the mixture thickens and becomes shiny add the oil in a thin, steady stream – stirring all the time – until the aïoli is very thick, then add enough of the lemon juice to thin the mixture. Continue adding the oil until all is incorporated, then add the remaining lemon juice. Taste and adjust the seasoning.

Grill the peppers under a hot grill, turning frequently, until the skin is charred on all sides. Alternatively, place one pepper in the flames of a gas ring (standing it on the hob). Turn it round, using long-handled

tongs, until the pepper is charred on all sides. Repeat with the other pepper. Wrap the hot peppers in a clean tea towel and leave until cold.

Holding the peppers under a cold tap or in a bowl of cold water, rub the blackened skins off with your fingers. Halve, core and seed the peppers, then cut the flesh into thick strips.

Drain the squid and reserve 2 tablespoons of the cooking liquid. Rinse the squid under cold running water, pat dry with absorbent kitchen paper, then place in a bowl.

Shell the mussels, reserving a few in their shells for garnishing. Add the shelled mussels to the bowl of squid with the strips of pepper, onion slices, prawns (if using), olives and capers. Toss gently to mix, then add half of the aïoli, and the reserved cooking liquid from the squid. Fold gently to mix, then taste and adjust the seasoning.

Line a salad bowl with lettuce, endive or radicchio. Put the fish salad in the bowl, then make an indentation in the centre and spoon in the remaining aïoli. Garnish with the reserved mussels. Serve at room temperature or chilled.

SUN-FILLED SALAD *The flavour of the Mediterranean is captured in a salad of squid, mussels, prawns, red and green peppers and black olives. It is dressed with aïoli – a garlic mayonnaise from the region of Provence in the south of France.*

BEEF & VEAL

RENDANG

Original recipes for rendang were made with water buffalo meat. Today, however, beef is more popular, even in West Sumatra in Indonesia where the dish originates.

Sambal oelek is a hot, spicy Indonesian seasoning, made from ground red chilli peppers and salt mixed with oil. It is available in small bottles from oriental stores and some delicatessens. Use it according to taste, adding a little at a time. If sambal oelek is difficult to obtain, the same seasoning can be made at home by crushing the flesh of 3 dried red chillies in a pestle and mortar with 1 level teaspoon of salt. Remove the seeds from the chillies before crushing – otherwise the sauce will be too fiery.

Rendang is a good dish to make in advance – the coconut milk is said to have a preserving effect on the meat. Store it in a covered container in the refrigerator for up to 2 days, then reheat with a few tablespoons of water to thin the sauce.

PREPARATION TIME: *20 minutes*
COOKING TIME: *1½ hours*

INGREDIENTS – *serves 4:*
1½ lb (700 g) top rump of beef or rump steak, trimmed of fat and cut into 2 in (50 mm) squares
1 medium onion, peeled and finely chopped
4 cloves garlic, peeled and crushed
1 in (25 mm) piece fresh root ginger, peeled and crushed
1 tablespoon sambal oelek (see introduction)
2 bay leaves
1 level teaspoon ground turmeric
1 level teaspoon salt
¾ pint (450 ml) coconut milk (see Lamb curry, page 82)

Put the beef in a wok or heavy-based saucepan. Stir in the remaining ingredients. Cook uncovered over a very low heat for 1-1¼ hours, stirring regularly until the meat is tender and the gravy quite thick.

Increase the heat and stir-fry (page 372) for about 10 minutes or until oil separates from the gravy. Lower the heat again and continue stir-frying until the gravy coats the meat in a dark crust. Taste and add more salt if necessary. Turn into a warmed serving dish and serve hot.

Rendang is rich, spicy and very filling, so portions need to be kept small. Serve with plain boiled rice and stir-fried vegetables such as carrots, mangetout and bean sprouts or with *Gado-gado* (page 103) made without the hard-boiled eggs.

65

STUFATO DI MANZO

Topside of beef cooked as a pot roast – *stufato di manzo* means 'beef cooked on a stove' in Italian – is a succulent joint. Lean brisket can be used instead of topside.

The stufato can be prepared and cooked 24 hours in advance. Store in the covered casserole in a cold place or the refrigerator. Bring to room temperature before reheating on top of the cooker for 20-30 minutes.

PREPARATION TIME: *30 minutes*
COOKING TIME: *2 hours*
OVEN TEMPERATURE: *preheat to 180°C (350°F, gas mark 4)*

INGREDIENTS – *serves 6:*
2½ lb (1.1 kg) piece of rolled topside of beef
8 rashers pancetta (see Meaty Minestrone, page 56) or smoked streaky bacon, chopped
1 large onion, peeled and roughly chopped
2 cloves garlic, peeled and crushed
1 level tablespoon plain flour
¼ pint (150 ml) red wine
½ pint (285 ml) beef stock (page 367)
1 bouquet garni
Salt and freshly ground black pepper
4 ripe tomatoes, skinned (page 389) and roughly chopped
GARNISH
Chopped fresh parsley

Put the beef in a heavy-based flameproof casserole and fry over a moderate heat until browned on all sides. The fat tied round the roll of beef will be sufficient for frying it. Remove the joint from the casserole and drain on absorbent kitchen paper.

Put the pancetta or bacon in the casserole and heat gently until the fat runs. Increase the heat and fry until it is crisp, then remove and set aside with the beef.

Lower the heat, put the onion and garlic in the casserole and fry gently for about 5 minutes until soft and lightly coloured. Sprinkle in the flour and cook for 1-2 minutes, stirring, then pour in the wine and stock and bring it slowly to the boil.

Return the beef and pancetta or bacon to the casserole. Add the bouquet garni, a little salt and plenty of pepper. Cover and cook in the oven for 1 hour.

Add the tomatoes to the sauce, then cook for a further hour, or until the beef is tender when pierced with a knife. Transfer the beef to a carving dish and leave to settle for 10-15 minutes.

Meanwhile, remove the bouquet garni from the gravy and discard. Skim or blot off any surplus fat. Place the casserole on top of the cooker and boil the gravy to reduce it slightly,

ITALIAN POT ROAST Topside of beef is cooked and served in a rich, thick gravy of red wine, bacon, onion, garlic and tomatoes.

then taste and add extra salt and pepper if necessary.

Carve the meat into thin, neat slices. Arrange, overlapping in a circle, on a warmed serving dish. Pour over a little of the gravy and sprinkle with chopped parsley. Serve hot, with the remaining gravy offered separately.

Italians serve the beef with balls of *Polenta* (page 229), but mashed potatoes or rice are good alternatives.

BARBECUED BEEF STEW

The flavour and tenderness of the beef in this stew will both improve the longer the meat is left in the marinade. The flavour will also improve if the meat is left to cool in the sauce overnight, then reheated. The stew must become bubbling hot, this will take 20-40 minutes.

For a fiery flavour, crush the seeds with the chilli flesh. Otherwise, omit them.

PREPARATION TIME: *30 minutes*
MARINATING TIME: *overnight or up to 5 days*
COOKING TIME: *2 hours*

INGREDIENTS – *serves 4-6:*
2-2½ lb (900 g-1.1 kg) chuck steak, trimmed of fat and cut into 1 in (25 mm) cubes
3 tablespoons vegetable oil
½ pint (285 ml) beef stock (page 367)
MARINADE
2 cloves garlic, skinned
2 fresh red or green chillies OR 1 dried red chilli
2 in (50 mm) piece fresh root ginger, peeled OR 2 level teaspoons ground ginger
2 tablespoons soya sauce
2 tablespoons clear honey
2 level tablespoons tomato purée
1 level tablespoon wine vinegar
Salt and freshly ground black pepper
1 small red pepper, cored and seeded
1 small green pepper, cored and seeded

To make the marinade first chop together the garlic, chillies and root ginger, if used, then pound with a pestle and mortar. Place in a bowl, then add the ground ginger, if used, soya sauce, honey, tomato purée and vinegar. Mix thoroughly.

Add the cubes of beef to the marinade, stir so that all the cubes are coated in marinade, then cover and place in the refrigerator. Leave at least overnight or for up to 5 days. Turn the meat in the marinade occasionally during this time.

When ready to cook, heat 2 tablespoons of the oil in a flameproof casserole. Add the beef in batches and fry briskly until browned on all sides.

Pour in any marinade remaining in the bowl then gradually stir in the stock. Bring slowly to the boil, stirring, then lower the heat and add 1 level teaspoon of salt, and pepper to taste. Cover and simmer for 1¾ hours or until tender.

Slice a few rings from each pepper and reserve for the garnish. Chop the remainder finely. Heat the remaining tablespoon of oil in a small frying pan, add the chopped pepper and fry for 1-2 minutes until softened. Add to the casserole and continue cooking for a further 15 minutes until the beef is very tender. Meanwhile, fry the reserved pepper rings in the oil left in the frying pan. Turn the stew into a warmed serving dish. Top with the pepper rings. Serve with plain boiled rice.

M E N U

American Supper for Four

CRISPY BAKED
POTATO SKINS
WITH AVOCADO AND
BLUE CHEESE DIP
page 60

❧

RUMP BURGERS
WITH MOZZARELLA
this page

LETTUCE AND TOMATOES

❧

FRESH FRUIT

ON THE DAY The dip can be made up to 4 hours in advance.

Allow about 1¾ hours to prepare the other recipes. First put the potatoes into the oven. While they are baking, prepare the burgers, wash and dry the lettuce and slice the tomatoes, and grill the bacon.

Finish off preparing the potato skins and grill them. At the same time cook the burgers. Keep the burgers warm while you serve the potato skins and dip.
TO DRINK Chilled lager or American beer.

RUMP BURGERS WITH MOZZARELLA

A hamburger made with good quality meat can be just as good as a steak. A mixture of rump steak and a cheaper cut of beef, such as chuck or shin, keeps the price down and provides just the right amount of fat for really juicy burgers. The meat can be chopped by hand, minced or processed, but take care when using a processor that the meat does not disintegrate into a purée.

MELTING MOZZARELLA Rump steak burgers conceal a rich surprise – a filling of Mozzarella cheese and chopped anchovies which runs out when a knife cuts into the centre.

PREPARATION TIME: *40 minutes*
COOKING TIME: *10-20 minutes*

INGREDIENTS – *serves 4:*
8 oz (225 g) rump steak
8 oz (225 g) chuck steak or shin of beef
8 tinned anchovies – about half a 1¾ oz (50 g) tin
A little milk
1 oz (25 g) butter or margarine
½ small onion, peeled and grated
1-2 oz (25-50 g) freshly grated Parmesan cheese
4 heaped tablespoons chopped parsley
1 level teaspoon dried mixed herbs
Salt and freshly ground black pepper
½ egg, beaten
4-6 oz (115-175 g) Mozzarella cheese
Vegetable oil, for shallow frying

Drain the anchovies and soak in milk for about 20 minutes.

Cut the meat into cubes, trimming off any large pieces of fat. Chop, mince or process and put into a bowl.

Melt the butter in a small pan, add the onion and fry gently for about 10 minutes until very soft and lightly coloured. Add to the beef with the Parmesan, parsley, herbs, and salt and pepper. Mix thoroughly with your hands, then bind with the beaten egg.

Divide the mixture into 8 equal portions and shape them into rounds with your hands. Place 4 of these on a board or work surface. Slice the Mozzarella cheese. Drain the anchovies, pat them dry with kitchen paper, then chop roughly.

Arrange the Mozzarella and anchovies on top of the 4 portions of meat on the board. Top with the remaining 4 portions of meat. Form into burger shapes making sure that the halves of each burger are pressed well together so that the stuffing does not come out.

Pour enough oil into a large, heavy-based frying pan just to cover the base. Heat until very hot, then put in the burgers and fry over high heat for 3 minutes on each side, until well seared. Lower the heat and continue cooking gently until the burgers are done. Lift out and drain.

Serve with a salad, and chipped potatoes or fresh, crusty bread. This dish is included in a menu on this page.

YOGHURT AND CASHEW A final trickle of yoghurt and a sprinkling of fried whole cashew nuts complete a casserole of beef spiced with aromatic cardamom, cloves, coriander and ginger. Natural yoghurt, added little by little during the initial cooking period, produces succulent, tender meat and a thick, rich gravy.

CASHEW SPICED BEEF

The secret of the creamy texture and rich flavour of this casserole lies in the way the yoghurt is very slowly added in the early stages. It is absorbed into the meat a little at a time, which makes it succulent and moist, and the sauce full of flavour. Do not be tempted to add more than 1 tablespoon of yoghurt at a time – although it may seem painstaking, the end result is well worth the trouble.

This casserole can be made up to 2 days in advance, or frozen, but in both cases leave the nut and yoghurt garnish until the reheating stage. Store in a tightly covered bowl in the refrigerator.

PREPARATION TIME: *40 minutes*
COOKING TIME: *1½ hours*

INGREDIENTS – *serves 4-6:*
2½ lb (1.1 kg) chuck steak
4 oz (115 g) unsalted cashew nuts
6 cardamom pods
4 whole cloves
2 level teaspoons coriander seeds
1 in (25 mm) piece of fresh root ginger, peeled and chopped
2 cloves garlic, peeled and roughly chopped
½ pint (285 ml) natural yoghurt
3 tablespoons vegetable oil
1 medium onion, peeled and finely chopped
4 celery sticks, trimmed and roughly chopped
2 level teaspoons ground turmeric
Salt and freshly ground black pepper

Trim the meat of fat and cut it into 1in (25mm) cubes.

Chop half of the cashew nuts roughly and place in a food processor or liquidiser. Split the cardamom pods open, then add to the nuts with the cloves, coriander seeds, ginger, garlic and about 3 tablespoons of the yoghurt. Blend to a paste. Alternatively, grind the nuts and spices, but not the yoghurt, with a pestle and mortar.

Heat 2 tablespoons of the oil in a large flameproof casserole. Add the chopped onion and fry gently for 5 minutes or until soft and lightly coloured. Add the chopped celery and the turmeric and fry for about 5 minutes more, stirring constantly.

Fry the beef over moderate heat, adding it to the casserole in batches, until browned on all sides and coated in the onion and celery mixture. Add the yoghurt paste 1 tablespoon at a time, stir-frying after each addition, then add the remaining plain yoghurt in the same way, reserving 2-3 tablespoons for the garnish. If you have ground the nuts and spices with a pestle add them to the meat and stir-fry for 2-3 minutes, then add the yoghurt, 1 tablespoon at a time as above. When all the yoghurt has been added, add salt and pepper to taste, cover the casserole and simmer gently for about 1½ hours or until the beef is tender.

Before serving, heat the remaining oil in a small frying pan, add the remaining whole cashew nuts and fry until browned. Watch them carefully – they burn very easily. Transfer the beef mixture to a warmed serving dish, trickle over the remaining yoghurt and sprinkle with the fried cashews. Serve immediately with boiled rice and a dish of stir-fried fresh spinach. Extra plain yoghurt can be handed round separately for those who like it.

CHILLI BEEF CABBAGE ROLLS

This quantity of chilli beef will fill 12 large cabbage leaves generously. If there is some left over, serve it separately. The filling can be made up to 24 hours in advance and kept in a covered container in the refrigerator. The cabbage, on the other hand, tastes better freshly cooked.

PREPARATION TIME: *45 minutes*
COOKING TIME: *40 minutes*

INGREDIENTS – *serves 4:*
2 lb (900 g) hard white cabbage
2 tablespoons vegetable oil
1 medium onion, peeled and finely chopped
1 clove garlic, peeled and crushed
10 oz (275 g) minced beef
2 level tablespoons tomato purée
1 level teaspoon chilli powder, or to taste
¼ teaspoon sugar
Salt and freshly ground black pepper
8 oz (225 g) boiled and drained long-grain rice – about 3 oz (75 g) uncooked rice
10 oz (275 g) tin red kidney beans, rinsed and drained
½ pint (285 ml) chicken stock (page 367)

With a strong, sharp knife, cut out and discard the core of the whole cabbage and any discoloured outer leaves, then put the rest of the cabbage in a deep bowl and pour over boiling water to cover. Leave the cabbage to stand for 20 minutes.

While the cabbage is soaking, make the filling. Heat the oil in a heavy-based saucepan. Add the onion and garlic and fry gently for about 5 minutes until soft and lightly coloured. Add the minced beef and fry until browned, stirring and pressing with the back of a wooden spoon to break up the meat.

Add the tomato purée, chilli powder, sugar, and salt and pepper to taste and stir well to mix. Cook gently for 15-20 minutes, stirring frequently.

Drain the cabbage. Remove the outer leaves and reserve. Carefully peel off 12 more large leaves. Any tears in the leaves will not be noticed once the rolls are cooked. Blanch the 12 leaves, in batches of three or four, in boiling salted water for 3 minutes. Run the leaves under cold water, then drain carefully and pat dry with absorbent kitchen paper. Cut away the base of the thick central stalks.

Remove the minced beef mixture from the heat and stir in the rice and kidney beans. Taste and adjust seasoning.

Place the cabbage leaves on a board or work surface and divide the chilli beef filling equally between them. Wrap the leaves around the filling — folding in the sides and tucking the ends over to make neat parcels. Squeeze gently to compress the parcels.

Line a well-buttered frying pan, into which the rolls will just fit, with the reserved outer leaves of the cabbage. Place the rolls seam side down in the pan, packing them closely together. Slowly pour in the stock and sprinkle with salt and pepper. Bring the stock slowly to the boil, then lower the heat, cover the pan with a lid or kitchen foil, and simmer for 40 minutes.

To serve, remove the rolls carefully from the pan with a slotted spoon and place on individual plates (discard the outer leaves that lined the pan). Serve with soured cream and a homemade tomato sauce (see *Vegetable moussaka*, page 102). Stir the pan juices from cooking the rolls into the tomato sauce, for extra flavour. Alternatively, make a simple sauce by mixing the pan juices with some soured cream. This dish is included in a menu on page 111.

A PANFUL OF CHILLI Blanched cabbage leaves make an excellent edible wrapping for a mixture of beef, rice and kidney beans spiced with hot chilli that is reminiscent of chilli con carne. The parcels are neatly fitted into a pan lined with more cabbage leaves and then braised in stock.

SOMERSET CIDER AND STEAK PIE

Root vegetables are one of the pleasures of the winter months. Either parsnips or turnips can be used in this very traditional English pie. The cooked filling can be stored for up to 2 days in the refrigerator. The filling alone, or the unbaked pie, can be frozen. The pie can be cooked from frozen allowing 20-30 minutes extra cooking time.

PREPARATION TIME: *45 minutes*
COOLING TIME: *2-3 hours or overnight*
COOKING TIME: *2½ hours*
OVEN TEMPERATURE: *preheat to 150°C (300°F, gas mark 2)*

INGREDIENTS – *serves 6:*
2 lb (900 g) stewing steak
2 tablespoons dripping or vegetable oil
1 large onion, peeled and thinly sliced
¾ pint (450 ml) beef stock (page 367)
½ pint (285 ml) dry cider
2 level teaspoons chopped fresh thyme OR 1 level teaspoon dried thyme
1 level teaspoon ground allspice
Salt and freshly ground black pepper
1 lb (450 g) carrots, peeled and thickly sliced
1 lb (450 g) turnips or parsnips, peeled and thickly sliced
12 oz (350 g) prepared weight puff pastry (page 394)
GLAZE
Beaten egg

Trim the meat of fat and cut it into bite-sized cubes. Heat the dripping or oil in a flameproof casserole. Add the meat, in batches if necessary, and fry over brisk heat until browned on all sides. Remove with a slotted spoon and leave to drain on absorbent kitchen paper.

Lower the heat under the casserole, add the onion and fry gently for about 5 minutes until softened. Return the meat to the casserole, add the stock, cider, thyme, allspice, and salt and pepper to taste. Bring to the boil, stirring, and cover. Transfer to the preheated oven and cook for 1 hour.

Blanch the carrots and the turnips or parsnips in boiling salted water for 3 minutes. Drain thoroughly. When the casserole has been in the oven 1 hour, add the blanched root vegetables to the casserole and stir well to mix. Cover again and return to the oven for a further hour, or until the meat is tender. Remove from the oven, turn into a bowl and leave until completely cold.

Preheat the oven to 220°C (425°F, gas mark 7). Roll out the pastry on a lightly floured surface and cut out a lid to fit a 3½ pint (2 litre) pie dish. Cut out a strip of the remaining pastry to go around the rim of the dish, and cut out decorative shapes, such as leaves or tassels (page 288), for the top of the pie.

Place a pie funnel in the centre of the pie dish, then spoon the cold beef and vegetable mixture around it. Brush the rim of the dish with water, and press the pastry strip into place. Brush the strip with water, then place the lid on top, cutting a hole over the pie funnel to let steam escape.

Press the edges of the pastry together to seal, then knock up and flute the edges (page 393). Moisten the pastry decorations and stick them on top of the pie, then brush all over the lid with beaten egg.

Bake the pie in the preheated oven for 30 minutes, or until the pastry is puffed up, crisp and golden-brown.

Serve hot, straight from the dish, with potatoes baked in their jackets, a green vegetable, and chilled cider.

CALF'S LIVER WITH LIME AND SAGE BUTTER

English or Dutch calf's liver is much more expensive than lamb's or pig's liver, but there is no comparison between them. Pale milky brown in colour, calf's liver has a much more delicate flavour, and is meltingly tender. Even staunch liver haters may be converted by this dish.

All liver tends to become tough if overcooked, but it is particularly important in the case of calf's liver not to exceed the cooking time otherwise the delicate fibres will be spoiled.

PREPARATION TIME: *20 minutes*
FREEZING TIME: *1-2 hours*
COOKING TIME: *8-10 minutes*

INGREDIENTS – *serves 4:*
4 thin slices calf's liver, each weighing about 3-4 oz (75-115 g)
4 oz (115 g) butter, softened
Finely grated rind and juice of 1-2 limes, according to taste
4 level teaspoons chopped fresh sage
Salt and freshly ground black pepper
2 level tablespoons plain flour
3 tablespoons dry sherry
GARNISH
Lime twists (page 286)
Fresh sage leaves

Put the softened butter into a bowl with the grated lime rind, 2 teaspoons of lime juice, the sage, and salt and pepper to taste. Beat with a wooden spoon until evenly mixed.

Lay the butter mixture between two sheets of greaseproof paper and press gently with a rolling pin until it is about ¼in (5mm) thick. Freeze for 1-2 hours until firm, then cut out 8 rounds using a fluted 2in (50mm) biscuit cutter. Set aside the butter trimmings. Place the pats of butter on a board or plate and return to the freezing compartment of the refrigerator or the freezer.

Season the flour with salt and pepper. Cut the liver into 8 neat, serving pieces, and then coat the pieces of liver thoroughly in the seasoned flour.

Melt the reserved butter trimmings in a large, heavy-based frying pan. Add the pieces of liver and fry over moderate heat for 2-3 minutes on each side, turning once. Place two pieces on each of four warmed dinner plates and keep hot.

Add the sherry to the sediment in the pan and mix them

MENU

French Bistro Supper for Six

COURGETTE SOUP WITH GARLIC
AND BLUE CHEESE *page 54*
with MELBA TOAST

CALF'S LIVER WITH LIME AND SAGE BUTTER
opposite page

NEW POTATOES

MANGETOUT, PETITS POIS *or*
FRENCH BEANS WITH CHOPPED FRESH HERBS

TARTE CLAFOUTIS
page 112

Make 1½ times the quantity of soup and liver given in the recipes.

IN ADVANCE The courgette soup can be made up to 2 days in advance. The clafoutis and the lime and sage butter can be made a day ahead.

ON THE DAY If you have made the soup, the tart and the butter in advance you will need about 20 minutes before the meal to reheat the soup, make the Melba toast (see *Potted trout*, page 20) and prepare the liver.

If you plan to cook everything in the evening, you will need to start about 2 hours before the meal. Make the lime and sage butter and put it in the freezer. Marinate the liver and soak the cherries for the tart. Make the pastry and, while it is chilling, make the soup.

Bake the pastry case and make the batter for the tart filling. About 40 minutes before you plan to start the meal, complete the tart and put it in the oven.

While the tart is cooking, finish the soup and make the Melba toast. Once the tart has cooked, leave it to stand in a warm place. Cook the vegetables, and prepare the liver. Cook the liver after you have finished the soup.

TO DRINK A light French red wine.

---

together, stirring vigorously. Add the remaining lime juice and allow to bubble for 1-2 minutes, stirring constantly. Taste and add more salt and pepper if necessary, then pour over the liver. Garnish each plate with lime twists and sage leaves, then top each piece of liver with one of the butter pats.

Serve immediately, before the butter melts.

Calf's liver should be eaten on its own to be appreciated fully. Follow with crisply cooked fresh vegetables in season such as broccoli, spinach, french beans or mangetout.

This dish is included in a menu on this page.

GOURMET LIVER Gently fried in butter flavoured with fresh limes and sage, thinly sliced calf's liver is unmistakably a delicacy. It is best eaten without any accompaniment that might conflict with the subtle flavours. Medallions of lime and sage butter are added just before serving, and fresh sage leaves and a twist of lime provide the simple garnish.

VEAL PAPRIKASH

Paprika is much milder and sweeter than chilli and can be used much more liberally. It is one of the staple flavourings in Hungarian cooking – goulash (a stew of beef, lamb or veal) is flavoured with paprika, so also are 'paprikash' (*paprikás*) recipes.

For a special occasion, use dry white wine or French dry cider instead of chicken stock. This dish can be made a day in advance. Reheat until bubbling hot, before serving.

PREPARATION TIME: *30 minutes*
COOKING TIME: *1 ½ hours*

INGREDIENTS – *serves 4:*
4 boneless veal steaks, each weighing 4-6 oz (115-175 g), trimmed of fat
2 level tablespoons plain flour
Salt and freshly ground black pepper
1 ½ oz (40 g) butter or margarine
2 tablespoons olive oil
1 lb (450 g) onions, peeled and finely chopped
1 clove garlic, skinned and crushed (optional)
1 level tablespoon paprika
½ teaspoon caraway seeds
4 ripe tomatoes, skinned (page 389), seeded and roughly chopped
About ¼ pint (150 ml) chicken stock (page 367)
Pinch of sugar
GARNISH
Soured cream
Snipped chives

Season the flour with salt and pepper and use to coat the veal steaks. Melt the butter or margarine with the oil in a large, heavy-based flameproof casserole. Add the steaks and fry in batches over moderate heat until golden-brown on both sides. Remove and set aside on a plate.

Add the onions and garlic to the pan and stir to coat in the butter and oil. Cover and cook over very gentle heat for 45 minutes, stirring frequently. The onions should turn into a very soft, light golden purée.

Sprinkle the paprika and caraway seeds into the casserole and stir for a few minutes. Add the tomatoes and stock, with the sugar and salt and pepper to taste. Bring slowly to the boil, stirring constantly, then return the steaks to the pan and spoon the onion mixture over them. Cover and cook gently for about 45 minutes, until the veal is tender. Taste and add salt and pepper if necessary, then transfer to a warmed serving dish. Trickle a little soured cream over the veal and sprinkle with chives. Serve extra soured cream separately.

The sauce is thick and pungent. Serve the dish, therefore, with fairly plain accompaniments such as tagliatelle noodles and a green side salad.

PRIDE OF HUNGARY Paprika, caraway seeds and plenty of soured cream give an authentic Hungarian flavour to veal steaks.

PORK

HONEY-GLAZED PORK CHOPS

Like many dishes of Chinese and Malaysian origin, these honey-glazed pork chops are cooked with five-spice powder. This is a reddish-brown mixture of anise, fennel, cloves, cinnamon and Szechwan pepper. It can be bought in oriental food shops and some supermarkets and delicatessens. Ground mixed spice can be used instead.

For an everyday meal, the white wine can be replaced either by half wine and half chicken stock, or by all chicken stock, with 1-2 tablespoons of dry sherry or vermouth.

PREPARATION TIME: *15 minutes*
COOKING TIME: *1 ¼ hours*
OVEN TEMPERATURE: *preheat to 190°C (375°F, gas mark 5)*

INGREDIENTS – *serves 4:*
4 thick loin pork chops
1 tablespoon vegetable oil
½ pint (285 ml) dry white wine
1 level teaspoon five-spice powder
Juice of 1 orange
2 tablespoons clear honey
Salt and freshly ground black pepper
GARNISH
Slices of orange

Heat the oil in a roasting tin. Add the chops and fry over moderate heat until browned on both sides. Pour in the wine, then sprinkle in the five-spice powder and bring to the boil. Remove the tin from the heat and cover with kitchen foil, then bake in the preheated oven for 1¼ hours until tender. During this time occasionally turn the chops in the liquid.

Remove the chops from the cooking liquid and cut off and discard the fat and rind. Place the chops on a warmed serving dish, cover with the foil from the roasting tin and keep them hot in the oven turned to its lowest setting.

Stir the orange juice, honey, and salt and pepper to taste, into the juices in the roasting tin. Bring to the boil and simmer, stirring all the time, until the liquid is reduced to a syrupy glaze – this should take about 5-10 minutes.

Spoon the glaze over the chops, garnish with orange slices and serve immediately.

The sauce is quite rich so provide a plain accompaniment such as Chinese egg noodles or boiled rice. *Chinese vegetable stir-fry* (page 104) would also go well with the chops, or alternatively, follow with a salad such as *Chinese salad* (page 275).

RED HOT RIBS

Chinese-style spare ribs – also called American ribs – can be bought at many large supermarkets. Most butchers will prepare them, although they do not normally display them. Hoisin sauce, sometimes labelled Chinese Barbecue Sauce, and chilli sauce (see *Duck with plum and ginger glaze*, page 88) can be bought at oriental food shops and some supermarkets.

PREPARATION TIME: *8-10 minutes*
COOKING TIME: *1½ hours*
OVEN TEMPERATURE: *preheat to 200°C (400°F, gas mark 6)*

INGREDIENTS – *serves 4-6:*
3-3½ lb (1.4-1.6 kg) Chinese-style pork spare ribs
2 cloves garlic, peeled and crushed
1-2 fresh green chillies, seeded and finely chopped OR ½-1 teaspoon chilli powder, to taste
½ in (15 mm) piece fresh root ginger, peeled and crushed
3 tablespoons clear honey
3 tablespoons dark, soft brown sugar
4 tablespoons tomato ketchup
4 tablespoons dry sherry or wine vinegar
2 tablespoons soya sauce
2 tablespoons Hoisin sauce
2 tablespoons French mustard
4 teaspoons chilli sauce, or to taste
Salt and freshly ground black pepper
GARNISH
Spring onion tassels (page 287)

Put all the ingredients, except the spare ribs and spring onion tassels in a jug and whisk well until thoroughly mixed.

Put the spare ribs in a large roasting tin and pour over the sauce. Turn the ribs to coat them in the sauce, brushing the sauce over with a pastry brush if necessary.

Bake, uncovered, in the preheated oven for 30 minutes, then turn the ribs over and roast for a further 30 minutes. Lower the oven temperature to 180°C (350°F, gas mark 4), turn the ribs over again and continue roasting for a further 30 minutes or until the pork is tender and the sauce is thick and syrupy.

Transfer to a large serving dish and garnish with spring onion tassels. Serve the ribs hot, on their own, with ice-cold beer or lager to drink. Provide plenty of napkins, and finger bowls too,

FIERY SPARE RIBS Red Hoisin sauce colours these baked spare ribs. A liberal hand with the chilli sauce ensures that they taste red hot too.

because spare ribs are always eaten with the fingers. Follow with boiled rice, and stir-fried vegetables or a raw mixed salad of bean sprouts, carrots, shredded white cabbage or Chinese leaf and cashew nuts.

ROAST LOIN OF PORK WITH CHEESE AND FIG STUFFING

In Denmark, where this recipe originates, roast loin of pork covered with crackling is a traditional Christmas dish. Ask the butcher to bone the loin and score its rind at close intervals. Do not have the joint rolled and tied, because it has to be stuffed.

PREPARATION TIME: *30 minutes*
COOKING TIME: *2½ hours*
OVEN TEMPERATURE: *preheat to 220°C (425°F, gas mark 7)*

INGREDIENTS – *serves 6:*
4½ lb (2 kg) loin of pork, boned
½ pint (285 ml) dry cider
Juice of 1 orange
STUFFING
6 oz (175 g) dried figs
4 oz (115 g) Wensleydale or Caerphilly cheese
1 dessert apple, cored
4 oz (115 g) fresh breadcrumbs
Finely grated rind of 1 orange
Salt and freshly ground black pepper
1 egg, beaten

DANISH CRACKLING Loin of pork is stuffed with dried figs, cheese, apple and orange rind, then cooked Danish-style to produce a crisp, light crackling. First the loin is cooked in cider and orange juice to soften the rind which then crisps up when sprinkled with salt and roasted. Here the joint is served with new potatoes glazed with butter and sugar.

First make the stuffing. Cut the woody stalks off the figs then cut the figs in small chunks and put them in a bowl. Grate the cheese into the bowl, then grate in the apple, including the peel. Add the breadcrumbs, orange rind and salt and pepper to taste. Mix well, then bind with the beaten egg. Set aside.

Put the pork, rind side down, on a board. With a sharp knife, make a horizontal cut between the meat and the outer layer of fat for the full length of the joint, cutting to within about 1in (25mm) of each edge, to make a pocket. Push the stuffing into the pocket, packing it in as firmly as possible. Roll up the joint lengthways and tie at regular intervals with string. Weigh the joint and calculate the roasting time, allowing 40 minutes per pound (450g).

Place the joint, rind side down, into a flameproof casserole into which it just fits. Pour in the cider and orange juice, then just enough water to cover the rind of the pork. Cook, uncovered, in the preheated oven for 30 minutes.

Remove the casserole from the oven and turn the joint over so that the rind is on top. Sprinkle with 1½ teaspoons salt. Return the casserole, uncovered, to the oven and roast for 1 hour until the crackling is crisp. Lower the oven temperature to 180°C (350°F, gas mark 4) and roast for a further hour, or, if the calculated roasting time comes to more than 2½ hours, until the full roasting time has been completed. Do not baste at all during roasting, or the crackling will not crisp.

Transfer the joint to a warmed serving dish, cover loosely with kitchen foil and set aside to settle in a warm place. Meanwhile, put the casserole on top of the stove and boil the cooking liquid to reduce slightly. Add salt and pepper to taste, then pour into a warmed jug. Carve the joint, not forgetting to remove the string, and serve with roast potatoes or Danish-style new potatoes tossed in melted sugar and butter until glazed, and another vegetable such as *Spiced red cabbage with juniper* (page 221).

SPICY PORK AND SAUSAGE RAGOÛT

Spicy continental sausages, obtainable from delicatessens, are best for this ragoût (stew). Use meaty frying sausages such as the Italian *luganega*; pork sausages from Romagna in the north of the country – *salsiccia al metro* – long, spicy sausages sold fresh by the metre; or *salamelle*, small, spicy sausages linked in a chain. Fresh French sausages, such as *saucisses de Toulouse*, are also suitable. Alternatively, use ready-cooked sausages such as the peppery Spanish *chorizo*; the minced pork *kabanos* from Poland; or the spicy Italian *pepperoni*. These sausages do not

need boiling, as the uncooked ones do.

The ragoût can be made up to 24 hours in advance, and improves in flavour with keeping. Cool, then store in the refrigerator overnight. Reheat for 15-20 minutes on top of the cooker, adding a few tablespoons of stock or water if the sauce has thickened.

PREPARATION TIME: *1¼ hours*
COOKING TIME: *1¼-1½ hours*

INGREDIENTS – *serves 4-6:*
1 lb (450 g) boneless pork spare rib, trimmed of fat and cut into bite-sized cubes
1 lb (450 g) continental-style sausage (see introduction)
5 tablespoons olive oil
1 large onion, peeled and thinly sliced
2 cloves garlic, peeled and crushed
1 level teaspoon paprika
14 oz (400 g) tin tomatoes, crushed or puréed with their juice OR *12 oz (350 g) fresh tomatoes, skinned (page 389) and roughly chopped*
½ pint (285 ml) chicken stock (page 367)
2 bay leaves
Salt and freshly ground black pepper
2 red peppers, cored, seeded and cut into thin strips
GARNISH
Chopped fresh continental (flat-leaf) parsley

Heat 2 tablespoons of the oil in a flameproof casserole or heavy-based saucepan, add the pork and fry over a brisk heat until

RICH RAGOÛT *Spicy continental sausages, cooked with pork, paprika and red peppers, give this stew its full, piquant flavour.*

lightly coloured on all sides. Remove with a slotted spoon and set aside. Heat another tablespoon of oil in the casserole. Add the onion and garlic and fry gently until soft and lightly coloured. Sprinkle in the paprika and fry for 1-2 minutes, then add the tomatoes and

simmer for about 10 minutes until the mixture is thick and reduced.

Add the stock, bay leaves and salt and pepper to taste. Bring to the boil, stirring, then return the pork to the pan, cover and simmer for 1 hour, until the pork is just tender.

While the pork is cooking, bring a large pan of water to the boil. Add the sausages and bring the water back to the boil, then cover and simmer for 10 minutes. Drain the sausages. Leave until cool enough to handle, then peel off the skins and cut the sausages into bite-sized pieces. If you are using ready-cooked sausages it is not necessary to boil them.

Heat 1 tablespoon of the remaining oil in a frying pan, add the pieces of sausage in batches and fry over moderate to high heat until crisp and golden-brown on all sides. Remove with a slotted spoon and drain on absorbent kitchen paper. Heat the remaining oil in the frying pan. Add the strips of pepper and fry over gentle heat for a few minutes until softened.

When the pork has been cooking for 1 hour, add the fried sausage and pepper to the casserole and simmer for a further 15 minutes, or until the pork is very tender. Remove the bay leaves before serving. Taste and add more salt and pepper, if necessary.

Serve hot, sprinkled with chopped parsley, and accompanied by a simple side dish such as boiled rice, pasta or mashed potatoes, and a simple green vegetable or salad.

ESCALOPES TAGINE

A *tagine* is a North African – particularly Moroccan – stew. It almost always includes dried fruits. In Morocco, which is a Moslem country, lamb, veal or chicken is usually the main ingredient. This recipe is made with pork, but the essential flavours of a tagine – sweet and savoury together – are kept.

Ready-beaten pork escalopes are available from some supermarkets. Veal escalopes, or even thin slices of rump steak, can be used instead of the pork.

PREPARATION TIME: *1 1/4 hours*
SOAKING TIME: *at least 30 minutes*
COOKING TIME: *10-15 minutes*

INGREDIENTS – *serves 4:*
4 pork escalopes, each weighing 3-4 oz (75-115 g), beaten very thin
1 1/2 oz (40 g) dried apricots
1 1/2 oz (40 g) dried apple rings
2 oz (50 g) prunes
1/4 pint (150 ml) dry white wine or chicken stock (page 367)
1 1/2-2 oz (40-50 g) risotto rice
1 1/2 oz (40 g) butter or margarine
1 medium onion, peeled and finely chopped
1 level teaspoon ground cinnamon
1 level teaspoon ground ginger
Finely grated rind and juice of 1 lemon
Salt and freshly ground black pepper
2 tablespoons vegetable oil
1 level tablespoon redcurrant jelly
1/2 pint (285 ml) chicken stock

NORTH AFRICAN ESCALOPES Strips of pork are stuffed with a Moroccan mixture of dried fruits and rice.

Put the dried fruit in a bowl. Heat the wine or stock to boiling point, then pour over the fruit. Cover and leave to soak for at least 30 minutes.

Cook the rice in a large pan of boiling water for 8-10 minutes or until it is tender, then drain.

Melt 1oz (25g) of the butter or margarine in a small frying pan, add the onion and fry gently for 5 minutes until softened. Stir in the cinnamon and ginger and cook for a few minutes more, then turn into a bowl. Add the cooked rice and lemon rind and mix well.

Drain the soaked fruit and set aside the liquid. Chop the fruit finely, discarding the prune stones. Mix the fruit with the rice mixture, adding salt and pepper to taste.

Lay the escalopes flat on a board or work surface and cut each one in two. Divide the stuffing equally between the eight pieces of pork, placing it at one end of the meat. Roll the meat up around the stuffing, then secure with wooden cocktail sticks, or string.

Melt the remaining butter with the oil in a flameproof casserole large enough to hold the rolled escalopes in a single layer. Add the escalopes and fry over moderate heat until golden-brown on all sides. Remove with a slotted spoon and set aside on a plate.

Pour off all but 1-2 teaspoons of fat from the casserole. Stir in the redcurrant jelly until melted, then add the reserved soaking liquid from the dried fruit, the lemon juice and chicken stock. Bring to the boil, stirring, then return the escalopes and their juices to the casserole. Lower the heat, sprinkle with salt and pepper to taste, then cover and simmer for 10-15 minutes until the pork feels tender when pierced with a skewer.

Remove the escalopes from the casserole and discard the cocktail sticks or string. Place the escalopes on warmed plates. Taste the sauce and adjust the seasoning, then pour it over the escalopes. Serve hot with rice and a mixed or green salad.

STIR-FRIED PORK WITH RED PEPPER AND CUCUMBER

Before cutting the pork fillet for this Chinese stir-fried dish, freeze it for a few hours. It will be much easier to cut into thin slivers while frozen, and it will defrost while marinating.

Vegetable oil can be used instead of sesame oil.

PREPARATION TIME: *20 minutes*
MARINATING TIME: *1 hour*
COOKING TIME: *15-20 minutes*

INGREDIENTS – *serves 4:*
1 1/4-1 1/2 lb (575-700 g) pork fillet (tenderloin), trimmed of fat and cut into thin strips
4 tablespoons sake (rice wine) or dry sherry
4 tablespoons soya sauce
1 1/2 tablespoons cornflour
1 level tablespoon tomato purée
1 level teaspoon sugar
3/4 pint (450 ml) chicken stock (page 367)
3 tablespoons vegetable oil
1 large red pepper, cored, seeded and cut into thin strips
1/2 large cucumber, seeded and cut into thin strips
1 tablespoon sesame oil
4 spring onions, trimmed and finely chopped
1 in (25 mm) piece fresh root ginger, peeled and finely chopped
1 clove garlic, skinned and crushed
Salt and freshly ground black pepper

Put the pork in a bowl with the sake or sherry and half of the soya sauce. Cover and leave to marinate for about 1 hour. The pork can be marinated for up to 2 days if stored in an airtight container in the refrigerator and turned occasionally.

In a jug, mix the cornflour to a paste with the remaining soya sauce and the tomato purée and sugar, then stir in the stock.

Heat 2 tablespoons of the vegetable oil in a wok or deep, heavy-based frying pan. Add the red pepper and stir-fry (page 372) over high heat for 1-2 minutes, then add the cucumber and stir-fry for 1 minute more. Remove with a slotted spoon and set aside on a plate.

Heat the remaining tablespoon of vegetable oil with the sesame oil in the wok, then add the spring onions, ginger and garlic. Stir-fry over moderate heat for 2 minutes, then add the pork with salt and pepper to taste. Increase the heat to high and stir-fry for about 5 minutes until all the strips have changed colour.

Pour the stock mixture into the pan and stir-fry vigorously to mix with the meat. Let the mixture bubble and thicken, stirring all the time, then simmer for a few minutes more until the meat is really tender. Return the strips of pepper and cucumber to the wok and heat through, stirring all the time. Taste and add salt and pepper if necessary. Serve immediately with Chinese noodles.

LAMB

SPICED LAMB PILAU

The rice in a pilau (or pilaf) is cooked in delicately spiced seasoned stock, often the liquid in which meat has been simmering. This gives the pilau a rich colour and flavour, far better than the literal meaning of its name – rice porridge – would indicate. Meat, vegetables, nuts and dried fruit are ingredients often added to the rice. Pilau itself comes from Turkey, but similar dishes, under other names – *polo* for example in Persian – are eaten throughout the Middle East.

The combination of lamb fillet and minced lamb varies the texture of this pilau, but you could use just lamb fillet or just minced lamb. The courgettes can be omitted if they are not in season, or replaced with green or red peppers.

The meat can be cooked up to 48 hours in advance, and will improve in flavour with keeping. Store it in the covered casserole in the refrigerator, and bring to the boil before adding the rice and courgettes. The cooked meat can also be frozen. Thaw completely at room temperature, then bring to the boil before completing the recipe.

PREPARATION TIME: *35 minutes*
COOKING TIME: *1¼ hours*

INGREDIENTS – *serves 4:*
1 lb (450 g) lamb fillet, trimmed of fat and cut into ¼-½ in (5-15 mm) cubes
8 oz (225 g) minced lamb
1 oz (25 g) butter
1 large onion, peeled and roughly chopped
2-3 cloves garlic, peeled and crushed
2 level teaspoons ground coriander
1 level teaspoon ground cumin
½ teaspoon ground ginger
½ teaspoon turmeric
1 cinnamon stick
1 level tablespoon tomato purée
1 pint (570 ml) chicken stock (page 367) or water
Salt and freshly ground black pepper
4 small courgettes
12 oz (350 g) long grain rice
2 oz (50 g) seedless raisins
2 oz (50 g) pine nuts
GARNISH
Fresh coriander leaves, chopped

Melt the butter in a large flameproof casserole, add the onion and fry gently for about 5 minutes until softened. Add the garlic, the lamb fillet and the minced lamb and fry, stirring constantly, until browned.

Add the spices and fry, stirring, for a few minutes more, then stir in the tomato purée, ¼ pint (150ml) of the stock or water, and salt and pepper to taste. Bring to the boil, stirring, then lower the heat, cover and simmer for 1 hour or until the cubes of lamb are tender.

Trim the courgettes and slice them into diagonal chunks ¼-½in (5-15mm) thick.

Add the remaining stock or water to the pan and bring to the boil, then add the rice and courgettes. Cover and simmer for 15 minutes or until the rice is tender. Fold in the raisins and pine nuts, and heat through for a few minutes. Taste and adjust the seasoning.

Turn the pilau onto a serving dish. Sprinkle with the coriander leaves and serve with a green salad, and plain yoghurt.

AROMATIC PILAU Coriander leaves decorate a dish fit for a sultan – a fragrant mixture of rice, lamb, raisins, pine nuts and spices.

MIDDLE-EASTERN DELICACY *A light combination of aubergine, beef, lamb and plenty of fresh mint in a sauce of yoghurt and tomato is a far remove from ordinary meatballs.*

MINTED MEATBALLS WITH YOGHURT SAUCE

Minced meat, usually beef or lamb, is one of the central ingredients in Middle-Eastern cooking. There are numerous varieties of meatball – these are flavoured with aubergine and allspice – but what all have in common is an even texture.

The meatballs can be cooked up to 24 hours in advance and kept in the refrigerator. The flavour improves on reheating.

PREPARATION TIME: *1½ hours*
CHILLING TIME: *2 hours or overnight*
COOKING TIME: *1 hour*
OVEN TEMPERATURE: *preheat to 200°C (400°F, gas mark 6)*

78

INGREDIENTS – *serves 4-6:*
2 medium aubergines
8 oz (225 g) minced lamb
8 oz (225 g) minced beef
1 onion, peeled and chopped
1-2 cloves garlic, peeled and chopped
4 oz (115 g) fresh white breadcrumbs
4 heaped tablespoons chopped fresh mint
1 level teaspoon ground allspice
Salt and freshly ground black pepper
Olive oil for shallow frying
¾ pint (450 ml) hot beef stock (page 367)
2 level tablespoons tomato purée
¼ pint (150 ml) natural yoghurt, at room temperature
1 level tablespoon cornflour

Thread the aubergines on skewers and grill under a preheated hot grill for 10-15 minutes, turning from time to time, until the skins wrinkle and char, and the flesh feels soft. Leave until cool enough to handle, then peel off the skins with a knife.

Chop the aubergine flesh roughly, then place in a food processor with the lamb, beef, onion and garlic. Blend to a fine paste. It may be necessary to do this in batches, depending on the capacity of the processor.

Put the mixture into a bowl and add the breadcrumbs, half of the mint, the allspice and salt and pepper to taste. Mix well with your hands, then chill in the refrigerator for at least 2 hours, or overnight.

With dampened hands, shape the mixture into 30 small balls. Pour oil into a heavy-based frying pan to a depth of about ¼in (5mm). Heat until very hot, then fry the meatballs in batches until browned on all sides. Remove with a slotted spoon and drain on kitchen paper.

Put the meatballs in an ovenproof dish. Mix the hot beef stock with the tomato purée, then pour over the meatballs. Cover (with foil if the dish does not have a lid) and cook in the preheated oven for 1 hour.

Drain the liquid from the meatballs into a jug. Cover the meatballs again and keep hot.

To make the sauce, whisk the yoghurt and cornflour together in a heavy-based saucepan, then very gradually whisk in the hot liquid in which the meatballs were cooked. Bring slowly to the boil, whisking vigorously, then lower the heat and simmer until thickened. Taste, and adjust the seasoning.

Pour some sauce onto each dinner plate and arrange the meatballs on top. Sprinkle with the remaining mint (or garnish with whole sprigs of mint instead). Serve the remaining sauce in a jug. Serve spinach and boiled rice with the meatballs.

The meatballs are excellent served cold on cocktail sticks for a drinks party (in which case form the mixture into 60 small balls) with a plain yoghurt dip, or a yoghurt, cucumber and mint raita (see *Khichri*, page 96).

M E N U

Spring Lunch for Four

LAMB CHOPS WITH TARRAGON AND CUCUMBER
opposite page

NEW POTATOES

FRESH PEAS WITH BACON AND SPRING ONIONS

MINTED APPLE SNOW
page 106

Two rashers of bacon and a small bunch of spring onions, chopped and sautéed in the bacon fat, make a good addition to fresh peas.
IN ADVANCE The purée for the apple snow must be made at least 2 hours in advance to give it time to cool. It can be made the day before and kept in a covered bowl in the refrigerator.
ON THE DAY Allow about an hour. First shell the peas, then prepare the potatoes and start to cook them. Prepare the cucumber for the lamb and leave it to drain while you cook the peas. While they are simmering, cook the lamb and complete the apple snow.

SPRING LAMB *New potatoes and fresh peas with bacon accompany lamb chops in a delicate tarragon and cucumber sauce. Minted apple snow is a light end to the meal.*

LAMB CHOPS WITH TARRAGON AND CUCUMBER

Tarragon has a distinctive, slightly bitter taste. It can be used either fresh or dried here, but this recipe is best made in early summer when home-produced lamb is on the market and fresh tarragon is available. The sauce can also be made with dillweed or parsley.

PREPARATION AND COOKING
TIME: *40 minutes*

INGREDIENTS – *serves 4:*
8 small lamb chops
½ cucumber
Salt
Freshly ground black pepper
1½ oz (40 g) butter
2 tablespoons chopped, fresh tarragon OR 1 tablespoon dried tarragon
¼ pint (150 ml) single cream
2 egg yolks
GARNISH
Whole sprigs of tarragon

Turn on the grill to medium heat.

Peel the cucumber, cut into thirds and remove the seeds, then cut each third lengthways into 8 sticks. Put the sticks into a colander over a bowl or the sink, and sprinkle with salt. Leave the cucumber for 10-15 minutes until the juices run out. Rinse under cold water and drain.

Trim about 1in (25mm) of fat off the long end of each chop and scrape the bone clean. Grind black pepper over the chops and dot both sides with half the butter. Grill them for 5 minutes on each side.

While the chops are cooking, melt the remaining butter in a pan over medium heat. Add the cucumber and the dried tarragon if used so that it softens. Cover and cook gently for about 5 minutes.

Lightly mix together the cream and the egg yolks. If you are using fresh tarragon add it at this point.

Lay the chops in a line on a warmed flat dish and garnish with the cucumber sticks. Keep warm. Reserve the juices from the grill pan and do not clean the pan in which the cucumber was cooked.

Spoon off most of the fat from the grill pan and scrape the remaining juices into the cucumber pan. Add the cream and egg mixture to the pan. Stir over a low heat until it has warmed through and thickened slightly. Do not allow the sauce to boil.

Garnish the chops with sprigs of fresh tarragon. Serve the sauce separately. Choose simple vegetables such as spring greens or french beans. This dish is included in a menu on the opposite page.

M E N U

Warming Winter Dinner for Four to Six

POT ROAST
LEG OF LAMB
opposite page

JACKET POTATOES

GREEN SALAD

MARMALADE
AND FIG SPONGE
page 110

IN ADVANCE It is necessary to start soaking the beans at least 8 hours in advance.

ON THE DAY Allow about 3 hours. Prepare the lamb and put it in the oven. Make the sponge and start steaming it about 1½ hours before the meal, so that it has completed 2 hours' steaming when you come to eat it. Allow 1-1½ hours for baking the potatoes, depending on their size.

Just before serving, make the green salad.

TO DRINK Either a dry red or dry white wine, depending on what has been used in cooking.

POT ROAST LEG OF LAMB

The meat, vegetables and haricot beans for this dish are all cooked together in a single pot.

PREPARATION TIME: *1 hour*
SOAKING TIME: *at least 8 hours*
COOKING TIME: *2 hours*
OVEN TEMPERATURE: *preheat to 180°C (350°F, gas mark 4)*

INGREDIENTS – *serves 4-6:*
3½-4 lb (1.6-1.8 kg) leg of lamb
8 oz (225 g) haricot beans
4 cloves garlic, peeled
2 level teaspoons fresh rosemary OR 1 level teaspoon dried rosemary
Salt and freshly ground black pepper
3 tablespoons olive oil
1 medium onion, peeled and roughly chopped
2 celery sticks, trimmed and roughly chopped
2 medium carrots, peeled and thinly sliced
1 dessert apple, cored and roughly chopped
14 oz (400 g) tin tomatoes
¼ pint (150 ml) dry red or white wine
½ pint (285 ml) water
1 bouquet garni
GARNISH
Chopped fresh parsley

COUNTRY LAMB A leg of lamb, spiked with garlic, is ready to be pot-roasted with haricot beans, vegetables and herbs.

Cover the haricot beans with cold water and leave to soak for at least 8 hours or overnight. Drain the beans and rinse under cold running water. Place in a large saucepan, cover with fresh cold water and bring to the boil. Skim off any scum with a slotted spoon, then half cover with a lid and simmer for 1 hour.

Meanwhile, make deep incisions in the flesh of the lamb with a pointed knife. Cut the garlic into thin slivers and insert them into the incisions, then rub the rosemary and plenty of salt and pepper all over the joint.

Heat the oil in a large, heavy-based flameproof casserole. Add the lamb and fry it over moderate heat for 30 minutes, turning it from time to time until it is well-browned on all sides. Remove the lamb and set aside, then pour off the excess fat from the casserole, leaving behind just enough to fry the vegetables.

Add the onion, celery and carrot to the casserole and fry gently for about 5 minutes until softened. Add the apple and tomatoes with their juice, then the wine and water. Bring to the boil, stirring.

Drain the beans and add to the casserole with the lamb. Tuck the bouquet garni among the beans, then cover the casserole with kitchen foil and place the lid on top. Cook in the preheated oven for 2 hours, turning the lamb over in the casserole every 30 minutes.

Remove the lamb from the casserole, place on a warmed serving dish and leave to settle for about 15 minutes.

Meanwhile, remove the bouquet garni and taste and adjust the seasoning of the beans and sauce in the casserole.

To serve, spoon some of the beans and sauce around the lamb and sprinkle with parsley. Serve the remaining beans and sauce in a jug or bowl.

Serve with potatoes, and a green vegetable, or green salad. This dish is included in a menu on the opposite page.

LAMB WITH LIME AND PERNOD

The flavour of aniseed, which is characteristic of Pernod, is also used to flavour French *pastis* and Greek *ouzo*. Either of these may be used instead of Pernod in this recipe.

PREPARATION TIME: *15 minutes*
MARINATING TIME: *at least 1 hour*
COOKING TIME: *10 minutes*

INGREDIENTS – *serves 4:*
8-12 thick loin lamb chops
3 tablespoons olive oil
2 cloves garlic, peeled and crushed
Finely grated rind and juice of 2 limes
Freshly ground black pepper
2 oz (50 g) butter
4 tablespoons Pernod
Salt
GARNISH
12 sprigs of rosemary, and lime twists (page 286)

Trim as much fat as possible off the chops. Curl the long end of the chop around the eye of the meat and the bone to make noisette shapes. Secure with wooden cocktail sticks or fine string. Place the chops in a single layer in a shallow dish.

Whisk together the olive oil, garlic, half of the lime rind and juice and plenty of black pepper. Pour over the lamb, cover and leave to marinate at cool room temperature for at least an hour. The chops can be left in the marinade for up to 3 days.

When ready to cook, melt the butter in a large, heavy-based frying pan. Remove the lamb from the marinade with a slotted spoon and place in a single layer in the pan (it may be necessary to use two pans). Fry over moderate to brisk heat for 5 minutes until sizzling and well browned on the underside. Turn over and fry on the other side.

With a slotted spoon, transfer the lamb to a warmed serving dish. Cover loosely and keep hot. Pour the Pernod into the pan juices, with any remaining marinade, and the remaining lime rind and juice. Stir vigorously over high heat, scraping up the sediment from the base and sides of the pan. Add salt and pepper to taste, then pour over the lamb.

Push a sprig of rosemary into each chop and garnish with lime twists. Serve immediately, with simple vegetables such as buttered new potatoes and mangetout, green beans or petits pois.

LAMB CURRY WITH COCONUT AND OKRA

A Caribbean touch is given to this curry by the combination of coconut, okra, tomatoes and chilli. Okra, sometimes also called ladies' fingers or bhindi, is a fairly new vegetable to this country. But the long, green pods can now be bought in many supermarkets. Be sure to buy okra that is young and crisp.

PREPARATION TIME: *50 minutes*
COOKING TIME: *1-1¼ hours*
OVEN TEMPERATURE: *preheat to 160°C (325°F, gas mark 3)*

INGREDIENTS – *serves 4-6:*
2-2½ lb (900 g-1.1 kg) lamb fillet, trimmed of fat and cut into 1 in (25 mm) cubes
½ pint (285 ml) coconut milk (see method)
3-4 tablespoons ghee or butter
1 medium onion, peeled and thinly sliced
1-2 cloves garlic, peeled and crushed
1 level tablespoon turmeric
2 level teaspoons ground coriander
½-1 teaspoon chilli powder
12 oz (350 g) ripe tomatoes, skinned (page 389) and roughly chopped
Finely grated rind and juice of 2 limes
Salt and freshly ground black pepper
8 oz (225 g) small, young okra
GARNISH
Toasted shredded coconut
1 lime, sliced

To make fresh coconut milk for this recipe, grate the flesh of half a coconut – or use 6oz (175g) desiccated coconut – pour in ¾ pint (450ml) boiling water, stir and leave to soak for 20-30 minutes. Strain thoroughly, squeezing the milky, coconut-flavoured liquid out of the coconut through a strong wire sieve with the back of a metal spoon. Coconut milk can also be made by dissolving 4-6oz (115-175g) block creamed coconut in ½ pint (285ml) boiling water; sieve before use. Use both types within 24 hours. Ready-made coconut milk is available in cans from delicatessens and some supermarkets. All three types are suitable for this recipe.

Heat 2 tablespoons ghee or butter in a large flameproof casserole. Add the cubed lamb in batches and fry over moderate heat until browned on all sides. Remove with a slotted spoon and set aside.

Add the onion, garlic and the remaining ghee or butter if necessary, and fry gently for about 5 minutes until soft and lightly coloured. Add the spices and fry for a few minutes more, stirring constantly.

Increase the heat and stir in the coconut milk. Add the tomatoes and stir to blend with the coconut and spices. Break them up with a wooden spoon so that the juices flow. Add half the lime rind and juice with 1 level teaspoon salt and pepper to taste, then return the lamb to the casserole. Bring slowly to the boil, stirring, then cover and transfer to the preheated oven. Cook for 1-1¼ hours until the lamb is tender.

While the lamb is cooking, prepare the okra. Wash them, then cut off the stalk ends, taking care not to break into the flesh or the okra will burst open during cooking and make the sauce slimy. Blanch in boiling salted water for 5 minutes, then drain and add to the curry 10 minutes before the end of the cooking time.

Taste the curry and add more salt and pepper if necessary, then stir in the remaining lime juice. Transfer to a warmed serving dish. Sprinkle with the remaining lime rind and the shredded coconut and garnish with the lime slices. Serve hot with plain boiled rice, a sambal (a side salad) of banana slices, lemon juice and grated fresh coconut tossed together, and dishes of pickles and chutneys.

Indians usually drink water with their meals – if they drink anything at all. Buttermilk or diluted yoghurt (*lassi*) are also sometimes served. Wines and spicy food do not go well together. Lager is probably the best alcoholic drink to serve with curry.

The curry can be made up to 2 days in advance, without the okra. Store in a covered container in the refrigerator. It can also be frozen for up to 3 months. In both cases, add the okra to the curry when the time comes to reheat it.

POULTRY
&
GAME

KOTOPOULO KAPAMA

In Greek cooking, the word *kapama* is applied to casseroles with thick pungent tomato sauces. In this recipe the meat in the casserole is chicken – *kotopoulo*.

PREPARATION TIME: *1 hour*
COOKING TIME: *45 minutes*

INGREDIENTS – *serves 4:*
4 large chicken portions, weighing about 10 oz (275 g) each
3 cinnamon sticks
8 cloves
10 allspice berries
2 level tablespoons plain flour
Salt and freshly ground black pepper
4 tablespoons olive oil
2 celery sticks, trimmed and finely chopped
2 medium carrots, peeled and finely chopped
1 medium onion, peeled and finely chopped
14 oz (400 g) tin tomatoes
½ pint (285 ml) chicken stock (page 367)
2 dried bay leaves, crumbled
2 heaped tablespoons chopped fresh coriander leaves or parsley

Halve each chicken portion. Crush the cinnamon, cloves and allspice to a powder with a pestle and mortar or coffee grinder, then mix the spices with the flour, and salt and pepper to taste, on a plate. Coat the chicken portions in the mixture.

Heat 3 tablespoons of the oil in a large flameproof casserole. Add the chicken pieces and fry over moderate heat, in batches if necessary, until golden-brown on all sides. Remove with a slotted spoon and set aside.

Lower the heat and add the remaining oil, then the celery, carrots and onion. Fry gently, stirring frequently, for 10 minutes until softened. Sprinkle in any remaining spiced flour mixture from the plate and stir for 1 minute. Add the tomatoes with their juice, and crush well with a wooden spoon. Add the chicken stock and bay leaves. Bring to the boil, stirring, then return the chicken to the casserole. Lower the heat, cover and simmer for 45 minutes or until the chicken is tender. Stir in the chopped coriander or parsley. Taste and add more salt and pepper if necessary.

Serve with plain boiled rice or new potatoes, and follow with a crisp green salad.

The flavour of the casserole is improved if it is cooked a day in advance and reheated. Rabbit joints can be used instead of chicken in the casserole.

YAKITORI

Grilled marinated chicken – *yakitori* – is one of Japan's most popular dishes.

Shoyu is Japanese soya sauce. It is lighter than its Chinese equivalent, and should, if possible, be used in all Japanese dishes where subtlety of flavour is important. It is available at oriental food shops, and at some health food shops, but a mild Chinese soya sauce can be used instead. Sake – Japanese rice wine – is also available at oriental shops, but a very dry sherry can be used as a substitute.

Traditionally, yakitori should be cooked on small wooden skewers, also available at oriental stores. Soak them in water for 15 minutes before use, this prevents them burning during cooking. Ordinary metal kebab skewers can be used instead, but they should be oiled first.

For the best flavour marinate the chicken for 24 hours or even longer. It can be left for up to 3 days. Turn it frequently during this time.

PREPARATION TIME: *15 minutes*
MARINATING TIME: *at least 4 hours*
COOKING TIME: *10-15 minutes*

JAPANESE CHICKEN A sauce of sake – rice wine – mixed with Japanese soya sauce is poured over pieces of marinated chicken grilled on wooden skewers, just before serving.

INGREDIENTS – *serves 4:*
4 boneless chicken breasts, total weight 1¼-1½ lb (575-700 g)
4 fl oz (115 ml) shoyu
4 fl oz (115 ml) sake
4 level tablespoons dark, soft brown sugar
3 cloves garlic, skinned and crushed
1 in (25 mm) piece of fresh root ginger, peeled and crushed or very finely chopped
Freshly ground black pepper

Cut the chicken into bite-sized cubes, discarding all skin. Put half of the shoyu, half of the sake and half of the sugar in a shallow dish with the garlic, ginger and black pepper to taste. Whisk well together until the sugar has dissolved.

Add the chicken pieces to the dish and stir well to coat in the marinade. Cover the dish tightly and marinate in the refrigerator for at least 4 hours. Turn the chicken occasionally.

When ready to cook, remove the chicken from the marinade and thread onto skewers. Cook over a charcoal barbecue or under a preheated moderate grill for 10-15 minutes, turning the skewers frequently and brushing with the marinade.

While the chicken is cooking put the remaining shoyu, sake and sugar in a small saucepan with pepper to taste and simmer for a few minutes. Serve the yakitori hot, with the sauce poured over it, accompanied by rice and stir-fried vegetables.

BONED CHICKEN WITH PISTACHIO STUFFING

A boned chicken is much easier to carve than a whole one. If pistachio nuts are difficult to find, walnuts or almonds may be substituted. Breast of chicken can be used instead of veal.

PREPARATION TIME: *45 minutes*
COOKING TIME: *1½ hours*
OVEN TEMPERATURE: *preheat to 190°C (375°F, gas mark 5)*

PISTACHIO CHICKEN Green pistachio nuts and green pepper give distinctive flavour and colour to the stuffing in this roast boned chicken.

INGREDIENTS – *serves 6:*
1 chicken, about 2½-3 lb (1.1-1.4 kg)
8 oz (225 g) veal shoulder
1 chicken liver
1 oz (25 g) butter
1 level tablespoon cornflour
¼ pint (150 ml) milk
2 egg whites
1 small green pepper, washed, seeded and chopped
1 oz (25 g) pistachio nuts, shelled and halved

Bone the chicken (page 378).

Chop the veal and liver very finely until almost a purée. This is best done in a food processor or by passing the meat twice through the finest blade of a mincer.

Melt the butter in a small saucepan over medium heat. Stir in the cornflour, then, stirring all the time, slowly add the milk. Bring to the boil and simmer for a minute until thick. Remove from the heat, cool for about 5 minutes and stir into the meat.

Beat the egg whites into the mixture, then fold in the green pepper and pistachio nuts.

Fill the chicken with the stuffing and sew up with fine string. Place in a roasting tin with a knob of lard or margarine in the bottom of the tin. Roast in the preheated oven for 1½ hours, basting at intervals.

Serve hot with new potatoes and a green vegetable such as french beans or spinach. Alternatively, allow the chicken to cool, then refrigerate until needed. Remove the string before carving.

POLLO AL CACCIATORE

The Italian title of this dish means 'chicken hunter's style' – that is, a simple dish which a hunter might prepare for his evening meal. Free-range chickens will give the best flavour. Corn or maize-fed birds, which have a yellow flesh, are most like the chickens sold in Italy.

The dish can be cooked up to 24 hours in advance and kept in the covered casserole in the refrigerator before reheating.

PREPARATION TIME: *30 minutes*
COOKING TIME: *45 minutes*

INGREDIENTS – *serves 4:*
3½-4 lb (1.6-1.8 kg) roasting chicken cut into 8 serving pieces (page 378)
2-3 level tablespoons plain flour
2 level teaspoons chopped fresh rosemary OR 1 level teaspoon dried rosemary
Salt and freshly ground black pepper
1½ oz (40 g) butter
3 tablespoons olive oil
1 medium onion, peeled and roughly chopped
1-2 cloves garlic, peeled and crushed
¼ pint (150 ml) dry white wine or chicken stock
2 bay leaves
1 tablespoon wine vinegar
2 level teaspoons tomato purée
Pinch of sugar
8 oz (225 g) button mushrooms, wiped and halved, or sliced if large

MENU

Cook Ahead Italian Dinner for Four

POLLO AL CACCIATORE
this page

BOILED RICE

GREEN SALAD

TORTA DI MELE
page 108

IN ADVANCE Allow 2 hours the day before. Make the torta di mele. While it is baking, cook the pollo al cacciatore.

ON THE DAY Allow about 30 minutes to cook the rice, reheat the pollo and make the salad.

TO DRINK A dry white Italian wine such as Soave or Verdicchio.

Mix the flour with the rosemary and salt and pepper. Coat the chicken pieces with the seasoned flour. Melt 1oz (25g) of the butter with 2 tablespoons of the oil in a large flameproof casserole. Add the chicken pieces (in batches if necessary) and fry over moderate heat until the skin is golden-brown on all sides. Remove from the casserole and set aside.

Lower the heat and add the onion and garlic to the casserole. Fry gently for about 5 minutes until softened, then add all the remaining ingredients except the mushrooms. Bring slowly to the boil, stirring, then return the chicken to the casserole. Lower the heat again and simmer for 30 minutes.

Heat the remaining butter and oil in a frying pan, add the mushrooms and toss over high heat for 1-2 minutes until lightly coloured. Add to the casserole and stir gently into the sauce. Continue cooking for a further 15 minutes until the chicken is tender. Remove the bay leaves, taste and adjust the seasoning before serving.

The traditional Italian accompaniment is *Polenta* (page 229), plain boiled brown rice is an alternative.

This dish is included in a menu on the opposite page.

CHICKEN HYMETTUS

Mount Hymettus in Greece has been famous for its honey since ancient times. The mountain is covered in thyme, from which the bees collect their pollen, giving the honey an exceptional flavour, said by some to be the best in the world. However, honey from Hymettus is not essential for the delicate honey sauce in this dish.

Marinating the chicken for 2-3 days in lime juice makes it very tender and full of flavour. The chicken can quite safely be left in the marinade for this length of time, but it must be very fresh when you buy it. If limes are unobtainable, lemons may be substituted, but you may only need the juice of 2 lemons.

Chicken Hymettus can be made up to 24 hours in advance and kept in the covered casserole in the refrigerator. On reheating, the casserole should be allowed to simmer for at least 10 minutes.

PREPARATION TIME: *25 minutes*
MARINATING TIME: *2-3 days*
COOKING TIME: *45 minutes*

INGREDIENTS – *serves 4:*
4 chicken portions
Finely grated rind and juice of
  3 limes
Good pinch of saffron strands
1 oz (25 g) butter
4 tablespoons corn oil or
  sunflower oil
2 tablespoons clear honey
2 level teaspoons chopped fresh
  thyme OR *1 level teaspoon dried*
  thyme
2 heaped tablespoons chopped
  fresh mint
Salt and freshly ground black
  pepper
1 oz (25 g) flaked almonds

Cut each chicken portion in half, then prick all over with the point of a fine skewer and place in a shallow dish. Sprinkle with the grated lime rind and the juice, then cover the dish and

marinate in the refrigerator for 2-3 days. Turn the chicken in the juice occasionally during this time, twice a day if possible.

When ready to cook, soak the saffron strands in 4 tablespoons of boiling water for 20 minutes, then strain, reserving the saffron-coloured liquid. Melt the butter with the oil in a large, heavy-based frying pan. Remove the chicken from the marinade with a slotted spoon. Add the chicken to the pan and fry over brisk heat until golden-brown on all sides.

Mix the honey with the saffron liquid and any of the marinade remaining in the dish, then pour over the chicken. Add thyme, half the mint and a good sprinkling of salt and pepper. Cover the pan and simmer gently for 45 minutes or until the chicken is tender, basting occasionally.

Just before serving, toast the almonds under the grill until golden-brown. Mix with the remaining mint. Transfer the chicken and juices to a warmed serving dish and sprinkle over the almonds and mint. Serve hot, with new potatoes, cooked in their skins, and a green vegetable such as french beans, spinach or courgettes.

FOOD OF THE GODS After lengthy marinating in lime juice, these sautéed chicken joints are tender and full of flavour. Honey, saffron, almonds and mint make a fragrant Greek sauce.

CHICKEN SALAD VERONICA

White grapes are one of the main ingredients of this salad as with French dishes cooked *à la véronique*.

The salad can be made up to 24 hours in advance, without the chicory. Store in a covered container in the refrigerator.

PREPARATION TIME: *30 minutes*
COOLING TIME: *about 2 hours plus chilling time*
COOKING TIME: *1-1 1/2 hours*

INGREDIENTS – *serves 4:*
3 lb (1.4 kg) chicken, with giblets
1 carrot, peeled and chopped
1 onion, peeled and stuck with about 6 cloves
2 celery sticks, trimmed and chopped
2 level tablespoons chopped fresh tarragon OR 2 level teaspoons dried tarragon
Salt and freshly ground black pepper
4 tablespoons dry white wine
Finely grated rind and juice of 1 lemon
1/4 pint (150 ml) thick homemade mayonnaise (page 369)
2 tablespoons fresh single or double cream (optional)
2 level teaspoons French (Dijon) mustard
4 oz (115 g) seedless white grapes, rinsed and dried
2 heads of chicory
GARNISH
Lemon twists (page 286)
Sprigs of tarragon

SALAD BOUQUET *Petals of chicory leaves hold diced chicken mixed with grapes and tarragon.*

Fill a large saucepan about one-third to half full of water. Put in the carrot, onion and celery, with half of the tarragon and salt and pepper to taste, then bring to the boil.

Immerse the chicken carefully in the liquid and add the giblets, except the liver which would make the stock taste bitter. Cover the pan with a lid and simmer for 1-1 1/2 hours or until the chicken is tender.

Leave the chicken to cool in the liquid, then remove and set aside. Strain 1/2 pint (285ml) stock into a smaller, heavy-based saucepan. Add the wine and lemon juice and boil vigorously to reduce to about 4fl oz (115ml). Leave to cool.

Meanwhile, remove the chicken flesh from the bones. Dice neatly, discarding the skin and any fat. Put the diced flesh in a bowl with the mayonnaise, cream (if using), mustard and grated lemon rind. Fold gently together, then gradually stir in the cold reduced stock. The sauce is quite thin at this point – it thickens with chilling. Reserve a few grapes for garnish then add the rest with the remaining tarragon and salt and pepper to taste. Mix gently again. Chill in the refrigerator for at least 30 minutes before serving.

To serve, line individual bowls with chicory leaves, then pile the salad in the centre. Garnish with the reserved grapes, lemon twists and tarragon sprigs. Serve chilled with crispbreads or French bread.

TURKEY GROUNDNUT STEW

'Groundnut' is another name for peanut – so called because the seed pods ripen below the ground. In this recipe the peanuts are deep-fried to give the stew extra colour and flavour, but they can be toasted under the grill or dry-fried in a non-stick frying pan instead.

PREPARATION TIME: *20 minutes*
COOKING TIME: *40 minutes*

INGREDIENTS – *serves 4:*
2 lb (900 g) boneless lean turkey meat, cut into 3/4 in (20 mm) cubes
2 tablespoons vegetable oil
1 medium onion, peeled and finely chopped
1 clove garlic, peeled and crushed
2 dried red chillies, finely chopped OR 1 level teaspoon chilli powder
1 level tablespoon tomato purée
1/2 pint (285 ml) turkey stock or chicken stock (page 367)
2 bay leaves
Salt and freshly ground black pepper
8 oz (225 g) shelled unsalted peanuts
Vegetable oil, for deep-frying
1 large green pepper, seeded and diced
Pinch of cayenne pepper or chilli powder, to taste

Heat the oil in a flameproof casserole, add the onion, garlic and chillies and fry gently, stirring, for about 5 minutes until softened. Add the turkey cubes, increase the heat and fry until browned on all sides. Stir and toss the turkey frequently, so that it combines with the onion mixture.

Stir in the tomato purée, then pour in the stock and add the bay leaves, with salt and pepper to taste. Bring slowly to the boil, stirring constantly, then cover and simmer for 40 minutes or until the turkey is tender.

Meanwhile, heat the oil in a deep-fat fryer to 190°C (375°F). Deep-fry (page 372) 6oz (175g) of the peanuts for about 5 minutes until the skins turn a rich, dark brown, then remove the peanuts with a slotted spoon and drain on kitchen paper.

When the turkey is tender, measure off ½ pint (285ml) of the cooking liquid. Discard the bay leaves. Blend the fried peanuts and measured cooking liquid together in a food processor or liquidiser to make a thick paste.

Add the peanut paste to the casserole, stir well to combine and heat through gently, stirring. Heat a little oil in a frying pan and fry the remaining peanuts and the diced green pepper with cayenne or chilli powder to taste. Taste the stew and adjust the seasoning, then turn into a serving dish and sprinkle with the fried peanuts and pepper. Serve immediately.

Groundnut stews are traditionally served with plain boiled rice and fried bananas.
, The stew can be made up to 48 hours in advance and kept in a covered casserole in the refrigerator, then reheated.

STIR-FRIED TURKEY WITH CELERY, WALNUTS AND ORANGE

A Chinese wok is not essential for this dish – a deep, heavy-based frying pan can be used instead – but it does make the stir-frying (page 372) much easier. However, aim to keep all the ingredients moving over high heat so that they cook quickly and evenly.

PREPARATION TIME: *20 minutes*
COOKING TIME: *25 minutes*

INGREDIENTS – *serves 4:*
4 turkey escalopes, or slices of breast, total weight about 1½ lb (700 g)
1 small orange
2 oz (50 g) shelled walnut pieces
4 celery sticks, trimmed
1 onion, peeled
Finely grated rind and juice (5 tablespoons) of 1 orange
2 level tablespoons soft brown sugar
3 tablespoons soya sauce
3 tablespoons vegetable oil
1 tablespoon sesame oil
Salt and freshly ground black pepper

First prepare the garnish. Remove the outer peel (zest) from half of the small orange, cut it into matchstick strips, then blanch them in boiling water for 2-3 minutes. Drain and leave to dry on absorbent kitchen paper. Divide the orange into segments, removing all peel, pith and membrane (page 398). Set aside.

Cut the turkey into thin strips, across the grain of the meat. Set aside a few whole pieces of walnut then chop the rest roughly. Cut the celery into diagonal, chunky slices. Slice the onion thinly. Put the grated orange rind and orange juice in a jug with the sugar and soya sauce. Whisk well to combine.

Heat 2 tablespoons of the vegetable oil in a wok or deep, heavy-based frying pan. Add the onion and fry gently for about 5 minutes until softened. Add the celery and stir-fry for a few minutes until lightly coloured but still crisp. Remove with a slotted spoon and set aside. Add the strips of turkey to the wok, increase the heat and stir-fry for 10 minutes until lightly coloured and just tender. Remove the wok from the heat. Heat the remaining tablespoon of vegetable oil with the sesame oil in a separate small pan until hot. Add the reserved whole pieces of walnut and the orange segments and toss over high heat to heat through.

Return the wok to the heat and add the onion, celery and chopped walnuts to the turkey. Pour in the orange juice mixture, add salt and pepper to taste and stir-fry over moderate heat for 2-3 minutes until all the ingredients are combined. Stir in the orange segments and reserved walnut pieces.

Turn into a warmed serving dish and sprinkle with the reserved blanched strips of orange zest. Serve immediately with Chinese egg noodles.

STIR-FRIED TURKEY Narrow strips of turkey meat are quickly cooked with celery, orange juice, chopped walnuts and segments of orange.

DUCK WITH PLUM AND GINGER GLAZE

When the Chinese cook duck they take particular care with the skin which is regarded as a delicacy. In this recipe the skin is glazed. To make the glaze, Chinese cooks would purée fresh plums, but plum jam makes a very good substitute. Low-sugar or reduced-sugar jam gives a fruitier flavour.

If duckling portions are unavailable, use a whole duck cut into quarters. Chilli sauce is available at most supermarkets as well as Chinese food shops. It has a pungent, fiery taste, and should be used sparingly. The amount suggested here makes the glaze quite hot.

PREPARATION TIME: *15 minutes*
COOKING TIME: *1 hour 25 minutes*
OVEN TEMPERATURE: *preheat to 180°C (350°F, gas mark 4)*

INGREDIENTS – *serves 4:*
4 duckling portions (leg, thigh, or breast and wing)
Salt
4 oz (115 g) plum jam
2 tablespoons lemon juice
1 clove garlic, peeled and crushed
2 level teaspoons ground ginger
2 teaspoons chilli sauce
Freshly ground black pepper
GARNISH
Spring onion tassels (page 287)

Prick the duckling portions all over with a skewer to allow the fat to drain off, then rub the skins with salt. Place the portions on a rack in a roasting tin and pour ¼ pint (150ml) of water into the tin. Roast in the preheated oven for 1¼ hours or until the flesh is tender and the juices run clear when the thickest part of the flesh is pierced with a knife.

Remove the duckling from the oven and pour off all the fatty juices from the tin. Raise the oven temperature to 220°C (425°F, gas mark 7).

Put the plum jam in a saucepan with the lemon juice, garlic, ginger, chilli sauce and salt and pepper to taste. Heat gently until the jam has melted, stirring all the time.

Place the duckling portions in a clean roasting tin and brush the jam glaze over the skin. It may be necessary to apply two coats to use up all the glaze. Return to the oven and roast for a further 10 minutes, until glazed. Transfer the duckling portions to a serving dish and garnish with spring onion tassels.

For a Sunday lunch, serve hot with crisp roast potatoes and vegetables in season. Alternatively, serve with the traditional Chinese accompaniments: egg noodles and stir-fried vegetables. The duck is also very good cold.

PLUM DUCK The secret is in the glazing – a blend of plum jam, lemon juice, garlic, ginger and chilli. The duck is served with stir-fried vegetables and egg noodles, and garnished with spring onion tassels.

GAMEKEEPER'S CASSEROLE

Rabbit reared for the table has a very mild flavour, unlike wild rabbit which is more gamey. Rabbit portions are available both fresh and frozen, but 4 chicken portions can also be used for this recipe.

PREPARATION TIME: *1 hour*
COOKING TIME: *2 hours*
OVEN TEMPERATURE: *preheat to 160°C (325°F, gas mark 3)*

INGREDIENTS – *serves 4:*
4 rabbit legs, thawed and thoroughly dried if frozen
4 oz (115 g) smoked streaky bacon, rind removed
2 oz (50 g) butter
2 tablespoons olive oil
1 medium onion, peeled and roughly chopped
1 celery stick, trimmed and roughly chopped
1 medium carrot, peeled and thinly sliced
2 cloves garlic, peeled and crushed
¼ pint (150 ml) dry white wine
2½ fl oz (75 ml) full-bodied red wine
2 fl oz (50 ml) red wine vinegar
2 level teaspoons chopped fresh rosemary OR 1 level teaspoon dried rosemary
5 juniper berries
2 whole cloves
2 bay leaves
Salt and freshly ground black pepper
GARNISH
Fresh bay leaves and rosemary sprigs

Cut each rabbit leg in half with a sharp knife. Make ½in (15mm) deep incisions in the rabbit flesh with the point of the knife. Cut the bacon into small pieces and insert them into the cuts in the rabbit flesh.

Melt the butter with the oil in a large flameproof casserole. Add the rabbit pieces in batches and fry over moderate heat until browned on all sides. Remove from the pan with a slotted spoon and set aside.

Add the onion, celery, carrot and garlic and fry over gentle heat for about 10 minutes, stirring frequently until softened and lightly coloured.

Return the rabbit pieces to the casserole. Add the remaining ingredients with salt and pepper to taste. Bring slowly to the boil, then cover and cook in the preheated oven for 2 hours, or until the rabbit is so tender that the meat comes away easily from the bones. Taste and adjust the seasoning of the sauce. Garnish with fresh bay leaves and rosemary sprigs.

Serve with *Polenta* (page 229), or creamed potatoes to absorb the abundant sauce. Rice or noodles could also be served. Accompany with crisply cooked green vegetables such as broccoli, brussels sprouts or french beans.

The casserole can be cooked in advance and kept in the covered casserole in the refrigerator for up to 24 hours before reheating. Allow it to simmer for at least 10 minutes.

EGGS & CHEESE

WATERCRESS AND RICOTTA QUICHE

The ingredients in this quiche give it a particularly piquant, peppery flavour. Italian Ricotta cheese is available at Italian shops, cheese specialists and some delicatessens. It is a fresh, soft, white cheese made from ewe's milk, with a slightly acid taste. For this recipe, curd cheese or sieved cottage cheese can be used instead. Single or double cream can be used instead of the soured cream. Milk can also be used instead of soured cream, but in this case the filling will have less body.

The quiche will keep fresh for up to 24 hours. Wrap it loosely in kitchen foil and store in an airtight container. Refresh the quiche, still in the foil wrapping in a moderate oven – 180°C (350°F, gas mark 4) – for about 10 minutes before serving.

PREPARATION TIME: *40 minutes*
COOKING TIME: *25 minutes plus standing time*
OVEN TEMPERATURE: *preheat to 190°C (375°F, gas mark 5)*

INGREDIENTS – *serves 4-6:*
Shortcrust pastry made with 6 oz (175 g) flour (page 392)
2 oz (50 g) butter or margarine
1 medium onion, peeled and finely chopped
2 bunches of watercress – about 6 oz (175 g) – trimmed and chopped
8 oz (225 g) Ricotta cheese
¼ pint (150 ml) soured cream
3 eggs, beaten
¼ teaspoon cayenne pepper
Salt

Line a deep 9in (230mm) loose-based metal flan tin with the pastry. Prick the base with a fork, line with foil and beans, then bake blind (page 393) in the preheated oven for 15 minutes. Remove the foil and beans and bake for a further 5 minutes.

To make the filling, melt the butter or margarine in a saucepan, add the chopped onion and fry gently for about 5 minutes until softened. Stir in the chopped watercress then remove from the heat.

Put the Ricotta cheese in a bowl and gradually beat in the soured cream until evenly mixed. Add the eggs, with the cayenne and salt to taste, and beat once again. Stir in the watercress and onion.

Pour the filling into the pastry case, return to the oven and bake for 25 minutes or until the filling is just set. Leave to cool for at least 15 minutes before removing from the tin and slicing. Serve warm or cold with a tomato salad.

PERSIAN EGGAH

There are countless variations on eggah made throughout the Middle East. It is a kind of filled omelette, served solid and flat like the Italian frittata or Spanish tortilla. In the Middle East, large eggahs such as this are served as main course dishes. Less substantial ones are eaten as snacks. Cold, they are good for cocktails or picnics.

PERSIAN OMELETTE The scent of cardamom suffuses this omelette filled with onions and noodles.

PREPARATION TIME: *50 minutes*
COOKING TIME: *20 minutes*

INGREDIENTS – *serves 4-6:*
2 oz (50 g) butter
4 tablespoons olive oil
2 large Spanish onions, peeled and thinly sliced
4-6 cardamom pods, according to taste, crushed
9 oz (250 g) Chinese noodles
6 eggs
Salt and freshly ground black pepper

Melt the butter with 2 tablespoons of the oil in a large, heavy-based frying pan. Add the onions and cardamom pods and fry very gently for 40 minutes until the onions are very soft. Stir frequently during this time, and take care that the onions do not catch on the base of the pan and burn. They should be a light golden colour at the end of the cooking time.

While the onions are cooking, plunge the noodles into a large pan of boiling salted water. Cover tightly and immediately remove from the heat. Leave for 5 minutes, then drain thoroughly and cut into short lengths with kitchen scissors.

Crack the eggs into a bowl and beat lightly with a fork, adding salt and pepper to taste. Remove the onions from the pan with a slotted spoon and add to the eggs together with the noodles. Mix well.

Add 1 tablespoon of oil to the frying pan and heat until moderately hot. Pour in the egg mixture, mix lightly with a fork, then cook, uncovered, for 15-20 minutes until the underside is golden-brown. Do not stir or shake the mixture.

Turn the eggah out of the pan, upside down, onto a plate. Heat 1 more tablespoon of oil in the pan, then slide the eggah back into the pan, cooked side uppermost. Cook over moderate heat for 5 minutes, until the underside is golden-brown. Alternatively, just slide the pan under a preheated grill to brown the uncooked side.

Serve hot with a mixed salad and a bowl of chilled natural yoghurt (page 12).

CAULIFLOWER BLUE CHEESE SOUFFLÉ WITH SAGE

One of the classic family recipes – cauliflower cheese – is given another variation as a light, fluffy soufflé. Danish Blue cheese gives the soufflé a good sharp flavour, but any blue cheese, such as Stilton, or Gorgonzola, can be used instead – as can Sage Derby, in which case no extra sage is needed.

A soufflé cannot be cooked in advance – it must be served immediately after baking because it starts to sink – but the cheese sauce base can be made the night before. Store it in a covered bowl in a cold larder or the refrigerator, then cook the cauliflower and continue with the recipe.

PREPARATION TIME: *40 minutes*
COOKING TIME: *35 minutes*
OVEN TEMPERATURE: *preheat to 200°C (400°F, gas mark 6)*

INGREDIENTS – *serves 3-4:*
1½ oz (40 g) butter
1½ oz (40 g) plain flour
8 fl oz (225 ml) milk
4 oz (115 g) Danish Blue cheese, grated
2 level teaspoons chopped fresh sage OR 1 level teaspoon dried sage
Salt and freshly ground black pepper
8 oz (225 g) cauliflower florets, divided into tiny sprigs
3 eggs, separated

Lightly butter the inside of a 5½in (140mm) or 1¾ pint (1 litre) capacity soufflé dish.

Melt the butter in a saucepan, add the flour and cook, stirring, over a low heat for 1-2 minutes. Remove from the heat and gradually blend in the milk, then return to the heat and bring to the boil, stirring constantly. Simmer until very thick, then add the cheese, sage, a little salt and plenty of black pepper. Stir over gentle heat until the cheese has just melted, then remove the pan from the heat and set aside to cool slightly.

While the sauce is cooling, bring a large pan of salted water to the boil. Plunge the cauliflower into the water, bring quickly back to the boil and blanch for 2 minutes only. Drain thoroughly.

Fold the egg yolks into the cheese sauce, then fold in the cauliflower. In a clean, dry bowl, whisk the egg whites until stiff and standing in peaks. With a large metal spoon, fold the egg whites carefully into the cauliflower cheese with a figure-of-eight motion until evenly incorporated.

Spoon the mixture into the prepared soufflé dish, then bake immediately in the preheated oven for 35 minutes until well risen, with a golden-brown crust. Do not open the oven door until the cooking time is up. The sudden rush of cold air will cause the soufflé to sink.

Serve immediately with a salad for a light main course.

CUCUMBER AND WATERCRESS MOUSSE

A summer evening meal, a dinner party or a buffet party are all occasions when this mousse can be served.

The mousse can be made up to 24 hours in advance and kept in its mould in the refrigerator, until ready to garnish.

PREPARATION TIME: *1 hour*
CHILLING TIME: *at least 4 hours, preferably overnight*

INGREDIENTS – *serves 6-8:*
1 small or 1/2 large cucumber
Salt
1 bunch watercress, about 3 oz (75 g)
4 hard-boiled eggs, shelled and chopped
1 lemon
1/2 oz (15 g) powdered gelatine
2 egg whites (save yolks for mayonnaise)
MAYONNAISE
2 egg yolks
3 level teaspoons Dijon mustard
Freshly ground black pepper
4 fl oz (115 ml) olive oil
4 fl oz (115 ml) vegetable oil or corn oil
5 teaspoons lemon juice
GARNISH
Slices of cucumber and hard-boiled egg OR sieved hard-boiled egg

Cut the cucumber in half lengthways and scoop out the seeds with a sharp-edged teaspoon. Finely chop the flesh, place in a colander and sprinkle lightly with salt. Cover with a plate, place heavy weights on top and leave to stand for 30 minutes to leach out the bitter juices from the cucumber.

Meanwhile, make the mayonnaise (page 369).

Finely chop half the watercress, discarding the stalks. Place in a bowl with the chopped hard-boiled eggs and cucumber, fold in the mayonnaise and grate in the rind of the lemon.

Squeeze the juice from the lemon into a small heatproof bowl. Sprinkle in the gelatine and leave to soak for 5 minutes until spongy. Stand the bowl in a pan of gently simmering water and stir until the gelatine has dissolved. Remove the bowl from the pan and leave to cool for about 5 minutes, then stir the gelatine into the mousse.

Whisk the egg whites until stiff and dry, then fold into the mousse until evenly mixed. Taste, and adjust the seasoning. Pour into an oiled 2 pint (1.1 litre) ring mould or kugelhopf tin. Cover and chill in the refrigerator for at least 4 hours, preferably overnight, until set.

When set, loosen the top edge of the mousse from the mould with the point of a knife. Dip the base of the mould in hot water very briefly, then turn the mousse out onto a serving plate.

COOL GREEN RING The yellow and white of a hard-boiled egg and crisp sprigs of watercress garnish a light watercress and cucumber mousse.

Fill the centre of the mousse with the remaining watercress, and garnish with slices of cucumber and hard-boiled egg, or sieved hard-boiled egg. Serve chilled, with brown bread or crispbread and butter.

MEXICAN EGGS

In Mexico, this colourful spicy egg dish is known also as *huevos rancheros* (ranch-style eggs). Each person helps himself to a tortilla, a kind of pancake made from *masa harina*, or maize flour, then spoons the egg and pepper mixture on top. Tortillas can be bought in some supermarkets and delicatessens, or this dish can be eaten with toast.

The pepper mixture, without the eggs, can be made up to 2 days in advance, and improves in flavour with keeping. Store it, covered, in the refrigerator. When reheating, add a little water because the mixture thickens while standing. The pepper mixture can also be frozen.

PREPARATION TIME: *20 minutes*
COOKING TIME: *45 minutes*

INGREDIENTS – *serves 4:*
4 tablespoons olive oil
1 large onion, peeled and roughly chopped
2 cloves garlic, peeled and crushed
½-1 level teaspoon chilli powder
2 green peppers, cored, seeded and thinly sliced
2 red peppers, cored, seeded and thinly sliced
14 oz (400 g) tin tomatoes
Pinch of sugar
Salt and freshly ground black pepper
4 large eggs
4 oz (115 g) strong Cheddar cheese, grated
4 heaped tablespoons freshly grated Parmesan cheese

M E N U

Family High Tea for Four

MEXICAN EGGS
this page

TORTILLAS or
HOT BUTTERED TOAST

AMERICAN
BUTTERSCOTCH PIE
page 108

Tortillas can be bought from some delicatessens.
IN ADVANCE The pie can be made up to 2 days ahead.
ON THE DAY Allow an hour to make the Mexican eggs. While they are cooking, make the toast or warm the tortillas in the oven.

Heat the oil in a deep, heavy-based frying pan which has a lid. Add the onion and garlic, and fry gently for about 5 minutes until softened. Add the chilli powder to taste and the sliced peppers, and fry for a further 10-15 minutes, stirring frequently, until soft. Add the tomatoes with their juice, the sugar, and salt and pepper to taste. Stir with a wooden spoon, crushing the tomatoes. Simmer gently,

uncovered, for 40 minutes. Taste, and add more salt and pepper if necessary.

Make 4 hollows in the mixture with the back of a spoon, then crack an egg into each hollow. Cover the pan tightly with a lid, then cook for 3 minutes. Mix together the Cheddar and Parmesan cheeses and sprinkle over the eggs. Cover the pan again and cook for a further 2 minutes, or until the eggs are cooked to your liking. Serve immediately with Mexican tortillas or triangles of hot buttered toast.

This dish is included in a menu on this page.

TORTA PASQUALINA

Legend has it that *Torta Pasqualina* is one of the oldest of Italian recipes. The name means 'Easter Pie' and it is said that the dough was originally rolled into 33 layers, to symbolise Christ's age when he died. Today it is usually made more simply, with puff pastry as in this recipe. Shortcrust pastry can also be used.

A variation on Torta Pasqualina from Genoa includes artichokes. If you wish to do so, use a 14oz (400g) tin of artichoke hearts, drained, quartered and folded into the filling.

Torta Pasqualina is a filling dish. It can be made less substantial by omitting the 6 whole eggs. It will keep in a cool place for 2-3 days.

PREPARATION TIME: *50 minutes*
COOKING TIME: *1¼ hours*
COOLING TIME: *at least 2 hours*
OVEN TEMPERATURE: *preheat to 200°C (400°F, gas mark 6)*

INGREDIENTS – *serves 6-8:*
2 lb (900 g) fresh spinach OR 1 lb (450 g) frozen leaf spinach, thawed and well drained
Salt
1 oz (25 g) butter
1-2 cloves garlic, peeled and crushed
1 level teaspoon dried marjoram
1 lb (450 g) Ricotta or curd cheese
8 eggs
3 oz (75 g) Parmesan cheese, freshly grated
¼ teaspoon freshly grated nutmeg
Freshly ground black pepper
14 oz (400 g) prepared weight puff pastry (page 394)
Vegetable oil, for brushing

Wash the spinach thoroughly, discarding any damaged or yellow leaves. Cut off and discard thick stalks and ribs.

Put the spinach in a large saucepan with only the water that clings to the leaves. Add ½ teaspoon of salt and cook over moderate heat for about 5 minutes until tender. Drain thoroughly, then chop finely.

Rinse the pan and melt the butter in it. Add the spinach, garlic and marjoram, then cook over moderate heat for about 5 minutes, shaking the pan constantly. Turn into a bowl and leave until cold.

While the spinach is cooling, put the Ricotta or curd cheese in another bowl and beat in 2 of the eggs. Add 2oz (50g) of the Parmesan cheese, the nutmeg, a little salt and plenty of pepper.

Line a 10in (250mm) loose-based cake tin with non-stick baking paper, or use a non-stick tin. Roll out two-thirds of the pastry on a floured surface, and use to line the base and right up the sides of the tin.

Mix the spinach and cheese mixtures together, then spoon into the tin. Make 6 large hollows in the mixture and break an egg into each. Sprinkle the eggs with salt and pepper then the remaining Parmesan.

Roll out the remaining pastry and cut out a lid for the top of the pie. Brush the edge of the lining pastry with water, then place the lid on top. Press the edges to seal, then crimp or flute (page 393). Prick the lid all over with a fork and brush with a little oil. If you wish, roll out the unused scraps of pastry and use a sharp knife to cut out the letters to spell TORTA PAS-QUALINA. Place the letters on top of the pie, then brush with oil. Bake in the preheated oven for 1¼ hours; do not worry if the pastry rises up above the rim of the tin. Cool in the tin. Serve cold, cut into wedges.

EASTER PIE The letters spell the name of this Italian pie. Serve with chilled white wine and a salad of tomatoes and sliced onions.

PASTA & RICE

PASTA MEXICANA

Avocado, tomatoes, onion, garlic and Tabasco are all common ingredients in Mexican cookery. The sauce can be made 2-3 days in advance. Store covered in the refrigerator. Add the avocado on reheating.

PREPARATION TIME: *20 minutes plus time to make pasta*
COOKING TIME: *40 minutes*

INGREDIENTS – *serves 4:*
Tagliatelle made with 11 oz (300 g) flour and 3 eggs (see recipe for fresh pasta, page 390) OR 14 oz (400 g) dried small pasta shapes
2 tablespoons olive oil
1 small onion, peeled and finely chopped
1 clove garlic, peeled and crushed
1 lb (450 g) ripe tomatoes
¼ pint (150 ml) vegetable stock (page 368) or water
4 tablespoons red or white wine (optional)
A few drops Tabasco sauce
Salt and freshly ground black pepper
1 large ripe avocado
2 teaspoons lemon juice

Heat the oil in a heavy-based saucepan, add the onion and garlic, and fry gently for about 5 minutes until softened.

Skin (page 389) and roughly chop the tomatoes. Add them to the onion, breaking them up with a wooden spoon, then add the stock or water and the wine, if used, with Tabasco and salt and pepper to taste. Bring to the boil, stirring, then lower the heat, cover and simmer very gently for 40 minutes, stirring occasionally.

Towards the end of the cooking time for the sauce, bring about 6 pints (3.4 litres) of water to the boil in a very large saucepan with 2 level teaspoons of salt. Add the tagliatelle or pasta shapes, a little at a time. Stir well until the water comes back to the boil, then simmer for 3 minutes for fresh pasta, 10-12 minutes (or according to the packet instructions) for dried pasta shapes.

Halve, peel and stone the avocado, then dice the flesh finely and toss in the lemon juice. Add the avocado to the tomato sauce and heat through gently for 1-2 minutes. Taste and add salt and pepper if necessary.

Drain the pasta thoroughly, then turn into a warmed serving bowl. Pour over the sauce and serve immediately with a simple green salad.

TUNA CANNELLONI

Cannelloni made with fresh pasta is a much lighter dish than cannelloni made with dried. This cannelloni dish is lighter still by having a fish filling instead of the heavier, though more usual, meat filling.

For cannelloni – literally *cannelle* are 'pipes'; *cannelloni* are 'large pipes' – the fresh pasta needs to be rolled very thinly, otherwise the dish will be too heavy. Do not try to make the dish with fresh pasta unless you have a pasta machine to do the necessary rolling. In this recipe the pasta is made with one less egg than usual, to make a firmer dough which rolls up easily around the filling.

If you are using dried cannelloni tubes, it is not necessary to pre-boil them.

This dish can be made to the stage before baking up to 24 hours in advance. Keep covered in the refrigerator. The dish can also be frozen at this stage. To cook from frozen, allow about 20 minutes extra and cover for half the cooking time.

FRESH CANNELLONI If you wish to make your own fresh pasta, cannelloni is the simplest kind to try. In this recipe the squares of pasta are rolled round a light filling of tuna fish, and cooked in layers of tomato sauce. The rich cheese topping is golden and bubbling when it is taken from the oven.

PREPARATION TIME: *1½ hours plus time to make pasta*
COOKING TIME: *40 minutes*
OVEN TEMPERATURE: *preheat to 190°C (375°F, gas mark 5)*

INGREDIENTS – *serves 6:*
18-20 sheets of fresh pasta (page 390) made with 9½ oz (265 g) flour and 2 eggs OR 18-20 dried cannelloni tubes
2 oz (50 g) freshly grated Parmesan cheese
TOMATO SAUCE
4 tablespoons olive oil
1 medium onion, peeled and finely chopped
1 large carrot, peeled and finely chopped
2 celery sticks, finely chopped
2 cloves garlic, peeled and crushed
3 × 14 oz (400 g) tins tomatoes
1 level tablespoon tomato purée
Salt and freshly ground black pepper
1 level teaspoon dried basil
1 level teaspoon dried oregano
FILLING
2 × 7 oz (200 g) tins tuna in oil or brine
4 oz (115 g) frozen peas, cooked and drained
4 level tablespoons fresh white breadcrumbs
1 level teaspoon dried oregano
½ teaspoon freshly grated nutmeg
CHEESE SAUCE
1½ oz (40 g) butter or margarine
1½ oz (40 g) plain flour
¾ pint (450 ml) milk
4 oz (115 g) Cheddar cheese, grated
Pinch of freshly grated nutmeg

First make the tomato sauce. Heat the oil in a heavy-based saucepan and add the onion, carrot, celery and garlic. Fry gently for about 10 minutes, until soft and lightly coloured.

Drain the tomatoes and reserve the juice. Chop the tomatoes roughly, then add to the pan with the tomato purée and salt and pepper to taste. Stir well to mix, then simmer for about 15 minutes until thick.

Pour one-third of the tomato sauce into a bowl and leave to cool. Add the reserved tomato juice, with the basil and oregano, to the sauce left in the pan. Cover and simmer for a further 10 minutes, then remove from the heat.

To make the filling, drain the tuna fish, place in a bowl and flake with a fork. Fold in the peas, breadcrumbs, oregano and nutmeg. Mix with the reserved tomato sauce in the bowl. Taste and adjust the seasoning.

Divide the filling equally between the squares of pasta, then roll them up around the filling. Seal the join with water. Alternatively, spoon the filling into the dried cannelloni tubes.

Pour half of the hot tomato sauce in the pan into a greased large ovenproof dish. Arrange the cannelloni, seam side down, in a single layer on top. Pour over the remaining sauce.

To make the cheese sauce, melt the butter or margarine in a saucepan, add the flour and cook gently for 1-2 minutes, stirring constantly. Remove from the heat and whisk in the milk a little at a time, then return to the heat and bring to the boil, stirring all the time. Simmer until thickened, then add the Cheddar cheese, nutmeg and salt and pepper to taste.

Pour the cheese sauce over the tomato sauce in the dish, then bake in the preheated oven for 30 minutes. Sprinkle the Parmesan over the top and bake for a further 10 minutes until golden-brown.

Serve hot, straight from the dish, with a green salad and crusty French bread or continental rolls.

MONKFISH AND MUSSEL PAELLA

There are many regional variations on Spain's most famous dish, paella. This one, made with seafood, is popular along the country's Mediterranean coast, but other versions use chicken, rabbit, spicy sausage (*chorizo*) and pork. This combination of seafood can be changed if you wish. In Spain, paella is often made with squid. For a special occasion, lobster can be substituted for the monkfish. Giant Mediterranean prawns could be used instead of, or with, the mussels to garnish the dish.

Paella is not a dish for cooking in advance, but the ingredients can be prepared and the mussels cooked several hours beforehand if you wish.

PREPARATION TIME: *45 minutes*
COOKING TIME: *25 minutes*

INGREDIENTS – *serves 4:*
2 lb (900 g) fresh mussels OR *8-12 oz (225-350 g) shelled, cooked mussels*
2 lb (900 g) monkfish fillets, skinned and cut into bite-sized pieces
¼ pint (150 ml) dry white wine or water
1 bouquet garni
About 1½ pints (850 ml) fish stock (page 367)
Pinch of saffron threads
6 tablespoons olive oil
1 medium onion, peeled and roughly chopped
2 cloves garlic, peeled and crushed
6½ oz (185 g) tin pimentos, drained and cut into strips
2 large ripe tomatoes, skinned and roughly chopped
12 oz (350 g) Valencia or risotto rice
Salt and freshly ground black pepper
4 oz (115 g) peas (fresh or frozen), cooked and drained
GARNISH
Lemon wedges
Sprigs of fresh parsley

Prepare the uncooked mussels (page 377), if you are using them. Put the mussels in a saucepan and pour in the wine or water. Add the bouquet garni and bring to the boil. Cover and cook over high heat for 5-8 minutes, shaking the pan frequently, until the mussel shells open. Drain the cooking liquid and mussel juices into a measur-

ing jug and make up to 2 pints (1.1 litres) with fish stock. Discard the bouquet garni. Reserve 12 mussels in their shells for garnish, and shell the rest.

Put the saffron threads in a small bowl and pour over 2-3 tablespoons of the hot stock. Leave to infuse for 20 minutes.

Heat the oil in a paella pan or a large, deep frying pan. Add the monkfish, and fry over moderate heat for 5 minutes. Remove with a slotted spoon and set aside. Add the onion, garlic and strips of pimento, increase the heat to high and fry for 10 minutes, stirring all the time. Add the tomatoes and fry, stirring, for a further 5 minutes, until the mixture is quite thick.

Add the rice to the pan and

stir until it is coated with the onion mixture. Return the monkfish to the pan, then pour in 1½ pints (850ml) of the fish stock and mussel cooking liquid (or just fish stock if you are using ready-cooked mussels). Add the saffron liquid, and salt and pepper to taste, and cook briskly for a few minutes. Lower the heat and cook, uncovered, for 15-20 minutes without stirring or shaking, until the fish and rice are both tender.

Add the peas and shelled mussels, and stir gently to mix with the rice and monkfish. Heat through, adding more fish stock, if necessary, to moisten the paella to the required consistency. The paella should not be as sticky as a risotto, but

SEAFOOD PAELLA Mussels in their shells, lemon wedges and sprigs of continental parsley garnish this traditional Spanish dish.

neither should it be as dry as an Indian pilau.

Taste and add salt and pepper if necessary and then turn off the heat. Cover the paella with a lid or a clean tea towel, and leave to stand for 3-4 minutes to allow the flavours to mingle and mature. Before serving, garnish with the reserved mussels in their shells, and lemon wedges and parsley.

Serve with crusty French bread, and a Spanish-style salad of shredded crisp lettuce and sliced or chopped raw onion.

KHICHRI

In Hindi, *khichri* means a 'hotch-potch'. It is a name given to several dishes, but most often to this dish of spiced rice and lentils. The British in India adopted khichri and turned it into kedgeree, leaving out the lentils and spices, and adding fish and hard-boiled eggs.

Split red lentils make a colourful contrast to the white rice, but brown or green lentils may be used instead. Basmati is long-grained Asian rice, sold in many supermarkets.

A *raita* is a relish of yoghurt mixed with cooked or raw vegetables and spices. This raita is made with cucumber. It provides a cool contrast to the khichri, but can be omitted.

PREPARATION TIME: *20 minutes*
SOAKING TIME: *20 minutes*
COOKING TIME: *15 minutes*

INGREDIENTS – *serves 4:*
8 oz (225 g) basmati rice
8 oz (225 g) split red lentils
4 oz (115 g) ghee or butter
*2 medium onions, peeled and
    thinly sliced*
2 cloves garlic, peeled and crushed
1 level teaspoon ground cumin
About 1½ pints (850 ml) water
2 bay leaves
1 cinnamon stick
4 cloves
4 cardamom pods, crushed
*Salt and freshly ground black
    pepper*
*2 level tablespoons chopped fresh
    coriander leaves*

RAITA
½ cucumber, chopped
½ pint (285 ml) plain yoghurt
*Salt and freshly ground black
    pepper*
¼ teaspoon ground cumin
Pinch of paprika

First make the raita. Mix together all the ingredients except the paprika. Turn into a serving bowl, and sprinkle with paprika.

INDIAN KEDGEREE Khichri is a spicy mix of rice and lentils, very different from the breakfast dish into which the British transformed it. Raita and lager are cool accompaniments.

Cover and then chill in the refrigerator until needed.

Put the rice in a sieve and rinse well under cold running water. Place in a bowl and cover with cold water. Wash the lentils, then place in a separate bowl and cover with cold water. Leave both rice and lentils to soak for 20 minutes.

Meanwhile, melt the ghee or butter in a large, heavy-based saucepan. Add the onions and garlic and fry over very gentle heat for 10-15 minutes, stirring frequently until pale golden. Remove with a slotted spoon and set aside.

Drain the rice and lentils. Add to the pan and toss to coat in the remaining fat. Add the ground cumin and toss again, then pour in 1½ pints (850ml) of water. Bring to the boil, stirring, then add the bay leaves, cinnamon stick, cloves and cardamoms, with 1 level teaspoon of salt and plenty of black pepper. Stir once, lower the heat, cover and simmer very gently for 15 minutes, or until the rice and lentils are tender and most of the liquid has been absorbed. Check the amount of liquid from time to time during cooking, and stir well. If the liquid is absorbed too quickly, before the rice and lentils are tender, stir in a little more water – the finished dish should be quite moist.

Before serving, fold the fried onions and half of the coriander into the rice and lentils. Adjust the seasoning. Turn into a warmed serving dish and sprinkle with the remaining coriander. Serve hot with the yoghurt and cucumber raita and wholemeal pitta bread. This dish is included in a menu on this page.

RISOTTO AI QUATTRO FORMAGGI

A properly made risotto should have a thick, creamy consistency which can only be obtained by using the right type of short grain rice. Many supermarkets now sell 'Italian risotto rice', but the rice labelled *arborio* from Italian delicatessens is better still. If the cheeses are not all available, the risotto can be made with just one or two, but the taste will not be quite as interesting.

PREPARATION AND COOKING
   TIME: *45 minutes*

INGREDIENTS – *serves 4:*
2 oz (50 g) butter
1 medium onion, peeled and
   finely chopped
14 oz (400 g) Italian risotto rice
4 fl oz (115 ml) dry white wine
About 2 pints (1.1 litres) well-
   flavoured chicken stock (page
   367)
2 oz (50 g) Fontina, rind
   removed
2 oz (50 g) Bel Paese, rind
   removed
2 oz (50 g) Dolcelatte, rind
   removed
1 oz (25 g) freshly grated
   Parmesan
2 heaped tablespoons finely
   chopped parsley, preferably the
   continental (flat-leaved)
   variety
Salt and freshly ground black
   pepper

Melt the butter in a heavy-based saucepan or flameproof casserole. Add the onion and fry gently for about 5 minutes, until soft and lightly coloured.

Add the rice and stir for about 2 minutes until thoroughly coated with the butter. Add the wine and stir until absorbed by the rice, then add ½ pint (285ml) of the stock. Bring to the boil, then lower the heat and simmer gently until the stock has been absorbed, stirring frequently during cooking.

Continue adding stock, ½ pint (285ml) at a time. (If the stock is added all at once, the rice will not absorb it properly.) Simmer very gently and stir frequently during cooking. Do not add more stock until the previous quantity has been absorbed. The total cooking time should be about 15-20 minutes, until the rice is creamy in consistency and *al dente* (tender but firm to the bite).

Slightly more or less than a total of 2 pints (1.1 litres) of stock may be needed, depending on the kind of rice and the exact level of heat used.

Dice the Fontina, Bel Paese and Dolcelatte and fold them gently into the rice with the Parmesan. Heat through for 1-2 minutes until the cheeses just begin to melt, then add the parsley and salt and pepper to taste. Turn into warmed serving bowls and serve immediately with crusty rolls and salad. As a dinner party starter, the risotto will serve 6-8 people.

'RISOTTO WITH FOUR CHEESES'
Sweet Fontina, hard, fresh Parmesan, mild, blue-veined Dolcelatte and creamy Bel Paese are stirred into the risotto with continental parsley.

DAL CROQUETTES WITH YOGHURT AND MINT SAUCE

Pulses are *dal* in Indian cooking. Yellow split peas are the main ingredient of these croquettes, which are suitable for vegetarians. The croquettes can be made up to the frying stage 2-3 days in advance, and kept in the refrigerator.

PREPARATION TIME: *50 minutes*
COOKING TIME: *10 minutes*

INGREDIENTS – *serves 4:*
8 oz (225 g) yellow split peas
2 tablespoons vegetable ghee or oil, plus vegetable oil, for shallow frying the croquettes
1 medium onion, peeled and finely chopped
1 level teaspoon turmeric
1 level teaspoon garam masala
1 level teaspoon caraway seeds
1/2 teaspoon chilli powder
4 oz (115 g) vegetarian Cheddar cheese, grated
4 oz (115 g) fresh wholemeal or granary breadcrumbs
Salt and freshly ground black pepper
3-4 tablespoons oatmeal or wholemeal flour
SAUCE
1/2 pint (285 ml) set natural yoghurt
About 6 heaped tablespoons chopped fresh mint
2-3 cloves garlic, peeled and crushed with 1 level teaspoon salt
Pinch of sugar

Put the split peas in a sieve and wash under cold running water. Tip the peas into a saucepan, cover with plenty of cold water and bring to the boil. Lower the heat, cover and simmer for 30-40 minutes, until tender.

While the peas are cooking, heat the oil in a separate small saucepan, add the onion and spices and fry very gently for about 10 minutes until softened. Remove from the heat.

Next make the sauce. Whisk all the ingredients for the sauce together in a bowl, with plenty of black pepper. Alternatively, blend the sauce ingredients in a liquidiser or food processor. Chill in the refrigerator.

Drain the split peas very thoroughly, pressing them in the sieve to extract the water. Turn them into a bowl and mash them roughly with a fork. Add the spiced onion, with the grated cheese, breadcrumbs and salt and pepper to taste. Mix with a fork until the ingredients are well combined.

With your hands, form the mixture into 12 rounded cakes and coat them with the oatmeal or wholemeal flour.

Pour enough oil into a heavy-based frying pan to cover the base thinly. Heat until very hot, then add 4 of the croquettes. Fry for 1-2 minutes on each side, until golden-brown. Drain on kitchen paper while frying the other croquettes. Add more oil if necessary.

Serve hot, with the chilled sauce and a salad.

SALADS & VEGETABLES

SPANISH HOT POTATO SALAD

The Spanish often have salads like this as *tapas*, or appetisers, before lunch and dinner. However, this combination of hot and cold vegetables and fish also makes a very good main course.

The *salsa verde*, or 'green sauce', can be made up to 24 hours in advance, but needs to be whisked vigorously before serving because it separates. Store in a covered container in the refrigerator. The salad ingredients are best freshly prepared.

PREPARATION TIME: *1 hour*

INGREDIENTS – *serves 4:*
2 lb (900 g) waxy new potatoes
Salt
3 peppers (preferably 1 red, 1 yellow and 1 green)
1¾ oz (50 g) tin anchovy fillets in oil, drained and separated
2 ripe Mediterranean (beefsteak) tomatoes, skinned (page 389) and sliced
1 Spanish onion, peeled and sliced into rings
7 oz (200 g) tin tuna fish, drained and flaked
SALSA VERDE
1 large bunch of fresh parsley, about 2 oz (50 g), very finely chopped
1 hard-boiled egg, shelled and very finely chopped
4 cloves garlic, peeled and crushed
5 tinned anchovy fillets, drained and finely chopped
1/4 pint (150 ml) olive oil
1/4 pint (150 ml) vegetable oil
3 tablespoons lemon juice
Freshly ground black pepper
GARNISH
A few black olives

Scrub the potatoes, then cook them in boiling salted water for 20 minutes or until tender.

While the potatoes are boiling, grill the peppers under a hot grill, turning frequently, until the skin is charred on all sides. Alternatively, place one pepper in the flames of a gas hob (standing it on the hob). Turn it round, using a set of long-handled tongs, until the skin chars. Repeat with the other peppers. Holding the peppers under a cold tap or in a bowl of cold water, rub off the blackened skins with your fingers. Cut in half and remove the cores and seeds, then tear or cut the flesh into thick strips.

Drain the potatoes, and leave until just cool enough to handle while making the salsa verde.

To make the salsa verde, put the parsley, egg, garlic and anchovies in a bowl and mix together. Whisk the olive oil and vegetable oil together in a jug, then gradually whisk them into the mixture in the bowl. Add the oil a little at a time to begin with, as though making mayonnaise, then start to add it in a thin, steady stream as the mixture becomes thick. Add the lemon juice, and pepper to taste – the sauce is unlikely to need salt because of the saltiness of the anchovies.

Skin the potatoes and slice thickly. Arrange the slices on a flat dish, with the whole anchovy fillets on top. Arrange the peppers, tomatoes, onion and tuna fish, each in a separate dish. Garnish with black olives – use as many or as few as you wish. Whisk the salsa verde vigorously if it has separated, then pour it into a serving bowl. Serve as soon as possible, while the potatoes are still warm and before the salsa verde begins to separate once more.

Serve for an informal lunch or early evening meal with crusty French bread and a full-bodied red or crisp dry white wine. Separate bowls of lettuce and cucumber, with a dressing of oil and vinegar or lemon juice, are the usual accompaniments.

SPANISH COMPOSITION Each ingredient for this mixed salad – tuna fish, strips of red pepper, sliced hot potatoes, Mediterranean tomatoes and onions – is carefully displayed on a separate plate so that each person can compose his own salad then pour over the rich green dressing. Lettuce and diced cucumber complete the arrangement.

HIGH-FIBRE SALAD

The ingredients for this healthy main meal salad can be varied. Red cabbage, florence fennel, cucumber, sweet red and green peppers, and cooked red kidney, haricot or cannellini beans can be included, for example, as can dried figs, dried apricots, prunes and fresh pineapple.

PREPARATION TIME: *40 minutes*
MARINATING TIME: *overnight*

INGREDIENTS – *serves 4-6:*
4 fl oz (115 ml) olive oil
4 fl oz (115 ml) red wine vinegar
1 level teaspoon paprika
*Salt and freshly ground black
   pepper*
*8 oz (225 g) hard white or red
   cabbage*
4 large carrots, peeled
6 celery sticks, trimmed
*6-8 oz (175-225 g) shelled
   mixed nuts*
6 oz (175 g) whole pitted dates
*3 oz (75 g) Stilton or Danish
   Blue cheese*
*6 heaped tablespoons chopped
   fresh parsley*
Radicchio, endive or lettuce

Pour the olive oil and wine vinegar into a large bowl. Add the paprika, salt and pepper, and beat vigorously with a fork.

Shred the cabbage finely, discarding any thick, hard stalks and damaged outer leaves. Place in the bowl. Grate the carrots, slice the celery thinly, and add both to the cabbage. Mix the vegetables together to coat in the dressing. Cover the bowl tightly, and leave overnight in the refrigerator.

When ready to serve, chop the nuts and dates roughly and fold into the salad. Crumble the cheese into the salad, reserving about 1oz (25g) for the garnish. Fold in two-thirds of the parsley and adjust the seasoning.

Line a large salad bowl with radicchio, endive or lettuce leaves and sprinkle lightly with salt and pepper. Spoon the salad into the bowl, piling it up in the centre. Mix the reserved cheese and parsley together, and sprinkle over the top.

Serve at room temperature with granary or wholemeal bread. This dish is included in a menu on the opposite page.

CHEESE NUTBURGERS

Chopping and grating the ingredients for this recipe by hand will produce a chunky, coarse-textured burger. With a food processor, the ingredients will be finer, resulting in a smoother burger, which can be made in just a few minutes.

Almost any hard cheese – such as Cheddar, Edam, Double Gloucester or Red Leicester – can be used as a substitute for Sage Derby.

These burgers can be made up to 48 hours in advance. Store, covered, in the refrigerator. They can be frozen uncooked, then fried from frozen, allowing extra frying time.

PREPARATION TIME: *15-25
   minutes*
COOKING TIME: *10 minutes*

INGREDIENTS – *serves 6:*
*8 oz (225 g) shelled mixed nuts,
   chopped*
*2 medium carrots, peeled and
   grated*
*4-6 oz (115-175 g) Sage Derby
   cheese, grated*
*3 oz (75 g) fresh wholemeal or
   granary breadcrumbs*
*1 small onion, peeled and finely
   chopped*
*1 celery stick, trimmed and finely
   chopped*
*1 level teaspoon chopped fresh
   sage OR ½ teaspoon dried sage*
1 dessert apple
*Salt and freshly ground black
   pepper*
3-4 tablespoons vegetable oil

COATING
*2 oz (50 g) shelled mixed nuts,
   very finely chopped*
*3-4 oz (75-115 g) dried
   breadcrumbs*

Put the nuts into a bowl with the carrots, cheese, fresh breadcrumbs, onion, celery and sage. Peel and core the apple, then grate into the bowl. Add a little salt and plenty of pepper. Mix well with your hands to combine all the ingredients. Divide the mixture into 6 equal portions and form each into a burger shape.

Mix together the nuts and the breadcrumbs for the coating, then spread on a flat plate. Place the burgers on the coating mixture, and press to cover evenly. Turn over the burgers and do the same with the other side.

Heat the oil in one or two frying pans. Add the burgers and fry over low to moderate heat for 5 minutes on each side until golden-brown. Lift out and drain on absorbent kitchen paper before serving.

Serve hot or cold with a salad such as *Winter slaw* (page 276), or a simple green or tomato salad. This dish is included in a menu on the opposite page.

WHOLEFOOD DINNER A healthy meal need not be a boring one. The combination of a chunky salad consisting of marinated raw vegetables, nuts, fruit and cheese, with cheese nutburgers is as delicious as it is full of fibre.

M E N U

*Wholefood
Dinner
for Six*

CHEESE NUTBURGERS
opposite page

HIGH FIBRE SALAD
opposite page

MINTED RASPBERRY
AND YOGHURT ICE
page 108

Make twice the quantity of raspberry ice given in the recipe. Any left over can be returned to the freezer.

IN ADVANCE The raspberry ice can be made up to 3 months in advance. If the nutburgers are to be served cold they can be cooked up to 2 days ahead. If they are to be served hot, they can be prepared, ready for cooking, the night before. Prepare the salad the night before.

ON THE DAY First transfer the ice from the freezer to the refrigerator so that it can soften slightly. If you have prepared the nutburgers in advance, you will only need 10-20 minutes to cook them. Complete the salad.

VEGETABLE SAMOSAS

Indian samosas are individual parcels of light, crisp pastry with a curried filling that are deep-fried. It is very important to have the oil at the right temperature, otherwise they will not be crisp.

The samosas can be prepared to the stage before deep-frying up to 24 hours in advance. Keep them in a cool place, covered with a damp tea towel.

PREPARATION TIME: *2 hours*
COOKING TIME: *25-30 minutes*

INGREDIENTS – *makes 16:*
FILLING
*12 oz (350 g) potatoes
(preferably new), scrubbed
Salt
2 tablespoons ghee, butter or
vegetable oil
1 medium onion, peeled and
finely chopped
2 dried red chillies, finely chopped
1 in (25 mm) piece fresh root
ginger, peeled and crushed
2 level teaspoons garam masala
2 level teaspoons mustard seeds
1-2 level teaspoons ground cumin
1/2 teaspoon ground turmeric
2 medium carrots, peeled and
finely diced
1/2 pint (285 ml) water
2 oz (50 g) frozen peas
Freshly ground black pepper*
PASTRY
*8 oz (225 g) plain flour
1/2 teaspoon salt
1 1/2 tablespoons solid ghee or
butter
About 3 1/2 fl oz (100 ml) water
Oil for deep-frying*

First make the filling. Boil the potatoes in salted water for 15 minutes, or until just tender.

While the potatoes are boiling, melt the ghee in a heavy-based frying pan. Add the onion, chillies and ginger and fry gently, stirring, for about 5 minutes until softened. Add the spices and fry for a further 5 minutes, stirring constantly. Add the carrots and water, bring to the boil, then simmer, uncovered, for 15 minutes.

Drain the potatoes, and when cool enough to handle, peel off the skins. Dice the potato flesh.

Add the peas to the frying pan, and simmer for a further 5-10 minutes, or until all the liquid has been absorbed. Remove from the heat and stir in the potatoes. Add salt and pepper to taste, and leave on one side until cold.

While the filling is cooling, make the pastry. Sieve the flour and salt into a bowl, then rub in the ghee or butter with your fingertips. Add the water a little at a time and work with your hands to a smooth, elastic dough. Cover the bowl with a damp, clean tea towel and leave to rest for at least 15 minutes.

Cut the dough into 16 equal pieces. Keeping the remaining pieces covered, dip a piece in a little vegetable oil, then roll out on a board to a 4in (100mm) square. Put 1-2 tablespoons of the filling near one corner of the square of pastry. Fold the square in half to form a triangle. Alternatively, roll the dough into

circles, 5in (130mm) across, and fold them in half over the filling. Press firmly to seal, then crimp or flute the edges if you wish. Repeat with the remaining pastry and filling until all are used up, making 16 samosas altogether. Keep the samosas covered with a damp cloth as they are made, to prevent the pastry from drying out.

When ready to cook, heat the oil in a deep-fat fryer to 190°C (375°F). Lower the samosas carefully into the hot oil one at a time. Deep-fry (page 372) in

SPICY PARCELS Crisp, deep-fried pastry encloses a filling of curried vegetables. Simple triangular samosas are much easier to make than the traditional cone-shaped ones.

batches of two or three, for 2-3 minutes, until golden on both sides, turning frequently. Drain on absorbent kitchen paper while frying the remainder.

Serve them hot with yoghurt and mint sauce (see *Dal croquettes,* page 98), or cold, in which case they are good for picnics.

GADO-GADO

The literal meaning of *gado-gado* is 'a mixture'. It is an Indonesian salad of vegetables – lightly blanched but still crisp – served with a hot, spicy peanut sauce.

Indonesians make the sauce spicier still by adding an ingredient called *trasi* or *terasi*, which is sold in small jars at Chinese and oriental food shops, sometimes by its Malaysian name of *blachan* or *balachan*. It is a very pungent shrimp paste, which gives the sauce a fishy flavour. *Trasi* is highly concentrated. If you choose to use it in the sauce, add only 1 level teaspoon.

Ingredients for gado-gado vary. Mangetout are sometimes used instead of french beans, and shredded firm cabbage is often included. Squares of deep-fried tofu (soya bean curd) can be added to provide protein.

PREPARATION TIME: *1 hour*

INGREDIENTS – *serves 4:*
4 medium-sized new potatoes, scrubbed
4 medium-sized young carrots, scrubbed or peeled, and very thinly sliced
8 oz (225 g) french beans, topped and tailed
4 oz (115 g) cauliflower florets
4 oz (115 g) bean sprouts
Salt
Leaves from the heart of 1 round lettuce
½ cucumber, thinly sliced
4 hard-boiled eggs, shelled and sliced

PEANUT SAUCE
Vegetable oil for deep-frying
4 oz (115 g) shelled unsalted peanuts
1 level tablespoon sambal oelek (see Rendang, page 65) OR *1 level teaspoon chilli powder*
2 cloves garlic, peeled and crushed
½ small onion, roughly chopped
2 level teaspoons soft brown sugar
2 oz (50 g) creamed coconut, grated or chopped
Juice of 1 lemon

First prepare the peanut sauce. Heat the oil in a wok or deep-fat fryer to 190°C (375°F). Deep-fry (page 372) the peanuts for about 5 minutes until the skins turn a rich, dark brown.

With a slotted spoon, transfer the peanuts to a liquidiser or food processor. Add the remaining sauce ingredients and blend to a paste. Transfer the peanut paste to a heavy-based saucepan and set aside.

Start preparing the vegetables by putting the potatoes in a large pan of salted water. Bring to the boil, cover and simmer for about 20 minutes until tender. Remove the potatoes from the water with a slotted spoon, and set them aside until they are cool enough to handle.

While the potatoes are cooling, add the carrots to the simmering potato water and blanch for 4 minutes. Remove with a slotted spoon and set aside. Blanch the french beans and cauliflower in the same water for 3 minutes, and then the bean sprouts for 1 minute.

Slice the potatoes into rounds, removing the skins if you prefer.

Measure out ¼ pint (150ml) of the blanching water and stir into the peanut paste. Simmer for about 5 minutes, stirring, until thickened. Remove the pan from the heat.

To arrange the vegetables, first place the lettuce leaves, stalks inwards, around the edge of a large serving dish. Top each leaf with a few slices of cucumber and hard-boiled egg. Place a circle of overlapping potato slices on top of the stalk ends of the lettuce leaves. Arrange the beans like the spokes of a wheel, with one end of each bean resting on the ring of potatoes and the rest of the bean pointing towards the centre. Next put a band of carrot slices and cauliflower florets, then fill in the centre with bean sprouts.

Reheat the sauce, stirring constantly, then taste and add salt if necessary. Trickle the sauce all over the central part of the salad. Arrange more slices of cucumber and hard-boiled egg over the top.

Serve immediately with prawn crackers, or with crusty bread or crispbreads. Gado-gado can also be served as a first course or side salad for an Indonesian or oriental meal, in which case the ingredients can be arranged on individual plates.

VEGETABLE MOUSSAKA

Of all Greek dishes, moussaka is the most widely eaten outside Greece. Classically it consists of layers of minced lamb and aubergines, crowned with a golden, crusty top of thick, white sauce. However, it adapts very successfully to being made with vegetables only rather than with meat.

The ingredients can be varied. Halumi – a hard, salty cheese – is obtainable from Greek and Cypriot shops and some supermarkets. It is very similar to Feta cheese – which can be used instead, or you can use a mature Cheddar. Sweet red and green peppers can be added to the tomato sauce, and the mushrooms or courgettes omitted.

PREPARATION TIME: *2-2¼ hours*
COOKING TIME: *1½ hours*
OVEN TEMPERATURE: *preheat to 180°C (350°F, gas mark 4)*

INGREDIENTS – *serves 6-8:*
2 lb (900 g) aubergines
Salt
1½ lb (700 g) potatoes, scrubbed and halved if large
2½ oz (65 g) butter or margarine
1 lb (450 g) mushrooms, wiped and sliced
1 lb (450 g) courgettes, trimmed and sliced
2 fl oz (50 ml) olive oil
2 fl oz (50 ml) vegetable oil
4 oz (115 g) Halumi cheese, crumbled

TOMATO SAUCE
2 tablespoons olive oil or vegetable oil
1 medium onion, peeled and finely chopped
1-2 cloves garlic, peeled and crushed
1 lb (450 g) tomatoes, skinned (page 389) and roughly chopped
¼ pint (150 ml) dry red or white wine OR *vegetable stock (page 368)*
1 level teaspoon dried mixed herbs
Freshly ground black pepper
TOPPING
14½ oz (410 g) tin evaporated milk
1½ oz (40 g) cornflour
1 oz (25 g) butter or margarine
1 oz (25 g) plain flour
4 oz (115 g) Halumi cheese, crumbled
1 large egg, beaten
¼ teaspoon grated nutmeg

Wipe and slice the aubergines and place in layers in a colander, sprinkling each layer with salt. Put a plate over the aubergines, then place heavy weights on top. Leave to stand for 30 minutes to allow the bitter juices in the aubergines to leak out. Parboil the potatoes in salted water for 10-15 minutes or until they just give when pierced with a knife. Drain and leave until cool enough to handle.

While the potatoes are cooking, start to make the tomato sauce. Heat the oil in a heavy-based saucepan, add the onion and garlic and fry gently for about 5 minutes until soft and lightly coloured. Add the tomatoes and increase the heat. Stir well with a wooden spoon to break up the tomatoes, then add the wine or stock, herbs and salt and pepper to taste. Bring to the boil, stirring, then lower the heat, cover and simmer gently for 20 minutes.

While the tomato sauce is cooking, melt 1½oz (40g) of the 2½oz (65g) of butter in a large, heavy-based frying pan, add the mushrooms and fry until the juices flow, tossing constantly. Stir the mushrooms and their juices into the tomato sauce.

Melt the remaining 1oz (25g) of butter in the frying pan, add the courgette slices and fry for a few minutes until lightly coloured on both sides. Add to the tomato sauce, then remove the sauce from the heat.

Rinse the aubergines under cold running water, drain and pat thoroughly dry with absorbent kitchen paper.

Mix together the olive oil and vegetable oil. Pour enough oil into the frying pan just to cover the base. Heat until quite hot, then add a layer of aubergine slices. Fry until golden-brown on the underside, pressing the slices flat with a spatula as they cook, then turn them over and fry until golden-brown on the other side. Transfer to absorbent kitchen paper to drain while frying the remaining aubergine slices in batches. Add more oil between each batch.

Slice the potatoes thinly, removing the skins if you wish.

Pour half of the tomato sauce into a large, deep casserole or baking dish. Arrange half of the potato slices over the sauce, then half of the aubergines. Sprinkle over 2oz (50g) of the Halumi cheese. Repeat these layers once more.

To make the topping, make up the evaporated milk with water to 1½ pints (850ml) as directed on the tin. In a separate jug cream the cornflour to a paste with a little of the milk. Melt the butter or margarine in a saucepan, add the plain flour and cook, stirring, for 1-2 minutes. Remove from the heat and gradually blend in the milk. Return to the heat and bring to the boil, stirring, then stir in the cornflour paste. Simmer until thickened and smooth, stirring all the time, then add the Halumi cheese and stir until melted. Remove the pan from the heat, leave to cool for about 5 minutes, then stir in the egg, nutmeg and salt and pepper.

Pour the topping over the moussaka. Bake in the preheated oven for 1½ hours, until the potatoes feel tender when pierced with a skewer. If the topping shows signs of overbrowning, cover with foil. Let the moussaka settle for 10 minutes before serving.

CLASSICAL ALTERNATIVE Vegetables replace meat in this moussaka. Retsina, sesame bread and a salad of tomatoes, onion, Feta cheese and mint continue the Greek theme.

103

CHILLI BEAN AND WHOLEWHEAT PIE

Whole grains of wheat make an excellent nutty substitute for meat in this vegetarian version of chilli con carne.

PREPARATION TIME: *1 ¼ hours*
SOAKING TIME: *overnight*
COOKING TIME: *1 hour*
OVEN TEMPERATURE: *preheat to 180°C (350°F, gas mark 4)*

INGREDIENTS – *serves 6:*
8 oz (225 g) dried red kidney beans, soaked in cold water overnight OR 15½ oz (440 g) tin red kidney beans, drained and rinsed
8 oz (225 g) wholewheat, soaked in cold water overnight
4 oz (115 g) carrots, peeled and thickly sliced
Salt
2 tablespoons vegetable oil
1 large onion, peeled and roughly chopped
3 celery sticks, trimmed and roughly chopped
1 green pepper, cored, seeded and cut into strips
1-2 cloves garlic, peeled and crushed (optional)
½-1 level teaspoon chilli powder, according to taste
14 oz (400 g) tin tomatoes
½ pint (285 ml) water
1 level tablespoon.tomato purée
1 level teaspoon soft brown sugar
Freshly ground black pepper
½ pint (285 ml) natural yoghurt
2 eggs, beaten
4-6 oz (115-175 g) Cheddar cheese, grated

Drain the soaked kidney beans, if used, and rinse under cold running water. Put them in a large saucepan and cover with fresh cold water. Bring to the boil, skim with a slotted spoon, then boil rapidly for 10 minutes. Drain and rinse again, then bring to the boil in fresh cold water. Lower the heat, half cover with a lid and simmer for 1 hour, or until the beans are tender.

Meanwhile, drain the wholewheat. Bring a large pan of water to the boil, add the wholewheat and boil rapidly for 15 minutes. Drain. Blanch the carrots for 3 minutes in boiling salted water.

Heat the oil in a heavy-based pan. Add the onion, celery, green pepper and garlic, if being used. Fry gently, stirring, for about 5 minutes until softened.

Add the chilli powder and fry for a few minutes more, then add the tomatoes, water, tomato purée, sugar, and salt and pepper to taste. Bring to the boil, stirring, then remove from the heat. Stir the wholewheat and carrots into the tomato mixture in the pan. Drain the cooked kidney beans and stir into the tomato mixture, or stir in the tinned beans. Transfer to a baking dish.

Whisk the yoghurt and eggs together in a bowl. Add two-thirds of the cheese and whisk again. Pour slowly over the bean mixture and sprinkle with the remaining cheese. Bake in the preheated oven for 1 hour, until puffed up and golden-brown. If necessary, raise the oven temperature to 200°C (400°F, gas mark 6) for the last 10 minutes of cooking time to brown the top. Serve hot, straight from the dish, with French bread and a green salad.

VEGETARIAN CHILLI A sizzling topping of yoghurt and cheese completes a spicy dish of wholewheat, kidney beans and vegetables. The recipe can be varied by using other vegetables such as mushrooms.

CHINESE VEGETABLE STIR-FRY

Soya bean curd – *tofu* – gives body to this combination of crunchy stir-fried vegetables. The dish must be eaten immediately, but the vegetables can be prepared in advance.

PREPARATION TIME: *45 minutes*
COOKING TIME: *20 minutes*

INGREDIENTS – *serves 4-6:*
1 lb 3 oz (530 g) tin bamboo-shoot halves in water OR 2 × 8 oz (225 g) tins
4 medium carrots, peeled and cut into matchstick strips
8 oz (225 g) cauliflower florets, divided into tiny sprigs
11 oz (300 g) packet of tofu (soya bean curd)
¼ pint (150 ml) vegetable oil
1 onion, peeled and thinly sliced
2 in (50 mm) piece of fresh root ginger, peeled and cut into matchstick strips
2 cloves garlic, peeled and crushed
4 tablespoons soya sauce
2 level tablespoons yellow bean sauce
2 tablespoons dry sherry
2 level teaspoons soft brown sugar
8 oz (225 g) mangetout, topped and tailed
8 oz (225 g) bean sprouts
1 red pepper, cored, seeded and cut into thin strips
Salt and freshly ground black pepper
1-2 tablespoons sesame oil

Drain the bamboo shoots, reserving 4fl oz (115ml) of the

liquid, then cut the shoots into thin strips. Blanch the carrots and cauliflower in boiling water for 2 minutes only. Drain well and set aside.

Drain the tofu and dry with absorbent kitchen paper. Cut into squares. Heat the oil in a wok or deep, heavy-based frying pan until moderately hot. Add the squares of tofu in batches and fry until lightly browned and slightly crisp on all sides. Remove with a slotted spoon and leave to drain on absorbent kitchen paper.

Drain off all but 1 tablespoon of the oil. Add the onion, ginger and garlic, and fry gently for about 5 minutes until softened.

Meanwhile, mix the bamboo-shoot liquid in a jug with the soya sauce, yellow bean sauce, sherry and sugar.

Add the blanched carrots and cauliflower to the wok, together with the mangetout, bean sprouts, bamboo shoots and red pepper. Increase the heat and stir-fry (page 372) for 5 minutes. Pour in the liquid and stir-fry to combine. Bring to the boil, stirring, then lower the heat and add the tofu, with salt and pepper to taste. Simmer for 1-2 minutes only, stirring all the time, then turn into a warmed serving dish. Sprinkle with sesame oil to taste.

Serve immediately with prawn crackers or poppyseed rolls, and sparkling mineral water. Alternatively, serve as a vegetable accompaniment to any Chinese main course, or to plain or barbecued meat or fish.

PUDDINGS & DESSERTS

LIME AND PINEAPPLE ICEBOX PUDDING

Icebox puddings originated in the United States and take their name from the American word for refrigerator.

Two tablespoons of vodka or white rum can be added to the ice cream with the crushed pineapple, and a further 2 tablespoons to the juice for soaking the sponges.

If you wish to freeze the pudding for more than a day or two, remove it from its tin, then wrap it first in kitchen foil and then in a freezer bag before returning it to the freezer.

PREPARATION TIME: *30 minutes*
FREEZING TIME: *overnight*

INGREDIENTS – *serves 6-8:*
8 oz (225 g) tin pineapple slices in natural juice
Finely grated rind and juice of 2 limes
6-8 trifle sponges
26 fl oz (750 ml) packet of vanilla ice cream (not soft-scoop), softened
DECORATION
Slices of lime (optional)

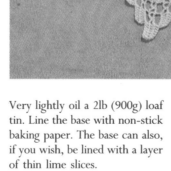

Very lightly oil a 2lb (900g) loaf tin. Line the base with non-stick baking paper. The base can also, if you wish, be lined with a layer of thin lime slices.

Drain the pineapple. Make the lime juice up to 6fl oz (175ml) with the pineapple juice. Pour it into a shallow dish.

Cut the trifle sponges horizontally into two layers. Dip half of them, one at a time, into the juice, and use to line the bottom of the prepared tin. Cut them so that they fit neatly. Reserve the remaining sponges and juice.

Chop the pineapple roughly, then crush with a wooden spoon. Place the pineapple in a sieve and press it to extract as much juice as possible.

Turn the ice cream into a bowl and fold in the crushed pineapple, with the lime rind. Spoon the mixture into the tin, packing it down on top of the trifle sponges. Level the top.

Dip the remaining trifle sponges in the remaining juice. Place on top of the ice cream, cutting to fit as before. Press down firmly, then cover the tin

TROPICAL ICEBOX PUDDING Lime and pineapple give a tropical tang to this sandwich of ice cream and sponge, lying in a pool of cream and decorated with twists of lime.

with foil. Freeze overnight.

When ready to serve, run a knife between the ice cream and the inside of the tin, then invert onto a chilled serving plate. Peel off the lining paper, then decorate with lime twists (page 286), if you wish. Serve the pudding immediately, cut into slices.

MINTED APPLE SNOW

One of the simplest desserts is varied by the addition of chopped mint and orange. The apple purée can be made the day before and kept in a covered dish in the refrigerator or, when there is a surplus of apples, it can be frozen.

PREPARATION AND COOKING
   TIME: *20 minutes*
COOLING TIME: *1-2 hours*

INGREDIENTS – *serves 4:*
1 lb (450 g) cooking apples
Finely grated rind and juice of
   1 large orange
2 egg whites
3 oz (75 g) caster sugar
3 level tablespoons finely chopped
   fresh mint
DECORATION
A few whole mint leaves
Thin strips of orange zest

Peel, core and slice the apples. Put them in a pan with the rind and juice of the orange, and simmer gently until the apple is pulpy. Sieve the apple mixture, or blend in a liquidiser or food processor, to produce a smooth purée. Leave to cool.

Just before the meal, whisk the egg whites until stiff, then whisk in the sugar. Fold the egg white and the chopped mint into the apple purée.

Heap the apple snow into tall glasses and decorate with a few mint leaves and strips of orange zest. This dish is included in a menu on page 78.

MOCHA CHOCOLATE CHEESECAKE

Moist and rich, this coffee and chocolate cheesecake is best served with natural yoghurt rather than cream.

The cheesecake will keep fresh for 3-4 days, stored in the refrigerator, or it can be frozen without the decoration.

PREPARATION TIME: *40 minutes*
COOKING TIME: *1¼ hours*
COOLING TIME: *overnight*
CHILLING TIME: *at least 2 hours*
OVEN TEMPERATURE: *preheat to*
   160°C (325°F, gas mark 3)

INGREDIENTS – *serves 8:*
BASE
2 oz (50 g) shelled hazelnuts
6 oz (175 g) coffee cream biscuits
3 oz (75 g) butter or margarine
FILLING
12 oz (350 g) curd cheese
¼ pint (150 ml) soured cream
2 eggs
4 oz (115 g) soft brown sugar
4-6 oz (115-175 g) plain
   chocolate (preferably
   unsweetened)
2 tablespoons very strong cold
   coffee or coffee and chicory
   essence
2 level tablespoons cornflour
DECORATION
Grated chocolate

To make the base, toast the hazelnuts under the grill, shaking the grill pan constantly so that they brown evenly. Turn the nuts into a clean tea towel and rub off the skins while still warm. Chop the nuts roughly.

Put the biscuits into a bowl and crush finely with a rolling pin or crush in a pestle and mortar. Stir in the nuts. Melt the butter or margarine, then mix with the biscuits and nuts.

With the back of a metal spoon, press the biscuit mixture into the base of a well-buttered 8in (200mm) springform or loose-based cake tin. Chill in the refrigerator.

To make the filling, put the cheese into a large bowl and beat until soft and light, then beat in the soured cream until evenly blended. Put the eggs and sugar in a separate bowl, beat until thick and light, then gradually beat the egg mixture into the cheese mixture. Set aside.

Break the chocolate in pieces and put them into a heatproof bowl set over a pan of simmering water. Add the coffee to the chocolate and heat very gently until the chocolate has melted, only stirring once or twice towards the end.

Stir the melted chocolate into the cheese mixture. Sieve in the cornflour. Mix until evenly blended, then pour into the tin and bake in the preheated oven for 1¼ hours. Turn the oven off and leave the cheesecake to cool in the oven overnight.

Remove the cheesecake carefully from the tin and place on a serving plate. Chill for at least 2 hours before serving sprinkled with grated chocolate.

This dish is included in a menu on page 61.

FRESH FRUIT PAVLOVAS

One of Australia's national dishes is a meringue cake first made for the Russian ballerina Anna Pavlova on a tour of Australia in the early years of this century. The meringue cases can be made up to 4 days in advance. The fruit topping can be made several hours in advance and kept covered tightly in the refrigerator.

PREPARATION TIME: *40 minutes*
CHILLING TIME: *at least 30*
   minutes
COOKING TIME: *1 hour*
OVEN TEMPERATURE: *preheat to*
   120°C (250°F, gas mark ½)

INGREDIENTS – *serves 6:*
MERINGUE CASES
4 egg whites
Pinch of salt
8 oz (225 g) caster sugar
1¼ level teaspoons cornflour
1¼ teaspoons vinegar
Non-stick baking paper

FRUIT PAVLOVAS Strawberry leaves adorn meringue cases filled with strawberries, mango, orange and melon marinated in Cointreau.

remove all pith and membrane (page 398), then cut each segment into two or three pieces, removing the pips. Add to the bowl and mix.

Cut the melon in half. Discard the seeds and scoop out the flesh with a melon baller. Alternatively, cut the skin off the melon and slice the flesh into cubes. Mix the melon with the mixture in the bowl.

Peel the mango, holding it over the bowl to catch the juices (page 398). Cut the flesh into cubes and add to the bowl. Halve or slice the strawberries if they are large, and add to the bowl. Mix the fruit together. Cover the bowl tightly, and chill in the refrigerator for at least 30 minutes to let the flavours mingle.

When ready to serve, place one meringue case on each dessert plate. Spoon the fruit on top, then pour over any juices from the bottom of the bowl. Serve immediately, or the juices will make the meringue soggy.

SWEET COCONUT RICE

Sweet and aromatic rice dishes are common in Indian cooking. This pudding can be served hot, or alternatively chilled when it is called *kheer* or *sheer*. This is

traditionally served decorated with very fine, delicate sheets of real silver or gold leaf, called *vark*, which are eaten, although the quantity is so small that it cannot be tasted. It is available only in Indian food shops.

PREPARATION TIME: *25 minutes*
COOKING TIME: *1 hour*
OVEN TEMPERATURE: *preheat to 180°C (350°F, gas mark 4)*

INGREDIENTS – *serves 4-6:*
4 whole cardamoms
4 cloves
4 oz (115 g) short grain rice
1¹/₂ pints (850 ml) milk
2 oz (50 g) granulated sugar
4 oz (115 g) creamed coconut, dissolved in ¹/₂ pint (285 ml) boiling water
2 oz (50 g) seedless raisins
¹/₂ oz (15 g) butter
1-2 teaspoons rosewater (optional)
DECORATION
Chopped pistachio nuts or toasted flaked almonds

Crush the cardamoms and cloves with a pestle and mortar or a spice grinder. Put in a large saucepan with the rice, milk and sugar. Strain in the coconut liquid, then bring to the boil, stirring all the time.

Pour the mixture into a baking dish and add the raisins and butter. Stir, then bake, uncovered, in the preheated oven for 1 hour, or until the rice is tender, stirring occasionally. If you wish, sprinkle with rosewater before serving, and scatter pistachios or almonds over the top.

FRUIT TOPPINGS
4 tablespoons Cointreau or other orange-flavoured liqueur
2 level tablespoons caster sugar
1 large juicy orange
1 small ripe honeydew melon
1 ripe mango
8 oz (225 g) strawberries, hulled

First, make the meringue cases. Line two baking sheets with non-stick baking paper and set aside. Put the egg whites and salt in a large bowl, and whisk until stiff and standing in peaks.

Add half of the sugar and continue whisking until glossy. With a large metal spoon, fold in the remaining sugar, the cornflour and vinegar.

Spoon three mounds of the meringue – each about 4-4¹/₂in (100-115mm) across – onto each sheet of baking paper. Hollow out the centre of the mounds with the back of a spoon to make nest shapes.

Bake the meringue cases in the preheated oven for 1 hour, until crisp on the outside – they

will still be soft on the inside. Swap the sheets over on the oven shelves halfway through the cooking time. Lift each meringue case off the baking paper with a fish slice, and place on a wire rack to cool. Once cool, they can be stored in an airtight tin with greaseproof paper between each layer.

To prepare the fruit topping, put the Cointreau and sugar in a bowl. Grate in the orange rind, then whisk well to mix. Divide the orange into segments, and

SWEET AND SHARP Sweet butterscotch contrasts with a sharp topping of cream and low-fat cheese.

the preheated oven for 15 minutes, then remove the foil and beans and return to the oven for a further 5 minutes or until the pastry is crisp and lightly golden. Set on one side.

Put the egg yolks, butter and soft brown sugar in a heavy-based saucepan. Mix the cornflour to a paste with a little of the evaporated milk, and then add to the pan with the remaining evaporated milk. Beat vigorously with a balloon whisk over moderate heat until the mixture is bubbling and very thick – this should take about 5 minutes. Pour into the pastry case. Leave until cold and set.

Whip the cream until it stands in soft peaks, then fold in the quark. Remove the pie from the tin. Spoon the topping over the pie and swirl it with a spoon or knife, then sprinkle with the demerara sugar. Serve chilled. This dish is included in a menu on page 92.

MINTED RASPBERRY AND YOGHURT ICE

The yoghurt base gives this ice cream a distinctively tangy flavour. This recipe can be made with other soft fruit, and a few tablespoons of liqueur can be added to the purée.

PREPARATION TIME: *20 minutes*
FREEZING TIME: *6 hours or overnight*

INGREDIENTS – *serves 4:*
8 oz (225 g) raspberries, fresh or frozen
4 oz (115 g) caster sugar
1-2 level teaspoons chopped fresh mint, to taste
¼ pint (150 ml) natural yoghurt
¼ pint (150 ml) soured cream
2 eggs, separated
2 level tablespoons icing sugar
DECORATION
A few frosted mint leaves (page 290)

Purée the raspberries, sugar and mint in a liquidiser or food processor. Alternatively, press the raspberries through a sieve, then beat in the sugar until dissolved and add the mint.

Pour the purée into a bowl and add the yoghurt, soured cream and egg yolks. Beat well to mix, then pour into a freezer container and freeze, uncovered, for about 2 hours, until just beginning to freeze at the edges.

Whisk the egg whites until thick and fluffy. Add the icing sugar, sieved, and whisk again until the meringue mixture stands in stiff peaks.

Beat the ice cream with a fork to break up the ice crystals, then fold in the meringue until evenly mixed. Return to the freezer for at least 4 hours, preferably overnight, until firm enough to scoop. Beat the mixture as often as possible during the freezing time, to help break up ice

crystals and give the mixture a smooth texture.

Serve the ice straight from the freezer. Scoop the ice into glass dishes and top with frosted mint leaves. This dish is included in a menu on page 101.

TORTA DI MELE

In Italy, this apple cake is usually served cold with strong coffee at the end of lunch or in the middle of the afternoon, but it is just as good warm as a pudding. It will keep for 1-2 days.

Golden Delicious apples are the nearest thing to Italian apples available here, but any dessert apple that is not too sharp or hard, such as Cox's Orange Pippin, can be used.

PREPARATION TIME: *40 minutes*
COOKING TIME: *40 minutes*
OVEN TEMPERATURE: *preheat to 180°C (350°F, gas mark 4)*

INGREDIENTS – *serves 6:*
1½ lb (700 g) dessert apples
1 tablespoon lemon juice
4 eggs
3 oz (75 g) caster sugar
3 oz (75 g) vanilla sugar
5 oz (150 g) self-raising flour
Pinch of salt
4 oz (115 g) unsalted butter, melted and cooled
1 teaspoon vanilla essence
3 tablespoons milk
2 tablespoons brandy
3 oz (75 g) Maraschino cherries, drained and dried
Non-stick baking paper

AMERICAN BUTTERSCOTCH PIE

Mixing quark (a low-fat soft cheese) with cream lowers the fat content of the topping for this pie. Thick natural yoghurt can be used as an alternative topping with or without cream.

The pie can be served as a dessert or, cut into thin wedges, with morning coffee. It can be made up to 2 days in advance and stored in the refrigerator.

PREPARATION TIME: *45 minutes*
COOLING TIME: *1 hour*
COOKING TIME: *20 minutes*
OVEN TEMPERATURE: *preheat to 190°C (375°F, gas mark 5)*

INGREDIENTS – *serves 6:*
Shortcrust pastry made with 6 oz (175 g) flour (page 392)
4 egg yolks
3 oz (75 g) unsalted butter
3 oz (75 g) dark, soft brown sugar
2 level tablespoons cornflour
14½ oz (410 g) tin evaporated milk
¼ pint (150 ml) double cream
¼ pint (150 ml) Quark or other low-fat cheese
2 level tablespoons demerara sugar

Line an 8in (200mm) loose-based flan tin with the shortcrust pastry. Prick the base and line with kitchen foil and baking beans. Bake blind (page 393) in

Grease the inside of a 9in (230mm) loose-based cake tin. Dust lightly with flour, shaking off the excess. Line the base with non-stick baking paper.

First prepare the apples. Fill a bowl with cold water and add the lemon juice. Peel, quarter and core the apples, then slice them thinly. Drop the slices into the bowl of water as you work, to prevent them turning brown. Set aside while preparing the sponge mixture.

Whisk the eggs and sugars together with an electric beater until thick and light. Alternatively, whisk the eggs and sugars with a hand whisk in a bowl set over simmering water. Remove the bowl from the heat.

Sieve in half the flour with the salt and whisk again, then whisk in the melted butter in a thin, steady stream. Stir in the vanilla essence, milk and brandy. Sieve in the remaining flour and beat well until evenly mixed.

Drain the apples well, then fold them gently into the sponge mixture. Pour into the prepared tin. Press the cherries into the mixture at random, then bake in the preheated oven for 40 minutes or until a skewer inserted into the centre comes out clean.

Leave the cake to settle in the tin for 10-15 minutes, then turn it out and peel off the lining paper. Stand the cake the right way up on a serving plate and serve while still warm, with vanilla ice cream or chilled cream. This dish is included in a menu on page 84.

INDIVIDUAL PEAR PUFFS

One of the best pears to use for this simple dessert is the sweet, juicy Conference pear. It received its name in 1885 when it won first prize in an International Pear Conference held in Chiswick, London. It won against some 10,000 other pear varieties. Other firm dessert pears, or ripe cooking pears, can be used instead of Conference.

Pears, like apples, are complemented by good cheese. In this recipe they are accompanied by cream cheese, but blue cheese can be used instead. Blue Brie and Dolcelatte (a mild, blue Italian cheese) both melt to the right consistency for the filling. As an alternative, soured cream can be used in the filling instead of cheese.

PREPARATION TIME: *30 minutes*
COOKING TIME: *15 minutes*
OVEN TEMPERATURE: *preheat to 220°C (425°F, gas mark 7)*

INGREDIENTS – *serves 4:*
2 Conference pears
7 oz (200 g) prepared weight puff pastry (page 394)
3-4 oz (75-115 g) cream cheese
1-2 oz (25-50 g) chopped mixed nuts
Finely grated rind and juice of ½ lemon
½ teaspoon ground cinnamon
4 heaped teaspoons caster sugar, or to taste
GLAZE
1 egg, beaten

Cut the pastry into 8 equal pieces. Roll out each piece to a 3in × 4in (80mm × 100mm) rectangle. Dampen a baking sheet and place 4 of the rectangles on it. Brush the edges of the rectangles with water.

Cut out the centre of the remaining rectangles, leaving a border or frame about ½in (15mm) wide. Place the borders on top of the rectangles on the baking sheet. Press to seal, then set the pastry frames aside.

Mix the cream cheese and nuts together. Peel and halve the pears. Carefully scoop out the cores with a sharp-edged teaspoon. Fill the cavities with the cream cheese and nut mixture. Place the pear halves, filled side down, inside the frames. With a sharp knife, make diagonal slashes in the pears, then brush the exposed pear flesh immediately with lemon juice.

Mix together the lemon rind, cinnamon and sugar to taste, then sprinkle over the pears. Brush the pastry frames with beaten egg to glaze, then bake in the preheated oven for 15 minutes until puffed and golden-brown. Serve hot with cream.

PICTURE PEAR A case of golden puff pastry frames a halved pear stuffed with cream cheese and nuts.

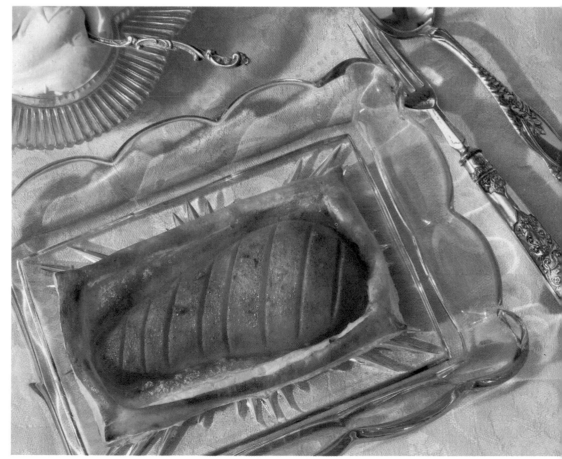

MARMALADE AND FIG SPONGE

Steamed puddings are particularly associated with dark winter evenings and schooldays. But properly made they can be as light and airy as any dinner party dessert. The flavour of this sponge is quite sharp, but it can be varied by using a different flavoured marmalade or jam.

Semi-dried figs, softer than dried figs, have the best texture for this pudding, but ordinary dried figs can be used instead.

PREPARATION TIME: *30 minutes*
COOKING TIME: *2 hours*

INGREDIENTS – *serves 8:*
6 oz (175 g) self-raising flour
Pinch of salt
4 oz (115 g) butter or margarine
4 oz (115 g) soft brown sugar
Finely grated rind of 1 orange
2 eggs, beaten
4 oz (115 g) semi-dried figs, chopped
2 oz (50 g) shelled walnuts or mixed nuts, roughly chopped
5 heaped tablespoons orange marmalade (page 32)

Prepare a steamer or double boiler, or put a large pan of water on to boil. The water in the pan should come halfway up the sides of the basin that the pudding is to be cooked in.

Sieve the flour and salt together. Put the butter, sugar and orange rind in a bowl and beat until light and fluffy. Add the beaten eggs gradually, adding a little of the flour if the mixture shows signs of curdling. Fold in the remaining flour evenly, then add the figs, walnuts and 2 tablespoons of the marmalade. Add 1-2 tablespoons of warm water, if necessary, to give a soft, dropping consistency.

Butter a 2 pint (1.1 litre) pudding basin, and put the remaining marmalade in the bottom. Spoon the pudding mixture into the basin, then cover the top of the mixture with a circle of buttered greaseproof paper. Cover the basin with kitchen foil, with a pleat folded in it to allow the pudding to expand. Tie with string.

Put the basin in the top of the steamer or double boiler, or in the large pan of boiling water. Cover and steam for 2 hours.

Remove the covers and run a knife between the pudding and the inside of the basin. Turn the pudding out onto a warm serving plate and serve immediately, with natural yoghurt, cream or custard. Alternatively, a quick sauce can be made by melting marmalade in freshly squeezed orange juice. This dish is included in a menu on page 80.

STEAMING PUDDING *Radiating warmth, this sponge packed with figs and nuts is served here with a sauce of orange juice and marmalade.*

GINGER AND KIWI ICE CREAM

The combination of preserved ginger, kiwi fruit and double cream makes this an exceptionally rich ice cream. Made in a pudding basin, and decorated with a sprig of holly, it could even be used instead of plum pudding at Christmas. The ice cream is soft enough to be served straight from the freezer.

This recipe can be used as a base for other fruit ice creams. Make ¼-½ pint (150-285ml) of lightly sweetened fruit purée. Many fruits can be used instead of ginger and kiwi – for example, gooseberries, apricots, plums, strawberries, raspberries or damsons – so long as the purée is well flavoured. Make the mousse as below but replace the ginger syrup with an extra tablespoon of icing sugar.

PREPARATION TIME: *40 minutes*
FREEZING TIME: *overnight*

INGREDIENTS – *serves 8-10:*
1 oz (25 g) stem ginger and 2 tablespoons of the preserving syrup
4 kiwi fruit
4 level tablespoons caster sugar
2 egg yolks
4 level tablespoons icing sugar
2 tablespoons water
7 fl oz (200 ml) double cream

Roughly chop the pieces of ginger and put in a liquidiser or food processor. Peel three of the kiwi fruit, slice the flesh and add to the machine. Blend to a smooth purée, then turn into a measuring jug. There should be about 7fl oz (200ml). Stir in the caster sugar, then chill in the refrigerator while preparing the egg and cream mousse.

Set a large heat-proof bowl over a pan of gently simmering water. Put the egg yolks in the bowl with the icing sugar, the reserved ginger syrup and water. Whisk vigorously with a hand-held electric beater or a balloon whisk for at least 10 minutes, until the mixture is thick enough for a ribbon-like trail to be left across the top when the beater or whisk is lifted.

Remove the bowl from the pan of hot water, stand it in another bowl and surround with ice cubes. Continue whisking until the mixture is cold.

Whip the cream until it is thick enough to hold its shape. Fold first the chilled fruit purée and then the cream into the egg mousse. Pour the mixture into a 1½ pint (850ml) mould, soufflé dish, cake tin or pudding basin, then cover and freeze overnight.

When ready to serve, peel and slice the remaining kiwi fruit. Dip the base of the mould very quickly – 1-2 seconds only – in a bowl of warm water. Turn the ice cream out onto a well-chilled serving plate and decorate the top with the slices of kiwi fruit. Serve immediately with crisp biscuits such as *Hazelnut crisps* (page 338). This dish is included in a menu on page 96.

MENU

*Supper
on a Shoestring
for Four*

CHILLI BEEF
CABBAGE ROLLS *page 68*
with TOMATO SAUCE

BOILED RICE

MIXED SALAD OF
LETTUCE, TOMATOES
AND CUCUMBER

∽

ST CLEMENT'S MOUSSE
this page

The rice can all be cooked in advance. Use some for the rolls, reheat the rest in a heavy-based saucepan. Add 1-2 tablespoons of water, cover and heat gently, shaking occasionally.

IN ADVANCE The mousse can be made up to 2 days ahead.

ON THE DAY Allow about 1½ hours. Prepare the cabbage rolls and while they are cooking make the tomato sauce (use the recipe in *Vegetable moussaka*, page 102). Cook the rice, and make the salad. Prepare the orange zest garnish for the mousse. Decorate the mousse just before serving.

'ORANGES AND LEMONS' A mousse named after a nursery rhyme appeals to adults as well as children.

ST CLEMENT'S MOUSSE

'Oranges and lemons, say the bells of St Clement's.' As befits a pudding named after a nursery rhyme, this orange and lemon mousse is a favourite with children. But for dinner party soufflés, substitute up to 4 tablespoons of an orange-flavoured liqueur, such as Grand Marnier or Cointreau, for the equivalent amount of orange juice.

The mousse can be made up to 2 days in advance. Cover the bowl tightly and store in the refrigerator.

PREPARATION TIME: *40 minutes*
CHILLING TIME: *at least 4 hours*

INGREDIENTS – *serves 6-8:*
*Finely grated rind and juice of
   2 oranges*
*Finely grated rind and juice of
   1 lemon*
4 eggs, separated
4 oz (115 g) caster sugar
*1 level tablespoon powdered
   gelatine*
½ pint (285 ml) whipping cream
DECORATION
*Julienne shreds of orange and
   lemon rind (see method)*

Pour the orange juice and lemon juice into a measuring jug and make up to ½ pint (285ml) with water, if necessary.

Put the egg yolks and sugar in a heatproof bowl standing over a pan of gently simmering water. Beat with an electric or balloon whisk until the mixture is thick enough to hold a ribbon trail when the beaters are lifted (this can take as long as 10-15 minutes). Remove the bowl from the heat and set aside.

Pour 4 tablespoons of the measured fruit juice into a small heatproof bowl and sprinkle in the gelatine powder. Leave to soak for 5 minutes until spongy, then stand the bowl in the pan of hot water and heat gently until the gelatine has dissolved.

Stir the dissolved gelatine into the egg yolk mixture, then stir in the remaining measured fruit juice and the grated orange and lemon rinds.

Whip the cream until it just holds its shape. Whisk the egg whites until standing in stiff peaks. Fold the cream into the mousse until evenly distributed, then fold in the egg whites.

Turn the mousse into a large glass serving bowl, and chill in the refrigerator for at least 4 hours until set.

To decorate, pare the rind of half an orange and half a lemon very thinly. Remove any white pith. Cut the rind into thin strips. Blanch the strips in boiling water for 3 minutes, rinse them in cold water, then drain and dry on absorbent kitchen paper. Sprinkle on top of the mousse just before serving. Serve chilled. This dish is included in a menu on this page.

TARTE CLAFOUTIS

Clafoutis is a traditional cherry batter pudding from the region of Limousin in central France. In this recipe the clafoutis is baked in a case of sweet almond pastry.

In Limousin, clafoutis is made with wild black cherries, but any ripe cherries will do. Tinned black cherries also work well – use two 15oz (425g) tins of stoned black cherries in heavy syrup. Drain them well before soaking in the kirsch.

PREPARATION TIME: 1¾ hours
COOKING TIME: 50-55 minutes
     plus standing time
OVEN TEMPERATURE: preheat to
     190°C (375°F, gas mark 5)

INGREDIENTS – serves 6-8:
12 oz (350 g) ripe cherries,
     pitted
4 tablespoons kirsch or cherry
     brandy
3 oz (75 g) plain flour
2 oz (50 g) caster sugar
3 eggs, beaten
½ pint (285 ml) double cream
2 tablespoons melted butter
Icing sugar for dredging

ALMOND PASTRY
6 oz (175 g) plain flour
Pinch of salt
3 oz (75 g) ground almonds
3 oz (75 g) caster sugar
3 oz (75 g) butter, diced
1 egg, beaten

Put the cherries into a bowl, sprinkle with 2 tablespoons of the kirsch and leave to soak for 1 hour.

Meanwhile, make the pastry case. Sieve the flour and salt onto a marble slab or cold work surface. Stir in the ground almonds and sugar, then make a well in the centre. Add the diced butter and rub in the flour with your fingertips until the mixture resembles breadcrumbs. Add the egg and stir with a fork to bind the dough together.

Gather the dough into a ball with one hand, then wrap in kitchen foil or a plastic bag and chill in the refrigerator for about 30 minutes.

Flatten the dough with a rolling pin, then place in the centre of a 9in (230mm) flan dish or tin. Press the dough with your fingertips to line the base and sides of the dish, then trim the edge with a knife. Prick the base with a fork and fill with kitchen foil and baking beans. Stand the dish on a baking sheet and bake blind (page 393) in the preheated oven for 15 minutes. Remove the foil and beans from the pastry case and bake for a further 5 minutes, until the pastry is set and light golden.

To make the filling, sieve the flour into a bowl, stir in the caster sugar, then gradually beat in the eggs and cream to make a smooth batter. Drain the cherries. Add the cherry juice to the batter, with the melted butter. Alternatively, blend all the ingredients together in a liquidiser or food processor.

Arrange the cherries evenly in the pastry case and slowly pour in the batter. Do not worry if it comes over the pastry around the edge of the tart, this will help protect the cooked pastry from overbrowning while the filling is cooking.

Bake in the oven for 30-35 minutes, until the filling is just set in the centre. Remove from the oven and sprinkle immediately with the remaining kirsch. Leave to stand for at least 30 minutes. Dredge the tart with icing sugar before serving warm or cold.

In France, tarts and pastries are almost always served plain. Fresh pouring cream can be served with this tart, but it is very rich served by itself. For those who like the contrast of sweet and sour, serve with soured cream, smetana or natural set yoghurt. This recipe is included in a menu on page 71.

CHERRY TART A case of almond pastry contains a filling based on an old French country recipe – cherries soaked in kirsch and baked in a rich custard. The tart can be made with other fruit including plums, apples and grapes, or dried fruit.

CHEESE

Cheese is among the most versatile of foods. It is equally appropriate at a children's tea party, an elegant dinner, in a picnic hamper for a day in the country or at the races, or in an everyday lunchbox.

TYPES OF CHEESE

The very variety of cheeses can be intimidating. There are hundreds of different varieties available in this country – even a modest supermarket may stock 15–20 kinds. Travel abroad has given many more people access to the thousands of cheeses which are rarely sold in Britain. France produces the greatest variety of different cheeses, Italy almost as many. Britain has recently undergone a revolution in cheesemaking and many new and rediscovered cheeses are now taking their place beside long-established varieties such as Cheddar and Stilton. Other countries tend to produce a more limited range but they all add up. Faced with a bewildering array of cheeses, many of them unfamiliar, it is often tempting simply to fall back on a few well-known favourites. In order to sample new cheeses with greater confidence, it is useful to be acquainted with the main groups into which most cheeses can be classified – according to the milk used, their texture, and whether the rind or any veining in the cheese has been produced by a mould.

Distinctive milks

Almost all cheeses are made from cow's milk, ewe's milk or goat's milk, and the distinctive flavour of each helps determine the flavour of the cheese. In some cases, a cheese owes its special flavour to a particular breed of animal – Larzac sheep in the case of Roquefort.

Most cow's milk cheese is made from pasteurised milk – milk heated to destroy potentially harmful microorganisms. Pasteurisation is essential for large-scale cheesemaking because it makes it possible to mix the milk from many different herds and yet still produce a uniform cheese. However, it is worth looking out for cheese made from unpasteurised milk because the flavour is almost always better than the same cheese made from pasteurised milk. Goat's milk and ewe's milk is only rarely pasteurised.

COW'S MILK CHEESES By far the majority of cheeses are made from cow's milk.

Cow's milk cheeses include all the most famous British cheeses – such as Cheddar and Stilton – French Camembert and Brie, and Italian Gorgonzola.

EWE'S MILK CHEESES Roquefort is possibly the best known ewe's milk cheese. Others include the Spanish Manchego and Italian Pecorino cheeses. Ewe's milk cheeses are generally sharper than cow's milk cheeses.

GOAT'S MILK CHEESES Cheese made from goat's milk has a coarser, more robust flavour than any other cheese. Goat's milk cheeses (given the generic name *chèvre* in France) include the tiny, hard Crottins de Chavignol and other *crottins de*

SOME SOFT CHEESES

1 RIGOTTES (in oil) *France,* cow's milk or cow and goat's milk
2 MOZZARELLA *Italy,* cow or buffalo's milk
3 MUNSTER *France,* cow's milk
4 ROQUEFORT *France,* ewe's milk
5 FROMAGE FRAIS *France,* cow, ewe or goat's milk
6 BRIE *France,* cow's milk
7 RICOTTA *Italy,* cow or ewe's milk
8 GOAT CHEESE (with herbs and paprika) *Britain*
9 GOAT CHEESE *Britain*
10 BANON (wrapped in chestnut leaves) *France,* goat or ewe's milk
11 TALEGGIO *Italy,* cow's milk
12 CHÈVRE *France,* goat's milk
13 PONT L'EVÊQUE *France,* cow's milk
14 VACHERIN MONT-D'OR *France,* cow's milk
15 CHÈVRE (with ash rind) *France,* goat's milk
16 CAMEMBERT *France,* cow's milk

chèvre, Banon from Provence and Valençay from Berry. There are also many British goat's milk cheeses now available.

OTHER MILKS The milk of the water buffalo is the only other milk used in Europe to make cheese – in Italy and the Balkans. Mozzarella was originally made from it, and some *Mozzarella di bufala* is still made in southern Italy. In Tibet, yak's milk is used and in Lapland, reindeer's milk.

Varied texture

The primary factors governing the texture of a cheese are the type of milk (whether it is full-fat or skimmed, for example), and the production process. Methods used to make cheese vary widely, but the basic stages are the same for most cheeses.

The milk from which the cheese is made is first 'started' – ripened to a certain degree of acidity, usually with the help of a culture of sour milk high in lactic acid. The milk is then coagulated, or curdled, usually by adding rennet, a substance found in the stomachs of young calves – to leave white curds and watery whey. (A non-animal rennet is used for making vegetarian cheeses.) The curds are then cut into pieces and drained to remove the whey.

The curds are next transferred to a perforated mould for the final drainage or, in a few cases, moulded by hand. Some cheeses are pressed at this stage. The final stage is ripening – the cheeses are removed from the moulds and stored in a controlled environment for anything from a few days to a few years. The length of the ripening period affects the texture. As a cheese matures it loses moisture, so the youngest cheeses are also the softest ones. During ripening the distinctive rinds, veining or holes develop. With many cheeses the flavour intensifies during ripening.

There are four main categories of cheese by texture: soft, semi-soft, semi-hard and hard.

SOFT CHEESES The very softest cheeses are the 'fresh' cheeses – in French, *fromage frais* – such as curd, cream and cottage cheeses. These cheeses are not ripened at all, or only for a few days. They do not keep and should be eaten as soon as possible.

Cheeses such as Camembert and Brie and the Italian Taleggio, although soft and creamy, are firmer than fresh cheeses. The curds are not pressed; and are ripened for about a month.

SEMI-SOFT CHEESES These are usually unpressed and left to ripen for up to six months. Semi-soft cheeses tend to be either crumbly or creamy. Many of the French blue cheeses come into this group – for example, Bleu d'Auvergne.

SEMI-HARD CHEESES The semi-hard cheeses form the largest group. They are first pressed, then ripened for anything from three to 18 months, and are firm and sliceable. Several of the classic British cheeses, such as Caerphilly, Wensleydale, Derby and Lancashire are semi-hard. So too are the Danish Samsø and Havarti, the Norwegian Jarlsberg, German Tilsit, Dutch Edam and a number of mountain-region cheeses such as the Swiss Appenzeller and Raclette, Italian Fontina, and Pyrenean ewe's milk cheeses. The flavour of these cheeses ranges from mellow for a young cheese to tangy for more mature varieties.

HARD CHEESES All hard cheeses are heavily pressed. Some are 'cheddared' – blocks of pressed curds are stacked on top of each other and turned several times to expel as much whey as possible. Others are 'cooked' – the curds are heated in the whey to make them shrink and harden so that the whey can drain off more easily. Some cheeses are both cheddared and cooked. Some cheeses, such as Italian Parmigiano (Parmesan), are ripened for up to four years.

Cheeses in this group include Cheddar and Double Gloucester, Swiss Emmental and Sbrinz, and French Cantal and Comté. Most can be eaten as dessert cheeses when young and used for cooking when fully matured or ripened.

Valuable moulds

The growth of moulds of various kinds is an important characteristic of some cheeses. The moulds usually develop from forms of the mould *penicillium* – from which penicillin is made.

BLUE CHEESES To make most of the blue cheeses a culture of *Penicillium roquefortii* – originally identified in Roquefort – is added to the curds. Occasionally the blue veining develops naturally. During ripening, the cheese is pierced with steel needles to allow the mould to spread more easily from the centre. Some blue cheeses, such as Stilton, have dry, crusty grey rinds formed as the curds at the edges of the cheese dry out; others, such as the French *bleu* cheeses and Roquefort, are closely wrapped in foil during ripening and have no rind.

Blue cheeses range in texture from the soft, spreadable Italian Gorgonzola to the semi-hard cheeses such as Stilton and blue Cheshire. French goat's milk and ewe's milk veined cheeses – such as Roquefort – are often described as *persillé* (literally 'parsleyed') rather than *bleu*, because their veins tend to be green rather than blue in colour.

SOFT WHITE RIND CHEESES After being moulded, some soft cheeses – the French Camembert and Brie, for example – are sprayed with the mould *Penicillium candidum*. This produces a soft white, bloom-like growth on the surface. The cheese ripens from the surface inwards.

WASHED-RIND CHEESES Another form of surface mould is produced by washing cheeses during ripening with water, brine, beer or a special bacterial culture. This produces soft, sometimes clammy rinds, ranging in colour from yellow to red and with a distinctively pungent smell and sharp taste. The pungency of the smell, however, is not necessarily a sign that the cheese itself will be very strong tasting. Washed-rind cheeses include Munster, Livarot, Port Salut, Reblochon and some kinds of Pont l'Evêque from France.

ARTIFICIAL RINDS Some kinds of cheese have coverings added that are not the result of the ripening process: these include Edam with a coating of bright red paraffin wax; Valençay which is covered with wood ash; and the Cornish Yarg which has a covering of nettles.

BUYING AND STORING CHEESE

Look for shops where pieces are cut from whole cheeses. A huge selection is not necessarily a good sign; a dozen cheeses in perfect condition are preferable to many more that have been on the shelf for too long. You should be able to taste a cheese before buying it. Cheeses can often be bought direct from farms or small dairies in cheesemaking regions.

The label

The amount of information given varies considerably, but sometimes a cheese label will indicate, for example, if the cheese was made in a factory or on a farm or small dairy, the type of milk, the milk's fat content and whether it was pasteurised or not. If the cheese is French, look for the words *non-pasteurisé*, or *fromage fermier* (farmhouse cheese), or *au lait cru* (with raw milk); these indicate that the cheese was made from unpasteurised milk.

A number of cheeses are becoming more and more international. Cheddar, for example, is now produced as far afield as Egypt and Japan. Nevertheless, it is still generally true that the best cheese of any particular kind is made in the country of its origin.

There are some labels or marks that distinguish authentic cheeses made by traditional methods in their countries of origin from foreign imitations: *Appellation d'origine*, for example, on a French cheese. Authentic Italian Parmesan has *Parmigiano Reggiano* stamped on its rind. Exported Swiss Emmental, Gruyère, Sbrinz, Royalp and Appenzeller should be stamped on the label or rind, or both, with the mark of the Swiss Cheese Union – a man blowing an alpenhorn – with Switzerland's name in four languages written around it.

In some cases – Stilton and the Italian cheeses Gorgonzola and Pecorino, for example – the name alone guarantees its authenticity.

The condition

Examine the cheese itself. Avoid any cheeses that are cracked and dry, crumbling, oozing sweat, collapsing or uneven in texture.

Soft cheeses, such as Brie and Camembert, should be neither chalky inside nor too runny. Do not try to ripen the cheese at home; the conditions in the shop are generally more favourable.

The veins in a blue cheese should be evenly distributed, and the paste between the veins should not be tinged brown.

Washed-rind cheeses should have an even colour and should

SOME SEMI-HARD AND SEMI-SOFT CHEESES

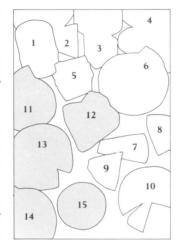

SEMI-HARD
1 STILTON (blue) *Britain*, cow's milk
2 LANCASHIRE *Britain*, cow's milk
3 BLUE SHROPSHIRE *Britain*, cow's milk
4 GOUDA *The Netherlands*, cow's milk
5 TILSIT *West Germany*, cow's milk
6 CAERPHILLY *Britain*, cow's milk
7 RACLETTE *Switzerland*, cow's milk
8 YARG *Britain*, cow's milk
9 STILTON (white) *Britain*, cow's milk
10 TOMME DE SAVOIE *France*, cow's milk

SEMI-SOFT
11 BEL PAESE *Italy*, cow's milk
12 GORGONZOLA *Italy*, cow's milk
13 BLEU D'AUVERGNE *France*, cow's milk
14 PORT SALUT *France*, cow's milk
15 REBLOCHON *France*, cow's milk

smell pungent but clean – not smell strongly of ammonia.

The holes in cheeses such as Emmental or Gruyère should be reasonably uniform in size, and there should be a slight glistening dampness in the eyes.

Keeping cheese fresh

Only buy as much cheese as you can eat within a few days. The temperature and humidity levels in modern homes are rarely suitable for keeping cheese for long periods. If you have a cool cellar or larder, store the cheese there. Otherwise, the best place to store it is the warmest part of the refrigerator.

Keep soft, fresh cheeses, such as curd cheese, in the sealed tubs in which they are sold. These are the only cheeses that actually need to be refrigerated.

Cheeses such as Brie and Camembert should be kept in their boxes or wrapped in grease-proof paper and clingfilm or foil. Take them out of the refrigerator about 30 minutes before serving. Eat within a week of purchase.

Semi-soft, semi-hard and hard cheeses tend to dry out and crack; so wrap them in several layers of foil or a damp cloth before putting them in the refrigerator. Remove them at least an hour before serving.

SERVING CHEESE

Whatever the occasion may be – whether it is a sophisticated dinner, a quick snack for unexpected guests or a large cheese and wine party – choose the best cheese you can afford and make sure it is in perfect condition. Provide a small selection of good cheeses rather than a huge array of bits and pieces.

DINNER PARTY The cheese course at a dinner party in Britain is generally served after the pudding. In France, however, it is served after the salad and main course but before the pudding. Most cheeses, in fact, taste better either immediately after or with something savoury. The lingering flavours of a sweet pudding will drown much of the subtlety of a cheese's flavour.

Provide four cheeses at most on a cheeseboard, and aim for a balanced selection. Generally, there should be one soft cheese (but not one of the fresh cheeses – these are eaten as desserts or used in cooking), one hard, semi-hard or semi-soft cheese, one blue cheese and one that is rare or seasonal. If possible, include a goat's milk or ewe's milk cheese and one at least that is reasonably well known – for unadventurous guests.

Arrange the cheese on a large wooden board or flat ceramic tray. Serve a variety of breads and plain, unsalted biscuits. If you serve butter, it should be unsalted.

CHEESE AND WINE PARTY A cheese and wine party provides a good opportunity to serve whole cheeses (such as Brie) rather than pieces. The only cheeses to avoid are the strongly flavoured washed-rind cheeses, like German Limburger, which become very pungent after a spell in a hot room.

EATING CHEESE Whether or not you eat the rind on the cheese is purely a matter of taste. The French do not usually eat the rind of a Brie or Camembert, for example, but many other people do. Some rinds are obviously inedible, such as the red wax on Edam, but generally, if the rind tastes good, eat it.

SOME HARD CHEESES

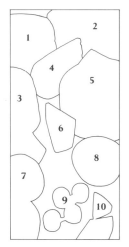

1 PARMIGIANO REGGIANO (Parmesan) *Italy,* cow's milk
2 DOUBLE GLOUCESTER *Britain,* cow's milk
3 CHEDDAR *Britain,* cow's milk
4 EMMENTAL *Switzerland,* cow's milk
5 RED LEICESTER *Britain,* cow's milk
6 PECORINO *Italy,* ewe's milk
7 PROVOLONE *Italy,* cow's milk
8 FETA *Greece,* ewe or cow's milk
9 CROTTINS DE CHAVIGNOL *France,* goat's milk
10 BORWICK *Britain,* ewe's milk (smoked)

Afternoon Tea

*T*EA AND CHINA TEAPOTS, *sugar bowls, silver salvers and all the beloved paraphernalia of the tea table blossomed all at once in England during the last half of the 17th century. Their rise in popularity was accelerated by the arrival of Charles II's queen, Catherine of Braganza, who brought the tea-drinking habit from the Portuguese court.*

Tea drinking swiftly became an epidemic in polite society, and in 1717 Thomas Twining opened a teashop for ladies in London, the first of many, in which women could meet and gossip as their husbands did in the exclusively male coffee-houses. ('Love and scandals are the best sweeteners of tea', commented the novelist Henry Fielding.)

The fashion for afternoon tea developed in the early part of the 19th century after Anna, Duchess of Bedford, no longer able to bear the mid-afternoon pangs of hunger, ordered some snacks to be served with a pot of tea. The idea quickly spread. Tea was accompanied by cream or sweetened milk, comfits (sweets) and bread and butter. The heyday of cress sandwiches, muffins, cakes, crumpets and toasting forks was yet to come, though it was fast maturing by 1889 when Jerome K. Jerome in 'Three Men in a Boat' spoke of 'a sixpenny tea, which includes bread and butter and cake ad lib., and is cheap at the price if you haven't had any dinner'.

The climax was the 'thé dansants' — afternoon tea dances — of the early decades of the 20th century, and the teashops with temptation beckoning from three-decker cake stands. Both dances and teashops were trampled under by the Second World War, but a few of them resurfaced afterwards to bring a touch of grace into the latter half of the 20th century.

Planning & Preparation

Afternoon tea is no longer the occasion it was in its Victorian and Edwardian heyday – as a social event, it died along with the lady of leisure. But there are still many opportunities for glorious, old-fashioned tea parties: Sunday afternoons with toasted crumpets and fruit cake; large family occasions such as christenings or birthdays; village fêtes and garden parties.

Making the tea

The tea itself should always be freshly brewed – whatever the occasion and however many guests. At a small party for no more than about 8-10 people this will not usually present difficulties. For a larger party it may be necessary to borrow or hire teapots. Look under Catering Hire in *Yellow Pages*. A large 8-10 pint (4.5-5.7 litre) teapot will make enough tea for 30-36 people. You will need about 10 heaped tablespoons of tea. Places such as village halls often have tea urns for heating large quantities of water or they can be hired. At home it may be necessary to boil the water up in some large saucepans.

Teas that are high in tannin, such as Assam, Ceylon and English Breakfast, should only be drunk very fresh. For parties, weaker, more subtly flavoured teas, such as Darjeeling, Earl Grey or the China teas Lapsang Souchong or Keemun, are more suitable. These teas can be left to brew for longer and they can also be made to go farther by adding more hot water to the pot. (See *Tea*, page 140.)

Planning the menu

Cakes, pastries and biscuits for afternoon tea parties should generally be delicate and decorative to complement the subtle flavour of the tea being served – exceptions to this rule are the traditional Scottish teas which tend to be very substantial, and high teas (see below).

Individual cakes and biscuits should be small enough to eat in two or three bites. Make sandwiches from thinly sliced bread and cut them into small rectangles or triangles with the crusts removed.

Include some plain cakes and biscuits, such as *Swedish cardamom cake* (page 131) or *Chocolate pretzels* (page 135), to balance rich ones. A small party is an opportunity to make elaborate cream cakes, but for larger teas, such as fêtes, the food should be more robust and fairly easy to eat.

In winter, serve warming, heavier food such as buttered crumpets and muffins, teabreads (such as *Irish tea brack*, page 124, and *Apricot and orange tea-bread*, page 134) and fruit cake. Lighter cakes and pastries, such as *Orange flower sponge cake* (page 133) and *Lemon curd cup cakes* (page 126), are more suitable for a summer tea.

Getting ahead

Prepare as much of the food as possible in advance. Most teabreads and fruit cakes stay fresh for several days in airtight containers. Sponge cakes, as long as they contain fat, can be made a day ahead and stored, wrapped, in a cool place.

Most sandwiches can also be assembled in advance (see page 137). Avoid damp fillings, such as tomatoes; they will make the sandwiches soggy. Make sure that each slice of bread is well buttered to protect the bread from any dampness in the filling. Brown bread stands up to moist fillings better than white bread.

China and cutlery

Keep your best china for parties indoors in your own home. Enhance it, and the food, with pretty tablecloths. Pastry forks are useful if you are serving cream cakes. Provide plenty of napkins. Lay the food on low tables or arrange it on a trolley. For a very large party, china and cutlery can be hired.

Tea in the garden

It is usually wisest not to use your best china outdoors – unless you have a very stable garden table. Arrange the food on trays lined with paper doilies, which are easier to pass around than plates, and can be rested on the grass. To avoid rushing between the garden and kitchen, take out with you plenty of napkins and some vacuum flasks of freshly boiled water to top up the teapot. With large numbers, it is a good idea to have a camping stove or two so that water can be boiled up on the spot. Clip down the corners of tablecloths with clothes pegs so that they do not blow about. You may need food covers if there are many flies.

Arranging the seating

For a party of up to about 12 people, try to provide seats for every one – if only rugs and cushions on the grass. For a larger party it is only necessary to ensure that there are enough seats for elderly people and others who cannot stand for long periods. Group the seats round tables. Seats for garden parties can be hired (see *Buffet parties*, page 250).

High tea

In the North of England and Scotland high tea is widely eaten. This meal is more substantial than afternoon tea, and is usually served at about six o'clock. A cooked dish, such as kippers or poached eggs, is followed by bread and butter and cake, all accompanied by strong Indian tea. Dishes suitable for high tea include *Egg and salmon cocottes* (page 16), *Fish cakes with egg sauce* (page 17), *Snipdoodle* (page 30) and *Sage sausages with mustard sauce* (page 21).

RECIPES FROM OTHER CHAPTERS

Many recipes from other chapters are suitable for tea parties. The following are some suggestions:

CAKES & PASTRIES

SHERRY GATEAU

Four layers of sponge cake are sandwiched together with a sherry butter cream and covered with chocolate cream to make this rich gateau. The sherry gateau can be made a day in advance and kept, covered, in the refrigerator.

The butter cream filling is best made with a hand-held electric beater because it requires lengthy beating.

PREPARATION TIME: *60 minutes plus chilling time*
COOKING TIME: *25 minutes*
OVEN TEMPERATURE: *preheat to 180°C (350°F, gas mark 4)*

INGREDIENTS — *makes one 9 in (230 mm) cake:*
CAKE
6 eggs
6 oz (175 g) caster sugar
6 oz (175 g) plain flour
BUTTER CREAM FILLING
8 oz (225 g) caster sugar
3 tablespoons cold water
4 egg yolks
10 oz (275 g) unsalted butter, softened
2-3 tablespoons sweet sherry

CHOCOLATE CREAM
7 oz (200 g) plain dessert chocolate
½ pint (285 ml) double cream, not chilled
2-3 tablespoons sweet sherry
DECORATION
5 or 6 plain chocolate thins, each cut into two triangles

Grease two 9in (230mm) sandwich tins and line each base. Sprinkle with caster sugar.

Whisk the eggs and sugar together with an electric beater, or in a large mixing bowl set over hot water, until the mixture is thick and foamy and the beater leaves a trail across the surface of the mixture. This may take as long as 10 minutes.

Sieve the flour twice. Fold it into the egg mixture in several additions. Divide the mixture between the prepared tins.

Bake in the preheated oven for 25 minutes until just starting to shrink from the tins. Cool in the tins for 2 minutes, then turn out onto a wire rack. When cold, halve each cake.

To make the butter cream, place the egg yolks into a mixing bowl and beat lightly with a fork. Dissolve the sugar in a pan with the water, stirring over low heat. Raise the heat and boil the syrup until it reaches 105°C (220°F) on a sugar thermometer, or a short-thread stage when a little of the syrup (cooled in a teaspoon) forms a short thread when pulled between thumb and forefinger. This will take 2-3 minutes. Remove from the heat.

Pour the syrup in a thin stream onto the egg yolks, whisking all the time until the mixture turns pale and thickens. This may take 5-10 minutes. Gradually whisk in the softened butter, adding it in small pieces. Continue to whisk the cream until it is smooth and fluffy and has thickened, then gradually whisk in the sherry.

Sandwich the layers of cake with butter cream.

To make the chocolate cream, break the chocolate into pieces and melt in a bowl over hot water. Whisk the double cream until stiff but still glossy. Gradually beat in the sherry and all but 1-2 tablespoons of the melted chocolate. The mixture may appear at first to separate, but it will thicken as you continue beating.

Spread the chocolate cream over the top and sides of the cake with a palette knife.

Trickle the remaining chocolate in many fine lines over the top of the cake to form a star-like decoration. A little vegetable oil added to the chocolate will make it more fluid. Arrange the chocolate triangles evenly around the top. Chill the gateau before serving.

CREAM SHERRY Lashings of sherry flavour the rich butter cream that fills this gateau and the chocolate cream that covers it. A starburst of melted chocolate, and triangles of plain chocolate, make a simple but impressive decoration.

BRANDY SNAPS FILLED WITH GINGER CREAM

The wafer-thin, rolled biscuits known as brandy snaps are a Yorkshire speciality. The unfilled biscuits will keep for 2-3 days in an airtight container.

PREPARATION TIME: *25 minutes*
COOKING TIME: *20-30 minutes*
OVEN TEMPERATURE: *preheat to 160°C (325°F, gas mark 3)*

INGREDIENTS — *makes about 30:*
4 oz (115 g) butter
4 oz (115 g) demerara sugar
4 oz (115 g) golden syrup
4 oz (115 g) plain flour
1 level teaspoon ground ginger
1 teaspoon lemon juice
1 teaspoon brandy
FILLING
¼ pint (150 ml) double cream
2 pieces preserved stem ginger, chopped
2 tablespoons stem ginger syrup from the jar of preserved ginger
1 egg white

Grease three very smooth baking sheets.

In a pan, set over medium heat, melt the butter with the sugar and syrup. Stir until the sugar is completely dissolved.

Remove the pan from the heat and sieve the flour and ginger into the butter mixture. Stir well and beat in the lemon juice and brandy until the mixture is completely smooth.

Drop well-spaced teaspoons of the mixture onto the greased baking sheets. Allow space for the biscuits to spread to about 4in (100mm) across.

Bake, one tray at a time, in the centre of the preheated oven for 8-10 minutes until deep golden-brown. Remove from the oven. Allow to cool for about a minute then, using a palette knife, carefully lift up a biscuit. Wrap the biscuit around the handle of a wooden spoon, with the smooth side of the biscuit on the inside. Leave the biscuit on the handle while it sets, then slide it onto a wire rack to cool. Repeat with the rest of the brandy snaps.

If the biscuits stiffen on the tray before they have all been rolled, put the tray back in the oven for a minute or so until the biscuits soften again.

To make the filling, whisk the cream until stiff but still glossy. Stir in the chopped ginger and the ginger syrup. Whisk the egg white until stiff, and fold into the cream. Pipe or spoon the ginger cream into both ends of each brandy snap, and then arrange them on a serving dish. The brandy snaps are included in a menu on this page.

RICH FRUIT CAKE

For festive occasions such as Christmas or a wedding, this dark and moist cake is excellent. It improves with keeping, and ideally should be made at least a month before eating. Wrap the cake in greaseproof paper, and keep it in an airtight container in a cool, dry place.

This recipe makes a square 8in (200mm) or a round 9in (230mm) cake. Halve the recipe to make a square 6in (150mm) or round 7in (180mm) cake. Cook the smaller cake for 1 hour at the higher temperature, followed by about 1½ hours at the lower temperature.

PREPARATION TIME: *1 hour plus soaking time*
COOKING TIME: *3-3½ hours*
OVEN TEMPERATURE: *preheat to 150°C (300°F, gas mark 2)*

INGREDIENTS — *makes one cake:*
8 oz (225 g) seedless raisins
2 oz (50 g) large, stoned raisins
8 oz (225 g) sultanas
8 oz (225 g) currants
4 tablespoons cream sherry
8 oz (225 g) butter
8 oz (225 g) dark muscovado sugar
2 tablespoons black treacle
4 eggs
10 oz (275 g) plain flour
¼ teaspoon bicarbonate of soda
½ teaspoon salt
1 level teaspoon ground mixed spice
4 oz (115 g) glacé cherries, quartered
4 oz (115 g) candied peel, chopped
2 oz (50 g) blanched almonds, slivered

Put the seedless and the stoned raisins, sultanas and currants into a bowl and stir in the sherry. Leave in a warm place for several hours to allow the fruit to absorb the sherry.

Grease the cake tin (see introduction), and line the base. If using an oven that tends to burn the edges of cakes, tie three layers of brown parcel paper around the tin, allowing the paper to project some way above the rim.

In a large mixing bowl, cream the butter and sugar together until light and fluffy. Beat in the treacle and gradually add the eggs, beating well between additions. Add a little flour to the mixture towards the end to prevent it from curdling.

Sieve the remaining flour with the bicarbonate of soda, salt and mixed spice. Fold into the egg mixture with the sherry-soaked fruit, cherries, candied peel and almonds. Stir well with a wooden spoon, but do not over-mix or the mixture will become too soft.

Turn into the prepared tin and smooth level.

Bake the cake in the preheated oven for 1½ hours, then lower the heat to 140°C (275°F, gas mark 1), and bake for 1½-2 hours more or until a fine knitting needle or skewer inserted into the centre of the cake comes out clean.

Remove the cake from the oven and leave in the tin until cool. Turn out and peel away the lining paper.

The cake can be iced for a special occasion (page 402) or eaten plain. This cake is included in a menu on this page.

M E N U

Christmas Day Tea for Eight

RICH FRUIT CAKE
this page
or BÛCHE DE NOËL
page 123

BRANDY SNAPS FILLED WITH GINGER CREAM
this page

MINCE PIES AND TARTS
page 122

Although Christmas cake is traditional, it can be very heavy on top of all the other Christmas food, and Bûche de Noël makes a lighter alternative.

IN ADVANCE The cake can be prepared several weeks in advance. The bûche, brandy snaps (unfilled) and mince pies and tarts can all be made a day ahead.

ON THE DAY Allow about 45 minutes just before the party to fill the brandy snaps.

CHRISTMAS AFTERNOON A rich fruit cake, decorated with marzipan and royal icing, is the centrepiece of a spread which also includes brandy snaps and mince pies and tarts.

MINCE PIES AND MINCE TARTS

Traditionalists may prefer a sugar-crusted lid over their Christmas mincemeat. But mince tarts with a trickled almond glacé icing are also very good. The same recipe can be used for both pies and tarts.

Ground almonds give this pastry a subtle flavour and crisp texture. The pastry bakes better and shrinks less if it is allowed to rest for 30 minutes between mixing and rolling.

Mince pies and tarts will keep for up to a week in the refrigerator or an airtight tin.

PREPARATION TIME: *45 minutes*
COOKING TIME: *15-20 minutes*
OVEN TEMPERATURE: *preheat to 200°C (400°F, gas mark 6)*

INGREDIENTS — *makes 12 mince pies and 12 mince tarts:*
8 oz (225 g) plain flour
4 oz (115 g) butter
1 oz (25 g) ground almonds
2 oz (50 g) caster sugar
A few drops almond essence
4-5 tablespoons milk
1-1½ lb (450-700 g) mincemeat (page 138)
A little extra milk
Caster sugar for dusting
1 tablespoon granulated sugar
3 oz (75 g) icing sugar
A little hot water

Sieve the flour into a mixing bowl and rub in the butter until the mixture resembles coarse breadcrumbs.

Stir in the ground almonds and sugar. Add the almond essence to the milk, pour onto the flour and mix to a dough. Shape the pastry dough into a ball, wrap in a butter paper, or place in a plastic bag, and rest in the refrigerator for 30 minutes.

Roll out the pastry until about ⅛in (3mm) thick. With fluted pastry cutters, cut out 24 circles 3in (80mm) across and 12 circles 2½in (65mm) across.

Grease 24 patty tins and line them with the larger pastry circles. Place 1 heaped teaspoon of mincemeat in each.

To make the pies, brush the underside of the smaller pastry circles with milk and use them to cover half the mincemeat tarts, pressing down the edges firmly. Brush the tops with milk and sprinkle with a little sugar. Prick the pastry tops with a fork two or three times.

Bake in the centre of the preheated oven for 20 minutes until the pastry is golden and crisp. Cool the mince pies in the tins for 5 minutes, then either serve while still warm or transfer to a wire rack until cold.

Bake the open tarts for 15 minutes in the preheated oven

or until the pastry is just starting to change colour. Cool in the tin for 5 minutes, then transfer to a wire rack to cool completely.

Sieve the icing sugar, add a drop of almond essence and mix with enough hot water to make a pouring consistency. Trail a little icing over the mincemeat in each tart, making a series of zigzags. Leave on one side until the icing has set.

These pies and tarts are included in a menu on page 120.

FROSTED GINGERBREAD

In medieval England gingerbread, sweetened with honey, was highly regarded for its medicinal properties. It was also often presented as a trophy at jousting tournaments, gilded and decorated with box leaves. Today, gingerbread is usually sweetened with treacle or golden syrup. This dark, moist gingerbread has a caramel frosting.

It is important not to open the oven door during the first half hour when baking gingerbread, otherwise the rush of cold air will cause it to sink in the middle. Gingerbread will keep for 3-4 days stored in an airtight tin.

PREPARATION TIME: *30 minutes*
COOKING TIME: *45 minutes*
OVEN TEMPERATURE: *preheat to 190°C (375°F, gas mark 5)*

INGREDIENTS — *makes 20 squares:*
4 oz (115 g) butter
1 tablespoon golden syrup
2 tablespoons black treacle
8 oz (225 g) plain flour
3 oz (75 g) muscovado sugar
½ teaspoon bicarbonate of soda
½ teaspoon salt
½ teaspoon ground cinnamon
2 level teaspoons ground ginger
1 egg
¼ pint (150 ml) buttermilk
4 oz (115 g) preserved stem ginger, drained and chopped
ICING
1 oz (25 g) unsalted butter
1½ oz (40 g) muscovado sugar
1 tablespoon syrup from the jar of preserved stem ginger
DECORATION
20 split blanched almonds

Grease and line a 7in (180mm) square cake tin.

In a small pan, melt the butter with the golden syrup and treacle. Sieve the flour, sugar, bicarbonate of soda, salt, cinnamon and ginger into a mixing bowl. Stir in the butter mixture, the egg, buttermilk and chopped, preserved ginger. Mix well and turn the mixture into the prepared cake tin.

Bake in the centre of the preheated oven for about 45 minutes — until a fine knitting needle or skewer inserted into the centre comes out clean. Cool in the tin for 2 minutes, then turn out onto a wire rack, ready for icing.

To make the icing, gently heat the butter with the sugar and

OPEN AND ENCLOSED Mincemeat tarts, with almond-flavoured icing trickled over the top, make a change from traditional mince pies.

ginger syrup until the sugar is dissolved. Raise the heat and boil the mixture for 1 minute. Remove from the heat and leave to cool slightly. Pour over the top of the gingerbread, allowing some to trickle down the sides. Arrange the split blanched almonds in rows on top of the icing, so that the gingerbread can be cut into 20 even squares when the icing has set.

This gingerbread is included in a menu on page 336.

BÛCHE DE NOËL

The traditional French Christmas cake is a chocolate swiss roll, iced to look like a Yule log, called Bûche de Noël (Christmas log). In the south of France, the roll is filled with a purée of chestnuts – its flavour enhanced with coffee and brandy. The roll can alternatively be simply spread with whipped cream or a vanilla-flavoured butter cream before rolling up. Instead of icing it, the roll can be left plain or just dusted with icing sugar. Bûche de Noël is best eaten on the day it is made, or it can be stored in the freezer for up to a month. Thaw overnight in the refrigerator, and sprinkle with a little extra caster sugar before serving.

PREPARATION TIME: *50 minutes*
COOKING TIME: *12-15 minutes*
OVEN TEMPERATURE: *preheat to 200°C (400°F, gas mark 6)*

INGREDIENTS:
SWISS ROLL
2 oz (50 g) self-raising flour
1 oz (25 g) cocoa powder
3 eggs
3½ oz (90 g) caster sugar
A little extra caster sugar
CHESTNUT FILLING
2 tablespoons freshly ground coffee and 6 tablespoons milk OR 1 tablespoon coffee essence mixed with 4 tablespoons hot milk
8 oz (225 g) unsweetened chestnut purée
2 oz (50 g) caster sugar
¼ pint (150 ml) double cream
2 tablespoons brandy
ICING
½ teaspoon coffee essence
1 level tablespoon cocoa powder
1½ tablespoons hot water
4 oz (115 g) icing sugar
2 oz (50 g) butter
GARNISH
Icing sugar

Grease and line the base of a swiss roll tin about 13in × 9in (330mm × 230mm). Allow the lining paper to project a little at each end, but do not line the sides of the tin.

Sieve the flour with the cocoa twice and set the mixture aside on a sheet of greaseproof paper in a warm place.

Whisk the eggs with the sugar using an electric beater, or in a mixing bowl set over hot water, until the mixture is thick and foamy. This may take as long as 10 minutes.

Gradually fold in the flour mixture. Pour the mixture into the prepared tin and spread level. Bake in the centre of the preheated oven for 12-15 minutes until well risen and springy to the touch. Turn out onto a teacloth sprinkled with caster sugar. Peel off the greaseproof paper and, with a sharp knife, trim away the edges of the cake to make it easier to roll.

Take one end of the cloth and fold it over one of the shorter sides of the cake. Now roll up the cake with the cloth so that the cloth is taking up the space where the filling will go later. Leave the cloth-covered roll on a wire rack to cool.

To make the filling, bring the ground coffee almost to the boil with the milk. Remove from the heat, leave for 5 minutes then strain through a very fine sieve. Alternatively, mix the coffee essence with the hot milk.

Sieve the chestnut purée into a bowl. Beat in the hot coffee milk and the sugar until the mixture is smooth. Whisk the cream until stiff, and fold into the purée with the brandy.

When the swiss roll is cool, unroll it carefully and spread the filling evenly over the cake. Re-roll carefully.

To make the icing, put the coffee essence, cocoa and hot water into a bowl and mix until smooth. Add the sieved icing sugar and the butter and beat

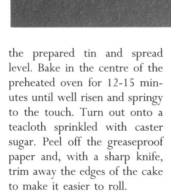

FRENCH LOG A chocolate swiss roll with chestnut, cream and brandy filling, and chocolate icing spread to look like bark, is the French alternative to fruit Christmas cake. Paper holly leaves and a sprinkling of icing sugar add to the illusion.

until thoroughly mixed.

Use a palette knife to spread the icing over the swiss roll. With the palette knife or a fork, mark lines to look like bark. Leave the icing to harden slightly, then give the cake a light dusting of icing sugar to look like snow on the log.

This cake is included in a menu on page 120.

RUM AND RAISIN CAKE

The raisins in this recipe are soaked in rum until they are plump. The resulting cake is moist and well-flavoured. Allow several hours for the raisins to swell, overnight is best. The cake is baked in a square tin for easy cutting, but a 9in (230mm) round tin may be used instead. The cake will keep for 1-2 weeks, wrapped in greaseproof paper and kitchen foil and stored in a cool place.

PREPARATION TIME: *20 minutes plus soaking time*
COOKING TIME: *1¼-1½ hours*
OVEN TEMPERATURE: *preheat to 160°C (325°F, gas mark 3)*

INGREDIENTS – *makes one 7½ in (190 mm) cake:*
1 lb (450 g) seedless raisins
¼ pint (150 ml) dark Jamaican rum
12 oz (350 g) plain flour
1½ level teaspoons baking powder
8 oz (225 g) demerara sugar
8 oz (225 g) butter or margarine
3 eggs, beaten
A little extra demerara sugar

Soak the raisins in half the rum for a few hours, or overnight, until the fruit has swollen.

Grease and line a 7½in (190mm) square cake tin.

Sieve the flour and baking powder into a mixing bowl and stir in the sugar. Cut the butter into the mixture and rub it in until the mixture resembles breadcrumbs. Stir in the raisins and beaten eggs, and mix well.

Turn the mixture into the prepared cake tin, and smooth level. Sprinkle with the extra demerara sugar.

Bake in the centre of the preheated oven for 1¼-1½ hours, or until a fine skewer inserted into the centre of the cake comes out clean.

Cool the cake in the tin for 15 minutes then turn out onto a wire rack. Trickle the remainder of the rum over the top of the cake and let it soak in. Leave the cake until it is quite cold before cutting.

IRISH TEA BRACK

In Gaelic, *brec* means 'speckled'. Hence the name of this traditional Irish tea cake – speckled with raisins and sultanas. Brack is usually made with yeast, but this version is raised with baking powder which shortens the preparation time considerably. However, allow time for the fruit to soak in tea. It can be left overnight.

The brack will keep, wrapped, in the refrigerator for up to a week.

PREPARATION TIME: *20 minutes*
SOAKING TIME: *4-5 hours or overnight*
COOKING TIME: *1¼-1½ hours*
OVEN TEMPERATURE: *preheat to 160°C (325°F, gas mark 3)*

INGREDIENTS – *makes one 6 in (150 mm) cake:*
6 fl oz (175 ml) warm tea without milk
5 oz (150 g) soft, dark brown sugar
6 oz (175 g) seedless raisins
6 oz (175 g) sultanas
6 oz (175 g) plain flour
1 level teaspoon baking powder
1 level teaspoon ground mixed spice
1 egg, beaten

Measure the tea, sugar, raisins and sultanas into a mixing bowl and stir well. Leave for 4-5 hours, or overnight, for the fruit to swell.

Grease a 6in (150mm) round cake tin and line the base.

Sieve the flour, baking powder and mixed spice onto the soaked fruit and tea. Add the egg and mix well. Beat for 1 minute. Turn the mixture into the prepared tin.

Bake in the centre of the preheated oven for 1¼-1½ hours, or until a fine skewer inserted into the centre of the cake comes out clean.

Cool the brack for 15 minutes in the tin, then turn out onto a wire rack.

Spread with butter, cream cheese or *Lime curd* (page 138), or eat plain. Brack is also very good toasted after a day or two.

IRISH TEATIME TREAT Raisins and sultanas, plump and juicy after soaking in tea, make Irish tea brack fruity enough to be eaten on its own, but creamy unsalted butter and the tang of homemade lime curd are the perfect addition.

MOCHA ECLAIRS

The Yemeni city of Mocha was considered the coffee capital of the world until the end of the 17th century. It produces coffee that tastes a little of chocolate. Today 'mocha' can mean either the variety of coffee or a flavouring of mixed coffee and chocolate. A blend of mocha and mysore coffee, with chocolate, is used to flavour the cream filling for these eclairs, but any good quality coffee can be used instead of this blend.

The eclairs should be served within 2-3 hours of filling, otherwise the choux pastry cases will start to soften. The choux paste can be made up to 24 hours in advance and stored, covered, in the refrigerator. The baked, unfilled cases will keep firm and dry for a day in an airtight tin if stored when completely cold. The baked cases can also be frozen, but in this case they should be thawed, then heated for a few minutes in a moderate oven – 180°C (350°F, gas mark 4) – to restore their crispness before filling.

PREPARATION TIME: *45 minutes*
COOKING TIME: *30 minutes*
OVEN TEMPERATURE: *preheat to 220°C (425°F, gas mark 7)*

INGREDIENTS – *makes 12:*
CHOUX PASTRY
3 oz (75 g) plain flour
¼ pint (150 ml) hot water
2 oz (50 g) butter
2 eggs, beaten

MOCHA CREAM
5 tablespoons creamy milk
1½ level tablespoons finely ground mocha/mysore coffee
3 oz (75 g) plain dessert chocolate
¼ pint (150 ml) double cream
ICING
5 oz (150 g) icing sugar
1 level tablespoon instant coffee powder
5 teaspoons hot water.

Grease two baking sheets.

Sieve the flour onto a sheet of greaseproof paper. Measure the water into a pan and bring to the boil over moderate heat. Add the butter in pieces and stir until melted. Bring the liquid back to the boil, then remove the pan from the heat and add the flour all at once.

Beat with a wooden spoon over moderate heat for a few minutes until the paste forms a ball and leaves the sides of the pan. Remove from the heat and allow to cool until you can comfortably hold your hand against the side of the pan.

Add the eggs little by little to the mixture, beating in each addition of egg well. Finally, beat the mixture to make a smooth, glossy paste.

Spoon the mixture into a piping bag fitted with a plain ½in (15mm) nozzle. Pipe six strips of the mixture about 4in (100mm) long onto each of the greased baking sheets.

Bake in the centre of the preheated oven for 25-30 minutes until golden and crisp. Do not open the oven door until the baking time is up.

Remove the eclairs to a wire rack and immediately make a short cut along one side of each to allow the steam to escape. Leave the eclairs to cool.

While the eclairs are cooling on the rack, make the mocha cream. Measure the milk into a small pan, sprinkle the coffee on top and slowly bring almost to the boil, stirring all the time. Remove from the heat and leave to infuse for 5 minutes. Pour through a very fine strainer, then allow to cool.

Break the chocolate into pieces and melt in a bowl over hot water. Whisk the cream until thick, lightly mix in first the coffee milk and then about two-thirds of the chocolate.

Make the cut in the side of each eclair a little longer and, using a spoon or piping bag, fill with mocha cream.

To make the icing, sieve the icing sugar, mix with the coffee powder and gradually stir in hot water to make a pouring consistency. Spoon the icing over each eclair. When the icing is almost set, trickle the remainder of the melted chocolate in a zigzag pattern over the icing. A little vegetable oil added to the chocolate will make it more fluid. Let the icing and chocolate set.

RICH AND DARK Melted chocolate, trickled over coffee icing, is the last touch to these eclairs filled with dark mocha cream.

POLISH HONEY CAKE

In Eastern Europe many cakes are made with breadcrumbs and ground nuts instead of flour. This results in a cake with a rich, unusual texture. Be prepared for the cake to rise during cooking and then sink as it cools – this is normal. The cake is made in a fluted brioche mould or a ring mould. It will keep for 2-3 days in an airtight tin.

PREPARATION TIME: *30 minutes plus cooling time*
COOKING TIME: *45-50 minutes*
OVEN TEMPERATURE: *preheat to 180°C (350°F, gas mark 4)*

INGREDIENTS:
A little caster sugar
6 oz (175 g) honey
4 eggs, separated
2 oz (50 g) light brown sugar
½ teaspoon vanilla essence
3½ oz (90 g) fairly dry breadcrumbs
3½ oz (90 g) walnuts, finely chopped
¼ pint (150 ml) whipped cream (optional)

Grease a 10in (250mm) fluted brioche mould, or a deep ring mould of similar volume – about 3¼ pints (1.9 litres) – and line the base. Sprinkle the inside of the mould with caster sugar.

Warm the honey by standing the jar in hot water for 15 minutes, then measure the warm honey into a mixing bowl. Add the egg yolks and the sugar, and whisk the mixture until light and foamy. Whisk in the vanilla essence.

Mix the breadcrumbs with the walnuts.

Whisk the egg whites until stiff. Using a metal spoon, alternately fold the egg whites and the breadcrumb mixture into the honey mixture in several additions.

Turn the mixture into the prepared mould. Bake in the centre of the preheated oven for 40-50 minutes until risen and golden-brown. Leave to cool in the tin for 3 minutes, then turn out onto a wire rack to cool. Serve cold.

The cake is rich enough to eat as a dessert, in which case, serve it with whipped cream.

POLISH SURPRISE The deceptively plain appearance of this Polish cake belies its honeyed moistness. In Poland it would be served with glasses of lemon tea.

M E N U

Easter Sunday Tea for Four to Six

SIMNEL CAKE
opposite page

LEMON CURD
CUP CAKES
this page

HOT CROSS BUNS
page 128

If you make a full batch of hot cross buns on Good Friday, half of them can be stored to be enjoyed on Easter Sunday.

IN ADVANCE The simnel cake can be made several weeks in advance. The hot cross buns can be made 1–2 days in advance.

ON THE DAY Allow about an hour in the morning to make the cup cakes. Decorate the cakes, and warm through the buns just before serving.

LEMON CURD CUP CAKES

Use edible crystallised spring flowers to decorate these little cakes. They are ideal for a tea in spring – Easter Sunday for example. The flowers can be made up to a week in advance, and kept in a warm, dry place. Without the flowers, the cakes freeze well for 1-2 weeks.

PREPARATION TIME: *30 minutes*
PREPARATION AND DRYING TIME FOR FLOWERS: *1½-2 hours*
COOKING TIME: *20 minutes*
OVEN TEMPERATURE: *preheat to 180°C (350°F, gas mark 4)*

INGREDIENTS – *makes 12:*
4 oz (115 g) softened butter or margarine
4 oz (115 g) caster sugar
Finely grated rind of ½ lemon
2 eggs, beaten
3½ oz (90 g) self-raising flour
8 oz (225 g) lemon curd (see Lime curd, page 138)
Paper cases
Icing sugar for dusting
CRYSTALLISED FLOWERS
Primroses, single blooms of pale-hued polyanthus flowers, violets
1 egg white
Caster sugar

Place fluted paper cases into 12 patty tins.

Cream the butter with the sugar and the grated lemon rind until light and fluffy. Gradually beat in the eggs. Sieve the flour and fold into the mixture. Spoon the mixture into the paper cases.

Bake in the centre of the pre-heated oven for 20 minutes until risen and golden. Remove from the oven and cool, still in the paper cases, on a wire rack.

When the cakes are cold use a very sharp, small knife to slice off the top of each cake. Cut the lid into quarters and set aside. Make a hollow in the top of the cake with a teaspoon, and spoon in lemon curd until level with the top of the cake. Place three of the reserved lid quarters on top of the lemon curd, evenly spaced. Discard the other quarter. Dust the cake with sieved icing sugar and set aside.

To make the crystallised flowers, select dry, perfect flower heads and remove the stalks. Slightly whisk the egg white. Gently brush the petals on both sides with the egg white. Sprinkle each flower generously with caster sugar and shake off the surplus. Place the sugar-coated flowers on a wire rack in a warm place for about an hour to dry completely.

Place a crystallised flower on each cake before serving.

These cakes are included in a menu on the opposite page.

SIMNEL CAKE

The present form of the simnel cake – a fruit cake iced with marzipan, and decorated with 11 balls of marzipan representing the disciples without Judas – is very recent. Early simnel cakes consisted of a case of hard pastry, coloured golden with saffron and filled with dried fruit. The name is derived from the Latin word *simila* – the finest quality of wheat flour – and must refer to the flour used for the pastry. Gradually the hard pastry has been replaced with lighter pastry, and finally by a coating of marzipan. However, the balls of marzipan are a 20th-century addition – the cake may instead be decorated with crystallised spring flowers or small Easter eggs.

This cake will keep for up to a month in an airtight tin.

PREPARATION TIME: *50 minutes*
COOKING TIME: *2¾-3 hours*
OVEN TEMPERATURE: *preheat to 150°C (300°F, gas mark 2)*

INGREDIENTS – *makes one 7 in (180 mm) cake:*
6 oz (175 g) butter
6 oz (175 g) light, soft brown sugar
3 eggs
Finely grated rind of 1 orange
Finely grated rind of 1 lemon
8 oz (225 g) plain flour
1 level teaspoon baking powder
1 level teaspoon ground mixed spice
1 lb (450 g) mixed dried fruit
2 oz (50 g) glacé cherries, quartered
2 oz (50 g) candied peel, chopped
2 tablespoons milk
1 tablespoon apricot jam
1 lb (450 g) marzipan (page 400)
2 oz (50 g) icing sugar
A little hot water

DECORATION
Crystallised flowers (see Lemon curd cup cakes), small Easter eggs, or marzipan balls (see method)
Gold or white ribbon

Grease and line a 7in (180mm) cake tin.

In a warmed bowl, cream the butter and sugar until light and fluffy. Gradually beat in the eggs and the grated orange and lemon rind. Sieve the flour with the baking powder and mixed spice. Fold into the egg mixture. Mix in the dried fruit, glacé cherries, candied peel and milk.

If you plan to decorate the cake with marzipan balls, set aside about 4oz (115g) of the marzipan. Divide the remaining marzipan in half and roll out one piece into a circle the same size as the cake tin.

Spoon half the cake mixture into the prepared tin, place the circle of marzipan on top and cover with the remaining mixture. Smooth the surface level.

Bake in the centre of the preheated oven for 2¾-3 hours, or until the centre of the cake is firm to the touch. Cool the cake in the tin for 45 minutes, then turn onto a wire rack.

When the cake is cold, brush the top with apricot jam. Roll out the remaining marzipan to cover the top of the cake. Press down gently and mark a pattern with the prongs of a fork around the edge.

Mix the icing sugar with a little hot water to make a stiff pouring consistency and run the icing over the centre of the cake, leaving a margin of marzipan around the edge. When the icing has set, decorate the cake with crystallised flowers or Easter eggs. Alternatively, make the reserved marzipan into 11 balls and arrange them around the edge of the cake.

Wrap a length of gold or white ribbon round the cake, and tie with a bow.

This cake is included in a menu on the opposite page.

EASTER FLOWERS Crystallised primroses decorate a simnel cake, and violets nestle in the centre of lemon curd cup cakes.

HOT CROSS BUNS

'One a penny, two a penny, hot cross buns', was the London street cry during the 19th century. But the tradition of eating buns marked with a cross goes back well before the Christian Church adopted the practice to mark Good Friday. To the Greeks and Romans a cross on a circle symbolised the four seasons, and both had festive cakes bearing a cross.

The buns will keep, wrapped, in the refrigerator for 1-2 days.

PREPARATION TIME: *30 minutes*
RISING TIME: *1-2 hours*
COOKING TIME: *25-30 minutes*
OVEN TEMPERATURE: *preheat to 200°C (400°F, gas mark 6)*

INGREDIENTS – *makes 12:*
1 oz (25 g) fresh yeast OR *2 level teaspoons dried yeast* OR *1 sachet easy-blend dried yeast*
1½ oz (40 g) caster sugar
2 tablespoons warm water
1 lb (450 g) plain flour
1 level teaspoon salt
1 level teaspoon ground mixed spice
½ teaspoon ground cinnamon
2 oz (50 g) butter
3 oz (75 g) mixed dried fruit, or currants
2 oz (50 g) candied peel, chopped
½ pint (285 ml) lukewarm milk
1 egg yolk mixed with 2 tablespoons milk

SHORTCRUST PASTRY
2 oz (50 g) plain flour
1 oz (25 g) butter
1 tablespoon cold water

GLAZE
1 tablespoon milk mixed with 1 tablespoon caster sugar

Cream the fresh yeast with 1 level teaspoon of the caster sugar and stir into the warm water. Or sprinkle the dried yeast onto the warm water. Set either yeast mixture in a warm place for 10-15 minutes until it becomes frothy. If using easy-blend dried yeast, follow the instructions on the packet.

Sieve the flour, salt and spices into a mixing bowl. Rub in the butter until the mixture resembles breadcrumbs, and stir in the sugar, dried fruit and candied peel. Mix in the yeast mixture and the milk. Beat the mixture with a wooden spoon until the dough leaves the sides of the bowl. Cover the bowl with a large plastic bag and leave in a warm place for 1-2 hours until double in bulk.

Meanwhile, make the pastry. Rub the butter into the flour, then mix to a dough with the cold water. Shape the pastry into a ball, wrap and keep in the refrigerator until needed.

Grease two large baking sheets.

Turn the dough out onto a floured surface and knead lightly for 1 minute. Divide into 12 pieces and shape each piece into a ball. Place on the baking sheets and brush with the mixture of egg yolk and milk.

Roll out the pastry thinly and cut into strips ¼in (5mm) wide. Place two strips on each bun to form a cross, making sure that the pastry strips extend right down the sides of the bun. Brush the pastry with the egg yolk mixture. Leave the buns in a warm place for 30 minutes to prove, until puffy.

Bake the buns in the preheated oven for 25-30 minutes until golden-brown. Brush the hot buns with the glaze and replace in the oven for 2 minutes. Serve immediately, or transfer to a wire rack to cool. Warm the buns through in a moderate oven when needed.

These buns are included in a menu on page 126.

GOOD FRIDAY BUNS One of the symbols of Easter, hot cross buns should be eaten warm from the oven.

GOLD AND SILVER MARBLE CAKE

Queen Victoria is supposed to have been particularly fond of a sponge cake recipe in which yolks of eggs were added to one half of a sponge mixture to make a golden cake, and stiffly whisked egg whites were folded into the other half to make a silver cake. That idea is used in this cake to produce a gold and silver marble effect by combining the two mixtures.

The cake will keep, in an airtight tin, for 4-5 days.

PREPARATION TIME: *50-55 minutes*
COOKING TIME: *50-60 minutes*
OVEN TEMPERATURE: *preheat to 180°C (350°F, gas mark 4)*

INGREDIENTS – *makes one 8 in (200 mm) cake:*

GOLD MIXTURE
3 oz (75 g) butter
3 oz (75 g) caster sugar
3 tablespoons warm water
3 egg yolks, lightly beaten
3 oz (75 g) plain flour
1½ level teaspoons baking powder
½ oz (15 g) ground almonds
A few drops almond essence

SILVER MIXTURE
3 oz (75 g) butter
3 oz (75 g) caster sugar
1½ tablespoons warm water
½ oz (15 g) ground almonds
A few drops almond essence
3 egg whites
3 oz (75 g) plain flour
¾ teaspoon baking powder

MARZIPAN
3 oz (75 g) ground almonds
1½ oz (40 g) icing sugar
1½ oz (40 g) caster sugar
1 egg yolk
1 teaspoon lemon juice
1 teaspoon brandy
1-2 drops almond essence
DECORATION
2 tablespoons apricot jam,
  warmed and sieved
1 level tablespoon icing sugar
1 paper doily (with large holes)
A few gold and silver dragees

Grease an 8in (200mm) cake tin, and line the base.

For the gold mixture, cream the butter in a warmed bowl until soft. Beat in half the sugar, then gradually beat in the rest of the sugar and the warm water alternately until the mixture is light and fluffy. Beat in the egg yolks. Sieve the flour and baking powder, and fold into the mixture with the ground almonds and almond essence.

Place spoonfuls of the mixture on the base of the prepared cake tin.

For the silver mixture, cream the butter until soft. Gradually beat in the sugar and warm water until the mixture is light and fluffy. Fold in the ground almonds and almond essence. Whisk the egg whites until stiff but not dry. Sieve the flour with the baking powder. Fold the beaten egg whites and flour into the mixture alternately in several additions.

Fill the gaps left in the cake tin between the spoonfuls of gold mixture with spoonfuls of the silver mixture. Use a cocktail stick or needle to pull streaks of the gold mixture into the silver mixture.

Bake the cake in the centre of the preheated oven for 50-60 minutes or until the centre of the cake is springy to the touch. Cool in the tin for 2 minutes then turn out onto a wire rack to cool.

To make the marzipan, mix together the ground almonds, icing sugar, caster sugar, egg yolk, lemon juice, brandy and almond essence in a bowl. Knead together until the mixture forms a ball. Dust a work surface or pastry board with a little sieved icing sugar, and roll out the marzipan to make a circle the same size as the cake.

Brush the top of the cake with apricot jam, and place the marzipan on top. Level gently with a rolling pin. Scallop the edges of the marzipan by pushing it in at intervals with your finger. Place a paper doily on the cake and dredge icing sugar over it. Carefully remove the doily to leave the lacy pattern. Decorate the top with a few gold and silver dragees.

HIDDEN MARBLING As the first slice is lifted from this almond cake, streaks of gold and silver appear. Two batches of mixture produce the pattern: one made with egg yolks, the other with egg whites. For a stronger effect, add a little yellow food colouring to the gold mixture.

M E N U

Summer Garden Tea for Six to Eight

ROLLED
SMOKED SALMON
SANDWICHES
page 138

EPICUREAN BUTTER
SANDWICHES
page 137

ALMOND MERINGUES
this page

CHOCOLATE
STRAWBERRY GATEAU
page 132

SWEDISH CARDAMOM
CAKE *opposite page*

IN ADVANCE The carda-mom cake, the sponge for the gateau and the almond meringues (unfilled) can all be made at least a day in advance.

ON THE DAY Allow about an hour to make the sand-wiches. In addition, reserve the hour before the party to fill the meringues and ice the gateau.

Ask the guests to help you carry the food to the table when they arrive. Do not put it out in the garden in advance, particularly if it is a hot day.

SUMMER AFTERNOON Spread out on a table in the garden are fluted cardamom cake, strawberry-pink chocolate gateau, meringues flecked with green-tinted almonds, and triangular epicurean butter sandwiches encircled by delicate rolled smoked salmon sandwiches.

ALMOND MERINGUES

An 18th-century Swiss pastry-cook called Gasparini is credited with creating the first meringue, from stiffly beaten egg whites mixed with sugar. The light, crisp confection spread quickly to the rest of Europe. Marie Antoinette is said to have been fond of meringues.

These almond meringues are decorated with fragments of green-tinted almonds and sand-wiched with whipped cream mixed with an almond-flavoured Italian liqueur, Amaretto di Saronno. Maraschino – flavour-ed with cherry kernels – could be used if Amaretto is unavailable.

Meringues are a very good way of using up egg whites, left over after making mayonnaise,

PREPARATION TIME: *35 minutes*

COOKING TIME: *3 hours*

OVEN TEMPERATURE: *preheat to 110°C (225°F, gas mark ¼)*

INGREDIENTS – *makes 7-8:*
¾ *oz (20 g) unblanched almonds*
A few drops green food colouring
2 teaspoons water
2 egg whites
4 oz (115 g) caster sugar
1 oz (25 g) ground almonds
¼ *pint (150 ml) double cream*
2 level teaspoons caster sugar
1 tablespoon Amaretto di Saronno
Non-stick baking paper

To remove the almond skins, cover the almonds with cold water in a small pan and bring to the boil. Remove from the heat as soon as the water boils, drain and cover with cold water. Peel away the skins and then finely chop the blanched almonds.

In a small bowl, mix a drop or two of green food colouring with the water and add the chopped almonds. Mix together until the almonds have taken up the colour and are a pale, delicate green. Turn them onto a piece of kitchen paper to dry.

Line a baking sheet with non-stick baking paper.

To make the meringue, whisk the egg whites in a very clean bowl until stiff. Add half the sugar, and whisk in briefly. Combine the remainder of the sugar with the ground almonds and, using a metal spoon, fold carefully and evenly into the egg-white mixture. Place rounded dessertspoons of the

meringue mixture onto the lined baking sheet. The mixture should make 14-16 meringues. Sprinkle each meringue with the green-tinted almonds.

Bake the meringues in the preheated oven for 2 hours. Switch off the oven and leave the meringues in the oven for 1 hour more.

Gently remove the meringues from the baking paper. Whisk the cream until stiff. Fold in the sugar and the Amaretto di Saronno. Sandwich pairs of meringues with the cream.

The meringues are very fragile and creamy. It is wise to give guests a fork and napkin when they eat them.

These meringues are included in a menu on the opposite page.

SWEDISH CARDAMOM CAKE

The fragrance of cardamom is a little like eucalyptus, but its taste is far more subtle. The spice comes from northern India, and travelling merchants brought it back to Scandinavia where it is widely used. It is possible to buy ready-ground cardamom, but the aroma of freshly crushed cardamom is much sweeter.

This cake looks very pretty baked in a cake tin with fluted sides, if one is available. A deep 8in (200mm) flan tin can also be used. It will keep 2-3 days in an airtight tin.

PREPARATION TIME: *20 minutes*

COOKING TIME: *45-50 minutes*

OVEN TEMPERATURE: *preheat to 180°C (350°F, gas mark 4)*

INGREDIENTS– *makes one 7-8 in (180-200 mm) cake:*
16 cardamom pods
6 oz (175 g) caster sugar
2 oz (50 g) butter, melted
1 egg, beaten
¼ *pint (150 ml) single cream*
8 oz (225 g) plain flour
1 level teaspoon baking powder
1 oz (25 g) flaked almonds
A little caster sugar

Grease and line a 7-8in (180-200mm) round cake tin.

Peel away the pale green outer husks from the cardamom pods and remove the tiny black seeds. Crush these to a fine powder with a pestle and mortar, or in a spice grinder.

Measure the sugar into the bowl and beat in the butter and egg. Mix in the ground cardamom and the cream. Sieve the flour with the baking powder and fold in with the flaked almonds. Pour the mixture into the prepared tin.

Bake in the centre of the preheated oven for 45-50 minutes, or until a fine skewer inserted into the centre of the cake comes out clean.

Cool in the tin for 2 minutes then turn out onto a wire rack. Just before serving, sprinkle the top of the cake lightly with caster sugar.

This cake is included in a menu on the opposite page.

for example. Egg whites cracked the day before whisk much better than freshly separated ones because the albumen is more concentrated after slight evaporation. Cover the egg whites to prevent them drying out completely, and keep in the

refrigerator. Take them out again, though, well before starting to make the meringues – egg whites should be at room temperature for whisking.

Unfilled, the meringues will keep for up to a week in an airtight tin.

CHOCOLATE STRAWBERRY GATEAU

The first strawberries ripen in the garden at the beginning of June, just as the weather gets warm enough to eat this gateau outdoors.

The sponge cake can be made a day ahead and frozen, or kept wrapped in foil in the refrigerator. The cake should not be iced more than 1-2 hours before serving or the moisture in the strawberries will cause the butter cream to separate.

PREPARATION TIME: *50 minutes*
COOKING TIME: *30–35 minutes*
OVEN TEMPERATURE: *preheat to 180°C (350°F, gas mark 4)*

INGREDIENTS — *makes one 7½ in (190 mm) cake:*
Finely grated rind and juice of 1 small orange
3 tablespoons cocoa powder
4 oz (115 g) muscovado sugar
4 oz (115 g) softened butter
3 oz (75 g) self-raising flour
1 level teaspoon baking powder
2 eggs
DECORATION
4 oz (115 g) firm, ripe strawberries with stalks
2 oz (50 g) plain dessert chocolate
Non-stick baking paper
MERINGUE BUTTER CREAM
5 oz (150 g) unsalted butter
2 small egg whites
4 oz (115 g) caster sugar
3 oz (75 g) ripe strawberries, hulled

Grease a 7½in (190mm) cake tin and line the base.

In a warmed mixing bowl, blend the orange rind and juice with the cocoa until smooth. Add the rest of the cake ingredients and beat everything together for 2 minutes. Turn the mixture into the prepared cake tin and smooth level.

Bake in the centre of a pre-heated oven for 30-35 minutes, until the centre of the cake is springy to the touch.

Cool the cake in the tin for 2 minutes, then turn out onto a wire rack. When cold cut the cake into two layers.

To prepare the decoration, wipe the strawberries with a damp cloth but leave the stalks intact. Melt the chocolate in a small bowl over hot water. Dip each strawberry in the melted chocolate until half covered. Place on non-stick baking paper to set while you prepare the butter cream.

Warm the butter in a small pan over low heat until it is runny but still cloudy. Set it on one side to cool.

Whisk the egg whites with the sugar in a bowl set over simmering water until the mixture stands in peaks. Now stand the bowl in cold water and whisk for 2-3 minutes more

STRAWBERRY DELIGHT Luscious strawberries, dipped in dark chocolate, decorate a chocolate sponge filled and covered with a soft strawberry icing.

until the meringue is cool. Purée the strawberries in a food processor or liquidiser, or mash them with a fork until smooth. Fold the cooled butter and the purée carefully into the meringue. Chill the butter cream in the refrigerator until you are ready to ice the cake, but do not leave it for more than about 30 minutes.

To assemble the cake, sandwich it with a thick layer of butter cream and spread the rest over the top and sides. Swirl the cream on top with a knife. Arrange the chocolate-dipped strawberries around the top of the cake. Serve at once, or chill in the refrigerator for not more than 1-2 hours.

This gateau is included in a menu on page 130.

SALLY LUNN TEA CAKES

There is a story that a Sally Lunn living in 18th-century Bath made these yeast cakes, which were eaten by visitors to the Pump Room. Alternatively the name may come from *soleil et lune* (sun and moon in French), because the golden crust of the baked cake, risen above the lighter lower half, often resembles the moon eclipsing the sun. The cakes should ideally be eaten warm from the oven. But they can be frozen and warmed through in a moderate oven after thawing.

PREPARATION TIME: *25 minutes*
RISING TIME: *1½-2 hours*
COOKING TIME: *20 minutes*
OVEN TEMPERATURE: *preheat to 200°C (400°F, gas mark 6)*

INGREDIENTS — *makes two 6 in (150 mm) cakes:*
½ oz (15 g) fresh yeast OR 1 level teaspoon dried yeast OR ½ sachet easy-blend dried yeast
1 level tablespoon caster sugar
2 tablespoons warm water
8 fl oz (225 ml) milk
2 oz (50 g) butter
12 oz (350 g) strong plain flour
1 level teaspoon salt
Finely grated rind of ½ lemon
1 egg, beaten
GLAZE
1 tablespoon milk mixed with 1 tablespoon caster sugar

Cream the fresh yeast with a little of the sugar and mix in the water. Or sprinkle the dried yeast onto the water. Leave either yeast mixture in a warm place for 10-15 minutes until frothy. If using easy-blend dried yeast, follow the instructions on the packet.

Grease two 6in (150mm) round cake tins.

Heat the milk gently with the butter until the butter has melted. Remove from the heat and cool to lukewarm.

Sieve the flour and salt into a bowl. Stir in the sugar and grated lemon rind. Add the yeast liquid, milk and egg and beat well with a wooden spoon until smooth. Place the bowl in a large plastic bag and leave in a warm place for an hour, or until double in volume.

Beat the dough again and divide it between the prepared cake tins. Leave in a warm place for 20-30 minutes until the dough has risen slightly.

Bake in the preheated oven for 20 minutes, or until golden. Remove from the oven and brush with the milk mixed with the sugar. Leave the tea cakes in the tins for 5 minutes, before turning them out onto a wire rack. Serve while still warm, split in half, spread with jam (such as *Peach conserve*, page 139) and filled with clotted cream.

ORANGE FLOWER SPONGE CAKE

Until well into this century, orange-flower water was found in almost every kitchen in England. Although much less common today, it is still available in most chemists and herbalists or from Middle-Eastern delicatessens. It gives an exotically scented taste to this feather-light sponge, which is decorated with fresh orange blossom or other small edible flowers. Make sure that the orange-flower water is triple distilled (also called triple strength), and suitable for cooking.

The cake is at its best eaten on the day it is made, but it can be kept for a day in a plastic box in the refrigerator.

PREPARATION TIME: *25 minutes plus cooling time*
COOKING TIME: *25-30 minutes*
OVEN TEMPERATURE: *preheat to 180°C (350°F, gas mark 4)*

INGREDIENTS — *makes one 7½ in (190 mm) cake:*
2½ oz (65 g) plain flour
1½ oz (40 g) cornflour
4 eggs
4 oz (115 g) caster sugar
1 teaspoon orange-flower water (triple distilled)
A little extra caster sugar
ICING
¼ pint (150 ml) double cream
½ teaspoon orange-flower water
A few drops orange food colouring (optional)
1 egg white
1 level tablespoon caster sugar
DECORATION
Fresh flowers — orange blossom or other small delicate flowers, or crystallised mimosa

Grease two 7½in (190mm) sandwich tins, and line each base. Sprinkle with caster sugar.

Sieve the flour and cornflour together twice, and then set aside on a piece of greaseproof paper in a warm place.

Whisk the eggs with the caster sugar using an electric beater, or in a mixing bowl set over hot water, until light and foamy and the whisk leaves a trail across the top of the mixture. This may take as long as 10 minutes.

Whisk in the orange-flower water and, using a metal spoon, fold in the sieved flour in a figure-of-eight movement. Divide the mixture between the two prepared tins.

Bake in the centre of the preheated oven for 25-30 minutes until the cakes are well risen and golden, and the centre is springy to the touch.

Cool in the tins for 2 minutes, then run the blade of a knife around the cakes and turn them out onto a wire rack to cool.

When the cakes are cold, make the icing. Whisk the cream with the orange-flower water until stiff but still glossy. Colour delicately with just a drop or two of food colouring. Whisk the egg white until stiff, then fold in the sugar. Fold the egg white into the cream. Sandwich the sponge cakes with half the icing and spread the rest over the top of the cake.

SCENTED SPONGE The heady scent of Philadelphus blossom — mock orange — matches exactly the fragrance of the orange-flower water which flavours this light sponge.

Chill the cake until ready to serve. Decorate around the base of the cake with fresh orange blossom and place a few more flowers on top.

APRICOT AND ORANGE TEA-BREAD WITH ORANGE HONEY BUTTER

Dried apricots soaked in orange juice make this tea-bread moist and fruity with a fresh flavour. The bread is eaten spread with butter that is flavoured with orange zest and sweetened with honey.

The loaf will keep, wrapped, for 4-5 days in the refrigerator. The stored bread is also good toasted.

PREPARATION TIME: *30 minutes*
SOAKING TIME: *3-4 hours*
COOKING TIME: *50-60 minutes*
OVEN TEMPERATURE: *preheat to 180°C (350°F, gas mark 4)*

INGREDIENTS — *makes one 1 lb (450 g) loaf:*
4 oz (115 g) dried apricots
¼ pint (150 ml) orange juice
4 oz (115 g) self-raising flour
4 oz (115 g) wholewheat flour
1 level teaspoon baking powder
2 oz (50 g) muscovado sugar
2 oz (50 g) butter
1 egg, beaten
Juice and finely grated rind of ½ orange
ORANGE HONEY BUTTER
4 oz (115 g) unsalted butter
4 oz (115 g) set honey
Finely grated rind of ½ orange

Gently heat the apricots in a pan with the orange juice for about 3 minutes. Remove from the heat, cover and leave to soak for 3-4 hours. Roughly chop the softened apricots and set aside with the orange juice.

Grease a 1lb (450g) loaf tin and line the base.

Stir the flours together in a mixing bowl and add the baking powder and sugar. Rub in the butter. Stir in the apricot and orange juice mixture, the egg, and the juice and grated rind of the half orange. Mix everything together well.

Turn the mixture into the prepared loaf tin and smooth level. Bake in the centre of the preheated oven for 50-60 minutes or until a fine skewer inserted into the centre of the loaf comes out clean.

Cool in the tin for 15 minutes then transfer to a wire rack. Serve sliced, spread with orange honey butter.

To make the orange honey butter, soften the butter in a warmed bowl and, with a wooden spoon, beat in the honey and the orange rind until the mixture is smooth and spreadable. Spoon into a small pot for serving with the sliced tea-bread.

As an alternative to orange honey butter the apricot and orange tea-bread could be spread with apricot jam (page 32), or simply with butter.

ORANGE DUET The tang of orange joins the freshness of apricot in a moist tea-bread which is spread with a mixture of honey and butter also flavoured with orange.

WHOLEWHEAT SPONGE CAKE WITH MANGO FILLING

Sponge cakes made with wholewheat flour can be every bit as light as those made with white flour, if the eggs are separated and the whites whipped. This sponge cake has a slightly nutty flavour and is sandwiched with a mango filling. Tinned mango purée can be used. Alternatively, purée the flesh of one small, very ripe mango.

The filled cake will keep for 1-2 days in an airtight tin.

PREPARATION TIME: *30 minutes*
COOKING TIME: *30-35 minutes*
OVEN TEMPERATURE: *preheat to 160°C (325°F, gas mark 3)*

INGREDIENTS — *makes one 8 in (200 mm) cake:*
3 oz (75 g) muscovado sugar
1 tablespoon clear honey
4 tablespoons warm water
A few drops vanilla essence
4 eggs, separated
4 oz (115 g) 100 per cent wholewheat flour
FILLING
3 oz (75 g) unsalted butter
3 oz (75 g) caster sugar
4 level tablespoons mango purée (see introduction)
A little extra caster sugar

Grease two 8in (200mm) sandwich tins, and line each base.

Measure the sugar, honey, water and vanilla essence into a mixing bowl. Add the egg yolks.

Whisk the mixture with an electric beater until thick and frothy. Alternatively, use a hand beater and whisk the mixture in a bowl set over a pan of hot water. This may take as long as 10 minutes.

In a separate bowl, whisk the egg whites until stiff. Fold carefully into the yolk mixture in two or three additions.

Sieve the flour onto the mixture (some bran will be left in the sieve). Fold the flour in gradually. Add half the bran left in the sieve, but return the remainder to the flour bag. Divide the mixture between the prepared tins, and smooth the surface level.

Bake in the centre of the preheated oven for 30-35 minutes until well risen and springy to the touch.

Cool in the tins for 2 minutes then turn the cakes out onto a wire rack.

To make the mango filling, cream the butter with the sugar in a warmed bowl until very light and fluffy. Gradually beat in the mango purée until the mixture is creamy and the sugar has dissolved.

Sandwich the cakes with the filling. Sieve a little caster sugar over the cake and leave in a cool place for an hour for the filling to firm up.

CHOCOLATE PRETZELS

The traditional German pretzel is shaped like a loose knot. It is not difficult to twist strips of dough into this shape, but these chocolate pretzels can also be baked in twisted sticks so that they look like maypoles for a May Day tea party. The combination of puff and shortcrust pastry gives the pretzels a ripply effect as the puff pastry swells with cooking.

These pretzels will keep for up to 2 weeks stored in an airtight tin.

PREPARATION TIME: *35 minutes*
COOKING TIME: *10-15 minutes*
OVEN TEMPERATURE: *preheat to 220°C (425°F, gas mark 7)*

INGREDIENTS — *makes about 20:*
6 oz (175 g) plain flour
2 oz (50 g) cocoa powder
½ teaspoon ground cinnamon
4 oz (115 g) caster sugar
4 oz (115 g) butter or margarine
1 egg, separated
2 tablespoons milk
8 oz (225 g) prepared weight
  puff pastry (page 394)
4 oz (115 g) icing sugar
A little hot water

CHOCOLATE KNOTS *Despite their intricate appearance, these pretzels are very simply made by twisting strips of sandwiched chocolate shortcrust pastry and puff pastry into the traditional loose knot shape. The final decoration is a thin trickle of white icing over the knots.*

Grease two baking sheets.

Sieve the flour, cocoa and cinnamon into a bowl and stir in the sugar. Cut the butter into the mixture and rub it in until the mixture resembles fine breadcrumbs.

Beat the egg yolk with the milk and pour onto the dry ingredients. Mix together to make a dough.

On a floured board, roll out the chocolate dough to make a rectangle measuring 16in × 10in (405mm × 250mm). Then roll out the puff pastry to make a rectangle the same size.

Brush the chocolate pastry with the egg white and place the puff pastry on top. Gently press the two layers together with a rolling pin.

Cut the pastry lengthways into strips about ½in (15mm) wide. To shape each pretzel, take an end of a pastry strip in each hand. Cross the ends and then join them to the middle of the strip about 1in (25mm) apart. It does not matter if they are not perfectly shaped. Place the pretzels on the greased baking sheets.

Bake the pretzels in the centre of the preheated oven for 10-15 minutes until the puff pastry is golden. Transfer to a wire rack to cool.

Sieve the icing sugar and mix with enough hot water to make a pouring consistency. Trickle the icing, zigzag fashion, across the pretzels. Leave the pretzels in a warm place to allow the icing to set before serving.

Clotted cream can be bought in some shops and supermarkets outside the West Country, or it can be ordered by post. If it is not available, plenty of stiffly whipped double cream or unsalted butter tastes just as good. Make twice the quantity of wholewheat scones given in the recipe.

IN ADVANCE The walnut layer cake can be made the day before the party.

ON THE DAY Allow about an hour just before the party to make the scones.

WHOLEWHEAT WEDGES A ring of scones made with wholewheat flour and sweetened with honey and dried fruit is as full of flavour as it is wholesome.

WHOLEWHEAT RAISIN SCONES

Quick and easy to make, these scones are best served warm from the oven. They are useful when unexpected guests arrive for tea. This wholewheat scone ring has a good nutty flavour, and is sweetened with honey.

PREPARATION TIME: *15 minutes*
COOKING TIME: *15-20 minutes*
OVEN TEMPERATURE: *preheat to 220°C (425°F, gas mark 7)*

INGREDIENTS — *makes 8:*
8 oz (225 g) 100 per cent wholewheat flour
1½ level teaspoons baking powder
¼ teaspoon salt
2 oz (50 g) butter
3 oz (75 g) seedless raisins
1 egg
1 tablespoon clear honey
A scant ¼ pint (125 ml) milk

Measure the flour into a bowl and stir in the baking powder and salt. Rub in the butter until the mixture resembles coarse breadcrumbs. Stir in the raisins.

Break the egg into a measuring jug and beat in the honey. Make up to ¼ pint (150ml) with the milk. Pour onto the dry ingredients and mix together to make a soft dough.

Turn the dough out onto a floured baking sheet and form into a round about 6in (150mm) in diameter. Use a knife to mark the top of the scone ring into eight wedges.

Bake in the centre of the preheated oven for 15-20 minutes, until risen and lightly browned. Transfer the scone ring to a wooden platter or basket and serve it warm cut into wedges.

Spread the scones with butter or cream cheese, and jam. If some scones are left to the next day, they are equally good split in two and toasted.

These scones are included in a menu on this page.

WALNUT LAYER CAKE WITH SEVEN-MINUTE FROSTING

For many, walnut layer cake — cloaked in white icing and studded with walnut halves — revives childhood memories of visits to tea shops. The icing is thick, white seven-minute frosting which, when set, has a surface like frozen snow with a softer marshmallow layer underneath. The cake should be eaten within 2 days.

PREPARATION TIME: *40-50 minutes plus cooling time*
SETTING TIME: *1-2 hours*
COOKING TIME: *25 minutes*
OVEN TEMPERATURE: *preheat to 180°C (350°F, gas mark 4)*

INGREDIENTS — *makes one 7 in (180 mm) cake:*
4 eggs
4 oz (115 g) caster sugar
4 oz (115 g) plain flour
1 level teaspoon baking powder
5 oz (150 g) walnuts, finely chopped
¼ teaspoon vanilla essence
1 oz (25 g) butter, melted
FROSTING
12 oz (350 g) caster sugar
2 egg whites
4 tablespoons hot water
¼ teaspoon cream of tartar
¼ teaspoon vanilla essence
8 walnut halves

Grease three 7in (180mm) sandwich tins. Line the base of each.

Whisk the eggs and sugar together using an electric beater, or in a mixing bowl set over hot water, until the beater leaves a trail across the surface of the mixture. This may take as long as 5-10 minutes.

Sieve the flour and baking powder together, and mix with the finely chopped walnuts. Using a metal spoon, gradually fold the flour and walnuts into the egg mixture with the vanilla essence and the melted butter, taking care not to drive the air out of the mixture.

Divide the mixture between the prepared tins.

SANDWICHES

Sandwiches for afternoon tea should be small and elegant. Use very fresh bread. Because it is difficult to cut this thinly, it is usually best to buy ready-sliced bread. Cut off the crusts after assembling the sandwiches.

Fillings can be very simple such as thinly sliced cucumber, pâté, chopped hard-boiled egg with cress, or thin slices of chicken, ham or tongue. Season the fillings with salt and freshly ground black pepper.

To keep sandwiches fresh before serving, cover the plate with clingfilm and store in the refrigerator. This way they will stay fresh for 6–8 hours. They can also be frozen, provided the ingredients for the filling have not previously been frozen.

PREPARATION TIME: *20 minutes*

INGREDIENTS – *makes 32:*
8 anchovy fillets
Yolks of 2 hard-boiled eggs
4 oz (115 g) unsalted butter, softened
½ teaspoon Dijon mustard
12 fresh or tinned green peppercorns, crushed
2 small gherkins, finely chopped
1 level teaspoon finely chopped capers
1 level tablespoon finely chopped chives
1 level tablespoon finely chopped tarragon or chervil
A squeeze of lemon juice
8 slices fresh thin wholemeal or white bread from a large loaf
GARNISH
Sprigs of tarragon or chervil, or chive flowers

Rinse the anchovy fillets in warm water, drain well and chop finely. Blend the anchovies in a food processor with the crumbled egg yolks, butter and mustard, or pound the ingredients in a bowl. Mix in the peppercorns, gherkins, capers, chives and tarragon. Add lemon juice to taste.

Cut the crusts from the bread, and spread half the slices with the savoury butter. Cover with the unbuttered slices and press gently together. Cut each sandwich into quarters, then cut each quarter in half diagonally.

Garnish with sprigs of tarragon or chervil, or chive flowers. These sandwiches are included in a menu on page 130.

Bake in the centre of the preheated oven for 25 minutes or until the cakes are just starting to shrink from the sides of the tins. Leave in the tins for 2 minutes, then turn out onto a wire rack to cool.

To make the frosting, set a large mixing bowl over simmering water. In the bowl, whisk together the sugar, egg whites, water and cream of tartar for about 7 minutes, or until the meringue thickens and forms soft peaks. Remove the bowl from over the hot water and continue to whisk until the frosting is cool. Whisk in the vanilla essence.

Sandwich the three cake layers with some of the frosting, and spread the rest thickly over the top and sides of the cake. Arrange the walnut halves on top when the frosting has begun to set, and leave the cake in a

WALNUT CAKE Generous swirls of snowy seven-minute frosting, marshmallow-soft beneath a crisp surface, envelop airy layers of walnut sponge. Be sure to space the walnuts evenly or someone may not receive a fair slice.

warm place for 1-2 hours for the frosting to finish setting.

This cake is included in a menu on the opposite page.

EPICUREAN BUTTER SANDWICHES

The name of the Greek philosopher Epicurus has come to be associated with those who appreciate good food and wine. Anchovies, herbs and spices are blended together to make this a savoury butter that should appeal to an epicure. It can also be spread on *Canape's* (page 172).

137

ROLLED SMOKED SALMON SANDWICHES

Smoked salmon is rolled around thinly sliced brown bread spread with a layer of dill-flavoured butter to make these tiny sandwiches, which look like pinwheels. If dill is not available, use chives instead. The bread should be very fresh, soft rather than dense, and sliced as thinly as possible: this helps the sandwiches to stay rolled up. Buy ready-sliced bread or cut the bread with a sawing motion and use a fine-toothed knife.

PREPARATION TIME: *20 minutes*

INGREDIENTS – *makes 24-32:*
2 oz (50 g) butter
2 level tablespoons finely chopped fresh dill
A squeeze of lemon juice
6-8 thin slices very fresh soft brown bread
3-4 oz (75-115 g) thinly sliced smoked salmon
Cayenne pepper

Soften the butter in a slightly warm bowl. Beat in the chopped dill with a squeeze of lemon juice to taste.

Cut the crusts from the slices of bread. Spread each slice generously with the herb butter.

With sharp scissors, cut the smoked salmon to fit the slices of bread, cutting it short by ½in (15mm). Lay the smoked salmon on the buttered bread, leaving one end of the bread uncovered.

Sprinkle the salmon with cayenne pepper. Roll up each slice of bread, starting to roll the slice from the end covered with smoked salmon.

Use a very sharp knife to cut each roll into four or five rounds.

Arrange the sandwiches on a plate, cut side up.

These sandwiches are included in a menu on page 130.

LUXURY ROLLS Soft fresh brown bread, butter mixed with finely chopped dill, and paper-thin slices of smoked salmon, are rolled and sliced into little pinwheel sandwiches.

PRESERVES

STRAWBERRY JAM

Ruby red and glistening with whole strawberries, this is a classic English jam. It can be difficult to get strawberry jam to set. Use fruit that is perfectly dry and only just ripe. This contains the most pectin.

PREPARATION TIME: *30 minutes*
COOKING TIME: *1¼-1½ hours*

INGREDIENTS – *makes about 5 lb (2.5 kg) jam:*
4 lb (1.8 kg) strawberries
Juice of 4 large lemons
3 lb (1.4 kg) sugar, warmed
A small knob of butter

Hull the strawberries and cut any very large fruit in half. Cook the strawberries with the lemon juice very gently in a heavy-based pan over low to moderate heat for 20-30 minutes.

Add the warmed sugar and stir over low heat until the sugar has dissolved. Then raise the heat and add the butter. Boil rapidly until the jam reaches setting point (page 399). Start testing for a set after about 15-20 minutes.

Use a slotted spoon to remove any scum from the surface of the jam. Leave the jam to stand for 5-10 minutes so that the fruit will be more evenly distributed in the jars. Stir once or twice.

Pour the jam into hot, dry jars. Seal either straight away, or when completely cold. (Sealing when the jam is lukewarm encourages the growth of mould.) Label when cold. Store the jam in a dry, cool place.

This jam is included in a menu on page 136.

LIME CURD

Homemade curd has a clean, citrus flavour that is much purer than that of commercially made varieties. The fresh sharpness of limes makes a change from lemon, but the limes may be replaced by 2 large lemons for a more traditional curd. Alternatively the curd may be made with 2 small oranges or 1 small grapefruit. It will keep in a cool place – the refrigerator is best – for about a month.

PREPARATION AND COOKING TIME: *30 minutes*

INGREDIENTS – *makes 1-1½ lb (450 g-700 g) curd:*
3 small limes
8 oz (225 g) caster sugar
4 oz (115 g) butter, cut into small pieces
3 eggs, lightly beaten

Finely grate the rind of the limes and squeeze the juice. Place the rind and strained juice in a bowl over simmering water with the sugar and butter. Stir with a wooden spoon until the butter has melted and the sugar has dissolved.

Strain in the eggs, and stir over barely simmering water until the curd thickens and coats the back of the spoon.

Remove from the heat and pour into small, hot, dry jars. Cover and label when cool.

Spread lime curd on warm *Sally Lunn tea cakes* (page 132) or *Irish tea brack* (page 124); or use the curd to sandwich sponge cakes or fill little sponge cakes (*Lemon curd cup cakes*, page 126).

WALNUT AND ORANGE MINCEMEAT

The spicy mixed-fruit preserve called mincemeat did originally contain minced meat, mixed with dried fruit. Today the meat is replaced by suet or butter. Mincemeat is much easier to make than jam, and it is possible to be creative with flavour combinations. This particular blend contains orange, walnuts and whisky in addition to the more usual dried fruits and apple.

Mincemeat should be left for at least 3-4 weeks to mature before use. Because the apples are cooked first, this mincemeat keeps specially well. It should stay fresh for 6-12 months stored in a cool, dry place.

PREPARATION TIME: *1 hour*
STANDING TIME: *overnight*
COOKING TIME: *10 minutes*

INGREDIENTS – *makes about 3 lb
(1.4 kg) mincemeat:*
1¼ lb (575 g) cooking apples
4 tablespoons water
Walnut-sized knob of butter
8 oz (225 g) sultanas
4 oz (115 g) walnut pieces
*4 oz (115 g) candied peel,
chopped*
8 oz (225 g) currants
8 oz (225 g) muscovado sugar
*Juice and finely grated rind of
1 large orange*
1 level teaspoon ground cinnamon
½ teaspoon grated nutmeg
½ teaspoon ground cloves
*6 oz (175 g) melted butter or
grated suet*
4 tablespoons whisky

Peel and core the apples and chop roughly. Cook gently over medium heat with the water and the knob of butter until mushy. Remove from the heat and mash with a fork. Turn into a large wide bowl and allow to cool.

Chop the sultanas and walnuts quite coarsely. Add to the apple with the candied peel, currants, sugar, juice and rind of the orange, cinnamon, nutmeg and cloves and mix well.

Stir in the melted butter or grated suet, and the whisky. Cover with a cloth and leave to stand overnight. The following day, spoon the mincemeat into dry, warm jars. Press it down well to exclude air, seal tightly (page 399) and label.

PEACH CONSERVE

The summery scent of fresh peaches is captured in this recipe. Conserves generally do not set as firmly as jams – the consistency is more syrupy. Choose peaches that are ripe but not bruised.

PREPARATION TIME: *50 minutes*
COOKING TIME: *1¼ hours*

INGREDIENTS – *makes 3-4 lb
(1.4-1.8 kg):*
3 lb (1.4 kg) ripe peaches
2 oranges
Juice of 2 large lemons
*2¼ lb (1 kg) granulated or
preserving sugar, warmed*

Cover the peaches with boiling water for 1 minute then carefully remove the skins. Cut the peaches in half and discard the stones. Slice the peaches thinly.

Finely grate the rind of one orange. With a sharp knife cut all trace of pith from both the oranges. Holding the oranges over the preserving pan to catch the juice, cut out the segments, discarding the membrane (page 398), and put them in the pan.

Put the grated orange rind and the lemon juice into the preserving pan. (No water is needed, enough liquid will come from the fruit.)

Add the sugar and dissolve it over a moderate heat, stirring from time to time. Once the sugar has completely dissolved, boil steadily for 4 minutes. Remove from the heat and stir in the peaches. Bring to the boil again and boil rapidly until setting point is reached (page 399). Skim and then leave to stand for 5-10 minutes.

Pour the conserve into hot, dry jars, and seal. Label when cold.

Peach conserve is perfect for serving with scones or tea cakes. It can also be used to fill open tartlets or be eaten with vanilla ice cream.

SOUVENIR OF SUMMER On bleak winter afternoons, peach conserve will recall the forgotten warmth of summer. Spread it on brown bread and butter, or sandwich it with cream in a Sally Lunn tea cake.

TEA

All tea plants are varieties of an evergreen – *Camellia sinensis* – native to Asia. The beverage is made from the leaves of the plant, steeped in boiling water.

Tea leaves contain oils which are the source of flavour, and tannin which gives the beverage pungency and colour. Most tea drunk in Britain is fermented ('black')–during the manufacturing process the leaves are oxidised. 'Green' tea, widely drunk in Asia, is not fermented. The resulting beverage is pale green with a delicate, slightly bitter taste. Some teas, including 'Oolong' teas, are partially fermented.

Oils, fragrant flowers and spices are used to flavour teas. Teas are also blended. Most of the popular brands are blends.

The tea imported into Britain comes mainly from India, China and Sri Lanka (Ceylon). In general, China teas have a more delicate flavour than Indian or Ceylon varieties. Tea is also grown in Africa, Japan, South America, Turkey and Russia.

Listed below are a few of the countless varieties of tea.

BLACK TEAS

ASSAM A pungent, malt-flavoured Indian tea.

CEYLON A delicate, mellow tea with a nutty flavour.

DARJEELING A delicate Indian tea with a muscatel flavour.

EARL GREY A blend of China teas flavoured with oil of bergamot, a small citrus fruit.

ENGLISH BREAKFAST A rich, full-bodied blend of Indian and Ceylon teas.

KEEMUN A mellow China tea.

KENYAN An African tea with a smooth mellow flavour.

LAPSANG SOUCHONG A powerful China tea with a distinctive, smoky flavour.

RUSSIAN (GEORGIAN) Fragments of twigs give an earthy flavour.

SEMI-FERMENTED AND GREEN TEAS

JASMINE Semi-fermented China tea. It is scented with jasmine flowers.

GREEN JAPANESE A rich tea with a distinctly bitter flavour.

GUNPOWDER A fruity yet bitter China tea. The small curled leaves resemble gunpowder.

TISANES (HERBAL TEAS)

Crushed herbs, flowers or hips – such as rosemary, camomile and rosehip – are infused in boiling water to make tisanes in much the same way as tea, but usually for a longer time.

Storing tea

Store tea in an airtight container in a dry place, away from direct light. Unopened packets of scented tea will keep for up to four months in peak condition and the more basic teas for up to eight months.

Making tea

The teapot should be made of china or glazed earthenware, which retains heat well. Metal teapots, including silver ones, do not make such good tea.

Warm the teapot by filling it with hot water. Leave it to stand. Bring freshly drawn water to the boil. Do not use water that has been left standing in the kettle: tea requires oxygen to brew properly, and much of the oxygen will have been boiled off.

Tip out the water in the pot and add the tea. It is usual to allow 1 rounded teaspoon for every person. When making tea for more than three people, add an extra spoonful 'for the pot'.

As soon as the water boils, pour it onto the tea leaves. Put the lid on the pot and leave to infuse for about 5 minutes.

Stir the tea once before pouring into cups through a fine strainer. If the tea is too strong, dilute it with hot water.

There is no 'correct' sequence for adding milk, but cold milk added first will protect bone china cups against the heat of the tea. Offer sugar separately.

Green tea is always served without any addition. China tea is usually served on its own or with a thin slice of lemon or lime. Indian tea can be served with sugar, lemon, milk or mint.

The leaves in the pot can be topped up once with freshly boiled water for a second brew. Do not top up more than once.

TEA FOR LARGE NUMBERS When making tea for 20 or more people, use either a small tea urn or two very large china teapots. See also page 118.

SERVING TEA It is usual to serve a delicate tea for afternoon tea, for example Darjeeling or Ceylon, or a blend such as Lady Londonderry. There are many blends of breakfast tea suitable for first thing in the morning. Green tea is a good accompaniment to Oriental food.

ICED TEA Strain hot tea – preferably an Indian or Ceylon variety which is neither very strong nor very dark – into a heatproof jug. Add sugar to taste and a little orange, lemon or lime juice. Stir until the sugar has dissolved. Cool, then cover and chill for at least 3 hours. Serve with ice.

RUSSIAN

GUNPOWDER

CEYLON

ASSAM

LAPSANG SOUCHONG

CAMOMILE TISANE

Children's Parties

CHILDHOOD as a separate and different part of the social scene — and with it children's parties — seems to be a fairly recent concept. For much of history, children were expected to dress and behave as small adults, and as such attended whatever festivities that were going. One mid-19th-century memoir of a New Year's Eve tells of 'a clutch of great-aunts, great-uncles and cousins...turkey and beef decked in holly, plum pudding flaming in brandy, punch in silver goblets...children romping and chasing a favourite aunt for a kiss under the mistletoe...'

A rather different picture was recalled by the daughter of a London clergyman who attended her first Children's Ball in 1873, when she was 14 years old. At the ball, the walls were lined with grown-ups, but only the children danced — waltzes and polkas — and they were regaled with roast chicken and champagne cup. But before she and her sister could get to the puddings, 10 o'clock struck, and their mother came to whisk them home.

Other times, other ways, but children always love parties. A local woman recalls V-E Day in 1945, when a Cardiff street gave a party for its children...'neighbours pooled their sweet rations and collected money, and our grocer gave his entire stock of sweets, fruit and jellies. The church lent the tables, the milkman lent his cart for the platform, and we lent our radiogram and records. Blackout curtains came down to make fancy dresses for the children. That evening, 94 children paraded around the streets, carrying lighted candles in jam jars, wearing all manner of weird dress and singing lustily... It was a brave sight, never to be forgotten'.

Planning & Preparation

Successful children's parties require careful planning, plenty of imagination and considerable organisation. Work out a timetable right at the start, including every job that needs to be done before the party.

Invitations

Do not let a children's party become too big. Small children, in particular, will be confused and unhappy in a crowd. Invite just five or six close three-year-old friends to a party for a three-year-old child. For a child of about five, invite a dozen friends at most. For six to nine-year-olds you may be put under pressure and have to invite more children – a whole class of 20-25, for example – but do not overdo it. Older boys, especially, will need constant supervision. Do not mix age groups at a party.

Send written invitations. State the times the party is to start and finish, and enclose clear directions, with a map if necessary, for getting to your house. Include your telephone number.

Where to hold the party

For an indoor party use two rooms if possible, one for games and one for eating; the kitchen can be used for eating. If only one room is available, separate the eating and playing areas. Alternatively, for a summer party, give the children a picnic in the garden or a nearby park – but be prepared to retreat indoors in case of showers. For a winter party for seven to nine-year-olds it might be worth hiring a local hall or community centre for a few hours.

Put up plenty of decorations. If the party is at home, remove any ornaments, furniture or pictures that might get damaged. Have ready cloths to wipe up any spills. If furniture is lockable, lock it and put the key in a safe place. Remove all keys from doors – particularly the bathroom and lavatory doors. Remove or secure any trailing electrical wires. Put all chemicals – household cleaners, for example – out of reach and preferably out of sight. Lock away all medicines.

Make up a first aid box and put it in a convenient place. Pin up the telephone number and address of the nearest casualty unit by the telephone.

What to eat

Children under five do not generally eat much. Offer them lots of brightly coloured food, cut into small pieces and served in small dishes. Provide a simple iced sponge, not a fruit cake. Provide plenty of crisps, soft drinks and water as well.

Children of five and over eat ravenously, so provide plenty of food and drink. Simple food is generally the most popular – burgers in baps, for example, sausages and other foods on sticks, interesting cakes and biscuits, peanuts and crisps. As a centrepiece to the table, make or buy an especially decorative cake. Serve fizzy drinks, orange juice, squash or flavoured milk with the meal.

Entertainment

It is essential to organise plenty of adults to help you during the party. Older teenagers, especially girls, often make good helpers. With very young children, you need one helper for every three or four children. With older children you can make do with fewer helpers – but a couple of strong young men are useful to cope with boisterous older boys. For children of five or over, it is often worth getting a professional entertainer or magician to occupy at least part of the time. They can be found in *Yellow Pages* and on many school notice boards.

The basic pattern for children's parties is the same for all age groups. The party should not be unduly long or elaborate. Some activity should be planned for every moment.

With young children, aim to start at 3 o'clock. Play organised games until tea at about 3.45. After tea let very small children play their own games until it is time to go home at 5.15. Five to seven-year-olds can be kept occupied by quieter games, a magic show or other entertainment until they go home at 6 o'clock. Parties for eight or nine-year-olds usually start and finish later.

Make sure you have a long list of games to play (remember when compiling the list that some take only a few minutes). You should also have plenty of prizes, such as small toys or crayons, for the winners. They need not be expensive.

Older children (eight and nine-year-olds) often enjoy theme parties – such as space-age or fireworks parties – where they dress up. Also popular with this age group are single-sex parties – football or cricket matches for boys, for example, or for girls, dressing up and having a dinner party. Alternatively, tape some current pop music and have a disco competition with children of both sexes. Parties where children are expected to sit quietly and watch video films are not generally successful.

Time to go home

At the end of the party, try to get the children into their coats before their parents arrive, so that they can be taken straight home. Presents are usually given to children as they leave, so that even the children who have not won prizes have something to take home. Give the same sort of thing as the prizes. Do not invite the parents in for tea. The party should end before the children get tired and fractious.

SAVOURIES

RABBIT FACES

Prepare all the ingredients for these rabbit faces in advance, but assemble them just before the party. Strips of liquorice can be used for whiskers instead of strips of carrot.

PREPARATION TIME: *20 minutes*

INGREDIENTS – *makes 8:*
4 medium bananas
Juice of ½ lemon
24 small lettuce leaves
8 tinned pear halves (1 large tin) in natural juice, drained
2-3 carrots, peeled and cut into 48 long, thin strips
24 raisins
8 small plastic or paper plates

Peel the bananas and cut each in two lengthways. Brush with lemon juice to prevent them from discolouring.

Place three lettuce leaves on each plate. Place one pear half on each plate. Cut each piece of banana in two and place two pieces of banana at the broad end of each pear to form ears. Make whiskers with the strips of carrot – three on each side of the face. Use the raisins for eyes and nose. This dish is included in a menu on page 148.

CRAFT AT SEA

Small dinghies sailing on a sea of lettuce are easily made with bridge rolls and thin slices of processed cheese.

The boats can be made 2-3 hours in advance of the party. Store them, lying on their sides and covered with clingfilm, in the refrigerator.

PREPARATION TIME: *20 minutes*

INGREDIENTS – *makes 20:*
10 small bridge rolls
About 2 oz (50 g) butter, softened
Yeast extract
20 cocktail sticks
20 triangles of processed cheese
1 round lettuce

Split the bridge rolls in half lengthways. Butter each half and spread lightly with yeast extract.

To make the sails, thread a cocktail stick through the centre of each cheese triangle to form a mast. Leave about ¼-½in (5-15mm) of the cocktail stick showing at the base of the triangle. Stick the base of the mast into a bridge roll.

Wash and dry the lettuce. Shred the leaves and spread them on a large, flat serving dish to form the 'sea'. Arrange the craft on the lettuce.

AT SEA A flotilla of tiny sailing boats, made from bridge rolls and slices of cheese, scud across a sea of lettuce, avoiding tomato buoys.

CAT'S WHISKERS

Stuffed eggs can be used as a base for a variety of animal faces. These are decorated as cats.

To ensure that the yolks are in the centre of the hard-boiled eggs, use very fresh eggs that have been stored with the pointed ends down.

PREPARATION TIME: *30 minutes*

INGREDIENTS–*serves 12:*
6 large fresh eggs
1 oz (25g) butter
1 tablespoon mayonnaise
1 level tablespoon finely chopped chives
Salt and freshly ground black pepper
3 black olives, stoned and cut into quarters OR 12 currants
½ small green pepper, cored and seeded
1 firm tomato, halved and seeded
Uncut chives for whiskers

Hard-boil the eggs and cool them under cold running water. Shell the eggs and cut them in half lengthways. Take out the yolks and mix them until smooth with the butter, mayonnaise, chopped chives, and salt and pepper to taste.

Stuff the centre of each egg white with the yolk mixture. Mound the stuffing up to form oval faces. Cover and chill the stuffed eggs in the refrigerator.

Make up the cats' faces just before the party. With the pointed end of each egg down, press pieces of black olive or currants into the yolk to make eyes. Cut the green pepper into triangles for ears. Cut the tomato into tiny triangles for noses and use chives, suitably trimmed, for whiskers.

BOBOTIE

Older children often prefer something more substantial, and savoury, than the cakes, jellies and sweets usually provided at parties for younger children. This is a South African dish of beef baked with a savoury egg topping. It appeals to children because it is both sweet and spicy. It can also be made with minced lamb, fresh or left over from a joint. It is important to use lean mince. Mustard can be used instead of curry powder for a slightly different flavour.

Bobotie may be cooked in advance and stored in the freezer for up to 1 month then reheated from frozen in a hot oven – 190°C (375°F, gas mark 5) – for 40-45 minutes.

PREPARATION TIME: *20 minutes*
COOKING TIME: *1 hour*
OVEN TEMPERATURE: *preheat to 160°C (325°F, gas mark 3)*

INGREDIENTS – *serves 4-6:*
1 lb (450 g) finely minced beef
1 slice white bread
¼ pint (150 ml) milk
2 tablespoons vegetable oil
1 onion, finely chopped
1 teaspoon mango chutney
1 level teaspoon turmeric
1 level teaspoon apricot jam
1 tablespoon vinegar or lemon juice
2 level teaspoons curry powder
1 oz (25 g) raisins
Salt and freshly ground black pepper
1 large egg, lightly beaten

Tear the bread roughly into pieces and soak it in 2 tablespoons of the milk.

Heat the oil in a pan. Cook the onion gently until transparent and just turning golden.

In a large bowl mix together the bread, onion and beef. Add the chutney, turmeric, apricot jam, vinegar or lemon juice, curry powder and raisins. Stir thoroughly until well blended and add salt and pepper to taste. Press the mixture into a lightly greased baking dish, cover with kitchen foil and bake in the preheated oven for 30 minutes.

Beat the remaining milk with the beaten egg and season lightly with salt and pepper. Remove the dish from the oven and raise the oven temperature to 180°C (350°F, gas mark 4). Pour the egg mixture over the meat and continue cooking, uncovered, for a further 30 minutes, until the egg mixture is set.

Follow the South African

MEANWHILE, BACK AT THE RANCH
Bean and bacon mess pot is served with baked potatoes and hot chocolate.

custom and provide small side dishes to go with the bobotie – grated coconut, sliced cucumber and banana, chopped tomatoes, chutneys and relishes. Serve with a salad – grated carrot with apples and raisins, for example. This dish is included in a menu on page 147.

BEAN AND BACON MESS POT

Cowboys on the cattle trail, soldiers deep in Red Indian country or settlers heading for the American West always finished the day with a steaming pot of beans and bacon eaten round the camp fire – at least in the Hollywood version. To achieve the 'right' atmosphere, serve this casserole on tin camping plates or out of large tin mugs – if you have them. The casserole can be made on the morning of the party and then thoroughly reheated.

For older children, put the hot casserole in wide-necked vacuum flasks and take them on an evening or winter picnic.

PREPARATION TIME: *30 minutes*
SOAKING TIME: *24 hours*
COOKING TIME: *2 hours*
OVEN TEMPERATURE: *preheat to 190°C (375°F, gas mark 5)*

INGREDIENTS – *serves 12:*
3½-4 lb (1.6-1.8 kg) joint of collar bacon
½ pint (285 ml) dry cider
6 oz (175 g) brown sugar
1 teaspoon prepared mustard
1 oz (25 g) butter
1 tablespoon oil
2 medium onions, roughly chopped
4 × 15.9 oz (450 g) tins baked beans in tomato sauce
2 tablespoons tomato purée
1 level teaspoon ground ginger
1 level teaspoon ground cumin
1 teaspoon Tabasco sauce

Soak the bacon joint in a large bowl of cold water for 24 hours. Change the water completely at least three times.

Put the bacon in a large pan and cover it with fresh cold water. Slowly bring the water to the boil, then simmer for 45 minutes.

Drain the bacon then run cold water over it, until it is cool enough to handle. With a sharp knife, cut off the skin and all but about ⅛in (3mm) of the fat. Place the bacon on a rack in a roasting tin, fat side up. Mix the cider with the brown sugar and mustard and pour the mixture over the bacon. Roast the bacon in the preheated oven for 1¼ hours, basting it frequently.

Heat the butter with the oil in a large flameproof casserole. Gently fry the onions until they are golden. Add the beans, tomato purée, ginger, cumin and Tabasco to the pan. Mix all the ingredients together thoroughly.

With a carving knife and fork, cut the bacon into bite-sized pieces, removing any fat or gristle. Add the bacon to the bean mixture in the casserole. Skim any fat from the juices in the roasting tin, and stir the juices into the bean and bacon mixture. Heat through in the preheated oven for 15 minutes (or longer if the casserole is being reheated from cold).

Serve hot with jacket potatoes topped with grated cheese, or with chunks of brown bread. This dish is included in a menu on page 151.

PUDDINGS

ORANGE CROWNS

Sparkling orange sorbet is presented in orange shells cut into crowns. For adults, leave the rims of the orange shells plain and decorate with crystallised violets and glossy green leaves. The sorbet is made with concentrated orange juice, which ensures a consistently good flavour not always guaranteed with fresh oranges.

PREPARATION TIME: *45 minutes plus freezing time*

INGREDIENTS – *serves 6:*
SORBET
6 oz (175 g) caster sugar
½ pint (285 ml) water
1 level teaspoon powdered gelatine
6 oz (175 g) tin frozen concentrated orange juice
2 egg whites
ORANGE CROWNS
6 medium oranges
Silver dragees
Jelly diamonds

Put the sugar and water in a pan, sprinkle in the gelatine and leave to soak for 10 minutes.

Gently heat the water and stir until the gelatine and sugar have dissolved into a clear syrup.

Remove the syrup from the heat and set it aside to cool.

Unwrap the frozen block of orange juice. Break it up with a fork or the handle of a wooden spoon and add it to the sugar syrup. Stir until the mixture is quite smooth. Pour the mixture into two shallow freezing trays or a single large plastic container. Freeze it, uncovered, for about 1½ hours until it is icy at the edges and slushy.

Whisk the egg whites in a bowl until they stand in soft peaks. Remove the orange mixture from the freezer, add it to the egg whites and whisk until smooth and light. Turn the mixture back into the trays or container and freeze for an hour.

Remove the sorbet from the freezer. Turn it into a bowl and whisk again until the mixture is smooth. Turn it back into the trays or container and freeze for about 4 hours until quite firm. Cover and leave in the freezer until needed.

ORANGE CROWNS Wipe over each orange and cut a thin slice from the bottom to expose the flesh. Carefully remove the flesh, using a grapefruit knife or a small sharp knife to loosen it, and a teaspoon to scoop it out.

With kitchen scissors make zigzag cuts around the edge to simulate the top of a crown. Cut a very thin slice from the base of each orange shell so that it will stand upright.

Place the orange shells upside down on a wire rack to drain. Transfer them to a tray, then freeze them uncovered until firm.

Remove the sorbet from the freezer and allow it to thaw for 2-3 minutes only. Spoon the sorbet into the frozen orange crowns and press it down firmly, mounding it up in the centre.

Decorate the crowns with silver dragees and jelly diamonds. Cut slits in the orange shells if necessary to hold the decorations. Freeze the filled crowns uncovered on a tray until completely firm, wrap them in freezer wrap and pack them in a rigid, freezerproof container. Store in the freezer until needed. This dish is included in a menu on page 151.

REGAL PUDDING Glittering crowns, filled with orange sorbet, are worth their weight in doubloons.

SUNSHINE RING

If you wish to make your own meringues to go with this simple homemade jelly, follow the recipe for *Almond meringues* (page 130) but omit the almonds and make smaller meringues.

PREPARATION TIME: *20 minutes*
DEFROSTING TIME: *45-60 minutes*
SETTING TIME: *2-3 hours*

INGREDIENTS – *serves 8:*
6 oz (175 g) tin frozen concentrated orange juice
4 level teaspoons powdered gelatine
¾ pint (450 ml) water
14 oz (400 g) tin pineapple chunks in natural juice, drained
10½ oz (290 g) tin mandarin oranges in natural juice, drained
4 oz (115 g) white mini meringues

SUNSHINE JELLY The sunny effect of an orange fruit jelly can be enhanced with a sunburst cut from card.

Open the tin of frozen orange juice and tip it into a large jug to thaw. Do not dilute it. Once the orange juice has thawed, put 3 tablespoons into a small bowl. Sprinkle in the gelatine and leave it to soften for 5 minutes. Stand the bowl in a pan of hot water and stir until the gelatine has dissolved.

Stir the gelatine mixture into the remaining orange juice. Stir in the water and half the pineapple chunks and mandarin oranges. Pour the mixture into a 2 pint (1.1 litre) ring mould. Leave the jelly in the refrigerator for 2-3 hours to set.

Just before the party, unmould the jelly. Loosen the edge with a knife, dip the mould very quickly into a bowl of hot water, cover it with a large flat serving plate, invert it and turn out the jelly. Pile the remaining pineapple and mandarin oranges into the centre. Arrange the meringues around the side.

BUTTERSCOTCH FROZEN YOGHURT

The smooth, rich taste of butterscotch combines very well with the tartness of yoghurt in this American recipe. The best results are obtained with homemade yoghurt (page 12).

PREPARATION TIME: *25 minutes*
FREEZING TIME: *3-4 hours*

INGREDIENTS – *serves 4-6:*
2 fl oz (50 ml) evaporated milk
1 level teaspoon gelatine
1½ oz (40 g) butter
6 oz (175 g) soft brown sugar
Pinch of salt
1 teaspoon vanilla essence
1 pint (570 ml) plain whole milk yoghurt
DECORATION
Grated chocolate

Put 1 tablespoon of the evaporated milk in a small bowl, sprinkle in the gelatine and leave to soak for 10 minutes.

Melt the butter gently in a small pan. Add the brown sugar and salt, and stir constantly over low heat until the mixture is smooth and just simmering.

Put the remaining evaporated milk in a bowl set over simmering water. Stir in the gelatine mixture, the vanilla, and the sugar mixture. Heat through, stirring, until all the ingredients have dissolved. Leave to cool until lukewarm.

Stir the sugar mixture evenly into the yoghurt. Turn it into a plastic container. Freeze for about an hour. Beat with a fork to break up any ice crystals. Return to the freezer for a further hour, then beat once more. Transfer the mixture to individual freezerproof pots or bowls. Cover and return to the freezer until needed.

Just before serving, sprinkle with grated chocolate.

BIG UGLY GREEN MONSTER CAKE

An ice cream meringue layer cake is much more interesting to children when covered with coloured ice cream and decorated to look like a monster. Green is good for ghost-monsters, but other colours – pink, blue and yellow – can be used.

PREPARATION TIME: *45 minutes*
COOKING TIME: *2 hours*
OVEN TEMPERATURE: *preheat to 110°C (225°F, gas mark ¼)*

INGREDIENTS – *serves 10-12:*
4 egg whites
8 oz (225 g) caster sugar
3 pints (1.7 litres) soft scoop ice cream and 2-3 teaspoons green food colouring OR 3 pints (1.7 litres) mint ice cream
Liquorice allsorts, shoelaces and strips
12 in (300 mm) cake board

Line three baking trays with greaseproof or non-stick baking paper. Draw an 8in (200mm) circle on each sheet of paper.

Whisk the egg whites in a large bowl until stiff. Whisk in half the sugar. Gently fold in the remaining sugar.

Spoon the meringue mixture into a large piping bag fitted with a large plain nozzle and pipe the meringue onto the circles marked on the baking sheets. Alternatively spoon the meringue onto the circles and spread it with a palette knife. Bake in the preheated oven for 1 hour. Turn off the oven but leave the meringue in the oven for a further hour to dry out then remove to cool. Peel off the backing paper.

While the meringue is cooking, beat 2-3 teaspoons of green food colouring into the plain ice cream, if used. Return it to the freezer.

Place one meringue disc on the cake board. Working quickly, spread the meringue with a layer of green ice cream. Cover with a second meringue disc and add another layer of ice cream. Top with the last disc.

Cover the entire cake with the remaining ice cream. Mound up the top and make the edges gently flow out. Use liquorice sweets for eyes and teeth, and liquorice strips and shoelaces for his mouth and eyebrows. He can also be decorated with strips of liquorice cut into bat shapes.

Freeze the monster, uncovered, until he is firm. Cover him with a tent of foil and keep in the freezer. Allow him to soften for about 10 minutes before serving. This cake is included in a menu on this page.

HALLOWEEN MONSTER Layers of meringue covered with green ice cream and decorated with liquorice make a monster to send agreeable shivers down the spine. Glasses of apple and ginger fizz, fudge and toffee apples, plus a bat or two, keep up the Halloween spirit.

MENU

Halloween Party for 12 Children aged 10 to 12

BOBOTIE *page 144*

CARROT AND ORANGE
SALAD *page 311*

OVEN CHIPS

BIG UGLY GREEN
MONSTER CAKE
opposite page

TOFFEE APPLES
page 154

FUDGE *page 153*

APPLE AND GINGER
FIZZ *page 154*

Make twice the quantity given in the recipes for carrot and orange salad and fizz, and two bobotie.

IN ADVANCE The monster cake and the fudge can be made several days in advance. The toffee apples can be made 1-2 days ahead.

ON THE DAY Allow about 2 hours in the afternoon to make the salad and prepare the bobotie and the apple mixture for the fizz.

WHISKED JELLY

A light, frothy jelly is a simple variation on a party favourite. Other flavours can be used instead of raspberry. The hundreds and thousands can be replaced by chocolate vermicelli or grated chocolate, but all decoration should be added at the last moment otherwise the colour might run.

Evaporated milk will whisk to a greater volume if it is chilled in the refrigerator first.

PREPARATION TIME: *20 minutes*
SETTING TIME: *2-2½ hours*

INGREDIENTS – *serves 10:*
1 packet raspberry jelly
¼ pint (150 ml) warm water
¼ pint (150 ml) cold water
6 fl oz (175 ml) tin evaporated milk
1 tablespoon lemon juice
Hundreds and thousands

Dissolve the jelly in the warm water then stir in the cold water. Chill the jelly in the refrigerator until it is almost set. This will take 1-1¼ hours. In a large bowl whisk the evaporated milk with the lemon juice until it is thick and frothy. Then gradually whisk in the thickened jelly. Pile the mixture into individual paper jelly cases or a single large bowl. Return to the refrigerator to set firm.

Just before serving, decorate the jelly with hundreds and thousands. This dish is included in a menu on this page.

M E N U

Birthday Party for Eight Children
aged 3 to 5

RABBIT FACES *page 143*

SANDWICH SHAPES

HAPPY MEN BISCUITS *page 151*

WHISKED JELLY *this page*

ROCKET CAKE
this page

CRISPS, SMARTIES,
SAVOURY BISCUITS

LEMONADE *page 154*

Arrange the food on plenty of small plates. The children will probably not eat much, but the important thing is that the table should look pretty and inviting.

Use very thinly cut bread for the sandwiches and familiar fillings such as sardine, egg and cress, cheese spread, honey or Marmite spread very thinly. To give the party a space theme, cut the sandwiches into moon and star shapes with biscuit cutters.

Make the whisked jelly in individual plastic or paper containers. Stick candles into the cake board for the birthday child to blow out.

Place bowls of crisps, Smarties and small savoury biscuits on the table.

IN ADVANCE Make the rocket cake, the happy men biscuits, the jellies and the lemonade the day before.
ON THE DAY Allow 1-2 hours before the party to make the rabbit faces and prepare the sandwiches.

Set a rabbit face at each child's place.
TO DRINK Milk or milk shakes and plenty of water in addition to the lemonade.

CAKES & BISCUITS

ROCKET CAKE

A tall rocket with a glistening nose cone is simple enough for an older child to make.

Although homemade swiss roll has the best flavour, this rocket is best made with a bought roll, which has the advantages both of convenience and of being firm enough to stand upright. You can arrange birthday candles and toy spacemen or Father Christmas around the base of the rocket. The colour and flavour of the roll and the icing can be varied.

The cake can be kept overnight covered with a tent of kitchen foil, in the refrigerator.

PREPARATION TIME: *35 minutes*

INGREDIENTS
Soft vanilla buttercream made with 1 lb (450 g) icing sugar (page 400)
Cake board about 10 in (250 mm) square
1 swiss roll
½ tablespoon granulated sugar
2 chocolate flake bars
Kitchen foil
Smarties

Colour half the buttercream and leave the rest plain.

Place a dab of plain buttercream in the middle of the cake board. Trim the ends of the swiss roll. Stick it upright on the board. The roll forms the body of the rocket. With a palette knife or a fork dipped in hot water, smooth coloured buttercream all over the rocket and plain buttercream over the cake board round it. Rough up the icing on the board with a knife so that it looks like a moonscape. Sprinkle the icing on the board with the granulated sugar (this is moon dust).

Cut the chocolate bars in half, and place the halves against the rocket as supports. Press Smarties into the sides of the rocket to represent rivets.

To make the nose cone, cut out a circle of kitchen foil about 6in (150mm) in diameter. Make a cut from the edge of the circle to the centre and form the foil into a cone with a base the same diameter as the end of the rocket. Stick the cone onto the end. Stick Smarties onto the nose cone with dabs of buttercream. Leave the cake in a cool place to set. The cake is included in a menu on this page.

STARSTRUCK PARTY A swiss-roll rocket with a gleaming nose cone stands ready for take off from a barren moonscape. It is the final treat in a birthday tea which opens with pear and banana rabbit faces and smiling happy men biscuits.

VICTORIA SPONGE

Because it makes a rich, quite firm cake, Victoria sponge can be used as the base for many different cakes, including cakes of unusual shapes. It also makes a simple, pretty birthday cake if iced in the child's favourite colour and decorated with candles, silver dragees, hundreds and thousands or crystallised flowers (see *Lemon curd cup cakes*, page 126).

The ingredients given below make up a basic quantity of cake mixture, which can be multiplied according to the size of tin that is to be used. Quantities for basic sandwich tins are given below. For more unusually shaped tins – squares, rectangles, hearts and numbers, for example – fill the tin you are going to use with water, to the depth you wish the cake to be. For every 1 pint (570ml) of water use the basic quantity of mixture. Multiply the amount accordingly. So for a tin that holds 2 pints (1.1 litres) of water, use 4oz (115g) fat, sugar and flour, and 2 eggs.

PREPARATION TIME: *25 minutes*
COOKING TIME: *depends on size of tin (see method)*
OVEN TEMPERATURE: *preheat to 180°C (350°F, gas mark 4)*

INGREDIENTS – *basic quantity:*
2 oz (50 g) butter or margarine
2 oz (50 g) caster sugar
1 egg, lightly beaten
2 oz (50 g) self-raising flour

All the ingredients must be at room temperature or the mixture will curdle.

Cream together the butter and sugar until light and fluffy. Gradually add the egg, beating continuously. Fold in the flour with a large metal spoon.

Turn the mixture into the tin and smooth the top with a knife. Bake in the centre of the preheated oven until golden-brown, springy to the touch and just beginning to shrink away from the sides of the tin. The cooking time will vary with the size and shape of the tin. For cakes baked in a sandwich tin, see below. The same quantity of mixture cooked in a loaf tin will take slightly longer.

CHOCOLATE SPONGE Add 1 level tablespoon of cocoa powder to the 2oz (50g) of flour in the basic mixture.

LEMON OR ORANGE SPONGE Add the finely grated zest of ½ lemon or ½ small orange to the basic mixture.

VICTORIA SANDWICH For a 7in (180mm) sandwich, make 3 times the basic quantity of mixture and divide between two 7in (180mm) sandwich tins. Bake in the preheated oven for about 25 minutes. Sandwich the cakes with raspberry jam, lemon curd, buttercream (page 400) or whipped cream and soft fruit. Then dredge with caster sugar or ice with glacé icing (page 400).

For an 8-9in (200-230mm) sandwich make 4 times the basic quantity of mixture, and bake for about 35 minutes.

TREASURE CHEST BIRTHDAY CAKE

Gold-covered chocolate money, pieces of chocolate wrapped in gold or silver foil (many bars of chocolate have a wrapping of foil underneath the paper wrapper), gold and silver dragees, and jewel-bright boiled sweets can all be used as treasure to fill this pirates' treasure chest.

As a variation especially suitable for girls, the same technique can be used to make a jewel box. Simply use lemon-flavoured buttercream, coloured pale pink, instead of chocolate buttercream, and fill the box with boiled sweets for jewels, and little necklaces that the children can take home.

The cake can be made a day in advance and kept, covered with a tent of kitchen foil, in the refrigerator.

PREPARATION TIME: *1½ hours*
COOKING TIME: *1½ hours*
OVEN TEMPERATURE: *preheat to 180°C (350°F, gas mark 4)*

INGREDIENTS
3 × basic quantity Victoria sponge mixture (page 149)
Chocolate buttercream made with 10 oz (275 g) icing sugar (page 400)
Vanilla buttercream made with 6 oz (175 g) icing sugar (page 400)
Cake board, about 10 in (250 mm) square
Treasure (see introduction)
Cake candles

BIRTHDAY TREASURE A pirates' hoard overflows from the chest — a simply made sponge cake decorated with buttercream. A hamper of stick-jaw toffee lies ready in case the treasure runs out.

Line a 2lb (900g) loaf tin with non-stick baking paper or greased greaseproof paper. Fill the tin with the Victoria sponge mix and bake in the preheated oven for 1¼-1½ hours until golden-brown and springy to the touch. Turn the cake out, right side up, onto a wire rack and leave until cold.

Cut horizontally through the cake with a bread knife to cut off the top third. This layer will be the lid. Place the bottom of the cake in the centre of the cake board and spread about two-fifths of the chocolate buttercream over the sides of the cake. Spread the top and sides of the lid with the remaining chocolate buttercream. Leave the bottom and lid in a cool place for the icing to set. If you are in a hurry you can put the cake into the freezer for a few minutes to set the icing.

Fit an icing bag with a star nozzle and fill it with the vanilla buttercream. Pipe a shell border round the base of the chest, down each of the four corners and round the top edge of the chest. Pipe a border round the bottom edge of the chest.

Arrange the treasure on the top of the chest, towards the front, to look as though it is overflowing. Put some of the treasure beside the chest on the cake board. If you have a lot of treasure, hollow out a little of the sponge to make room for it in the base of the chest. Pipe a little buttercream along the back edge of the bottom of the chest to stick the lid in place. Fix the lid on the chest, slightly open, supported by the treasure.

Pipe a border of buttercream round the bottom edge of the lid and pipe two bands of shells across the top to represent the straps. Leave to set.

Arrange the candles on the board. Pipe a little buttercream round each to hold it in place.

This cake is included in a menu on the opposite page.

Provide small or medium, rather than large, potatoes and plenty of different fillings, such as grated cheese, sweetcorn and chopped grilled bacon.

Make twice the quantity given in the recipe for orange crowns.

IN ADVANCE The crowns and the toffee can both be made well in advance. Allow a day to soak the ham for the mess pot. Make the cake the day before.

ON THE DAY Make the mess pot in the morning ready to be reheated. Allow 1-1½ hours to cook the potatoes.

TO DRINK Cola and squash.

HAPPY MEN BISCUITS

Only very simple decoration is needed to make round biscuits look like broadly smiling faces. The biscuits will keep for 2-3 days in an airtight tin.

The biscuit mix has exactly the same ingredients as shortbread, only the method is different. Instructions for making shortbread petticoat tails are also given below.

PREPARATION TIME: *30 minutes
plus setting time*
COOKING TIME: *15-20 minutes*
OVEN TEMPERATURE: *preheat to
190°C (375°F, gas mark 5)*

INGREDIENTS – *makes 12-16:*
4 oz (115 g) butter
2 oz (50 g) caster sugar
6 oz (175 g) plain flour, sieved
Currants for eyes
2-3 oz (50-75 g) milk chocolate

Line a large baking sheet with non-stick baking paper, or use a non-stick baking sheet.

Cream together the butter and sugar until light and fluffy. Gradually work in the flour and mix to a loose dough. Knead the dough lightly until smooth. Roll out the dough on a lightly floured pastry board or work surface to a thickness of about ¼-⅜in (5-10mm), then cut into rounds with a 2in (50mm) fluted biscuit cutter. Transfer to the baking sheet. Score a smile on each biscuit. Press in two currants to make the eyes.

Bake in the preheated oven for 15-20 minutes until just beginning to brown. Leave on the baking sheet for about 5 minutes, then transfer to a wire rack and leave to cool.

Break the chocolate into pieces, then melt it gently, without stirring, in a bowl set over simmering water. Dip the top edge of each biscuit in the chocolate so that each happy man has a line of hair. Lay the biscuits on a piece of non-stick baking paper and leave until set.

PETTICOAT TAILS Preheat the oven to 150°C (300°F, gas mark 2). Line a baking sheet with a sheet of greaseproof or non-stick baking paper.

Sieve the flour and sugar together into a bowl. Rub in the butter until the mixture resembles coarse breadcrumbs, then knead lightly until smooth. Roll it out to a circle about ½in (15mm) thick. Transfer to the baking sheet. Score the top deeply into 8 sections, then prick on a pattern with a fork. Cook in the preheated oven for 1 hour.

These biscuits are included in a menu on page 148.

HAPPY SMILE Beaming shortbread biscuits have eyes made with currants and milk chocolate hair.

CHOCOLATE HEDGEHOGS

Children can make these rich little hedgehogs themselves, although it is not a recipe for a hot day – melting chocolate goes everywhere. Even if you are making them yourself, try to keep your hands as cool as possible. Roll an ice cube between your hands once or twice while shaping the hedgehogs. They can be made up to 24 hours in advance and stored in the refrigerator.

For older children, coloured dragees can be used for the hedgehogs' eyes instead of pieces of angelica or glacé cherry, which are safer for younger children who might choke.

PREPARATION TIME: *20 minutes*

INGREDIENTS – *makes 20:*
*8 oz (225 g) plain chocolate
    biscuits
5 oz (150 g) caster sugar
3 oz (75 g) cocoa powder
3 oz (75 g) butter, softened
3 fl oz (90 ml) tepid milk
40 small pieces of angelica or
    glacé cherry – for eyes
2 oz (50 g) blanched almonds,
    cut into strips*

Crush the biscuits in a food processor or liquidiser. Alternatively, place them in a plastic bag, or between two sheets of greaseproof paper, and crush them with a rolling pin. Mix the biscuit crumbs in a bowl with the sugar and 2oz (50g) of cocoa powder. Gradually stir in the softened butter and the milk. Mix all the ingredients together until evenly blended.

Divide the mixture into 20 pieces. Form the pieces into balls and then roll in the remaining cocoa powder. Shape each ball at one end to form the hedgehog's nose. Press on pieces of angelica or glacé cherry to make the eyes. Stick almond strips all over the hedgehog's body to represent spines.

Chill in the refrigerator until just before serving.

WELCOME GUESTS Hedgehogs with chocolate bodies have strips of blanched almond for spines, and bright glacé-cherry eyes.

CHOCOLATE DOMINOES

Iced brownies – halfway between a biscuit and a cake – are an American teatime treat. In this recipe they are decorated to look like giant dominoes – complete with spots.

For older children, stir 4oz (115g) of chopped walnuts into the mixture with the flour.

PREPARATION TIME: *35 minutes*
COOKING TIME: *25-30 minutes*
SETTING TIME: *about 1 hour*
OVEN TEMPERATURE: *preheat to
    180°C (350°F, gas mark 4)*

INGREDIENTS – *makes 10:*
*4 oz (115 g) butter
3 oz (75 g) self-raising flour
1/2 teaspoon baking powder
1 1/2 oz (40 g) cocoa powder
2 eggs, lightly beaten
8 oz (225 g) caster sugar
Finely grated rind of 1 orange*
CHOCOLATE FUDGE ICING
*1/2 oz (15 g) cocoa powder
8 oz (225 g) icing sugar
2 oz (50 g) butter
1 tablespoon milk
2 tablespoons hot water*
GLACÉ ICING
*2 oz (50 g) icing sugar
1-2 dessertspoons water*

Grease a 10in (250mm) square cake tin.

Melt the butter in a small pan and leave it until lukewarm. Sieve together the flour, baking powder and cocoa powder.

Beat the eggs and sugar together until light and fluffy. Fold in the flour and cocoa, melted butter and orange rind. Mix until evenly blended.

Turn the mixture into the prepared cake tin and spread it smoothly. Bake in the preheated oven for 25-30 minutes until springy to the touch. Remove from the oven and leave to cool in the tin. Once cold, turn out onto a wire rack for icing.

To make the fudge icing, sieve the icing sugar and cocoa powder together into a bowl. Gently melt the butter in a small pan with the milk and water. Bring just to the boil then immediately pour onto the sieved icing sugar and cocoa powder. Stir with a wooden spoon until smooth. Continue stirring until just thick enough to spread.

Spread the chocolate icing smoothly over the top of the cake with a broad-bladed knife. Leave for about an hour to set.

Cut the cake into 10 rectangles, each measuring 2in × 5in (50mm × 130mm). Score a line across the centre width of each rectangle with a knife to mark the dividing line of a domino.

To make the glacé icing, sieve the icing sugar into a bowl. Beat in enough water to make a stiff icing. Make a cone with greaseproof paper, cut off the tip, fill the cone with the icing and pipe dots to form the numbers on the dominoes.

PARTY GAMES Pipe the right numbers on these chocolate dominoes and they can be set out in a game.

SWEETS & DRINKS

FUDGE

Perfect fudge is creamy and smooth. This is a basic recipe which can be varied (see below). Fudge involves boiling sugar and should not be made by children without adult supervision.

PREPARATION AND COOKING
TIME: *30 minutes*

INGREDIENTS – *makes 64 squares:*
1 lb (450 g) caster sugar
8 fl oz (225 ml) milk
4 oz (115 g) unsalted butter
1 teaspoon vanilla essence

Butter a tin about 8in (200mm) square and 2in (50mm) deep.

Put the sugar, milk and butter in a large saucepan. Stir over low heat until the sugar has completely dissolved.

Bring the mixture to the boil, stirring constantly. Continue boiling, for about 20 minutes, until the mixture reaches 114°C (238°F) – when measured with a sugar thermometer – or the soft ball stage when a teaspoon of the mixture dropped into a bowl of cold water forms a soft ball which can be squashed flat.

Remove from the heat and stir in the vanilla essence. Leave in the pan to cool.

When the fudge is lukewarm, beat it until the mixture becomes creamy and loses its gloss. Pour the fudge into the prepared tin and leave until it is firm enough to retain the mark of a knife, then mark it into 1in (25mm) squares. Leave it to set.

Break the fudge into squares and store in an airtight tin or jar.
FRUIT FUDGE Follow the basic recipe until the mixture is creamy, then stir in 4oz (115g) of raisins, or very finely chopped glacé pineapple or dried apricot.
NUT FUDGE Follow the basic recipe until the mixture is creamy, then stir in 4oz (115g) of finely chopped nuts, such as walnuts, almonds, pecans or hazelnuts.

This fudge is included in a menu on page 147.

STICK-JAW TOFFEE

Although children will enjoy helping to make toffee, they should never be allowed to make it unsupervised, because the mixture gets exceedingly hot.

PREPARATION TIME: *30 minutes*

INGREDIENTS – *makes about*
1½ lb (700 g):
6 oz (175 g) unsalted butter
8 oz (225 g) soft brown sugar
8 oz (225 g) golden syrup
7 oz (200 g) tin condensed milk

Grease a swiss roll tin or baking tin measuring about 11in × 7in (280mm × 180mm) and at least ½in (15mm) deep.

Melt the butter gently in a large heavy-based saucepan. Be careful not to let the butter burn. Brush the butter up the sides of the saucepan.

Add the sugar and stir it over low heat until it has completely dissolved. Stir in the golden syrup and gradually bring the mixture to the boil. Stir in the condensed milk.

Boil the mixture steadily for about 20 minutes, stirring all the time. It will thicken and darken slightly. The toffee is ready when the mixture reaches 114-118°C (238-245°F) on a sugar thermometer, or the soft ball stage when a teaspoon of the mixture dropped into a bowl of cold water forms a soft ball which can be squashed flat.

Pour the toffee quickly into the prepared tin. Leave it until it is lukewarm, then mark it into squares by cutting it with a greased or oiled knife. If any oil from the knife adheres to the toffee, wipe it off with kitchen paper. Leave the toffee until it is quite cold and firm.

Cut the toffee into squares with kitchen scissors, then twist the squares individually in plain or coloured Cellophane or foil.
FRUIT AND NUT TOFFEE Stir 4oz (115g) warmed dried fruit and chopped nuts into the mixture before pouring it into the tin.

Stick-jaw toffee is included in a menu on page 151.

TOFFEE APPLES

With a nut topping these are a little more sophisticated than ordinary toffee apples, and so are a perfect treat for children aged 8-9 and older. Peanuts make the best topping. Because of the high temperatures reached during the cooking this recipe is too dangerous for children to attempt on their own.

Wrapped in Cellophane and stored in a cool, dry place, the apples will keep for 3-4 days.

PREPARATION TIME: *30 minutes*
SETTING TIME: *20-30 minutes*

INGREDIENTS – *serves 12:*
4 oz (115 g) finely chopped nuts
12 bright green crisp apples
12 wooden sticks (chopsticks or
   narrow dowelling)
1½ lb (700 g) demerara sugar
½ pint (285 ml) water
3 oz (75 g) butter
2 tablespoons golden syrup

Line a tray with buttered greaseproof paper, or set out three large jam jars. Spread the chopped nuts out on a large flat dish. Impale the apples securely on the wooden sticks.

Dissolve the sugar in the water over low heat, then add the butter and golden syrup. Keep stirring until the mixture is well blended. Boil the mixture rapidly until the syrup reaches the small crack stage – 143°C (290°F), or the point at which a blob of the mixture put into a bowl of cold water forms a brittle thin film which cracks or snaps cleanly.

Remove from the heat and allow the bubbles in the caramel to subside. Working quickly, dip each apple into the caramel and swirl it around for a few seconds until evenly coated.

Dip the top of each apple in the nuts, then lay it on the buttered paper to set, or stand it in one of the jam jars – this results in a more regular-shaped apple. These toffee apples are included in a menu on page 147.

LEMONADE

One of the most refreshing of summer drinks is lemonade, made from the juice of fresh lemons. The syrup can be kept for up to 2 weeks in a covered jug in the refrigerator.

PREPARATION TIME: *20 minutes*
   plus chilling time

INGREDIENTS – *makes about 6½*
   pints (3.7 litres), 20 glasses:
6 lemons, scrubbed
½ pint (285 ml) water
1 lb (450 g) caster sugar
Still or sparkling water
Ice cubes
Slices of lemon

Peel the rind thinly from the lemons with a potato peeler, taking care to discard any white pith. Put the rind into a large pan and add ½ pint (285ml) water. Cover the pan and simmer for 5 minutes – but do not let it boil. Remove from the heat. Squeeze the lemons into a large bowl. Add the sugar, then strain the liquid from the pan over the juice. Stir until the sugar has dissolved.

Keep the lemonade syrup in a covered jug or a clean bottle in the refrigerator. Before serving, dilute the lemonade with still or sparkling water, allowing approximately 1 part lemonade

SPECIAL LEMON Fresh, homemade lemonade and sandwiches cut out with duck-shaped biscuit cutters will appeal to any child.

to 5 parts water per glass.

Put ice cubes in the jug with the lemonade if the children like them, and decorate with slices of lemon. This drink is included in a menu on page 148.

APPLE AND GINGER FIZZ

Although apple and cinnamon may be the more familiar partners in cooking, apple and ginger can be combined with equal success. Apple juice and ginger ale – the non-alcoholic variety is used in this recipe – produce a bubbling fruit cup.

Do not prepare the apple mixture more than 1-2 hours in advance, or the apple slices will begin to discolour.

PREPARATION TIME: *15 minutes*

INGREDIENTS – *makes 4 pints*
   (2.3 litres), 10-12 glasses:
2 pints (1.1 litres) unsweetened
   apple juice
Juice of 1 lemon
4 apples
Ice cubes
2 pints (1.1 litres) ginger ale
Sprigs of mint or slices of lemon

Pour the apple juice and lemon juice into a large jug – a glass jug will look the most attractive. Core and thinly slice the unpeeled apples and add them immediately to the juice, stirring them in to make sure they are covered by the liquid. Cover the jug and chill in the refrigerator until required.

Before serving, add the ice cubes and the ginger ale. Float a few sprigs of mint or slices of lemon on the top of the fizz. Pour into tall tumblers.

This drink is included in a menu on page 147.

Drinks Parties

THE CASE WAS BEST PUT by the writer Andrew Boorde, in 1542. 'Water,' he said, 'is not wholesome, sole by itself, for an Englishman.' He was echoing an opinion long held by his countrymen, most especially in regard to festive occasions.

In the late Middle Ages, to help the evening along, there were all kinds of concoctions: hippocras, for example, a blend of red wine, cinnamon, ginger and honey which was strained through a cloth before drinking; or wine flavoured with sage, or other aromatic herbs, probably to disguise the awful taste.

Spirits came late to Britain, probably in the 15th century, when genever (gin) was imported from Genoa or Holland. Italian and French monks had been making medicinal herbal distillations since at least 1200.

The drinks party is really a 20th-century phenomenon. It makes entertaining for large numbers possible for those with no servants and little space, and the most popular mainstay of such parties is the cocktail.

The name was most curiously derived from the hunter, a horse whose tail is cocked or docked and is not quite a thoroughbred. By association, 'cocktail' also came to be applied to someone who is not quite a gentleman, a person of mixed antecedents. Thence, it was but a short slip to a mixed drink, so that by 1806, in the USA, the term had come to mean a drink composed of spirits of any kind, flavoured with sugar, water and bitters. The most glamorous cocktails were a product of Prohibition in the USA (1920-33) when, as in the Middle Ages, all kinds of additives were included to disguise the unpleasant taste of the liquor, in this case the bathtub gin of the speakeasies.

Planning & Preparation

Of all kinds of party, a drinks party is among the simplest to give. Conventions about times or food and drink are far from rigid, and you can usually arrange the party to suit your own convenience and pocket.

Invitations

In the country, morning drinks parties at weekends usually start at 12 noon, so that guests can get home for lunch at about 1.30. Evening drinks parties in the country usually start at 6.30, finishing by 8.00. Drinks parties in the town tend to start later and go on longer. Evening parties are more common, often starting at 7.00 and going on to 9.00 or later. Make it quite clear in the invitations what kind of party you are giving. State both the time it will start and the time it will finish.

There will always be some last-minute cancellations, and guests who just fail to turn up, at any party. Invite more people than you actually expect to come. There should be enough guests to fill the room where the party is held without overcrowding it, and guests should be able to mingle and move unobtrusively from group to group. If, by any chance, all the guests do turn up, it is better to have a slightly overcrowded room than an empty one.

To enable guests to circulate freely, push all large furniture against the walls before the party. Store away small tables, delicate chairs or rugs and any precious china. Provide plenty of deep ashtrays – they are useful for discarding olive stones and cocktail sticks as well as cigarettes. Make sure that the room is well ventilated.

Organising the drinks

When deciding on what drinks to serve, remember that spirit-based cocktails or other drinks are both expensive and time-consuming to mix. If you are going to serve them – at an open bar, for example – it is an advantage to hire professional help (this can be found in *Yellow Pages*). With a limited budget, it is better to have plenty of reasonably priced, drinkable wine, or a punch. For a morning party serve sherry. Provide soft drinks for those who do not want to drink alcohol. Organise in advance a few friends to help to keep glasses topped up.

Do not take the risk of running dry. Most wine merchants will take back unopened bottles (though check first), so buy more than you think you will need. As a rough guide, allow a bottle of spirits, five bottles of wine or a gallon of punch for every ten guests. A bottle of spirits yields 30 single measures, a bottle of wine 6 glasses and a gallon of punch 30 glasses. A guest at an evening party will usually have three drinks. However only you know your friends and exactly how much they are likely to drink at a party. Much also depends on how long the party lasts.

Hiring glasses

Glasses can be hired from your local wine merchant – free, if he also provides the drink. If you are buying the drink from a supermarket which does not hire glasses, hire them and any other equipment you need from one of the firms listed in *Yellow Pages* under Catering Equipment. Order as many glasses as there are guests and then half as many again. In this way, there will be plenty of clean glasses for guests who put glasses down and lose them.

Planning the food

It is essential to serve some kind of food at a drinks party. Since they are usually held before lunch or dinner most people will be drinking on empty stomachs. The food should be light, nourishing and small enough to eat in one or two bites at most. Allow about eight pieces of food per person of which half should be reasonably substantial. Avoid food that is likely to drip over guests' clothes. Remember slimmers and provide lots of fresh crudités and fruit. In addition to the specially prepared foods, distribute bowls of different kinds of nuts, savoury biscuits and crisps around the room.

The selection of food at a drinks party need not be vast but should look fresh and appetising. Do not over-garnish the food or mix together several different sorts of food on the same plate. If the guests have to make a choice it will hold up the conversation.

Before the party begins, arrange the food on the serving plates. Keep hot food on an electric hotplate or in a hostess trolley; hire or borrow one if necessary. Offer the guests drinks as they arrive. Do not expect them to help themselves. If you are serving only one or two types of drink, pour out glasses in advance to be handed round on trays. Add ice to glasses just before serving. Let the first arrivals eat the nuts and crisps, and do not bring in the rest of the food until about half the guests have arrived. Serve the cold canapé-style food first, then hot snacks. Only offer one or two plates of food at a time. When the plates get more than half empty, return to the kitchen for more; a plate that has been picked over is unattractive.

Shy guests will often be pleased to hand food round because it gives them an excuse to circulate and mingle.

Stop offering either food or drink about half an hour before the party is due to finish, or the guests will simply stay on, whatever the invitation says.

SAVOURIES

SPICY ALMONDS

A few almonds taken before a meal, according to Andrew Boorde – a 16th-century writer on cooking and health – 'preserveth a man from drunkenship'. This recipe makes no such claim, but spicy, toasted almonds have been an accompaniment to cocktail drinks ever since they were invented.

Golden-brown, the almonds are shown to their best in blue and white bowls – or set against the gleam of silver and glass. Sprinkle a few flakes of dried red pepper over the nuts for an added dash of colour.

They are best prepared the morning of the party. Other nuts, walnuts and pecans, for example, can be prepared in the same way as these almonds.

PREPARATION TIME: *10 minutes*
COOKING TIME: *25 minutes*
OVEN TEMPERATURE: *preheat to 150°C (300°F, gas mark 2)*

INGREDIENTS – *makes 8 oz (225 g):*
8 oz (225 g) whole, unblanched almonds
1 oz (25 g) sea salt
2 heaped teaspoons ground cumin
1 level teaspoon sugar

Lightly grease a baking sheet.

Put the almonds in a bowl, cover with boiling water and allow to stand for a minute or two. Peel off the skins – they should come away easily. Dry the nuts with kitchen paper.

Spread the nuts out on the baking sheet and cook them in the preheated oven until they are a very pale biscuit colour. Check the nuts regularly, because they burn easily. Sprinkle a sheet of greaseproof paper with the salt, cumin and sugar. Empty the nuts onto the paper and swish them around in the seasoning.

Gathering up the corners of the paper, twist it into a bundle and fasten with string. Leave the almonds wrapped up until they are needed.

The almonds are included in a menu on page 158.

SOLE CEVICHE

The Peruvians claim to have invented *ceviche* – but raw fish marinated in fresh lime juice is popular throughout South America. The fish is traditionally garnished with onions, tomatoes, sweetcorn, peppers or sweet potatoes, and served on a bed of lettuce. Adapted as a cocktail snack, the small cubes of fish are skewered on cocktail sticks. Lemon juice can be used instead of lime. Any firm white fish can be used instead of sole, but it must be very fresh.

PREPARATION TIME: *30 minutes*
MARINATING TIME: *overnight*

INGREDIENTS – *makes about 35 pieces:*
1 lb (450 g) lemon or Dover sole
2 fl oz (50 ml) fresh lime juice (2-3 limes)
2 shallots, very finely chopped
1 fresh green chilli, very finely chopped
1 tablespoon white rum
1½ tablespoons olive oil or sunflower oil
1 red pepper
1 green pepper
Salt and freshly ground black pepper
Cocktail sticks

Fillet and skin the sole (page 374). Cut the flesh into ½in (15mm) squares.

Put the lime juice, chopped shallots and chilli, rum and oil into a glass or ceramic mixing bowl (using metal bowls or spoons may mar the flavour of the fish). Add the fish. Stir the ingredients together, making sure the fish is well coated with the marinade. Season to taste with salt and pepper. Cover the bowl tightly and store in the refrigerator overnight.

Remove the seeds from the two peppers, and slice into ½in (15mm) strips, lengthways. Cut the strips into squares, each measuring about ½in (15mm).

Drain the fish cubes, reserving the marinade. Onto one end of each cocktail stick first thread a piece of red pepper then a cube of fish, and then a piece of green pepper. Put the reserved marinade and ceviche into a bowl that is quite deep, and just large enough to hold all the sticks. Cover the bowl and chill in the refrigerator until needed.

This dish is included in a menu on page 179.

PERUVIAN PARTY PIECE Vivid squares of red and green pepper sandwich cubes of raw fish threaded on cocktail sticks. A lime-juice marinade based on traditional South American recipes, 'cooks' and flavours the fish, leaving it firm and white with a tang of chilli and a hint of rum.

157

```
M   E   N   U
```

Evening Cocktail Party
for 16 to 20

BAKED OYSTERS
this page

SMOKED SALMON CANAPÉS
page 174

ROQUEFORT FRUIT AND NUTS
page 170

SPICY ALMONDS
page 157

MARINATED OLIVES
page 170

DRY MARTINI
page 177

BLOODY MARY
page 178

Allow 2 oysters, 2-3 canapés and 2-3 Roquefort fruit and nuts per person. Make the full quantity of marinated olives and double the quantity given in the recipe for spicy almonds.

Spread the bases for the smoked salmon canapés with green butter (page 173). Fill black grapes and walnuts with Roquefort cheese.

IN ADVANCE Make the olives up to 3 weeks ahead. Prepare the flavoured butters for the oysters and canapés the night before.

ON THE DAY Make the almonds in the morning.

Allow about 2 hours before the party. Stuff the grapes and walnuts and make the canapés. Arrange them on trays, cover and leave in a cool place. Prepare the oysters so that they are ready to be baked during the party.

TO DRINK Mix jugs of the cocktails. Alternatively, serve champagne or white wine.

BAKED OYSTERS

A considerable mystique has built up around the art of eating oysters. Should they be eaten raw or cooked, spiced or plain? Should they be chewed or swallowed whole? Here the oysters are baked in a herb butter and finished with a topping of Parmesan cheese.

Prepare the butter in advance, and open the oysters just before serving to keep them fresh. They are then cooked briefly and served warm in their shells.

Choose an elegant dish to display the oysters, adding only a simple garnish of watercress and lemon wedges.

Allow 2-3 oysters per person, to be chewed or swallowed to taste. Provide small forks with which to eat them, and napkins.

PREPARATION TIME: *20 minutes*
COOKING TIME: *8 minutes*
OVEN TEMPERATURE: *preheat to 180°C (350°F, gas mark 4)*

INGREDIENTS – *serves 8-12:*
24 fresh oysters
2 cloves garlic, crushed
2 oz (50 g) butter, softened
1 level tablespoon finely chopped parsley
1 level teaspoon finely chopped chives
2 tablespoons dry white wine
2 teaspoons Worcestershire sauce
Salt
1-2 oz (25-50 g) freshly grated Parmesan cheese
GARNISH
Lemon wedges

Mix together the garlic, butter, parsley and chives to form a paste. Add the wine and Worcestershire sauce, and season with salt to taste.

Discard any oyster shells that are not tightly closed or do not close when tapped.

To remove all the sand, scrub the oysters with a stiff brush under cold running water. Take each oyster in one hand, flat shell down. Work the point of a sharp, short-bladed knife into the hinge and cut the muscles which secure the oyster to its shell. Turn the oyster over. Run the blade between the shells to prise them apart, and separate them with a final twist of the knife. Discard the flat shell. Loosen the oyster, leaving it in its rounded half shell with as much liquid as possible. See also page 377.

Place the oysters in an oven-proof dish and spread each one with the butter. Sprinkle with Parmesan cheese and bake for about 8 minutes until the cheese is just starting to brown. Serve immediately, garnished with lemon wedges. This dish is included in a menu on this page.

IN THE COOL OF THE EVENING
Oysters baked with herb butter add an unforgettable masterstroke to a party already graced by smoked salmon canapés, black grapes and walnuts filled with Roquefort cheese, marinated olives and spicy almonds. The final touch is a pitcher of well-chilled martinis — stirred, not shaken.

GORGONZOLA BITES

The Italian cheese Gorgonzola is named after a small town near Milan, where cowherds wintered with their cattle and developed this smooth, lightly spiced blue cheese. It gives these cheese pastry biscuits a rich flavour and light, melting texture. Other blue cheeses such as Stilton, Dolcelatte, Mycella or Danish Blue can be substituted for Gorgonzola.

The pastry is quite difficult to handle, and is easier to roll out if placed between sheets of non-stick baking paper. Floured greaseproof paper may also be used for this purpose.

PREPARATION TIME: *25 minutes*
CHILLING TIME: *30 minutes*
COOKING TIME: *8-10 minutes*
OVEN TEMPERATURE: *preheat to 200°C (400°F, gas mark 6)*

INGREDIENTS – *makes about 60:*
6 oz (175 g) butter
4 oz (115 g) Gorgonzola cheese
1 egg, beaten
Salt and freshly ground black pepper
8 oz (225 g) plain flour, sieved
Non-stick baking paper
TOPPING
1 egg, beaten
Chopped nuts or poppy seeds

Line two or three baking sheets with non-stick baking paper, or use non-stick baking sheets.

Cream the butter in a bowl until soft and fluffy. Mash the cheese separately and then mix it with the butter. Stir in the beaten egg and season with salt and pepper.

Gradually work the sieved flour into the egg and cheese mixture. Add a very little water if necessary to bind the mixture. Knead the mixture lightly to a smooth dough. Wrap it in greaseproof paper and chill in the refrigerator for 30 minutes.

Roll out the dough between two sheets of non-stick baking paper, making a rectangle approximately ⅛in (3mm) thick.

Cut into squares, triangles and rectangles, or make simple shapes with floured biscuit cutters. Make crescent shapes by cutting the pastry into strips, 3in × 2in (80mm × 50mm), roll them into logs and bend them into curves.

Place the pastry shapes on the baking sheets. Glaze each shape with beaten egg and sprinkle with chopped nuts or poppy seeds. Bake in the preheated oven for 8-10 minutes until the pastry is light golden.

Cool on a wire rack. The Gorgonzola bites break easily and should be stored with great care in an airtight container, stacked between sheets of greaseproof paper. They will keep for 5-6 days.

The bites can either be served cold or they can be warmed before serving in a moderate oven – 180°C (350°F, gas mark 4) – for about 5 minutes.

The bites are included in a menu on page 169.

SAVOURY STUFFED PRUNES AND DATES

Prunes and dates, which are naturally sweet, make very good cocktail snacks when combined with savoury ingredients – here a cream cheese and bacon filling.

Make a slit along the length of each date to remove the stone. This leaves the fruit intact while making room for the filling. Choose the best large, juicy prunes. Softened ready-to-eat varieties are widely available. The recipe can be made entirely with prunes or dates.

Prepare the stuffed dates and prunes a few hours before the party and store, covered, in the refrigerator.

PREPARATION TIME: *30 minutes*

INGREDIENTS – *makes about 30:*
8 oz (225 g) dates and prunes, stoned (about 30)
2 oz (50 g) streaky bacon
6 oz (175 g) cream cheese
8 walnuts, shelled
Salt and freshly ground black pepper

Grill the bacon until crisp, and cool on kitchen paper to absorb any fat. Chop the bacon finely in a food processor. Add the cream cheese and walnuts and blend for 5 seconds. Season to taste with salt and pepper. Pipe the mixture into the dates or prunes using an icing bag fitted with a broad star nozzle.

MINI CHOUX WITH SAVOURY FILLINGS

Small choux puffs can be filled with smooth meat or fish pâtés and pastes, cheeses and savoury butters. Some suggestions are given here, but you can experiment with other fillings that are soft but not moist. Do not fill the choux more than 3 hours in advance.

PREPARATION TIME: *15 minutes plus time to make the fillings*
COOKING TIME: *15-20 minutes*
OVEN TEMPERATURE: *preheat to 200°C (400°F, gas mark 6)*

INGREDIENTS – *makes about 40:*
CHOUX
5 oz (150 g) plain flour
Pinch of salt
4 oz (115 g) butter
½ pint (285 ml) water
3 large eggs, lightly beaten
GLAZE
1 egg beaten with 1 teaspoon water
SAVOURY FILLINGS
(see below)

Grease 2-3 baking sheets.
Make the choux pastry (page 395). Using a teaspoon or icing bag drop small mounds of paste onto the baking sheet. Brush each mound lightly with glaze.
Bake the choux balls in the centre of a preheated oven for 15-20 minutes, until they are pale golden in colour and have doubled in size.

LIGHT AND SAVOURY Choux puffs are filled with cream cheese mixed with walnuts or red lumpfish roe (left), and tapénade (right) – a rich blend of olives, capers and anchovies.

Remove them from the oven and make a small slit in each choux to let the steam escape. Return them to the oven for a few minutes longer to dry out. Cool completely on a wire rack.
Widen the slit in each choux and add the fillings with a teaspoon. Pipe in the creamier fillings with an icing bag.

SAVOURY FILLINGS

CHEESE AND WALNUT – *fills about 20:*
Beat together 6oz (175g) of cream cheese and 2oz (50g) finely chopped walnuts.

CHEESE AND LUMPFISH ROE – *fills about 20:*
Beat together 6oz (175g) of cream cheese and 2 tablespoons of lumpfish roe (red or black).

SMOKED TROUT BRANDADE – *fills about 15:*
Make half the quantity, about 6oz (175g), of the recipe on page 167 (Cherry tomatoes with three fillings).

RED PEPPER BUTTER – *fills about 20:*
Make the full quantity, about 6oz (175g), of the recipe on page 173 (Canapés – savoury butters).

TAPÉNADE – *fills about 15:*
Make a quarter of the quantity, about 4oz (115g), of the recipe on page 166, and blend with 2oz (50g) butter.

CHEESE AND SPINACH – *fills about 15:*
Process 2oz (50g) cottage cheese with 2oz (50g) Feta cheese and 2oz (50g) cooked, finely chopped spinach.

SHARP CHEESE SAUCE – *fills about 20:*
Melt 2oz (50g) butter in a pan over low heat and stir in 2oz (50g) plain flour. Cook for 2-3 minutes then gradually stir in ½ pint (285ml) milk until the sauce is smooth and has thickened. Bring to the boil and simmer for 3-4 minutes. Stir in 2oz (50g) grated Gruyère cheese and mustard to taste. Do not allow to boil again. Season with salt and a pinch of cayenne pepper. Cool slightly before filling.

These choux are included in a menu on page 164.

MINI QUICHES WITH THREE FILLINGS

Individual quiches look much more attractive for a cocktail party than a large quiche cut into small slices, and are easier to eat. Other fillings can be used instead of the following three.
The quiches are best freshly cooked, but they can be baked in advance and then warmed through in a moderate oven – 180°C (350°F, gas mark 4) – for about 5 minutes.

PREPARATION TIME: *40 minutes*
COOKING TIME: *18-20 minutes*
OVEN TEMPERATURE: *preheat to 180°C (350°F, gas mark 4)*

INGREDIENTS – *makes 36:*
PASTRY
12 oz (350 g) plain flour
¼ teaspoon salt
3 oz (75 g) butter
3 oz (75 g) lard
2-3 tablespoons water
EGG MIXTURE – *for 36:*
6 eggs, beaten
½ pint (285 ml) milk
Salt and freshly ground black pepper
PRAWN AND MUSHROOM FILLING – *for 12:*
1 oz (25 g) butter
3 oz (75 g) mushrooms, sliced
1½ teaspoons chopped fresh thyme
6 oz (175 g) peeled, cooked prawns, roughly chopped
Salt and freshly ground black pepper

COURGETTE AND TARRAGON
FILLING – *for 12:*
2 oz (50 g) butter
*1 level tablespoon finely chopped
fresh tarragon OR 1 level
teaspoon dried tarragon*
*6 oz (175 g) courgettes, cut into
¼ in (5 mm) cubes*
*Salt and freshly ground black
pepper*
*About 2 level tablespoons grated
Parmesan cheese*
TUNA AND BLACK OLIVE FILLING
– *for 12:*
7 oz (200 g) tin tuna
8 black olives, stoned

To make the pastry, sieve the
flour and salt into a bowl. Chop
the butter and lard, and rub
them into the flour, until the
mixture resembles fine breadcrumbs. Mix in enough water to
make a stiff dough. Chill in the
refrigerator for 30 minutes.

While the dough is chilling
prepare the fillings. To make the
prawn and mushroom filling,
melt the butter in a pan, then
fry the mushrooms and thyme
over moderate heat for 2-3 minutes. Leave to cool then stir in
the prawns and season to taste
with salt and pepper.

To make the courgette and
tarragon filling, melt the butter
in a heavy-based pan. Stir in the
tarragon and cook it gently for a
few seconds to soften it. Add the
courgettes and fry them gently
until just beginning to turn
golden. Season with salt and
pepper, then leave to cool.

To make the tuna and black
olive filling, drain and flake the

tuna and slice the olives. Set
aside until needed.

Roll out the pastry thinly.
Using a 3in (80mm) fluted biscuit cutter, cut out 36 circles
and line three trays of 12 shallow patty tins or 36 fluted
tartlet tins – measuring 2-2½in
(50-65mm) in diameter.

Divide the prawn and mushroom filling between 12 of the
pastry cases, and divide the
courgette and tarragon filling
between another 12 cases.
Divide the flaked tuna between
the remaining cases, and lay
slices of olive on top of the tuna.

Whisk together the eggs,
milk, and salt and pepper to
taste. Carefully pour enough of
the egg mixture into each pastry
case to cover the filling. Sprinkle
each of the courgette quiches
with Parmesan cheese.

Bake (in batches if you are
serving them immediately) in
the centre of the preheated oven
for 18-20 minutes until the
filling is set and golden-brown.

Transfer the quiches to a wire
rack, allow them to cool a little
then transfer them to warm (but
not hot) serving dishes. If you
are going to reheat them later,
leave them until cold then pack
them in plastic boxes interleaved
with greaseproof paper.

*BABY QUICHES Individual quiches are
much easier to eat with fingers than
slices from a large one. These are
filled with courgettes and tarragon
(top), tuna and olives (centre) and
prawns and mushrooms (bottom).*

DEVILS

Prunes wrapped in bacon and served on toast – devils on horseback – are a classic dinner party savoury, but without the toast they also make a very good hot snack especially suitable for a winter drinks party.

Use the ready-to-eat variety of prunes, or soak them overnight in tea which will give added flavour as well as softening the flesh. As a variation, dates can be used instead of prunes, and pieces of walnut instead of almonds.

For a savoury, serve on fried bread or hot buttered toast.

The devils can be prepared a few hours before the party and kept, covered, in the refrigerator. Once cooked, they can be kept warm in a low oven, covered with kitchen foil, for up to 30 minutes.

PREPARATION TIME: *30 minutes*
COOKING TIME: *15 minutes*
OVEN TEMPERATURE: *preheat to 200°C (400°F, gas mark 6)*

INGREDIENTS – *makes about 30:*
8 oz (225 g) prunes, stoned (about 30)
2 oz (50 g) almonds, shelled and skinned
8 oz (225 g) streaky bacon (about 10 rashers)

Line a baking sheet with foil.
Stuff each prune with an almond. Remove the rind and any gristle from the bacon. Stretch each rasher by laying it flat on a board and running the blade of a knife along its length. Cut each rasher into three. Wrap a piece of bacon round each prune and secure it with a wooden cocktail stick. Put the rolls on the baking sheet and cook in the preheated oven for 15 minutes. Drain the rolls on a wire rack and serve warm.

This dish is included in a menu on page 169.

DEVILS AND DOGS Prunes stuffed with almonds and wrapped in bacon – dismounted devils – and miniature hot dog sausages glazed in redcurrant and mustard sauce yield welcome warmth on a cold evening.

GLAZED FRANKFURTERS

A long-standing rivalry exists between the *frankfurter* and the *wienerwurst* – contenders for the title of original hot-dog sausage. The frankfurter from Germany and the Austrian wienerwurst contain finely ground lean meat – traditionally pork, but now often beef – or a mixture of meats. Both are lightly smoked.

In this recipe, small frankfurters served warm in a sweet-sour sauce are elevated from street-corner food to elegant cocktail snacks. Provide a container of cocktail sticks to spike them with. Decorate with redcurrants when they are in season.

PREPARATION AND COOKING TIME: *20 minutes*

INGREDIENTS – *makes about 40:*
1 lb (450 g) cocktail frankfurters
6 oz (175 g) redcurrant jelly
1 tablespoon prepared mustard
1 fl oz (25 ml) lemon juice (about 1 lemon)

With a wire whisk, stir the redcurrant jelly, mustard and lemon juice together in a medium-sized saucepan, over a moderate heat, until the redcurrant jelly has dissolved. Add the frankfurters to the redcurrant sauce and heat through gently for 3-4 minutes.

Transfer the frankfurters and sauce to a warmed serving dish and serve immediately.

This dish is included in a menu on page 169.

M E N U

Morning Sherry for 12 to 16

MINI CHOUX
page 160

STUFFED MUSHROOMS
opposite page

FRUIT AND VEGETABLE KEBABS
page 170

PANFORTE DI SIENA
page 49

Make the full quantity given in the recipes for mini choux and stuffed mushrooms. Make 24-32 fruit and vegetable kebabs and 2 panforte di Siena.

IN ADVANCE Make the panforte up to 3 weeks ahead. The night before, make the choux puffs, but do not fill them until the day.
ON THE DAY Allow about 2½ hours. Prepare the stuffed mushrooms and the fruit and vegetable kebabs. Fill the choux puffs. Cut the panforte into thin wedges. During the party, bake the mushrooms.
TO DRINK Sherry.

STUFFED MUSHROOMS

In her manual of modern household management, *Superwoman*, published in 1975, the writer Shirley Conran adopted the motto: 'Life is too short to stuff mushrooms.' However, with these stuffed mushrooms the trouble is minimal and the results well worth the effort.

The mushrooms can be prepared on the morning of the party. Keep them covered in a cool place and bake them just before they are needed.

PREPARATION TIME: *20 minutes*
COOKING TIME: *10 minutes*
OVEN TEMPERATURE: *preheat to 200°C (400°F, gas mark 6)*

INGREDIENTS – *makes about 30:*
1½ lb (700 g) medium mushrooms (about 30)
5 oz (150 g) butter
1 fl oz (25 ml) dry white wine
1 oz (25 g) smoked ham, finely chopped
1 oz (25 g) Parmesan cheese, grated
1 oz (25 g) Gruyère cheese, grated
½ teaspoon dried oregano
3 level tablespoons finely chopped parsley
2 eggs, hard-boiled and finely chopped
1 tablespoon lemon juice
Salt and freshly ground black pepper
GARNISH
Small sprigs of watercress
Small wedges of lemon

Grease a baking tray. Wipe the mushrooms. Remove the stalks and chop them roughly.

Melt 4½oz (130g) butter in a small pan and gently sauté the chopped stalks. Add the wine and ham to the pan, and cook for a few minutes. Add the grated cheese, herbs, hard-boiled eggs and lemon juice. Season to taste with salt and pepper and mix well. Fill the mushroom caps with the mixture and put them on the baking tray. Dot them with the remaining butter. Bake in the preheated oven for 10 minutes.

Serve warm, garnished with watercress and small lemon wedges. This dish is included in a menu on the opposite page.

SHERRY PARTY Baked mushrooms, stuffed with a mixture of butter, wine, smoked ham, cheese and herbs; wedges of panforte; mini choux filled with tapénade; and kebabs of cucumber, avocado and melon are worthy partners to sherry.

CUCUMBER FILLED WITH TAPÉNADE

Tapénade was invented only a century ago in Marseilles. It is a rich paste of capers (*tapéno* in Provençal) pounded with tuna, anchovies, olives, lemon juice, brandy and olive oil. It is used here as a filling for cucumber.

PREPARATION TIME: *35 minutes*
CHILLING TIME: *1 hour*

INGREDIENTS – *makes about 48 pieces:*
4 medium cucumbers
TAPÉNADE – *makes about 1 lb (450 g)*
10 oz (275 g) black olives, pitted
1 teaspoon lemon juice
1 fl oz (25 ml) brandy
4 oz (115 g) tinned tuna fish in brine, drained and flaked
3 oz (75 g) bottled capers, drained
6 anchovy fillets, drained
1 clove garlic, crushed
1 level tablespoon dry mustard
¼ teaspoon ground cloves
¼ teaspoon ground ginger
¼ teaspoon freshly grated nutmeg
1 fl oz (25 ml) olive oil
Freshly ground black pepper
GARNISH
Watercress

Peel the cucumbers and cut them in half lengthways. Scoop out the seeds with a teaspoon and sprinkle the cut surfaces with salt. Leave the cucumber shells in a colander for about 30 minutes to drain. Pat dry with absorbent kitchen paper.

To make the tapénade, put the olives in a food processor with the lemon juice, brandy, tuna, capers, anchovy, garlic, mustard and spices. Blend to a smooth paste. Continue blending and gradually add the olive oil in a thin trickle as though making mayonnaise. Season to taste with black pepper. Spoon the tapénade into a plastic box or a bowl, cover and refrigerate.

Dry the cucumber halves with kitchen paper and fill them with the tapénade. Mound the mixture up slightly above the level of the cucumber. Put the cucumber halves in the refrigerator for an hour to allow the cucumber to become crisp and the tapénade firm.

Cut the cucumber into 1in (25mm) lengths. Serve chilled, garnished with watercress.

MANGETOUT AND CUCUMBER MÉLANGE

The cool flavours of mangetout and cucumber mingle here with richer flavours of prawn, smoked salmon and smoked trout in a subtle combination of crisp green vegetables and delicate pink fillings.

As its name implies in French, *mangetout* – also called sugar peas – are eaten whole. The tender pod is regarded as a greater delicacy than the insignificant pea. In 17th-century France, the fashion for eating mangetout among the ladies of Louis XIV's court bordered on obsession, according to the king's mistress, Madame de Maintenon.

Offcuts of smoked salmon – much cheaper than slices – are sold in some delicatessens, and can be used for the smoked salmon mousse. The vegetables and fillings can be prepared up to 6 hours in advance and kept in the refrigerator until needed. Assemble the parts of the mélange no more than an hour before the party, to keep the vegetables crisp.

MÉLANGE OF PINK AND GREEN
Slices of cucumber are topped with smooth smoked trout brandade, and crisp mangetout are either wrapped round prawns or filled with a mousse of cream cheese and smoked salmon.

PREPARATION TIME: *1½ hours plus chilling time*

INGREDIENTS – *makes about 150 pieces:*
2 cucumbers (40 slices)
Salt
8-12 oz (225-350 g) large mangetout (90-100 pods)
60 large peeled prawns, about 8 oz (225 g)
Lemon juice
Paprika
10-12 oz (275-350 g) smoked trout brandade (make the full quantity given in Cherry tomatoes with three fillings, opposite page)
1-2 tablespoons double cream
SMOKED SALMON MOUSSE
3 oz (75 g) smoked salmon
8 oz (225 g) cream cheese
2 fl oz (50 ml) double cream
2 teaspoons lemon juice

Score the cucumbers lengthways with a fork and cut them into slices ¼in (5mm) thick. Sprinkle the cucumber with salt and leave to drain in a colander. Pat dry with kitchen paper. Cover and store in the refrigerator until required.

Wash and top and tail the mangetout. Unless they are young and very fresh, string them as well. Blanch them for

30 seconds in boiling water and drain. Rinse in a bowl of cold water containing several ice cubes. Drain again. Pat dry with a clean tea towel or kitchen paper, wrap and store in the refrigerator.

To make the smoked salmon mousse, put the smoked salmon, cream cheese, double cream and lemon juice in a food processor or liquidiser and blend until smooth. Chill in a covered container in the refrigerator for at least an hour.

Toss the prawns in lemon juice and sprinkle lightly with paprika. With a sharp, pointed knife, split 30 mangetout in half lengthways, making 60 halves. Wrap one mangetout half round each prawn and secure with a wooden cocktail stick.

Soften the smoked salmon mousse with a wooden spoon. Split each of the remaining mangetout down its curved edge with a sharp pointed knife. Make sure the other edge remains intact. Pipe the mousse into each pod. A leaf nozzle gives the most decorative result.

With a star nozzle, pipe each slice of cucumber with brandade. If the brandade is too stiff to pipe add a little double cream. Garnish each slice with a small frond of dillweed.

Arrange the mélange on a tray, or on a baking sheet covered in silver foil. Decorate it with fresh watercress, fronds of dillweed or a small bunch of flowers. This dish is included in a menu on page 179.

CHERRY TOMATOES WITH THREE FILLINGS

Hollowed-out cherry tomatoes can be filled with pâtés, mousses or other savouries. They are only 1-1½in (25-40mm) in diameter – small enough to be eaten in one or two bites.

The tomato cases can be prepared the night before the party and kept in the refrigerator. The fillings can be made, and the tomatoes filled, up to 6 hours in advance. Store them, covered, in the refrigerator.

PREPARATION TIME: *55 minutes*

INGREDIENTS – *makes about 30:*
1 lb (450 g) cherry tomatoes (about 30)
FILLINGS
(see below)

Wash and dry the tomatoes and remove the stalks. Cut a thin slice off the bottom of each one. Remove the seeds and pulp with a coffee spoon or small melon baller. (The pulp can be saved for use in a sauce or soup.) Place the tomatoes cut side down on a rack or large plate and leave them to drain in the refrigerator until needed.

A TEMPTATION OF TOMATOES Three different fillings transform little cherry tomatoes – piped smoked trout brandade, prawns topped with dill, and crab mayonnaise.

SMOKED TROUT BRANDADE
 – for about 30 tomatoes:
1 smoked trout
2 oz (50 g) cream cheese
1 oz (25 g) butter
2 teaspoons lemon juice
Salt and freshly ground black pepper
GARNISH
Small sprigs of parsley

Skin and bone the trout. Put the trout, cream cheese, butter and lemon juice in a food processor or liquidiser. Process until smooth, then season with salt and pepper. Pipe the mixture into the tomatoes, using a star nozzle. Garnish with parsley.

PRAWN AND DILL FILLING – *for about 30 tomatoes:*
6 oz (175 g) peeled prawns
1½ level tablespoons fresh dillweed
3 teaspoons lemon juice
Salt and freshly ground black pepper
GARNISH
1 sprig of dill

Chop the prawns and the dill, and mix with the lemon juice in a bowl. Season to taste with salt and pepper.

Spoon the prawn and dill mixture into the tomato cases. Garnish each tomato with a small frond of dillweed.

CRAB MAYONNAISE FILLING – *for about 30 tomatoes:*
5-6 oz (150-175 g) white crab meat
1½ tablespoons lemon mayonnaise (page 369)
1½ tablespoons finely chopped parsley
Salt and freshly ground black pepper
GARNISH
Fine strips of lemon zest

Mix the crab meat, mayonnaise and parsley in a bowl, and season to taste with salt and pepper. Spoon the mixture into the tomato cases and garnish with strips of lemon zest.

LEMON DIP

Ground almonds give body and texture to this summer dip of soured cream and lemon, served with an array of the season's most delicate vegetables – mangetout, french beans and tender young asparagus. When asparagus is not in season, sticks of seeded cucumber can be used.

The dip can be stored for up to 4 hours in the refrigerator. The crudités can be prepared a day in advance and stored in the refrigerator.

Ready-ground almonds can be used, but the flavour is not as good as that of almonds freshly ground.

PREPARATION TIME: *40 minutes*

INGREDIENTS – *serves about 10:*
DIP
4 oz (115 g) unblanched almonds
½ pint (285 ml) soured cream
3-4 tablespoons lemon juice
2 level teaspoons finely grated lemon zest
Salt and freshly ground black pepper
CRUDITÉS
1 lb (450 g) french beans
1 lb (450 g) mangetout
1 lb (450 g) young asparagus

Blanch the almonds in boiling water for 2-3 minutes. Rub off the skins and grind the nuts in a food processor or liquidiser.

Add the soured cream, lemon juice and zest, blend to a smooth cream and season with salt and pepper. Pour the dip into a

serving bowl. Cover and chill.

To prepare the crudités, top and tail the french beans and mangetout and blanch them in boiling water for 1-2 minutes. Plunge them into cold water and dry carefully on absorbent kitchen paper. Blanch the asparagus in boiling water for 4 minutes (see page 386). Plunge into cold water and dry.

This dip is included in a menu on page 179.

PRAWN AND GINGER DIP

Two of the flavours of Southeast Asian cooking are combined here with cream cheese, lemon and chives. The dip can, as an alternative, be piped straight onto small radicchio leaves, using a wide nozzle. Decorate the dip with chopped chives or small watercress leaves.

PREPARATION TIME: *10 minutes*

INGREDIENTS – *serves about 10:*
8 oz (225 g) peeled prawns
4 oz (115 g) cream cheese
¼ pint (150 ml) double cream
1 fl oz (25 ml) lemon juice (about 1 lemon)
2 level teaspoons ground ginger
Salt and freshly ground black pepper
1 level teaspoon chopped chives

Remove any dark veins from the prawns and then put the prawns into a food processor or liquidiser and blend briefly until finely chopped. Add the cream cheese, cream, lemon juice and ginger. Blend for a further few seconds until all the ingredients are combined. Season with salt and freshly ground black pepper. Alternatively chop the prawns as finely as possible by hand then beat together with the cheese, cream, lemon juice and ginger. Serve chilled, sprinkled with chopped chives.

Serve crisp green vegetables as crudités – blanched broccoli florets and french beans, or courgette sticks (see also *Crudités with dips*, page 320). Do not choose vegetables with too strong a taste, however, because they will dominate the dip.

This dip is included in a menu on the opposite page.

SUBTLE SPICE *Crudités – broccoli florets, sticks of courgette, french beans and radishes – make a crisp contrast to a prawn and ginger dip.*

ALMOND OLIVES

Traditionally, olives are served in the Middle East as part of the sociable ritual of sampling *mezze* – small appetisers eaten before a main meal.

PREPARATION TIME: *45 minutes*

INGREDIENTS – *makes 30:*
6 oz (175 g) almonds, shelled
About 30 pimento-stuffed olives, 7 oz (200 g) jar
4 oz (115 g) cream cheese
30 petit fours paper cases

Place the almonds in a small bowl and cover with boiling water. Leave them for 2-3 minutes, then rub away the skins. Toast the almonds under a moderately heated grill until golden. Watch them, because they burn easily. Chop them finely and spread them on a plate.

Drain the olives and pat them dry with absorbent paper.

Beat the cream cheese to soften it. With your hands, coat the olives in the cheese and roll them into neat balls. Keep your hands as cold as possible by dipping them in cold water every so often. Roll the olives in the chopped almonds.

Lay them on a large plate or baking sheet and chill in the refrigerator. They can be stored overnight. Just before the party, put each almond olive in a paper case and arrange them on a shallow serving plate.

This dish is included in a menu on the opposite page.

Allow 2-3 pieces of smoked ham and fruit per person. Make the full quantities of frankfurters and Gorgonzola bites, double the quantities of dip, almond olives, devils and mince pies and 2-3 times the quantity given in the recipe for glögg.
IN ADVANCE The day before, make the olives, dip and Gorgonzola bites. Prepare the devils and the glögg.
ON THE DAY Allow 2-2½ hours for preparing the food and reheating the glögg.

QUICK COCKTAIL SNACKS

Too often the effort required to make a cocktail snack seems to be out of all proportion to its small size. However, there are many simple snacks which take only a few minutes to make. Aim to provide variety in both flavour and colour.

MEAT, FISH AND EGGS

ASSORTED SALAMIS AND COLD MEATS
Arrange a selection of thinly sliced different salamis and cold meats on a large serving dish. Fold or roll up the slices. Garnish with radish roses (page 287) and lengthways slices of dill-pickled cucumber.

HONEY SAUSAGES
Preheat the oven to 180°C (350°F, gas mark 4). Place 1lb (450g) cocktail sausages or chipolatas twisted into shorter lengths (about 15-20) in a baking dish. Mix 1 tablespoon clear honey with 1 tablespoon whole grain mustard or half English mustard and half whole grain mustard. Spread it over the sausages so they are evenly coated. Bake in the preheated oven for 30 minutes.

SMOKED HAM AND FRUIT
Wrap very thinly sliced smoked ham (such as parma ham) cut into pieces about 3in × ¾in (75mm × 19mm) around segments of fresh figs; tinned, drained palm hearts or asparagus spears; slices of avocado (brushed with lemon juice to prevent discoloration); peeled segments of kiwi fruit; or cubes of melon or papaya. Impale the pieces on cocktail sticks. About 4oz (115g) ham will wrap 15-20 pieces of fruit.

SMOKED SALMON AND MONKFISH
Poach 8oz (225g) monkfish in fish stock for about 10 minutes until tender. Leave to cool in the stock, then skin and bone the fish and cut into ¾in (20mm) cubes. Wrap each cube in a piece of smoked salmon – you will need about 4oz (115g) – and secure with a cocktail stick.

QUAIL'S EGGS
Boil quail's eggs for 4 minutes, then plunge them into cold water. Serve shelled or un-shelled, with celery salt.

DISHES OF DELIGHTS Quail's eggs, morsels of monkfish wrapped in smoked salmon, cubes of melon, papaya, kiwi fruit or avocado wrapped in parma ham, and assorted salamis and cold meats are all quick to prepare.

CHEESE

CELERY LOGS

Mash 4oz (115g) blue cheese (Danish Blue will do) with 1 dessertspoon of mayonnaise and 3 level teaspoons finely chopped capers. Spoon the mixture into sticks of celery (use 1 large head of celery). Cut the filled sticks into 1in (25mm) lengths. This makes about 30 logs.

ROQUEFORT FRUIT AND NUTS

Mash 4oz (115g) Roquefort or other blue cheese to a smooth paste with a wooden spoon. Halve 8oz (225g) green or black grapes (about 25) and remove the pips. Sandwich the halves together with the cheese and thread on cocktail sticks. This amount of cheese will alternatively fill about 16 apricot or plum halves, or can be used to sandwich about 30 pairs of walnut or pecan halves.

CREAM CHEESE BALLS

Mix 4oz (115g) cream cheese with 1 level tablespoon chopped chives and one of the following: 2 teaspoons anchovy paste, 2 teaspoons tomato purée, or 1 level teaspoon curry powder. Chill the mixture in the refrigerator for about 30 minutes, then shape with your hands into balls the size of a large grape. Roll the balls in about 2oz (50g) finely chopped walnuts and chill in the refrigerator. This makes about 10 balls. Serve in petit-four paper cases.

MOZZARELLA TOASTS

Preheat the oven to 200°C (400°F, gas mark 6). Spread 20 mini Melba toasts (available in packets) very sparingly with tomato ketchup. Cut about 6oz (175g) thinly sliced salami and about 6oz (175g) thinly sliced Mozzarella cheese into pieces the same size as the toasts. Lay a slice of salami and a slice of Mozzarella on each toast. Lay the toasts on a baking sheet and bake in the preheated oven for 5 minutes only, until the cheese has started to melt. The toasts may be grilled for 3 minutes instead of baked. Serve hot.

HOT BRIE OR CAMEMBERT

Preheat the oven to 180°C (350°F, gas mark 4). Cut off the rind from the top of a whole small Brie, Camembert or other creamy cheese – these are usually about 4-6in (100-150mm) in diameter. Cover it thickly with toasted almonds. Place it on a small ovenproof dish and warm in the preheated oven for about 10 minutes until soft and runny. Serve with small crisp biscuits or tortilla chips for dipping into the runny cheese.

STUFFED ARTICHOKE HEARTS OR CUCUMBER CUPS

Drain a 14oz (400g) tin of artichoke hearts (about 8). Fill the depression in the top with 2-3oz (50-75g) cream cheese mixed with 1 level teaspoon chopped chives. Garnish each heart with a peeled prawn. Alternatively, mix the cream cheese with about 1 level tablespoon finely chopped walnuts and garnish with pieces of walnut.

The same fillings can be used to stuff cucumber cups. Cut a cucumber into 1½in (40mm) lengths and scoop out the centre. Turn the cups upside down on a wire rack to drain before stuffing. A large cucumber should yield about 8 cups.

ASSORTED CHEESE CUBES

Cut a variety of firm cheeses into cubes and arrange them on a large plate with fresh crudités (see *Crudités with dips*, page 320), or thread the cubes of cheese onto cocktail sticks with pieces of fruit such as melon, pineapple, grape or kiwi fruit.

PÂTÉS

GARLIC PÂTÉ BALLS

Shape 4oz (115g) of any stiff garlic pâté into small balls and roll them in 3-4 finely chopped gherkins. Chill in the refrigerator. Serve in petit-four cases. This makes 10-12 balls.

APPLE AND PÂTÉ SLICES

Choose crisp apples and slice thinly. Brush each slice with lemon juice to prevent discoloration, then spread the slices with smooth chicken liver pâté. Two apples yield about 25–30 slices, for which you will need about 4oz (115g) pâté. Decorate each apple slice with a small piece of parsley or thyme.

STUFFED MUSHROOMS

Wipe 6oz (175g) button mushrooms with a damp cloth and remove the stalks then brush the surface with lemon juice. Stuff the mushroom cups with about 4oz (115g) smooth pâté and garnish with a piece of gherkin or green pepper or a sprinkling of chopped parsley.

PASTRIES

CROUSTADES

Fill ready-made croustade cases (made of fried or baked bread), or pastry cases which can be bought in some delicatessens, with black or red lumpfish roe and garnish with a thin wedge of lemon or a sprig of fresh dill or parsley. They can also be used as cases for most of the fillings suggested in this chapter.

PUFF PASTRY SAVOURIES

Preheat the oven to 220°C (425°F, gas mark 7). Use ready-made puff pastry. Roll it out to about ⅛in (3mm) thick and cut it into triangles about 2½in × 2½in × 2in (65mm × 65mm × 50mm). Place half an anchovy fillet on each one. Roll it up from the base and then bend to form a crescent. Place on a baking tray, brush with beaten egg, and bake in the preheated oven for about 7 minutes until puffy and golden. Serve hot or cold. A 7-8oz (200-225g) packet of pastry will make about 30.

FRUIT AND VEGETABLE KEBABS

Thread a colourful variety of raw vegetables and fruit onto cocktail sticks. Use squares of green and red peppers; cubes of cucumber, avocado and melon, or anything else in season. Brush anything likely to discolour – such as avocado or apple – with lemon juice.

MARINATED OLIVES

Drain 8oz (225g) black olives preserved in brine and rinse them in warm water. Prick the olives, place them in a sterilised jam jar and cover with a marinade of 2 tablespoons of lemon juice, 4 tablespoons olive oil, 1 level teaspoon finely chopped rosemary or oregano, and salt and pepper to taste. A clove of garlic, crushed, can be added if you wish. Seal the jar and store until required. The olives will keep for 2-3 weeks.

QUICK VARIETY Mushrooms stuffed with pâté (top left) are joined in the top row by hot Mozzarella toasts and a baked whole Camembert served with tortilla chips. Below, from the left, are cubes of cheese with grapes and pieces of kiwi fruit; pâté and cream cheese balls; croustades filled with red and black lumpfish roe, and puff pastry savouries; celery logs and apple and pâté slices.

CANAPÉS

Canapé comes from the French for 'couch' and, translated into culinary terms, it describes a miniature open sandwich. The couch is the base of bread or pastry on which is spread flavoured butters and toppings.

Bases, butters, toppings and garnishes can all be prepared several hours before the party and kept covered in a cool place. Assemble the canapés no more than 1-2 hours before required, to prevent the bases from softening. Pastry cases can be made crisp again by heating them in a moderate oven – 180°C (350°F, gas mark 4) – for 10 minutes. Allow an average of 6-8 canapés per person.

BASES

BREAD BASES

Canapé bases should never be soggy. The bread used can be ordinary white or brown, but they need to be toasted, sautéed or baked to make them crisp. Close-textured breads – like rye bread, or the dark Westphalian *pumpernickel* – are firm enough to use without toasting, and provide a sharp but pleasant undertone to canapés of cheese and flavoured savoury butters. Mini Melba toasts – sold in packets by some supermarkets – provide a light, dry foundation for small savouries. If more substantial canapés are required, use thinly sliced French bread, or *baguettes*.

Pitta, the thin unleavened bread of the Middle East, can now be bought in many food shops and works well as a simple base. Cut each pitta into quarters then separate the two layers with your fingers. Butter one side of each piece then bake the pieces in a moderate oven – 180°C (350°F, gas mark 4) – for 10 minutes. If you wish to use pitta unbaked, it should be just warmed through before serving. Plain pizza dough (see *Pizza alla casalinga*, page 59) can also be used for simple bases.

CUTTING THE BASES Canapé bases are traditionally either square or rectangular, and should be no more than ¼in (5mm) thick and 1½in (40mm) in diameter. Shapes can be varied to suit individual occasions and tastes by using biscuit or petits-fours cutters.

Loaf sizes vary considerably, but as a general rule a small straight-sided loaf will give about 50 rectangular canapé bases, a large one 108. Ready-sliced loaves are by far the most convenient. Use thinly sliced loaves, remove the crusts and then cut each slice into 4 (or 6 if you are using a large loaf). If the shapes are irregular you may get fewer bases from each slice.

PREPARING THE BASES The way in which the bread base is treated affects the flavour and texture of the canapé.

Delicate 'green' butters of watercress and spinach, or parsley and lemon (opposite page) are delicious spread on a richer base of sautéed bread. Cut out the shapes, and fry them gently in a mixture of butter and olive oil. For a small loaf you will need about 4 tablespoons of butter and 4 tablespoons of olive oil. Add the butter and oil to the pan as you need it, rather than all at once. Drain the bases on kitchen paper then leave them to cool on a wire rack.

Baked bread is less dry than toast, yet lighter than the sautéed variety. Brush the slices of bread with melted butter – 6oz (175g) for a small loaf – cut out the bases, and place them on a baking tray. Bake in a very hot oven – 230°C (450°F, gas mark 8) – for 8 minutes. Watch them carefully and shake the tray so that the bases on the edge of the tray do not burn. This type of base can be stored for 1-2 weeks in an airtight container.

PASTRY BASES

Plain or cheese-flavoured pastry can be used (see page 392). For a richer cheese pastry make the recipe for *Gorgonzola bites* (page 159), with a milder cheese, such as Cheddar. Try cheese pastry biscuits spread with anchovy butter or walnut cream cheese (opposite page), garnished with slices of olive or walnut.

VEGETABLE BASES

Slices of potato or cucumber adapt very well as canapé bases. Use potatoes with a smooth, waxy texture such as 'Majestic'. Boil them in their skins until cooked through, but still firm, and peel them carefully. Cut them into slices ¼in (5mm) thick. Each slice can then be shaped into flowers, hearts or rounds with biscuit cutters.

Score cucumbers lengthways with a canelle knife or a fork, then cut them into ¼in (5mm) slices. Cucumber flowers or hearts, cut out of the slices with petits-fours cutters, are an attractive alternative.

CHEESE BASES

Waxy cheeses, such as Edam or Gouda, also make bases, sliced and shaped in the same way as potatoes or cucumbers.

DAINTY CANAPÉS On the silver tray are toast rectangles topped with almond butter, smoked chicken and cranberry sauce; and cheese pastry rounds topped with walnut cream cheese spread and radish slices.

On the black dish are rounds of rye bread topped with green butter and carpaccio; and triangles of black bread topped with prawn butter and asparagus tips.

On the black tray are slices of canelled cucumber topped with curry butter and ham; and diamonds of Gouda cheese topped with watercress and chive butter and avocado slices. Cool White Lady cocktails are as elegant as the canapés.

SPREADS

Savoury butters and cream cheese spreads act as a bond, securing the garnish to the canapé, and sealing the base against any moisture from the garnish. With a very rich topping only a very thin layer of butter or cheese spread, if any, is needed to make the topping stick. Small quantities of spreads can also be piped onto canapés as a final decoration.

Prepare all spreads at least 2 hours before making up the canapés and store in a cool place – this allows the flavours to mingle. Let the spreads come to room temperature before spreading, however, or the base may break.

To make savoury butters or cheese spreads, cream the butter or cheese with a wooden spoon or with an electric beater, to make it smooth and fluffy. Purée the ingredients used for flavouring or chop them very finely. Add them to the butter or cheese and mix well. Press the mixture through a fine sieve to make sure the ingredients are thoroughly blended, then season to taste with salt and black pepper. Beat the spread again until smooth and fluffy.

As a rough guide, 6oz (175g) of butter or cream cheese spread will be enough for 30-40 canapés, depending on the size. The following recipes consist of 4oz (115g) of butter or cream cheese mixed with varying quantities of flavouring, and will cover 20-30 canapés.

The spreads can be stored, covered, for up to 2 days in the refrigerator.

SAVOURY BUTTERS
Mix 4oz (115g) of unsalted butter with any of the following flavourings:

ALMOND

2oz (50g) of finely chopped, blanched almonds, and the juice and zest of ½ an orange.

ANCHOVY

4 anchovy fillets, soaked overnight in milk, then mashed to a paste with a pestle and mortar.

BLUE CHEESE

2oz (50g) of Stilton, Roquefort or other crumbly blue cheese, mashed with a wooden spoon.

CURRY

2 level teaspoons of curry powder.

GREEN

2oz (50g) of watercress, chives or fresh, blanched spinach, finely chopped.

MAÎTRE D'HÔTEL

2 level teaspoons of chopped parsley, ½-1 teaspoon of lemon juice and ½ teaspoon of mustard powder.

RED PEPPER

Half red pepper roasted under a hot grill for about 5 minutes until the skin has blackened and blistered, then peeled, chopped roughly and puréed.

PRAWN

2oz (50g) of finely chopped, peeled, cooked prawns, and a pinch of nutmeg.

SAFFRON

2 level teaspoons of saffron strands soaked in 1 teaspoon of water. Flavour the butter with the water.

CREAM CHEESE SPREADS
Mix 4oz (115g) of full fat cream cheese with any of the following flavourings:

ANCHOVY

2 teaspoons of anchovy paste.

WATERCRESS AND CHIVES

2 level teaspoons of finely chopped watercress leaves, 2 level teaspoons of finely chopped chives and ½ teaspoon of finely grated onion.

SMOKED SALMON

2oz (50g) of finely chopped smoked salmon (use pieces of smoked salmon rather than the more expensive slices) and lemon juice to taste.

TUNA

2 level tablespoons of mashed tinned tuna fish, with a dash of vinegar or lemon juice and 1 level tablespoon of mayonnaise.

WALNUT

2oz (50g) of finely chopped walnuts.

TOPPINGS AND GARNISHES

There is great scope for imaginative combinations of toppings and garnishes, and the suggestions made here are only a beginning. The quantities given will garnish 20-30 canapés.

FISH
PRAWN

6oz (175g) of peeled, cooked prawns. Top each canapé with 2 whole prawns and garnish with a drop of mayonnaise.

SMOKED EEL

4oz (115g) of smoked eel, blended to a smooth paste with 2 tablespoons of single cream and 1 tablespoon of olive oil. Pipe the mixture onto the canapés and decorate with small leaves of parsley or chervil.

KIPPER

3oz (75g) of tinned flaked kipper fillet, 1 apple and 1fl oz (25ml) of soured cream. Top each canapé with a small slice of apple brushed with lemon juice, a few flakes of kipper and a drop of soured cream.

SARDINE

4oz (115g) of tinned sardines, drained and mashed together with 1 tablespoon of lemon juice. Top each canapé with a teaspoon of the mixture and sprinkle with chopped herbs.

SMOKED SALMON

4oz (115g) of thinly sliced smoked salmon, 2oz (50g) of red or black lumpfish roe and 2 tablespoons of soured cream. Cut the smoked salmon to fit the canapé shapes or roll up strips of salmon and place them on top. Just before serving, garnish with lumpfish roe and a drop of soured cream.

CRAB

4oz (115g) of flaked crab, mixed with 1 level tablespoon of mayonnaise. Top each canapé with a teaspoon of the mixture and garnish with red pepper.

WHITEBAIT

8oz (225g) of very small whitebait, coated in 1oz (25g) of seasoned flour and deep-fried (page 372). Top each canapé with 1-2 fish, and decorate with segments of orange or lemon.

FISH FLOURISHES Whitebait and maître d'hôtel butter top rounds of fried bread; prawns and prawn butter top black bread; kipper and watercress and chive cream cheese spread top crescents of toast; smoked eel and saffron butter top cheese pastry; and sardine and red pepper butter top rye bread.

MEAT AND POULTRY
CARPACCIO

4oz (115g) of very thinly sliced raw fillet steak (see *Carpaccio with fresh fig purée*, page 201) and 2-3 tablespoons of lightly whipped double cream flavoured with creamed horseradish. Just before serving, cut the slices of steak to fit the canapés and top each canapé with a little of the horseradish-flavoured cream.

BEEF

4oz (115g) of wafer-thin slices of cold roast beef, ½ tablespoon of prepared mustard or creamed horseradish and 15 grapes – about 5oz (150g) – or pieces of dill-pickled cucumber or gherkin. Spread the canapés lightly with mustard or horseradish. Cut the beef to fit the canapés and garnish each with half a grape or a piece of pickled cucumber or gherkin. This combination is very good on a pumpernickel base.

SALAMI

4oz (115g) of thinly sliced salami and 3-4 fresh figs. Cut the slices of salami to fit the canapé bases, top each with a thin wedge of fresh fig.

SMOKED HAM

4oz (115g) of thinly sliced smoked ham, and 2oz (50g) of button mushrooms, thinly sliced and sautéed lightly in olive oil. Cut the smoked ham to fit the canapés, top each with a slice of mushroom and a sprinkling of finely chopped parsley.

CHICKEN

3oz (75g) of cooked chicken, chopped with 1oz (25g) of apple and 1oz (25g) of walnuts, and mixed with 2 level tablespoons of double cream.

SMOKED CHICKEN OR TURKEY

3oz (75g) of breast of smoked chicken or turkey and 2-3 tablespoons of cranberry sauce, grape jelly or *Greengage jelly* (page 32). Spread each canapé base with cranberry sauce or jelly, top with a thin slice of chicken or turkey and garnish with leaves of mustard and cress.

DUCK

3oz (75g) of cold roasted duck breast. Top each canapé with a small slice of duck and garnish with a segment cut from thin slices of orange, or with half a fresh cherry.

TURKEY

4oz (115g) of cooked turkey, diced and moistened with vinaigrette (page 371). Divide the turkey between the canapés and garnish with sprigs of parsley, watercress or, if available, coriander.

VEGETABLES AND FRUIT

Thin slices of tomato, cucumber, avocado or apple (brushed with lemon juice to prevent discoloration), radish, mango, kiwi fruit, peach and olive; cherries; tinned asparagus tips; and leaves of watercress and mâche (lamb's lettuce), garnished with fresh herbs, can all be used as toppings.

COCKTAILS

Cocktails were developed in America during the Prohibition years of the 1920s and early 1930s, largely in an attempt to make bootleg liquor palatable. Hundreds of concoctions have been created since then, and the recipes on the following pages are only a small sample.

Cocktails can be made individually, but for a party it is easier and more economical to serve just one or two varieties and to make them up in larger quantities. Some can be made in advance and kept in the refrigerator, but leave adding the ice until just before serving.

Some recipes require a cocktail shaker. This shakes all the ingredients with ice so that they are thoroughly mixed and very cold. Shakers usually incorporate a strainer as well. If you do not have a cocktail shaker, you can instead mix the ingredients vigorously together in a large jug with a spoon or fork, but the result will not be quite as good, nor the procedure as impressive.

SWEET AND SOUR Sugar-frosted tumblers take the edge off a classic 'sour' cocktail — whisky, lemon and sugar, shaken together and then mixed with soda water.

WHISKY SOUR

A 'sour' is a combination of spirits, sugar and the astringent juice of fresh lemons. The white of an egg gives the light froth characteristic of sours.

PREPARATION TIME: *10 minutes*

INGREDIENTS – *makes 4 glasses:*
1 egg white, lightly beaten
Bowl of caster sugar
Ice cubes
8 fl oz (225 ml) whisky
Juice of 2 lemons
4 level teaspoons caster sugar
Soda water (optional)
4 maraschino cherries
4 slices of orange

Dip the rims of four 'Old Fashioned' short tumblers briefly in egg white, and then dip them into the bowl of sugar so that the rims are frosted.

Put the ice cubes in a cocktail shaker and add the whisky, lemon juice, sugar and 4 teaspoons of the remaining egg white. Shake well and strain the liquid into the tumblers.

Add soda water to taste, and decorate with the cherries and orange slices, skewered on a cocktail stick.

MINT JULEP

A part of the romance of America's Deep South is the mint julep. The name comes from the Persian *gūlab*, or 'rose water', and was used in Europe and America to describe sweet, syrupy drinks – often of the medicinal kind. In America the julep evolved into a combination of crushed ice soaked in wine or spirits, suffused with the flavour of mint. They were served in special silver julep cups, or in tall glasses cloudy with cold.

PREPARATION TIME: *10 minutes*
CHILLING TIME: *15 minutes*

INGREDIENTS – *makes 4 glasses:*
10 sprigs of fresh mint
4 level teaspoons caster sugar
8 fl oz (225 ml) Bourbon or rye whiskey
Crushed ice

Reserve four sprigs of mint for the decoration.

Crush one or two sprigs lightly, and rub against the insides of the glasses. Take the four remaining sprigs and put one into each glass, with a level teaspoon of sugar and a teaspoon of whiskey. Bruise the mint gently with the handle of a wooden spoon and stir it gently until the sugar has dissolved.

Fill the glasses to the brim with crushed ice, tamp the ice down hard with the wooden spoon and add 1fl oz (25ml) of whiskey to each glass. Put the glasses in the freezing compartment of the refrigerator or the freezer for 15 minutes.

Top up the glasses once more with crushed ice and add the remaining whiskey. Do not stir. Decorate with the reserved sprigs of mint, and serve at once.

BRANDY ALEXANDER

Although most cocktails are drunk before a meal, rich, creamy, Brandy Alexander is very good at the end of a dinner party. Crème de cacao is a chocolate-flavoured liqueur. Serve the cocktail immediately

AFTER-DINNER COCKTAIL Brandy, cream and crème de cacao liqueur, sprinkled with nutmeg, makes a rich partner to dark chocolates.

after mixing or the ingredients will begin to separate.

PREPARATION TIME: *5 minutes*

INGREDIENTS – *makes 4 glasses:*
Ice cubes
4 fl oz (115 ml) brandy
4 fl oz (115 ml) crème de cacao
4 fl oz (115 ml) double cream
Freshly grated nutmeg

Place the ice cubes in a cocktail shaker with the brandy, crème de cacao and cream. Shake well, then strain into cocktail glasses. Sprinkle a little nutmeg over each one before serving.

PUSSYFOOT

'Pussyfooter' is a slang expression for the cautious type. During the Prohibition years of the 1920s in America, it came to mean someone who supported the ban on alcohol – hence this non-alcoholic cocktail.

PREPARATION TIME: *10 minutes*

INGREDIENTS – *makes 4 glasses:*
4 fl oz (115 ml) orange juice
4 fl oz (115 ml) lemon juice
4 fl oz (115 ml) lime juice
1 teaspoon Grenadine
1 egg yolk
Crushed ice
4 cocktail cherries

Blend the orange, lemon, lime, Grenadine and egg yolk in a liquidiser. Put the crushed ice in a jug and pour the cocktail mixture over it. Leave it to chill for a few minutes. Alternatively, put the crushed ice in a cocktail shaker and pour over the orange, lemon and lime juices. Add the Grenadine and the egg yolk and shake well.

Strain the mixture into wine glasses, add a cocktail cherry on a stick to each glass and serve.

BUCK'S FIZZ

Buck's Club of London takes the credit for devising this invigorating combination of chilled fresh orange juice and champagne. Although true Buck's fizz should be made with champagne a delicious compromise between authenticity and expense can be reached using sparkling white wine.

PREPARATION TIME: *5 minutes*

INGREDIENTS – *makes 8 glasses:*
8 fl oz (225 ml) fresh orange juice, chilled
1 bottle champagne, chilled

Pour the orange juice into a large glass jug, add the champagne or sparkling white wine and pour immediately into champagne flutes.

KIR

The favourite drink of the Abbé Kir, mayor of Dijon in central France and Resistance hero during the German occupation, was a mixture, popular in the region, of crème de cassis (blackcurrant liqueur) and dry white wine. Since that time the mixture has been known as Kir.

For Kir Royale, champagne (or sparkling white wine) replaces still white wine.

PREPARATION TIME: *5 minutes*

INGREDIENTS – *makes 6-8 glasses:*
6-8 teaspoons crème de cassis
1 bottle (750 ml) chilled dry white wine

Chill the wine glasses in the refrigerator first. Put a teaspoon of crème de cassis into each glass and top up with wine. If necessary, stir briefly to mix.

GIN SLING

At least since the early 19th century, Americans have fended off the heat of long summer days with cool drinks known as slings. One early traveller, Charles W. Janson, wrote in *The Stranger in America* (1807): 'The first craving of an American in the morning is for ardent spirits mixed with sugar, mint, or some other hot herb, and which are called slings.

One of the most famous versions is the Singapore sling – a concoction attributed to the Raffles Hotel of Singapore.

PREPARATION TIME: *10 minutes*

INGREDIENTS – *makes 4 glasses:*
8 fl oz (225 ml) gin
Juice of 4 small lemons
1 level tablespoon sugar
Ice cubes
Soda water
4 slices of lemon
Sprigs of fresh mint

Put the gin, lemon juice and sugar in a jug and stir. Put a cube of ice in each of four tall tumblers and pour in the gin sling. Add soda water, or water, to taste and decorate with lemon slices and sprigs of mint. SINGAPORE SLING Omit the sugar from the recipe, use the juice of 2 large lemons rather than 4 small ones, and add 4fl oz (115ml) of cherry brandy.

Mix together the gin, cherry brandy and lemon juice in a jug. Continue as for gin sling.

WHITE LADY

Cool and elegant, the White Lady emerged in Paris after the First World War. This blend of gin, fresh lemon juice and the orange-flavoured liqueur Cointreau became one of the smart drinks for ladies throughout Europe and America in the 1930s and 1940s.

Egg white can be added to give more body.

PREPARATION TIME: *5 minutes*

INGREDIENTS – *makes 4 glasses:*
Ice cubes
4 fl oz (115 ml) gin
2 fl oz (50 ml) fresh lemon juice
2 fl oz (50 ml) Cointreau
White of 1 egg (optional)
4 maraschino cherries
4 orange slices

Put the ice in a cocktail shaker and add the gin, lemon juice, Cointreau and egg white if used. Shake well and strain into cocktail glasses.

Put a cherry and a slice of orange, skewered on a cocktail stick, into each glass.

PINK GIN

There is a long-established tradition in the British navy that pink gin – chilled gin flavoured with red Angostura bitters – is beneficial to health. The tradition is founded on a degree of truth, for the bitters come from the bark of the South American angostura tree – which is used in medicine to reduce fevers.

PREPARATION TIME: *5 minutes*
CHILLING TIME: *5 minutes (for the glasses)*

INGREDIENTS – *makes 4 glasses:*
2 teaspoons Angostura bitters
Ice cubes
8 fl oz (225 ml) dry gin
Water or soda water

Chill four wine glasses for 5 minutes in the freezer, or the ice compartment of a refrigerator.

Put about ½ teaspoon of bitters in each glass and swirl it around to coat the sides. Tip out the dregs. Add an ice cube and about 2fl oz (50ml) gin to each glass, and top up with water or soda water to taste.

If you prefer a stronger flavour, stir the bitters into the gin.

DRY MARTINI

A recipe for dry martini is like a stolen spell – you have discovered the ingredients, but the magician still holds the secret combination. No two dry martini enthusiasts will agree on the proportion of gin to vermouth, and whether to shake the cocktail or to stir. In America it is said that if you are lost in a desert, just mix a dry martini and ten people will appear from nowhere to show you a better way. The following recipe is offered only as a guideline.

PREPARATION TIME: *10 minutes*

INGREDIENTS – *makes 4 glasses:*
4 green olives
8 fl oz (225 ml) dry gin
4 fl oz (115 ml) dry vermouth
Ice cubes
4 strips of lemon rind

Put an olive, impaled on a cocktail stick, into each glass. Put the gin and vermouth into a jug or large mixing glass with a generous handful of ice, and stir gently. Strain into cocktail glasses. Twist a strip of lemon rind over each glass to release the oils, and then drape it over the edge of the glass. This cocktail is included in a menu on page 158.

MARGARITA

In Mexico, tequila is drunk neat, after a lick at a pinch of salt placed on the back of the hand and a suck at a slice of lime. The Margarita is based on this ritual combination.

PREPARATION TIME: *15 minutes*

INGREDIENTS – *makes 4 glasses:*
Slice of lime
Finely ground salt
8 fl oz (225 ml) tequila
2 fl oz (50 ml) Cointreau
2 fl oz (50 ml) fresh lime juice
Ice cubes

Chill four cocktail glasses in the refrigerator. Rub a slice of lime round the rims, then press the rims into the salt so that they

appear frosted. Put the tequila, Cointreau and lime juice into a jug or mixing glass with ice and stir. Strain carefully into the frosted glasses.

MEXICAN MARGARITA Tequila – the fermented sap of a cactus – is the basis of a cocktail drunk from glasses frosted with salt and here served with almond olives.

BLOODY MARY

The prototype of the Bloody Mary emerged in Paris in the 1920s, in Harry's New York Bar. The basic mixture of vodka and tomato juice was enlivened with various flavourings. The name Bloody Mary seems to have become established in the 1940s. It has been linked by some writers on cocktails with the name of Mary, Queen of Scots who was beheaded, or to Mary Tudor, the original Bloody Mary who had many put to death on religious grounds.

The proportion of the various ingredients can be varied to suit individual tastes. The same drink made with tequila is called a Bloody Maria.

PREPARATION TIME: *10 minutes*

INGREDIENTS – *makes 4 glasses:*
Ice cubes
8 fl oz (225 ml) vodka
16 fl oz (475 ml) tomato juice
2 tablespoons lemon juice
1 tablespoon Worcestershire sauce
2-3 dashes of Tabasco
Pinch of celery salt
Salt and freshly ground black
pepper

Put the ice cubes in a large glass jug. Pour in the vodka and tomato juice. Add the lemon juice, Worcestershire sauce, Tabasco and celery salt. Season to taste with salt and pepper. Stir well and strain into medium tumblers. This cocktail is included in a menu on page 158.

HARVEY WALLBANGER

An American surfing enthusiast had this cocktail named in his honour. Pancho's Bar in Manhattan Beach, California, was the setting in which Harvey – whose surname has not survived as part of the legend – drank vodka and orange laced with Galliano, an Italian liqueur flavoured with herbs. He had lost a surfing tournament, downed several of these cocktails by way of consolation, and on leaving the bar walked into a wall. The Harvey Wallbanger cocktail is supposed to commemorate this event.

PREPARATION TIME: *10 minutes*

INGREDIENTS – *makes 4 glasses:*
Crushed ice
8 fl oz (225 ml) vodka
16 fl oz (475 ml) fresh orange
juice
4 tablespoons Galliano liqueur

Put about 2 heaped tablespoons of crushed ice into each of four tall tumblers.

Mix the vodka and orange in a jug or cocktail shaker and pour it over the ice. Float 1 tablespoon of Galliano liqueur on top by pouring it carefully over the back of a spoon, held just above the surface of the liquid.

The cocktail is usually drunk through long straws.

PUNCHES

Serve hot punches in heatproof bowls or jugs. Cold summer punches can be served in traditional glass punch bowls. Chill a summer punch for a few hours in the refrigerator. Afterwards, keep it cold, either by putting a large block of ice into the bowl (a block does not melt as quickly as ice cubes) or by standing the punch bowl in a larger bowl filled with ice cubes.

STRAWBERRY BOWLE

Champagne's dry and heady effervescence enhances any fruit cup. A number of different fruits can be used, including peaches, pineapples and plums, but the blend of champagne and strawberries reigns supreme. Dry sparkling white wine can be substituted for champagne.

The origin of bowle is obscure, but it may be an old form of 'bowl' – meaning a large drinking cup and, by association, the drink itself. In some old recipes a sprig of fresh, sweet-smelling woodruff is added to the bowle while the fruit is soaking in the champagne. Woodruff can be hard to find, but if it is available it enhances the flavour of the bowle, and the punch bowl can be decorated with garlands of woodruff.

Do not add ice. Chill the champagne first. If possible, serve the bowle in a punch bowl, set in another bowl filled with ice.

PREPARATION TIME: *20 minutes*
CHILLING TIME: *6 hours*

INGREDIENTS – *makes 5¼ pints*
(3 litres), about 20 glasses:
2 lb (900 g) strawberries
3-4 oz (75-115 g) caster sugar
4 bottles champagne

Make the full quantity of mélange and spinach rolls; three times the quantity given in the recipes for ceviche, dip and petits fours, and four times the quantity of fruit and savoury tartlets (use lobster and asparagus filling).

Allow at least a full day for preparations.

IN ADVANCE Make the wedding cake at least a month in advance, and ice it a week ahead. Make and freeze the spinach rolls and the pastry cases for the tartlets.

The day before, make the ceviche, the petits fours and the fillings for the lobster tartlets and mélange.

ON THE DAY First thing, chill the strawberries and champagne for the bowle. Prepare the vegetables for the mélange and the crudités for the dip.

Make the lemon dip, fill the tartlets and assemble the ceviche and the mélange.

During the reception, heat through the spinach rolls.

TO DRINK If you wish to make enough bowle to last the wedding, make about 6-8 times the quantity. Otherwise, make enough for one glass each and then serve champagne or dry white wine.

Set aside a few strawberries for decoration. Wash and hull the remaining strawberries. Put them in the punch bowl, add the sugar and pour in one bottle of champagne. Cover the bowl and leave in the refrigerator for 6 hours to chill and allow the fruit to flavour the champagne.

Just before serving, put the punch bowl on a bed of ice and pour in the remaining 3 bottles of champagne. Add the reserved strawberries to the bowle.

This punch is included in a menu on this page.

SUMMER RECEPTION The sweet fragrance of strawberries steeped in chilled champagne fills each glass of strawberry bowle. Iced petits fours, and lobster and asparagus tartlets echo the pastel tones of a wedding cake decorated with icing roses blushed with pink.

PLANTERS' PUNCH

One of the longest established punches is planters' punch – a rum-based concoction devised by early planters (landowners) in the Americas. The recipe is enshrined in the formula – 1 part sour (lime juice), 2 parts sweet (sugar), 3 parts strong (rum), and 4 parts weak (water). These proportions may be adapted to suit individual tastes.

REFRESHING RUM A West Indian rum punch and spicy almonds refresh at the end of a long, hot day.

PREPARATION TIME: *10 minutes*

INGREDIENTS – *makes about 2 pints (1.1 litres), 6 glasses:*
1 orange
12 fl oz (340 ml) rum
4 fl oz (115 ml) fresh lime juice (2 or 3 limes)
8 oz (225 g) caster sugar
A dash of Angostura bitters or Grenadine
16 fl oz (475 ml) soda water
Crushed ice

Cut the orange into 6 thin slices. Make a small slit in each slice, from centre to rind.

Pour the rum and lime juice into a large jug, and stir in the sugar. Add a dash of Angostura bitters or Grenadine to taste. Pour in the soda water.

Half fill tall tumblers with the crushed ice, then pour on the punch. Decorate the rim of each glass with a slice of orange.

GLÖGG

The source of the word *glögg* gives the key to the character of this excellent Scandinavian punch. It comes from the Old Swedish *glöth* – meaning 'ember' or 'glowing coal' – and conjures up images of warm gatherings by the fire, drinking this potent mix of wines and spirit.

You will need a 10 pint (5.6 litre) pan or two 5 pint (2.8 litre) pans for this recipe. Use a steel or enamel pan, not a preserving pan.

PREPARATION TIME: *15 minutes*
STANDING TIME: *8 hours*

INGREDIENTS – *makes 8¼ pints (4.6 litres), about 24 mugs:*
2 bottles full-bodied red wine
2 bottles Sauternes or muscatel
1½ bottles sweet (Italian) vermouth
6 fl oz (175 ml) aquavit
1 in (25 mm) piece of fresh ginger
6 cardamom seeds, crushed
6 cloves
2 in (50 mm) stick of cinnamon
1 tablespoon Angostura bitters
Thinly pared rind of 1 orange
8 oz (225 g) seedless raisins
8 oz (225 g) caster sugar
8 oz (225 g) whole almonds, blanched and peeled

Peel the ginger and bruise it slightly. Tie the ginger and other spices loosely but securely in a piece of muslin.

Pour the red wine, Sauternes (or muscatel), vermouth and Angostura bitters into the pan. Add the bag of spices to the wine, together with the orange peel and raisins. Heat gently until just steaming, then remove from the heat, cover the pan with kitchen foil if it does not have a lid, and leave the wine and spices to stand for 8 hours.

Before serving, remove the spice bag and orange peel, and add the aquavit and sugar. Reheat the punch but do not let it boil. Remove from the heat, add the almonds and ladle into mugs. This punch is included in a menu on page 169.

MULLED WINE

An undistinguished dry, red table wine can be transformed into a special treat for autumn and winter parties by mulling – heating and spicing it. Other 'sweet' spices (allspice, ginger or mace, for example) can be substituted for those used here.

PREPARATION TIME: *15 minutes*
STANDING TIME: *10 minutes*

INGREDIENTS – *serves 12:*
4 bottles (3 litres) dry red table wine
Rind of 2 lemons, thinly pared
Juice of 4 lemons
12 cloves
1 level teaspoon grated nutmeg
1 cinnamon stick
6 oz (175 g) granulated sugar
4 fl oz (115 ml) brandy (optional)
1 thinly sliced lemon

Pour the wine into a large saucepan and add the lemon rind and juice, cloves, nutmeg, cinnamon stick and sugar.

Heat gently until the mixture is just steaming, stirring occasionally to dissolve the sugar. Remove from the heat, cover and stand for 10 minutes.

Heat once more, then remove from the heat, discard the lemon rind, cloves and cinnamon stick. Stir in the brandy, if used, and pour into a warmed punch bowl or large jugs. Garnish with the lemon slices and serve hot, in mugs. This punch is included in a menu on page 336.

WINE

In the last 20 years or so the range of wines on sale in Britain has increased enormously. It is now possible to buy excellent wines from no fewer than 40 countries – a wider range than that offered in any other country. Wines have also become easier to buy; good wines can be bought in supermarkets and off-licences as well as traditional wine merchants.

When choosing a wine, do not simply consider well-known names. With improvements in wine-making techniques, wines from the lesser-known areas of countries such as France and Germany, or from less familiar wine producers such as Australia, Portugal and Bulgaria are often of excellent quality and much cheaper than those from the best-known 'classic' regions, such as Bordeaux and Burgundy in France.

Ultimately, the only way to judge a wine is by tasting it. But even if you cannot taste a wine before you buy it, there are a number of ways to predict its taste, character and quality:

*RIPE UNTO HARVEST The leaves'
autumn tints and a silvery bloom
signify grapes ready for picking.
These Nebbiolo grapes are used to
make two of Italy's greatest red
wines, Barolo and Barbaresco.*

knowing the grape or grapes from which a wine is made, for example, and the system of quality control used in the country of origin.

Wine making

Wines are almost exclusively made from the species of grape, *Vitis vinifera*. All the ingredients for making wine are contained within grapes. When they are crushed so that these ingredients come into contact with each other, fermentation starts naturally. The yeast present as the bloom on the skins of the grapes, attacks the sugar in the juice and converts it into alcohol.

Most fine wines and a number of cheaper ones are made from the grapes of a single year's harvest, or vintage. These wines are known as 'vintage' wines. Some cheap table wines, however, and most champagnes are blends of different wines from different vintages.

STYLES OF WINE

RED WINE One of the most important ways of categorising red wine is according to 'body'. Full-bodied wines fill the mouth with flavour, and the flavour lingers in the mouth for a long time after you have swallowed the wine. The fullest-bodied table wines include Californian Cabernet Sauvignons, Italian Barolo and French Châteauneuf-du-Pape.

Light-bodied wines have purer, simpler flavours. The best-known is Beaujolais.

WHITE WINE The simplest way to classify white wine is according to its sweetness or dryness. As a rule, dry white wines are lighter in body with a crisp, fresh taste and smell. Sweeter white wines generally have greater breadth of flavour and are richer and fuller in body. But there are some aromatic wines – such as the Alsace Gewürztraminers – which, though dry, have the spiciness and pungency of sweeter wines.

A number of supermarket and off-licence chains use a numbered code for white wines: the driest wines are labelled 1 and the sweetest 9.

GRAPE VARIETIES

Since most of the flavour and style of any wine depends on its primary ingredient, the grape, knowing the variety or varieties of grape used can tell you a lot about the wine.

Some wines – varietal wines – are made from just one variety of grape. Others, such as French Châteauneuf-du-Pape, may be made from as many as a dozen or so different varieties.

Red-wine grapes

Most red wines are made with black grapes only. The skins of the grapes are left with the juices throughout fermentation. The pigmentation in the skins gives the wines their colour. The skins also yield tannin which gives depth of flavour.

Rosé wines are generally made with black grapes, but the

skins are removed after the initial stages of fermentation.

The principal red-wine grapes are the Cabernet Sauvignon, Gamay, Merlot, Pinot Noir, Syrah and Zinfandel grapes (see below). Other grapes include the Cabernet Franc grape (used in many Loire and Bordeaux wines); the Grenache grape (used in a number of the Rhône Valley and Provence wines); the Carignan grape (grown in vast quantities in southern France); the Italian grapes Nebbiolo (used in Barolo and Barbaresco) and Sangiovese (used in Chianti); and the Spanish Tempranillo grape (used in Rioja and Penedès wines).

CABERNET SAUVIGNON

Some of the finest wines in the world – the greatest clarets from Bordeaux, for example – are made with the Cabernet Sauvignon grape. Its principal characteristic is an aroma and flavour of blackcurrants.

In Bordeaux, the Cabernet Sauvignon is generally blended with other grapes, particularly the softer-flavoured grapes, Cabernet Franc and Merlot (see below). Traditionally this blend has produced hard, tannic wines, with great depth of flavour, which mature magnificently. But now most cheaper Bordeaux reds are lighter and fruitier and should be drunk while still young.

In hotter areas, such as California or Australia, Cabernet Sauvignon wines are more fruity

and lush. Australian wine makers often blend Cabernet Sauvignon with Shiraz grapes (see Syrah, below) to make rich, robust wines.

In cooler New Zealand, the Cabernet Sauvignon wines are lighter and drier, and in Italy they are softer-flavoured.

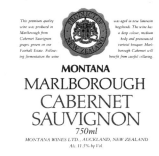

MONTANA MARLBOROUGH CABERNET SAUVIGNON
750ml

MONTANA WINES LTD., AUCKLAND, NEW ZEALAND
Alc. 11.5% by Vol.

NEW ZEALAND CABERNET In a cool climate the Cabernet grape makes light, dry, red wines.

GAMAY

All red Beaujolais wines are made from the Gamay grape. It makes uniquely fresh, light red wines, which can be served chilled. Beaujolais wines are a light purple-crimson, with a pungent, fruity aroma and a light, fruity, slightly acidic taste.

The Gamay grape is also grown in other parts of France – such as the Ardèche and the Auvergne – and in eastern Europe, where it is used to make reliable, light, fresh, red wines known simply as Gamays. In California, the grape is known as Napa Gamay – after one of the region's principal wine-making areas, the Napa Valley.

Most Gamay wines are best

drunk within a year or two of being made, and Beaujolais Nouveau should be drunk within a few months of harvest. But the 'cru' Beaujolais, those from named villages such as Fleurie or Juliénas, may be kept for a few years.

MERLOT

This grape is best known as part of the classic Bordeaux blend, especially in the St-Emilion and Pomerol districts. On its own, Merlot makes a mid-red wine, soft and slightly sweet.

CLOS DU BOIS

Merlot
SONOMA COUNTY
(75% Merlot/25% Cabernet Sauvignon)

VINTED & BOTTLED BY CLOS DU BOIS WINERY
HEALDSBURG, CALIFORNIA USA • ALCOHOL 12.8% BY VOLUME

CALIFORNIAN MERLOT The soft Merlot grape is often blended with the harsher Cabernet Sauvignon.

PINOT NOIR

The grape of all the great red Burgundies, Pinot Noir makes a wine that is inimitably soft and velvety in texture. When young, the flavour of Pinot Noir wines is reminiscent of raspberries. As they mature, they take on a pungent, slightly gamey flavour.

In Burgundy, Pinot Noir is made into a fruity, gently

scented wine without the hard edge of tannin tasted in Cabernet Sauvignon wines. The juice of Pinot Noir grapes is also used in making most champagnes (see opposite page).

In hotter climates, such as California and Australia, it makes wines that are very rich and plummy. It is also grown in the Tyrol, where it is known as Blauburgunder. In Italy, Pinot Noir is sometimes known as Pinot Nero.

PRODUCE OF YUGOSLAVIA
e 70cl SLOVIN

Pinot Noir
FROM THE VINEYARDS OF KRAJINA

QUALITY WINE
KVALITETNO VINO

Bottled by TELTSCHER BROTHERS LTD · PRESTONS RD · LONDON E.14

YUGOSLAV PINOT NOIR Wines made from Pinot Noir are soft and velvety in texture.

SYRAH (or Shiraz)

The classic grape of the Rhône Valley, the Syrah produces dark, long-lived, tannic wines with considerable depth of flavour and a curious smoky taste. The weighty, long-lived luscious red Hermitage wines of the northern Rhône, for example, are made exclusively from Syrah.

It is also used outside Europe to make notable heavyweight wines of considerable individuality. In Australia, the grape is known as Shiraz and is made into a pungently spicy wine, which locals unglamorously liken to a 'sweaty saddle'.

ZINFANDEL

California's only successful native grape, Zinfandel makes unusual inky dark, heavily tannic and full-bodied red wines.

Zinfandel grapes are also used to make 'white' wines. In fact, these 'white' Zinfandels are pink because the pigmentation in the skins is so strong that even the briefest contact with the juice gives the wine a pink colour.

White-wine grapes

Most white wines are made from white grapes only, but white wine can be made from black grapes if the skins are removed before fermentation. The black grapes Pinot Noir (see above) and Pinot Meunier, for example, are used in making most champagnes. Wines, particularly sparkling wines, made from white grapes only, can be labelled *blanc de blancs*.

The principal white-wine grapes are Chardonnay, Chenin

PRINCELY GRAPES Champagne, Pouilly-Fuissé and Chablis are some of the great white wines made from Chardonnay grapes.

Blanc, Gewürztraminer, Muscat, Riesling and Sauvignon Blanc (see below). Other important, though less widely grown, white-wine grapes include the Semillon grape (used in the sweet wines from Bordeaux, Sauternes and Barsac); the Muscadet grape (used to make wines of the same name around Nantes in the Loire Valley); the Aligoté grape (used in the cheaper white Burgundy wines); the Müller-Thurgau and Silvaner grapes (widely used in German wines); and the Trebbiano grape (used in many central Italian wines, both red and white, such as Orvieto, Chianti and Soave).

CHARDONNAY

From its native Burgundy, Chardonnay has spread throughout the world. The grapes are golden in colour with a heady, weighty bouquet.

The grape's pleasantly balanced acidity is brought out best in Burgundy's cool climate. There it makes complex wines (such as Chablis), voluptuous, well-rounded and full, but with a refreshing astringence. Chardonnay is also used in making almost all champagnes; *blanc de blancs* champagnes are made exclusively from Chardonnay.

Pure Chardonnay wines are almost always full and rich. In hot regions, such as California and Australia, they become exceptionally weighty with a high degree of alcohol. They are sometimes so rich that they seem almost to be sweet. Good

Chardonnays from Bulgaria, Italy, the Loire and New Zealand can usually be bought at reasonable prices.

FRENCH CHARDONNAY This is a still Chardonnay wine, although made in the Champagne region.

CHENIN BLANC

The European home of the Chenin Blanc grape is the Loire Valley. There it is made into Anjou blanc, Saumur and Vouvray. The grape has a faintly honeyed smell – some say that it smells more of wet straw – and makes essentially fresh wines with some body and depth.

It is also widely grown in California; South Africa, where it is sometimes known as Steen and makes more full-bodied wines; Chile and Argentina; and Australia.

GEWÜRZTRAMINER

The Gewürztraminer grape has a uniquely exotic, spicy, slightly sweet smell, reminiscent of tropical fruit. Gewürztraminer wines are full and fruity, yet most of them are also bone dry, creating an unusual sweet and sour impression in the mouth. Alsace, in north-eastern France,

is Gewürztraminer's home; but it also flourishes now in Yugoslavia, Austria, Italy, Australia and California. In these regions and countries it is used to make wines of all characters – dry, medium and sweet. Gewürztraminer wines are labelled simply Gewürztraminer or occasionally Traminer.

MUSCAT

Spicy, headily scented and with a pungently fruity taste, Muscat grapes are generally used to make sweet dessert wines – such as the Italian Asti Spumante, Muscat de Beaumes-de-Venise from Southern France and some good Muscats from Australia and Portugal. However, there are also some excellent dry Muscat wines – notably those made in Alsace.

RIESLING

Ninety-five per cent of Germany's best wines are made from the Riesling grape (pronounced 'reesling') – also known as Rhine or Johannisberg Riesling. It has a distinctive bouquet, reminiscent of Alpine flowers, and a refreshing acidity. It makes very light-bodied wines, either dry or, in Germany, medium to sweet. The best European Rieslings come from Germany and Alsace; hotter climates tend to subdue the grape's distinctive acidity.

Other grapes known as Riesling (the Olasz, Laski and Wälsch Riesling and Riesling Italico) are distinct from the

Rhine Riesling grape and are generally less well thought of. In northern Italy and eastern Europe, they are used to produce aromatic wines, pungent, fruity and slightly sweet. They are likeable and very reasonably priced, but they lack the fresh acidity of Rhine Rieslings.

AUSTRALIAN RIESLING Rieslings can be dry, medium or sweet. This one is lusciously sweet.

SAUVIGNON BLANC

The Sauvignon Blanc grape has a distinctive, strongly catty or gooseberry smell and an astringent, acid taste. It makes dry, crisp wines best drunk young.

Most dry white Bordeaux wines are made with the Sauvignon Blanc grape – often blended with Semillon. Also made with Sauvignon Blanc are the Sancerres and Pouilly Fumé wines of the Loire. In sunnier climates, such as Yugoslavia and California, Sauvignon Blanc makes softer-flavoured wines with a more flowery, grassy taste. These wines can also be known as Fumé Blanc wines.

BULGARIAN SAUVIGNON In warmer climates Sauvignon Blanc makes dry, flowery-flavoured wines.

SPARKLING WINES

All wines would become sparkling if they were fermented in a tightly sealed container, leaving the carbon dioxide which is a natural by-product of fermentation nowhere to go except to dissolve itself back into the wine. Champagne is the best-known sparkling wine, though others of varying quality are made in every wine-producing country.

Pink *rosé* champagne has a slightly fuller more fruity flavour than white champagne and may be slightly sweet.

MÉTHODE CHAMPENOISE The most painstaking – and expensive – method of introducing the sparkle into sparkling wine is the méthode champenoise.

To make any sparkling wine – except for those made by carbonation (see below) – the wine is fermented twice. The first fermentation produces a normal still wine. A solution of wine and sugar is then added to the wine with special yeasts to provoke the second fermentation. In the champagne method, the second fermentation takes place inside the bottles.

To remove the sediment produced by the second fermentation, the bottles are placed neck downwards and the sediment is gently shaken down onto the corks. The wine and sediment in the necks is then frozen and removed. The bottles are topped up with wine, usually laced with liquid sugar, and recorked.

Only sparkling wines from the Champagne region northeast of Paris are allowed to call themselves champagne in Europe. At present, other sparkling wines made by the same method have 'Méthode Champenoise', or 'Champagne Method' on the label. But in the future, it will be illegal in EEC countries to sell sparkling wine labelled either Méthode Champenoise or Champagne Method. American wines are labelled 'fermented in this bottle' and Spanish wines 'Cava'.

The other French champagne method sparkling wines are those of Saumur, Vouvray, Burgundy and Alsace, Blanquette de Limoux from the south and the sweet Clairette de Die from the Rhône Valley.

TANK METHOD Also known as the *cuve close* ('sealed vat') method, the tank method was invented by the French winemaker, Eugène Charmat. The wine is put through its second fermentation in large sealed tanks instead of individual bottles. It is then chilled and filtered under pressure. It is topped up with more wine and some sugar, then bottled.

The tank method produces huge quantities of sparkling wine, but the bubbles are larger and disperse more quickly than in champagne method wines.

Sparkling wines made using the tank method include almost all the *Deutscher* (German) *Sekt* wines and the sweet, muscat-based Asti Spumanti and Moscato Spumanti from Italy.

TRANSFER METHOD This is a popular method in America. The wine's second fermentation takes place in bottles, but the wine is then removed to tanks and filtered under pressure. American wines made in this way are labelled 'fermented in the' (as opposed to *this*) 'bottle'.

CARBONATION The lowest grade of sparkling wine is one that has simply been carbonated like fizzy lemonade. These wines have very short-lived bubbles.

Dry or sweet

The label on most sparkling wines will declare the wine's degree of dryness or sweetness.
BRUT ZERO, BRUT INTÉGRALE or BRUT SAUVAGE: bone dry. Such wines are very rare.
BRUT: dry.
EXTRA SEC or EXTRA DRY: marginally less dry.
SEC: less dry again.
DEMI-SEC: medium, or half dry.
DOUX or RICH: sweet.

Opening a bottle of sparkling wine

Handle a bottle of sparkling wine as little as possible in the hours before serving – otherwise the cork may fly out dangerously as it is removed. When opening the bottle, have a cloth and a glass handy – the cloth to grasp the cork and the glass to catch any wine that might bubble over when the cork comes out.

1 Stand the bottle on a table and tear off the foil. Grasp the neck of the bottle in one hand with your thumb held firmly over the top of the cork. Carefully undo the wire muzzle.

2 Take the bottle in both hands, one holding the base, the other grasping the cork in the cloth. Tilt the bottle at an angle of 45 degrees and gently twist the base – not the cork. The cork will gradually ease out.

3 Keeping the bottle tilted, pour out the first glass of wine. The bottle can then be set down on the table.

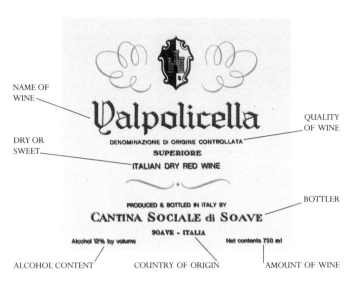

NAME OF WINE
DRY OR SWEET
QUALITY OF WINE
BOTTLER
ALCOHOL CONTENT
COUNTRY OF ORIGIN
AMOUNT OF WINE

USEFUL LABEL Even if you cannot taste a wine, its label should yield enough information to judge its style and quality.

UNDERSTANDING THE LABEL

By law the label on a wine must tell you the wine's country of origin, the amount of wine in the bottle or container (in litres and centilitres or millilitres), and the name and address of the bottler or brand owner. For wines from EEC countries, the label must also give the quality, assessed according to the system of quality control used in the country of origin.

Most labels will also give much more information – the region, for example, the vintage year if any, the grape variety if a single one predominates, and sometimes the alcohol content. It will also often be indicated if the wine is sweet or dry, on a neck label possibly, or with serving suggestions on the back.

COUNTRY BY COUNTRY

Most important wine-producing countries have systems of grading wine according to quality. How the wines are graded, however, and how the grade of a particular wine is indicated on its label varies considerably from country to country.

FRANCE

It is generally agreed that France produces the world's greatest wines – though not all French wines are superb. The better wines are labelled 'appellation contrôlée', a guarantee that a wine has been made in a particular region or district indicated on the label and using the grape varieties and wine-making methods traditional to the region. A red wine labelled 'appellation Bordeaux contrôlée', for example, has been made in the Bordeaux region from the traditional Bordeaux grapes.

The regions that are entitled to label their wines appellation contrôlée are strictly defined by law. They include, for example, Bordeaux and Burgundy. In addition there are many smaller districts, villages or even single vineyards within the larger regions which have traditions of producing distinctive wines of exceptional quality, and these too are entitled to their own appellations contrôlées. The Médoc, Graves, St-Emilion and Pomerol districts are included in the 90 or so different appellations within the Bordeaux region. Burgundy with over 200 different appellations contrôlées is the largest region.

The more specific the appellation, the better the wine. A wine labelled 'appellation Clos de la Roche contrôlée' (made on the 38 acre Clos de La Roche vineyard near the village of Morey-St-Denis in Burgundy) will be better than a wine simply labelled 'appellation Bourgogne contrôlée', made somewhere in Burgundy (Bourgogne).

Not all the wine-producing regions are entitled to an appellation. Second-ranking regions

which, nonetheless, have traditions of producing distinctive wines of reasonable quality can label their wines 'VDQS', *vin délimité de qualité supérieure*. *Vins de pays* come lower down the scale and are everyday wines from a specified area, while the most ordinary wines – accounting for about 65 per cent of France's total production – are the *vins de tables*, anonymous blends of wines coming mainly from southern France.

Generally in France, the more northerly the region and the cooler its climate, the fresher, fruitier and more fragrant the wine. The best-known, and generally most expensive, red wines are the reds of Bordeaux – known in Britain as 'clarets' – and those of Burgundy. The most famous still, dry white wines come from Burgundy. There are also, however, many excellent but much cheaper French wines.

GERMANY

The ripeness of the grapes from which German wines are made is the crucial factor in determining the wines' quality and style. The riper the grapes (and so the higher the level of sugar in them), the better the resulting wine. The best German wines are rich and sweet.

Lying so far north, German vineyards do not always have enough sunshine for their grapes to ripen fully. When this happens, sugar may be added – but only to make ordinary wines,

INFORMATIVE BOTTLE SHAPES A *wine can often be identified initially by its bottle. Certain bottle shapes are traditionally associated with particular European wine regions. Here, from left to right, are a high-shouldered bottle of the kind used for Bordeaux wines, a sloping-shouldered Burgundy bottle, a tall thin brown* German hock bottle, a similar but taller green Alsace bottle, a club-shaped bottle of the kind used for Provence wines, and a champagne bottle especially strong to withstand the pressure.

French and German wine makers also follow some colour conventions: sweet white Bordeaux wines are in clear bottles, red wines (clarets) and dry white wines in green bottles; German Moselle wines have green bottles, those from the Rhine Valley (hocks) have brown bottles.

Wine makers in other parts of the world use these traditional shapes, but they are not necessarily a guide to the type of wine.

not when making quality ones.

The most ordinary German wines are the *tafelweins*, equivalent to France's vins de table. If buying a tafelwein, check the label for the country of origin. Make sure that it is a *Deutscher* (German) *tafelwein*, not a blend of wines from other countries in the EEC: the EEC blends tend to be inferior. Slightly finer than the ordinary tafelwein is *landwein*, equivalent to France's vin de pays. Landweins are usually dry or medium dry and come

from a specific area; they are comparatively rare.

Quality wines of the lowest grade are labelled '*Qualitätswein bestimmter Anbaugebiete*' ('quality wine from a designated area'), usually abbreviated to QbA. The most common QbA wine is Liebfraumilch. This comes from certain specified regions, indicated on the label, and must be made predominantly with the Riesling, Müller-Thurgau or Silvaner grapes. Liebfraumilchs are not always remarkable in their

quality and it is best to avoid the cheaper ones.

The best German wines are labelled '*Qualitätswein mit Prädikat*' (QmP) – 'quality wine with special attributes'. They are further subdivided into QmP Kabinett wines, made simply with ripe grapes; Spätlese wines, made with late-gathered, very ripe grapes; Auslese wines, made with specially selected late-gathered grapes; and the most expensive and sweet Beerenauslese and Trockenbeerenauslese wines, made only from the ripest grapes with the highest concentration of sugar. Eisweins – literally 'ice wines' – are wines made from grapes that have been left on the vine until the winter frosts begin. The grapes are harvested and pressed while they are still frozen and produce intensely sweet wines.

Most of Germany's vineyards lie on either the Rhine or Moselle rivers. The labels on the better wines will generally indicate the grape varieties from which the wines are made. Look out for Rieslings. Wines made from Müller-Thurgau and Silvaner tend to be softer.

ITALY

In theory, the classification *Denominazione di origine controllata* (DOC) on an Italian wine should be equivalent to the French appellation contrôlée. In practice, the situation is not so simple because in the past controls have not been tight enough. DOCG – *Denominazione di origine controllata e garantita*

('and guaranteed') – is a more reliable sign of a wine of real quality. It indicates a wine from one of Italy's greatest wine-producing areas – a Chianti, for example, or a Barolo. Alternatively, choose a DOC wine labelled 'Classico', indicating that the wine comes from the heart of its region. *Riserva* means that the wine has been matured for longer.

Most Italian red wines are warm and round to the taste; the whites tend to lack refreshing acidity and need to be served very cold.

An Italian wine that is popular in this country but varies in quality is Lambrusco, traditionally from the region around Modena in northern Italy. Lambrusco can be red or white. Choose red Lambruscos in corked – not screw-topped – bottles, labelled DOC and indicating the district of origin. The best come from Sorbara and Grasparossa di Castelveltro. Most Lambrusco sold in this country is semi-sparkling.

SPAIN

Increasing amounts of good Spanish table wine are being sold in Britain. The classification *Denominación de origen* (DO) is equivalent to appellation contrôlée in France. *Reserva* indicates a wine that is at least five years old and has spent part of that time maturing in oak *barricas*, or barrels. *Gran Reserva* means that the wine has been aged even longer in wood.

The principal regions for red wine are Rioja (pronounced 'ree-ókha') and Penedès which both produce big, robust wines. Many of these wines are stored for a while in oak and have a distinctive oaky, vanilla flavour. Both areas also produce good white wines, most of which are light and fresh; but a few of the more traditional ones, which may also be matured in oak (Rioja's Marqués de Murrieta whites, for example), have a rounder and fuller flavour. Generally, with modern methods, Spanish wines are becoming lighter, fruitier and fresher.

PORTUGAL

The best-known Portuguese white table wines are the *vinhos verdes* ('green wines'), which are very light and slightly sparkling. Well-chilled, they are both refreshing and festive. The best-known reds are the full-bodied, mature reds from the Dão (pronounced roughly 'down') region. Also good are the slightly richer reds from the Bairrada region, west of Dão. The best-known Portuguese rosés, such as Mateus Rosé, are slightly sparkling like vinhos verdes.

Look out for wines labelled *reserva* or *garrafeira*, which have been matured longer. Portuguese wines can be excellent value for money.

OTHER COUNTRIES

Eastern European and New World wines are becoming increasingly popular. Look for the grape variety, or varieties, from which they are made to judge their character.

Recently, England has started producing wine commercially – all white wine. At their best, English wines have an attractively fresh, flowery flavour. They are generally named after their grape variety – Müller-Thurgau, for example.

STORING WINE

Wines used to be sold too young to drink, and customers were expected to mature them at home. Now, however, most wines are sold ready to drink straight away. Nonetheless, all

but the lightest-bodied and cheapest red wines will improve if you keep them.

The ideal place for storing wine is somewhere away from direct light or sun and with a constant, cool temperature. Store bottles on their sides to keep the corks moist. If the corks dry out, air will get into the bottle and spoil the wine. Special racks for storing wine bottles are widely available.

Do not keep wine long after opening the bottle. Most table wine will taste positively unpleasant after 24 hours. To lengthen its life a little, transfer any leftover wine into a clean half bottle leaving the wine in contact with as little air as possible. Even cooking wine should be kept in this way and will not last more than a few days.

For sparkling wines, special champagne stoppers are available which can be used to keep the sparkle in a partly empty bottle for 24 hours. Alternatively, cut two wedges at right angles to one another from the bottom of the original cork and force it back into the bottle.

Wine containers

Wine used to come only in bottles of standard size. Now you can buy it in bottles and containers of every conceivable size and shape, from those containing a single glass to wine boxes and huge 3 litre bottles.

When buying wine for a party, do not assume that huge, party-sized bottles are the best

		EUROPEAN WINE GRADINGS		
COUNTRY	ORDINARY TABLE WINE	REGIONAL TABLE WINE	QUALITY WINE	TOP-QUALITY WINE
FRANCE	Vin de table	Vin de pays	Vin délimité de qualité supérieure (VDQS)	Appellation contrôlée
GERMANY	Deutscher tafelwein	Landwein	Qualitätswein (QbA)	Qualitätswein mit Prädikat (QmP)
ITALY	Vino da tavola		Denominazione di origine controllata (DOC)	Denominazione di origine controllata e garantita (DOCG)
SPAIN	Vino de mesa		Denominación de origen (DO)	
PORTUGAL			Denominação de origen	

value for money. Large bottles are not always sold in sufficient quantities to cut the price significantly. On the other hand, a wine in standard-sized bottles – 70–75cl (about 1¼ pints) – may be a shop's best-selling wine and, per glassful, the most reasonably priced. Allow half to three-quarters of an ordinary bottle of wine per person. See also *Drinks parties* (page 156).

For a dinner party, buy wine in ordinary bottles or two-bottle magnums. Allow half to three-quarters of an ordinary bottle per person.

Wine in wine boxes tends to be more expensive because of the sophisticated technology that keeps the wine fresh for up to three months after it has been broached. But they are good for people who like a glass of wine every once in a while even though they are never a good buy for parties.

SERVING WINE

Wine has always been surrounded by much unnecessary mystique. But there are some basic rules designed to make the most of any wine.

TEMPERATURE
White, sparkling and rosé wines can become positively numbed by being served too cold. If one of these wines has been stored at room temperature, an hour or two in the door of the refrigerator usually chills it enough – or, for more rapid chilling, 10 minutes in a bucket or basin of

cold water and ice. In dire emergencies, put the wine very briefly in the freezer – but for no more than 5 minutes.

When the term 'room temperature' was coined to describe the ideal serving temperature for red wines, there was no central heating and houses were much cooler. Red wine kept anywhere other than the refrigerator or cellar will be quite warm enough to serve. If it is stored in a cellar, bring it into the main part of the house at least 2 hours before it will be needed.

Corkscrews
Choose a corkscrew with an open spiral – not one with a screw-like spiral on a solid shaft. Solid shaft corkscrews tend simply to push bits of the cork, or worse still the whole cork, down into the bottle. Try also to get a corkscrew with some form of leverage to help you pull the cork out of the bottle such as the waiter's friend, Screwpull or double-action corkscrew (often made in boxwood).

If, in spite of everything, the cork disintegrates and falls into

IDEAL SPIRAL A corkscrew should be strong with an open spiral rather than a screw-like solid shaft, which is liable to split the cork.

GLASSES FOR WINES A wine glass should be narrower at the rim than in the body, to retain the bouquet of the wine. It should be clear so that you can see the colour of the wine, and have a stem so that the heat of your hand does not affect the temperature of the wine.

Here, from left to right, are: two glasses suitable for either red or white wine, although white wine is usually drunk from the smaller glass so that it does not lose its chill in the glass; a champagne flute (tall, to retain the bubbles); a hock glass, from the Moselle Valley in Germany; and a

Paris goblet, which is suitable for all types of table wine.

Champagne glasses are generally filled to near the rim so that the bubbles do not disperse quickly. With all other wines, however, the glass should be half filled. If it is full the wine's bouquet will be lost.

the bottle, it will not do the wine any harm. But the wine will look better if you decant it, straining off the bits of cork with a sieve or tea strainer.

Letting wine breathe
Almost all medium to full-bodied red wines will grow softer and develop a more mellow bouquet if exposed to the air for a while before being served. Open the bottle 2 hours or so before serving and leave the wine to breathe inside its own bottle. If you are short of time you can open the bottle about 15 minutes before serving and either transfer

the wine to another clean container, or simply pour out two or three glasses of wine.

Old wines also, occasionally need decanting to separate them from any sediment. Leave the bottle upright for a few hours to let the sediment settle at the bottom. Then, keeping the shoulder of the bottle in a beam of light from a torch or candle, pour the wine carefully and in one movement into another container. As soon as the light shows sediment appearing in the neck, stop pouring.

If a bottle of wine has a rotten cork, this will affect the wine

making it taste flat, lacking any distinctive smell or in some cases have a sharp, chlorine smell. Such wine is said to be 'corked', and should be returned to the wine shop.

WINE WITH FOOD

There are few hard-and-fast rules about which wine goes with which food. Generally, you should match like with like – a light wine with a delicate dish, for example. If you are having fish in a light creamy sauce, a big, powerful red wine will be inappropriate – it will simply overpower the food and drown its flavours. Instead, you might serve, for example, a medium-weight dry white wine. But do not be afraid to experiment, trying different wines with different foods.

Certain types of food kill the flavour of any wine served with them. They include strong vinaigrette dressings which make wine taste sour; eggs and chocolate, both of which coat the mouth and so make the appreciation of wine almost impossible; and strongly spiced dishes and curries, which are too strong for any wine. If you include these foods in a menu, just omit the wine with that particular course.

If you are serving more than one wine with a meal, the usual order is first white wine, then red wine and finally sweet white wine. A delicate white wine would be swamped if it came after a stronger red wine, which in its turn would be swamped after a sweet white wine.

As an apéritif before a meal, serve a dry white wine, a dry sherry or vermouth, or a chilled light-bodied red such as Beaujolais. After a meal, it is traditional to drink sweeter fortified wines such as port or Madeira. If you have been drinking medium or full-bodied red wine with the meal, you can continue drinking that.

Fine sparkling wines, such as champagne, can be drunk before, after or even during the meal; they go well with most foods. Full-bodied red wines are not good for drinks parties.

TYPES OF WINE

These are well-known examples of different styles of wine, but it is worth trying some of the many lesser-known wines that are available.

LIGHT-BODIED REDS: Beaujolais, young Chianti, Valpolicella, Gamay, Merlot.

MEDIUM-BODIED REDS: 'cru' Beaujolais, young Bordeaux, young Burgundy, Rioja, Penedès, Eastern European and Californian Cabernet Sauvignons.

FULL-BODIED REDS: older Bordeaux, older Burgundy, Barbaresco, Barolo, Dão, Syrah, Californian Zinfandel, Australian Shiraz.

LIGHT DRY WHITES: Alsace Pinot Blanc and Riesling, Bourgogne Aligoté, Entre-Deux-Mers, Loire white (such as Anjou, Muscadet and Saumur), Soave, new-style Rioja and Penedès white, vinho verde.

FULL DRY WHITES: older Burgundy, Gewürztraminer, old-style white Rioja, most Californian and Australian whites.

MEDIUM-DRY WHITES: German tafelweins and QbA and QmP Kabinett wines, Laski, Olasz and Wälsch Riesling, Riesling Italico, English whites.

SWEET WHITES: Barsac, sweet Sauternes, Muscat, Monbazillac, German QmP wines, Hungarian Tokay.

ROSÉS: Anjou, Provence and Tavel.

CHOOSING THE WINE FOR YOUR MEAL

KIND OF FOOD		LIGHT-BODIED RED	MEDIUM-BODIED RED	FULL-BODIED RED	LIGHT DRY WHITE	FULL DRY WHITE	MEDIUM-DRY WHITE	SWEET WHITE	ROSÉ
PASTA	With fish sauce				•		•		
	With meat sauce	•	•	•					
	With cream sauce					•	•		
FISH	Shellfish				•				•
	On own or with bland sauce	•			•	•	•		
	With strong sauce	•			•	•			
WHITE MEAT (Chicken, turkey, pork or veal)	Grilled, fried, poached	•			•	•	•		•
	Roast	•			•	•			
	With bland sauce				•	•	•		
	With strong sauce		•				•		•
RED MEAT (Beef, mutton or lamb)	Roast		•	•					
	Stews or pies			•					
OTHER MAIN COURSES	Cold meat	•			•	•	•		•
	Game		•	•					
	Egg dishes	Do not serve wine							
	Mild spicy food				•				
	Strongly spicy food	Serve lager							
	Chinese food					•	•	•	•
SALAD	With vinaigrette	Do not serve wine							
	With other dressings	•					•		•
DESSERTS	Chocolate desserts	Do not serve wine							
	Other desserts							•	
CHEESE	Soft cheese	•			•	•	•	•	
	Hard or blue cheese		•	•				•	

Dinner Parties & Lunch Parties

IN 1817 the Prince Regent gave a dinner at the Brighton Pavilion. It began with four different kinds of soup, and proceeded via a fish stew, trout, turbot and eel to ham, goose, truffled chicken and veal. These were pursued by 36 entrées, which included salmon, partridges and sirloin of beef. That was the first course. There followed eight pastry reproductions of famous buildings, then roasts of goose, duck and partridge. Close behind came lobster, oysters, cakes and soufflés – a further 32 courses in all. However, no one was really expected to eat this formidable array. It was a relic of the kind of dinners served in great houses since the Middle Ages, in which a different dish was set before each person present, who then shared it with his neighbours.

By Victoria's reign, this custom had been largely replaced by the 'service à la russe', in which a first servant offered meat from the sideboard, a second vegetables, a third sauces and so on. Old-fashioned people complained that this was the death-knell of conversation, but it forms the pattern of our meals today.

As the number of dishes offered has changed down the centuries, so has the hour of dinner – meaning the main meal of the day. In early medieval courts it was at 9am, while Louis XIII in the 17th century ordained it should be two hours later. Elizabeth I thought 2pm was a suitable hour, and nowadays it may be almost any time at all. Each age, however, probably agrees with Lord Byron:

Albeit all human history attests
That happiness for Man – the hungry
  sinner –
Since Eve ate apples, much depends on
  dinner.

Planning & Preparation

A special dinner or lunch party is like a small-scale theatrical production – food, setting and guests coordinated so that everyone feels comfortable, entertained, and well-fed but not over-fed. It provides the cook with an opportunity to be a little extravagant in a way which is not practical at larger parties. As with most entertaining the secret lies in thorough advance planning so that when the time of the party arrives, everything runs without a hitch and – most important – the cook can join in the party rather than being an absent member spending long stretches in the kitchen.

Invitations

Resist the temptation to invite more people than you can fit comfortably round your table – eight is usually the maximum. Bear in mind also that cooking for more than eight is a chore requiring extremely efficient organisation. Family are the exception to the rule. They do not usually mind being crammed around a table or being asked to help with the cooking.

Invite people to arrive about an hour before the time you plan to eat. This allows time for introductions and aperitifs, and for latecomers. When you issue the invitation, tell the guests what time you plan to eat: 7.30 for 8.30 for example, or 12.00 for 1.00. Do not allow much longer than an hour for pre-dinner drinks – the guests will start to become restless, and it will also throw your timing.

If you issue the invitation by telephone more than a few days in advance it is wise to send a written reminder.

Planning the menu

Take into account time of day, season and the number of guests when planning the menu. It is not too early to do this as soon as your guests have accepted.

For a weekend dinner party you will probably have a whole day to prepare. For a lunch party or weekday dinner party you will have to allow for some preparation the day before. Select at least one course that can be prepared completely in advance. Do not plan a meal that leaves you with too much to do at the last minute – making a temperamental sauce, for example.

The usual number of courses for a dinner party in this country is three or four – first course, main course, pudding and maybe cheese. But there is nothing to prevent you adding a salad course, for example, or leaving out the pudding, or serving only two courses. If you work slowly, or are easily confused by inter-ruptions, plan a menu with few courses. Do not be tempted to be overambitious. The menus in the chapter that follows all have first courses and puddings that require some preparation, but you could always replace a first course with half an avocado or a slice of melon, or the pudding with a bowl of cherries or fresh peaches.

If you serve a salad as a separate course, the best stage in the meal is after the main course where it refreshes the palate, and before the pudding. In France, cheese is often served before the pudding as well (see *Cheese*, pages 113-116).

It is usual to provide bread with the first course unless something similar – Melba toast, for example – is included.

Choose the main course first. It is safest to choose one that you can be reasonably sure will be liked by most guests. Liver dishes, for example, and curries are best avoided unless you are cooking for people you know well. While it is sensible not to serve an untried dish for a dinner party in case it goes wrong, part of the fun of giving a dinner party is the chance to try a dish that is a bit more expensive or time-consuming than you would usually cook. Few people can afford to give such a dish a trial run. It is a better policy to stick to tried techniques. Do not launch on a soufflé, for example, unless you have made one before.

Once you have chosen the main course, fit the other courses round it. Balance colour and texture and ingredients. See also the *Menu planner* (page 407).

Think each course through carefully as you plan. Take into account how you will keep it hot or chilled, and what china and cutlery will be needed. If you do not have enough plates and cutlery to avoid washing up between courses, borrow some.

Organisation

Once you have fixed the menu write it out clearly, together with a preparation checklist and timetable, and pin it up in a prominent position in the kitchen. Tick off each item on the list as you go along.

Aim to have all preparation in advance completed well before the guests are due to arrive – this includes laying and decorating the table (see *The table*, pages 246-248), setting out the drinks, warming the plates, chilling or uncorking the wine (see *Wine*, pages 181-188), clearing up the kitchen and putting ready everything you need for any last-minute cooking.

Keep plates and dishes hot in a warming drawer of the oven, a hostess trolley, a low oven, or – failing that – immersed in a sink of very hot water.

At the end of the meal, coffee and liqueurs can either be served at the table or used as an opportunity to move people into another room. If coffee is served at table encourage the guests to change places.

SOUPS, STARTERS & SAVOURIES

QUAIL EGGS IN SHERRY JELLY

It is important not to overcook quail eggs. They are less than one-third the size of a hen egg and need only 30 seconds for soft-boiling, otherwise they will be too hard. The mottled beige and brown eggs are often sold in delicatessens, butchers' shops and fishmongers.

Quail eggs in jelly can be made a day in advance and kept in the refrigerator. Bring them out into room temperature 15 minutes before serving and add the topping of soured cream and lumpfish roe.

PREPARATION TIME: *20 minutes*
CHILLING TIME: *2-3 hours*

INGREDIENTS – *serves 8:*
1¼ *pints (725 ml) beef*
  consommé
5 *tablespoons medium dry sherry*
3 *level teaspoons powdered*
  gelatine
24 *quail eggs*
¼ *pint (150 ml) soured cream*
4 *level teaspoons black lumpfish*
  roe

Heat the consommé gently in a pan until it melts, then remove from the heat.

Put 2 tablespoons of the sherry into a small bowl and sprinkle into the gelatine. Stand the bowl in a saucepan of hot water and stir until the gelatine has dissolved. Stir into the consommé with the rest of the sherry and then leave to cool.

While the consommé is cooling, bring a pan of water to a steady boil. Lower the quail eggs into the water – a chip basket makes it possible to lower them all at once – bring back to the boil and cook for just 30 seconds. Remove the eggs and run them quickly under a cold tap to cool them and stop them cooking any further. Allow to cool for a few minutes. Carefully shell the eggs, then place 3 eggs in each of 8 deep ramekin dishes, and fill up the dishes with the consommé. Chill in the refrigerator for 2-3 hours until set.

Carefully spread a dessertspoon of soured cream over the top of each dish and garnish with a ½ teaspoon of lumpfish roe. Serve with fingers of brown bread and butter.

This dish is included in a menu on page 245.

BURIED TREASURE Dainty beige and brown quail eggs, very lightly boiled, are shelled, then hidden in ramekins beneath sherry-flavoured jelly. Once the jelly has set, each dish is topped with soured cream and garnished with lumpfish roe.

ARTICHOKE AND MARTINI SOUP

Martini is a variety of vermouth – a fortified wine flavoured with herbs and spices. The name vermouth is derived from the German word *Wermut*, meaning 'wormwood' – an aromatic plant which is used for flavouring the liqueur absinthe, as well as in vermouth. There are different vermouths – each company closely guards the secret of its particular blend – but if Martini is not available another dry vermouth can be used instead.

Tinned artichoke hearts give just as good a flavour as the hearts of fresh globe artichokes and save time and trouble.

For a very special occasion, present the soup in bowls set inside other slightly larger bowls containing crushed ice. This keeps the soup ice cold.

PREPARATION AND COOKING
   TIME: *45 minutes*
CHILLING TIME: *3-4 hours or
   overnight*

INGREDIENTS – *serves 8:*
1 small onion, finely chopped
1 oz (25 g) butter
*2 × 15 oz (425 g) tins
   artichoke hearts*
*1½ pints (850 ml) chicken stock
   (page 367)*
*Salt and freshly ground black
   pepper*
½ pint (285 ml) double cream
6 tablespoons dry Martini
*2 level tablespoons coarsely
   chopped parsley*
GARNISH
2-3 tablespoons double cream OR
   *about 1 level tablespoon
   chopped parsley*

In a large pan, fry the onion gently in the butter for 4 minutes until transparent.

Thoroughly drain the artichoke hearts. Chop roughly, then add them to the onion and continue to fry gently for a further 2 minutes. Add the chicken stock and salt and pepper to taste. Bring to the boil, then simmer gently for 5 minutes. Blend in a liquidiser or food processor until smooth, or press through a sieve, then leave in a bowl to cool.

Whip the cream lightly until it has thickened but is not yet standing in peaks. Mix it into the cool soup. Stir in the Martini and the chopped parsley. Chill for 3-4 hours, or overnight.

To serve, pour into small bowls. Swirl a little cream into each bowl, or sprinkle with chopped parsley, and serve immediately. This dish is included in a menu on page 208.

GLITTERING BOWL *A fresh, creamy soup of artichoke hearts, flavoured with vermouth, can be sprinkled with chopped parsley, and served on a bed of crushed ice.*

CHESTNUT SOUP

Fresh chestnuts usually begin to appear in the shops towards the beginning of October. Some are easy to peel, but with others it can be a very tedious process. Roasting is usually all that is needed to loosen the shiny outer shell and the brown inner skin. However, the inner skins of some chestnuts are very stubborn. In this case, put the chestnuts into a pan of cold water with a little cooking oil, after removing the shells. Bring the water to the boil then turn the heat down very low so that the water is barely simmering. Remove a few chestnuts at a time, so that they stay warm, and rub off the skins.

Tinned whole chestnuts, well drained, can be used instead of fresh chestnuts. They do not need peeling. Parsley can be used if chervil is unavailable.

PREPARATION TIME: *1 hour*
COOKING TIME: *20 minutes*
OVEN TEMPERATURE: *preheat to
   180°C (350°F, gas mark 4)*

INGREDIENTS – *serves 6:*
1 lb (450 g) fresh chestnuts
*1 pint (570 ml) chicken stock
   (page 367)*
4 tablespoons brandy
1 pint (570 ml) milk
*Salt and freshly ground black
   pepper*
1 level tablespoon chopped chervil
1 oz (25 g) butter
¼ pint (150 ml) single cream

Using a sharp knife, make a short cut in the shell of each chestnut. Put the chestnuts onto a baking tray and roast them in the preheated oven for about 6 minutes. While they are still warm, peel off the shells and rub off the brown inner skins. If the chestnuts get cold and difficult to peel, return them to the oven for a few minutes.

Put the chestnuts into a pan with the chicken stock and simmer for 20 minutes until tender when pierced with a knife. Blend the chestnuts and stock to a smooth purée in a liquidiser or food processor, or push them through a food mill or coarse sieve.

Put the purée into a saucepan and stir in the brandy, milk, salt and pepper to taste and the chervil. Bring to the boil, stirring continuously. Beat in the butter and the cream and heat through gently. Serve piping hot with croutons (page 286).

GARLIC AND PINE KERNEL TARTLETS

Pine kernels are extracted from the cones of the stone pine – the tall umbrella-shaped tree of Italian Renaissance paintings. They can be bought in delicatessens, Italian food shops, and some health food shops.

The tartlets can be assembled the night before, ready to be baked. Let the pastry cases go cold before filling them.

PREPARATION TIME: *30 minutes*
COOKING TIME: *30-35 minutes*
OVEN TEMPERATURE: *preheat to 190°C (375°F, gas mark 5)*

INGREDIENTS – *serves 4:*
8 oz (225 g) rich shortcrust pastry (page 392)
5 oz (150 g) unsalted butter
6 cloves garlic, peeled
4 level tablespoons grated Parmesan cheese
1 level tablespoon chopped fresh basil
4 level tablespoons pine kernels, roughly chopped
Freshly ground black pepper
Beaten egg
GARNISH
Sprigs of fresh basil

Roll out the pastry and use it to line four individual fluted flan tins, about 4in (100mm) in diameter. Press the pastry well up the edges of the tins. Chill the pastry cases in the refrigerator for 30 minutes.

To make the filling, put the butter, garlic, Parmesan cheese and chopped basil into a liquidiser or food processor and blend until smooth. The ingredients can alternatively be pounded with a pestle and mortar until smooth. Mix in the pine kernels and add pepper to taste. Chill the filling in a covered container in the refrigerator.

Line the pastry cases with kitchen foil and baking beans. Bake blind (page 393) in the preheated oven for 10 minutes.

Remove the foil and beans, and brush the rims of the pastry cases with beaten egg. Divide the garlic butter filling between the pastry cases. Bake in the preheated oven for 20–25 minutes until the pastry is golden-brown. The hot filling may seep into the pastry – this gives the

PINE PERFECT *Tartlets of melting shortcrust pastry are filled with chopped pine kernels, Parmesan cheese, garlic, butter and basil.*

tartlets their characteristic rich flavour and appearance.

Remove from the tins and serve immediately, garnished with fresh basil. This dish is included in a menu on this page.

Use wholemeal flour and free-range eggs.

IN ADVANCE The night before, make the vinaigrette and prepare the tartlets.

ON THE DAY Allow 1½-2 hours for preparations, plus time to soak the beans for the dal. Prepare the roulade ingredients and the filling in advance, but do not bake it until after the first course has been eaten.

TO DRINK A white wine that is not too dry, such as a Moselle or Hock.

M E N U

Spring Lunch for Four

MANGETOUT
AND
BRIE MOUSSE
this page

CHAMPAGNE
SHRIMP RISOTTO
page 206

GREEN SALAD

GERANIUM CREAM
page 243

IN ADVANCE The day before, make the geranium cream and the mangetout and Brie mousse.

ON THE DAY Allow about 1½ hours to make the risotto. While it is cooking prepare the salad and the dressing but do not toss them together until just before serving. When the risotto is cooked, keep it covered over very low heat while you eat the mangetout and Brie mousse.

TO DRINK Pink champagne or dry pink sparkling wine.

MANGETOUT AND BRIE MOUSSE

Tender *mangetout* – the name means 'eat all' in French – are baby peas in baby pods. They are also known as sugar peas. Frozen mangetout can be used. Blue Brie or Cambazola can be used instead of ordinary Brie. The mousse can be made up to 24 hours in advance.

PREPARATION AND COOKING
   TIME: *45 minutes*
CHILLING TIME: *3-4 hours*

INGREDIENTS – *serves 4:*
4 oz (115 g) mangetout
*6 oz (175 g) Brie, weighed after
   the rind has been cut off*
8 oz (225 g) curd cheese
1 small clove garlic, peeled
¼ pint (150 ml) single cream
¼ teaspoon French mustard
*Salt and freshly ground black
   pepper*
2 eggs, separated
4 tablespoons water
*3 level teaspoons powdered
   gelatine*
GARNISH
Lemon slices

Top, tail and string the mangetout if necessary. Rinse and put them into a saucepan with 4 tablespoons of water. Cover with a lid and bring just to the boil, then simmer gently for 4 minutes. Drain them and rinse under cold running water.

Carefully slit down one side of each mangetout and open it out flat, removing the peas

inside. Keep the peas on one side. Line a small greased terrine or 1lb (450g) loaf tin with the best pods. Discard the rest.

Put the Brie, curd cheese, garlic, cream, mustard and salt and pepper into a liquidiser or food processor and blend until smooth. Blend in the egg yolks.

Put the water into a small bowl and sprinkle in the gelatine. Stand the bowl in a pan of hot water and stir until the gelatine has dissolved. Mix the gelatine evenly into the cheese and egg yolk mixture.

Whisk the egg whites until

EMERALD MANTLE A brilliant green layer of tender mangetout pods cloaks a mousse of Brie and curd cheese, served here with lemon mayonnaise.

stiff but not dry. Fold them lightly but thoroughly into the cheese mixture, with the reserved peas from the mangetout. Spoon the mousse into the lined terrine or loaf tin. Chill for 3-4 hours until set.

Carefully unmould the set mousse onto a dish. Garnish with lemon slices. This dish is included in a menu on this page.

BASIL AND MOZZARELLA PANCAKES

Fresh basil gives the best flavour to these pancakes, it can easily be grown in a pot on the windowsill. The pancakes can be made up to 2 days in advance and kept, wrapped, in the refrigerator ready for filling.

PREPARATION TIME: *1 hour*
STANDING TIME: *30 minutes*
COOKING TIME: *15 minutes*
OVEN TEMPERATURE: *preheat to
   190°C (375°F, gas mark 5)*

INGREDIENTS – *serves 6:*
4 oz (115 g) plain flour
1 egg
¼ pint (150 ml) milk
¼ pint (150 ml) water
*Salt and freshly ground black
   pepper*
*2 level tablespoons chopped fresh
   basil OR 2 level teaspoons dried
   basil*
Oil for cooking
Anchovy paste
*8 oz (225 g) Mozzarella cheese,
   thinly sliced*
6 slices Parma ham
½ pint (285 ml) single cream
*2 level tablespoons grated
   Parmesan cheese*

Sieve the flour into a bowl. Make a well in the centre, add the egg and half the milk and beat to a smooth paste. Beat in the remaining milk and the water. Season with salt and pepper to taste, and stir in the basil. Cover the batter and leave to stand for 30 minutes.

Using a 6-7in (150-180mm) pancake pan or heavy-based frying pan, make 12 pancakes (page 390). Slide the first pancake out of the pan onto a plate lined with non-stick baking paper, then stack the other pancakes on top, as they are made, interleaved with sheets of non-stick baking paper.

Spread each pancake with about a mustard spoon of anchovy paste. Top with Mozzarella and half a slice of ham, and roll up. Lightly grease an ovenproof dish. Place the filled pancakes in the dish, spoon over the cream, sprinkle with the Parmesan cheese and season with salt and pepper.

Bake in the preheated oven for 15 minutes, until the Parmesan cheese has melted and the top is lightly golden.

SOFT CHEESE GALETTE

Any similar combination of soft cheeses can be sandwiched between the layers of puff pastry in this galette.

The puff pastry can be baked up to 48 hours in advance and kept wrapped in kitchen foil.

PREPARATION TIME: *35 minutes plus cooling time*
COOKING TIME: *25-30 minutes*
OVEN TEMPERATURE: *preheat to 200°C (400°F, gas mark 6)*

INGREDIENTS – *serves 6:*
14 oz (400 g) prepared weight puff pastry (page 394)
Beaten egg
2 level tablespoons freshly grated Parmesan cheese
3 oz (75 g) butter, softened
1 large clove garlic, crushed
Salt and freshly ground black pepper
1 level tablespoon chopped fresh tarragon
3 oz (75 g) Bleu de Bresse, softened
3 oz (75 g) Montrachet, softened
2 oz (50 g) Petit-Suisse, softened

Roll out the puff pastry to a rectangle about 9in × 16in (230mm × 405mm). Cut it into 4 even-sized rectangles about 9in × 4in (230mm × 100mm). Place the pastry rectangles on two dampened baking sheets. Glaze with beaten egg and sprinkle with the grated Parmesan cheese. Bake in the preheated oven for 15-20 minutes, until crisp and golden. Remove from the oven and leave it until it is quite cold. If the pastry rectangles have lost their shape, trim them.

Mix the softened butter with the garlic, salt and pepper to taste, and the chopped tarragon. Spread three of the pastry layers evenly with the flavoured butter. Spread one buttered layer with the Bleu de Bresse, one with the Montrachet, and one with Petit-Suisse. Assemble the layers one on top of the other, finishing with the plain pastry layer. Wrap carefully but securely in kitchen foil. The galette can be assembled up to 3 hours in advance.

Cook in the oven – still heated to 200°C (400°F, gas mark 6) – for 8-10 minutes to soften the cheeses and warm the pastry through. Serve piping hot. Cut it into slices with a sharp serrated bread knife.

This dish is included in a menu on page 217.

GRILLED HALUMI CHEESE WITH MINT

Throughout Greece, and in many parts of the Middle East, there are street cafés which sell aromatic grilled or fried cheese like this. If Halumi cheese is not available, Feta, which is similar, can be used instead.

PREPARATION TIME: *30 minutes*
COOKING TIME: *3-4 minutes*

INGREDIENTS – *serves 6:*
1 bunch of fresh mint (see method)
Cooking oil
1 lb 2 oz (500 g) Halumi cheese
4 tablespoons olive oil
2 cloves garlic, crushed
Freshly ground black pepper
GARNISH
Wedges of lemon

Turn on the grill to medium heat.

Strip the leaves from the bunch of mint. Chop enough of the leaves to give you 2 level tablespoons of chopped mint. Set it aside. Lay the mint stalks in the base of the grill pan and lay the rack over the top. Brush the rack well with cooking oil.

Cut the Halumi cheese into cubes of about 1in (25mm). It is often rather crumbly, and it is easier to cut if you use a damp knife. Place the cubes of cheese on the oiled rack, and sprinkle with half the chopped mint.

Place under the preheated grill, and cook until the cheese softens and colours slightly – about 3-4 minutes. Do not overcook or it may lose its shape.

While the cheese is cooking, mix the remaining chopped mint with the olive oil, garlic and black pepper to taste.

To serve, spoon the grilled cheese onto small serving plates and sprinkle with the flavoured oil. Garnish with wedges of lemon and serve with warm pitta bread. This dish is included in a menu on page 219.

MEMORIES OF GREECE Cubes of grilled Halumi cheese are sprinkled with fresh mint, olive oil and garlic.

SPIEDINI DI TALEGGIO E FRUTTI DI MARE

The Italians have a number of dishes cooked on little skewers, or *spiedini*. In this one seafood (*frutti di mare*) is interspersed with cubes of Taleggio cheese and then deep-fried.

If Taleggio is difficult to find, Bel Paese can be used instead. Ordinary prawns can be used, but you will need to substitute 4 for each of the large Mediterranean ones used in this recipe.

PREPARATION TIME: *40 minutes*
MARINATING TIME: *4 hours or overnight*
COOKING TIME: *3 minutes*

INGREDIENTS – *serves 6:*
12 Mediterranean prawns, cooked and shelled
24 cooked mussels, shelled (page 377)
12 oz (350 g) Taleggio cheese, cut into cubes about ³/₄ in (20 mm)
Oil for deep-frying
MARINADE
4 tablespoons olive oil
Juice and grated rind of ¹/₂ lemon
1 level tablespoon chopped fresh rosemary
1 clove garlic, crushed
Salt and freshly ground black pepper
COATING
A little flour for dusting
2 eggs, beaten
4 level tablespoons fine dry breadcrumbs

SAUCE
2 oz (50 g) butter
Grated rind of 1 lemon
1 level tablespoon chopped fresh rosemary
1 clove garlic, crushed

Cut medium-sized prawns in half across, large prawns into three pieces. Put the prawns, mussels and cubes of cheese into a shallow dish.

FRUITS OF THE SEA Prawns and mussels are deep-fried with cubes of Taleggio cheese then sprinkled with hot lemon and butter sauce.

In a small bowl, mix the olive oil with the lemon rind and juice, rosemary, garlic and salt and pepper to taste. Spoon the marinade evenly over the seafood and cheese. Cover and leave in the refrigerator for 4 hours, or overnight.

Drain the seafood and cheese thoroughly, reserving all the marinade. Thread the seafood and cheese alternately onto 6 small kebab skewers – about 6in (150mm) long. Sieve a light, even coating of flour over each skewer. Dip each one into the beaten egg and then roll evenly in the fine breadcrumbs.

Deep-fry in oil heated to 180°C (350°F) for just 3 minutes (page 372). Drain thoroughly on kitchen paper. Keep warm.

To make the sauce, melt the butter in a small saucepan with the lemon rind, rosemary, garlic, and remaining marinade.

Arrange the cooked spiedini on a serving plate and spoon over the hot butter sauce. Serve immediately with crusty bread.

FEUILLETÉS D'ASPERGES

A perfect feuilleté should be so light that you scarcely know you are eating it. The name for these pastries comes from the French word *feuille* – a leaf.

Instead of six heart-shaped pastries, you can make 12 round pastries, cooked in bun tins. Pesto is an Italian basil sauce which can be bought ready-made from delicatessens.

The pastries can be shaped and filled 24 hours in advance. Do not make the sauce more than about 4 hours in advance.

PREPARATION TIME: *30 minutes*
COOKING TIME: *15 minutes*
OVEN TEMPERATURE: *preheat to 200°C (400°F, gas mark 6)*

INGREDIENTS – *serves 6:*
2-2¹/₂ lb (900 g-1.1 kg) young fresh asparagus OR 12 oz (350 g) tinned asparagus tips or spears
1 clove garlic, crushed
2 level tablespoons chopped pine kernels
2 level tablespoons roughly chopped parsley
Salt and freshly ground black pepper
2 egg yolks
13 oz (375 g) prepared weight puff pastry (page 394)
GLAZE
Beaten egg
SAUCE
¹/₄ pint (150 ml) plain yoghurt
1 clove garlic, crushed
1 teaspoon pesto sauce
2 oz (50 g) chopped walnuts
GARNISH
6 small cooked asparagus tips (see method)
Twists of lemon (page 286), lemon leaves, or small sprigs of basil

Prepare and cook the fresh asparagus (page 386). Drain it and cut off the tender green tips – discard the stems. If using tinned asparagus, drain it thoroughly. Set aside 6 asparagus tips for garnish. Beat the remaining asparagus tips in a bowl with the garlic, pine kernels, parsley, salt and pepper to taste, and the egg yolks.

Roll out the puff pastry on a lightly floured board to a thickness of about ¼in (5mm). Using a heart-shaped cutter, about 3½in (90mm) across, cut 12 hearts from the pastry. Line six heart-shaped tartlet tins with half the pastry shapes, pressing the pastry well up the edges of the tins. Brush the pastry edges with beaten egg.

Divide the asparagus filling between the pastry cases. Lay the remaining heart-shaped pieces of pastry over the filling, and press the edges together so that they are tightly sealed. Decorate the edge of the pastry by notching it with a knife or a fork. Glaze the pastry with beaten egg, then bake in the preheated oven for about 15 minutes, until puffed up and golden-brown.

To make the sauce, blend all the ingredients in a liquidiser or food processor until smooth. Add salt and pepper to taste.

Carefully remove the baked feuilletés from their tins and place each one on a small warmed plate. Spoon a small amount of the sauce beside each one. Garnish with asparagus tips and lemon twists or leaves, or sprigs of basil. This dish is included in a menu on this page.

LIGHT OF HEART Asparagus and pine kernels fill feather-light puff pastry hearts. They are served with a sauce of yoghurt and chopped walnuts, and garnished with lemon leaves and asparagus tips.

MENU

Midsummer Dinner for Eight

FEUILLETÉS D'ASPERGES
opposite page

SAUTÉED VEAL WITH REDCURRANTS AND CREAM
page 211

MANGETOUT

NEW POTATOES

RASPBERRY AND RATAFIA TERRINE
page 238

Increase the quantity of feuilletés by one-third and make eight.

IN ADVANCE The day before, make the terrine and the feuilletés (do not glaze them).

ON THE DAY Allow about an hour. Cook the vegetables and keep them warm. Cook the veal to the point before adding the redcurrants and cream. Glaze and cook the pastries.

After the first course, complete the veal.

TO DRINK Dry white wine.

LOBSTER PÂTÉ WITH ROSÉ SAUCE

Lobster makes a very rich and extravagant pâté. The meat can sometimes be bought loose, or it may be necessary to buy a whole lobster (page 376). A lobster weighing about 1½-1¾lb (700-800g) should yield about 12oz (350g) meat. Both the pâté and the sauce can be made a day in advance and then kept in the refrigerator.

PREPARATION TIME: *1 hour*
CHILLING TIME: *3-4 hours*

INGREDIENTS – *serves 8:*
12 oz (350 g) cooked lobster
meat, free of shell and
membrane
6 oz (175 g) full fat cream
cheese
2 tablespoons orange lumpfish roe
Yolks of 3 hard-boiled eggs
3 tablespoons dry vermouth
Salt and freshly ground black
pepper
½ pint (285 ml) double cream
2 tablespoons water
3 rounded teaspoons powdered
gelatine
2 level tablespoons chopped chives
8 small cooked asparagus spears,
fresh (page 386) or tinned
SAUCE
½ pint (285 ml) rosé wine
1 small shallot, finely chopped
1 level tablespoon chopped fresh
dillweed
½ pint (285 ml) soured cream
3 level tablespoons orange
lumpfish roe
Yolks of 2 hard-boiled eggs, sieved

GARNISH
8 small cooked asparagus spears,
fresh or tinned
Finely diced cucumber (either raw
or lightly poached)

Put the lobster meat (if you are using a whole lobster with roe include that as well) into a liquidiser or food processor with the cream cheese, lumpfish roe, egg yolks and vermouth and blend until smooth. Pour the mixture into a bowl, add salt and pepper to taste, and stir in the double cream until it is evenly blended.

Put the water into a small bowl and sprinkle in the gelatine. Stand the bowl in a pan of hot water and stir until the gelatine has dissolved. Stir into the lobster mixture and then leave on one side until it starts to thicken – this will take only 4-5 minutes, if the gelatine is not too hot. Fold in the chives.

Lightly grease 8 small individual moulds, ramekins or coffee cups, about 4-5fl oz (115-150ml)

LOBSTER WITH ROSÉ A creamy pink sauce flavoured with rosé wine, and flecked with orange lumpfish roe, accompanies a lobster pâté pierced with tender asparagus spears.

capacity, or one medium-sized terrine or loaf tin, about 2 pints (1.1 litres) capacity. Spoon half the mixture into the moulds or terrine, then lay the asparagus spears – whole or cut into shorter lengths – on top. Spread the remaining lobster mixture evenly over the asparagus. Chill in the refrigerator for 3-4 hours until set.

To make the sauce, put the rosé wine, shallot and dillweed into a small pan. Bring to the boil and simmer until the wine has reduced to about 2 tablespoons. Strain the wine and then leave to cool.

Mix the wine with the soured cream, lumpfish roe and sieved egg yolks. Chill in the refrigerator until needed. (Do not blend the sauce in a liquidiser or food processor – this will make it too thin.)

Remove the individual patés from their moulds. If you find you cannot remove them easily, dip the base of each mould very briefly in hot water to loosen it. If you have chosen to make one big paté, cut it into 8 slices and lay each slice on a plate. Trickle over a little of the pink sauce and garnish with the asparagus spears and diced cucumber. Serve the remaining sauce separately in a small jug.

SWEET AND SOUR FISH BALLS

Fish balls, poached in stock, are served with sweet and sour sauce. The fish balls can be shaped, and the sauce prepared, up to 6 hours in advance.

PREPARATION TIME: *1 hour*
CHILLING TIME: *1 hour*
COOKING TIME: *5-10 minutes*

INGREDIENTS – *serves 6:*
2 lb (900 g) white fish fillet,
skinned, boned and flaked
2 level tablespoons chopped
parsley
1 large clove garlic, peeled
1 tablespoon soya sauce
2 level tablespoons cornflour
2 egg yolks
Salt and freshly ground black
pepper
About 3-4 pints (1.7-2.3 litres)
chicken stock (page 367)
SAUCE
4 tablespoons white wine vinegar
1 tablespoon tomato purée
4 tablespoons orange juice
1 tablespoon soya sauce
4 tablespoons dry sherry
6 tablespoons chicken stock (page
367)
2 cloves garlic, cut into strips
1 slice fresh root ginger, cut into
thin strips
2 level tablespoons soft brown
sugar
1 level tablespoon cornflour
3 tablespoons olive oil
1 red pepper, seeded and cut into
thin strips
1 green pepper, seeded and cut
into thin strips

GARNISH
Shreds of spring onion or a few unshelled prawns

Put the flaked fish into a food processor, with the parsley, garlic, soya sauce, cornflour, egg yolks and salt and pepper, and blend until smooth, light and fluffy. It will probably be necessary to blend half the ingredients in one batch and then blend the remaining ingredients in a second batch. Chill the mixture for 30 minutes.

Line a baking sheet with lightly greased greaseproof paper or kitchen foil and fill a bowl with iced water. Dip your hands into the iced water and shape the fish mixture into even-sized balls, about 1in (25mm) in diameter. Place the fish balls on the prepared baking sheet, then cover with another layer of lightly greased greaseproof paper or foil. Chill for at least 30 minutes before cooking.

While the fish balls are chilling make the sauce. Put the wine vinegar, tomato purée, orange juice, soya sauce, dry sherry, stock, garlic and ginger into a pan. Bring to the boil and simmer for 3 minutes. Stir in the brown sugar until dissolved. Blend the cornflour to a paste with a little of the sauce. Stir into the hot sauce, then continue stirring over a gentle heat until the sauce has thickened and cleared.

Heat the olive oil in a frying pan and stir-fry (page 372) the strips of pepper for 2-3 minutes.

They should still be slightly crisp. Drain with a slotted spoon and add to the sauce.

Put enough chicken stock in a deep frying pan to give a depth of 1½in (40mm). Heat it to simmering point. Add the fish balls and poach gently for 3 minutes. (The stock must not boil.) Turn over and poach for a further 3-4 minutes.

Drain the fish balls well. Spoon them into a serving dish and cover with the prepared sauce. Serve immediately, garnished with the spring onion, or prawns. This dish is included in a menu on page 224.

MARINATED HALIBUT WITH WATERCRESS MOUSSELINE

Provided it is very fresh, raw fish is quite safe to eat. Monkfish can be substituted for halibut. Both the sauce and the fish can be prepared up to 24 hours in advance.

PREPARATION TIME: *25 minutes*
CHILLING TIME: *2 hours*

INGREDIENTS – *serves 4:*
1½ lb (700 g) boned halibut, skinned
Juice of 3 limes
Juice of 3 lemons
1 large clove garlic, crushed
1 tablespoon chopped fresh tarragon
Salt and freshly ground black pepper

WATERCRESS MOUSSELINE
1 bunch watercress, 3-4 oz (75-115 g)
¼ pint (150 ml) good mayonnaise, homemade (page 369) or ready-made
¼ pint (150 ml) double cream
GARNISH
Endive leaves

Cut the halibut into small cubes, about ¾in (20mm). Put them into a shallow dish and pour over the lime juice and lemon juice. Add the garlic, tarragon, and salt and pepper to taste. Turn the halibut in the mixture so that it is evenly coated. Cover and chill for 2 hours.

To make the sauce, separate the watercress into sprigs and cut off the stalks. Put the watercress sprigs, mayonnaise and double cream into a liquidiser or food processor and blend until smooth. Alternatively, chop the watercress very finely and beat it together with the mayonnaise and cream in a bowl.

Remove the fish from the refrigerator about 15 minutes before serving. Arrange on small plates on a bed of endive. Spoon a little of the marinating juices over each portion. Serve with the sauce, handed separately in a sauceboat, and warm pitta bread. This dish is included in a menu on page 204.

FRESH HALIBUT The tang of halibut marinated in lime and lemon juice contrasts with the smoothness of a pale green watercress sauce.

PRAWN MOUSSE WITH AVOCADO SAUCE

The moulds for this mousse should be about 6fl oz (175ml) in capacity. Metal sponge pudding moulds, or large coffee cups or ramekin dishes, will all be suitable. Double fillets are the two fillets from one side of a flatfish. The mousse can be made up to 24 hours in advance. The sauce can be made 4-6 hours in advance.

PREPARATION AND COOKING
    TIME: *2 hours*
CHILLING TIME: *2-3 hours*

INGREDIENTS – *serves 10:*
5 double fillets of lemon sole
2 level tablespoons finely chopped
    parsley
Salt and freshly ground black
    pepper
¾ pint (450 ml) dry white wine
12 oz (350 g) plaice fillets,
    skinned
8 oz (225 g) peeled prawns
Grated rind of 1 lemon
¾ pint (450 ml) single cream
6 level teaspoons powdered
    gelatine
10 medium-sized slices smoked
    salmon, about 1-1¼ lb (450-
    575 g)
SAUCE
2 small ripe avocado pears
14 fl oz (400 ml) fish stock, or
    light chicken stock (page 367)
1 clove garlic, peeled
GARNISH
Black lumpfish roe

MYSTERY MOUSSE Little rolls of sole fillet are concealed inside moulds lined with smoked salmon and filled with prawn mousse. The mousses are served with avocado sauce.

Cut each double fillet of sole in half lengthways. Remove the skin if this has not already been done. Sprinkle the skinned sides of each fillet with chopped parsley, and salt and pepper to taste, then roll it up like a swiss roll with the parsley on the inside. Secure each fillet with a wooden cocktail stick.

Lay the rolled fillets in a shallow pan and pour over the white wine. Bring it just to the boil, then cover the pan and simmer for 4-5 minutes until the sole is just tender. Lift the fillets from the pan with a slotted spoon and leave them to cool. Remove the cocktail sticks.

Lay the plaice fillets in the liquid remaining in the pan, simmer for 3 minutes then lift them out with a slotted spoon.

Put the cooked plaice into a liquidiser or food processor with the prawns, lemon rind and cream. Blend until smooth, then transfer to a bowl.

Strain ½ pint (285ml) of the fish cooking liquid into a bowl. Sprinkle in the gelatine. Stand the bowl in a saucepan of hot water and stir until the gelatine has dissolved. Stir the dissolved gelatine into the fish mixture then leave on one side until it starts to thicken (this will take about an hour). Add extra salt

and pepper if it is necessary.

Lightly grease 10 individual moulds. Line each with a slice of smoked salmon, cutting it to fit inside the mould. Do not cut off the excess salmon round the edges. Spoon in a little of the mousse mixture, add a rolled sole fillet, then fill the mould up to the top with more mousse. Fold any overlapping pieces of smoked salmon over the mousse. Chill for 2-3 hours until set.

To make the sauce, halve and stone the avocados and scoop out the flesh into a liquidiser or food processor. Add the stock and garlic. Blend until smooth, adding a little extra stock if necessary – the sauce should be quite thick. Season to taste with salt and pepper.

To serve, turn each mousse onto a small plate. Surround it with a pool of the avocado sauce. Garnish with lumpfish roe. This dish is included in a menu on page 236.

SWEETBREAD TERRINE WITH CREAM CHIVE SAUCE

Soft and white, with a fine, subtle taste, sweetbreads have for centuries been regarded as a delicacy. They come from the thymus glands, or sometimes the pancreas, of calves and lambs. Calf's sweetbreads are generally considered the choicer, but they can be difficult to find. Lamb's sweetbreads are more readily available and less expensive, but smaller.

For a less rich sauce, make it with single cream instead of soured cream, or half single cream and half yoghurt. The terrine can be made 24 hours in advance and kept in the refrigerator.

PREPARATION TIME: *50 minutes plus soaking, marinating and cooling time*
COOKING TIME: *40 minutes*
OVEN TEMPERATURE: *preheat to 160°C (325°F, gas mark 3)*

INGREDIENTS – *serves 6:*
6 oz (175 g) sweetbreads (calf's or lamb's)
3 tablespoons brandy
Salt and freshly ground black pepper
6 oz (175 g) lean veal
4 oz (115 g) boneless chicken
1 small onion, finely chopped
1 clove garlic, chopped
1 oz (25 g) butter
¼ pint (150 ml) single cream
Freshly grated nutmeg
2 egg yolks
1 level tablespoon finely chopped walnuts
SAUCE
¼ pint (150 ml) soured cream
2 level tablespoons chopped fresh chives
Salt and freshly ground black pepper

Soak the sweetbreads in lightly salted water for 30 minutes. Drain and put them into a pan with fresh cold water. Bring to the boil and simmer for 3 minutes, then rinse the sweetbreads under cold running water. Remove all skin and membrane and cut into even-sized pieces, about ¾in (20mm) square. Put the sweetbreads into a dish with the brandy, and salt and pepper to taste. Cover and leave to marinate in the refrigerator or a cool place for 1 hour.

Finely mince the veal and the chicken. Put them into a large bowl. Fry the onion and garlic gently in the butter for 3-4 minutes. Then mix them with the veal and chicken, cream, nutmeg, egg yolks, walnuts and salt and pepper to taste. Drain the sweetbreads and add the marinade to the mixture in the bowl.

Grease a small earthenware terrine or 1lb (450g) loaf tin and line with greaseproof paper. Spoon half the veal and chicken mixture into the terrine. Cover with the pieces of sweetbread and press them in. Spread with the remaining mixture. Smooth the surface level. Cover with a piece of greased foil, then stand the terrine in a roasting tin. Pour hot water into the roasting tin to come halfway up the sides of the terrine. Cook in the preheated oven for 40 minutes. Remove the terrine from the water bath and leave until cold.

While the terrine is cooling, make the sauce. Mix the soured cream with the chives, and add salt and pepper to taste.

Unmould the terrine carefully. Serve it cut in slices on individual plates with the sauce poured around each portion.

CARPACCIO WITH FRESH FIG PURÉE

Although slices of raw beef may sound more suited to a weight-lifter's diet than a dinner party, it in fact makes a lovely, light elegant first course.

The beef should be of the finest quality. Chilling it tightens the fibres and makes it easier to cut it into the very thin slices that are necessary. The beef should be sliced as close to serving time as possible because it darkens rapidly, losing its bright fresh colour.

PREPARATION TIME: *15 minutes*
CHILLING TIME: *30 minutes*

INGREDIENTS – *serves 4:*
8-12 oz (225-350 g) fillet of beef
4 large fresh figs
4 tablespoons Marsala or sweet sherry
GARNISH
4 tablespoons virgin green olive oil
4 fresh figs, cut into segments (page 397)

Trim the beef of any fat, then put it in a plastic bag and put it into the freezer, or the freezing compartment of the refrigerator, for just 30 minutes.

STEAK WITH FRESH FIGS *The subtle flavour of paper-thin slices of raw beef – carpaccio – is enhanced by a purée of fresh figs and Marsala.*

Blend the figs and Marsala together in a liquidiser or food processor until smooth.

Using a very sharp knife, cut the beef across the grain into paper-thin slices. Remove any sinews. Arrange the slices, over-lapping, on four plates and spoon some of the fig purée onto each portion. Trickle a little olive oil on top, and garnish with sections of fresh fig. Serve immediately. This dish is included in a menu on page 239.

FISH & SHELLFISH

BUTTERFLY SALMON

The salmon steaks for this dish are split and opened out (butterflied), then cooked in a heart-shaped papillote – a wrapping of foil which seals in all the flavours and aromas. These are released when the papillote is opened at the table. A food processor or liquidiser is needed to make the shrimp butter.

PREPARATION TIME: *45 minutes*
COOKING TIME: *15 minutes*
OVEN TEMPERATURE: *preheat to 200°C (400°F, gas mark 6)*

INGREDIENTS – *serves 4:*
2 large salmon steaks, about 1 in (25 mm) thick
1 leek, cut into long, narrow (julienne) strips
1 large carrot, peeled and cut into long, narrow strips
4 sprigs of fresh dillweed
Kitchen foil

SALMON VALENTINE Salmon steaks, split and opened out, are cooked together with prawn butter, leeks, carrots and dill, wrapped in a heart-shaped parcel of foil.

SHRIMP BUTTER
4 oz (115 g) peeled shrimps or prawns
2 small shallots, peeled and roughly chopped
3 oz (75 g) butter
Grated rind of ¼ lemon
2 tablespoons brandy
1 level tablespoon chopped fresh dillweed
Salt and freshly ground black pepper

Make the shrimp butter first. Put the shrimps, shallots, butter, lemon rind, brandy and chopped dillweed into the liquidiser or food processor and blend them together until smooth. Add salt and pepper to taste.

Lay the salmon steaks on a board. Cut each one in half, cutting down vertically along the line formed by the ribs, backbone and fin. Carefully remove the bones. Turn each piece of salmon onto the curved side with skin on it. Using a very sharp knife, cut down through each piece to within ½in (15mm) of the skin all along the curve, so that it is nearly divided into two. Carefully open out each salmon piece, gently pressing down both sides so that they lie flat on the board.

The salmon looks even more impressive if it is prepared without the skin, but this is more difficult to do.

Melt 1 tablespoon of the blended shrimp butter in a small

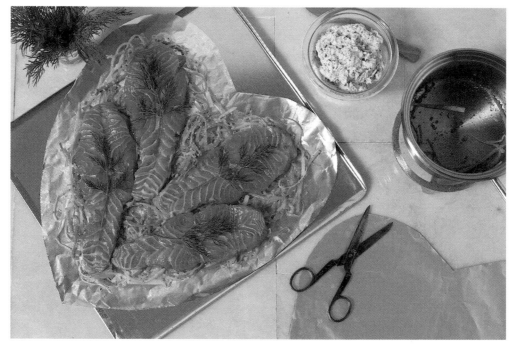

pan. Add the strips of leek and carrot and fry very gently for 4 minutes.

While the vegetables are frying, cut off about 30in (760mm) of kitchen foil and fold in half. Cut out two large heart shapes – about 14in (355mm) from top to bottom. Lightly oil the shiny side of one of the heart shapes of foil and place it on a baking sheet.

Spread the fried vegetables over the top of the foil heart, leaving a border of foil 1in (25mm) deep all the way round. Lay the butterfly salmon steaks on top, with a piece of dillweed on each. Dot all over with the rest of the shrimp butter. Cover with the other heart-shaped

piece of foil, dull side up. Fold the edges over to seal the pieces of foil together.

Place on a large baking sheet and bake in the preheated oven for 15 minutes. Carefully lift the papillote onto a flat serving dish and take it to the table still sealed. Cut open the papillote at the table and lift out each portion. Serve with plain boiled new potatoes, and a light green vegetable such as asparagus.

SALMON WITH CUCUMBER AND GREEN PEPPERCORNS

The early summer, from May to July when salmon is at its best, is the time to serve this dish. The sauce is delicate in flavour so that it does not overwhelm the flavour of the fish. If chervil is unavailable use tarragon or parsley instead.

PREPARATION AND COOKING TIME: *25 minutes*

INGREDIENTS – *serves 4:*
4 salmon steaks
4 fl oz (115 ml) water
4 fl oz (115 ml) dry white wine
2 bay leaves
12 green peppercorns
½ cucumber, peeled, seeded and diced
2 tablespoons double cream
2 oz (50 g) butter, cut into small pieces
GARNISH
Sprigs of chervil

Put the water, wine, bay leaves and peppercorns in a large frying pan and bring to the boil. Reduce the heat, put in the salmon and cucumber, cover loosely and simmer gently for about 10 minutes until the salmon flakes when pressed near the bone.

Remove the salmon and the cucumber from the pan and arrange on a warm serving dish. Keep them warm while you make the sauce.

Boil the liquid in the pan briskly until it has reduced in quantity by just over half. Remove the bay leaves. Reduce the heat and stir in the cream, then whisk in the butter pieces one by one until it is all blended smoothly into the sauce.

Pour the sauce around the fish and garnish with the sprigs of chervil. Serve immediately with new potatoes and a simple green salad or a green vegetable such as spinach or french beans.

SALMON IN RASPBERRY VINEGAR AND PINK PEPPERCORN SAUCE

The tartness of raspberries adds a refreshing tang to lightly poached salmon. Pink peppercorns can be bought from specialist grocers and delicatessens. If they are not available use green peppercorns instead.

The pink peppercorn sauce

can be prepared in advance. Just before serving, reheat the sauce and poach the salmon.

PREPARATION TIME: *30 minutes*
COOKING TIME: *15—20 minutes*

INGREDIENTS – *serves 4:*
4 small, thick salmon steaks
1 lb (450 g) raspberries, fresh or frozen
1 pint (570 ml) dry white wine
4-6 teaspoons redcurrant jelly
2 level teaspoons pink peppercorns
1 level tablespoon chopped fresh dillweed OR *1 1/2 teaspoons dried dillweed*
Salt

Cut each salmon steak in half, vertically, cutting right through the bone. Carefully remove all the bones and skin.

Put a few raspberries to one side for the garnish. Put the remaining raspberries into a pan with the white wine. Simmer for 10 minutes. Strain the liquid through a sieve.

Put the strained raspberry liquid into a large shallow pan. Add the redcurrant jelly, pink peppercorns, chopped dillweed and salt to taste. Stir over a gentle heat until the jelly has dissolved. Lay the pieces of salmon in the sauce. Cover and poach gently for 5-6 minutes.

Lift the cooked salmon onto a warm serving dish. Turn up the heat slightly and allow the sauce to bubble briskly for 1 minute. Spoon the sauce around the salmon and garnish with the reserved raspberries. This dish is included in a menu on page 239.

ROUGET À LA PROVENÇAL

Red mullet (*rouget de roche* in French) is of a different family from the cheaper grey mullet and has a much better flavour. It is a Mediterranean fish and is at its best during the summer. Red mullet is usually cooked whole, with all its multitude of tiny bones. In this recipe fillets are used, which are much easier to eat. The glorious, iridescent pale red skin should be left on the

FLAVOUR OF PROVENCE Shimmering red mullet are cooked with orange, wine, garlic, anchovies and thyme.

fillets. It is not difficult to fillet the fish (page 373) but fiddly, so it is often best to ask the fishmonger to do it. If only large fish are available, buy four and serve one fillet per person.

PREPARATION AND COOKING
TIME: *25 minutes plus cooling time*
CHILLING TIME: *3-4 hours*

INGREDIENTS – *serves 8:*
8 small red mullet, about 6 oz (175 g) each, filleted but unskinned
6 tablespoons olive oil
2 shallots, thinly sliced
2 cloves garlic, finely chopped
1 level tablespoon chopped fresh thyme
Finely grated rind and juice of 1 large orange
4 anchovy fillets, finely chopped
Salt and freshly ground black pepper
4 tablespoons red wine
GARNISH
Orange segments, pith removed (page 398)
Chopped fresh thyme

Trim the red mullet fillets to a neat shape.

Heat the olive oil in a large shallow frying pan. Add the shallots and garlic and fry gently for 4 minutes. Add the thyme, orange rind, anchovy fillets and salt and pepper to taste and fry for a further minute. Lay the red mullet fillets on the top and then add the orange juice and red wine. Cover the pan and simmer gently for 6 minutes.

Leave the mullet to cool in its liquid for 30 minutes. With a fish slice carefully lift the fillets out onto a plate. Spoon the sauce from the pan onto a shallow serving dish, then lay the mullet on top. Cover and chill for 3-4 hours.

Garnish with the orange segments and sprinkle with chopped fresh thyme. This dish is included in a menu on page 230.

BURGUNDY FISH CASSEROLE

The Burgundy region of eastern France is rich in river fish and in wine, and with these the Burgundians have contrived to enliven the diet of a Catholic population who eat fish at many meals. A particular speciality is a casserole – traditionally made with freshwater fish, but here adapted for shellfish. Shelled mussels can be used. If you cannot get crab claws use more mussels or scallops.

PREPARATION AND COOKING
TIME: *2 hours*

INGREDIENTS – *serves 4-6:*
1 lb (450 g) unshelled prawns
4 oz (115 g) butter
3 red peppers, seeded and chopped
3 large leeks, cleaned and chopped
Salt and freshly ground black pepper
2 medium onions, finely chopped
3 large carrots, chopped
3 sticks celery, chopped
2 level teaspoons chopped fresh thyme
2 cloves garlic, crushed
¾ pint (450 ml) dry white wine
¾ pint (450 ml) fish stock (page 367)
1 lb (450 g) shelled scallops
24 unshelled mussels, scrubbed (page 377)
6 crab claws
½ teaspoon saffron strands
4 egg yolks
½ pint (285 ml) double cream

Shell the prawns and reserve the shells.

Melt half the butter in a large, heavy-based pan. Add the red peppers and half the leeks. Season to taste with salt and pepper. Cover and cook very gently until the vegetables are quite soft but not browned – this should take 25-30 minutes. Remove the lid from the pan and cook for a further 10 minutes until most of the moisture has evaporated and a thick vegetable purée remains. Cool for a few minutes, then blend in a liquidiser or food processor until smooth, or rub through a coarse sieve. Chill in the refrigerator. The purée can be made up to 24 hours in advance.

Melt the remaining butter in a large pan. Add the remaining leeks, and the onions, carrots, celery, thyme and garlic. Cover and cook gently for 10 minutes. Add the reserved prawn shells, white wine, fish stock and salt and pepper to taste. Simmer gently for 20 minutes.

Strain the liquid through a sieve into a large pan, pressing down well on the vegetables to extract all the flavour. Discard the contents of the sieve. Bring the strained liquid just to the boil. Add the scallops, mussels and crab claws and simmer gently for 4 minutes. Add the peeled prawns and simmer for a further 2-3 minutes. Remove from the heat.

Pour 1 tablespoon of boiling water over the saffron threads, leave to steep for a few minutes, then strain. Beat the egg yolks with the cream, then add the saffron liquid. Gradually stir a little of the hot liquid from the pan of shellfish into the egg mixture, then add the egg mixture to the pan of shellfish. Stir over a very gentle heat for 4-5 minutes, until the sauce thickens slightly. Do not overheat the sauce or it will curdle.

Ladle the casserole into large, shallow soup bowls and top each portion with a spoonful of the chilled pepper and leek purée. Serve immediately with plenty of hot, crusty bread. Serve the remaining purée separately so that the guests can help themselves. Provide finger bowls for use after removing the mussels from their shells and prising out the crabmeat.

SAFFRON SHELLFISH A spoonful of red pepper and leek purée tops a succulent casserole of mussels, prawns, scallops and crab claws, rich with wine, cream and saffron.

SCALLOPS IN PASTRY SHELLS

Instead of their natural shells, the scallops in this dish are served in edible shells made of pastry. It saves time to buy the scallops out of their shells, cleaned and prepared for cooking, but you do need 4 scallop shells in which to cook the pastry cases. Scallops are in season throughout the winter, and generally the colder the month, the better they are. The pastry shells can be filled, ready for baking, up to 4 hours in advance.

PREPARATION TIME: *45 minutes*
COOKING TIME: *20 minutes*
OVEN TEMPERATURE: *preheat to 200°C (400°F, gas mark 6)*

INGREDIENTS – *serves 4:*
1 lb (450 g) prepared weight puff pastry (page 394)
4 clean scallop shells
Vegetable oil
12 medium scallops, off their shells
¼ pint (150 ml) dry white wine
1 tablespoon chopped fresh chives
Salt and freshly ground black pepper
4 tablespoons double cream
2 egg yolks
1 egg, beaten
Hollandaise sauce (page 370)

Roll out the pastry quite thinly. Cut out 8 squares, each the size of a scallop shell. Lightly oil the scallop shells and line each one with a piece of pastry. Press the pastry well into the shell so that it takes on the natural marking. Trim off excess pastry.

Poach the scallops in the white wine for 6 minutes, with the chives and salt and pepper to taste. Remove the scallops from the pan. Cut each one in half and drain well on absorbent kitchen paper.

Divide the cooked scallops between the four pastry-lined shells, and brush the pastry rims of the shells with beaten egg.

Beat the cream and egg yolks together, and spoon over the scallops. Cover with the remaining squares of pastry, trim off excess pastry and pinch the edges together to seal. Score lines on top of the pastry with a sharp knife to give a shell-like appearance. Glaze with beaten egg and make a small hole in the top of the pastry.

Bake in the preheated oven for 20 minutes. Carefully ease the pastry cases out of the shells and place on individual plates. Spoon a little Hollandaise sauce through the hole in each pastry crust – make the hole larger if necessary – and serve immediately with the remaining sauce handed separately in a sauceboat. This dish is included in the menu on the opposite page.

GIFT FROM THE SEA Scallop shells of pastry enclose real scallops poached in white wine. Hollandaise sauce poured through a hole in the top moistens the contents. The shells are served with sorrel and lemon purée.

LANGOUSTINES IN GINGER BUTTER

French *langoustines* are sometimes sold in this country as Dublin Bay prawns. They are usually frozen but their flavour is much better when fresh. Pacific king prawns or freshwater crayfish can also be used in this recipe. If you wish to serve this dish as a first course, provide two or three prawns each depending on what is to follow.

PREPARATION TIME: *15 minutes*
COOKING TIME: *4-5 minutes*

INGREDIENTS – *serves 4:*
16-20 uncooked langoustines (Dublin Bay prawns)
3 oz (75 g) butter
½ in (15 mm) piece of fresh root ginger, peeled and finely chopped
2 cloves garlic, crushed
2 level tablespoons chopped fresh coriander leaves
Salt and freshly ground black pepper
Long sprigs fresh coriander leaves

Turn on the grill to medium heat.

With a sharp knife, split the langoustines in half lengthways,

PRIZE CATCH *Langoustines, or Dublin Bay prawns, are grilled in a piquant butter containing ginger, garlic and chopped coriander. They are served on a bed of fresh coriander with homemade mayonnaise.*

cutting along the underside so that when they are opened out the prawns hinge along the back. Lay them in a shallow ovenproof dish.

Mix the butter with the ginger, garlic, chopped coriander and salt and pepper to taste. Dot the langoustines with knobs of the flavoured butter, then cook under the preheated grill for 4-5 minutes only.

Lay the langoustines on a bed of fresh coriander, and serve with homemade mayonnaise (page 369) or Hollandaise sauce (page 370).

CHAMPAGNE SHRIMP RISOTTO

Most risottos are rightly regarded as basic everyday dishes, but this one rises into a class of its own on the bubble of pink champagne. Unlike most Italian risottos, this one is not meant to be creamy. The grains of rice stay much drier and more separate because long grain rice is used instead of round grain Italian risotto rice, and the risotto is cooked without stirring.

PREPARATION TIME: *15 minutes*
STANDING TIME: *30 minutes*
COOKING TIME: *40 minutes*

INGREDIENTS – *serves 4:*
12 oz (350 g) cooked, unshelled shrimps or prawns
1 medium onion, finely chopped
1 oz (25 g) butter
1 pint (570 ml) water
1 clove garlic, finely chopped
1 level tablespoon chopped fresh fennel OR 1 level teaspoon dried fennel seed
Thin strip of lemon peel
Salt and freshly ground black pepper
2 tablespoons olive oil
8 oz (225 g) long grain rice
½ pint (285 ml) pink champagne, or sparkling pink wine
GARNISH
Radicchio leaves
Feathery sprigs of fennel

Peel the shrimps or prawns, reserving the shells. Fry the onion gently in the butter for 3 minutes. Add the shrimp shells, water, garlic, fennel, lemon peel and salt and pepper to taste. Bring to the boil and simmer for 10 minutes. Remove from the heat and leave to stand for 30 minutes, then strain the stock through a fine sieve.

Heat the oil in a large pan. Stir in the rice so that all the grains are coated with oil, and fry gently for 3-4 minutes until the rice turns opaque. Gradually stir in the strained shrimp stock and the pink champagne. Bring to the boil and simmer gently, covered, for 20 minutes. Add salt and pepper to taste and fold in the peeled shrimps. Simmer gently for a further 5 minutes, by which time all the stock will have been absorbed by the rice.

Serve piping hot, garnished with radicchio leaves and sprigs of fennel. This dish is included in a menu on page 194.

MEAT

NOISETTES OF PORK WITH PRUNES AND CALVADOS

The prune and Calvados sauce for this dish can be prepared in advance. The noisettes can be fried just before the meal. Before serving, combine the noisettes and the sauce, reheat, and complete the dish.

PREPARATION TIME: *15 minutes*
COOKING TIME: *35 minutes*

INGREDIENTS – *serves 4:*
8 small slices pork fillet, each 1 in (25 mm) thick OR 4 large pork loin chops
10 oz (275 g) stoned ready-to-eat prunes
1/2 pint (285 ml) apple juice
1 small onion, finely chopped
1/4 pint (150 ml) chicken stock (page 367)
4 tablespoons Calvados
Salt and freshly ground black pepper
1 1/2 oz (40 g) butter
1 clove garlic, crushed
Pinch of ground ginger
4 tablespoons soured cream
8 or 4 croûtes of fried bread (see Eggs Soubise, page 16)
GARNISH
Thin slices of orange

First prepare the noisettes. Trim excess fat off the pork fillets or chops and remove any bones. Then shape into neat rounds and, if necessary, tie firmly with string. Put on one side.

Set aside 8 of the prunes, then put the remaining prunes into a pan with the apple juice and onion. Bring to the boil and simmer gently for 10 minutes until soft. Cool slightly. Blend in a liquidiser or food processor, or

FRENCH BLEND Specialities of Tourraine and Normandy – pork, prunes, Calvados and cream – simmer together just before serving.

sieve, until smooth, then mix in the chicken stock, Calvados, salt and pepper to taste.

Fry the noisettes in the butter in a deep frying pan for 5 minutes on each side. Add the garlic, ginger, and the prune sauce. Slowly bring to the boil, then simmer for 5 minutes. Stir in the soured cream and then the reserved prunes, and heat through gently for 5 minutes.

Place a noisette on each croûte of fried bread, spoon over a little of the sauce, and garnish with a slice of orange. Serve with boiled potatoes and a green vegetable.

STIR-FRIED BEEF AND BROCCOLI

In some Chinese food shops it is possible to obtain Chinese broccoli, which has flatter leaves than the European varieties and a rather more pronounced flavour – rather like asparagus. But if it cannot be found, ordinary broccoli is just as good.

PREPARATION TIME: *30 minutes*
COOKING TIME: *10-15 minutes*

INGREDIENTS – *serves 6:*
1 1/2 lb (700 g) fillet of beef
Salt and freshly ground black pepper
4 level teaspoons cornflour
1 lb (450 g) broccoli
6 tablespoons olive oil
1 large onion, finely chopped
6 tablespoons chicken stock (page 367)
3 level teaspoons soft brown sugar
2 tablespoons soya sauce
4 tablespoons dry sherry
1 slice fresh root ginger, 1/2 in (15 mm) thick, finely chopped
2 cloves garlic, peeled and finely chopped
GARNISH
3 level tablespoons chopped, toasted cashew nuts
Spring onion tassels (page 287)

Cut the fillet of beef into thin slices across the grain, about 1/8in (3mm) thick. Then cut each slice into strips, 3in × 1/2in (80mm × 15mm). Your butcher may do this for you if asked. Mix together the salt, pepper and cornflour and then rub them into the pieces of beef.

Trim the broccoli florets from the stalks. Halve the florets and cut the stalks lengthways into slices 1/8in (3mm) thick. If the stalks are tough, peel away the outer skin.

Heat 3 tablespoons of the oil in a large, deep frying pan, or a wok. Add the strips of beef and chopped onion, and stir-fry (page 372) over a brisk heat for 3 minutes. Remove the beef and onion and keep warm.

Add the remaining oil to the pan. Add the broccoli and stir-fry for 3 minutes. Add the stock and brown sugar and allow to bubble for 1 minute. Return the beef and onion to the pan, stir-fry for 1 minute and then add the soya sauce, sherry, ginger and garlic. Cook over a moderate heat for a further 2-3 minutes.

Spoon onto a warm serving dish, sprinkle with the chopped cashew nuts and spring onion tassels. Serve immediately while piping hot, with plain, boiled rice. This recipe is included in a menu on page 224.

M E N U

New Year's Eve Dinner for Eight

ARTICHOKE AND MARTINI SOUP
page 192

BEEF STUDDED WITH SMOKED OYSTERS
this page

POTATO AND CHIVE GALETTE
page 226

BRUSSELS SPROUT, ORANGE AND
CINNAMON PURÉE *page 223*

PORT AND STILTON SALAD
page 230

CHILLED BANANA SOUFFLÉ WITH
BURNT ORANGE SAUCE *page 240*

The tartlets that accompany the beef can be filled with puréed asparagus tips for this menu.

IN ADVANCE The night before, make the soup and the chilled banana soufflé.

ON THE DAY Allow 4-5 hours. Start to cook the beef. Make the tartlets. Prepare the galette, the purée and the ingredients for the salad.

Prepare the sauce for the beef to the point just before adding the cream. Grill the galette and keep it warm. Reheat the purée. Make the sauce for the pudding.

After eating the soup, warm through the tartlets and stir the cream into the sauce for the meat.

After the main course assemble the salad.

TO DRINK A fine red wine, such as Hermitage or Margaux, with the beef. A sweet white wine such as a Sauternes with the soufflé.

BEEF STUDDED WITH SMOKED OYSTERS

Both fore-rib and wing-rib of beef are suitable for this dish. For a 'standing' rib roast, ask the butcher not to remove the chine bone at the base of the joint, so that the joint stands upright. If artichoke purée is unavailable, purée about half a tin of artichoke hearts instead. A purée of tinned asparagus tips can be used as an alternative. Red wine can be used in the sauce instead of soured cream.

The pastry cases can be cooked 1-2 days in advance and stored in an airtight box.

PREPARATION TIME: *45 minutes*
COOKING TIME: *2-4 hours (see method)*
OVEN TEMPERATURE: *preheat to 190°C (375°F, gas mark 5)*

INGREDIENTS – *serves 8:*
Standing rib roast of beef – 3 ribs, 8-10 lb (3.6-4.5 kg)
Salt and freshly ground black pepper
2 × 3½ oz (90 g) tins smoked oysters
Small sprigs of parsley
3 oz (75 g) butter
Shortcrust pastry made with 4 oz (115 g) flour (page 392)
Beaten egg
3 tablespoons artichoke purée
2 level tablespoons plain flour
¼ pint (150 ml) beef stock (page 367)
½ pint (285 ml) soured cream
GARNISH
Sprigs of watercress

Rub the joint all over with salt and pepper. Drain the smoked oysters, and set aside 8 for the garnish. Make small deep cuts at regular intervals in the flesh of the beef (not the outside covering of fat). Tuck an oyster and a sprig of parsley into each cut.

Stand the beef upright in a roasting tin. Spread the butter all over the joint, then cover it loosely with kitchen foil.

Calculate the roasting time for the joint: allow 15 minutes per pound (450g) plus an extra 15 minutes for underdone beef; 20 minutes per pound plus 20 minutes for medium beef; and 25 minutes per pound plus 25 minutes for well-done beef.

Roast in the preheated oven for 1 hour. Remove the foil, then complete the roasting time, basting every so often. Because the time taken to cook will vary from joint to joint, according to the thickness of the joint and the quality of the meat, test the beef before the calculated cooking time is up by sticking a skewer into it near the bone. When the beef is slightly underdone the juices will be pink. With well-cooked meat the juices run clear.

While the beef is cooking, make the tartlet cases. Roll out the pastry and use it to line eight small tartlet (or bun) tins. Press the edges well up the sides of the tins. Line with small circles of greaseproof paper and baking beans. Bake blind (page 393) in the preheated oven for 10 minutes until the pastry has set.

Remove the paper and beans. Brush the rims of the pastry cases with beaten egg and return to the oven for a further 5 minutes. Remove from the oven and leave to cool.

Once the pastry cases are cool, fill each one with a little artichoke purée and top with a smoked oyster. Cover the tin of tartlets with kitchen foil.

Transfer the cooked beef to a serving dish and cover with a double thickness of kitchen foil to keep it warm. Pour all the juices from the roasting pan into a bowl, pour off the fat, then return 3 tablespoons of the remaining juices to the tin. Stir the flour into the juices over moderate heat and cook to a brown paste (roux). Gradually stir in the stock and the soured cream and simmer for 2-3 minutes. Season with salt and pepper.

Warm the tartlets through in the oven (this will take only 4-5 minutes). Arrange the tartlets round the beef and garnish with sprigs of watercress. Serve the soured cream sauce separately. This dish is included in a menu on this page.

BEEF OF OLD ENGLAND Roast ribs of beef make one of the finest sights to be seen on any dinner table. Here the joint is studded with smoked oysters and surrounded by small tarts filled with artichoke purée and topped with more smoked oysters. Rich gravy, potato and chive galette, and a purée of brussels sprouts and orange are served with the joint.

STEAK IN HORSERADISH PANCAKES

Unless you have a root in your garden, or can find it in the wild, fresh horseradish is difficult to obtain. Jars of grated horseradish can sometimes be bought, but failing that, a strong horseradish sauce can be used instead of the freshly grated root to flavour these pancakes. Tinned consommé can be used.

PREPARATION TIME: *30 minutes*
MARINATING TIME: *6 hours or overnight*
COOKING TIME: *20-30 minutes*

INGREDIENTS – *serves 6:*
6 fillet steaks, each about 1 in (25 mm) thick
2 oz (50 g) butter
2 tablespoons vegetable oil
7 fl oz (200 ml) beef consommé
MARINADE
1 small onion, cut into thin rings
1 clove garlic, crushed
1 level tablespoon chopped chives
7 fl oz (200 ml) red wine
Salt and freshly ground black pepper
PANCAKE BATTER
4 oz (115 g) plain flour
½ teaspoon salt
1 egg
¼ pint (150 ml) milk
¼ pint (150 ml) brown ale
1 level teaspoon grated fresh horseradish
Oil for frying
GARNISH
Small sprigs of watercress

Lay the fillet steaks in a shallow dish with the onion, garlic, chives, red wine and salt and pepper to taste. Cover the dish and leave in the refrigerator to marinate for at least 6 hours or overnight. Turn the steaks in the marinade two or three times.

To make the pancake batter, sieve the flour and salt into a

bowl. Make a well in the centre and put in the egg and half the milk. Beat together to make a smooth paste, then gradually beat in the remaining milk, the brown ale and the horseradish.

Using a lightly oiled pan, make 6 large pancakes (page 390). As you make each pancake, lay it on a lightly oiled

work surface to cool. When all the pancakes are made, stack them interleaved with waxed paper, then wrap the stack in kitchen foil and chill in the refrigerator until needed.

Before assembling the pancakes and steak, warm the pancake stack, still wrapped in foil, in a cool oven – 150°C (300°F, gas mark 2) – for 15 minutes. The pancakes will not come to any harm if left in the oven for as long as 30-40 minutes.

Drain the steaks, reserving the marinade. Heat the butter in a large frying pan with the oil. Fry the steaks over high heat for about a minute on each side to seal in the juices, then lower the heat and continue cooking until the steaks are cooked to the desired degree. Put the steaks in a dish, cover with foil, and keep warm.

Add the marinade and the consommé to the juices remaining in the pan. Boil the liquid briskly until it has reduced by about one-third.

Just before serving, warm through the sauce, then wrap each steak in a pancake and place it on a warmed serving dish. Pour over the sauce, garnish with watercress and serve immediately with a green vegetable and new potatoes.

STEAK PANCAKE Juicy fillet steaks, marinated in red wine, are fried in butter then wrapped in hot pancakes flavoured with fresh horseradish and brown ale.

FEGATO ALLA FRUTTA SECCO

Calf's liver (*fegato di vitello* in Italian) is here served in a rich sauce of dried fruit (*frutta secco*).

PREPARATION TIME: *10 minutes*
STANDING TIME: *30 minutes*
COOKING TIME: *4-5 minutes*

INGREDIENTS – *serves 6:*
3 oz (75 g) raisins
4 oz (115 g) dried peaches, chopped
½ pint (285 ml) dry white wine
4 tablespoons brandy
12 small thin slices calf's liver, about 1¼ lb (575 g)
Plain flour seasoned with salt and freshly ground pepper
3 oz (75 g) butter
GARNISH
3 level tablespoons chopped parsley

Put the raisins, peaches and white wine into a pan. Bring them to the boil and simmer for 5 minutes, then remove the pan from the heat and stir in the brandy. Leave on one side to steep for 30 minutes.

Dust the slices of liver lightly in seasoned flour. Heat the butter in a large shallow pan until it is bubbling. Add the slices of liver and fry them briskly for 1-1½ minutes on each side. Add the marinated fruit and the juices and simmer for 1 minute. Spoon onto a warm serving dish, sprinkle with the chopped parsley, and serve immediately.

SAUTÉED VEAL WITH REDCURRANTS AND CREAM

Fillet of veal is a small sausage-shaped joint which comes from the top of the leg – above the part from which escalopes are cut. It is very tender and easy to cut into the very thin slices – or scallops – that are needed for this recipe, so that the meat will cook very quickly. Use a sharp knife and cut the fillet against the grain of the meat into slices no more than ¼in (5mm) thick. The Italians call these slices of fillet *scallopine* – 'little escalopes'.

Frozen redcurrants can be used instead of fresh. The dish can be prepared, to the point just before the cream and redcurrants are added, up to 45 minutes in advance. Just before serving, reheat and complete the recipe.

PREPARATION TIME: *15 minutes*
COOKING TIME: *10-15 minutes*

INGREDIENTS – *serves 8:*
*2 lb (900 g) veal fillet, cut into
    very thin, small scallops*
*Salt and freshly ground black
    pepper*
2 level tablespoons plain flour
2 oz (50 g) butter
*6 spring onions, cut lengthways
    into thin strips*
½ pint (285 ml) dry white wine
3 tablespoons crème de cassis
½ pint (285 ml) single cream
*8 oz (225 g) redcurrants,
    stripped from their stalks (page
    397)*

GARNISH
*Small sprigs of fresh redcurrants,
or redcurrant leaves*

Season the scallops with salt and pepper, and dust with flour.

Heat the butter in a large frying pan and fry the strips of spring onion over a brisk heat for 2 minutes. Add the scallops of veal and fry quickly for 4 minutes, turning once. Add the white wine and cassis, and allow to bubble briskly for 1 minute. Stir in the single cream and the redcurrants and heat through.

Spoon onto a warm, shallow serving dish, and garnish with small sprigs of fresh redcurrants or redcurrant leaves. Serve immediately with a light green vegetable, such as mangetout, and new potatoes. This dish is included in a menu on page 197.

SUMMER BOUNTY Redcurrants bring flavours of high summer to delicate slices of veal. Strips of spring onion, blackcurrant liqueur (crème de cassis) and cream complete the dish, and redcurrant leaves add the final touch. Mangetout make a crisp, seasonal accompaniment.

211

LAMB CUTLETS WITH GREENGAGE SAUCE

A glaze of vermouth, greengage jam and green peppercorns adds interest to grilled lamb cutlets.

Venison cutlets, from the best end of neck, can be used instead of lamb, but they need basting and slightly longer cooking.

PREPARATION TIME: *20 minutes*
COOKING TIME: *10 minutes*

INGREDIENTS – *serves 4:*
8 lamb cutlets
7 fl oz (200 ml) dry white vermouth
Juice of 1 lemon
1 level tablespoon green peppercorns
3 level tablespoons greengage jam
Salt and freshly ground black pepper
2 oz (50 g) butter, melted
16 small mangetout

Trim the long bone of each cutlet so that it looks neat.

Put the vermouth, lemon juice and 2 level teaspoons of the green peppercorns into a pan. Simmer gently until the liquid is reduced by half. Stir in the greengage jam over a gentle heat until the jam is dissolved. Add salt and pepper to taste.

Place the cutlets on the rack of the grill pan. Brush with some of the melted butter and season to taste with salt and pepper. Grill for 2-3 minutes. Turn the cutlets over. Brush again with butter and then return to the grill for a further 2 minutes.

Cook the mangetout with the remaining butter and green peppercorns, in a covered pan, for 3 minutes.

Brush the cutlets on both sides with a little of the vermouth and greengage glaze and return to the grill for 1-2 minutes, turning once.

Arrange the cutlets on a serving dish, spoon over the remaining glaze, and garnish with the mangetout and peppercorns.

OLIVE-STUDDED LAMB WITH OLIVE AND PEPPER PURÉES AND GARLIC CREAMS

Some of the best Mediterranean flavours – olives, anchovies, red peppers, olive oil and garlic – are combined in this dish. The purées can be made, and the garlic creams and the lamb can be prepared ready for cooking, up to 24 hours in advance.

PREPARATION TIME: *1 hour plus chilling time*
COOKING TIME: *see method*
OVEN TEMPERATURE: *preheat to 160°C (325°F, gas mark 3)*

INGREDIENTS – *serves 6:*
1 small leg of lamb, about 3½ lb (1.6 kg)
10 plump, stoned, black olives, halved
4 anchovy fillets, roughly chopped
1 spray fresh rosemary, divided into small sprigs
6 tablespoons olive oil

RED PEPPER PURÉE
2 medium-sized red peppers, seeded and chopped
¼ pint (150 ml) double cream
¼ pint (150 ml) chicken stock
1 teaspoon lemon juice
Salt and freshly ground black pepper
BLACK OLIVE PURÉE
4 oz (115 g) plump, stoned, black olives
2 cloves garlic
6 anchovy fillets
2 oz (50 g) unsalted butter
1 teaspoon lemon juice
Pinch of paprika
GARLIC CREAMS
10 cloves garlic, peeled and crushed
¾ pint (450 ml) double cream
4 egg yolks
1 whole egg
Salt and freshly ground black pepper

First make the purées. For the red pepper purée, put the chopped red peppers, cream and stock into a heavy-based pan. Bring to the boil. Cover and simmer for 15 minutes until the peppers are very soft. Add the lemon juice and simmer uncovered for a further 5-10 minutes, until thick. Leave to cool slightly, then purée in a liquidiser or food processor until smooth. Season to taste with salt and pepper. Store in a covered container in the refrigerator.

To make the black olive purée, put the black olives and garlic into a pan with ⅓ pint (190ml) water. Cover the pan and simmer for 15 minutes until the olives are very soft. Leave to cool slightly, and then put the olives and the cooking liquid into the liquidiser or food processor with the anchovy fillets, butter, lemon juice and paprika. Blend to a smooth purée. Store in the refrigerator in a covered container.

To make the garlic creams, put the garlic and cream into a small pan. Simmer gently for 20 minutes until the garlic is very soft and the cream has reduced to about ½ pint (285ml). Blend in the liquidiser or food processor until smooth. Beat in the egg yolks, whole egg, and salt and pepper to taste. Keep the mixture in a covered container in the refrigerator until you are ready to cook the garlic creams.

To prepare the lamb, make about 20 short, deep cuts all over the leg of lamb. Press half a black olive, a piece of anchovy fillet and a small sprig of rosemary into each cut. Rub the olive oil all over the surface of the meat. Cover and chill in the refrigerator for at least 2 hours, or overnight.

Just before roasting the meat, cook the garlic creams. Pour the prepared mixture into six small, lightly greased ramekin dishes, or small ovenproof bowls. Stand them in a deep ovenproof dish and pour enough hot water into the dish to come halfway up the sides of the ramekins. Cook in the preheated oven for 25-30 minutes, until just set. Remove the ramekin dishes from the water, and put on one side.

Keep the water bath for reheating the garlic creams and purées.

Turn the oven up to 190°C (375°F, gas mark 5). Calculate the roasting time for the lamb, allowing 15 minutes per pound (450g) and 15 minutes extra. Put the prepared leg of lamb into a roasting tin and roast in the preheated oven. To test whether the lamb is cooked, pierce it with a skewer. The juices from the centre should still run slightly pink.

A little over 10 minutes before the meat is due to come out of the oven, put the pepper and olive purées into two small ovenproof dishes and stand them in the water bath with the ramekins of garlic cream. Cover with a piece of kitchen foil, and heat through in the oven with the lamb for about 10 minutes.

Carve the leg of lamb. Arrange two or three slices of lamb on each plate, with a spoonful of each of the two purées. Place each garlic cream on a small plate lined with a paper doily. Any accompanying vegetables, such as *Tian de legumes* (page 227), can be served onto side plates if necessary.

ALFRESCO LUNCH Tender slices of roast lamb are the centrepiece of a sunny open-air meal to linger over. They are carved from a leg of lamb studded with black olives, anchovy fillets and sprigs of rosemary, and served with purées of black olive and red pepper and a ramekin of baked, garlic-flavoured cream.

POULTRY & GAME

CHICKEN WITH WALNUT AND TARRAGON SAUCE

Mixing chicken with nuts – especially walnuts – is common in the Middle East. This recipe is a richer version of Turkish Circassian chicken.

PREPARATION TIME: *45 minutes*
COOLING AND CHILLING TIME:
 4-6 hours or overnight
COOKING TIME: *1½ hours*

INGREDIENTS – *serves 10:*
2 oven-ready chickens, about
 3½ lb (1.6 kg) each
1 bunch tarragon stalks
1 small onion, stuck with 4 cloves
2 stems celery, roughly chopped
1 level teaspoon crushed
 peppercorns
Piece of blade mace
½ lemon
Salt
12 oz (350 g) shelled walnuts
1 pint (570 ml) natural yoghurt
 or soured cream
4 cloves garlic
3 level tablespoons chopped fresh
 tarragon
2 slices wholemeal bread

GARNISH
3 tablespoons olive oil
1 level tablespoon paprika
Sprigs of fresh tarragon

Put the chickens into a large pan with the tarragon stalks, onion, celery, peppercorns, mace, lemon, and salt to taste. Add enough water to come halfway up the chickens. Bring to the boil, cover, and simmer gently for 1½ hours until the chickens are just tender. Allow the chickens to cool in the cooking liquid.

Skin the chickens and remove the flesh in largish strips. Strain the liquid through a fine sieve.

To make the sauce, put the walnuts into a liquidiser or food processor with half the yoghurt, all the garlic and tarragon, and the bread, crumbled. Blend to a smooth paste. Alternatively, pound the ingredients to a paste with a pestle and mortar.

Turn the walnut paste into a bowl and mix with the remaining yoghurt and about ½ pint (285ml) of the strained stock. The sauce should be just thick enough to coat the chicken. Mix the prepared sauce with the pieces of chicken and put into a covered container. Chill for at least 4 hours, or overnight.

Spoon the chicken and sauce onto a large shallow serving dish. Mix the olive oil with the paprika and trickle it over the chicken. Garnish with sprigs of fresh tarragon.

Serve with fresh bread and a crisp salad. This dish is included in a menu on page 236.

DUCK BREASTS WITH BLACKBERRY AND APRICOT SAUCE

Duck is a rich and succulent meat with a marked flavour of its own. Traditionally it is accompanied by tart fruit sauces, commonly orange or cherry. This is a rich alternative for late summer. The sauce is made with blackberries and dried apricots. At other times of the year the sauce can be made with frozen blackberries or tinned ones, well drained.

Duck breasts are the most economical way to buy duck – most of their weight is meat, unlike the whole duck which has a large proportion of fat and bone. Once cooked, the duck breasts and sauce can be kept warm in a covered dish for up to 30 minutes.

PREPARATION TIME: *15 minutes*
COOKING TIME: *about 45 minutes*
SOAKING TIME: *overnight*

INGREDIENTS – *serves 6:*
6 boneless duck breasts
4 oz (115 g) dried apricots
¼ pint (150 ml) water
4 oz (115 g) fresh blackberries
2 level teaspoons soft brown sugar
1½ oz (40 g) butter
½ pint (285 ml) dry white wine
1 level teaspoon green peppercorns
Salt and freshly ground black pepper
1 duck liver or chicken liver, finely chopped

GARNISH
6 fresh apricots, blanched, halved and stoned
Sprigs of watercress
A few whole blackberries

Cover the dried apricots with water and soak them overnight.

Drain the apricots and put them into a pan with the ¼ pint (150ml) of water. Cover and simmer gently for 20 minutes, until soft. Blend the cooked apricots to a purée in a liquidiser or food processor, or rub them through a sieve. Add the blackberries and sugar, and blend or sieve again until smooth.

Fry the duck breasts gently in the butter for 5-10 minutes, until evenly coloured on all sides. Add the white wine, green peppercorns, and salt and pepper to taste, and simmer for 5 minutes. Stir in the blackberry and apricot purée and the chopped liver. Simmer gently for 10-15 minutes until the duck is quite tender.

Remove the duck breasts to a warm serving dish, spoon over the sauce, and garnish with the apricot halves, watercress and whole blackberries.

LAST DAYS OF SUMMER Blackberries puréed with dried apricots make a rich sauce for breasts of duck.

POT ROAST PHEASANT WITH CLARET AND ORANGE SAUCE

The season for pheasant runs from October 1 to February 1, but they are best in November and December. As with all game, pheasant is allowed to hang before being eaten, to tenderise the flesh and intensify its gamey flavour. Hen pheasants have a better flavour than cock pheasants, but are not as plump. Young pheasants, up to a year old, are the most tender.

Pheasant can be dry if it is cooked too fast or without enough moisture. When roasting a pheasant the breast must be covered with bacon or barding fat and the bird must be basted frequently. When pot roasting, however, as here, it is only necessary to check occasionally that there is still enough liquid in the pot. A pan large enough to hold three pheasants is needed. Use a reasonably good claret for the sauce; it draws out the full gamey flavour of the pheasant.

PREPARATION TIME: *35 minutes*
COOKING TIME: *1¼-1½ hours*

INGREDIENTS – *serves 8:*
3 medium pheasants, about 2 lb (900 g) each, trimmed ready for cooking
Salt and freshly ground black pepper
Finely grated rind of 1 orange
2 oz (50 g) butter

2 tablespoons olive oil
1 medium onion, finely chopped
2 cloves garlic, finely chopped
3 carrots, peeled and thinly sliced
3 stems celery, chopped
Sprig of fresh rosemary
1 pint (570 ml) claret
About 1-1½ pints (570-
*   850 ml) good brown stock*
*   (page 367), more if the pan is*
*   very large*
¾ oz (20 g) plain flour
3 level tablespoons redcurrant
*   jelly*
GARNISH
Segments of unpeeled orange
*   scored with a canelle knife*
Sprigs of rosemary and celery
*   leaves*
Cooked fresh cranberries

Check that the pheasants have been thoroughly cleaned. Wipe out the body cavity with kitchen paper. Singe them if necessary to remove any remaining stubbly pieces of feather.

Season the birds inside and out with salt and pepper, and rub the grated orange rind well into the skin.

Heat half the butter and the olive oil in a large pan. Put the pheasants in the pan and brown evenly on all sides in the hot fat. Transfer the pheasants to a plate. Add the onion, garlic, carrots and celery to the fat remaining in the pan. Fry for 3-4 minutes.

Replace the pheasants in the pan, on the bed of vegetables, and add the rosemary and claret. Pour in enough stock to come almost halfway up the birds.

Cover the pan with a lid and bring to the boil. Simmer gently for about an hour – young tender birds will be cooked within this time, but slightly older pheasants may take 10-15 minutes longer. Transfer the cooked pheasants to a serving dish, cover loosely with kitchen foil, and keep warm.

Skim the cooking liquid and strain through a fine sieve, then measure off 1 pint (570ml). If necessary, make the liquid up to quantity with a little extra stock. Put the measured liquid into a pan and heat through over moderate heat. Blend the remaining butter with the flour to make a smooth paste – beurre manié (page 371). Stir the redcurrant jelly into the hot liquid. Add the beurre manié in small lumps, whisking continuously over the heat to produce a smooth sauce.

Spoon some of the sauce over the pheasants, and serve the remainder separately in a sauce boat. Garnish with orange segments, sprigs of rosemary and celery leaves, and cranberries.

Serve with simple vegetables such as small jacket potatoes or boiled potatoes, and brussels sprouts. This dish is included in the menu on page 245.

FESTIVE PHEASANT Pot roasting in claret ensures that these birds are moist and tender. They are garnished with fresh cooked cranberries, orange segments, sprigs of rosemary and celery leaves, and served with an orange and claret sauce.

WILD DUCK WITH KUMQUATS

The mallard is the commonest – and one of the tastiest of wild ducks. It is in season from September to February but is at its best in November and December. Wigeon and teal are also good to eat, but are much smaller and not as readily available. Mallard is usually hung for only a day – wigeon and teal are not hung at all.

Wild duck must never be overcooked. Its flesh is almost entirely free of fat, and even slight overcooking will dry it out and cause it to lose much of its flavour and texture. Indeed some people cook it for only 10 minutes – but at this stage it is barely heated through.

In this dish, the duck is cooked with kumquats – small, oval, orange-like fruit, originally from Japan but now imported from North Africa. They have a slight tanginess that goes particularly well with wild duck. A dash of brandy prevents the kumquat sauce from being too sharp. Kumquats are eaten whole – skin, pips and all.

The watercress butter used in the garnish can be made in advance and kept in the freezer. It also goes well with many cooked vegetables.

PREPARATION TIME: *50 minutes*
COOKING TIME: *40-50 minutes*
OVEN TEMPERATURE: *preheat to 190°C (375°F, gas mark 5)*

INGREDIENTS – *serves 6:*
3 wild ducks, prepared for cooking
3 duck livers
6 level tablespoons chopped parsley
4 oz (115 g) smoked ham, chopped
Salt and freshly ground black pepper
20 kumquats
3 oz (75 g) butter
2 level tablespoons flour
½ pint (285 ml) red wine
4 tablespoons brandy
1-2 tablespoons apricot jam, sieved
WATERCRESS BUTTER
1 bunch watercress, about 3 oz (75 g)
3 oz (75 g) butter, softened
1 clove garlic, crushed
Salt and freshly ground black pepper
GARNISH
Fried croutons (page 286) cut into heart shapes

Check that the inside of each duck has been properly cleaned. If necessary, wipe it out with a damp cloth or kitchen paper.

To make the stuffing, chop the duck livers, mix them with the parsley and smoked ham, and add salt and pepper to taste. Chop 12 of the kumquats and mix them into the stuffing. Stuff the body cavity of each bird with one-third of the mixture. Place the ducks in a roasting tin and rub them with the butter. Roast in the preheated oven for 40-50 minutes (depending on the size of the

ducks) until the juices run clear brown – not pink – when the thickest part of the thigh is pierced with a skewer. Remove the ducks to a warm serving dish and keep warm.

Pour off all but about 2 tablespoons of the cooking juices from the roasting tin. Stir the flour into the juices in the tin with a wooden spoon. Gradually add the wine, brandy and apricot jam – stirring over a gentle heat until the jam has dissolved and the sauce is smooth. Thinly slice the remaining 8 kumquats, stir them into the sauce and heat through.

Cut the ducks in half using poultry shears, a sharp knife or strong kitchen scissors and replace them on the serving dish. Spoon the hot sauce over the top. Garnish with the croutons spread with watercress butter and serve with a green vegetable such as peas, broccoli or spinach. This dish is included in a menu on the opposite page.
WATERCRESS BUTTER Trim the stalks off the watercress and finely chop the leaves. Mix with the butter, garlic, and salt and pepper to taste.

AUTUMNAL DUCK The subtle gamey flavour of wild duck is joined with the tartness of the kumquats which flavour both the stuffing and the sauce. The dish is garnished with heart-shaped croutons spread with watercress butter, and served with almondine potatoes. An abundance of frosted fruit decorates the table.

M E N U

Autumn Dinner for Six

SOFT CHEESE GALETTE *page 195*

WILD DUCK WITH KUMQUATS *opposite page*

SPICED RED CABBAGE WITH JUNIPER
page 221

ALMONDINE POTATOES *page 220*

CHEESE

STEAMED COFFEE SOUFFLÉS WITH
HOT CHOCOLATE SAUCE *page 237*

The soufflés need careful timing. A salad such as *Cos lettuce with tomato and tarragon vinaigrette* (page 232) can be served instead of cheese, or the guests can wait and digest their duck while the soufflés are cooking.

IN ADVANCE The night before, cook the puff pastry for the galette, prepare the potatoes, make the watercress butter for the croutons and make the chocolate sauce.

ON THE DAY Allow 3-3½ hours. Prepare and start to cook the cabbage and prepare the galette. Make the stuffing for the ducks. Turn the oven up, put the cabbage at the bottom and start to cook the ducks. Make the croutons and prepare the soufflés.

Once the ducks are cooked, make the sauce and keep warm. Cook the galette (it is not necessary to turn up the oven – allow 2-3 minutes extra) and the potatoes.

After eating the duck, complete and cook the soufflés and warm through the chocolate sauce.

TO DRINK Wild duck can be served with white or red wine. Suitable whites would include an Australian Chardonnay or a good Rheinhessen, suitable reds would include a Pomerol or an Italian Barolo. Do not serve wine with the pudding. Chocolate kills the flavour.

RABBIT AND SAGE FRICASSÉE

A fricassée is almost invariably made of white meat – chicken, turkey, veal, or, in this case, rabbit – swathed in a light, pale sauce. Too often it can be a disappointing dish, made with reheated leftovers – Christmas turkey, for example. But freshly cooked and flavoured with fresh herbs, if possible, it makes an elegant meal.

The fricassée can be kept warm, if necessary, in a covered pan over very low heat, for about 30 minutes.

PREPARATION TIME: *10 minutes*
COOKING TIME: *50 minutes*

INGREDIENTS – *serves 4:*
4 large rabbit joints, or 8 smaller ones
1½ oz (40 g) butter
1 medium onion, finely chopped
½ pint (285 ml) dry white wine
7 fl oz (200 ml) chicken stock (page 367)
1½ level tablespoons chopped fresh sage OR 1½ level teaspoons dried sage
2 level tablespoons chopped parsley
Salt and freshly ground black pepper
½ tablespoon plain flour
½ tablespoon butter
3 tablespoons single cream
1 egg yolk
GARNISH
Heart-shaped croutons (page 286)
Small sprigs of fresh sage

Melt the butter in a large pan and fry the chopped onion gently for 4 minutes. Add the rabbit joints and brown them evenly on all sides.

Add the white wine, stock, chopped sage and parsley, and season to taste with salt and pepper. Bring to the boil, cover and then simmer for about 30 minutes or until the rabbit is just tender.

Remove the rabbit joints from the pan and keep warm.

Cream the flour and butter together to a smooth paste – beurre manié (page 371). Boil the juices in the pan for 3 minutes. Beat in the beurre manié, a small knob at a time, until the sauce has thickened slightly and is smooth. In a small bowl, beat the cream with the egg yolk then stir it into the sauce. Heat the sauce through but do not allow it to boil.

Return the rabbit joints to the pan and heat through, then transfer to a warm serving dish and garnish with the heart-shaped croutons and sprigs of fresh sage.

BSTILLA

When the Moors were driven out of southern Spain in the 15th century, they are said to have taken back with them to North Africa a pigeon pie called *bstilla* – pronounced puh-STEE-yah. The pie is served on special occasions in Morocco and also Algeria, such is the high regard in which it is held. It is traditionally made with pigeons – which are at their best from March to October – but it is also sometimes made with chicken.

Phyllo pastry requires great expertise to make, but is available ready-made from delicatessens or from Greek and Middle-Eastern shops. It is sometimes sold as 'strudel pastry'. It comes in rectangular sheets, stacked together, rolled up and sealed in polythene to keep it moist. The paper-thin sheets usually measure approximately 18in × 12in (455mm × 300mm).

The pie can be prepared up to 4 hours in advance and kept in the refrigerator, but do not brush it with the egg until just before putting it in the oven.

PREPARATION TIME: *45 minutes*
COOKING TIME: *1¾-2 hours*
OVEN TEMPERATURE: *preheat to 190°C (375°F, gas mark 5)*

INGREDIENTS – *serves 6:*
3 tender pigeons, cleaned
2 bay leaves
1 bunch parsley stalks
Sprig of fresh mint
½ lemon
½ teaspoon crushed black peppercorns
Salt and freshly ground black pepper
½ teaspoon ground cinnamon
½ teaspoon mixed spice
½ teaspoon ground ginger
2 cloves garlic, finely chopped
2 level tablespoons chopped fresh mint
6 eggs
4 oz (115 g) butter, melted
12 sheets phyllo pastry
4 oz (115 g) chopped toasted almonds
1 egg yolk, beaten
Pinch of saffron strands, dissolved in 1 tablespoon boiling water
2 in (50 mm) piece cinnamon stick, flaked
1 level tablespoon granulated sugar

Put the pigeons into a pan with the bay leaves, parsley stalks, mint, lemon, crushed peppercorns, and salt to taste. Add enough water to come halfway up the pigeons. Cover the pan and bring to the boil. Simmer gently for 1 hour until the pigeons are tender. Allow to cool in the cooking liquid.

Skin the pigeons and remove all the bones. Tear the flesh into pieces. Mix the pigeon flesh with the ground cinnamon, mixed spice, ground ginger, chopped garlic and mint.

Beat the eggs with salt and pepper to taste and 6 tablespoons of the strained stock from cooking the pigeons. Put 1 tablespoon of the melted butter into a pan. Add the beaten egg mixture and stir over a gentle heat until the egg mixture lightly scrambles.

Brush a large, rectangular ovenproof dish, about 12in × 9in (300mm × 230mm), with melted butter. Fit one sheet of phyllo pastry in the bottom of the dish, allowing the edges to come up the sides of the dish. (Keep the other sheets covered with a damp cloth while you are working.) Brush the sheet of phyllo pastry with melted butter, and then add another 3 sheets of phyllo pastry, brushing each one well with melted butter before adding the next. Sprinkle with the chopped toasted almonds and spread with half the egg mixture. Lay a further 4 sheets of phyllo pastry on top, brushing between each one with melted butter. Lay the pieces of cooked pigeon on top and spread with the remaining egg mixture. Cover with the remaining 4 sheets of phyllo pastry, brushing each one with melted butter. Tuck the top phyllo sheets down and under the bottom ones.

Mix the beaten egg yolk with the strained saffron liquid and brush all over the top of the pie. Sprinkle with the flaked cinnamon and the sugar.

Bake in the preheated oven for 40 minutes – then raise the oven temperature to 220°C (425°F, gas mark 7) and cook for a further 10-15 minutes, until the top is really crisp and deep golden in colour. Cut into large squares and serve very hot with a salad. This dish is included in a menu on the opposite page.

PIGEON PIE Bstilla is a North African dish of spiced pigeon, mixed with almonds and egg, and encased in paper-thin sheets of phyllo pastry. The pie is topped with flaked cinnamon and served with bemuelos (deep-fried potato cakes), and orange, avocado and coriander salad.

*Middle-
Eastern
Lunch for Six*

GRILLED HALUMI
CHEESE WITH MINT
page 195

❧

BSTILLA *opposite page*

BEMUELOS *page 228*

ORANGE, AVOCADO AND
CORIANDER SALAD
page 232

❧

ATAÏF *page 242*

❧

CANDIED DATES *page 236*

IN ADVANCE The night be-
fore, prepare the candied
dates, the oranges for the
salad, and the ataïf.
ON THE DAY Allow about
4½ hours. Prepare and cook
the bemuelos and the bstilla,
then prepare the Halumi
and complete the salad.
Reheat the bemuelos and
grill the Halumi cheese.

During the main course,
heat through the ataïf.
TO DRINK A dry, crisp white
wine, such as Demestica or a
good dry Muscadet.

PINTADE AUX QUARANTE GOUSSES D'AIL

The guinea fowl (*pintade* in French) is native to West Africa where it still lives in the wild. In Europe it has been domesticated – and eaten – since Roman times at least. Until Shakespeare's time and even after, it was known in England as the turkey – because it was believed to come from Turkey. The American turkey was later named after it.

This dish, cooked with '40 cloves of garlic' (*quarante gousses d'ail*), sounds alarming. But, surprisingly enough, it does not taste strongly of garlic – even though the cloves are eventually blended into the sauce.

PREPARATION TIME: *45 minutes*
COOKING TIME: *1¼ hours*

INGREDIENTS – *serves 8:*
2 plump guinea fowl, 2½-3 lb (1.1-1.4 kg) each, prepared for cooking
6 oz (175 g) goat cheese
Salt and freshly ground black pepper
40 cloves garlic (about 5 bulbs), peeled
About 1 oz (25 g) fresh basil or tarragon
1 pint (570 ml) dry white wine
3 egg yolks
¼ pint (150 ml) green ('virgin') olive oil
GARNISH
Hearts of 2 cos lettuce, quartered
Sprigs of fresh basil

Beat the cheese with a wooden spoon to soften it, and mix it with salt and pepper to taste.

Starting at the neck end of one of the birds, insert your fingers carefully between the skin and the breast flesh. Then run your fingers along the length of the bird to separate the skin and flesh, taking care not to puncture the skin. Repeat with the other bird.

Insert the cheese between the skin and flesh of each guinea fowl, spreading it evenly, then mould the skin back into place.

Put the birds into a large, deep pan with the garlic, basil, white wine and ½ pint (285ml) water. Bring to the boil and simmer gently for 1 hour, until the birds are tender and a skewer penetrates the thigh easily.

Lift the guinea fowl onto a serving dish and cover with a double thickness of kitchen foil to keep them warm. Strain the cooking stock. Put the garlic cloves and basil into a liquidiser or food processor with ½ pint (285ml) of the cooking stock. Blend until smooth, then add the egg yolks and blend once again. Very gradually blend in the olive oil, as though making mayonnaise. Add salt and pepper to taste. Warm the sauce in the top of a double saucepan, or in a basin set over a pan of hot water.

Cut off the leg and wing joints of the guinea fowl and carve the breast. Arrange the pieces on a warm serving dish. Spoon half the sauce evenly over the top. Garnish with the quartered hearts of cos lettuce and sprigs of basil. Serve immediately, with the remaining sauce handed separately in a sauceboat. This dish is included in a menu on page 230.

FRENCH GUINEA FOWL Forty cloves of garlic give the sauce for this dish a surprisingly delicate flavour. Goat cheese inserted under the skin keeps the flesh of the bird moist during cooking. It is served with haricots verts au gratin.

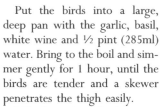

VEGETABLES

ALMONDINE POTATOES

The almond, which is a native of the Mediterranean, was enjoyed by Romans and Arabs alike. They spread its use throughout Europe, the Middle East and northern India. It is now grown also in California, South Africa and Australia. Almonds can be added to both sweet and savoury dishes. In this recipe, ground almonds are mixed with mashed potatoes, then rolled into balls and coated with finely chopped almonds.

The potato balls can be shaped and coated up to 24 hours in advance, and kept in the refrigerator until required.

PREPARATION TIME: *1 hour*
CHILLING TIME: *at least 4½ hours*
COOKING TIME: *15-20 minutes*
OVEN TEMPERATURE: *preheat to 190°C (375°F, gas mark 5)*

INGREDIENTS – *serves 6:*
2 lb (900 g) potatoes
Salt and freshly ground black pepper
3 level tablespoons ground almonds
1 egg
2 egg yolks

COATING
Plain flour
1 egg, beaten
4-6 oz (115-175 g) finely
 chopped almonds
Melted butter or cooking oil

Peel the potatoes and chop them roughly into ¾in (20mm) pieces. Cook them in boiling salted water until just tender. Drain the potatoes thoroughly and mash them. Beat the mashed potato with the ground almonds, whole egg, egg yolks and salt and pepper to taste. Leave to cool slightly.

Flour your hands and shape the potato mixture into small balls, about the size of small plums. Chill in the refrigerator for about 30 minutes.

To coat the potato balls, dust them lightly with flour and dip in beaten egg. Roll the dipped potato balls in the chopped nuts until evenly coated. Chill again, this time for at least 4 hours (or put the potato balls into the freezer for about 30 minutes).

To cook, lightly grease a shallow ovenproof dish. Arrange the balls in a single layer in the dish and brush with melted butter. Bake in the preheated oven for 15-20 minutes until they are lightly golden.

Alternatively, shallow-fry the potato balls in hot oil for about 5 minutes, turning them once. Drain them on absorbent paper. Serve with dishes that have plenty of sauce or gravy.

This dish is included in a menu on page 217.

SPICED RED CABBAGE WITH JUNIPER

Red cabbage is rarely, if ever, boiled, instead it is shredded and cooked in a casserole – preferably an earthenware one – often with apples, wine and spices. The richest, most mellow flavour is produced by long, slow cooking. The best results are achieved in a stored-heat stove, such as an Aga, when the cabbage can be left to cook for the whole day. Red cabbage is in season during the autumn and winter months.

PREPARATION TIME: *25 minutes*
COOKING TIME: *2½ hours*
OVEN TEMPERATURE: *preheat to*
 150°C (300°F, gas mark 2)

INGREDIENTS – *serves 6:*
1 medium-sized red cabbage,
 finely shredded
4 oz (115 g) piece streaky bacon,
 cut into small cubes
2 dessert apples, such as Cox's or
 Russets, cored and sliced but
 not peeled
1-2 level teaspoons crushed
 juniper berries
2 bay leaves
A large sprig of fresh rosemary
8 fl oz (225 ml) red wine
3 tablespoons brandy
Salt and freshly ground black
 pepper

Place the shredded cabbage, cubed bacon, sliced apple and juniper berries in layers in a large deep casserole. Press the bay leaves and rosemary into the centre. Mix the red wine with the brandy and salt and pepper to taste and pour over the cabbage. Lay a piece of buttered greaseproof paper on top of the cabbage, and then cover the casserole with a lid.

Cook in the preheated oven for 2½ hours. Check two or three times during cooking to see that the liquid has not evaporated completely. Add a little extra red wine or some stock if necessary. Serve hot.

Red cabbage is particularly good with game and fatty meat

UNCOMMON CABBAGE *Shredded red cabbage is cooked long and slowly with apple, rosemary and juniper berries for a full, mellow flavour.*

or poultry, such as pork, goose or duck. This dish is included in a menu on page 217.

221

GRATIN OF PARSNIPS AND POTATOES

Dishes cooked *au gratin* are dressed with a mixture of breadcrumbs and grated cheese. In gratins of vegetables, the vegetables are usually thinly sliced. For this recipe they are grated into long thin strands which give a different, more even, texture to the finished dish. The gratin can be prepared up to 2 hours in advance. Keep it, covered, in a cool place.

PREPARATION TIME: *45 minutes*
COOKING TIME: *40-45 minutes*
OVEN TEMPERATURE: *preheat to 190°C (375°F, gas mark 5)*

INGREDIENTS – *serves 8:*
1½ lb (700 g) potatoes
1½ lb (700 g) parsnips
1 small onion, peeled and finely chopped
1 oz (25 g) butter
1 clove garlic, crushed
¾ pint (450 ml) single cream
2 level tablespoons chopped chives
Salt and freshly ground black pepper
3 oz (75 g) finely grated cheese
3 level tablespoons fresh dry breadcrumbs

Peel the potatoes and the parsnips. Shred them into long thin strands, either using the shredder blade on a food processor or the coarse blade on a grater. Wrap the grated vegetables in a clean cloth and squeeze lightly to remove any excess moisture.

Fry the chopped onion gently

SUNNY PAIR The golden crust of a dish of shredded parsnips and potatoes prepared au gratin is matched by the flaming orange of a spicy carrot and ginger soufflé.

in the butter for 4 minutes. Remove the pan from the heat and stir in the garlic, cream and chives. Mix together the onion mixture, the shredded parsnips and potatoes, salt and pepper to

taste, and 2oz (50g) of the grated cheese. Spoon the mixture into a large greased gratin dish or shallow ovenproof dish. Mix the remaining grated cheese with the breadcrumbs and sprinkle over the top.

Bake in a preheated oven for 40-45 minutes, until the top of the gratin has a golden crust. Serve hot with roast meat, game and poultry. This dish is included in a menu on page 245.

CARROT AND GINGER SOUFFLÉ

The inconveniences normally associated with a soufflé are lessened with this slightly more robust type, but careful timing is still required. The carrot and ginger base can be made up to an hour in advance. The whisked egg whites can then be mixed in at the last moment.

PREPARATION TIME: *50 minutes*
COOKING TIME: *35-40 minutes*
OVEN TEMPERATURE: *preheat to 190°C (375°F, gas mark 5)*

INGREDIENTS – *serves 8:*
2 lb (900 g) carrots
Finely grated rind of ½ orange
Pinch of ground nutmeg
Salt and freshly ground black pepper
¼ pint (150 ml) soured cream
4 eggs, separated
4 level tablespoons soft white breadcrumbs
¼ teaspoon ground ginger
1 level tablespoon finely chopped preserved stem ginger
2 level tablespoons chopped parsley OR 2 level teaspoons dried parsley

Peel the carrots and chop them roughly. Cook them in boiling salted water until they are just tender. Drain the carrots well and mash them to a purée, press them through a food mill, or blend thoroughly in a food processor.

Put the carrot purée into a bowl and beat in the orange rind, nutmeg and salt and pepper to taste, soured cream, egg yolks, breadcrumbs and ground ginger. Butter a 2 pint (1.1 litre) soufflé dish.

Whisk the egg whites until stiff but not dry. Fold them lightly but thoroughly into the carrot mixture, together with the chopped stem ginger and the chopped or dried parsley.

Transfer the mixture carefully to the prepared soufflé dish.

Bake in the preheated oven for 35-40 minutes, until the mixture is just set, well risen and light golden in colour. Serve immediately. This dish is included in a menu on page 245.

STEAMED VEGETABLE JULIENNE IN VINE LEAVES

In the eastern Mediterranean vine leaves are often used to wrap meat, rice or vegetables. In this dish, they are stuffed with vegetables chopped into julienne – matchstick – strips.

In Britain, vine leaves can be bought preserved in brine. In early summer, fresh ones are available in Greek and Middle-Eastern food shops. The leaves of British vines can also be used.

The stuffed leaves can be prepared up to 1 hour in advance, ready to be steamed during the first course.

PREPARATION TIME: *45 minutes*
COOKING TIME: *20-25 minutes*

INGREDIENTS – *serves 4:*
8 large vine leaves or 16 medium ones
4 medium carrots, peeled
2 sticks celery
24 french beans
16 mangetout
Salt and freshly ground black pepper
8 tablespoons double cream
2 level tablespoons chopped fennel or dill

Soak vine leaves preserved in brine in warm water for 10 minutes. Blanch fresh vine leaves for 2-3 minutes in boiling water. Drain and lay well spread out on absorbent kitchen paper. If medium-sized leaves are used, arrange them in pairs with the leaves in each pair overlapping.

Cut the carrots and celery into matchstick strips, about ¼in × 3in (5mm × 80mm). Trim the stalk ends of the beans. Leave the mangetout untrimmed.

Divide the carrot and celery sticks between the vine leaves or pairs of leaves. Add 3 french beans and 2 mangetout to each vine leaf or pair of leaves, and season with salt and pepper. Wrap the leaves around the vegetables and make into parcels tied with fine string.

Put the vine leaf parcels into the top of a steamer, or into a colander over a pan of simmering water. Cover and steam for 20-25 minutes.

Transfer the parcels to a warm serving plate, and remove the strings. Keep the parcels warm while you heat the cream gently in a small pan. Spoon the cream over the parcels and sprinkle with the herbs.

Serve with light dishes such as *Fegato alla frutta secco* (page 210) or *Sautéed veal with redcurrants and cream* (page 211).

This dish is included in a menu on page 239.

BRUSSELS SPROUT, ORANGE AND CINNAMON PURÉE

Vegetable purées are very useful for a dinner party because most of them can be prepared several hours in advance, and then reheated. The sprouts can be puréed with a food mill instead of a processor and then mixed with the other ingredients.

PREPARATION AND COOKING
TIME: *40 minutes*

INGREDIENTS – *serves 8:*
2½ lb (1.1 kg) brussels sprouts
Salt and freshly ground black pepper
1 pint (570 ml) chicken stock (page 367)
4 oz (115 g) cream cheese
Finely grated rind of 1½ oranges
¼ teaspoon ground cinnamon
3 egg yolks
4 tablespoons double cream

GARNISH
Segments from 2 oranges, peel and pith removed (page 398)
Ground cinnamon

Wash and trim the sprouts. Cut them in half, and put them into a pan with a generous pinch of salt and the chicken stock. Cover and bring to the boil. Simmer gently, still covered, for about 10 minutes until the sprouts are just tender. Drain thoroughly.

Put the sprouts into a food processor with the cream cheese, orange rind, ground cinnamon and egg yolks. Blend to a smooth purée and beat in the cream, then season to taste with salt and pepper. Alternatively, press the sprouts through a food mill and then mix with the other ingredients. Heat the purée through in the top of a double saucepan, or in a bowl over a pan of gently simmering water.

Turn into a warm serving dish, and decorate the top with a knife or fork. Garnish with orange segments and a sprinkling of cinnamon.

The purée can be served with almost any fish, meat or poultry. This dish is included in a menu on page 208.

SPICED SPROUTS *Zest of orange and a dash of cinnamon enliven a purée of brussels sprouts enriched with cream cheese, eggs and cream. The purée makes an excellent accompaniment to roast rib of beef studded with smoked oysters.*

M E N U

Chinese Dinner for Six

SWEET AND SOUR FISH BALLS
page 198

STIR-FRIED BEEF AND BROCCOLI
page 207

LOTUS-WRAPPED RICE
this page

MUSHROOMS IN OYSTER SAUCE
opposite page

BOILED RICE

COCONUT AND GINGER JELLY
WITH LYCHEES *page 242*

If you wish to serve this menu in the Chinese style, provide each person with a rice bowl, saucer and chopsticks. An extra side plate will make it easier to eat the lotus-wrapped rice.

ADVANCE PREPARATION Make the jelly the night before. ON THE DAY Allow about 3 hours. Prepare the fish balls and sauce. Prepare the rice parcels, soaking the mushrooms in the meantime. Prepare the ingredients for the mushrooms in oyster sauce, then those for the stir-fried beef. Turn out and cut up the jelly.

About 15-20 minutes before the meal, boil the plain rice, cook the fish balls and reheat the sauce. Just before the meal, put the rice parcels on to steam.

After you have finished eating the fish balls, stir-fry the mushrooms and keep them warm, then stir-fry the beef and broccoli.

TO DRINK The Chinese traditionally drink warm rice wine or nothing with the meal, and tea afterwards. However, green tea, dry white wine or rosé wine all complement Chinese food.

LOTUS-WRAPPED RICE

The lotus is a sacred plant in much of the Far East, similar to a water lily. When the lotus is in full bloom in China, street vendors selling little parcels of steamed rice wrapped in lotus leaves are to be found on almost every corner. The leaf gives the rice a distinctive flavour, and can be eaten with it. Lotus leaves can be bought dried from Chinese supermarkets and some delicatessens.

This dish can be made with vine leaves rather than lotus leaves, but because vine leaves are quite small it is necessary to make smaller parcels or to use several overlapping leaves for each parcel (see *Steamed vegetable julienne in vine leaves*, page 223). The parcels can be prepared up to 2 hours in advance.

PREPARATION TIME: *40 minutes*
SOAKING TIME: *20 minutes*
COOKING TIME: *30 minutes*

INGREDIENTS – *serves 6:*
6 large lotus leaves about 10 in (250 mm) square
3 tablespoons olive oil
1 medium onion, finely chopped
2 cloves garlic, crushed
4 oz (115 g) cooked ham, finely chopped
1½ lb (700 g) cooked, drained rice – about 11 oz (300 g) uncooked rice
Salt and freshly ground black pepper
Fine string or raffia

Soak the lotus leaves in warm water for 20 minutes.

Heat the oil in a large pan and fry the onion over medium heat for 3 minutes. Add the garlic and ham, and fry for a further minute. Remove from the heat and mix in the cooked rice and salt and pepper to taste.

Thoroughly drain the lotus leaves and pat them dry with a clean cloth. Spread the leaves out flat. Divide the rice mixture between the leaves, placing each portion of rice just above the bottom edge of each leaf. Beginning at the bottom edge, carefully roll up each leaf until the rice is just covered. Fold in the two side edges then continue to

INGREDIENTS – *serves 6:*
14 large Chinese dried
 mushrooms
2 medium leeks, split and cleaned
3 tablespoons olive oil
1 medium onion, very thinly
 sliced
1 clove garlic, peeled and cut into
 thin strips
4 tablespoons dry sherry
1 level teaspoon cornflour
2 tablespoons oyster sauce
1 tablespoon soya sauce
Salt and freshly ground black
 pepper

Soak the mushrooms in warm water for 30 minutes. Drain them then slice them into thin strips, discarding the stalks. Cut the leeks lengthways into thin strips about 2in (50mm) long.

Heat the olive oil in a wok or a deep frying pan over high heat and stir-fry (page 372) the onion for 3 minutes. Add the strips of leek and garlic and stir-fry for a further 3 minutes. Add the sliced mushrooms and stir-fry for 2 more minutes.

Blend the sherry with the cornflour, then stir into the mixture in the pan, together with the oyster sauce, soya sauce, and salt and pepper to taste. Simmer for a further 2-3 minutes, until the mushrooms are just tender and the sauce has thickened slightly. Serve hot. This dish is included in a menu on the opposite page.

roll the leaf into a neat sausage shape. Repeat with the remaining lotus leaves. Tie up each parcel with fine string or lengths of raffia.

Place the parcels either in a steamer, or in a metal colander covered with a lid, set over a pan of simmering water. Steam for 30 minutes. Transfer to a

CHINESE PARCEL Cut the string on the lotus leaf and out pours fragrant rice, served here with stir-fried beef and mushrooms in oyster sauce.

warm serving dish, snip the strings and serve immediately.

This dish is included in a menu on the opposite page.

MUSHROOMS IN OYSTER SAUCE

Chinese dried mushrooms are a common ingredient in Chinese cooking. There are a number of different kinds; Chinese shops usually sell bags of mixed varieties and sizes. Select large ones for

this recipe. Any mushrooms you do not use immediately will keep for several months in a closed container.

Oyster sauce is made largely from oyster juice and soya sauce. It is thick and brown with a sweet-sour flavour. It can also be bought in Chinese shops and in some delicatessens.

POTATO AND CHIVE GALETTE

Potato *galettes* – potato cakes – are eaten throughout France, and almost every region has its own variation. This galette comes from the area around Lyons in south-eastern France. The flesh of baked potatoes is mashed with chives, onions and butter, then fried.

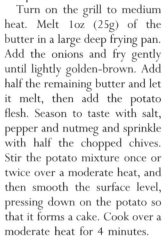

PREPARATION TIME: *35 minutes*
COOKING TIME: *1½ hours*
OVEN TEMPERATURE: *preheat to 200°C (400°F, gas mark 6)*

INGREDIENTS – *serves 8:*
6 medium baking potatoes
4 oz (115 g) butter
3 medium onions, thinly sliced
Salt and freshly ground black pepper
Ground nutmeg
3 level tablespoons chopped chives

Scrub the potatoes well. Dry them and bake in the preheated oven for about 1¼ hours, until just tender. Let the potatoes cool slightly, then split them and scoop the flesh into a bowl.

Turn on the grill to medium heat. Melt 1oz (25g) of the butter in a large deep frying pan. Add the onions and fry gently until lightly golden-brown. Add half the remaining butter and let it melt, then add the potato flesh. Season to taste with salt, pepper and nutmeg and sprinkle with half the chopped chives. Stir the potato mixture once or twice over a moderate heat, and then smooth the surface level, pressing down on the potato so that it forms a cake. Cook over a moderate heat for 4 minutes.

Dot the surface of the galette with the remaining butter. Place the pan under the preheated grill. Cook until the top of the potato forms a golden crust, rotating the pan if necessary so that the potato browns evenly. Carefully slide the galette onto a warm serving plate. Garnish by sprinkling with the remaining chives.

Serve hot, cut into wedges, with dishes that will not conflict with the flavour of chives. It is especially good with grilled oily fish. This dish is included in a menu on page 208.

LYONNAISE GALETTE A potato cake from south-eastern France, flavoured with chives, goes very well with grilled fish such as salmon trout.

HARICOTS VERTS AU GRATIN

Refreshing french beans quickly in cold water after cooking preserves their bright colour and crisp texture. This dish can be prepared ready for cooking up to an hour in advance.

PREPARATION TIME: *30 minutes*
COOKING TIME: *20 minutes*
OVEN TEMPERATURE: *preheat to 190°C (375°F, gas mark 5)*

INGREDIENTS – *serves 8:*
1½ lb (700 g) french beans
Salt and freshly ground black pepper
½ pint (285 ml) double cream
2 egg yolks
2 oz (50 g) butter
2 level tablespoons flaked hazelnuts or flaked almonds
2 level tablespoons fresh dry breadcrumbs
2 level tablespoons grated Parmesan cheese

Trim the stalks from the beans if you wish. Rinse the beans and put them into a pan. Add enough boiling water to half cover them, and a generous pinch of salt. Bring to the boil, cover and cook for 3-4 minutes, depending on the size of the beans – they should remain slightly crisp. Drain the beans thoroughly and then plunge them into a bowl of iced water. Drain once again and season to taste with salt and pepper.

Beat the cream lightly with the egg yolks. Spread the beans in a shallow, ovenproof dish. Dot all over with small knobs of butter and spoon the cream mixture over the top. Sprinkle with the flaked nuts, then the breadcrumbs and finally the grated Parmesan cheese. Cover with kitchen foil.

Cook in the preheated oven for 20 minutes. Remove the foil and return the dish to the oven for a further 5 minutes to brown the top. This dish is included in a menu on page 230.

SORREL AND LEMON PURÉE

Clumps of bright green sorrel are found growing in gardens throughout France. One of the many dishes it is used for is a sharp-flavoured purée. Although sorrel is rarely found in greengrocers in this country, it is very easy to grow. The leaves are best used when still young.

PREPARATION AND COOKING TIME: *25 minutes*

INGREDIENTS – *serves 4:*
2 lb (900 g) good young sorrel leaves
1½ oz (40 g) butter
1 level teaspoon caster sugar
Finely grated rind of 1 lemon
Salt and freshly ground black pepper
1-2 tablespoons single or double cream (optional)
1-2 egg yolks (optional)
GARNISH
A few thin wedges of lemon

Wash the sorrel well and shake dry. Discard any discoloured or blemished leaves. Roll the leaves up, 6 together at a time, and cut across the rolled sorrel leaves with scissors to produce thin strips (called a chiffonade).

Melt the butter in a pan. Add the prepared sorrel, sugar, lemon rind, and salt and pepper to taste. Cover the pan and cook until the sorrel has lost its crispness – with young sorrel this will only take a few minutes. Remove from the heat and beat to a purée with a wooden spoon. For a richer purée, a little cream, or an egg yolk or two, can be added at this stage.

Turn the purée into a warm serving dish and garnish with lemon wedges. The purée is a very good accompaniment to lamb and fish. This dish is included in a menu on page 204.

TIAN DE LEGUMES

Strictly speaking, a *tian* is a fairly deep earthenware gratin dish from Provence in the South of France. However, the word has also come to be applied to the wide variety of dishes traditionally cooked in a tian.

This tian can be prepared the night before and kept, covered, in the refrigerator.

PREPARATION TIME: *30 minutes*
COOKING TIME: *35-40 minutes*
OVEN TEMPERATURE: *preheat to 190°C (375°F, gas mark 5)*

INGREDIENTS – *serves 6:*
8 tablespoons olive oil
2 medium onions, thinly sliced
1 red pepper, seeded and sliced
1 green pepper, seeded and sliced
1 large aubergine, thinly sliced
2 cloves garlic, finely chopped
Salt and freshly ground black pepper
8 medium courgettes, sliced into rings
6 firm tomatoes, sliced
1 level tablespoon chopped fresh thyme
4 level tablespoons grated Parmesan cheese

Heat 4 tablespoons of the oil in a large frying pan. Add the sliced onion and fry gently until lightly browned. Add the sliced peppers, aubergine and garlic to the onions, and fry gently until soft. Add salt and pepper to taste and then spoon the mixture into the base of a large gratin dish. Arrange the sliced courgettes and tomatoes in overlapping rows on top. Sprinkle with 2 tablespoons of olive oil and the chopped thyme, and season once again with salt and pepper.

Bake in the preheated oven for 25 minutes. Sprinkle with the remaining 2 tablespoons of olive oil and the Parmesan cheese, and return to the oven for a further 10-15 minutes.

TIAN DE PROVENCE The combination of tomatoes, peppers, aubergines, courgettes and olive oil, is cooked in a traditional, earthenware tian, typical of the French region of Provence.

SPINACH AND BOURSIN ROULADE

Serve this roulade as soon as possible after filling it, or the cream cheese mixture will melt completely and ooze out. If it has to be kept for long, turn it out of its tin onto a clean tea towel. Peel off the baking paper then roll up the roulade with the towel in place of the filling. Wrap loosely in foil and keep warm in the oven turned down very low. Just before serving, unwrap the roulade, fill it and roll it up again. For a less rich dish, use herb-flavoured Quark instead of Boursin.

PREPARATION TIME: *45 minutes*
COOKING TIME: *10-12 minutes*
OVEN TEMPERATURE: *preheat to 200°C (400°F, gas mark 6)*

INGREDIENTS – *serves 4:*
6 oz (175 g) fresh spinach OR
4 oz (115 g) frozen spinach
1½ oz (40 g) butter
1½ oz (40 g) plain or wholewheat flour
¾ pint (450 ml) milk
Salt and freshly ground black pepper
Generous pinch ground nutmeg
3 eggs, separated
2 × 2¾ oz (70 g) packets Boursin, flavoured with garlic and herbs
3 tablespoons soured cream
2 level tablespoons chopped chives
2 tablespoons melted butter
2 level tablespoons roughly chopped parsley
Non-stick baking paper

Wash the spinach and put it in a pan without any water other than that which clings to the leaves. Cook for about 8 minutes until tender. Drain thoroughly, squeezing out as much moisture as possible, then chop finely. If using frozen spinach, follow the cooking instructions on the packet, drain and chop finely.

Grease a large swiss roll tin, about 10in × 13in (250mm × 330mm), and line it carefully with non-stick baking paper or lightly greased and floured greaseproof paper.

Melt the butter in a large pan. Stir in the flour and cook for half a minute. Gradually stir in the milk, beating between each addition. Stir over a gentle heat until the sauce has thickened and is smooth. Remove from the heat and beat in the spinach, salt, pepper and nutmeg to taste, and the egg yolks.

Whisk the egg whites until stiff but not dry, and fold lightly but evenly into the sauce. Pour the mixture into the prepared

HOT SPINACH ROLL Creamy Boursin cheese flavoured with herbs and garlic is mixed with soured cream and chives to fill a light spinach roulade.

tin, spreading it evenly into the corners. Bake in the preheated oven for 10-12 minutes, until pale golden and lightly set.

While the roulade is cooking, beat the Boursin cheese with the soured cream, chives, and salt and pepper to taste.

Turn the cooked roulade out carefully onto a sheet of non-stick baking paper. Peel the lining paper from the roulade. Spread the filling evenly over the roulade, to within about ¾in (20mm) of the edges. Roll up like a swiss roll. It does not matter if it cracks slightly. Brush with melted butter and sprinkle generously with chopped parsley. Carefully lift the roulade onto a long, flat serving dish with the seam side underneath, and serve. This dish is included in a menu on page 193.

BEMUELOS

A Jewish Passover dish, bemuelos are traditionally made with matzo meal – ground up unleavened bread. This can be replaced by flour, but the flavour will be slightly different. The bemuelos can be fried an hour in advance. Wrap in foil and reheat in a moderate oven for 10-15 minutes.

PREPARATION AND COOKING
  TIME: *50 minutes*
CHILLING TIME: *at least 2 hours*

INGREDIENTS – *serves 6:*
2 lb (900 g) potatoes
2 eggs, lightly beaten
4 oz (115 g) finely grated cheese such as a mature Cheddar
Salt and freshly ground black pepper
3 level tablespoons chopped parsley
About 4 oz (115 g) matzo meal
Oil for deep frying

Peel the potatoes and chop them roughly. Cook them in boiling salted water until just tender. Drain the potatoes thoroughly and mash them. Put the mashed potato into a heavy-based pan and stir over a gentle heat for 2-3 minutes to dry it out. Remove from the heat and beat in the eggs, cheese, salt and pepper to taste, parsley and 2 tablespoons of matzo meal.

Taking a tablespoon of the mixture at a time, shape it into small flat cakes, dusting each with matzo meal. Chill them in

the refrigerator for at least 2 hours so that they do not lose their shape during frying. Heat the oil to 190°C (375°F). Deep-fry (page 372) for 4-5 minutes until golden. Drain thoroughly on absorbent kitchen paper and serve hot.

Serve with rich dishes or with dishes with plenty of sauce. This dish is included in a menu on page 219.

MUNG BEAN DAL

Dal is the Hindi term for pulses – such as mung beans – and dishes made with them. Ready-grated tenderised coconut, or unsweetened desiccated coconut, may be used in this recipe instead of creamed coconut.

PREPARATION TIME: *35 minutes*
COOKING TIME: *20 minutes*
SOAKING TIME: *2-3 hours*

INGREDIENTS – *serves 4:*
8 oz (225 g) split mung beans
2 tablespoons olive oil
1 medium onion, finely chopped
¾ in (20 mm) piece root ginger, peeled and finely chopped
1 level teaspoon ground cardamom
1 level teaspoon turmeric powder
2 oz (50 g) creamed coconut, grated
½ pint (285 ml) vegetable stock (page 368)
Salt and freshly ground black pepper
1 medium red pepper, seeded and cut into matchstick strips

Wash the mung beans. Put into a bowl and add enough cold water to cover generously. Soak for 2-3 hours, then drain well.

Heat the oil in a deep frying pan. Add the onion and ginger and fry gently for 3-4 minutes. Add the cardamom and turmeric and stir over the heat for 1 minute. Add the drained mung beans and stir over a moderate heat for 3 minutes.

Blend the creamed coconut with a little of the stock and add to the mung beans, together with the rest of the stock. Add salt and pepper to taste, then bring to the boil. Cover the pan and simmer for about 15 minutes, or until soft. Stir in the strips of red pepper and simmer for a further 5 minutes. Serve hot. The dal is particularly good with fish. This dish is included in a menu on page 193.

POLENTA

Special Italian polenta flour – coarse ground maize – can be bought, but ordinary coarse cornmeal can be used instead.

In this recipe, the polenta is baked in the oven. It can also be made into different shapes, coated in egg and breadcrumbs and shallow-fried.

PREPARATION TIME: *25 minutes*
COOKING TIME: *50-55 minutes*
CHILLING TIME: *at least 1 hour*
OVEN TEMPERATURE: *preheat to 190°C (375°F, gas mark 5)*

INGREDIENTS – *serves 6:*
1¾ pints (1 litre) water
Salt
8 oz (225 g) polenta flour
Freshly ground black pepper
3 oz (75 g) melted butter
4 tablespoons grated Parmesan cheese

Bring the water and ½ teaspoon of salt to a rolling boil. Shower the polenta flour slowly but steadily into the water, stirring continuously to prevent the mixture becoming lumpy. After all the flour has been added, continue stirring until the mixture is quite smooth. Simmer gently for 25-30 minutes until the polenta is thick enough to stand a spoon in it, but not dry. Add salt and pepper to taste.

Grease a shallow ovenproof dish with a diameter greater than 9in (230mm), and spoon the polenta into it. Using a dampened spatula, shape the polenta into a cake about 9in (230mm) in diameter so that it does not quite reach the edges of the dish. Mark out 6 equal, wedge-shaped sections on the top of the cake. Chill for at least an hour. If you are chilling the polenta for longer than an hour it is necessary to cover it.

Cut along the marked sections easing them gently apart. Spoon over the melted butter and sprinkle with the grated Parmesan. Bake in the preheated oven for 20-25 minutes until a light golden-brown.

Serve hot instead of rice or potatoes.

SALADS

SALADE AUX CROTTINS DE CHÈVRES

Crottins de chèvres are little rounds of strongly flavoured French goat cheese. The name means,

unpoetically, 'goat's droppings'. They can be bought in specialist cheese shops and some delicatessens and supermarkets. Other French goat cheese can be used instead, as can British goat cheese although this tends to have a milder flavour. See *Cheese*, pages 113-116.

As an alternative this salad may be served as a first course with the crottins grilled (see method). If endive is difficult to find, use a crisp lettuce, such as an Iceberg or Webb's, or one of the continental red lettuces – oak leaf lettuce, for example.

PREPARATION TIME: *30 minutes*

INGREDIENTS – *serves 8:*
4 crottins de chèvre, about 2 oz (50 g) each
1 small head endive
Centre leaves of 1 cos lettuce
2 level tablespoons split, blanched almonds, lightly toasted
2 level tablespoons coarsely chopped parsley
DRESSING
3 tablespoons white wine vinegar
3 tablespoons walnut oil
3 tablespoons olive oil
1 teaspoon coarse grain mustard
1 clove garlic, crushed
Salt and freshly ground black pepper

Mix the white wine vinegar with the oils, mustard, garlic, and salt and pepper to taste.

Crumble the crottins. Wash the endive and the cos lettuce leaves and shake dry. Arrange on 8 small dinner plates or dessert plates. Scatter the crumbled crottins, almonds and parsley over the top. Sprinkle with the dressing, and serve.

To serve with grilled cheese, buy one small crottin per person. Cut each crottin into 3 slices and grill until golden. Arrange the slices on each plate of salad, then sprinkle with the dressing and serve immediately.

This dish is included in a menu on page 245.

GOAT CHEESE SALAD A walnut oil dressing complements goat cheese, almonds, crisp cos lettuce and endive.

PORT AND STILTON SALAD

Although Stilton should never be soaked in port, a glass of port with Stilton is a very good combination. The combination also works well in this salad in which a port-flavoured dressing is served with the Stilton. Radicchio looks like a small red and white lettuce – though it is in fact a kind of radish.

The salad can be served between the main course and dessert, or as a savoury course. All the ingredients can be prepared earlier in the day to be assembled later, but keep the lettuce and radicchio in a plastic bag in the refrigerator.

PREPARATION TIME: *20 minutes*

INGREDIENTS – *serves 8:*
1 oz (25 g) butter
4 oz (115 g) walnuts, chopped
2 cloves garlic, finely chopped
1 large radicchio, or 2 small ones
1 medium-sized crisp lettuce
8 oz (225 g) Stilton cheese,
*   coarsely crumbled*
DRESSING
8 tablespoons olive oil
2 teaspoons French mustard
Juice of 1 orange
Juice of ½ lemon
3 tablespoons tawny port
Salt and freshly ground black
*   pepper*

Heat the butter gently in a small pan. Add the walnuts and garlic and fry over a moderate heat for 2 minutes. Drain on absorbent kitchen paper.

Separate the leaves of the radicchio and lettuce. Wash them and shake dry.

To make the dressing, mix the olive oil with the French mustard, orange juice and lemon juice, port and salt and pepper to taste.

Arrange the radicchio leaves and lettuce leaves on eight salad plates. Sprinkle them with the crumbled Stilton, fried walnuts, then the port dressing. Serve immediately. This dish is included in a menu on page 208.

TAWNY SALAD Port dressing and red radicchio make a rich combination with crumbled Stilton and walnuts.

M E N U

Provençal Dinner for Eight

ROUGET À LA PROVENÇAL
page 203

❧

PINTADE AUX QUARANTE GOUSSES
D'AIL *page 220*

HARICOTS VERTS AU GRATIN
page 226

NEW POTATOES

❧

SALADE DE MÂCHE TIÈDE
opposite page

❧

SYMPHONIE DE TROIS COULEURS
page 240

Serve small red mullet or single fillets.

IN ADVANCE Make all the parts of the symphonie de trois couleurs the night before.

ON THE DAY Prepare the rouget about 4-5 hours in advance of the meal so that it has time to chill. Allow about 2½ hours to prepare the rest of the meal.

Prepare the haricots verts, the pintade and the ingredients for the salad.

Once the pintade is cooked, make the sauce and boil the potatoes. Put the haricots in to cook. Just before serving, garnish the rouget.

After the first course, reheat the sauce and cut up and garnish the pintade.

After the main course, boil the eggs, reheat the bacon and onions and assemble the salad.

After the salad, complete the symphonie.

TO DRINK A good medium-bodied white wine such as a white Bordeaux with the pintade, and a sweet white such as a Monbazillac with the pudding.

SALADE DE MÂCHE TIÈDE

Mâche – lamb's lettuce or corn salad – is best in early spring. If it is unavailable, use endive or a loose-leaved lettuce. Quail's eggs can be used instead of hen's eggs; allow one per person and boil for 30 seconds. The cold ingredients, apart from the herbs, can be prepared 1-2 hours ahead. Cook the bacon and eggs just before the meal. Wrap the eggs in a towel to keep warm until served. Warm the bacon before serving.

PREPARATION AND COOKING
TIME: *45 minutes*

INGREDIENTS – *serves 8:*
6 oz (175 g) mangetout
4 oz (115 g) lamb's lettuce
2 heads chicory
1 bunch watercress, 3-4 oz (75-115 g), washed and drained
4 medium courgettes
2 level tablespoons chopped fresh herbs (such as chives, parsley, chervil, basil, tarragon)
Young spinach leaves, sorrel leaves, or the centre leaves from a cos lettuce (see method)
6 rashers lean bacon, chopped
4 spring onions, chopped
6 tablespoons olive oil
4 eggs
Juices of 1 lemon
Salt and freshly ground black pepper

Top and tail the mangetout. Wash and drain them. Put them into a pan with 4 tablespoons of cold water. Cover the pan and simmer for 3 minutes. Drain the mangetout, refresh them under cold running water, then drain them once again.

Separate the leaves of lamb's lettuce. Wash them thoroughly and shake dry. Cut the chicory crosswise into thin slices. Separate the watercress into small sprigs. Top and tail the courgettes and slice them very thinly, diagonally.

Mix together the mangetout, lamb's lettuce, chicory, watercress, courgettes and chopped herbs. Line eight salad plates with spinach, sorrel or cos lettuce leaves and arrange the salad in the centre of each.

Put a pan of water on to come to the boil. Meanwhile, fry the chopped bacon and spring onions gently in the olive oil for 3 minutes. Boil the eggs for just 1½ minutes. Rinse them quickly in cold water to stop them cooking any further.

Stir the lemon juice into the bacon mixture and add salt and pepper to taste. Spoon the mixture over each portion of salad. Carefully break the eggs in half. Scoop the contents of half an eggshell over each salad. Serve immediately.

This dish is included in a menu on the opposite page.

HOT AND COLD Soft-boiled eggs and warm bacon are mixed with cold spinach leaves, lamb's lettuce, mangetout and courgettes to make a French warm salad (or salade tiède).

TOMATO VINAIGRETTE *Pale green, crisp cos lettuce hearts are set off by a fruity pink dressing made with tomatoes and tarragon.*

Add the chopped tarragon and blend again, very briefly. Taste, and adjust the seasoning.

Just before serving, cut both lettuce hearts into quarters lengthways. Arrange two pieces on each plate and spoon the tomato vinaigrette over the top. Garnish each portion with sprigs of tarragon. This dish is included in a menu on page 193.

PREPARATION TIME: *40 minutes plus chilling time*

INGREDIENTS – *serves 6:*
6 thin-skinned oranges
2 avocado pears, ripe but firm
DRESSING
6 tablespoons olive oil
2 cloves garlic, finely chopped
Juice of 2 limes or lemons
2 level tablespoons chopped fresh
  coriander
Finely grated rind of 1 orange
Salt and freshly ground black
  pepper
GARNISH
$^{1}/_{2}$-1 level tablespoon sesame
  seeds, toasted.

ORANGE, AVOCADO AND CORIANDER SALAD

Fresh coriander leaves give this salad its special flavour. Coriander, which is similar in appearance to parsley but much stronger in taste, is said to be the world's most widely used herb. It is an essential ingredient in many dishes in the Middle East, where it originated, and also in South America and the Caribbean. The peppery leaves are used like parsley as a garnish and the fruit – incorrectly called seeds – are used in, for example, curry powder. Fresh coriander leaves can be found in some supermarkets or in ethnic food shops.

The oranges for this salad can be prepared the night before.

First make the dressing. In a large bowl or jug mix the olive oil with the garlic, lime or lemon juice, coriander and orange rind. Add salt and pepper to taste.

With a sharp knife, cut all the peel and pith from each orange, then cut the oranges into thin slices and lay them in a shallow dish. Spoon over the prepared dressing. Cover and chill in the refrigerator for at least 2 hours or overnight.

Before serving, peel the avocados, being careful not to remove too much of the darker green flesh. Halve and remove the stones. Cut each avocado half lengthways into thin slivers.

Remove the orange slices from the dressing. Arrange them with the avocado slices on a shallow serving dish and spoon over the dressing. Sprinkle with the sesame seeds. This dish is included in a menu on page 219.

COS LETTUCE WITH TOMATO AND TARRAGON VINAIGRETTE

The tomato dressing on this salad has a fresh, fruity flavour. It can be kept for 3-4 days in the refrigerator. The heart of one Webb's lettuce, cut into 8 pieces, can be used if cos lettuce hearts are unavailable.

PREPARATION TIME: *25 minutes*

INGREDIENTS – *serves 4:*
2 cos lettuce hearts
VINAIGRETTE
8 oz (225 g) tomatoes
1-2 cloves garlic, peeled
3 tablespoons red wine vinegar
$^{1}/_{2}$ teaspoon coarse grain mustard
Salt and freshly ground black
  pepper
6 tablespoons olive oil
1 level tablespoon chopped fresh
  tarragon

GARNISH
Sprigs of fresh tarragon

First make the vinaigrette. Chop the tomatoes roughly. Put them into a liquidiser or food processor with the garlic, red wine vinegar, mustard, and salt and pepper to taste. Blend for a few seconds until the tomatoes have been reduced to a pulp but still have some texture. Gradually blend in the oil, in a fine trickle as though making mayonnaise.

TABBOULEH WITH LIME AND MARINATED RED PEPPERS

Burghul salad – tabbouleh – is eaten in all parts of the Middle East, but it is a particular speciality of the Lebanon. It can be eaten by itself or as an accompanying salad. Burghul – also called cracked wheat, bulgur wheat or, in Greek food shops, *pourgouri* – is wheat that has been boiled until it cracks open, then dried and ground.

PREPARATION TIME: *1 hour plus chilling time*

INGREDIENTS – *serves 10:*
1 lb (450 g) fine burghul
4 large red peppers
12 tablespoons olive oil
Juice of 2 limes
Salt and freshly ground black pepper
3 cloves garlic, crushed
4 spring onions, finely chopped
4 level tablespoons chopped fresh parsley
4 level tablespoons chopped fresh mint
Juice of 2 lemons
GARNISH
Vine leaves (optional)
10 stoned black olives, halved
Fresh coriander or parsley

Put the burghul into a large bowl. Add enough cold water to cover it by at least 1½in (40mm). Leave to soak for about 30-40 minutes, until the burghul has absorbed a lot of the water.

While the burghul is soaking, cut the peppers in half lengthways and remove the core, white membrane and seeds. Grill the pepper halves, cut sides down, under moderate heat until the skins blister and char, and the flesh softens. Skin the peppers, holding them under cold water to prevent you burning your fingers. Dry the skinned peppers thoroughly with absorbent kitchen paper. Cut them into thin strips and put them into a shallow dish.

Mix 4 tablespoons of the olive oil with the lime juice, salt and pepper to taste, and one-third of the crushed garlic. Spoon the dressing over the pepper strips, cover and leave to chill in the refrigerator.

Drain the soaked burghul thoroughly and squeeze it in a clean cloth to dry it further.

Mix the burghul with the chopped spring onions, remaining crushed garlic, chopped parsley and mint. Mix the remaining olive oil with the lemon juice and salt and pepper to taste. Stir into the burghul.

Spoon the tabboulch onto a shallow serving dish, lined, if you choose, with vine leaves and mound it in the centre. Spoon the marinated red peppers around the tabbouleh and stud it with the halved black olives. Garnish with sprigs of coriander or parsley and serve with warm pitta bread. This dish is included in a menu on page 236.

SALAD OF LEBANON *Marinated red peppers, juicy black olives and fresh coriander are the final additions to a dish of tabbouleh – a cracked-wheat salad dressed with olive oil, lemon juice, garlic, parsley and mint.*

PUDDINGS & DESSERTS

TORTA DI ALBICOCCHE CON ZABAGLIONE ALL'AMARETTO

Two of the best Italian desserts combine to create a lavish tart of fresh apricots (*albicocche*) and almond-flavoured zabaglione. *Torta di albicocche* has a base of rich and crumbling pastry, made with eggs, cream and a dash of Amaretto liqueur. Zabaglione – a froth of eggs whisked with sugar and sweet wine – is here made with Amaretto rather than the more traditional Marsala wine.

The tart can be made up to 24 hours in advance and warmed again in a moderate oven – 180°C (350°F, gas mark 4) – for 5-10 minutes only. It should be warm but not hot. Assemble the ingredients for the zabaglione in advance, but do not make it until just before serving.

PREPARATION TIME: *55 minutes*
CHILLING TIME: *30 minutes*
COOKING TIME: *40-45 minutes*
OVEN TEMPERATURE: *preheat to 190°C (375°F, gas mark 5)*

APRICOT TART *Fresh fruit, rich pastry and toasted pine kernels are bathed in a heady froth of zabaglione made with Amaretto liqueur.*

INGREDIENTS – *serves 6:*
8 oz (225 g) plain flour
5 oz (150 g) butter
2 egg yolks
2 tablespoons single cream
1 tablespoon Amaretto di Saronno
4 level tablespoons pine kernels, lightly toasted
12 fresh apricots
GLAZE
3 level tablespoons apricot jam
2 level tablespoons icing sugar

ZABAGLIONE
4 egg yolks
1½ oz (40 g) caster sugar
3½ fl oz (100 ml) dry white wine
2 tablespoons Amaretto di Saronno
2 egg whites

Sieve the flour into a bowl. Add the butter, chop it roughly with a knife and then rub it into the flour until the mixture resembles fine breadcrumbs.

In a separate bowl mix the egg yolks with the cream and Amaretto and then beat them into the flour and butter mixture to make a smooth dough.

Cover the bowl and chill for 30 minutes in the refrigerator.

Grease a 9in (230mm), loose-based flan tin. Roll out the chilled dough and use it to line

the flan tin. Chop 2 tablespoons of the pine kernels and sprinkle them over the base of the pastry case. Halve and stone the apricots and arrange them on top, rounded sides up.

Bake the tart in the preheated oven for 20 minutes. Remove the tart from the oven, cover it loosely with kitchen foil and return it to the oven for a further 20-25 minutes.

To make the glaze, melt the apricot jam, then sieve it into a bowl. Sieve the icing sugar and beat it into the jam until completely dissolved, then trickle the glaze over the warm tart. Sprinkle the remaining 2 tablespoons of pine kernels on top.

Keep the tart warm in a very low oven while making the zabaglione.

Put the egg yolks into a bowl over hot water with half of the caster sugar, the white wine and the Amaretto. Whisk them together until the mixture is thick, light and fluffy. Whisk the egg whites in a separate bowl until stiff but not dry and fold in the remaining caster sugar. Fold the egg whites and sugar lightly into the zabaglione, making sure they are thoroughly incorporated.

Pour the zabaglione into a warmed jug and serve immediately, poured over wedges of the warm tart.

FROMAGE À LA CRÈME WITH CHARENTAIS MELON

In France a rich meal may be followed by cheese and fruit, or a combination of both in a dessert of sweet cream cheese – *fromage à la crème*.

Perforated moulds (plain or heart-shaped) which allow the whey to drain away from the cheese are available from kitchen equipment shops. However, you can improvise by piercing holes in the base of a deep plastic carton or yoghurt pots.

PREPARATION TIME: *35 minutes*
CHILLING TIME: *5-6 hours or overnight*

INGREDIENTS – *serves 6:*
8 oz (225 g) curd cheese
8 oz (225 g) Quark or low-fat cream cheese
¼ pint (150 ml) double cream
2 oz (50 g) caster sugar
1 egg white
1 Charentais melon
4 tablespoons Beaumes-de-Venise or other dessert white wine
DECORATION
Fresh nasturtium flowers

Line a 1 pint (570ml) perforated mould, or six individual moulds, with muslin. To line the mould, take a square of muslin large enough to cover the base and sides. For deep moulds it may be necessary to make a slit in the muslin from one side to the centre point to ensure a neat fit.

Scald the muslin with boiling water, then press it into the mould, overlapping the slit edges. Leave the excess cloth hanging over the rim of the mould. Stand the mould on a rack over a tray or shallow dish.

Beat the curd cheese in a bowl with the Quark or cream cheese until smooth. Lightly whip the cream until it stands in soft peaks and mix with 1oz (25g) of the caster sugar and the cheeses. Whisk the egg white with the remaining 1oz (25g) of sugar until it stands in soft peaks. Fold the egg white into the cheese mixture.

Spoon the mixture into the prepared mould. Smooth off the surface and fold over the edges of the muslin to cover the cheese mixture. Chill in the refrigerator for 5-6 hours or overnight.

Halve the melon and scoop out the seeds. Using a 'parisienne' cutter – a melon baller – scoop the melon flesh into balls. Put the melon into a shallow dish, pour over the wine and mix well. Cover the dish tightly and chill for 2 hours.

Turn the fromage à la crème out onto a serving dish (or individual plates) and arrange the marinated melon balls around it with the marinade wine. Decorate with nasturtium flowers.

SWEET HEART Vivid nasturtium flowers and balls of Charentais melon soaked in Muscat wine decorate a heart of sweetened cheese and cream.

CANDIED DATES

Fresh dates are usually available from September to March. However, good plump boxed dates can be used instead. They do not require skinning. The stuffed dates will keep for up to 2 weeks, packed in an airtight box.

PREPARATION TIME: *45 minutes*
STANDING TIME: *2-3 hours*

INGREDIENTS – *makes 24:*
8 oz (225 g) marzipan
  (page 400)
2 level tablespoons shelled,
  chopped pistachio nuts, about
  1 oz (25 g)
1 teaspoon rose water
24 fresh dates, skinned
3 oz (75 g) granulated sugar
1 level teaspoon ground cinnamon

Knead the marzipan to soften it. Mix it with the chopped pistachios and rose water. Split the dates lengthways along one side and remove the stones. Stuff each date generously with the marzipan and pistachio mixture, shaping each one neatly.

Mix the sugar with the cinnamon. Roll each stuffed date in the cinnamon-flavoured sugar. Leave in a warm place for 2-3 hours until the sugar coating has hardened slightly. This dish is included in a menu on page 219.

MIDDLE-EASTERN SWEETMEATS
Fresh dates, with a fragrant marzipan, pistachio and rosewater filling, are rolled in sugar and cinnamon.

M E N U

Celebration Lunch for Ten

PRAWN MOUSSE WITH AVOCADO SAUCE
page 200

CHICKEN WITH WALNUT AND
TARRAGON SAUCE *page 213*

TABBOULEH WITH LIME AND MARINATED
RED PEPPERS *page 233*

FRENCH BEAN, FENNEL AND
WATERCRESS SALAD

CHERRY AND ALMOND CHEESECAKE
this page

Use about 1lb (450g) of french beans, 2½-3lb (1.1-1.4kg) of Florence fennel, and 2 bunches of watercress for the salad and toss it in vinaigrette (page 371).
IN ADVANCE Allow at least 5-6 hours the day before the party. Put the chickens on to cook. Cook the fish for the mousse, then make the cheesecake and the tabbouleh. Complete the mousse. Make the walnut and tarragon sauce and mix it with the chicken.
ON THE DAY Allow about 1½-2 hours. Boil the french beans for the salad. Cut the fennel into strips and wash and dry the watercress. Make the vinaigrette.

Make the avocado sauce and decorate the cherry and almond cheesecake. Just before serving, turn out and garnish the salmon mousses.

After the first course, toss the salad in the dressing and garnish the chicken.
TO DRINK A good dry or medium dry white wine. If you wish, a medium sweet sparkling white wine may be served with the pudding.

CHERRY AND ALMOND CHEESECAKE

The flavours of almond and cherry filter through all the different layers of this luxurious cheesecake.

Fresh cherries give the best results, but tinned cherries – very well drained – can be used instead. You will need two 15oz (425g) tins. The flavour of the cheesecake improves with chilling, but add the crushed praline just before serving.

PREPARATION TIME: *45 minutes*
CHILLING TIME: *6-24 hours*
COOKING TIME: *1¼ hours*
OVEN TEMPERATURE: *preheat to*
  180°C (350°F, gas mark 4)

INGREDIENTS – *serves 10:*
BASE
8 oz (225 g) digestive biscuits
2 oz (50 g) unblanched almonds
3 oz (75 g) butter
2 level tablespoons soft brown
  sugar
2 tablespoons kirsch
FILLING
4 oz (115 g) homemade
  marzipan (page 400)
3 oz (75 g) caster sugar
2 level tablespoons plain flour
1½ lb (700 g) full fat cream
  cheese
6 tablespoons kirsch
4 eggs
TOPPING
½ pint (285 ml) soured cream
12 oz (350 g) fresh cherries,
  pitted (page 396)
2 level tablespoons crushed
  praline (page 289)

Lightly grease a 10in (250mm) springform cake tin with removable base and opening side.

To make the base, put the biscuits in a large plastic bag and crush them with a rolling pin. Grind the almonds (with their skins) in a food processor, liquidiser or coffee grinder.

Melt the butter in a pan. Put the biscuits, almonds, sugar and kirsch in a bowl with the melted butter and mix well. Press the mixture evenly over the bottom and up the sides of the tin. Chill in the refrigerator.

While the base is chilling, make the filling. Crumble the marzipan into a bowl. Add the sugar, flour and 2oz (50g) of the cream cheese, and beat them together until smooth. In a separate bowl beat together the remaining cream cheese and the kirsch until light and fluffy, then beat into the marzipan mixture. Gradually beat in the eggs.

Pour the filling into the tin and bake in the preheated oven for 50 minutes. Remove the cake from the oven and spread the soured cream evenly over the top. Cook it for a further 25 minutes. The surface usually cracks slightly.

Allow the cheesecake to cool in its tin on a wire rack. Chill it thoroughly (still in its tin) for at least 6 hours or overnight.

Remove the cheesecake from the tin and arrange the pitted cherries on the top. Sprinkle crushed praline over the cherries. This dish is included in a menu on the opposite page.

STEAMED COFFEE SOUFFLÉS WITH HOT CHOCOLATE SAUCE

For perfect results, these steamed soufflés should be served as soon as they have finished cooking. This is best achieved by serving cheese before the dessert. This both revives the palate and allows the cook to put the finishing touches to the soufflé.

The chocolate sauce can be made up to 24 hours in advance and then heated through. Before the meal prepare the soufflé up to the point at which it is ready to have egg whites folded in and put into the oven.

PREPARATION TIME: *35 minutes*
STANDING TIME: *30 minutes*
COOKING TIME: *20-25 minutes*
OVEN TEMPERATURE: *preheat to 180°C (350°F, gas mark 4)*

INGREDIENTS – *serves 6:*
2 level tablespoons medium ground coffee
6 tablespoons boiling water
½ pint (285 ml) double cream
6 level tablespoons fresh white breadcrumbs
4 eggs, separated
2 oz (50 g) soft brown sugar
2 tablespoons Tia Maria liqueur
SAUCE
6 tablespoons water
6 level tablespoons granulated sugar
2 tablespoons Tia Maria liqueur
4 oz (115 g) plain chocolate, grated

Put the coffee into a small jug, pour over the boiling water and leave it to infuse for 30 minutes. Strain the coffee through a fine sieve or paper filter and press the grounds down well to extract the full flavour.

To make the chocolate sauce, put the water and sugar into a pan and stir over a gentle heat until the sugar has dissolved. Boil for 1 minute and remove from the heat. Beat in the Tia Maria and chocolate. Stir over a gentle heat for 30 seconds, or until the chocolate has dissolved. Remove the sauce from the heat and set aside until needed.

Lightly grease 6 large dariole moulds, or deep ramekin dishes about 7fl oz (200ml) in capacity.

Whip the cream in a large bowl until just thick enough to hold its shape. Lightly beat in the strained coffee, breadcrumbs, egg yolks, brown sugar and Tia Maria.

Whisk the egg whites until they are stiff but not dry. Fold them lightly into the coffee mixture until they are thoroughly blended. Spoon the mixture into the dariole moulds or ramekin dishes. Stand them in a roasting tin and add enough hot water to come halfway up their sides.

LIGHT AND DARK A cloud of steam raises these coffee soufflés. They are then turned out and enveloped in smooth chocolate sauce.

Cook in the preheated oven for 20-25 minutes, until just set and springy to the touch.

Heat the chocolate sauce in a double saucepan or a bowl set over hot water.

Carefully turn out the soufflés onto warmed serving plates, trickle a little of the hot chocolate sauce over each one and serve immediately. This dish is included in a menu on page 217.

PÊCHES À LA BELLE SANDRINE

La Belle Sandrine is a blend of Armagnac brandy and passion fruit. Its summery flavour is combined in this simple dish with that of ripe, fresh peaches. Fruit liqueurs can be used instead; apricot, peach or orange-flavoured liqueurs will all go well with the peaches.

Some varieties of peach discolour. It is therefore safer to prepare them as close to the time of the meal as possible. It is important that the peaches are all evenly ripe. Almonds ready cut into thin strips – 'stripped' almonds – can be bought in some delicatessens and grocers shops, and will be quicker than using blanched almonds.

PREPARATION TIME: *30 minutes*
CHILLING TIME: *30 minutes*

INGREDIENTS – *serves 4:*
4 large ripe peaches
2 oz (50 g) blanched almonds
4 fl oz (115 ml) La Belle
  Sandrine liqueur
¼ pint (150 ml) double cream
Small silver dragees
4 chocolate leaves (page 290)

Peel the peaches. If this is difficult, cover them with boiling water for 1-2 minutes, immerse in cold water then skin them.

Cut the almonds into thin strips, and stud each peach with almonds. Stand the peaches in a shallow dish, and spoon over the liqueur. Cover and chill in the refrigerator for 30 minutes.

Spoon a pool of cream onto each of four dessert plates and place a peach in the centre of each one. Decorate each with a chocolate leaf. Trickle a little of the marinade liqueur over the peaches, then scatter with silver dragees. This dish is included in a menu on page 204.

BELLE PÊCHE A fresh ripe peach is soaked in passion fruit liqueur, studded with almonds and decorated with a single chocolate leaf.

RASPBERRY AND RATAFIA TERRINE

Crème de cassis which flavours this terrine is a liqueur made from blackcurrants – *cassis* in French – in the Dijon area of central France.

The terrine, the sauce and the ratafia decoration can all be made 1-2 days in advance. The terrine is best made in a long loaf tin or terrine. This shape gives good slices when it is cut. The terrine can be made with other soft fruit such as blackberries, loganberries, or strawberries. If you do not like pips, sieve the fruit to make the purée rather than liquidising it. If you use strawberries, roughly chop the whole fruit before folding it into the mixture.

PREPARATION TIME: *1 hour*
CHILLING TIME: *at least 4 hours*
  or overnight

INGREDIENTS – *serves 8:*
1¾ lb (800 g) raspberries, fresh,
  or frozen and thawed
4 tablespoons crème de cassis
½ pint (285 ml) double cream
3 tablespoons water
4 level teaspoons powdered
  gelatine
32 ratafia biscuits
2 oz (50 g) plain chocolate
4 tablespoons orange juice or dry
  white wine

Put 8oz (225g) of the raspberries into a liquidiser or food processor with 2 tablespoons of the cassis and blend until smooth.

Turn the raspberry purée into a large bowl and mix with the double cream.

Put the water in a small bowl and sprinkle in the gelatine. Stand the bowl in a pan of hot water and stir until the gelatine has dissolved. Add to the raspberry purée and leave in a cool place until it starts to thicken – about 10 minutes. Fold in 8oz (225g) of the remaining raspberries. Break 16 of the ratafias coarsely and fold them into the raspberry mixture.

Lightly oil a long loaf tin or a terrine – about 2 pints (1.1 litres) capacity – and line it with greaseproof paper or non-stick baking paper. Spoon in the mixture and smooth the surface. Chill for at least 4 hours or overnight until set.

Melt the chocolate in a bowl set over a pan of gently simmering water. Sandwich pairs of the remaining ratafias with a little of the chocolate. Then dip each sandwich halfway into the chocolate and leave on a piece of non-stick paper, or greased greaseproof paper, to set.

Purée the remaining raspberries and cassis with the orange juice in a liquidiser or food processor.

Carefully invert the terrine onto a plate and cut it into neat slices. Place one slice on each dessert plate and spoon a pool of the raspberry purée around it. Decorate with the chocolate-dipped ratafias.

This dish is included in a menu on page 197.

MENU

*Pink Dinner
for Two*

CARPACCIO WITH
FRESH FIG PURÉE *page 201*

SALMON IN RASPBERRY
VINEGAR AND PINK
PEPPERCORN SAUCE
page 203

STEAMED VEGETABLE
JULIENNE IN
VINE LEAVES *page 223*

RADICCHIO SALAD

STRAWBERRY
AND CASSIS SORBET
this page

Make half the quantity given in all the recipes.

Use one medium head of radicchio for the salad and toss it in a simple vinaigrette (page 371).

IN ADVANCE The strawberry sorbet can be made several weeks ahead.

ON THE DAY Allow about 1½-2 hours for preparation. Prepare the salmon steaks and the sauce so that everything is ready for you to poach the salmon after the first course has been eaten.

TO DRINK Pink champagne or a dry rosé wine.

STRAWBERRY AND CASSIS SORBET

Fresh fruit gives a more summery flavour to sorbets and water ices than cooked fruit or fruit syrups. A sorbet should be almost slushy – not liquid, but not frozen hard. Because this sorbet contains a large proportion of alcohol – wine, and the blackcurrant liqueur crème de cassis – it will never freeze as hard as a plain water ice. The freezing point of alcohol is lower than that of water. The sorbet can be made well in advance. About 30 minutes before serving transfer it from the freezer to the refrigerator so that it can soften.

PREPARATION TIME: *20 minutes
    plus freezing time*

INGREDIENTS – *serves 4:*
1 lb (450 g) ripe strawberries
*4 tablespoons crème de cassis
    liqueur*
14 fl oz (400 ml) dry white wine
2 level tablespoons caster sugar
2 egg whites
DECORATION
4 perfect whole strawberries
*4 teaspoons crème de cassis
    liqueur*

Hull the strawberries and chop them roughly. Put them into a liquidiser or food processor with the cassis, white wine and sugar, and blend until smooth. Alternatively, press the strawberries through a sieve then mix the purée with the cassis, wine and sugar. Pour the mixture into a shallow container and freeze until ice crystals form around the edge of the container. This will take about 2 hours.

Tip the mixture into a bowl and beat well with a fork. Whisk the egg whites lightly and fold them into the strawberry mixture. Pour the mixture back into the container and return to the freezer until the sorbet is almost firm. This will take 3-4 hours.

Spoon the sorbet into tall, stemmed glasses. Trickle a teaspoon of crème de cassis over each portion, and decorate with a whole strawberry.

This dish is included in a menu on this page.

COOL PINK A strawberry sorbet laced with dry white wine and cassis makes a reviving end to a summer meal.

SYMPHONIE DE TROIS COULEURS

When fresh peaches are out of season, the peach purée, or *coulis*, for this dish can be made with peaches tinned in natural juice or apple juice. As an alternative to feathering, the coulis can be spooned over the mousse. All parts of the dish can be prepared the night before.

PREPARATION TIME: *45 minutes*
CHILLING TIME: *overnight*

INGREDIENTS – *serves 8:*
PISTACHIO MOUSSE
6 oz (175 g) shelled pistachio nuts – about 12 oz (350 g) unshelled
3 eggs, separated
3 oz (75 g) caster sugar
¾ pint (450 ml) double cream
¼ pint (150 ml) dry vermouth
4 tablespoons water
3 level teaspoons powdered gelatine
PEACH COULIS
4 large fresh peaches
Juice of ½ orange
2 tablespoons brandy
VANILLA CREAM
½ pint (285 ml) single cream
¼ pint (150 ml) soured cream
1 teaspoon vanilla extract
DECORATION
Chopped pistachio nuts

To make the pistachio mousse, grind 4oz (115g) of the pistachio nuts in a food processor or coffee grinder until fine. Chop the remaining pistachio nuts finely and put to one side.

Whisk the egg yolks with the caster sugar until thick and light. Gently mix in the cream, vermouth and ground pistachios.

Put the water into a small bowl and sprinkle in the gelatine. Stand the bowl in a pan of hot water and stir until the gelatine has dissolved. Mix the dissolved gelatine into the egg and cream mixture, and leave on one side until the mixture is on the point of setting. This will usually take 30-40 minutes.

Lightly oil 8 small moulds or coffee cups, about 6fl oz (175ml) in capacity. Whisk the egg whites until stiff but not dry. Fold them evenly into the egg and cream mixture with the chopped pistachios. Divide the mousse between the moulds, and leave overnight in the refrigerator to set.

PASTEL SYMPHONY A green pistachio mousse is set in a pale pool of vanilla-flavoured cream, feathered with peach purée.

To make the peach coulis cover the peaches with boiling water for 1-2 minutes, then immerse them in cold water. Remove the skins. Halve and stone the peaches, then put the peach flesh into a liquidiser or food processor with the orange juice and brandy and blend until smooth. Put the mixture into a small bowl, cover and chill.

To make the vanilla cream, stir together the single cream, soured cream and vanilla essence and chill for at least an hour.

Just before serving, unmould each pistachio mousse onto a plate. Sprinkle with a few of the

pistachio nuts. Surround with a pool of vanilla cream and trickle some of the peach coulis round it and feather with a knife. Serve the remaining coulis separately. This dish is included in a menu on page 230.

CHILLED BANANA SOUFFLÉ WITH BURNT ORANGE SAUCE

There are many recipes for cold fruit soufflés, but this one is unusual in that it is served with a hot sauce.

The soufflé can be made up to 24 hours in advance. The sauce can be made just before the meal and kept warm in a double saucepan, or a bowl set over a pan of hot water.

PREPARATION TIME: *1¼ hours*
SETTING TIME: *4 hours*
COOKING TIME: *20 minutes*

INGREDIENTS – *serves 8-10:*
1 pint (570 ml) milk
¼ teaspoon freshly ground nutmeg
5 eggs, separated
3 oz (75 g) caster sugar
3 ripe bananas, peeled and mashed
Grated rind and juice of ½ lemon
6 level teaspoons powdered gelatine
½ pint (285 ml) double cream
Icing sugar (optional)
Non-stick baking paper or greaseproof paper

BURNT ORANGE SAUCE
3 oz (75 g) granulated sugar
4 oz (115 g) butter
Finely grated rind and juice of 3 oranges
Juice of 2 lemons
1 level teaspoon cornflour

Lightly grease a 2½ pint (1.4 litre) soufflé dish. Tie a collar of double-thickness greased greaseproof paper or non-stick baking paper round the dish so that it projects 2in (50mm) above the rim of the soufflé dish.

Put the milk and nutmeg into a saucepan and heat to simmering point. Beat the egg yolks with the caster sugar until thick, light and fluffy. Gradually pour the hot milk onto the egg yolk mixture, beating until smooth. Pour the mixture into the top of a double saucepan, or set the bowl over a pan of simmering water. Stir over a moderate heat until the mixture thickens enough to coat the back of a wooden spoon, then beat in the mashed banana, lemon juice and rind. Remove from the heat.

Put 6 tablespoons of water in a small bowl and sprinkle over the gelatine. Stand the bowl in a saucepan of simmering water until the gelatine has dissolved. Add the gelatine to the egg and banana mixture and leave it on one side for about 15 minutes until it starts to thicken.

Lightly whip the cream and fold it into the mixture. Beat the egg whites until stiff and fold them into the mixture. Pour the mixture into the prepared dish and chill until set – this will take about 4 hours.

Just before the meal, make the sauce. Put the granulated sugar and half the butter into a pan. Stir the mixture over a moderate heat until it develops a toffee-like consistency. Stir in the orange juice and rind and lemon juice and allow the sauce to simmer briskly for 1 minute. Blend the cornflour with 2 tablespoons of water then blend in a further 4 tablespoons of water. Stir the cornflour into the sauce and continue stirring until it has thickened to the consistency of double cream. Divide the remaining butter into small pieces and beat the pieces, one by one, into the sauce.

Remove the collar from the soufflé. Dust the soufflé with icing sugar. Serve the hot sauce in a jug. This dish is included in a menu on page 208.

VACHERIN AUX FRAISES

Strawberries (*fraises*) are mixed with the cream that fills this dessert, but other fruit, such as raspberries or peaches, can be used instead. The baked meringue will keep for several weeks in an airtight container.

PREPARATION TIME: *1 hour*
COOKING TIME: *1 - 1¼ hours*
COOLING TIME: *overnight*
OVEN TEMPERATURE: *preheat to 140°C (275°F, gas mark 1)*

INGREDIENTS – *serves 8:*
8 egg whites
1 lb (450 g) caster sugar
1 teaspoon vanilla essence
FILLING
8 oz (225 g) strawberries
1 pint (570 ml) double cream
1 level tablespoon caster sugar
1 teaspoon vanilla essence

Draw one 7in (180mm) circle and three 6in (150mm) circles on non-stick baking paper. Lay the paper on two baking sheets. Line another baking sheet with non-stick baking paper.

In a large bowl whisk the egg whites until stiff. Gradually whisk in the caster sugar, until the mixture is stiff and glossy. Fold in the vanilla essence. Fill a piping bag fitted with a 1in (25mm) plain nozzle with meringue. Pipe 16 fingers of meringue about 4in (100mm) long onto the sheet of baking paper. Spread or pipe the remaining meringue over the four marked-out circles, keeping just inside the drawn line for the 6in (150mm) circles.

Bake in the preheated oven for 1-1¼ hours until crisp and dry. Turn off the oven and leave the meringue in the oven overnight to dry out. Peel off the baking paper.

To assemble the vacherin (not more than 1½-2 hours before serving), reserve a few whole strawberries for decoration. Hull and roughly chop the rest.

Whip ½ pint (285ml) of the cream with the sugar until stiff. Fold the chopped strawberries

and the vanilla essence into the cream. Spread one-third of the mixture over the 7in (180mm) disc of meringue. Lay the smaller discs on top layered with the cream mixture, finishing with a disc of meringue.

Whip the rest of the double cream until stiff. Spread about half the cream over the sides and

top of the 6in (150mm) discs. Do not cover the base disc.

Press meringue fingers against the sides of the vacherin so that they rest on the bottom disc with rounded sides facing outwards. You may not need to use all the fingers. Put the remaining cream into the piping bag fitted with a ½in (15mm) star nozzle.

Pipe lines of cream between the meringue fingers and around the top. Decorate with the reserved whole strawberries.

FRENCH DELIGHT Layers of meringue, sandwiched with strawberries and cream, are encased in meringue fingers.

COCONUT AND GINGER JELLY WITH LYCHEES

Lychees have been cultivated in China for at least 2000 years. The main season for lychees is December to February, but they sometimes appear in summer. Drained, tinned lychees can be used when fresh ones are out of season. If sake (Japanese rice wine) is difficult to obtain, use dry sherry instead.

PREPARATION TIME: *45 minutes*
STANDING TIME: *20-30 minutes*
CHILLING TIME: *6 hours*

INGREDIENTS – *serves 6:*
1/2 pint (285 ml) boiling water
2 oz (50 g) desiccated coconut
1 pint (570 ml) milk
3 tablespoons preserved stem ginger syrup
5 level teaspoons powdered gelatine
3 tablespoons finely chopped preserved stem ginger
18 fresh lychees, shelled
4 tablespoons sake (optional)

Pour the boiling water over the desiccated coconut and leave to steep for 30 minutes. Drain through a sieve, pressing on the coconut to extract as much flavour as possible.

Mix the resulting coconut liquid with the milk and the stem ginger syrup. Put 4 tablespoons of the mixed liquid into a small bowl and sprinkle in the powdered gelatine. Stand the bowl in a saucepan of hot water and stir until the gelatine has dissolved.

Stir the dissolved gelatine into the coconut mixture and leave in a cool place until syrupy – about 20-30 minutes. Stir in the chopped ginger. Pour into a dampened shallow dish. Use a dish which the jelly fills to a depth of about 1½in (40mm). Chill in the refrigerator for about 6 hours, or overnight.

Turn out the set jelly with care onto a flat tray and cut it into diamonds or ¾in (20mm) cubes with a dampened sharp knife. Divide the pieces of jelly between six shallow dessert dishes. Add the shelled lychees and trickle over a little sake.

This dish is included in a menu on page 224.

ORIENTAL FRUIT Fresh lychees – juicy and white beneath brittle pink shells – accompany a variation on one of the few Chinese desserts. A jelly flavoured with coconut and preserved stem ginger is cut into diamonds and a little rice wine is trickled over each portion.

ATAÏF

Spiced pancakes (*ataïf*), dipped in syrup or filled with cream, fruit and nuts are an essential part of Middle-Eastern festivities. The long fast of Ramadan is broken with the feast of Id es-Saghir, and ataïf are passed around among the guests to celebrate the end of abstinence.

The pancakes can be made in advance and stored for up to 4-5 days in the refrigerator, sandwiched between sheets of waxed paper or non-stick baking paper, and loosely wrapped in kitchen foil. Fill the pancakes up to 24 hours before the party, arrange them in an ovenproof dish and keep them covered in the refrigerator. Just before serving, pour over the butter and warm them in a moderate oven – 180°C (350°F, gas mark 4) – for 12-14 minutes.

PREPARATION TIME: *40 minutes*
STANDING TIME: *30 minutes*
COOKING TIME: *6-8 minutes*
OVEN TEMPERATURE: *preheat to 190°C (375°F, gas mark 5)*

INGREDIENTS – *serves 6:*
PANCAKES
4 oz (115 g) plain flour
Generous pinch of salt
1/4 teaspoon mixed spice
1/4 pint (150 ml) natural yoghurt
1 egg
6 fl oz (175 ml) milk
Finely grated rind of 1/2 lime or 1/4 lemon
Oil or butter for frying the pancakes

FILLING
3 oz (75 g) ground almonds
1 egg white, lightly beaten
2 oz (50 g) caster sugar
2 tablespoons clear honey
Finely grated rind of 1/2 lime or 1/4 lemon
4 oz (115 g) pitted dates, chopped
TOPPING
3 oz (75 g) butter
Juice of 1 lime or lemon
6 passion fruit

To make the pancakes, sieve the flour, salt and mixed spice into a bowl. Make a well in the centre, add the yoghurt and egg and beat until smooth. Gradually beat in the milk and add the lime or lemon rind. Cover the bowl and leave on one side to stand for 30 minutes.

To make the filling, mix together the ground almonds, egg white and caster sugar until the mixture is smooth. Add the honey, grated lime or lemon rind and the chopped dates.

Lightly oil or grease a 6-7in (150-180mm) heavy-based pancake pan and place it over a high heat. When it is very hot, reduce the heat to medium.

For each pancake, pour a tablespoon of batter onto the pan and spread it slightly by tilting the pan. Cook the pancake for 1 minute, then flip it over using a palette knife or spatula. Fry the pancake for a further minute then lift it onto a clean work surface or onto a sheet of non-stick baking paper. Lay all the pancakes out, or pile them up interleaved with non-stick baking paper. Make 12 pancakes in this way.

Put 1 heaped teaspoon of filling in the centre of each pancake, and fold over one edge. Fold in the sides, then continue to roll up the pancake.

Arrange the stuffed pancakes in a greased ovenproof dish.

To make the topping, melt the butter in a pan. Remove from the heat and add lime or lemon juice. Spoon the mixture over the pancakes. Cover with kitchen foil and bake them in the preheated oven for 6-8 minutes.

While the pancakes are cooking, halve the passion fruit and scoop out the pulp into a bowl with a teaspoon. Serve the pancakes topped with the passion fruit pulp. This dish is included in a menu on page 219.

TARTE AU SUCRE

There are several different kinds of *tarte au sucre* – it simply means 'tart with sugar' in French. In some recipes the sweet ingredient is sugar alone, or syrup. In this case the tart is filled with dried figs steeped in white wine and orange juice.

PREPARATION TIME: *30 minutes*
STANDING TIME: *4 hours or overnight*
COOKING TIME: *35-40 minutes*
OVEN TEMPERATURE: *preheat to 190°C (375°F, gas mark 5)*

INGREDIENTS – *serves 4:*
6 oz (175 g) plump dried figs
7 fl oz (200 ml) dry white wine
Pinch of ground cinnamon
Finely grated rind and juice of 1 orange
8 oz (225 g) prepared weight puff pastry (page 394)
1 egg white, beaten
1 level tablespoon icing sugar
3 tablespoons honey

Put the figs into a shallow bowl. Heat the white wine gently with the cinnamon and orange juice. Pour over the figs, then cover the bowl and leave to stand for 4 hours or overnight.

Roll out the puff pastry on a lightly floured board and use to line a loose-based flan tin, 8in (200mm) in diameter. Press the pastry well up the edges of the tin. Brush the pastry all over with beaten egg white.

Drain the steeped figs – they will have absorbed almost all the liquid. Arrange them in the pastry case, brush them with beaten egg white, then sprinkle with icing sugar.

Bake in a preheated oven for 35-40 minutes – until the pastry is well risen and golden-brown.

While the tart is cooking, gently heat the honey with the orange rind in a small pan. Trickle the syrup over the hot tart as soon as it comes out of the oven. Serve the tart either hot or cold, with cream if you wish. This dish is included in a menu on page 193.

GERANIUM CREAM

The heady perfumes of scented-leaf geraniums impart an elusive quality to foods. Leaves of rose geraniums give this cream an exotic, attar-of-roses flavour. Red and deep pink rose petals can be used for a similar result. Use rose petals that have not been sprayed.

PREPARATION AND COOKING TIME: *20-30 minutes*
CHILLING TIME: *overnight*

INGREDIENTS – *serves 6-8:*
½ pint (285 ml) crème fraiche or double cream
1 oz (25 g) caster sugar
5 fresh rose geranium leaves, bruised
8 oz (225 g) cream cheese
DECORATION
Pink rose petals

Place the crème fraiche or double cream in a double saucepan or in a bowl set over a pan of hot water. Stir in the sugar and bruised geranium leaves.

Heat gently, stirring, until the

FRAGRANT BLOSSOM *Pale pink rose petals decorate a dish of chilled cream scented with geranium leaves.*

cream is hot, but not boiling. Leave to cool. Put the cheese into a bowl. Beat in the cream. Cover and chill overnight.

Remove the geranium leaves and transfer the cream to a serving dish or small glass bowls. Scatter with rose petals.

Serve with soft summer fruits. This dish is included in a menu on page 194.

CHRISTMAS PUDDING WITH FOAMING COINTREAU SAUCE

This pudding is made with butter, which gives a lighter result than suet, and served with a whisked sauce flavoured with Cointreau. Dried apricots can be used instead of crystallised ones. The puddings can be kept in a cool dry place for up to a year. The flavour improves with time.

The sauce can be made 1-2 hours in advance. Reheat it in a basin set over a pan of hot water – be very careful not to leave it too long and let it scramble – then give it a final whisk just before serving.

PREPARATION TIME: *35 minutes*
COOKING TIME: *6 hours plus 2 hours reheating*

INGREDIENTS – *makes two 2 lb (900 g) puddings:*
4 oz (115 g) self-raising flour
1 level teaspoon mixed spice
1 level teaspoon ground ginger
1 level teaspoon salt
6 oz (175 g) chilled unsalted butter
4 oz (115 g) wholemeal breadcrumbs
4 oz (115 g) ground almonds
4 oz (115 g) sultanas
4 oz (115 g) raisins
4 oz (115 g) crystallised pineapple, chopped
3 oz (75 g) crystallised ginger, chopped
3 oz (75 g) crystallised apricots, chopped
3 oz (75 g) glacé cherries, chopped
3 oz (75 g) chopped mixed peel
Grated rind of 1 orange
Grated rind of 1 lemon
6 oz (175 g) dark muscovado sugar
3 eggs
6 tablespoons Cointreau
7 fl oz (200 ml) medium sweet white wine
SAUCE
3 eggs
2 oz (50 g) caster sugar
Finely grated rind of ½ orange
4 tablespoons double cream
4 tablespoons Cointreau

Sieve the flour, spices and salt into a large mixing bowl. Grate in the butter, then add the breadcrumbs, almonds, sultanas, raisins, pineapple, ginger, apricots, glacé cherries, mixed peel, orange and lemon rind and muscovado sugar. Beat the eggs lightly with the Cointreau and the white wine. Mix with the ingredients in the bowl.

Grease two 1¾ pint (1 litre) pudding basins and fill with the mixture. Lay a piece of greased greaseproof paper on top of the mixture in each basin, then cover the basins with pudding cloths or circles of kitchen foil, with a pleat across the centre, and tie down securely. Steam for 6 hours. Check the level of the water from time to time and top up with boiling water.

Leave the puddings until cold, then overwrap with kitchen foil and store in a cool, dark place.

Before serving, steam the puddings for a further 2 hours.

To make the sauce, put the eggs, caster sugar and orange rind into a bowl. Stand it over a pan of hot water and whisk until the mixture is thick and fluffy and the whisk leaves a trail when lifted out of the mixture. Whisk in the cream and Cointreau.

Turn the pudding out onto a warm plate and decorate with a sprig of holly. Serve the sauce separately in a jug or bowl. This dish is included in the menu on the opposite page.

CHOCOLATE MARZIPAN FINGERS

No matter how lavish the meal that has gone before, many guests still appreciate some form of sweetmeat after dinner. These fingers made with layers of chocolate and marzipan will keep in a cool place, covered loosely in greaseproof paper, for up to 36 hours. Do not store them in the refrigerator because the chocolate will sweat.

PREPARATION TIME: *40 minutes*
SETTING TIME: *3-4 hours*

INGREDIENTS – *makes 24:*
12 oz (350 g) homemade marzipan (page 400)
4 oz (115 g) white chocolate
8 oz (225 g) dark plain chocolate
2 oz (50 g) unblanched almonds, finely chopped
Icing sugar

Lightly dust a work surface with icing sugar. Roll out the marzipan into a rectangle measuring 12in × 6in (300mm × 150mm). Cut it in half lengthways to make two rectangles, each measuring about 12in × 3in (300mm × 80mm).

Melt the white and plain chocolate in separate bowls set over gently simmering water. Using a table knife, spread one rectangle of marzipan evenly with the white chocolate, then sprinkle with the chopped almonds. Leave to stand for 5 minutes, then spread half the plain chocolate over the nuts.

When the plain chocolate coating becomes tacky (after 5-6 minutes) and is on the point of setting, lay the second rectangle of marzipan on top to make a sandwich. Press the two layers of marzipan lightly together.

Spread the remaining plain chocolate over the top and comb swirling patterns in the chocolate with a fork. Leave for 3-4 hours until completely set.

When it is set, trim the edges of the marzipan sandwich neatly. Cut it lengthways into 4 strips, and then crossways into 6 strips to give 24 pieces, each measuring about 2in × ¾in (50mm × 20mm). This dish is included in a menu on the opposite page.

SWEET ENDING A festive meal should end on a sweet note – fingers of marzipan layered with white and dark chocolate and almonds.

M E N U

Christmas Lunch for Eight

QUAIL EGGS IN SHERRY JELLY
page 191

❧

POT ROAST PHEASANT WITH CLARET
AND ORANGE SAUCE *page 214*

GRATIN OF PARSNIPS AND POTATOES
page 222

CARROT AND GINGER SOUFFLÉ
page 222

❧

SALADE AUX CROTTINS DE CHÈVRES
page 229

❧

CHRISTMAS PUDDING WITH FOAMING
COINTREAU SAUCE *opposite page*

❧

CHOCOLATE MARZIPAN FINGERS
opposite page

One Christmas pudding is usually enough.
IN ADVANCE The night before, prepare the quail's eggs in sherry jelly and the chocolate marzipan fingers.
ON THE DAY Allow 4-5 hours. Prepare the salad ingredients, the purée for the soufflé and the gratin. Start to cook the pheasants, then make the sauce for the pudding. Start to steam the pudding.

Remove the pheasants from the oven and make the sauce. Put the gratin into the oven then the soufflé. The soufflé will not spoil with a few extra minutes in the oven. Garnish the quail eggs.

After eating the pheasants, assemble the salads, and start to reheat the pudding sauce.
TO DRINK A good red Bordeaux (claret). A sweet white wine will go well with the pudding.

THE TABLE

An attractively and imaginatively laid table should set the scene for a meal, whatever the occasion – whether a simple lunch, an elaborate dinner party, a buffet or a children's party. Even for a barbecue or picnic, carefully chosen plates, knives, forks, napkins and cloths will make the food and wine taste all the more delicious.

Cloths and mats

A table with a fine surface needs to be protected against spillages and heat from plates. An unattractive table may need disguising. In either case, the table can be covered with a cloth.

A tablecloth should be large enough to overhang the table by at least 9in (230mm) on all sides. Check when buying one that it has been treated to prevent stains penetrating the cloth. It may be necessary otherwise to lay a protective mat (which should be heatproof as well if the dishes are hot) beneath it.

White cloths are conventional for formal meals but for other occasions plain-coloured, lace, or patterned cloths can be used. For a dinner party, however, when the table is already covered with extra knives, plates, glasses, flowers and candlesticks, a patterned cloth can produce a very cluttered appearance.

There is no necessity to stick to conventional tablecloths. Patterned rugs, sheets or antique shawls could all be used, depending on the occasion.

If a table surface is particularly beautiful, mats can be used instead of a cloth. Many kinds of heatproof mat are available – rigid, plain or patterned, woven or rush. Mats should also be non-slip. Cloth mats, especially fine ones, often lacy or with embroidery, will not protect the table unless a heatproof mat is placed underneath. Small mats (coasters) are used for glasses.

Setting the table

The same pattern is always used to lay a table – whether for a formal banquet or a family supper. The difference lies in the number of knives, forks, spoons and glasses.

CUTLERY When setting the cutlery, two rules apply: the knives and spoons should be on the right of each place setting and the forks on the left; and the diner starts from the outside on both sides and works inwards.

Small spoons for eating avocado or ice-cream, for example, or specialist equipment for eating dishes such as snails or lobster should all take their place on either side of the plate. However, it is sometimes more convenient to bring them onto the table with the dish.

The prongs of the forks should point upwards, and the knife blades should face inwards.

The only usual variation is to put the pudding spoon and fork across the top of the place setting, spoon above with the handle to the right, and the fork beneath, pointing in the other direction. This is quite correct and saves space if the table is crowded with cutlery.

If there is a dessert course of fruit to be eaten with a knife and fork, these are brought on with the fruit.

CHINA The side plate is placed on the left of the place setting. If there is to be a cold first course it is often set at each place before the diners come in. Otherwise, plates are brought in with each course.

Finger bowls filled with warm water should be provided if any dish – spare ribs or shellfish, for example – has to be eaten with the fingers.

GLASSES Provide a separate glass for each wine. If only one wine is served at a dinner party the glass is placed just above the tip of the meat knife.

If there is more than one glass these should be arranged in the order in which they are to be used – from the outside on the knife side inwards towards the plate, or in a triangle. If possible, use distinctive glasses for each wine (see *Wine*, pages 181-188).

Port glasses can be placed on the table from the start, or brought in with the port. Liqueur glasses and brandy balloons are brought in with the liqueurs.

NAPKINS If the napkin is arranged in a complicated fold (see page 248) it is usually set in the centre of the place setting –

unless the first course has already been laid out, in which case it should be on the side plate. A simply folded napkin is laid on the side plate or to one side of the glasses.

BUFFET PARTIES It is usually most convenient to wrap each set of knife and fork in a napkin

for the guests to pick up with their plates before moving on to the food. Place the pudding spoons near the pudding plates. See *Buffet parties* (page 250).

Table decoration

A collection of beautiful glass, china and silver rarely needs anything but the simplest decoration. Anything more would detract from the effect. However, with less perfect materials, more effort has to be made in decorating a table.

When deciding on the decoration, bear in mind not only the size of your table and your resources of china, silver and glass, but also the furnishing and decoration of the room, and the food. Choose a colour scheme and decorations that will complement the room, reflect the occasion and the seasons and, above all, enhance the food –

TABLE SETTING No matter how many pieces of cutlery there are at a place setting they are always arranged from the outside in – the order in which they are used. This table is set for a meal consisting of soup, fish, meat, pudding and cheese. On the left of the plate, from the left, are the fish fork, meat fork and pudding fork. On the right, from the right, are the dessert knife (used for buttering bread as well as for cheese), soup spoon, fish knife, meat knife and pudding spoon. A glass for red wine, a smaller glass for white wine, and a water glass are arranged above the tip of the meat knife.

but not make it difficult to eat or talk by cluttering the table.

CANDLES The soft light of candles is very flattering both to the food and to people's faces. If necessary, supplement it with discreet electric lighting so that the diners can see to eat.

When selecting candles and candlesticks, the only general guideline is that the taller the candlestick the shorter the candle. The light cast by the candles should be on the food and the faces of the guests, not on the tops of their heads.

Candles should be of the non-drip variety to avoid damage to the table or cloth. Candles now come in many different colours. The candles you choose need not be uniform in colour, they can be chosen to complement each other – white and pale green for example.

Single candlesticks look best if they are collected in small groups on the table. They can form the centrepiece of a round or square table. Decorate them with flowers or ribbons tied to the base. On a large table the ribbons can be trailed to the edge of the table. At Christmas time, glass Christmas tree balls in different colours and sizes arranged around the base reflect the light of the candles.

Position the candles safely so that they cannot be knocked over. On a buffet table, any candles should be placed right at the back of the table – well out of the way of anyone reaching for one of the dishes.

FLOWERS AND LEAVES Arrangements of flowers on a dining table should not be so large or tall that they obscure people's view. Use either small vases with simple posies or single blooms, or low trailing arrangements, set in shallow containers and held by wire or florists' plastic foam. Bowls of water with blooms floating in them – such as camellias – reflect the light from the candles. Choose flowers with a delicate scent. A very strong perfume will conflict with the aroma of the food.

When there are not many flowers in the garden, leaves, branches or fir cones (sprayed gold or silver at Christmas) can also be used in arrangements.

A centre arrangement is most suited to a round or square table. A long table can be decorated with a long trailing arrangement or a series of bowls of flowers. Garlands of flowers or leaves can be trailed across a large table.

Position the flowers carefully so that there is plenty of space to lay down serving dishes.

Arrangements of flowers and other decorations for a buffet table should be much larger than those for a dining table, so that they will look effective from a distance.

FRUIT Bowls of fruit or low fruit stands can also be used as centrepieces. Decorate arrangements of carefully polished fruit with shiny orange, lemon, camellia or bay leaves, or stud them with silver or gold dragees –

hard sugar or chocolate sweets used for decorating cakes. See the illustration on page 245.

Single pieces of fruit or whole bunches can be frosted (see page 290, and the illustration to *Wild duck with kumquats*, page 216). NAPKINS The range of napkins is wide – from starched damask for a formal dinner to patterned paper for a children's party.

It is well worth the effort of laundering linen napkins for a dinner party, but paper napkins are increasingly used especially for large buffet parties. They come in a huge variety of colours often with candles to match. They should be as large and thick as possible.

Napkins can be folded very simply into triangles or rectangles, rolled up and placed in a glass, or tied with a ribbon instead of a napkin ring. A single flower or small bunch of flowers can be laid on each napkin.

Napkins can also be folded into intricate designs. These are not difficult, but to be effective you need large square napkins at least 15in × 15in (380mm × 380mm). Lightly starched linen napkins give the best result but paper ones will do.

The water lily fold is particularly pretty and deceptively intricate. With practice each napkin will take only a minute or two to fold. The fan fold is very simple.

WATER LILY FOLD

1 Open out the napkin. Fold the four corners to the centre with the points meeting.

2 Fold the four corners of the newly formed square to the centre with the points meeting.

3 Turn the newly formed square over. Fold each corner to the centre of the napkins as before.

4 Place a glass in the centre of the napkin. Press it down with one hand to keep the points and folds in place. Pull the loose section out from underneath one of the corners.

5 As you pull out the section, press in the point on the upperside to hold it in place. Repeat with all four corners.

6 Pull up the triangles on the underside. Turn over the corner of each.

THE FINISHED WATER LILY

FAN FOLD

1 Open out the napkin, then fold it in half.

2 Starting at one end, make widthwise folds, about 1in (25mm) wide, in the napkin – like concertina pleats – until about two-thirds of the napkin has been pleated.

3 Fold the pleated napkin in half so that the pleats are on the outside.

4 Hold the napkin with the fold at the top. Fold up the bottom left-hand corner of the unpleated half of the napkin so that it overlaps the fold.

5 Fold the overlap behind the triangular section of napkin, then place the napkin with the folded overlap and the base of the pleats on the table.

6 Open out the pleats to form a fan.

THE FINISHED FAN FOLD

Buffet Parties

STRICTLY SPEAKING, a buffet is more an article of furniture than a meal – a long table with one or more tiers on which an abundance of food, fruit and flowers can be decoratively displayed to tempt appetites on such occasions as ball suppers and wedding breakfasts.

Presenting these vast cornucopias, spilling over with game, meats, vegetables, fish, lobsters, truffles and edible fungi in a three-dimensional still-life, was a practice very dear to the hearts of the fashionable in 19th-century Paris and London. The master of the grand buffet was Marie-Antoine Carême, chef to many of the great houses of Europe including the Prince Regent. He created architectural confections of pastry and cream for his royal patron's table.

Yet, says Mrs Beeton, 'much may be done in the arrangement of a supper table, at a very small expense, provided taste and ingenuity are exercised'. On this principle she plans a buffet which has a boar's head in aspic at one end, a larded capon at the other, and is bordered with roast fowls and lobster salad. In between are mayonnaise of fowl, galantines of veal, tongues, game pies, Charlottes russes, trifles, meringues, iced Savoy cake, tipsy cake and other delicacies, all kept apart by heaps of fruit in tall metal bowls. In all buffets, she feels – quite rightly – that 'the eye, in fact, should be as much gratified as the palate'. The signal to the hungry guests that the feast has begun is provided by servants as they ladle soup into plates from a tureen.

How much of this life of indulgence was enjoyed by Mrs Beeton herself is uncertain. She died in 1865, of overwork and childbearing, at the age of 29.

Planning & Preparation

A buffet party makes it possible to give a lunch or dinner for a much larger number of people than can be fitted round an average dining table, without having to worry about seating and serving. However, as the number of guests increases so too does the importance of careful planning.

Arranging space

First consider the amount of space available. As a rough guide, a sitting room about 15ft × 15ft (4.6m × 4.6m) will hold 15-20 people if food and drink are situated elsewhere.

When arranging the party rooms aim to retain as much seating as possible while still leaving enough space for people to move about freely. It is not essential, however, to ensure that there is enough seating for everyone. Many young people are quite happy standing or sitting on a cushion on the floor. Provide groups of chairs for elderly people. Tables, cupboards or sideboards, cleared of ornaments, must be left for guests who are eating standing up to put down their drinks. Make sure that there is plenty of ventilation.

Put the food and drink in separate rooms, if possible, otherwise, put them at different ends of one large room. Put different courses on different tables, or failing that at opposite ends of the same table. Try to stagger the time at which people eat. This will help avoid congestion. Either the food or the drinks can, if you are short of space, be served in the kitchen.

Buffet food looks very attractive and so should be the focal point of the room. Decorate the tables with plenty of flowers, ribbons and pretty cloths. Tablecloths can be pinned up into swags and decorated with bows. If you are holding an evening party, make sure that the food is well lit.

To cut queueing for food to a minimum, lay the buffet tables so that the guests can first pick up a plate, together with a knife and fork wrapped up in a napkin (unless these are already placed on tables), and then move on to the food. It is better to have several smaller serving dishes of each item rather than one or two large ones so that more people can serve themselves at a time. Always keep some food in reserve so that dishes can be replenished.

China and cutlery

Finding enough glasses, china, cutlery, tables and chairs can sometimes be difficult.

For an informal cold buffet, strong paper plates (which also save on washing up) can be used. If you can obtain them, there are some paper plates available in cash and carry stores which are designed for caterers and are made of very strong cardboard. Unlike most other paper plates they are strong enough to hold hot food. Plastic knives, forks and glasses can also be used, but plastic knives are rarely strong enough to cut slices of meat.

For a buffet with hot food or a more formal occasion you will need china plates and metal cutlery. While you can often borrow from friends, the most convenient solution may be to hire equipment. Glasses can usually be hired from the wine supplier (see *Drinks parties*, page 156). China, cutlery, cloths, specialist kitchen equipment, tables, chairs and even marquees can all be hired. In addition to the hire shops in some larger towns, there are also a number of companies specialising in catering hire which are listed under 'Catering equipment hire' in *Yellow Pages*. Telephone several in order to get competitive quotes as they vary in what they offer and charge.

Arranging help

If you are giving a large party, you will be able to enjoy it more if you employ some assistance. Professional waitresses can be contacted through *Yellow Pages*. For a less formal occasion, there may be some responsible girls in the 15 to 17-year-old age group who will be very pleased to have the opportunity to earn some money helping out.

Planning the menu

Choose the food not only for flavour and appearance, but also with the practicalities of preparing and eating it in mind.

Any form of poultry or game on the bone, except for chicken drumsticks, is difficult to handle unless you are actually sitting down at a table, so if you are expecting people to eat, either standing up or balancing a plate on their knees, bite-sized, boneless pieces should be served. Similarly lettuce leaves and other salad vegetables should be torn into small pieces, and cold meats should be sliced thinly.

As you plan the menu, work out what you are going to serve the food in. You can even stick little self-adhesive labels on the dishes to remind you, so that you do not get confused at the last minute.

Keep food hot on an electric hot plate (these can be hired), otherwise have smaller dishes on the tables and replenish them frequently from large pans kept on the cooker in the kitchen.

If you have a microwave, this can be used to keep a continuous flow of hot food. Earlier in the day, arrange the food in serving dishes (remember most microwave ovens are not very large, so check that the dishes will fit in), cover them and then reheat them when they are required during the course of the party.

SOUPS & STARTERS

ICED FENNEL SOUP

Chilled soups first appeared in England in the late 18th century. The taste for them was spread by French aristocrats fleeing the Revolution. This soup, however, made with Florence fennel, has an Italian flavour.

The soup can be made up to 2 days in advance. If you wish to freeze it, leave out the cream.

PREPARATION TIME: *20 minutes*
CHILLING TIME: *overnight*
COOKING TIME: *30 minutes*

INGREDIENTS – *serves 12:*
3 lb (1.4 kg) fennel bulbs
3 oz (75 g) butter
2 large onions, peeled and chopped
3 pints (1.7 litres) chicken stock (page 367)
Salt and freshly ground black pepper
½ pint (285 ml) soured cream

Remove the green, feathery leaves from the fennel bulbs, and put them into a basin of cold water in the refrigerator to keep fresh. Peel off and discard the outer layers if they appear to be tough, then chop the bulbs roughly.

Melt the butter in a large saucepan. Add the fennel and onions, cover and cook gently for 10 minutes, stirring and shaking the pan several times. Pour on the stock and season to taste with salt and pepper. Bring to the boil, then cover the pan and simmer gently for about 20 minutes, or until the fennel is tender. Do not overcook the fennel or it will lose its delicate flavour.

Purée the soup in a liquidiser or food processor – it may be necessary to do this in several batches. Put the purée into a bowl, then beat in the cream. Add salt and pepper to taste and leave to cool. Chill overnight.

FINE FENNEL The delicate, slightly aniseed flavour of Florence fennel makes a tempting chilled soup.

Taste and adjust the seasoning.

Serve the soup ladled into individual bowls and garnished with the reserved fennel leaves.

This dish is included in a menu on page 283.

ICED APPLE SOUP

Curry adds spice to this soup. It can be made a day ahead, but do not add the apple more than 1-2 hours before serving.

PREPARATION TIME: *30 minutes*
CHILLING TIME: *3-4 hours*
COOKING TIME: *10 minutes*

INGREDIENTS – *serves 12:*
1½ oz (40 g) butter
1½ oz (40 g) plain flour
3 level tablespoons medium-hot curry powder
3 pints (1.7 litres) chicken stock (page 367)
1 pint (570 ml) single cream
Salt and freshly ground black pepper
3 dessert apples
Juice of 1 lemon
GARNISH
12 small sprigs of mint

Melt the butter in a large pan, add the flour and curry powder and cook for 1 minute, stirring continuously. Gradually add the stock and bring to the boil, still stirring. Remove from the heat. Leave to cool, whisking from time to time to prevent a skin from forming. Cover and chill for at least 3-4 hours.

Skim off any fat. Whisk in the cream and add salt and pepper to taste. Peel the apples and grate them into a basin. Add the lemon juice and toss well, then mix into the soup.

Garnish each bowl with a sprig of mint. This soup is included in a menu on page 261.

EGGS TONNATO

Tuna, or tunny fish, a relative of the mackerel, is popular with cooks throughout the Mediterranean, but no nation has exploited its delicate flavour and texture more fully than the Italians. They serve tuna, or *tonno*, in many combinations – mixed with potatoes, as part of a dish of white beans, made into a sort of sausage and above all in *maionese tonnata*.

This tuna mayonnaise or sauce is perhaps best known in the Italian summer dish *vitello tonnato*, where it accompanies cold veal, but it can be served with a number of cold dishes –

ITALIAN EGGS A classic sauce of tuna, anchovies, capers and mayonnaise cloaks hard-boiled eggs.

chicken for example. Here it is served with hard-boiled eggs.

Only one egg per person has been allowed in this recipe, but there is plenty of sauce if you wish to cook more eggs.

The eggs can be hard-boiled, and the sauce made up to 24 hours in advance. Shell the eggs and store them whole, submerged in a bowl of cold water. Do not assemble the dish until 2-3 hours before serving.

PREPARATION AND COOKING TIME: *30 minutes*

INGREDIENTS – *serves 12:*
12 eggs
7 oz (200 g) tin of tuna in oil
1/2 pint (285 ml) homemade mayonnaise (page 369)
2 tablespoons lemon juice
1 3/4 oz (50 g) tin anchovies
1 level tablespoon capers
4-6 tablespoons milk
Salt and freshly ground black pepper
GARNISH
Lemon wedges or parsley

Boil the eggs for 10 minutes, plunge them in cold water, and then remove the shells. Cut them in half lengthways. Arrange the halved eggs on a serving plate.

Finely mash the tuna, together with the oil from the tin, then stir in the mayonnaise and lemon juice. Finely chop half the anchovies and capers, reserving the remainder for garnishing, and add to the tuna mixture. Stir in enough milk to give the sauce the consistency of thick

double cream, and season with plenty of black pepper. Salt will probably not be necessary because of the saltiness of the anchovies.

Spoon the sauce over the eggs. Cut the remaining anchovy fillets in half lengthways, and arrange them in a crisscross fashion. Place a caper in the centre of each diamond, and garnish with lemon wedges or sprigs of parsley. This dish is included in a menu on page 258.

ESCABECHE DE PESCADO FRITO

The Spanish word *escabeche* derives from the Arabic *sakbay*, meaning 'meat or fish preserved in vinegar'. Escabeche dishes first appeared in Britain in the 18th century, since when the word has been anglicised as 'caveach'.

Escabeches are dishes of fried fish (*pescado frito*), or occasionally fried meat, marinated in a mixture of oil and vinegar, with added aromatics such as onions, ginger, pepper or herbs. This version, with a marinade which includes garlic, mushrooms and red pepper, is a speciality of Peru. It can be prepared 1-2 days in advance.

PREPARATION TIME: *30 minutes*
MARINATING TIME: *24 hours*
COOKING TIME: *20 minutes*

INGREDIENTS – *serves 12:*
3 lb (1.4 kg) haddock fillet
Salt and freshly ground black pepper
6 tablespoons olive oil
2 onions, peeled and sliced
2 cloves garlic, crushed
1 in (25 mm) piece of root ginger, peeled and finely chopped
6 oz (175 g) mushrooms, sliced
1 red pepper, seeded and chopped
1/2 pint (285 ml) white wine vinegar
1/4 pint (150 ml) water
1 1/2 level tablespoons sugar

Skin the fish and cut it into 12 portions. Season with salt and pepper.

Heat 2 tablespoons of the oil in a large frying pan, and quickly fry a few of the pieces of fish until just cooked through. Remove them from the pan with a slotted spoon and place in a serving dish. Repeat with the remaining fish. Add a little more oil as necessary.

Add the remaining oil to the pan and gently fry the onions and garlic for 5 minutes. Stir in the ginger and fry for 1 minute, then add the mushrooms and pepper and cook for a further 2-3 minutes. Add the wine vinegar, water and sugar and bring to the boil. Season with salt and pepper. Reduce the heat and simmer gently for 5 minutes. Pour over the fish, cover, and leave to marinate for 24 hours.

Serve with granary rolls. This dish is included in a menu on the opposite page.

Make double the quantity given in the cabbage recipe.
IN ADVANCE The ice cream loaf can be made up to 3 weeks in advance. The day before, make the escabeche and cook the meat and the pastry lid for the pie.
ON THE DAY About 3-3½ hours before the party, start to cook the cabbage. About 30 minutes before the meal, take the cabbage out of the oven and keep it warm. Turn up the oven temperature and reheat the meat. Turn out the ice cream loaf. Add the lid to the pie and complete the cooking.
TO DRINK A full-bodied red wine, such as a Barolo.

BROCCOLI MOUSSE

Florets of broccoli can be purple, green or white. Calabrese, from Calabria in the toe of Italy, which is fat and generally green is the kind to use for this recipe. If fresh broccoli is unobtainable, frozen spears can be used instead for this dish.

The mousse can be made 1-2 days in advance.

PREPARATION TIME: *45 minutes*
CHILLING TIME: *overnight*
COOKING TIME: *12 minutes*

INGREDIENTS – *serves 12:*
*2 lb (900 g) broccoli spears
    (calabrese)*
Salt
14 oz (400 g) tin consommé
8 oz (225 g) curd cheese
½ pint (285 ml) soured cream
2-3 tablespoons lemon juice
6 tablespoons water
*6 level teaspoons powdered
    gelatine*
Freshly ground black pepper
2 large red peppers
GARNISH
*Sliced radishes or radish roses
    (page 287)*

Lightly oil a 3½ pint (2 litre) mould. Trim off and discard any very coarse stalks from the broccoli. Cook it in a little boiling salted water, with the spears standing upright, for about 12 minutes or until it is just tender. Drain it well, then purée it, in batches, in a liquidiser or food processor together with the consommé and curd cheese.

Turn the mixture into a large bowl and beat in the soured cream and lemon juice to taste.

Put the water in a small basin and sprinkle in the gelatine. Leave to soften for 5 minutes, then set the basin over a pan of hot water. When the gelatine has dissolved, beat it into the broccoli mixture. Add salt and pepper to taste.

Halve the peppers lengthways and remove the seeds. Lay them, cut side down, on the rack of a grill pan. Roast them under a moderately hot grill, rotating them a couple of times, until the skin blisters and chars. Alternatively, scorch the peppers, one at a time, in the flames of a gas ring (standing them on the hob). Using long-handled tongs, turn each pepper round until it is charred on all sides.

Holding the peppers under a running cold tap or in a bowl of cold water, rub off the blackened skin with your fingers. Chop the flesh into ¼in (5mm) pieces. Beat it into the broccoli mixture then pour into the prepared mould. Chill overnight in the refrigerator.

To unmould, dip in hot water for a few seconds to loosen the mixture and invert onto a serving dish. Garnish with sliced radishes or radish roses.

FLORAL MOUSSE Clusters of radish roses and radish leaves make a flamboyant garnish for a savoury mousse of broccoli, red peppers, curd cheese and soured cream.

STILTON AND GRAPE PASTRIES

Because they are very rich, only one of these pastries has been allowed for each person. Other blue cheeses can be used instead of Stilton. The pastries can be prepared up to 24 hours in advance and stored, uncooked, in the refrigerator.

PREPARATION TIME: *50 minutes*
COOKING TIME: *12 minutes*
OVEN TEMPERATURE: *preheat to 230°C (450°F, gas mark 8)*

INGREDIENTS – *serves 12:*
12 large grapes
5 oz (150 g) Cheddar cheese, finely grated
5 oz (150 g) Stilton, finely crumbled
2 oz (50 g) walnuts, finely chopped
4 tablespoons single cream
14 oz (400 g) prepared weight puff pastry
Beaten egg, for glazing

Peel the grapes and remove the pips (page 397). Mix the Cheddar with the Stilton and the walnuts, then gradually beat in the cream. Take a little of the cheese mixture, flatten it in your hand, then wrap it round a grape, to make a ball slightly smaller than a golf ball. Repeat until all the grapes are covered.

Roll the pastry out thinly and cut it into 12 circles about 5in (130mm) in diameter.

Place one of the cheese balls in the centre of each pastry circle. Brush the edges of the circle with beaten egg, then fold them up together to form a neat, triangular-shaped package. Brush beaten egg all over the pastries and place them on two greased baking trays.

Bake in the preheated oven for about 12 minutes or until golden-brown. Serve as soon as possible. This dish is included in a menu on this page.

GRAPES AND CHEESE Whole grapes are encased in a mixture of Stilton, Cheddar, cream and walnuts then baked in puff pastry.

IN ADVANCE The day before, cook the turkey and make the charlotte malakoff and the winter slaw.
ON THE DAY Set aside an hour early in the day to prepare the Chinese salad and dressing and complete the turkey in crab sauce.

Allow about an hour before the party to decorate the charlotte, garnish the turkey and mix the Chinese salad with its dressing.
TO DRINK Dry white wine, such as a white Chianti, or rosé wine.

CHEESE ÉCLAIRS STUFFED WITH AVOCADO AND BACON

The avocado filling for these éclairs should not be made more than 3 hours in advance because it is likely to discolour. However, if you bury one of the avocado stones in the mixture, it will retard discoloration. The éclairs can be cooked a day ahead and stored in an airtight tin, but do not fill them more than an hour before serving.

PREPARATION TIME: *40 minutes*
COOKING TIME: *30 minutes*
OVEN TEMPERATURE: *preheat to 200°C (400°F, gas mark 6)*

INGREDIENTS – *serves 12:*
CHOUX PASTRY
2½ oz (65 g) plain flour
Pinch of salt
Freshly ground black pepper
2 oz (50 g) butter
¼ pint (150 ml) water
4 oz (115 g) Gruyère cheese, very finely grated
1 egg yolk
2 eggs
FILLING
12 rashers streaky bacon
2 large ripe avocados
½ pint (285 ml) mayonnaise
2 tablespoons lemon juice
3 level tablespoons chopped chives
A dash of Tabasco
Salt and freshly ground black pepper
GARNISH
Sprigs of watercress
Quartered tomatoes

Grease two or three large baking trays. Make the choux pastry (page 395). Beat in the grated cheese before beating in the egg yolk and the eggs, one at a time.

Put the pastry into a piping bag fitted with a ½in (15mm) plain nozzle and pipe out 12 éclairs, about 3in (80mm) long on the baking trays. Allow room for the éclairs to rise.

Bake in the preheated oven for 20-25 minutes or until golden-brown. Remove from the oven, make a slit in the side of each one to allow the steam to escape and return to the oven for a further 5 minutes to dry out. Remove from the oven and leave to cool on a wire rack.

Grill the bacon rashers until they are crisp. Halve and stone the avocados and scoop out the flesh into a liquidiser or food processor. Add the mayonnaise, lemon juice, chives, Tabasco and salt and pepper to taste. Blend until smooth. Then taste and add more Tabasco and salt and pepper, if necessary. Alternatively, mash the avocado flesh with a fork and mix it with the other ingredients.

Lengthen the slit in the side of each of the cooled éclairs and place a bacon rasher in each. Spoon the avocado mixture into a piping bag, fitted with the same nozzle that was used for piping the éclairs, and pipe some of the mixture into each éclair.

Arrange the éclairs on a large flat serving dish and garnish with sprigs of watercress and quarters of tomato.

MINTED FRUIT SALAD

Although fruit salads are generally thought of as desserts, they also make very refreshing first courses for winter or summer.

The ingredients in the salad can be varied to achieve particular colour effects. Papaya (papaw) has orange-pink flesh and a heady, exotic scent. Pink grapefruit, for example, are slightly sweeter than the ordinary variety with a delicate coloured flesh. If a melon with yellow or orange flesh such as Charentais is used as well, then the whole salad takes on a glorious orange-pink colouring which contrasts with the flecks of green mint. If papaya is unavailable, fresh peaches or nectarines can be used instead.

The oranges and grapefruit can be prepared a day in advance. Keep them in a covered bowl in the refrigerator. Complete the salad not more than 3-4 hours before serving.

PREPARATION TIME: *40 minutes*
CHILLING TIME: *at least 1 hour*

INGREDIENTS – *serves 12:*
6 large oranges
3 grapefruit
1 large melon (such as Honeydew) OR 2 small melons (such as Charentais or Ogen)
2 papaya (papaw)
2 level tablespoons chopped fresh mint
GARNISH
Sprigs of fresh mint

Peel the oranges and grapefruit with a small, sharp knife, removing all the white pith. Holding the fruit over a bowl, cut out each segment of fruit, discarding all the white pith and membrane (page 398). Squeeze the membrane over the bowl to extract as much juice as possible.

Halve the melon, remove the seeds, then cut off the skin and dice the flesh. Add to the orange and grapefruit. Repeat with the papaya (page 398). Add the mint and toss the salad lightly together. Turn into a serving dish. Cover tightly with a double wrapping of kitchen foil (melon can taint other food in the refrigerator), and chill for at least an hour before serving.

Garnish the bowl with sprigs of fresh mint.

A TOUCH OF MINT Orange, grape-fruit, melon and tropical papaya make a luscious fruit salad. Seasoned with plenty of freshly chopped mint it becomes a refreshing first course.

HOT MAIN COURSES

CURRIED EGGS IN CREAM SAUCE

The eggs for this curry can be hard-boiled, and the sauce made up to 24 hours in advance. Shell the eggs and store them submerged in a bowl of cold water. Before serving, gently reheat the sauce, then add the eggs and heat through.

PREPARATION TIME: *25 minutes*
COOKING TIME: *20 minutes*

INGREDIENTS – *serves 12:*
24 hard-boiled eggs, shelled
¼ pint (150 ml) vegetable oil
2 medium onions, peeled and finely chopped
3 in (80 mm) piece of fresh ginger, peeled and grated
2 large green chillies, seeded and finely chopped
2 pints (1.1 litres) single cream
3 tablespoons lemon juice
1 level tablespoon cumin seeds
¼ teaspoon cayenne pepper
2 level teaspoons garam masala
3 tablespoons tomato purée
½ pint (285 ml) vegetable stock (page 368)
6 level tablespoons chopped coriander leaves

Heat the oil in a large shallow saucepan, and gently fry the onions for 5 minutes. Add the ginger and chillies and cook for 1 minute, then add all the remaining ingredients except the eggs and coriander and bring just to simmering point.

Halve the eggs, then add them, in batches if necessary, to the sauce. Cook gently for 5 minutes, stirring occasionally to prevent the sauce sticking to the pan. Lift the eggs out carefully with a slotted spoon and place them in a serving dish. Pour over the sauce and sprinkle with the coriander. Serve with plain boiled basmati rice and a green salad.

SEAFOOD LASAGNE

Fresh and smoked haddock are combined with shellfish to make a rich sauce for this lasagne – a change from the more traditional meat sauce.

Green lasagne gives the best colour to the dish, but plain lasagne can be used instead. Always cook the lasagne for this dish in boiling salted water before baking with the seafood filling – even if the packet says that pre-cooking is unnecessary.

This dish can be made completely a day in advance and reheated. It can also be frozen, without the topping, if fresh mussels and prawns are used. Thaw completely (allow at least 8 hours) before adding the topping and reheating.

PREPARATION TIME: *1 hour plus cooling time*
COOKING TIME: *1 hour*
OVEN TEMPERATURE: *preheat to 190°C (375°F, gas mark 5)*

INGREDIENTS – *serves 12:*
3 pints (1.7 litres) milk
2 bay leaves
2 onions, peeled and quartered
1½ lb (700 g) smoked haddock fillet
1 lb (450 g) fresh haddock fillet
4 oz (115 g) butter
4 oz (115 g) plain flour
1 lb (450 g) cooked, shelled mussels (page 377)
6 oz (175 g) cooked, shelled prawns
2 level tablespoons chopped fresh dillweed OR 2 level teaspoons dried dillweed
Salt and freshly ground black pepper
2-3 tablespoons oil
1¼ lb (575 g) green lasagne
TOPPING
6 eggs
¼ pint (150 ml) single cream
Salt and freshly ground black pepper
1 oz (25 g) butter
4-6 oz (115-175 g) Cheddar cheese, grated

Put the milk, bay leaves and onion into a pan and bring to the boil. Remove from the heat, add the smoked and fresh haddock, cover the pan and leave until cool. Remove the haddock from the milk, skin, bone and flake it. Strain the milk and set it on one side.

Melt the butter in a large pan, add the flour and cook gently for 1 minute. Gradually stir in the reserved milk and bring to the boil over a low heat, stirring all the time to make sure that the bottom of the sauce does not burn. Remove from the heat and stir in the haddock, mussels, prawns and dillweed. Add salt and pepper to taste and set on one side.

Bring a large pan of salted water to the boil. Add the oil – to help to keep the pieces of lasagne separate – then add either a third or a half of the lasagne, depending on the size of the pan. Cook for about 8 minutes or until the lasagne is cooked but still has a bite to it – *al dente*. Drain and leave to drain in a single layer on a damp tea towel, so that they do not stick together. Repeat with the remaining lasagne.

Put a layer of fish and sauce in the base of an 8 pint (4.5 litre) ovenproof dish or roasting tin. Cover with a layer of lasagne and put another layer of fish on top of the lasagne. Add further layers of lasagne and fish until all the fish has been used up. Finish off with a final layer of lasagne.

To make the topping, beat the eggs with the cream and salt and pepper. Melt the butter in a pan and scramble the eggs gently until they are almost set, then spoon them over the top of the lasagne. Sprinkle with the cheese. Bake in the preheated oven for 45 minutes until bubbling and browned on top.

SALMON EN CROÛTE WITH DILL SAUCE

The salmon for this dish can be wrapped in pastry ready for baking a day in advance. Store it in the refrigerator. Baked, it can be kept hot in a low oven for 30 minutes or so. The sauce must be freshly made.

PREPARATION TIME: *1½ hours*
COOKING TIME: *1¼ hours*
OVEN TEMPERATURE: *preheat to 230°C (450°F, gas mark 8)*

INGREDIENTS – *serves 12:*
3 lb (1.4 kg) piece of salmon
¾ pint (450 ml) water
A few parsley stalks
Finely pared rind of 1 small lemon
1 teaspoon peppercorns
Salt
2¼ lb (1 kg) spinach
4 oz (115 g) butter
Freshly ground black pepper
Good pinch of grated nutmeg
2 level tablespoons chopped parsley
2 level tablespoons chopped fresh dillweed OR 2 level teaspoons dried dillweed
8 oz (225 g) peeled prawns
14 oz (400 g) prepared weight puff pastry (page 394)
1 egg, beaten

DELECTABLE PARCEL All the succulence of fresh salmon, spinach and prawns is contained in puff pastry and enhanced by a dill sauce.

SAUCE
6 egg yolks
Freshly ground black pepper
4 tablespoons lemon juice
12 oz (350 g) unsalted butter
4 level tablespoons fresh dillweed OR 1 level tablespoon dried dillweed
Salt
GARNISH
Sprigs of fresh dill
Whole prawns

Skin and fillet the salmon (page 373). Place the skin and bones in a pan with the water, parsley stalks, lemon rind, peppercorns and salt. Bring to the boil and remove any scum with a slotted spoon. Cover and simmer gently for 30 minutes. Strain and boil rapidly until the stock is reduced to about 6 tablespoons. Set on one side.

Thoroughly wash and drain the spinach and remove the stalks. Melt 1oz (25g) of the butter in a large pan, and add the spinach with about a teaspoon of salt. Cover and simmer, stirring occasionally, for about 5 minutes until the spinach is just tender. Drain and squeeze out the excess liquid. Chop roughly and season to taste with salt, if necessary, pepper and nutmeg.

Cream the remaining butter, then beat in the parsley, dillweed, and salt and pepper to taste. Stir in the prawns.

Roll out the pastry to a rectangle large enough to enclose the fish completely. Lay one of the fillets of salmon in the centre

of the pastry and season with salt and pepper. Spread half the spinach on top of it, then place the prawn mixture on top of the spinach. Cover with the remaining spinach. Season the other fillet of salmon and place on the top to form a sandwich.

Brush the pastry edges with beaten egg and fold the pastry up over the fish so that it is completely enclosed. Seal the edges well and trim off any excess pastry.

Line a baking tray with non-stick baking paper. Carefully lift the fish parcel onto the tray with the join underneath. Decorate with pastry leaves (page 288). Brush the pastry all over with beaten egg and bake in the preheated oven for 45 minutes. If the pastry browns too quickly, cover with a tent of foil.

To make the dill sauce, place the egg yolks, pepper and lemon juice in a heat-proof bowl with a good tablespoon of the butter. Stand the bowl over a pan of gently simmering water and stir with a wire whisk until the egg yolks start to thicken, then gradually beat in the remaining butter a tablespoon at a time. When all the butter has been incorporated, stir in the fish stock and dillweed. Taste and adjust the seasoning, if necessary. Keep the sauce warm over the pan of water. Do not let it get too hot or it will curdle.

Transfer the salmon to a serving dish and garnish with sprigs of fresh dill and whole prawns. Serve the sauce separately.

IRISH TAVERN PIE

Plenty of Guinness gives this steak pie a rich, malty flavour, conjuring up something of the atmosphere of the old pubs and drinking places of Dublin. A meat pie, steam rising and carrying with it the mouth-watering aroma, is a particularly welcome dish on a chilly evening.

Pies such as this can be prepared well in advance and so are good for buffet parties. Because of the need for a very large pie dish, the crust is baked separately and then placed on top of the filling. This way, any oven-proof serving dish of the right size can be used. For 12 people, use a serving dish that holds at least 6 pints (3.4 litres). Do not use one more than about 3in (80mm) deep – otherwise it is difficult to serve the pie.

The meat and the pastry can both be cooked 2-3 days in advance. Cover the meat and keep it in the refrigerator. Wrap the pastry lightly in foil or keep it in an airtight box.

Allow the meat to come to room temperature, then reheat until bubbling (20-30 minutes) in an oven preheated to 180°C (350°F, gas mark 4), then add the pastry lid and cook for a further 15 minutes.

PREPARATION TIME: *45 minutes*
COOKING TIME: *3-3¼ hours*
OVEN TEMPERATURE: *preheat to 220°C (425°F, gas mark 7)*

INGREDIENTS – *serves 12:*
5 lb (2.3 kg) braising steak
6 tablespoons oil
4 large onions, peeled and chopped
4 oz (115 g) plain flour
1½ pints (850 ml) Guinness
1½ pints (850 ml) beef stock (page 367)
2 level teaspoons dried thyme OR 4 sprigs fresh thyme
3 level teaspoons sugar
Thinly pared rind of 2 oranges, in large pieces
Salt and freshly ground black pepper
1 lb 5 oz (600 g) prepared weight puff pastry (page 394)
1 egg, beaten

Cut the beef into 1in (25mm) cubes. Heat 4 tablespoons of the oil in a large pan and fry the meat in batches until browned on all sides. Remove the meat from the pan with a slotted spoon and put on one side.

Heat the remaining 2 tablespoons of oil in the pan and fry the onions gently for about 5 minutes. Sprinkle the flour over them, stir in and cook over a low heat for 3–4 minutes, stirring frequently until the flour starts to brown. Gradually stir in the Guinness and stock and bring to the boil, stirring all the time. Add the thyme, sugar, orange rind, salt and pepper, and return the meat to the pan. Cover and simmer gently for 2 hours or until the meat is tender, stirring from time to time. Remove the orange rind, taste and adjust the seasoning.

To make the pastry lid for the pie, spread kitchen foil or non-stick baking paper over a large, flat baking tray. Place the pie dish upside down on the foil or paper and mark out an area ½in (15mm) larger than the top of the dish all the way round; this allows for the slight shrinkage of the pastry during cooking. Take a third of the pastry, roll it out and cut it into strips 1in (25mm) wide. Lay these round the edge of the marked-out area just inside the line, and brush with beaten egg. Roll out the remaining pastry until large enough to cover the marked-out area, and place on top of the strips.

Trim the edges of the pastry lid so that they line up with the pastry strips round the marked-out area. Seal the lid and strips together all the way round. Knock up with the back of a knife and then flute (page 393). Brush the top with beaten egg. Roll out the pastry trimmings and cut into leaf shapes to decorate the lid (page 288). Glaze the decorations with egg. Bake in the preheated oven for 15-20 minutes or until golden-brown, then remove from the oven. Turn the oven down to 180°C (350°F, gas mark 4).

Turn the meat into the serving dish, cover and reheat in the oven for 45 minutes. Using two fish slices, carefully lift the pastry lid onto the dish. Return to the oven for 10 minutes to heat through.

This dish is included in a menu on page 253.

Make 1½–2 times the quantities given in the recipes for eggs tonnato, salad and cider sorbet (depending on the appetites of the guests). Make three pancake stacks.
IN ADVANCE The sorbet and the ice bowl can be made 1–2 weeks ahead. Allow about 2½–3 hours the evening before or in the morning to make the pancake stacks and prepare the hard-boiled eggs and the sauce for the eggs tonnato.
ON THE DAY Allow about an hour before the meal to prepare the salad, assemble the eggs tonnato, and reheat the pancake stacks.
TO DRINK Cider and fruit juices or tomato juice.

CENTRAL AMERICAN SPICE Hot, spicy Mexican chilli con carne fills a savoury layer cake of pancakes, masked in cheese sauce and baked in the oven until bubbling hot. A mixed green salad of endive, lettuce, spinach, sorrel, french beans, broad beans and herbs provides the necessary cool contrast.

INGREDIENTS – *serves 6:*

FILLING

1½ lb (700 g) minced beef
1 large onion, peeled and chopped
2 cloves garlic, crushed
1 green pepper, seeded and
  chopped
2 tablespoons tomato purée
8 fl oz (225 ml) beef stock (page
  367)
1 level teaspoon mixed dried herbs
2 level teaspoons ground cumin
14 oz (400 g) tin red kidney
  beans
½-1 level teaspoon chilli powder

PANCAKES

6 oz (175 g) plain flour
½ teaspoon salt
2 eggs, beaten
¾ pint (450 ml) milk
Oil for frying

CHEESE SAUCE

1½ oz (40 g) butter
1½ oz (40 g) flour
¾ pint (450 ml) milk
6 oz (175 g) Cheddar cheese,
  grated
Salt and freshly ground black
  pepper

First make the meat filling. Fry the meat in a large pan, stirring frequently, until browned – but do not add any fat to the pan – there should be enough fat in the meat, unless it is exceptionally lean. Add the onion, garlic and green pepper and continue to cook, stirring frequently, for 5 minutes. Add the tomato purée, beef stock, mixed dried herbs, cumin, kidney beans and a pinch of chilli powder. Taste and add more chilli powder, if necessary – the exact amount of chilli powder will depend on the brand used. Bring the mixture to the boil, lower the heat, cover and simmer gently for 30 minutes.

Next make the pancakes. Sieve the flour and salt into a bowl. Break in the eggs, add half the milk and beat until smooth, then gradually beat in the remaining milk. Using a pan about 7in (180mm) in diameter, make 12 pancakes (page 390).

Lay one of the pancakes in the base of an ovenproof dish, about 9in (230mm) across and about 1in (25mm) deep, so that the sauce does not run over the edge as it cooks. Spread with some of the meat mixture, then place another pancake on top and spread that with more meat mixture. Continue adding layers of meat mixture divided by pancakes, finishing with a pancake. Set on one side.

To make the cheese sauce, melt the butter in a large pan. Add the flour and cook over a low heat for 1 minute. Gradually stir in the milk and bring to the boil, stirring all the time. Remove from the heat, stir in the cheese and add salt and pepper to taste.

Pour the sauce over the pancakes and put on one side until ready to reheat. Cover the stack with kitchen foil. Reheat in the preheated oven for 20 minutes then remove the foil and return to the oven for another 20 minutes or until golden-brown.

Serve with a simple salad. This dish is included in a menu on the opposite page.

MEXICAN PANCAKE STACK

The pancake is a versatile dish. In this recipe it is given a Mexican flavour by a meat filling spiced with chilli and garlic.

Instead of filling and rolling each pancake individually, the pancakes are stacked on top of one another with the meat filling in between. Do not try to make a stack with more than 12 pancakes – or it will be difficult to serve. If there are more than six people, make more stacks.

The pancake stack can be assembled a day in advance. Keep it covered in the refrigerator, then heat through before serving.

PREPARATION TIME: *30 minutes*
COOKING TIME: *1½ hours*
OVEN TEMPERATURE: *preheat to*
  190°C (375°F, gas mark 5)

LAMB IN WINE AND ANCHOVY SAUCE

Anchovies used to be much more widely used in cooking than they are today. In the 19th century, for example, anchovy sauces were often served with meat and fish.

In this recipe, the distinctive salty flavour of anchovy enhances a rich dish of lamb cooked in its own stock. Use the tubes of anchovy purée which can be bought in supermarkets and delicatessens.

The casserole will improve in flavour if made in advance and reheated. It can be made up to 2-3 days in advance and kept in the refrigerator.

PREPARATION TIME: *1½ hours*
COOKING TIME: *2¾ hours*

INGREDIENTS – *serves 12:*
2 lean shoulders of lamb, weighing about 3¼ lb (1.5 kg) each
1 large onion, peeled and quartered
2 sticks celery, chopped
¼ teaspoon dried rosemary
3 pints (1.7 litres) water
1 lb (450 g) button onions, peeled
4 oz (115 g) plain flour
1 pint (570 ml) red wine
4 tablespoons anchovy purée
8 oz (225 g) button mushrooms
2 oz (50 g) walnuts, chopped
Salt and freshly ground black pepper
GARNISH
Chopped parsley

With a sharp knife, cut all the meat off the two shoulders of lamb, reserving the bones. Trim off any fat then cut the meat into 1in (25mm) cubes. Put the fat into a frying pan over a gentle heat to melt it down.

Place the lamb bones in a large pan with the quartered onion, celery, a good pinch of rosemary and the water. Bring to the boil, cover and simmer gently for 1½ hours, then strain the stock into a bowl.

Heat 4 tablespoons of the lamb fat in a large pan and fry the button onions over brisk heat until browned. Remove the onions with a slotted spoon and set them aside on a plate.

Fry the lamb cubes in two or three batches until browned on all sides. Set the batches on one side with the onion. Remove the last batch from the pan then sprinkle the flour into the remaining fat, adding a little extra lamb fat if necessary. Cook over a very gentle heat, stirring frequently until the flour is browned, then gradually stir in the wine and 2 pints (1.1 litres) of the lamb stock. Bring to the boil, stirring all the time. Add the remaining rosemary and stir in the anchovy purée with a wire whisk. Return the meat and onions to the pan. Cover and simmer gently for 1 hour stirring from time to time.

Add the mushrooms and walnuts, cover and simmer gently for a further 15 minutes. Season to taste with plenty of pepper and salt, if necessary. Turn into a serving dish and sprinkle generously with parsley. Serve with new potatoes.

PORK WITH WATERCRESS SAUCE

The creamy and slightly peppery watercress sauce and the pork strips and mushrooms for this dish can be prepared 1–2 hours in advance if you wish. Before serving, reheat the pork strips and mushrooms thoroughly, then pour over the sauce and bring to the boil.

SUCCULENT LAMB Anchovy, rosemary, red wine and button onions impart rich flavours to lamb.

PREPARATION TIME: *30 minutes*
COOKING TIME: *10 minutes*

INGREDIENTS – *serves 12:*
4 lb (1.8 kg) boneless lean pork from the shoulder or leg
6 shallots
3 large bunches watercress
6 oz (175 g) butter
1½ pints (850 ml) double cream
Salt and freshly ground black pepper
12 oz (350 g) button mushrooms
GARNISH
Sprigs of watercress

First make the sauce. Peel and finely chop the shallots. Trim the watercress, then roughly chop it. Melt half the butter in a large pan, add the shallots and gently fry for 5 minutes. Add the watercress and cook for a minute or until it starts to wilt. Add the cream and bring to the boil. Turn the mixture into a liquidiser or food processor and purée until smooth.

Cut the pork into strips about ¼in (5mm) thick and 2in (50mm) long, and season with salt and pepper.

Slice the mushrooms. Heat the remaining butter in a large pan and lightly fry batches of the pork strips and mushrooms for 4-5 minutes. Return all the pork and mushrooms to the pan, and pour over the watercress sauce. Raise the heat and boil for 2-3 minutes. Taste and adjust the seasoning.

Turn into a warm serving dish, garnish with sprigs of watercress, and serve as soon as possible.

Make twice the quantity given in the recipes for apple soup and turkey meatballs. However, make only 1½ times the quantity of tomato sauce. Cook medium-sized potatoes and about 4lb (1.8kg) of runner beans.

IN ADVANCE The day before, make the soup (without adding the apple).

ON THE DAY Make the meatballs in the morning. Allow about 1-1½ hours before the meal to complete the preparations and reheat the meatballs.

TO DRINK Cider or a fruity red wine, such as a Rioja.

SPICED TURKEY MEATBALLS IN TOMATO SAUCE

Fresh turkey meat from either the breast or legs can be used for these light meatballs. If you use a whole turkey you will need a bird weighing about 7lb (3.2kg). Do not use ready-prepared frozen turkey joints, their water content is too high.

The dish can be prepared 2 days in advance and reheated.

PREPARATION TIME: *1 hour*
COOKING TIME: *1½ hours*

INGREDIENTS – *serves 12:*
TOMATO SAUCE
4 tablespoons oil
2 large onions, peeled and chopped
4 cloves garlic, peeled and crushed
4 lb (1.8 kg) tomatoes, skinned (page 389) and chopped
2 level teaspoons sugar
2 level teaspoons dried oregano
Salt and freshly ground black pepper
MEATBALLS
3 lb (1.4 kg) turkey meat
9 oz (250 g) fresh white breadcrumbs
3-4 eggs, beaten
Salt and freshly ground black pepper
4 level teaspoons ground ginger
2 level teaspoons ground cumin
About ½ teaspoon chilli powder
36 stuffed olives
Oil for frying
GARNISH
A few sprigs fresh coriander

First make the tomato sauce. Heat the oil in a pan and gently fry the onions and garlic for 5 minutes. Add the tomatoes, sugar, oregano and salt and pepper. Cover the pan and simmer gently for 30 minutes. Sieve the sauce, or liquidise it. Set it on one side.

To make the meatballs, finely mince the turkey meat or chop it in a food processor. Put it in a bowl with the breadcrumbs, eggs, salt, pepper, ginger, cumin and chilli powder – the exact amount of chilli powder will depend on the brand used, be guided by the manufacturer's description on the jar. Mix the ingredients well with your hands. Shape the mixture into 36 balls and push a stuffed olive into the centre of each one.

Heat some oil in a large frying pan and gently fry the meatballs, a few at a time, until they are golden-brown and sealed all over. Drain on kitchen paper.

Put the tomato sauce into a large shallow pan, add the meatballs and simmer together gently for 30 minutes. Taste and, if necessary, adjust the seasoning. Turn onto a serving dish and garnish with fresh coriander. This dish is included in a menu on this page.

OLIVE STUFFING Minced turkey meat spiced with ginger, cumin and chilli makes unusually light meatballs. A stuffed olive is pressed into the centre of each and they are cooked in fresh tomato sauce.

COLD MAIN COURSES

FISH AND PRAWN TERRINE

The fish for this terrine can be varied: smoked haddock fillets could replace the prawns and salmon, for example. The terrine can be made a day in advance and kept in the refrigerator.

PREPARATION TIME: *25 minutes*
COOKING TIME: *40 minutes*
CHILLING TIME: *2 hours*
OVEN TEMPERATURE: *preheat to 180°C (350°F, gas mark 4)*

INGREDIENTS – *serves 12*:
8 oz (225 g) salmon fillets
8 oz (225 g) peeled prawns
2 lb (900 g) cod fillets
½ pint (285 ml) white wine and water mixed
4 level tablespoons chopped, fresh tarragon OR 1 level tablespoon dried tarragon
4 egg whites
¾ pint (450 ml) double cream
Salt and freshly ground black pepper
Juice of 1 lemon
¼ pint (150 ml) soured cream
GARNISH
Whole leaves of tarragon or bay
3 large prawns in their shells

If dried tarragon is being used, pour a little hot water over the herbs, leave for a few minutes and drain.

Cut the salmon into thin strips. Put the wine and water into a pan and bring to the boil. Drop the salmon strips into the boiling liquid and leave for 1-2 minutes. Drain and cool.

Mix the peeled prawns gently with the tarragon.

PASTEL SLICE Layers of salmon, cod, prawns and herbs are revealed as stripes of white, pale pink and green when this terrine is cut.

Cut the cod into pieces and purée until smooth. If you use a food processor or liquidiser, keep the machine running and slowly pour on the egg whites and then the cream. Add salt,

pepper and lemon juice to taste. Alternatively, put the fish twice through the fine blade of the mincer, or until smooth. You can chop the fish very finely and press it twice through a sieve, but this is very laborious. If you have not used a liquidiser, beat in the egg whites, cream, salt, pepper and lemon juice with a wooden spoon.

Lightly oil a 2lb (900g) loaf tin, and line with oiled grease-proof paper. Put a quarter of the cod purée in a layer in the bottom, and cover with half the tarragon prawns and another quarter of the purée. Lay the salmon strips on this and cover with a further quarter of purée. Put on the remaining tarragon prawns and finish with purée. Cover with foil.

Stand the loaf tin in a large roasting tin. Add enough boiling water to come halfway up the sides of the loaf tin. Bake in the preheated oven for about 40 minutes, or until it is firm to the touch. Remove the loaf tin from the oven, take off the foil and leave in the roasting tin for 5 minutes. Then stand the loaf tin on a rack to cool.

Chill in the refrigerator for at least 2 hours or until needed. Turn the terrine out onto a flat dish. Beat the soured cream gently with a fork until smooth and then spread it over the top of the terrine. Decorate with unpeeled prawns, and tarragon or bay leaves.

This dish is included in a menu on this page.

Make two terrines and two croquembouches and double the quantity given in the recipes for the salads.

IN ADVANCE The day before, cook the ham and prepare the fish terrine, the puffs and filling for the croquembouches, the salad dressings and the potato salad.

ON THE DAY Allow about 4 hours to complete the ham and croquembouches and make the salads.

TO DRINK Dry sparkling or still white wine.

TROUT IN ASPIC WITH SMOKED COD'S ROE

The aspic jelly for this dish is made with fish stock and powdered gelatine. The flavour is much more delicate than jelly made with powdered aspic, which would dominate the subtle taste of the trout.

This dish can be prepared a day in advance.

PREPARATION TIME: 1¼ hours
plus cooling time
COOKING TIME: 40 minutes

INGREDIENTS – *serves 12:*
6 pink rainbow trout weighing at least 12 oz (350 g) each
2½ pints (1.4 litres) water
1 onion, chopped
A few parsley stalks
2 sprigs of tarragon
Pared rind of 1 small lemon
Salt
1 level teaspoon black peppercorns
¼ pint (150 ml) dry white wine
1½ oz (40 g) powdered gelatine
2 egg whites
Crushed shells of 2 eggs
STUFFING
2 oz (50 g) fresh white breadcrumbs
8 oz (225 g) skinned smoked cod's roe
8 oz (225 g) curd cheese
Juice of ½-1 lemon
Freshly ground black pepper
GARNISH
Tarragon leaves
Pieces of lemon rind
Black olives, stoned and sliced

Fillet the fish (page 373). Do not worry about the small bones – they are easier to remove after the fish has been cooked.

Place the fish heads and bones in a large pan with the water, onion, parsley stalks, tarragon, lemon rind, salt and peppercorns. Bring to the boil. Remove any scum with a slotted spoon. Cover and simmer gently for 30 minutes, then strain into a large, wide pan.

Bring the stock back to the boil, then remove from the heat and add the trout fillets. Cover and leave, off the heat, until completely cold.

To make the stuffing, put the breadcrumbs and the skinned cod's roe into a food processor and blend until smooth. Alternatively, pound them together with a pestle and mortar. Add the curd cheese and lemon juice and mix well. Season with plenty of pepper.

When the trout fillets are cold, lift them carefully out of the stock, one by one, and lay them, skin side down, on a chopping board. With the tip of a sharp knife, gently scrape any remaining bones out of the flesh of the fillets. Fill the slight hollow to one side of each fillet with the cod's roe stuffing. One fillet at a time, lay a fish slice on top of the fish and stuffing and slide another slice, or a palate knife, underneath. Turn the fish over onto the slice and carefully peel off the skin. Transfer the fish to a serving dish and slide away the fish slice. Arrange the

fillets on large serving plates. Cover with foil and chill.

Boil the fish stock rapidly until it is reduced to 1½ pints (850ml). Pour the wine into a pan and sprinkle in the gelatine. Add the fish stock, egg whites and crushed egg shells. Bring to the boil, whisking all the time.

Once the mixture starts to boil, stop whisking. Let it boil until the foam rises to the top of the pan. Remove from the heat immediately and allow the liquid to subside. Return to the heat

and let it boil up once again. Remove it from the heat to subside. Repeat the process twice more. Pour the mixture into a jelly bag or piece of muslin tied to the legs of an upturned kitchen stool (see *Greengage jelly*, page 32), and allow it to drip through into a bowl. Leave it until it has thickened to the consistency of unbeaten egg white.

Spoon a little of the aspic jelly over the trout fillets. Dip the tarragon leaves, pieces of lemon

and black olives into the jelly and arrange them decoratively on the fish and around the serving dish. When the jelly has set, spoon over the remaining aspic. Chill in the refrigerator until just before serving.

This dish is included in a menu on page 283.

FIXED IN ASPIC Lemon and olive flowers and tarragon leaves, set in aspic, lend old-fashioned elegance to stuffed rainbow trout.

MONKFISH IN SORREL SAUCE

Sorrel gives this sauce a pleasantly sharp taste – a change from the usual, often bland, dishes of fish and mayonnaise. It also contributes to the delicate colour combination of pale green sauce, white fish and yellow lemons. See also *Tomato and sorrel soup* (page 294).

The dish can be made a day in advance and kept in a covered bowl in the refrigerator. Just before serving, stir the mixture then transfer it to a shallow dish and garnish.

PREPARATION AND COOKING
TIME: *20 minutes plus cooling time*

INGREDIENTS – *serves 12:*
5 lb (2.3 kg) monkfish
2 pints (1.1 litres) fish stock (page 367)
8 oz (225 g) sorrel
½ pint (285 ml) single cream
Juice of ½ lemon
Salt and freshly ground black pepper
GARNISH
Lemon wedges

Skin and bone the monkfish and cut it into 1½in (40mm) cubes. Bring the fish stock to the boil. Remove from the heat and add the cubes of monkfish. Leave until quite cold.

Drain the monkfish, reserving the stock, and arrange it on a serving dish.

Remove the stalks from the sorrel and wash the leaves in cold water. Bring ½ pint (285ml) of the reserved fish stock to the boil. Add the sorrel and cook gently for 5 minutes. Remove the pan from the heat and leave to cool.

Purée the sorrel and stock in a liquidiser or food processor, or press it through a sieve. Add the cream and lemon juice, mix well and season to taste with the salt and pepper.

Pour the sauce over the monkfish and garnish with lemon wedges.

CRAB AND ASPARAGUS FLAN

Asparagus – or 'sparrow grass' to give it its old-fashioned English name – is a member of the lily family. If left to grow, its tender edible shoots sprout large, feathery but inedible leaves. The season for fresh British asparagus is May and June, but it freezes well and frozen spears can be used for this flan, if fresh ones are not available. Do not drink red wine with asparagus – there is sulphur in asparagus which makes the wine taste metallic.

The flan can be made up to 24 hours in advance and kept in a cool place.

PREPARATION TIME: *30 minutes*
COOKING TIME: *1¼ hours*
OVEN TEMPERATURE: *preheat to 190°C (375°F, gas mark 5)*

INGREDIENTS – *serves 10-12:*
Shortcrust pastry made with 12 oz (350 g) flour (page 392)
8-10 oz (225-275 g) asparagus spears, fresh or frozen
Salt
1 oz (25 g) butter
4 spring onions, finely chopped
6 eggs, beaten
1 pint (570 ml) single cream
12 oz (350 g) white and brown crabmeat (page 375)
Freshly ground black pepper
A dash of Tabasco

Roll out the pastry and line a 12in (300mm) flan tin. Line the pastry with greaseproof paper weighted down with baking beans and bake blind (page 393) in the preheated oven for 20 minutes. Remove the paper and beans and bake for a further 5-10 minutes to dry out the base. Remove from the oven and lower the oven temperature to 180°C (350°F, gas mark 4).

Cook the asparagus spears in boiling salted water for 10-15 minutes until they are just tender, then drain (page 386).

Melt the butter in a small pan and gently fry the spring onions for about 5 minutes. Beat the eggs in a bowl, add the cream and beat again, then stir in the fried onions and the crabmeat. Season with plenty of salt and pepper and a little Tabasco. Lay the asparagus spears in the base of the flan dish. Pour over the crabmeat mixture and bake in the oven for 45 minutes or until just set. Serve cold.

CAPPON MAGRO

The many ingredients which go to make up this Genoese salad mean that it is only really worth preparing for a large number of people. *Cappon* refers to the pieces of bread (traditionally ship's biscuit) which form the base on which layers of fish, shellfish, vegetables and sauce are arranged. *Magro* means that it is a fasting dish. Although it contains no meat, today this seems a singularly inappropriate name for so rich a dish.

All the individual ingredients, including the sauce, can be prepared and cooked earlier in the day, or the day before. Do not assemble the salad more than about an hour before serving.

PREPARATION TIME: *2-3 hours*
SOAKING TIME: *at least 2 hours or overnight*
COOKING TIME: *2½ hours*
OVEN TEMPERATURE: *preheat to 120°C (250°F, gas mark ½)*

INGREDIENTS – *serves 12:*
BASE
1 large bloomer loaf
2 cloves garlic
6 tablespoons olive oil
4 tablespoons wine vinegar
STOCK
1 lb (450 g) fish bones
2 pints (1.1 litres) water
1 onion, peeled and quartered
A few parsley stalks
Pared rind of 1 lemon
Salt
1 level teaspoon black peppercorns

SALAD
12 oz (350 g) cleaned squid (page 375)
2 lb (900 g) huss
1½ lb (700 g) mixed, cooked shellfish (page 377) including some, or all, of the following: mussels, prawns, white crabmeat, cockles, winkles, shrimps and scallops
12 oz (350 g) carrots
1 small cauliflower
12 oz (350 g) french beans
2 tablespoons lemon juice
1 tablespoon olive oil
1 head celery
8 oz (225 g) button mushrooms
14 oz (400 g) tin artichoke hearts, drained
Whites of 3 hard-boiled eggs (see yolks below)
4 oz (115 g) black olives
2 oz (50 g) green olives
SAUCE
4 oz (115 g) crustless white bread
1 bulb fennel
4 oz (115 g) parsley
1½ level tablespoons capers
2-3 cloves garlic
2 × 1¾ oz (50 g) tins anchovy fillets
Yolks of 3 hard-boiled eggs
½ pint (285 ml) olive oil
Juice of 1 lemon
Freshly ground black pepper

To make the base, cut the crusts off the bread, cut it in half lengthways and put it into the preheated oven for 2 hours or until crisp. Peel the cloves of garlic, cut them in half and rub half a clove of garlic onto both sides of each slice of bread. Lay the baked bread on a large flat serving dish, and pour 3 table-spoons of olive oil and 2 table-spoons of vinegar onto each piece. Leave to soak for at least 2 hours or overnight.

To make the stock, put the fish bones, water, onion, parsley stalks, lemon rind, salt and peppercorns into a pan, bring to the boil and simmer gently for 20 minutes. Strain the stock.

Cut the squid into rings about ¼in (5mm) wide and cut the huss into ½in (15mm) cubes.

Bring the strained fish stock to the boil, add the squid, bring back to the boil and simmer gently for 5 minutes. Remove from the heat, and add the cubes of huss. Cover and leave to cook in the cooling stock off the heat.

Prepare the shellfish, removing any shells.

Peel and slice the carrots, break the cauliflower into florets and top and tail the beans. Bring a small pan of salted water to the boil, add the carrots and cauliflower and cook for 5 minutes. Then add the beans and cook all the vegetables for a further 3 minutes. Do not overcook the vegetables, they should be crisp.

Drain the vegetables, then return them to the pan with the lemon juice and the olive oil.

Chop the celery, discarding the coarse outer stalks. Slice the mushrooms, quarter the artichoke hearts and chop the egg whites. The black and green olives can be stoned if you wish, but this is not essential.

To make the sauce, cut the

4oz (115g) of white bread into two or three pieces and soak in cold water for about 5 minutes. Drain the bread, then squeeze it dry in your hands. Cut the fennel into quarters, discarding any tough outer stalks. Chop the fennel in a liquidiser or food processor. Add the parsley and chop again. Add the capers, garlic, anchovy fillets and their oil. Continue to blend until the mixture is smooth. Add the egg yolks and bread and blend again.

Add the oil very gradually, as if making mayonnaise, keeping the machine running all the time, then add the lemon juice. Season to taste with pepper. Salt may not be necessary because the anchovies are salty.

To assemble the dish, drain the squid and huss. Build a pyramid of layers of fish, shellfish, vegetables and sauce on top of the bread base. Aim for a good mixture of different ingredients throughout. Keep back some of the more colourful ingredients to garnish the dish at the end. Chill the dish in the refrigerator until ready to serve.

Serve the salad first. When that is finished, the bread base can be broken up and dipped into any sauce left on the plates.

FASTING SALAD Cappon magro – an Italian dish originally made for eating on fast days – must not contain meat. But it more than compensates for any loss with an abundance of fish, shellfish, vegetables and rich sauce.

FRENCH ROAST BEEF A French cut of beef is ready to be cooked with red wine, thyme and garlic, but an English sirloin will do just as well.

ROAST BEEF WITH MUSTARD SAUCE

Only the best beef should be used for this elegantly simple dish. Entrecôte steak or the traditional English sirloin joint are both suitable. Alternatively, use one of the joints prepared in the French way by some butchers – *côtes de boeuf* or *rôti de boeuf*, for example.

The meat can be cooked 1-2 days in advance. Keep the beef in the refrigerator, wrapped in the foil with the juices. The sauce can be made up to 12 hours in advance. Keep covered, in the refrigerator.

PREPARATION TIME: *20 minutes plus cooling time*
COOKING TIME: *1 hour*
OVEN TEMPERATURE: *preheat to 200°C (400°F, gas mark 6)*

INGREDIENTS – *serves 12:*
5 lb (2.3 kg) joint of lean sirloin or entrecôte steak
3 cloves garlic
Salt and freshly ground black pepper
¼ pint (150 ml) red wine
Sprig of thyme
¼ pint (150 ml) double cream
4 tablespoons Meaux mustard or French wholegrain mustard
GARNISH
Sprigs of thyme

Peel the garlic and cut it into fine slivers. With the tip of a sharp knife, make a number of deep cuts in the joint and insert the slivers of garlic into them. Season the joint with salt and pepper. Lay a large piece of kitchen foil, folded double for strength, in a roasting tin. Place the joint in the centre of the foil, then fold up the foil edges and pour the red wine over the joint making sure that all the wine is contained by the foil. Lay the sprig of thyme on top of the joint of meat.

Enclose the meat completely with the foil and roast in the preheated oven for 1 hour. This results in a rare joint. If you prefer it medium or well done allow 10-15 minutes extra time. Remove from the oven and leave in the foil until cold.

Open the foil and take out the meat, leaving all the juices in the foil. Skim any fat from the juices then pour them into a small pan. Bring them to the boil and boil rapidly until they are reduced to ¼ pint (150ml). Leave to cool.

Whip the cream until it just holds its shape, then gradually whisk in the meat juices, and then the mustard. Taste, add more salt and pepper if necessary and turn into a large serving bowl or jug.

Carve some of the meat in advance and arrange the slices on a serving dish. The rest can be carved at the table. Garnish with sprigs of thyme.

This dish is included in a menu on page 270.

STUFFED BREAST OF VEAL WITH RED PEPPER SAUCE

Veal tends to be expensive, but the breast is one of the cheaper cuts. It may be necessary to order the joint from the butcher. The veal and the sauce can be prepared up to 2 days ahead.

PREPARATION TIME: *45 minutes plus cooling time*
COOKING TIME: *2½ hours*
OVEN TEMPERATURE: *preheat to 180°C (350°F, gas mark 4)*

INGREDIENTS – *serves 12:*
6 lb (2.7 kg) boned breast of veal
1¾ oz (50 g) tin anchovy fillets
3 oz (75 g) pitted green olives, halved
Freshly ground black pepper
2 level teaspoons finely chopped fresh rosemary OR 1 level teaspoon dried rosemary
Juice of 1 lemon
Salt
SAUCE
2 lb (900 g) red peppers
5 cloves garlic, crushed
8 fl oz (225 ml) olive oil
1½ tablespoons lemon juice
Salt and freshly ground black pepper
GARNISH
Black olives
Lemon quarters

With a sharp knife, trim as much of the visible fat from the veal as possible. Lay the breast out flat with the skin down and make two long slits along its entire length, cutting almost through to the skin. Pack these slits with the anchovies and olives, then sprinkle plenty of black pepper and half the rosemary all over the veal. Roll it up lengthways and tie in several places with string.

Place the veal on a large piece of kitchen foil and pour over the lemon juice. Season with salt and freshly ground black pepper and sprinkle with the remaining rosemary. Enclose the joint completely in the foil and roast in the preheated oven for 2½ hours. Remove from the oven and allow to cool completely.

While the meat is cooling, prepare the sauce. Cut the peppers into quarters, discarding the core, ribs and seeds. Lay them cut side down on the rack of the grill pan and place under a moderate grill until their skins blacken and blister, and their flesh becomes very soft – it may be necessary to grill the peppers in two batches.

Remove the peppers from the pan and peel off the blackened skins when they are cool enough to handle. Put them in a food processor with the garlic, and purée until smooth.

Keep the motor running slowly and gradually pour in the oil as if making mayonnaise. Add the lemon juice and season to taste with salt and pepper.

Cut the veal into thin slices and arrange on a serving plate. Garnish with olives and lemon quarters. Serve the red pepper sauce separately.

BEAUNE HAM

The town of Beaune, just south of Burgundy's ancient capital Dijon, gives its name to this dish – a simplified version of *jambon persillé*, a traditional Burgundian Easter dish.

PREPARATION TIME: *30 minutes plus cooling and chilling time*
SOAKING TIME: *5 hours or overnight*
COOKING TIME: *2 hours*

INGREDIENTS – *serves 12:*
5 lb (2.3 kg) boned and rolled joint of lean shoulder or forehock of bacon
Small bunch of parsley stalks
1 onion, peeled and quartered
1 small bay leaf
2 cloves garlic, peeled
1 level teaspoon black peppercorns
4 tablespoons white wine
3 rounded teaspoons powdered gelatine
2-3 oz (50-75 g) chopped parsley

Soak the bacon joint in a large bowl of cold water for 5 hours or overnight. Drain, then place in a pan with the parsley stalks, onion, bay leaf, garlic and peppercorns. Cover with cold water and bring to the boil. Cover and simmer gently for 2 hours.

Remove the pan from the heat and leave the joint to cool in the cooking liquid. Once it has cooled, remove the joint then taste the stock. If it seems to be a little tasteless, boil it to reduce it slightly. Set aside to cool.

Put the wine into a measuring jug and make up to 1 pint (570ml) with the stock. Spoon about 4 tablespoons of this mixture into a small basin. Sprinkle in the gelatine and leave to soften for 5 minutes, then stand the bowl over a pan of gently simmering water and leave until the gelatine has dissolved. Stir the mixture into the wine and ham stock and put on one side until the jelly is beginning to set and is about the consistency of unbeaten egg white.

Cut the skin and fat off the ham. Cut it into thin slices and arrange them on serving dishes. Sprinkle each slice of ham with some of the parsley. Carefully spoon some ham jelly over each slice, then chill for at least an hour or until ready to serve.

This dish is included in a menu on page 262.

PARSLEY HAM Slices of ham are sprinkled with parsley and glazed with jelly made from ham stock.

Put the prunes into a bowl with the salt and pepper, sage, garlic and juniper berries. Pour over the red wine and leave to soak for 8 hours or overnight.

First score deep, even incisions in the skin of the pork with a sharp knife. Then cut between the ribs and the meat until only the long bone at the base of the ribs holds them together and the ribs on one side and the meat on the other can be opened out like a book.

Drain the prunes, reserving the liquid in which they were soaked. Stuff the prunes between the ribs and meat. Tie the ribs and meat together, with the prunes sandwiched between them, in two or three places with string.

Place the joint in a small roasting tin, skin side up. Pour the liquid in which the prunes were soaked over the joint and sprinkle with plenty of salt. Bake in the preheated oven for 2 hours. Remove from the oven, then lift the pork out of the liquid in the tin and set aside to cool. If the pork is to be left overnight, cover it loosely with kitchen foil once it is quite cold, and store it in a cool place.

Scrape the juices from the roasting tin into a bowl and leave on one side until cool,

PORK STUFFED WITH PRUNES

Belly, the meat covering the lower part of the pig's rib cage, is one of the cheapest cuts of pork. Much of it tends to be fatty, but the thick end has plenty of lean meat, making it an economical yet well-flavoured joint. It may be necessary to order the joint in advance from the butcher in case he has to prepare it specially.

If you have to use unpitted prunes remove the stones after soaking rather than before. Use a few more prunes to allow for the weight of the stones.

Start preparations at least a day in advance. It is best to start 2 days ahead and to cook the pork and make the sauce the day before the party.

PREPARATION TIME: *20 minutes plus cooling time*
SOAKING TIME: *8 hours or overnight*
COOKING TIME: *2 hours*
OVEN TEMPERATURE: *preheat to 190°C (375°F, gas mark 5)*

INGREDIENTS – *serves 12:*
6 lb (2.7 kg) joint of thick end of pork belly on the bone
12 oz (350 g) pitted prunes
Salt and freshly ground black pepper
¼ teaspoon dried sage
3 cloves garlic, crushed
6 juniper berries, crushed
¾ pint (450 ml) red wine
¾ pint (450 ml) natural yoghurt

but not set. Skim all the fat off the cooking juices and then blend the juices evenly with the yoghurt to make the sauce. Store the sauce in a covered container in the refrigerator until needed.

Not more than 2 hours before serving, place the pork, skin side down, on a chopping board. Cut off the string. With a sharp knife completely separate the bones from the meat and discard them. Cut the meat, with the prune stuffing on top, into thin slices and arrange on a serving dish. Cover with foil until needed. Serve the yoghurt sauce separately in a bowl or jug.

CHINESE PORK SLICES WITH GARLIC SAUCE

Spices and herbs from the East combine with garlic to make something special out of this very simple pork dish. Coriander stalks add their slightly citrus taste; ginger brings a fiery touch; and sesame oil, widely used throughout the Far East, imparts its distinctive, toasted flavour. Sesame oil can be bought in many supermarkets, but if it is unavailable, use a good corn oil blended with toasted sesame seeds instead.

Made in smaller quantities this dish can be served for family meals and is a good way of using up any leftover pork.

PREPARATION TIME: *20 minutes*
MARINATING TIME: *4 hours or overnight*
COOLING TIME: *1 hour*
COOKING TIME: *2½ hours*

INGREDIENTS – *serves 12:*
5 lb (2.3 kg) joint of lean, boneless pork
3-4 pints (1.7-2.3 litres) chicken stock (page 367)
Small bunch coriander stalks
7 cloves garlic
4 tablespoons soya sauce
2 in (50 mm) piece of root ginger, finely chopped
4 spring onions, finely chopped
2 tablespoons sesame oil
GARNISH
Spring onion tassels (page 287)

Place the pork in a large pan. Pour over the stock and add the coriander and 3 of the cloves of garlic, peeled. Bring to the boil, cover the pan and simmer gently for 2½ hours. Remove from the heat and leave for about an hour until the pork is cool enough to handle.

Take out the pork, cut it into thin slices and arrange them on a serving plate.

Crush the remaining cloves of garlic. Mix thoroughly with ½ pint (285ml) of the cooking liquid, the soya sauce, and the ginger, onions and sesame oil. Pour the sauce over the pork and leave to marinate for at least 4 hours, or preferably overnight. Baste it with the marinade two or three times.

Garnish the dish with spring onion tassels.

SMOKED CHICKEN AND MANGO SALAD

Whole smoked chickens can be bought in some supermarkets and delicatessens. For this dish, smoked duck or turkey breasts – both of which are increasingly available in this country – can be used as a variation instead of smoked chicken.

This salad can be made a day in advance and kept, covered, in the refrigerator.

PREPARATION TIME: *1 hour*

INGREDIENTS – *serves 12:*
2 smoked chickens, 2½ lb (1.1 kg) each
3 ripe mangoes
2 green peppers, seeded and diced
1 bunch radishes, sliced
14 oz (400 g) tin water chestnuts, drained and sliced
¾ pint (450 ml) mayonnaise (page 369)
Salt and freshly ground black pepper

Remove and discard the skin of the smoked chickens. Cut the flesh into bite-sized pieces and place in a large bowl.

Peel the mangoes (page 397) and cut the flesh into slices, removing the stone. Reserve the best slices of mango for garnishing the dish and chop the remainder roughly.

Mix together the mango, chicken, green peppers, radishes and water chestnuts. Add the mayonnaise, mix well and season to taste with salt and pepper.

Turn the salad onto a serving dish and garnish with the reserved mango slices.

GOLDEN CONTRAST *Ripe mango – sweet and smooth – brings out the mild pungency of smoked chicken and the crispness of raw green peppers, radishes and water chestnuts.*

M E N U

Noon Wedding for Forty Eight

TURKEY GALANTINE *this page*

ROAST BEEF WITH MUSTARD SAUCE *page 266*

PASTA SALAD WITH BROAD BEANS *page 276*

LETTUCE HEARTS WITH CREAM DRESSING *page 274*

TOMATO SALAD

ALSACE CHOCOLATE GATEAU *page 280*

STRAWBERRY GALETTE *page 284*

WEDDING CAKE *page 402*

Allow at least 2 full days before the wedding for the preparations. Cook one galantine, and two joints of beef. Make three times the quantity given in the recipes for pasta salad and lettuce hearts, two chocolate gateaux and three galettes. Make a tomato salad with 8lb (3.6kg) of tomatoes, sliced and dressed with olive oil, salt and pepper and chopped chives.

IN ADVANCE Make the wedding cake at least a month in advance, and ice it a week ahead. The turkey galantine and chocolate gateaux can, if you wish, be frozen undecorated. Cook the turkey and the chocolate gateaux 2 days in advance. The beef can be cooked 2 days ahead, or the day before.

The day before the wedding, decorate the galantine, ice the gateaux, make the pasta salad and the dressing for the lettuce hearts, and cook the pastry cases for the strawberry galettes.

On the morning of the wedding, assemble the galettes, decorate the gateaux, make the mustard sauce for the beef and the tomato salad.

TO DRINK Champagne, a good dry white wine, and a light to medium-bodied red wine.

TURKEY GALANTINE

The highly decorative appearance of galantines – white meat, usually poultry, boned, stuffed and glazed with aspic – recalls the opulence of the Edwardian era when they were very popular.

The galantine can be cooked 2 days in advance, and decorated the day before. Store it in a cool place or the refrigerator. It can be frozen before glazing.

PREPARATION TIME: *2-3 hours*
SOAKING TIME: *6 hours or overnight*
CHILLING TIME: *8 hours or overnight*
COOKING TIME: *4 hours*
OVEN TEMPERATURE: *preheat to 180°C (350°F, gas mark 4)*

INGREDIENTS – *serves 24:*
1 oven-ready turkey with giblets, about 10 lb (4.5 kg)
STUFFING
2 lb (900 g) lean bacon joint
4 oz (115 g) dried apricots
2 lb (900 g) lean pork or veal, minced
2 level tablespoons chopped parsley
Grated rind of 1 lemon
2 level teaspoons dried marjoram
1 level teaspoon dried thyme
1 level teaspoon dried tarragon
Salt and freshly ground black pepper
1½ lb (700 g) boneless chicken or turkey breast fillets
4 tablespoons white wine
3 oz (75 g) butter
2 medium onions, peeled and grated

DECORATION
1 pint (570 ml), or 500 ml, packet aspic jelly powder
¾ pint (450 ml) mayonnaise
Cucumber peel, tarragon leaves and peeled lemon rind
Tomato roses (page 287) and sprigs of chervil
1 pint (570 ml) aspic jelly, chopped (page 288)

If the turkey is frozen allow to defrost overnight at room temperature or for 24 hours in the refrigerator. Soak the bacon joint in a bowl of cold water for at least 6 hours or overnight. Soak the apricots for 4 hours or overnight in cold water.

Bone the turkey (page 378), then prepare the stuffing.

WEDDING SPREAD Turkey galantine and roast beef, with salads of lettuce hearts in cream dressing, pasta and broad beans, and tomatoes, flank the white wedding cake.

---

tin with foil and roast in the preheated oven for 4 hours, removing the cover for the last 30 minutes. Take out of the oven and leave to become quite cold. Chill overnight.

When the turkey is chilled, make up the aspic jelly according to the instructions on the packet and allow to cool, but not set. Carefully stir about half the jelly into the mayonnaise. Place the galantine on a wire rack with a tray underneath to catch all the drips. When the mayonnaise and aspic mixture is just beginning to stiffen, spoon carefully all over the turkey. Leave this to set, then scoop up the drips from the tray, place in a basin over a pan of hot water and heat very gently until melted. Pour over the turkey once more.

Cut the cucumber peel, tarragon and lemon rind into decorative shapes, such as flowers and leaves. Dip each piece in the remaining liquid aspic and place on the galantine. Allow to set, then pour the last of the aspic over the top and allow to set. Place the tomato roses, each with a pair of chervil leaves, on the galantine. Place the galantine on a plate and surround with chopped aspic.

This dish is included in a menu on the opposite page.

Finely mince the turkey liver and heart. Mix in a bowl with the pork, parsley, lemon rind, dried herbs and salt and pepper.

Cut the chicken or turkey fillets into strips about ½in (15mm) wide. Season with salt and pepper and put into a small dish with the white wine. Marinate for at least 30 minutes.

Remove the bacon joint from the water in which it has been soaking. Dry well, and cut off the skin, then mince finely. Melt 1oz (25g) of the butter in a pan and gently fry the onions for 5 minutes. Add to the bacon and season with plenty of black pepper. Drain the apricots.

Lay the turkey out flat with

the skin underneath and season all over with salt and pepper. Spread half the pork mixture down the centre of the turkey, then lay half the chicken strips on top, and cover with half the bacon mixture. Lay the apricots in a line on top of the bacon, then cover with the rest of the bacon mixture, then the chicken

and then the pork. Bring the edges of the skin together, forming the mixture inside into a roll. Do not pull the skin too tight or it will split during cooking. Sew the turkey up.

Place the turkey in a roasting tin, spread all over with the remaining butter and season with salt and pepper. Cover the

TURKEY IN CRAB SAUCE

The sauce for this dish can be made 8-12 hours ahead if frozen crabmeat is used, 24 hours ahead if it is fresh.

PREPARATION TIME: *30 minutes plus cooling time*
COOKING TIME: *4 hours*
OVEN TEMPERATURE: *preheat to 180°C (350°F, gas mark 4)*

INGREDIENTS – *serves 12:*
1 turkey, about 8 lb (3.6 kg)
Salt and freshly ground black pepper
Sprig of thyme
2 oz (50 g) butter
1 pint (570 ml) mayonnaise (page 369)
½ pint (285 ml) soured cream
2 tablespoons lemon juice
1 lb (450 g) crabmeat, half white and half brown (page 375)
4 spring onions, finely chopped
2 oz (50 g) flaked almonds, toasted
GARNISH
Watercress leaves

Season the turkey with salt and pepper. Put the sprig of thyme inside the bird and place it on a large sheet of kitchen foil. Rub the bird all over with the butter, then close the foil round it. Place in a roasting tin and cook in the preheated oven for 4 hours. Remove from the oven and leave until cold (wrapped).

Mix the mayonnaise with the soured cream and lemon juice in a large bowl. Add the crabmeat

and spring onions and set aside.

Skin the turkey and cut the flesh into bite-sized pieces. Mix into the sauce, and season.

Spoon onto a serving dish. Sprinkle over the almonds and garnish with watercress. Cover and store in the refrigerator.

This dish is included in a menu on page 254.

HARE PIE

Hare is in season from September to March. If you buy a hare in its fur, it should weigh about 6lb (2.7kg) – to leave 2½-3lb (1.1-1.4kg) of meat when skinned. The meat of two rabbits or two pheasants can be used instead of hare. The pie can be made 2-3 days ahead.

PREPARATION TIME: *1-2 hours plus cooling and chilling time*
COOKING TIME: *2¾ hours*
OVEN TEMPERATURE: *preheat to 200°C (400°F, gas mark 6)*

INGREDIENTS – *serves 12:*
FILLING
1 hare, weighing about 2½-3 lb (1.1-1.4 kg) skinned
2 tablespoons Madeira (or port)
Salt and freshly ground black pepper
1½ lb (700 g) pork belly
1½ lb (700 g) pie veal
1 large onion
3 cloves garlic, crushed
10 dried juniper berries, crushed
3 level tablespoons chopped parsley
2 level teaspoons dried thyme

2 pints (1.1 litres) water
A few parsley stalks
1 medium onion, chopped
2 level teaspoons powdered gelatine
PASTRY
6 oz (175 g) lard
1¼ lb (575 g) plain flour
1½ level teaspoons salt
½ pint (285 ml) water
GLAZE
Beaten egg

Using a small, very sharp knife, bone the hare. Save the bones and put them on one side. Take the meat from the back and cut it carefully into lengthways strips about ¼in (5mm) thick. Place in a bowl, pour over the Madeira and season with salt and pepper. Put on one side.

Mince the remaining hare meat with the pork, veal and onion. Mix with the garlic, juniper berries, parsley and thyme and season with salt and pepper.

Next make the pastry case. Grease a 9in (230mm) loose-based cake tin thoroughly with a little melted lard. Use a tin with a single rather than double layered base. Sieve the flour and salt into a bowl. Put the rest of the lard and the water into a saucepan. Bring slowly to the boil, and as soon as it is boiling rapidly, pour it into the centre of the flour. Beat with a wooden spoon until the mixture clings together, leaving the sides of the bowl clean.

Turn the pastry onto a lightly floured surface and knead well

to a smooth dough. Roll out just over two-thirds of the pastry and carefully line the inside of the cake tin. Make sure that the pastry is as even as possible and that there are no holes in it, through which the meat juices could seep. Keep back a little pastry to plug any small holes that appear.

Put half the minced mixture into the pastry-lined tin, then lay the strips of hare meat, together with the liquid in which they have been soaking, on top. Cover with the remaining minced mixture. Do not pack the meat too tightly – otherwise, when the mixture expands during cooking, it may make holes in the pastry.

Brush the pastry edges with beaten egg. Roll out the remaining pastry to a circle for the lid. Place on top and pinch the edges together to seal them, trimming off any excess. Make a small slit in the top for the steam to escape. Decorate the top with pastry leaves.

Place the tin on a baking tray and bake in the preheated oven for 15 minutes. Lower the heat to 160°C (325°F, gas mark 3) and continue baking for a further 1¼ hours.

Take the pie out of the oven and allow to cool for about 5 minutes, then very carefully remove the pie from the tin,

GAME PIE A traditional raised pie – the hare filling flavoured with Madeira and juniper – is served with chicory, orange and almond salad.

pushing it up out of the tin from the base. Brush all over with beaten egg and return to the oven for another 1¼ hours. Remove the pie from the oven and allow to cool.

While the pie is cooking, boil the hare bones with the water, parsley stalks, chopped onion and salt and pepper for 2 hours, to make stock.

Pour ½ pint (285 ml) of the stock into a basin and sprinkle in the gelatine. Set the bowl over a pan of gently simmering water. When the gelatine has dissolved, set the mixture aside until it is cool and syrupy. Carefully pour it into the hole in the top of the pie. If there are any holes in the pastry, it may help to let the jelly cool further until it is half set, so that the jelly will not escape from the holes as readily. However, the resulting pie will not have quite as good a texture. Chill overnight.

MEDITERRANEAN TERRINE WITH HUMMUS SAUCE

An earthy yet sharply flavoured sauce of chick peas – *hummus* in Arabic – mixed with sesame-meal paste (*tahina*) accompanies a mould of aubergine, tomato and onion. The dish can be served as a starter or as a light main course.

The terrine and the sauce can be made 1-2 days in advance.

PREPARATION TIME: *1 hour*
SALTING TIME: *45 minutes*
CHILLING TIME: *overnight*
COOKING TIME: *45 minutes*

INGREDIENTS – *serves 12:*
3 lb (1.4 kg) aubergines
4 level teaspoons salt
2½ fl oz (75 ml) olive oil
2½ fl oz (75 ml) vegetable oil
2 lb (900 g) onions, peeled and sliced
1 lb (450 g) tomatoes, skinned (page 389) and chopped
Freshly ground black pepper
1½ level teaspoons dried oregano
SAUCE
15½ oz (440 g) tin chick peas
2 tablespoons lemon juice
2 cloves garlic, crushed
4 tablespoons tahina
4 tablespoons olive oil
Salt and freshly ground black pepper
1 oz (25 g) parsley, chopped
GARNISH
Lemon slices
Parsley

Cut the aubergines into thin slices. Lay them on trays, sprinkle with salt and leave for 45 minutes to draw out the bitter juices. Rinse the slices under cold water, drain and dry thoroughly with kitchen paper.

Mix the olive oil and vegetable oil together in a measuring jug. Heat about 1fl oz (25ml) of the oil in a large pan and gently fry the onions for 10 minutes. Remove from the pan with a slotted spoon and set them aside on a plate. Pour about a quarter of the remaining oil into the pan

and heat. Add a quarter of the aubergines and fry briefly over a high heat. Remove from the pan with a slotted spoon and put them on the plate with the onions. Repeat with the remaining oil and aubergines, frying them in 4 batches altogether.

Remove the pan from the heat and add the tomatoes. Replace the aubergines and onions. Season with a little extra salt and plenty of black pepper. Stir in the oregano.

Cover the pan and place over a very gentle heat for 45 minutes. Stir occasionally. Remove from the heat and allow to cool for about an hour. Taste and adjust the seasoning.

Lightly oil a 9in (230mm) cake tin – without a loose base. Select a few of the best aubergine slices from the mixture and arrange them in the base of the tin, overlapping slightly. Spoon the remaining mixture on top. Place a plate on top of the mixture to press it down. Chill overnight in the refrigerator.

To make the sauce, tip the chick peas, together with their liquid, into a liquidiser or food processor and blend until smooth. Keeping the motor running, add the lemon juice, garlic and tahina, then add the olive oil a little at a time. Season to taste with salt and pepper. Stir in the parsley, then turn into a bowl.

Turn the terrine out onto a serving dish with a lip – to catch the liquid. Garnish with lemon slices and parsley. Serve with hot pitta bread.

WEST COAST SALAD

The crisp Iceberg lettuce, beloved of Californians, is used in this salad. It is served with a rich American-style blue cheese dressing and makes a substantial main course. The ingredients can be varied according to season and taste. Tuna, ham or tongue can be used instead of salami, for example, and Chinese leaf, endive, Webb's or cos lettuce can be used instead of Iceberg lettuce.

Both the salad and the dressing should be prepared on the day they are to be eaten. But they can be made several hours in advance and kept in the refrigerator.

PREPARATION TIME: *50 minutes*

INGREDIENTS – *serves 12:*
2 Iceberg lettuces, shredded
1 cucumber, diced
11 oz (300 g) tin sweetcorn, drained
1 head of celery, chopped
2 green peppers, seeded and chopped
2 red peppers, seeded and chopped
8 oz (225 g) salami, sliced and cut in thin strips
6 hard-boiled eggs, quartered
4 oz (115 g) stoned black olives
4 tablespoons chopped parsley
Salt and freshly ground black pepper
DRESSING
½ pint (285 ml) mayonnaise (page 369)
8 fl oz (225 ml) vinaigrette (page 371)
8 fl oz (225 ml) single cream
8 oz (225 g) Danish Blue cheese, crumbled

Put all the ingredients for the salad into a large bowl. Cover and chill until ready to serve.

Mix together all the ingredients for the dressing. Pour over the salad before serving and toss together. Season to taste with salt and pepper.

Serve as a main course with warm French bread.

CALIFORNIAN SALAD Eggs, salami, peppers, olives and sweetcorn are substantial elements in a salad based on Iceberg lettuce. They are all tossed in a rich blue cheese dressing.

SALADS

MIXED GREEN SALAD

The combination of green salad vegetables can be varied according to what is available in the shops or your garden.

PREPARATION TIME: *20 minutes*

INGREDIENTS – *serves 12:*
1 Iceberg lettuce
12 oz (350 g) fresh spinach
Heart of 2 heads of endive
1½ lb (700 g) french beans
1 lb (450 g) shelled broad beans
A large handful of chopped sorrel
A large handful of chopped mixed fresh herbs such as tarragon, basil, chives and parsley
½ pint (285 ml) vinaigrette (page 371)

Chop the lettuce, spinach and endive roughly. Wash in cold water and drain. Top and tail the french beans and boil in lightly salted water for 3 minutes. Rinse under the cold tap. Boil the broad beans in lightly salted water for 5 minutes. Drain and remove the skins.

Put all the salad ingredients in a large bowl with the herbs. Toss with the vinaigrette. This salad is included in menus on pages 262 and 258.

LETTUCE HEARTS WITH CREAM DRESSING

Use crisp lettuces such as cos or Webb's for this salad. It may be necessary to vary the number of hearts depending on size. Lettuce hearts can sometimes be bought ready-prepared.

The dressing can be prepared the day before.

PREPARATION TIME: *10 minutes*

INGREDIENTS – *serves 12:*
6 lettuce hearts
DRESSING
¾ pint (450 ml) single cream
4 tablespoons wine vinegar
6 tablespoons olive oil
Good pinch of chilli powder
Salt and freshly ground black pepper
GARNISH
Paprika
Continental parsley

Wash and dry the lettuce hearts. To crisp them, place them in a plastic bag and chill them in the refrigerator.

To make the dressing, pour the cream into a bowl. Beat in first the wine vinegar, a tablespoon at a time, then the olive oil. Season to taste with chilli powder, salt and pepper.

Halve the lettuce hearts and arrange on a dish. Spoon over the dressing and sprinkle with paprika before serving. Garnish with parsley. This dish is included in a menu on page 270.

POTATO SALAD WITH GREEN DRESSING

The dressing for this salad can be made 2–3 days ahead and kept covered in the refrigerator.

PREPARATION TIME: *30 minutes plus cooling time*

INGREDIENTS – *serves 12*:
4 lb (1.8 kg) new potatoes
6 oz (175 g) spinach leaves, fresh or frozen
1 bunch watercress
A large handful of parsley
1 pint (570 ml) mayonnaise (page 369)

Scrub the potatoes. Boil them in their skins in lightly salted water for 10-15 minutes until tender. Drain and cut into even-sized pieces – unless they are very small, in which case leave them whole. Leave to cool.

Wash the spinach, watercress and parsley and drop them into a pan of lightly salted boiling water. Simmer for about 2 minutes until the leaves are soft. Drain thoroughly, saving the cooking water. Purée the vegetables in a liquidiser or food processor or by pressing them through a sieve.

Stir the purée into the mayonnaise, adding some of the cooking water if the mixture is too thick. Pour the dressing over the potatoes and mix well. This dish is included in a menu on page 262.

CHICORY, ORANGE AND ALMOND SALAD

The yoghurt dressing for this salad can be kept overnight, covered in the refrigerator.

PREPARATION TIME: *20 minutes*

INGREDIENTS – *serves 12*:
6 tablespoons sunflower oil
6 oz (175 g) flaked almonds
6 tablespoons lemon juice
½ pint (285 ml) natural yoghurt
6 level tablespoons finely chopped fresh parsley or lemon balm
8 large oranges
5 heads chicory
3 bunches watercress

Heat the oil in a pan. Add the almonds and fry gently until golden-brown. Remove from the heat, cool slightly then pour the lemon juice over the almonds. Leave to cool completely. Stir in the yoghurt, and parsley or lemon balm.

Remove the peel and pith from the oranges, then segment them (page 398), catching any juice in the bowl of yoghurt and almonds. Mix half the orange segments into the yoghurt and almond mixture. Reserve the rest for decoration.

Wash and dry the chicory and watercress and arrange round the outside of a large flat serving dish. Pile the yoghurt and almond mixture into the centre and decorate with the remaining orange segments.

CHINESE SALAD

Chinese leaf – also known as Chinese or Shantung cabbage – is an oriental variety which has become increasingly popular in Britain in recent years. Chinese water chestnuts, or *pi-tsi*, are not nuts, but the tubers of a plant related to the bulrush. They are available tinned, at supermarkets and Chinese grocers.

The salad and the dressing can be prepared a day in advance and kept separately in covered containers in the refrigerator. Mix them together just before serving.

PREPARATION TIME: *20 minutes*

INGREDIENTS – *serves 12*:
3 lb (1.4 kg) Chinese leaf
1 lb (450 g) fresh bean sprouts
11 oz (300 g) tin water chestnuts, drained and sliced
1 large green pepper, seeded and thinly sliced
Salt and freshly ground black pepper
DRESSING
6 fl oz (175 ml) vegetable oil
6 tablespoons wine vinegar
3 tablespoons soya sauce

Finely shred the Chinese leaf, then wash it and dry well. Pick over the bean sprouts, and wash

ORIENTAL ALLIANCE Chinese leaf, bean sprouts, water chestnuts and strips of green pepper are tossed in a light soya sauce dressing.

and dry thoroughly. Pile the leaf and bean sprouts into a large bowl with the water chestnuts and green pepper. Mix lightly together. Season well with salt and pepper. Cover and chill in the refrigerator until shortly before serving.

Put all the ingredients for the dressing in a screwtop jar and shake well. Pour over the salad and toss well. This salad is included in a menu on page 254.

ALTERNATIVE SLAW Finely shredded brussels sprouts, tossed with walnuts and a mustard dressing, make a change from cabbage coleslaw.

PREPARATION TIME: *30-60 minutes*

INGREDIENTS – *serves 12:*
2 lb (900 g) brussels sprouts
1 lb (450 g) carrots
1 small head of celery
3 oz (75 g) walnuts, chopped
Salt and freshly ground black pepper
DRESSING
½ pint (285 ml) natural yoghurt
¼ pint (150 ml) mayonnaise (page 369)
1 teaspoon Meaux mustard
Salt and freshly ground black pepper

Discard any very tough outer leaves from the sprouts and trim the bases. Wash them well in cold water and dry thoroughly. Finely shred the sprouts, either in a food processor or by hand, and put them into a bowl. Peel and grate the carrots and finely chop the celery. Add to the shredded sprouts with the walnuts. Mix well and season to taste with salt and pepper.

To make the dressing, mix the yoghurt with the mayonnaise and mustard and season to taste with salt and pepper. Mix with the vegetables.

Spoon the salad into a serving dish. Cover and chill until ready to serve. This dish is included in a menu on page 254.

WINTER SLAW

Coleslaw first became popular in the United States. It derives its name from the Dutch *koolsla*, meaning 'cabbage salad'. This slaw uses brussels sprouts instead of cabbage. It is a good way of using large sprouts, which are often cheaper.

The dressing is given a slightly sharp, spicy flavour by adding mustard. If possible, use *moutarde de Meaux* which is made from whole grains of mustard mixed with spices and herbs.

Both vegetables and dressing can be prepared a day in advance. Keep them covered in the refrigerator, either separate or mixed together.

SPICY BROWN RICE SALAD

The rice for this salad is spiced with turmeric, which also colours it yellow, cardamom pods and *garam masala*, an Indian mixture of spices. The salad is best made a day in advance.

PREPARATION TIME: *15 minutes plus cooling time*
COOKING TIME: *30 minutes*

INGREDIENTS – *serves 12:*
1 lb (450 g) brown rice
Salt
2 level teaspoons ground turmeric
8 cardamom pods
3 level teaspoons garam masala
¼ pint (150 ml) vinaigrette (page 371)
2 oz (50 g) sunflower seeds
2 red peppers, seeded and diced
½ cucumber, diced
Freshly ground black pepper

Put a large pan of salted water onto the heat. Whisk in the turmeric and add the cardamoms and rice. Bring to the boil. Cover the pan and cook gently, following the instructions on the rice packet. When the rice is tender remove it from the heat and drain well. If it is very sticky, rinse it with boiling water then drain it again. Put it in a large bowl. Mix the garam masala with the vinaigrette. Pour it over the rice and mix well, then leave to cool.

Remove the cardamom pods from the rice, then stir in the sunflower seeds, red peppers and cucumber, and mix well. Taste and adjust the seasoning.

This dish is included in a menu on page 283.

PASTA SALAD WITH BROAD BEANS

Use one of the numerous shaped pastas – such as shells – for this salad, they are easier to manage than the long varieties. It can be prepared a day ahead and kept in a cool place.

PREPARATION TIME: *45 minutes plus cooling time*
COOKING TIME: *15 minutes*

INGREDIENTS – *serves 12:*
8 lb (3.6 kg) broad beans in their pods OR 1 lb (450 g) frozen beans
Salt
1 lb (450 g) pasta shapes
8 fl oz (225 ml) vinaigrette (page 371)
4 level tablespoons chopped chives
GARNISH
Chives

Shell the broad beans, and, unless they are very young, remove the pale green skins from each bean (frozen beans do not usually need skinning). Cook them in a very little boiling salted water for 2 minutes, or until they are just tender, then drain. Follow the cooking instructions on the packet of frozen beans.

Bring a large pan of lightly salted water to the boil. Add the

pasta and cook, uncovered, for 5-10 minutes, according to the instructions on the packet, until the pasta is tender but still firm to the bite, *al dente*.

Drain the pasta well then toss it in a large bowl with the vinaigrette. Add the broad beans and chives and mix lightly together. Cover and leave to cool. Garnish with a few chives before serving. This dish is included in a menu on page 270.

TOMATO AND ONION SALAD WITH AVOCADO DRESSING

The large, mild onions known as Spanish onions should be used for this salad. Ordinary onions are too sharp. The avocado dressing can be prepared 3-4 hours in advance, and kept covered closely. The tomatoes and onions can be prepared up to 2 hours in advance.

PREPARATION TIME: *20 minutes*

INGREDIENTS – *serves 12:*
2 large Spanish onions
Salt
3 lb (1.4 kg) Mediterranean (beefsteak) tomatoes
Freshly ground black pepper
DRESSING
2 ripe avocados
1/4 pint (150 ml) soured cream
1/4 pint (150 ml) French dressing
2 cloves garlic, crushed
Salt and freshly ground black pepper

Peel the onions, cut them into thin rings and then blanch for 1 minute in boiling salted water. Drain them thoroughly and put them on one side to cool.

Slice the tomatoes and arrange them overlapping with the cooled onions round a large, shallow serving dish, leaving the centre clear. Season lightly with salt and pepper.

To make the dressing, halve and stone the avocados and scoop out the flesh into a liquidiser or food processor. Add the soured cream, French dressing, garlic and salt and pepper to taste. Purée until smooth, then adjust the seasoning.

Alternatively, mash the avocado flesh with a fork, then beat in the other dressing ingredients

RED, WHITE AND GREEN Rings of sweet Spanish onions and thinly sliced Mediterranean tomatoes, encircle a pool of avocado dressing, to make a vivid tricolour salad.

until the mixture is smooth.

Shortly before serving, spoon the avocado dressing into the centre of the salad.

FLAGEOLET BEAN SALAD

In France, dried flageolets are considered to be the choicest variety of haricot bean. They are pale green, and have a more delicate flavour than other haricot beans. This salad can be prepared 1-2 days in advance.

PREPARATION TIME: *15 minutes plus cooling time*
SOAKING TIME: *overnight*
COOKING TIME: *1 1/2 hours*

INGREDIENTS – *serves 12:*
1 lb (450 g) flageolet beans
Salt
2 bouquets garnis
1/2 pint (285 ml) mayonnaise (page 369)
4 level tablespoons chopped parsley
1 medium onion, very finely chopped
GARNISH
Small sprigs of parsley

Put the beans in a large bowl. Cover them with cold water and soak overnight. Drain, then put them into a saucepan with salt and the bouquets garnis. Cover with fresh cold water. Bring to the boil, then cover and simmer gently for about 1 1/2 hours or until just tender.

Drain the beans thoroughly and, while they are still warm, stir in the mayonnaise, parsley and onion. Leave to cool. Turn into a serving dish and garnish with sprigs of parsley. This dish is included in a menu on page 283.

277

PUDDINGS & DESSERTS

CIDER SORBET

Sorbet looks very attractive presented in an ice bowl – which also serves the practical purpose of keeping the sorbet chilled on the buffet table. To make an ice bowl, half fill a large heatproof and freezer-proof bowl with water and some ice cubes. Float another smaller bowl on top of the water. Put some weights into the smaller bowl so that the water is forced into a shape that will make a suitably sized bowl when frozen. The aim is to make a bowl of ice with sides about 1in (25mm) thick. Tape the bowl in place with freezer tape if necessary.

Put the bowls in the freezer until the water has frozen solid.

Pour some hot water into the smaller bowl to loosen it from the ice, then remove it. Turn the larger bowl upside down and pour hot water over it to free the ice bowl. Put this in the freezer until required. Stand it on a large deep plate for serving and fill it with the sorbet. The bowl should remain frozen for at least 1-2 hours, but do not leave it out all night.

FROZEN CHALICE A bowl of ice – easily made in the freezer – is a striking container for cider sorbet.

PREPARATION TIME: *10 minutes*
FREEZING TIME: *at least 6 hours*
COOKING TIME: *5 minutes*

INGREDIENTS – *serves 12:*
2 pints (1.1 litres) strong dry cider
1 lb (450 g) granulated sugar
½ pint (285 ml) water
DECORATION
Thin slices of apple, dipped in lemon juice to prevent discoloration

Pour the cider into a large bowl. Place the granulated sugar and water in a pan over a gentle heat and leave until the sugar has dissolved, stirring once or twice. Bring to the boil and boil rapidly for about 5 minutes until a thick syrup is formed. If you have a sugar thermometer, boil the syrup until it reaches 110°C (225°F). Remove from the heat and beat into the cider.

Put the mixture into a container and freeze, uncovered, until the mixture is slushy (this should take 2-3 hours). Beat well with a fork to break up the ice crystals. Return to the freezer and leave once again until slushy (this should take another 1-2 hours). Remove from the freezer and beat thoroughly once more. Cover, return to the freezer and freeze until firm.

Scoop the sorbet into the prepared ice bowl (see introduction) or into stemmed glasses. Decorate with slices of apple.

This dish is included in a menu on page 258.

CROQUEMBOUCHE

Literally translated from French, *croquembouche* – or *croque-en-bouche* – means 'crunch in the mouth'. It is a name usually given to a tall pyramid of choux puffs dipped in caramel.

The pyramid is easily made by piling the puffs one on top of the other, but a conical metal croquembouche tin can be used to achieve a more perfect shape. Butter the inside of the tin, then fill it loosely with the choux puffs dipped in caramel. When the caramel has dried, invert the tin and lift it off the croquembouche. Alternatively, construct the croquembouche around a tall cone of thin gold card.

The croquembouche can be decorated with rosettes of piped cream and crystallised flowers.

Assemble the croquembouche as near to the time to be eaten as possible – it cannot be kept in the refrigerator because the caramel will go soft and lose its shine. The puffs, however, can be made a day ahead and kept in an airtight tin. They also freeze well, but will benefit from a couple of minutes in a hot oven after defrosting to crisp them. The cream filling will keep for 2-3 days in a covered bowl in the refrigerator.

PUFF PYRAMID A pile of light, custard-filled choux puffs glazed with caramel is decorated with cream and crystallised violets.

PREPARATION TIME: *1¼ hours*
COOKING TIME: *10-15 minutes*
OVEN TEMPERATURE: *preheat to 220°C (425°F, gas mark 7)*

INGREDIENTS – *serves 8-12:*
PUFFS
Choux pastry (page 395) made with 4 oz (115 g) flour
FILLING
2 eggs, separated
4 oz (115 g) caster sugar
1½ oz (40 g) plain flour
½ pint (285 ml) milk
¾ oz (20 g) butter
1 teaspoon vanilla essence
Pinch of salt
1-2 tablespoons Grand Marnier (optional)
CARAMEL
8 oz (225 g) granulated sugar
6 fl oz (175 ml) water

Using a teaspoon or a piping bag with a ½in (15mm) nozzle, put walnut-sized mounds of the choux pastry onto wet baking sheets, leaving 2in (50mm) between each one. Bake in the preheated oven for 10-15 minutes until well risen and golden-brown. Pierce each puff with a sharp knife to let the steam escape. Return the puffs to the oven for 2-3 minutes to dry out. Leave to cool on a wire rack.

Next make the filling for the puffs. In a mixing bowl, beat the egg yolks with 3oz (75g) of the caster sugar until thick and pale yellow in colour. Beat in the flour and a little of the milk. Bring the remaining milk to the boil in a large pan. Pour slowly onto the egg yolks, beating all the time. Return the egg yolk mixture to the pan and stir over moderate heat until thick and boiling. Lower the heat and boil for 2-3 minutes, stirring continuously. Remove the pan from the heat and stir in the butter and vanilla essence.

Beat the egg whites with the salt until stiff. Fold in the remaining caster sugar. Stir a large spoonful of egg white into the custard, then add the Grand Marnier, if used, and stir again. Fold in the remaining egg white. Leave to cool. Fill the puffs (page 395).

To make the caramel, put the sugar and water in a pan and stir over low heat until the sugar has dissolved. Raise the heat and boil fiercely until it turns a golden-brown or reaches the 'small crack' stage 138-152°C (305-325°F) – when ½ teaspoon of the syrup dropped into a bowl of cold water separates into brittle threads. Remove from the heat and dip the base of the pan into cold water to stop the caramel cooking.

Quickly dip the top of each filled puff into the caramel. Be very careful not to burn your fingers. Arrange in a pyramid on a dish, sticking them together with the caramel. If the caramel starts to harden, melt it over a low heat. If necessary, make more caramel using half quantities of sugar and water.

Keep the croquembouche in a cool place (not the refrigerator) until required. This dish is included in a menu on page 262.

ALSACE CHOCOLATE GATEAU

One of the specialities of a little coffee shop just opposite the cathedral in the old town of Colmar in eastern Alsace is this rich chocolate gateau.

PREPARATION AND COOKING
    TIME: *1½ hours plus setting
    time*
OVEN TEMPERATURE: *preheat to
    200°C (400°F, gas mark 6)*

INGREDIENTS – *serves 12:*
FILLING
*6 tablespoons water
1 oz (25 g), or 2 level
    tablespoons, powdered gelatine
6 eggs, separated
3 oz (75 g) caster sugar
1½ pints (850 ml) single cream
12 oz (350 g) plain chocolate*
CAKE
*4 eggs
4 oz (115 g) caster sugar
4 oz (115 g) self-raising flour*
ICING
*8 oz (225 g) plain chocolate
½ pint (285 ml) double cream*
DECORATION
*¼ pint (150 ml) double cream,
    whipped
Chocolate leaves (page 290)
Crystallised rose petals*

To make the filling, put the water in a small basin and sprinkle in the gelatine. Leave to soften. Whisk the egg yolks and sugar together until they are thick and creamy.

Bring the cream to the boil in a large, heavy pan. Remove from the heat and whisk in the egg yolk mixture. Stir in the gelatine until it has dissolved. Break the chocolate into small pieces and stir into the mixture until it has melted. Leave to cool, stirring frequently.

Line a roasting tin, about 12in × 13in (300mm × 330mm) in size, with greaseproof or non-stick baking paper.

To make the cake, whisk the eggs and sugar together until they are thick and creamy. Sieve the flour and fold in. Turn the mixture into the prepared tin. Bake in the preheated oven for 12 minutes, or until golden-brown and springy to touch. Remove from the oven and turn out onto a wire rack to cool.

Cut out a circle from the slab of cake to fit the base of a 5 pint (2.8 litre) pudding basin or mixing bowl. Cut the rest of the cake into wedges and line the sides of the bowl completely.

Whisk the egg whites until they form soft peaks, then fold them into the chocolate filling mixture. Pour the filling into the cake-lined bowl and leave to set for at least 4 hours, or overnight. Unmould the mousse onto a large serving plate.

To make the icing, break the chocolate into small pieces, and put it into a small pan with the cream. Heat gently until the chocolate has melted, beating well. Remove from the heat and allow to cool slightly. Spoon carefully over the cake to give it

*CHOCOLATE CONFECTION Ribbons
of whipped cream, chocolate leaves
and crystallised roses garland a dome
of rich chocolate mousse encased in
sponge and chocolate icing.*

a smooth coating. Any icing which runs onto the plate can either be removed when it is set, or covered with cream.

Chill the gateau in the refrigerator until the icing has set, then pipe with whipped cream and decorate with chocolate leaves and rose petals. Return to the refrigerator until the party.

Remove the gateau at least 15 minutes before serving so that the chocolate icing softens slightly. This dish is included in a menu on page 270.

AMARETTI AND ICE CREAM LOAF

Italian *amaretti* biscuits are like small macaroons but with a more pronounced taste, because they are made with apricot kernels or bitter almonds rather than ordinary almonds. Ratafia biscuits are a good alternative. Other fruit liqueurs that will complement the almond flavour of the biscuits if Poire William (pear liqueur) is unavailable, include Amaretto di Saronno, Grand Marnier or slivovitz.

The loaf will keep in the freezer for 2-3 weeks.

PREPARATION TIME: *45-60
    minutes*
CHILLING TIME: *1½-2 hours*
FREEZING TIME: *overnight*

INGREDIENTS – *serves 12:*
*6 eggs separated
9 oz (250 g) icing sugar
7 fl oz (200 ml) Poire William
    liqueur
1 teaspoon vanilla essence
¾ pint (450 ml) double cream
18 amaretti biscuits*
DECORATION
*Whole hazelnuts
2-3 fl oz (50-90 ml) double
    cream, whipped*

Whisk together the egg yolks, half of the sugar, 4 tablespoons of the liqueur and the vanilla essence in a large bowl until the mixture is thick and creamy.

Whisk the egg whites until

they are very stiff, then gradually whisk in the remaining sugar, a teaspoon at a time. When all the sugar has been added, gradually whisk in the egg yolk mixture.

Whip the cream until it just holds its shape, then fold it into the egg mixture.

Pour a third of this mixture into a large loaf tin measuring approximately 10½in × 5½in (265mm × 140mm) at the top, and chill in the freezer for about 45 minutes or until it is just firm. Put the remaining mixture into the refrigerator.

Lay 9 of the amaretti biscuits in a shallow dish, sprinkle with half the remaining liqueur and leave to steep for 5 minutes. Arrange these biscuits over the ice cream in the loaf tin, then replace the tin in the freezer for 15 minutes.

Remove the tin from the freezer and pour half the remaining ice cream over the biscuits. Replace the tin in the freezer for a further 45 minutes or until the ice cream is just firm. Repeat the above process with the remaining biscuits, liqueur and ice cream.

Leave to freeze overnight. To unmould, quickly dip the tin in a bowl of very hot water, then invert onto a freezer-proof serving plate. Return to the freezer and freeze until firm. Just before serving, decorate the top and sides with a few whole hazelnuts and a little piped cream, if you wish. This dish is included in a menu on page 253.

CHARLOTTE MALAKOFF

According to tradition, this coffee charlotte was invented to celebrate the capture by the French of the Russian fortress of Malakoff in September 1855, at the height of the Crimean War. It can be made up to 2 days in advance and kept in the refrigerator. Decorate on the day.

PREPARATION TIME: *1 hour*
CHILLING TIME: *overnight*

INGREDIENTS – *serves 12:*
8 oz (225 g) butter, softened
7 oz (200 g) caster sugar
Scant ¼ pint (125 ml) Tia Maria or other coffee liqueur
6 fl oz (175 ml) very strong cold black coffee
6 oz (175 g) ground almonds
½ pint (285 ml) double cream
¼ pint (150 ml) single cream
4 tablespoons water
About 40 Boudoir or sponge finger biscuits
DECORATION
¼ pint (150 ml) double cream
Whole roasted coffee beans

Line the base of an 8in (200mm) loose-based cake tin with buttered greaseproof paper or non-stick baking paper. Cream the butter and sugar together in a large bowl until light and fluffy.

Mix together the liqueur and strong black coffee. Set aside half the mixture, then beat a little of the remainder into the butter and sugar mixture, then beat in some of the almonds.

Repeat, beating in the coffee mixture and almonds alternately, until both are used up.

Whip the double and single cream together until it holds its shape, then fold the cream into the butter and almond mixture.

Add the water to the remaining coffee and liqueur mixture. Trim the sponge fingers so that when they are standing upright they are the same height as the tin. Dip each trimmed sponge finger quickly in the coffee mixture and use to line the sides of the cake tin, standing them with the rounded end down and the sugar-coated side out. Soak the trimmed ends of the biscuits, together with any leftover biscuits, in the remaining coffee mixture.

Spread half the butter and almond mixture over the base of the prepared tin, and cover with the soaked sponge fingers. Spread the remaining butter and almond mixture on top. Lay a piece of buttered greaseproof paper or non-stick baking paper over the charlotte. Cover with a small plate that will just fit inside the tin and place a weight on top to press it down. Chill overnight in the refrigerator until the mixture is quite set.

Turn out the charlotte onto a serving plate. Whip the double cream until it is stiff and spread it over the top of the charlotte. Decorate with the whole coffee beans. This dish is included in a menu on page 254.

MARTIAL DESSERT A French victory in the Crimean War at the fortress of Malakoff inspired this coffee charlotte.

PLUM TART

Most plums, whether dessert varieties or cooking ones, can be used in this tart - the large red and gold Victoria, for example, or the blue Czar. Greengages or apricots are also suitable.

The flan can be made a day in advance, but do not spread the cream over until the day it is to be served.

PREPARATION TIME: *30 minutes plus cooling time*
COOKING TIME: *45 minutes*
OVEN TEMPERATURE: *preheat to 190°C (375°F, gas mark 5)*

INGREDIENTS – *serves 10-12:*
Shortcrust pastry (page 392) made with 12 oz (350 g) flour
8 oz (225 g) plum jam
2½ lb (1.1 kg) plums
About 2 oz (50 g) soft brown sugar
½ pint (285 ml) double cream
¼ pint (150 ml) single cream
1 oz (25 g) plain chocolate

Roll out the pastry and use it to line the base of a 12in (300mm) flan tin or dish. Prick the base lightly with a fork, then spread it with the jam – this helps to seal the pastry and prevents the plum juice from soaking into it. Halve and stone the plums and arrange them cut side down on top of the jam. Sprinkle with the sugar – the exact amount of sugar used depends on the tartness of the plums.

Bake in the preheated oven for about 45 minutes or until the plums are tender and the pastry is golden-brown. Remove the tart from the oven and set it on one side to cool.

Pour the double and single cream into a bowl and whip until thick. Spread over the top of the plums. Grate the chocolate coarsely and scatter it over the cream. This dish is included in a menu on page 261.

LIME AND MINT CHEESECAKE

A circle of shortbread forms the base of this cheesecake, instead of pastry or a biscuit mixture. The base and the cheese filling are made separately, then the shortbread is placed on top of the filling and the cake is turned out, upside down.

If possible, make the cheesecake a day in advance and then turn it out and decorate it on the day it is to be served. It can also be frozen, but without the decoration.

PREPARATION TIME: *40 minutes*
CHILLING TIME: *at least 6 hours*
COOKING TIME: *30-35 minutes*
OVEN TEMPERATURE: *preheat to 160°C (325°F, gas mark 3)*

INGREDIENTS – *serves 12:*
SHORTBREAD BASE
4 oz (115 g) plain flour
2 oz (50 g) cornflour
2 oz (50 g) caster sugar
4 oz (115 g) butter, preferably unsalted
Non-stick baking paper

FILLING
12 fresh mint leaves
Grated rind and juice of 5 limes
2 lb (900 g) curd cheese
¾ oz (20 g), or 1½ level tablespoons, powdered gelatine
2 eggs, separated
6 oz (175 g) caster sugar
DECORATION
¼ pint (150 ml) double cream, whipped
Mint leaves

To make the base, sieve the flour and cornflour into a bowl. Add the sugar, then rub in the butter with your fingers. The mixture will become crumbly at first, but then it clings together in heavy lumps. Turn onto a lightly floured work surface and knead lightly to a smooth round ball.

Mark out a 9in (230mm) circle on a piece of non-stick baking paper (use a cake tin as a guide). Butter the paper lightly on both sides and place it on a baking tray. Place the ball of dough in the centre of the circle and roll out evenly to fit the circle. Trim the edges, then prick all over with a fork.

Bake the shortbread in the preheated oven for 30-35 minutes until cooked, but not browned. Remove from the oven. Leave to cool for a couple of minutes, then lift it off the baking paper with a fish slice and place carefully on a wire rack to cool. When the shortbread is cold, trim it with a sharp knife to fit easily inside a 9in (230mm) cake tin then put it on one side. Oil the cake tin

very lightly, then put it aside.

To make the filling, blanch the mint leaves in boiling water for 5 seconds, then chop finely. Place in a bowl with the lime rind, half the juice and the curd cheese and beat well. Put the remaining lime juice in a small basin, sprinkle in the gelatine, and leave to soften for 5 minutes. Stand the basin in a pan of hot water and stir until the gelatine has dissolved.

Whisk the egg yolks and sugar until thick and creamy, then beat them into the cream cheese mixture. Beat the dissolved gelatine into the cream cheese mixture. Whisk the egg whites until they form soft peaks, then fold them into the cheese mixture. Turn into the prepared cake tin and spread evenly. Chill until set.

When the mixture has set, carefully lay the shortbread on top of it. Press the shortbread down lightly and chill for at least 4 more hours.

To turn out the cheesecake, dip the tin quickly into hot water and invert it onto a serving plate so that the shortbread is on the bottom. Decorate with spoonfuls of whipped cream, topped with mint leaves.

This dish is included in a menu on the opposite page.

SILVER CELEBRATION An elegant, pale-hued lime and mint cheesecake – decorated with cream and fresh mint leaves – is a fitting dessert for a silver wedding party.

Echo the silver-green colour theme of the food in any decorations and flowers.

Make twice the quantity given in all the recipes.

IN ADVANCE All the dishes can be made at least a day in advance. It is best, however, to allow the trout to cool overnight and to make the bean salad on the day.

ON THE DAY Allow about 3 hours to complete the trout, decorate the cheesecakes and make the bean salad.

TO DRINK Champagne or sparkling dry white wine.

ORANGE AND APPLE BOODLE

An orange fool, first served in the 1920s at Boodle's, one of London's oldest gentlemen's clubs, is the basis of this simple dessert. The orange mixture can be prepared a day in advance. Add the apple about 2 hours before serving.

PREPARATION TIME: *30 minutes*
CHILLING TIME: *2 hours*

INGREDIENTS – *serves 12:*
36 Boudoir or sponge finger biscuits
1½ pints (850 ml) soured cream
Grated rind and juice of 6 oranges
Juice of 1 small lemon
3 oz (75 g) caster sugar
4 crisp tart eating apples
GARNISH
12 orange slices

Crumble 1 sponge finger into the bottom of each of 12 large glasses and place 2 more sponge fingers down the inside of each glass. Put the soured cream into a bowl, then add the grated orange rind. Gradually beat in the orange juice and lemon juice, then the sugar.

Core the apples but do not peel them. Dice them and stir them into the orange mixture.

Spoon the mixture into the glasses, then chill in the refrigerator for about 2 hours before serving. Decorate each glass with a slice of orange before serving.

STRAWBERRY GALETTE

'Galette' is a very general French term applied to many different sweet and savoury dishes, from confections of puff pastry, fruit and cream like this dish, to ship's biscuit. However, all galettes tend to be some kind of cake or biscuit. The best known

sweet galette is the *galette des rois*, 'cake of kings', which is served on Twelfth Night.

If Grand Marnier is not available, another orange-flavoured liqueur such as Cointreau or Curaçao can be used.

The galette can also be made with raspberries; in this case use raspberry jam for the glaze.

The galette should be assembled on the day it is to be eaten,

but the pastry case can be made a day ahead and wrapped in foil.

PREPARATION TIME: *30 minutes*
COOKING TIME: *12-15 minutes*
OVEN TEMPERATURE: *preheat to 220°C (425°F, gas mark 7)*

GLISTENING GALETTE Perfect glazed strawberries rest on a fluffy, orange-flavoured cream filling.

INGREDIENTS – *serves 12:*
14 oz (400 g) prepared weight puff pastry (page 394)
¾ pint (450 ml) double cream
1 oz (25 g) caster sugar
3 tablespoons Grand Marnier
Grated rind and juice of 1 large orange
1½ lb (700 g) strawberries
12 oz (350 g) strawberry jam

Roll out the pastry to a rectangle measuring about 15in × 11in (380mm × 280mm) and line a 13in × 9in (330mm × 230mm) swiss roll tin. Press up the edges well. Prick all over the base of the pastry with a fork. Bake in the preheated oven for 7-8 minutes. Remove from the oven and prick the base again. Return to the oven and cook for another 5-6 minutes until golden-brown. Remove from the oven. Transfer the pastry case to a wire rack and leave it to cool.

Whip the double cream until it just holds its shape, then slowly whip in the sugar, Grand Marnier and orange rind. Spread the mixture evenly over the base of the pastry case.

Hull the strawberries and arrange on top of the cream.

Sieve the jam into a small pan. Add the orange juice and heat gently until the jam has melted, then boil rapidly for about 3-4 minutes. Remove from the heat and allow to cool, stirring frequently to prevent a skin forming. Spoon evenly over the strawberries and leave to set.

This dish is included in a menu on page 270.

RED FRUIT SALAD

Choose your own combination of soft red fruits for this salad using strawberries, raspberries, blackberries, blueberries, cherries, loganberries, redcurrants or blackcurrants according to what is available. The salad is best made an hour or two in advance and chilled so that the flavours can develop.

PREPARATION TIME: *15 minutes*
COOLING TIME: *30 minutes plus chilling time*

INGREDIENTS – *serves 12:*
4-5 lb (1.8-2.3 kg) mixed red soft fruits
2 small oranges
7 fl oz (200 ml) water
8 oz (225 g) granulated sugar

If using cherries, wash and stone them (page 396). Hull and carefully wash the other fruit.

Next make the syrup. Finely pare the oranges. Put the rind and juice of the oranges with the water and sugar into a pan. Stir over low heat until the sugar has dissolved, then bring to the boil. Boil for 3-4 minutes. Remove the orange rind from the syrup. If using cherries, blueberries, blackcurrants or redcurrants, add them to the syrup. Leave the syrup to cool for 30 minutes.

Put the prepared fruit into a serving bowl, pour over the cooled syrup and mix well. Cover and chill until needed. This dish is included in a menu on page 262.

PRESENTATION & GARNISHING

'It looks good enough to eat' – the appetite may be quickened by a delicious aroma wafting from the kitchen, but the first real impression of a dish is created by its appearance. Good food deserves to be carefully and thoughtfully presented so that it appears at its best and is truly a feast for the eyes.

French cuisine has had more influence in the West than any other. During the 19th and early 20th centuries it was characterised by an elaborate style of presentation, but recently it has been through a revolution. The new approach – *nouvelle cuisine* – uses traditional methods but the style is simpler and lighter with a distaste for heavy food or thick floury sauces that tend to overwhelm other ingredients.

Presentation is very important – strongly influenced by Oriental cuisine. Although the chefs in the restaurants where nouvelle cuisine developed have many assistants to help them with the intricate garnishing, many of the ideas can be applied in the home with little trouble and ample reward.

Presentation

Presenting food is more than just the way an individual dish is arranged on the plate: it starts when the menu is planned, and involves the shopping and the preparation, the way the table is laid, the plates you choose and the way each portion is served.

Planning the menu

Many different factors have to be reconciled when the dishes are chosen for a meal. There must be a balance of different tastes and textures and the meal should be nutritionally balanced (see *Menu planner*, page 407).

The preparation must be considered (see *Dinner parties and lunch parties*, page 190), not only to ensure that the meal is ready on time, but also to ensure that the food itself looks its best. It must not be allowed to deteriorate through being kept warm for too long, nor must the quality suffer because the preparation was hurried. Hot food must be served hot and cold food cold. Vegetables should be crisp. Sauces should be glossy with no trace of a skin.

Use fresh, seasonal produce wherever possible. Not only will you get a better result; it is often less expensive. Buy ingredients that are fresh and unblemished.

Think of the appearance of the whole meal. Much cooked food is naturally bland in colour and shapeless. There is no difficulty with a whole fish, for example, or a pie, or a standing rib of beef, or a globe artichoke – these all have colour and an interesting shape. A stew on the other hand, or a meat loaf, or a piece of meat swathed in a pale or brown sauce all need help from pretty garnishes or colourful vegetables. Balance garnished dishes on the menu with other bold, straightforward dishes, and simple bright vegetables so that the meal as a whole does not look fussy.

Choose colours that are both varied and complementary. Just as a meal of bland colours can look dull – so a meal of too many colours can be unsettling.

Serving

How you serve the meal should depend on the food itself. Rustic, provincial food, such as *Pot roast leg of lamb* (page 81), requires bold, generous presentation. Carve or serve the food at the table and put the vegetables in bowls on the table so that guests can help themselves. The same cut of meat, however, prepared in the style of nouvelle cuisine, such as *Olive studded lamb* (page 212), is better carved and arranged on plates in the kitchen so that you can be sure of just the right visual effect. Vegetables can be arranged on the plate or on a side plate.

It is rarely possible with ethnic dishes to reproduce exactly the manner in which they would be served in the country of origin, but you can improvise. Serve Chinese food, for example, in small individual dishes. If you have them, use chopsticks and eat out of small bowls rather than off large plates (see the *Chinese dinner*, page 224). Garnishes should be flamboyant, but they need not be complicated (see *Duck with plum and ginger glaze*, page 88).

Garnishing and decoration

The purpose in garnishing a dish is to make it look more appetising and attractive by the addition of trimmings or decoration.

● If possible use one of the ingredients from the recipe. The flavours will not conflict and nobody will be misled about the taste of the dish that he is about to eat. Most dishes include something that will make a good garnish – herbs being the obvious but not the only choice. Tomatoes, mushrooms, whole prawns, lemon, whole fruit, celery, sweet peppers and nuts, are just a few ingredients that can be used to garnish.

● Plan the garnishes so that there are neither too many similar garnishes, nor simple and flamboyant garnishes together.

● Do not let the garnish dominate the food either in flavour or size. It should bring out the best qualities in the dish, not camouflage them.

● Garnishes should usually be edible. Even the garnishes which would not normally be eaten, bay leaves or paper cutlet frills for example, should be non-poisonous or easily removed.

SIMPLE SAVOURY GARNISHES

FRESH HERBS

Herbs such as parsley, sage, chives or tarragon can easily be grown in the garden or a window box, and the leaves or flower heads make a natural garnish for many dishes. They are also available from many supermarkets and greengrocers. Some herbs complement the flavour of certain foods better than others – see *Herbs*, page 382.

Use small sprigs or single leaves on individual plates (see *Garlic and pine kernel tartlets*, page 193). On larger serving dishes, small bunches can be used or small bouquets of mixed herbs.

Chopped herbs can be sprinkled over dishes, particularly those with little natural colour of their own (see *Artichoke and Martini soup*, page 192).

FRESH HERBS Sage, winter savory and marjoram make a bouquet.

FLOWERS

Many flowers are edible and make very pretty garnishes for savoury and sweet dishes. Either separate the flower heads into petals and sprinkle them over the dish (see *Geranium cream*, page 243), or use the entire bloom. Some suitable varieties are carnations, chives, cowslips, dahlias, elderflowers, freesias, nasturtiums (see *Fromage à la crème*, page 235), philadelphus (see *Orange flower sponge cake*, page 133), pinks, primroses, roses or violets.

LEAVES

Individual leaves from one of the ingredients can garnish a dish. See *Sautéed veal with redcurrants and cream* (page 211). Salad leaves such as watercress and radicchio also make good garnishes.

Fig, vine, nasturtium and currant leaves can line fruit baskets and cheese boards, or a dish for serving a tart.

Garnish a fruit bowl with leaves from one of the fruits or with glossy green leaves such as bay, rose or camellia.

LEAVES A bowl of clementines is decorated with bay leaves.

CROÛTES AND CROUTONS

Bread cut into various shapes can be used as base on which to serve food – croûtes – (see *Eggs soubise*, page 16, and *Canapés*, page 172) or as a decoration – croutons.

Cut to shape slices of bread with the crusts removed. Fry the pieces in butter until golden-brown, then drain on absorbent kitchen paper.

As a base for small game birds and noisettes of meat, cut the bread into a square or round croûte. As a crouton garnish for soups and salads, either cut the bread into ½in (15mm) cubes or stamp out with a canapé cutter. To decorate pâtés, mousselines, quenelles, fish or meat dishes, cut the bread into triangles or use crescent, fish or heart-shaped biscuit cutters (see *Wild duck with kumquats*, page 216). The edges can be dipped in finely chopped herbs for additional colour.

Croutons can also be made from other ingredients such as slices of sausage (see *Split pea and sausage soup*, page 55).

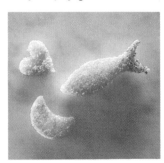

CROUTONS Shapes cut with canapé cutters are dipped in parsley.

FRUIT AND VEGETABLES

Whole small fruit and vegetables make striking, simple garnishes. See *Chilled cherry soup* (page 11).

JULIENNE These are uniformly cut 'matchstick' strips of vegetables, fruit or fruit peel about ⅛in (3mm) across and 1-2in (25-50mm) long. They can either be raw or cooked, but they should always be crisp. They can be sprinkled over food or tied in bundles held together with a sliver of pimento or lemon rind, or a ring of cucumber or chilli pepper.

JULIENNE A crisp bundle is held by a ring of chilli pepper.

WEDGES Avocado or apple (dipped in lemon juice to prevent discoloration), tomato, peach, pear, melon, lemon (see *Grilled Halumi cheese*, page 195), orange (see *Pot roast pheasant with claret and orange sauce*, page 214), and hard-boiled egg all add colour and texture. If the wedges are small, they can be arranged as petals of a flower with a little sprig of a herb such as parsley or coriander in the centre. Thin wedges can be arranged in a fan shape.

WEDGES A leaf of continental parsley enhances a fan of lime wedges.

SLICES Thin, even slices of cucumber, hard-boiled egg, lemon or lime, or lightly sautéed young vegetables such as courgettes or carrots can, for example, be grouped together at the side of a plate, arranged in an overlapping ring around a mousse on a serving dish, or used to decorate an aspic or jelly.

The slices will look more interesting if you score down the length of the fruit or vegetable at regular intervals with a cannelle knife before slicing.

SLICES A courgette can be scored with a cannelle knife before slicing.

TWISTS Make one cut from the centre of a thin slice to the outer edge, then twist the two edges in opposite directions. Twists are best made with slices of cucumber, lemon, lime or orange (see *Sardine pâté*, page 346, and *Lime and pineapple icebox pudding*, page 105). Another form of twist used to decorate cocktails is made by cutting a thin strip of lemon or orange peel. Twist the peel between your fingers over the cocktail to release the oils into the drink, then drop it into the glass (see *Evening cocktail party*, page 158).

BUTTERFLIES Cut a small 'vee' on opposite sides of a thin slice, almost meeting at the centre and discard the sections.

SPIRALS Using a sharp knife or cannelle knife, cut the skin in a spiral from fruit and vegetables such as apples (see *Danish apple pudding*, page 359), pears, lemons, limes, oranges or cucumber and twist into a spring shape.

PATTERNING

Making a pattern of the food itself is one of the simplest forms of decoration. You can, for example, draw the prongs of a fork or the back of a knife across a vegetable purée (see *Brussels sprout, orange and cinnamon purée*, page 223) or potato topping. The crisscross pattern of a barbecue rack can be simulated on an omelette, grilled or pan-fried steak or fish by heating a metal skewer over a gas flame and laying it across the surface of the food at regular intervals.

MORE ELABORATE SAVOURY GARNISHES

FRUIT AND VEGETABLES
BASKETS These can be made with fruit, such as lemons, oranges, pineapple, grapefruit or kiwi, or vegetables such as tomatoes or peppers. The baskets can be used as containers for sweet or savoury mixtures.

The most popular basket – usually filled with fruit salad – is made with a melon. Remove a thin slice from the base of a small melon to allow it to stand upright. Cut halfway down each side, leaving a 1in (25mm) wide 'handle' in the centre, then at right angles to the handle cut out the two wedge-shaped pieces on either side. Discard the seeds. Scoop out all the flesh and use it for your filling.

Large mushrooms can also be used as edible containers (see *Pâtés*, page 170).

BASKETS A melon basket can be filled with fruit salad.

CHILLI FLOWERS Cut the tip off a green or red chilli pepper. Using scissors, make vertical cuts almost to the base to form petals, trimming the tips to a point. Remove the seeds and place the chilli in iced water for an hour so that the flower opens out and the petals curl.

FLUTED MUSHROOMS (This technique is also called turning.) Use very white, completely round button mushrooms of a uniform size. With a small, pointed paring knife, score the mushroom cap from the centre to the edge at regular intervals, removing a narrow strip of flesh each time. Remove the stem. To prevent the mushrooms from discolouring, cook them in water with a few drops of lemon juice for about 3 minutes. Fluted mushrooms are a good garnish for fish dishes and cold salads.

FLUTED MUSHROOMS Shallow cuts create a spiral decoration.

GHERKIN FANS Slice a gherkin lengthways three or four times, keeping it joined at the base. Ease the slices apart to form a fan. Strawberries and cooked baby courgettes can be prepared the same way.

GHERKIN FANS Strawberries can be cut into fans as well as gherkins.

ONION CHRYSANTHEMUMS Peel a small onion and, using a very sharp knife, cut into quarters, lengthways, stopping just short of the base. Make several more cuts – the more you make, the more effective the flower will be – and gently press the onion open to form petals. Immerse in iced water for an hour.

ONION CHRYSANTHEMUMS Fine cuts open out in iced water.

RADISH ROSE Remove the stalk and cut a slice off the base so that the radish will stand upright. Starting near the base, cut a row of scallop shapes with a sharp knife, keeping them joined at the base. Continue to cut rows of scallops to the top of the radish. Place in iced water for an hour during which time the rose will open out.

RADISH ROSES Scallop cuts turn into petals in iced water.

RADISH WATERLILY Cut off the radish stalk then make six to eight crossing cuts through the centre of the radish. Place in iced water for an hour. See *Quick cocktail snacks* (page 169).

SPRING ONION TASSELS Trim the bulb base and cut the green shoot so that you end up with a 3in (75mm) length. Shred to within 1in (25mm) of the base and place in iced water for an hour. Alternatively, cut through the length of spring onion from both ends towards the centre (see *Duck with plum and ginger glaze*, page 88). Celery tassels can be made the same way with 3in (75mm) lengths of celery.

TOMATO ROSE Using a short sharp knife, cut a continuous spiral strip of skin about ½in (15mm) wide from a firm medium-sized tomato, starting at the base. With the flesh side inside, roll into a tight scroll. A smaller rose can be made with a ¼in (5mm) strip of skin cut from a cherry tomato (see *Turkey galantine*, page 270). Single leaves of watercress, chervil or parsley can be used as leaves.

TOMATO ROSES Leaves of continental parsley set off tomato roses.

VANDYKE TOMATOES Using a small, sharp knife, cut a zigzag pattern around the centre of a small tomato, cutting right through to the core. Separate the two halves. This method can be used with lemons as well and makes an alternative to quartered lemons with fish. The tomatoes or lemons can be scooped out to be used as containers for pâtés, mousses or salads.

VANDYKE TOMATOES Diced peppers and cucumber fill tomato cups.

TURNED VEGETABLES This technique can be used with most root vegetables – such as carrots, potatoes and turnips. Peel the vegetable and cut into even-sized pieces, then trim the pieces into barrel shapes. The 'turned' vegetables can then be

TURNED VEGETABLES Swede and carrot can be neatly shaped.

288

boiled, roasted, or parboiled and then deep-fried. As an additional decoration for roasting, make several crosswise cuts in the pieces, almost to the base.

ASPIC
This is one of the classic forms of garnish. It is used chiefly to give a glossy coating, inset with decorations, to cold buffet dishes (see *Turkey galantine*, page 270, and *Trout in aspic with smoked cod's roe*, page 263). It can also be used to decorate savoury mousses set in moulds.

Making aspic jelly is time-consuming, and aspic powder will normally be just as good. With very delicately flavoured dishes, however, it may be necessary to make your own. Blanched pieces of carrot, red, green or yellow pepper, orange, lemon and lime rind, sliced olives and fresh herbs can all be used for decorations, cut geometrically or in flower designs.

To decorate a mousse set in a mould, allow the aspic to cool to a syrup. Run a little aspic over the base and sides of the mould. Leave until set. Dip the pieces for decoration in the syrupy aspic then arrange them in the prepared mould. Leave until set, then cover with another thin layer of aspic. Allow to set, then fill the mould with the mousse.

Aspic can also be poured into a tray ½-1in (15-25mm) deep and then, when set, cut into cubes or roughly chopped to use as a border garnish (see *Turkey galantine*, page 270).

PIPING
Broad nozzles, either plain or rosettes, can be used to pipe mashed potato and vegetable purées as well as cream (see page 290).

Simple mashed potato can be piped into rosettes to decorate large dishes, or potato toppings can be piped. Combinations of different coloured vegetable purées (such as brussels sprout and carrot) give a striking result. Mashed potato can also be piped to form cases to hold, for example, peas. Brown the cases in the oven or under a hot grill.

PIPING A nest of mashed potatoes holds a clutch of green peas.

PASTRY DECORATIONS
Some decorative touches to a pie such as knocking up and fluting (see page 393) also serve the practical function of fixing the lid more securely. However, pastry also lends itself to more purely decorative treatments.

Canapé or biscuit cutters can be used to cut out pastry shapes, such as crescents or fish, to decorate pies or tarts (see *Hare pie*, page 272). Tartlet tins can be bought in many different shapes.

LATTICE Interwoven strips of pastry crisscross a jam tart.

LATTICE A lattice can be used to finish an open pie or tart. Cut about 10 strips of pastry ¼-½in (5-15mm) wide and slightly longer than the diameter of the tart. The exact number of strips will depend on the size of the tart. For a simple lattice, lay half the strips in one direction and the remainder at right angles, leaving space between each strip for the filling to show through. Trim off the excess pastry round the edges, and moisten the ends with water to help them adhere to the edge of the tart.

For a more professional touch, interweave the lattice. Lay half the strips in one direction. Lay the remaining strips at right angles, lifting up alternate lengths of the original set of strips as necessary to weave them in and out (see *Apple and redcurrant lattice*, page 314).

Special lattice cutters can also be used to create a latticed effect. Roll out a circle of pastry the same diameter as the tart. Press the cutter into the pastry and then carefully lift the shaped lattice over the filling.

PASTRY LEAVES Cut leaf shapes from rolled out pastry with a sharp knife, marking the veins with the back edge of the knife.
PASTRY TASSELS Cut a rectangular strip of pastry about 1½in (40mm) wide and about 6in (150mm) long. Make a series of thin cuts to within ½in (15mm) of the long edge. Roll up the strip and stand it upright with the cuts at the top so that the strips open out into a tassel.

LEAVES AND TASSELS A pastry tassel and pastry leaves crown a pie.

BUTTER DECORATIONS
A block of butter can be made more attractive by shaping it with a butter mould, or scoring patterns on the top with a fork. The butter can also be shaped into individual portions.
CURLS Special straight or curved butter curlers with crinkle-cut edges pulled across the surface of a block of cold butter create curls. As you make each curl, drop it into iced water. Keep chilled until needed. See *Pecan waffles* (page 31).
BALLS Smooth butter balls can be made with a melon baller. Scoop out balls of butter from a

SAVOURY BUTTERS A sausage of herb butter is sliced into savoury pats.

block of cold butter and drop them into iced water.

Textured butter balls can be made by rolling cubes of chilled butter, dipped in cold water first, between ridged butter pats. See *Irish tea brack* (page 124).

Butter balls can be rolled in chopped herbs, paprika or poppy seeds for extra effect.

SAVOURY BUTTERS Some dishes are garnished with pieces of flavoured butter (see *Calf's liver with lime and sage butter*, page 70). They can also garnish simple grilled or fried meat and fish.

Beat the flavouring (for example, chopped fresh herbs or garlic, lemon rind, paprika or anchovy essence) into some softened butter. Shape it into a sausage about 2in (50mm) across. Roll it up in greaseproof paper, twisting the ends. Chill until firm, then slice thinly into pats.

Alternatively, roll the butter out to a thickness of about ¼in (5mm) between sheets of greaseproof or non-stick baking paper. Chill until firm, then cut out shapes with a canapé or small biscuit cutter.

DESSERT DECORATIONS

Many of the savoury decorations mentioned before can also be used to decorate sweet dishes – flowers, leaves, pastry and fruit, for example.

CANDIED FRUIT
Glacé cherries and candied angelica, pineapple, and citrus peel, can be used whole or cut into leaves and flowers to decorate trifles, iced cakes or cheesecakes, for example.

CARAMEL
Caramel can be used for some of the most spectacular garnishes.

To make the caramel, dissolve granulated sugar in water – in the proportion 1lb (450g) sugar to ½ pint (285ml) water – in a heavy-based pan, stirring all the time, over low heat. Raise the heat and boil fiercely until the syrup turns golden-brown or reaches the 'small crack' stage –

138-152°C (280-305°F) on a sugar thermometer – when half a teaspoon of the syrup dropped into cold water separates into brittle threads. Remove the pan from the heat and dip the base briefly into cold water to stop it cooking further.

CARAMEL DIPPING Nuts, pieces of fruit or choux puffs (see *Croquembouche*, page 278) can all be dipped in caramel to give them a crisp golden, shining coating. Hold the items to be dipped with forks (be careful when dipping fruit because it may spatter). Leave to set on greaseproof paper. Do not dip items in caramel too far in advance or store them in the refrigerator, the caramel will soften and lose its shine.

CRUSHED CARAMEL Pour the caramel onto an oiled baking sheet. When cold, crush it with a food processor or rolling pin.

SPUN SUGAR Fine, brittle caramel strands form a glistening cloud..

PRALINE Crushed praline (a mixture of caramel and unblanched almonds) can be sprinkled over puddings and ice cream.

Put equal quantities of granulated sugar and unblanched almonds in a heavy-based pan and stir with a wooden spoon over a moderate heat until the sugar has melted and turned golden-brown. Watch it carefully because it burns very easily if cooked too quickly and for too long. Pour the mixture onto a lightly oiled baking tray and leave it to cool.

When the praline is cold and hard, break it into pieces, then crush the amount you need with a rolling pin or food processor. Store the remaining pieces in an airtight tin or jar.

PRALINE Caramel and almonds are crushed to make praline.

SPUN SUGAR Light and elaborate desserts, including special ice creams, can be decorated with a cloud of spun sugar. Bring the syrup to the 'hard crack' stage – 152-163°C (305-325°F) on a sugar thermometer – when the syrup dropped into cold water forms hard, brittle threads. Lay

a large piece of greaseproof paper nearby. Dip a fork into the syrup and then wave the fork backwards and forwards through the air over the paper. The contact of the sugar with the air forms it into a mist of crystalline strands.

Alternatively, wave the syrup backwards and forwards directly over the dish that is to be decorated, pulling the strands round with the fork to form a fine nest shape. Do not decorate a dish with spun sugar more than about 30 minutes before serving, because it will pick up moisture from the air and soften.

CHOCOLATE
Use the best plain dessert chocolate or good quality unsweetened cooking chocolate for decorations. Melted chocolate looks very effective trickled over cakes and desserts. If you use dessert chocolate it may help to add a little vegetable oil to make it flow more easily (see *Sherry gâteau*, page 119, and *Mocha éclairs*, page 125). Chocolate chips and chocolate flake can also be used as decorations.

CARAQUE Spread melted, plain chocolate to a depth of approximately ⅛in (3mm) on a clean glass, stainless steel or marble surface. When it has set, but before it has become brittle, use a paint scraper or the blade of a knife to strip off the chocolate as though removing paint. It will form long ragged curls. (See *Chocolate cream torte*, page 42.)

Shorter curls can be scraped

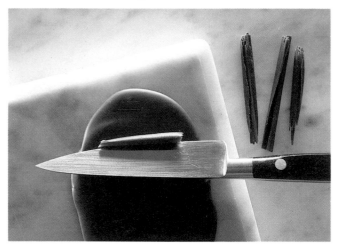

CARAQUE *A layer of chocolate is scraped into ragged curls.*

off a block of cold, plain chocolate with a vegetable peeler (see *Chocolate and ginger fridge cake*, page 362).

CUPS Chocolate cups can be used as edible containers for mousses, ice creams and sorbets. Pour melted plain chocolate into fluted paper cases (three cases thick for strength). Coat the base and sides, making sure the base is well covered, and pour out any excess chocolate. Leave to set. Apply a second thin coat of chocolate to the base and sides and leave to set. When com-

pletely set, peel away the paper.
DIPPING Whole blanched almonds, brazil nuts, hazelnuts and walnuts can be dipped with forks into melted plain chocolate. Leave on greaseproof or non-stick baking paper for the chocolate to set.

Strawberries (see *Chocolate strawberry gâteau*, page 132), fruit segments, grapes and cherries can be half-dipped in chocolate in the same way.

LEAVES Using washed and dried bay or rose leaves, brush the back of the leaf with a thin, even

CUPS *Strawberry mousse fills chocolate cases.*

LEAVES *A rose leaf is painted with chocolate then peeled away.*

layer of melted plain chocolate. Allow to set, then apply a second coat of chocolate. When completely set, carefully peel the original leaf off the chocolate one. See *Pêches à la Belle Sandrine* (page 238).

SQUARES Spread melted plain chocolate evenly on a flat, oiled surface. Leave until set then cut into squares. These can be halved to make triangles (see *Sherry gateau*, page 119).

CREAM

Rather than handing cream in a jug to accompany a dessert, it can be poured round the dessert.
FEATHERING Coffee or chocolate sauce or a brightly coloured fruit purée can be trickled onto a pool of cream and 'feathered' (see *Glacé icing*, page 400, and *Symphonie de trois couleurs*, page 240). Cream can also be trickled and feathered onto pools of dark sauce or purée.

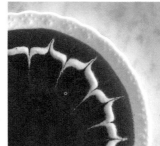

FEATHERING *A final flourish of cream decorates a raspberry purée.*

WHIPPED CREAM Decorative rosettes and scrolls of whipped cream can be piped singly onto desserts, or to cover the surface

of a dessert completely, or in a ring around the base of a moulded dessert. See *Alsace chocolate gateau* (page 280).

Defects, such as cracking, in sponges and meringues, can be hidden with whipped cream.

Whipped cream masking a dessert can be patterned with the blade of a rounded knife or the prongs of a fork.

Cream can be flavoured before it is whipped with icing or caster sugar, vanilla, almond, coffee or orange essence or a liqueur such as Grand Marnier.

FROSTING

Whole fruit or segments of fruit (see *Wild duck with kumquats*, page 216), flowers (see *Simnel cake*, page 127) and leaves can all be frosted with sugar. Choose small, perfect specimens. Violets, primroses, rose petals, mint leaves, and clusters of grapes or cherries are all suitable.

Rinse the item to be frosted and dry with kitchen paper. Brush with beaten egg white, then sprinkle evenly with caster sugar. Leave to dry on greaseproof paper for about an hour.

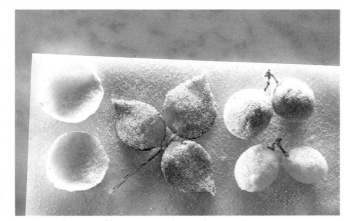

FROSTING *Sugar sparkles on rose petals, rose leaves and grapes.*

DRAGEES

Hard sugar sweets or pieces of chocolate, coated in silver or gold, can be used to decorate trifles (see *Ginger trifle*, page 334), cakes and other desserts (see *Pêches à la Belle Sandrine*, page 238). Small round dragees can be bought in supermarkets. Larger, irregularly shaped ones can be bought from specialist grocers and confectioners.

ICING SUGAR

A simple dusting of icing sugar can be used to decorate cakes and pastries.

Icing sugar, sieved through a paper doily with large holes, creates an intricate design on a plain cake (see *Gold and silver marble cake*, page 128). Place the doily on the area to be patterned and sieve the sugar over it. Carefully lift off the doily.

Picnics

LONG AGO, when Greek gentlemen met to exchange epigrams and the like, each one attending was expected to contribute a share of the food and drink as well as a share of the entertainment.

Some 2000 years later, a group of fashionable and well-read Londoners decided to follow their example and met in one another's houses, drawing lots for the items of refreshment they should supply. They called themselves the Pick-Nick Club for reasons not entirely clear, but it is certain that at the beginning at least, their feasts were held indoors. Nevertheless, by the time that William Wordsworth attended a huge 'picnic' on the top of Skiddaw to celebrate the defeat of Napoleon at Waterloo, the word had come firmly to mean a meal taken outdoors.

However named, one of the chief joys of eating under the sky is the informality of the occasion, which is probably why it has always had such a strong appeal to royalty who, for a short time, feel able to behave like anyone else. When Henry VIII and Anne Boleyn went a-Maying, they were brought pasties by players dressed as Robin Hood and his Merrie Men. Marie Antoinette, disguised as a milkmaid, served her friends with what she believed to be peasant fare in the gardens of Versailles. In contrast to the luxury of the French court, Queen Victoria and Prince Albert were made of sterner stuff and liked roughing it, enjoying many a dram and bannock in the company of ghillies in Highland deer forests.

Modern and humbler picnickers seek none of these elaborations and ask only that the weather, viewpoint, beach or river bank should match the perfection of their picnic fare.

Planning & Preparation

A picnic can be highly organised and sophisticated with china plates and silver, or the result of a spur-of-the-moment decision on a beautiful day with a rug on the grass and paper plates. The pleasure of eating outdoors is the same. Whatever the occasion, however, a clear head and some careful planning are needed if you are to arrive at the picnic spot with the food intact and edible, and nothing missing.

Planning the menu

Simple food survives a journey better than anything elaborate. Choose dishes that are not too fragile, will stand up to the hot weather and, if possible, can be prepared in advance.

Sandwiches are convenient for an impromptu picnic. You can take the bread and fillings and assemble them on the spot.

For salads, use crisp ingredients such as spinach, carrots or courgettes rather than soft lettuces which go very limp in warm weather. Unless the recipe states otherwise, pack the salad dressing separately in a screw-top jar or bottle and toss salad and dressing together just before you eat, so that the crispness of the ingredients is preserved.

Do not take fizzy drinks – including sparkling wine – on a picnic unless there will be plenty of time for them to settle after

the journey before the bottle or cans have to be opened.

Choose food for a walking trip which can be eaten with your hands.

Packing the food

Rigid plastic boxes or biscuit tins keep food fresh, and protect delicate food from squashing so that you can stack it. Lids help to keep the flies away. Salads packed in plastic boxes can be served from the containers.

Kitchen foil also protects food from damage. It is good for packing food which needs close wrapping, such as meat, pâtés or pastries. However, acid food may cause slight pitting of the foil. Greaseproof paper overwrapped with clingfilm is better in this case. This is also good for wrapping foods, such as sandwiches or cakes, which dry out easily.

Vacuum flasks are essential for keeping drinks hot or cold. Wide-necked flasks can be used for carrying food such as stews, thick soups or ice cream.

Both tea and coffee can be carried ready-made in vacuum flasks. Carry milk in a separate flask. Boiling the milk first will prevent it going sour or curdling. For freshly made tea or coffee, take a small camping stove to boil water on the spot. Instant coffee can be made with hot water carried in a flask.

Keep bottles of wine or beer chilled in coolboxes. Transfer fruit juices from cartons to leak-proof containers which can be re-closed if there is any left over.

Traditional hampers are good for carrying plates and cutlery, but there is rarely any room for food. Pack food that does not need to be kept cool in cardboard boxes or shopping bags that will stand upright in the back of a car; carrier bags are usually too squashy. Insulated coolboxes or coolbags fitted with ice packs are a good investment if you regularly go on picnics. Leave the food in the refrigerator right up to the last minute before packing it. If you do not have a coolbox, improvise by packing a large box with crumpled newspaper or bubble-wrap packing (the kind often used for delicate china) which is an efficient insulating material.

Plastic plates, glasses and mugs are unbreakable, weigh less than china and are more practical than paper. However, food tastes better off china plates, so you may prefer to take old plates that you will not miss if they are broken. If you take plastic knives and forks, take a few kitchen knives as well and a bread knife, because plastic cutlery is not very strong.

Packing the picnic

Before packing, make a checklist of everything you are likely to need, including the food.

The car boot is usually the coolest place in a car. Pack the

food firmly, so that it does not slide around at every corner. On a hot day, park the car in the shade if you are not going to eat immediately. If you have a hatchback car, do not remove the luggage shelf – it will protect the food from the sun. Cover food in an estate car with a rug.

Pack picnic food that is to be carried in a knapsack securely, preferably in lightweight containers that are leakproof and squash-resistant.

Pack all the elements of a picnic in the order you will need them. If possible, pack the first course at the top and the pudding at the bottom. Tape the corkscrew to a bottle.

Wrap napkins round cutlery, and between plates to stop them rattling. When you have packed all the food, cover it with the tablecloth. Pack rugs and chairs around the food so that they can be removed first.

Take plenty of paper napkins, kitchen roll, a damp sponge in a plastic bag, and a large plastic dustbin liner for putting all the rubbish into afterwards. Take a good supply of plain water – plastic fruit-squash bottles are good containers. It is also wise to take a basic first aid kit.

Choosing the picnic site

Select a spot with level ground and a little shade. On the beach, look for some shelter as well, otherwise sea breezes will blow sand into the food. Keep to footpaths, always close gates and clear away your litter.

SOUPS

JAMAICAN PUMPKIN SOUP

Pumpkin makes a deep yellow soup. It can be served chilled, but it is better hot for a picnic lunch in the British autumn when pumpkin is most widely available. For other times of the year, pumpkin can be diced and frozen, and the soup itself freezes well without the cream. Some pumpkin can be quite watery, in which case reduce the amount of stock.

PREPARATION TIME: *20 minutes*
COOKING TIME: *20 minutes*

INGREDIENTS – *serves 6:*
2 lb (900 g) pumpkin
1 medium onion
1 medium carrot
2 cloves garlic
1 oz (25 g) butter
*1¾ pints (1 litre) chicken stock
   (page 367)*
¼ pint (150 ml) single cream
*Salt and freshly ground black
   pepper*
Chopped parsley
Freshly grated nutmeg

Using a sharp knife, cut away the skin from the pumpkin and scoop out the seeds. Chop the flesh into 1in (25mm) chunks. Peel and slice the onion and carrot. Skin and crush the garlic.

Melt the butter in a large saucepan over medium heat and sauté the onion for 5 minutes, until it is soft and just beginning to brown. Add the chopped pumpkin, carrot and garlic and cook for a further 5 minutes.

Stir in the stock and bring to the boil. Reduce the heat, cover and simmer for about 20 minutes, stirring occasionally until the pumpkin is tender.

Cool slightly, then purée in a liquidiser or press through a sieve. Return to the pan and stir in the cream with salt and pepper to taste. Reheat thoroughly, but do not allow to boil again, then sprinkle in the chopped parsley and a good sprinkling of grated nutmeg. Pour into a vacuum flask. Serve with crusty bread. This recipe is included in a menu on page 312.

CREAMY BEETROOT SOUP

In Britain, beetroot tends to be confined to salads or pickles, which is a pity because it also makes rich-flavoured, glorious pink soups.

Freshly pulled beetroot gives the best flavour and colour to this soup, but pre-cooked beetroot can be used instead. Make sure the skins are intact before boiling fresh beetroot, otherwise the beetroot may start to 'bleed' and some of the colour and flavour will be lost.

PREPARATION TIME: *20 minutes*
COOKING TIME: *1 hour*

INGREDIENTS – *serves 8:*
1 lb (450 g) uncooked beetroot
8 oz (225 g) celery
2 oz (50 g) butter
*2 pints (1.1 litres) chicken stock
   (page 367)*
1½ oz (40 g) flour
*½ pint (285 ml) creamy milk or
   single cream*
2 oz (50 g) cooked ham
*Salt and freshly ground black
   pepper*
GARNISH
*Finely chopped beetroot tops or
   celery leaves*

Trim off the beetroot leaves, leaving the top and roots intact. Scrub the beetroot clean, taking care not to damage the skins. Cook in a large pan of boiling water for about 30 minutes – the cooking time will vary depending on the age and size of the beetroot. Do not pierce with a fork to test whether the beetroot is cooked because it will bleed, just check whether the skins will rub away easily.

Skin and chop the beetroot, then trim and chop the celery. Melt half the butter in a large pan and sauté the chopped celery for 2-3 minutes, to soften. Add the chopped beetroot and stock. Bring to the boil, then cover the pan and simmer for about 15 minutes, until the celery is tender.

Cool slightly, then turn into a liquidiser or food processor and blend until smooth. It may be necessary to do this in batches. The vegetables can be pressed through a sieve instead.

Melt the remaining butter in a saucepan over a medium heat and stir in the flour. Gradually stir in the milk or cream. Continue stirring over a gentle heat until the sauce thickens and is of a smooth consistency. Chop the ham very finely, then add to the pan with the puréed vegetable mixture. Add salt and pepper to taste, and bring to the boil. Simmer the soup very gently for 5 minutes, stirring occasionally. Pour into a vacuum flask.

If you are serving the soup at home, garnish with chopped beetroot tops or celery leaves. Serve with fresh bread, such as *Cashew nut rolls* (page 308).

VIVID WARMTH Beetroot makes a glowing, creamy soup which takes the chill off a cool day. Cashew nut rolls complete a filling snack.

TOMATO AND SORREL SOUP

The tart, refreshing taste of sorrel has been much admired for hundreds of years.

The bright green, spade-shaped leaves are occasionally seen in specialist greengrocers, but it is an easy plant to grow in the garden, providing an abundance of leaves almost the year through. The preferred cultivated variety is French sorrel, *Rumex scutatus*.

A delicious version of this soup can be made using watercress instead of sorrel.

PREPARATION TIME: *20 minutes*
COOKING TIME: *30 minutes*

INGREDIENTS – *serves 6:*
1 bunch sorrel leaves, about 2-3 oz (50–75 g)
1 lb (450 g) tomatoes OR 14 oz (400 g) tin tomatoes, drained
4 oz (115 g) shallots or spring onions
2 tablespoons olive oil
¾ pint (450 ml) chicken stock (page 367)
¼ pint (150 ml) dry white wine
1 level tablespoon chopped fresh tarragon
Salt and freshly ground black pepper
GARNISH
Croutons (page 286)

Cut off the stems and wash the sorrel thoroughly. Drain well. Wipe the tomatoes and cut them into quarters. Skin and roughly chop the shallots, or

trim and chop the spring onions.

Heat the oil in a large heavy pan and add the vegetables. Stir over a moderate heat for 2 minutes, then reduce the heat to very low. Cover with a lid and cook, shaking the pan occasionally, for about 20 minutes. Add the stock and simmer for a further 10 minutes.

Press through a fine sieve then add the wine, tarragon, and salt and pepper to taste.

To serve hot, return to the heat and bring almost to the boil, then pour into a vacuum flask. To serve cold, chill thoroughly in the refrigerator then pour into a vacuum flask.

Serve sprinkled with crisp bread croutons. For serving chilled at home, garnish each bowl of soup with a cube of ice floating in the middle.

CHILLI BEAN SOUP

Spicy and chunky, this soup is warming and filling on a frosty day. Adjust the chilli to taste – this amount makes quite a fiery soup. It is best eaten with a spoon, so carry it in wide-necked food flasks.

Dried kidney beans must be soaked overnight and then boiled for at least 10 minutes to eliminate poisons. For a quicker version of the soup, use tinned red kidney beans – which need no pre-soaking or cooking. Add the drained kidney beans with the garlic sausage.

PREPARATION TIME: *20 minutes*
SOAKING TIME: *overnight*
COOKING TIME: *30 minutes*

INGREDIENTS – *serves 6:*
4 oz (115 g) dried red kidney beans
1 oz (25 g) dripping or lard
8 oz (225 g) onions
1 level tablespoon chilli powder
1 carrot
1 stick celery
1 pint (570 ml) chicken stock (page 367)
¼ pint (150 ml) tomato juice
7 oz (200 g) garlic sausage
Salt

Place the dried kidney beans in a bowl and cover with cold water. Leave to soak for several hours or overnight.

Heat the dripping or lard in a heavy pan. Peel and finely chop the onions, then sauté in the fat until soft. Stir in the chilli powder and cook, stirring over a medium heat for 1 minute more.

Peel and finely chop the carrot, trim and finely chop the celery, and add to the pan with the beans, chicken stock and tomato juice, then bring to the boil, stirring. Cover the pan and boil rapidly for 10 minutes, then simmer gently for about 20 minutes or until the kidney beans are tender.

Dice the garlic sausage and add to the soup. Heat through thoroughly and season to taste with salt. Pour into a warmed wide-necked vacuum flask. Serve with fresh, crusty wholemeal rolls or French bread.

SAVOURY DISHES

FRESH COCONUT CHUTNEY

Britons returning from India in the 18th and 19th centuries brought back recipes for chutneys – highly spiced fruit or vegetable relishes. The type of chutney that became widespread in this country is cooked, and then matured for weeks. In India, however, uncooked chutneys, eaten on the day they are made, are equally popular.

This chutney is quite spicy, but the amount of fresh chilli can be varied to taste. Carry the chutney in a plastic box or in half a coconut shell tightly wrapped.

PREPARATION TIME: *15 minutes*

INGREDIENTS – *serves 6:*
¼ fresh coconut
1 small onion
1 fresh green or red chilli
Juice of 1 lemon

Coarsely grate the coconut flesh. Peel and finely slice the onion. Remove the seeds from the chilli and slice. Mix the lemon juice with the grated coconut, sliced onion and chilli. Spoon the chutney into a serving dish and cover until needed.

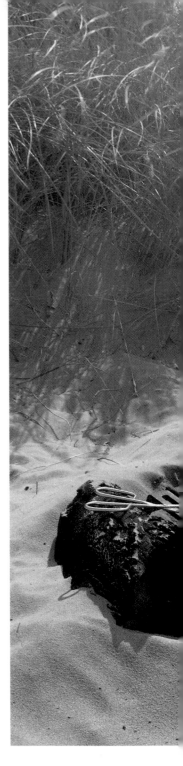

BEACHED PRAWNS *It takes only a few minutes to grill marinated prawns on a driftwood fire. Cooked in advance they can be eaten chilled instead. Fresh coconut chutney adds a flavour of the south seas.*

SPICED BUTTERFLY PRAWNS

Dublin Bay prawns (scampi) are the largest British prawn – about 4in (100mm) long. Pacific King prawns are even larger. They are usually frozen, but fresh Dublin Bay prawns occasionally appear.

Carry the chilled, cooked prawns in plastic boxes. The prawns may also be cooked on an open fire or barbecue. Take them in the marinade, then cook them threaded on skewers, or lay them on a rack over the fire and turn them with tongs.

PREPARATION TIME: *20 minutes*
MARINATING TIME: *1 hour*
COOKING TIME: *12 minutes*

INGREDIENTS – *serves 4:*
2 lb (900 g) uncooked Dublin Bay or Pacific King prawns
MARINADE
4 fl oz (115 ml) olive oil
2 tablespoons lemon juice
1 small onion
2 cloves garlic
1 in (25 mm) piece fresh ginger
1 green chilli
¼ teaspoon ground turmeric
Salt and freshly ground black pepper
GARNISH
Lemon wedges

If the prawns have been frozen, make sure they are thoroughly drained. Cut off the heads, then peel them, leaving on the tails, and remove the vein. To do this, make a shallow incision with a sharp knife down the length of the back of the prawn, all the way from head to tail. This exposes a dark threadlike tube – remove and discard it. Rinse the prawns and pat them dry on absorbent kitchen paper. With the knife, slit the prawns with care down the length of the back about three-quarters of the way through, and then open them out, so that they are butterfly shaped. Place them in a large shallow dish. If the prawns are to be cooked at the picnic site, put them in an unbreakable dish or a plastic box.

To make the marinade, whisk together the oil and lemon juice. Peel and finely chop the onion, peel and crush the garlic, peel and finely chop the ginger and seed and finely chop the chilli. Stir all these into the oil mixture with the turmeric and salt and pepper to taste. Pour the marinade over the prawns. Cover and leave in a cool place for at least an hour.

Turn on the grill to moderate heat. Line the grill pan with foil and put in the prawns and marinade. Grill, turning once, for about 12 minutes, until golden, basting occasionally.

Serve hot or allow to cool then chill. Garnish with lemon wedges and serve with *Fresh coconut chutney* (opposite page).

MINI STARGAZY PIES

Pilchards are the traditional filling for stargazy pie, one of Cornwall's most famous dishes. In the full-size pie, the fishes' heads poke out of the pastry, gazing at the stars – hence the name. These smaller versions of the original are made with sardines – young pilchards – and are easier to carry for a packed lunch or picnic. Use the freshest fish possible, and eat within a day of making. Wrap the cold pies in kitchen foil, or pack in plastic boxes to carry them.

PREPARATION TIME: *50 minutes*
COOKING TIME: *30 minutes*
OVEN TEMPERATURE: *preheat to 200°C (400°F, gas mark 6)*

INGREDIENTS – *serves 4:*
16 small fresh sardines – about 1¼ lb (575 g)
PASTRY
12 oz (350 g) plain flour
3 oz (75 g) margarine or butter
3 oz (75 g) lard
Cold water to mix
FILLING
1½ oz (40 g) fresh white breadcrumbs
5 tablespoons dry cider
2 oz (50 g) onion, finely chopped
2 oz (50 g) streaky bacon, diced
Finely grated rind of 1 lemon
1 hard-boiled egg
1 level tablespoon chopped parsley
Salt and freshly ground black pepper
GLAZE
Milk

Clean the fish (page 373) – sardines have large scales which must be removed. Cut off the heads, but leave the tails on.

To make the pastry, sieve the flour into a large mixing bowl and rub in the margarine and lard evenly until the mixture resembles breadcrumbs. Mix in just enough cold water to make a firm dough. Chill the pastry in the refrigerator while preparing the filling.

Mix the breadcrumbs with the cider. Add the onion and bacon to the breadcrumbs with the lemon rind. Roughly chop the egg and stir into the bread-crumbs together with the parsley, salt and pepper.

Divide the pastry into 8 pieces and roll out each to a circle about 7in (180mm) in diameter – a saucepan lid or a plate can be used as a guide. Take 4 of the circles, and on each one, arrange 4 sardines, meeting in the centre and radiating outwards so that the tails overlap the edges of the pastry slightly. Pile the bread-crumb mixture over the sardines. Moisten the edges of the pastry, and cover with the 4 remaining pastry rounds. Press and crimp the edges to seal. Pierce a small steam hole in the top of each pie and place on baking sheets. Brush with milk, and bake in the preheated oven for about 30 minutes until firm and golden-brown.

Serve the pies warm or cold, by themselves or with whole tomatoes or salad.

M E N U

*Stately
Summer Picnic
for Eight*

WATERCRESS AND
SMOKED HADDOCK
ROULADE *this page*

BONED STUFFED
DUCKLING *page 303*

SPINACH, ROQUEFORT
AND POMEGRANATE
SALAD *page 310*

POTATOES WITH BASIL
page 309

STRAWBERRIES
BEAUMES-DE-VENISE
page 311

Make twice the amount of the spinach salad and the strawberries.
IN ADVANCE Allow 4 hours the day before to prepare the duckling and roulade. The evening before, prepare the strawberries and the potatoes with basil.
ON THE DAY Allow about 40 minutes to make the spinach salad and the dressing.
TO DRINK Champagne, dry white wine, or light-bodied dry red wine. Muscat de Beaumes-de-Venise with the strawberries.

WATERCRESS AND SMOKED HADDOCK ROULADE

Roulade – meaning literally 'a rolling' in French – is a term traditionally applied to a piece of meat rolled round a stuffing. But it is also used for other rolled dishes. This roulade is very like a savoury swiss roll. It is equally suitable as a starter or as a main course. The quantities given here are for a main course.

Watercress can be bought either in bunches or, in many supermarkets, in packets, trimmed of its tough stalks.

Make the roulade the day before the picnic. Carry it still wrapped in the greaseproof paper in which it is rolled up, and overwrap with kitchen foil.

PREPARATION TIME: *45 minutes*
COOKING TIME: *10-15 minutes*
OVEN TEMPERATURE: *preheat to 200°C (400°F, gas mark 6)*

INGREDIENTS – *serves 8:*
4 level tablespoons grated Parmesan cheese
2 oz (50 g) fresh white breadcrumbs
4 oz (115 g) Gruyère cheese, coarsely grated
1 bunch watercress, about 3 oz (75 g)
4 large eggs, separated
¼ pint (150 ml) single cream
Salt and freshly ground black pepper
2 tablespoons hot water
Non-stick baking paper

FILLING
8 oz (225 g) smoked haddock
¼ pint (150 ml) milk
1 bay leaf
Sprig of parsley
1 stick celery, or celery leaves
1 oz (25 g) butter
1 level tablespoon flour
Freshly ground black pepper
GARNISH
Lemon wedges
Watercress

Line the base and sides of a swiss roll tin, measuring about 12in × 8in (300mm × 200mm) and about 1in (25mm) deep, with non-stick baking paper. Butter the paper well and sprinkle with half the Parmesan cheese.

Mix the breadcrumbs with the grated Gruyère cheese. Wash and dry the watercress. Discard the stalks and chop the leaves very finely. Stir the water-cress into the cheese and bread-crumb mixture. Stir in the egg yolks, cream, and salt and pepper to taste. With a metal spoon, fold in the hot water to soften the mixture. Whisk the egg whites until stiff, then fold carefully into the mixture. Turn into the prepared tin and spread evenly. Bake in the preheated oven for 10-15 minutes, until well risen and just firm.

Remove the roll from the oven and cover it with a damp tea towel to prevent it from drying out, and cracking when it is rolled. Sprinkle a sheet of greaseproof paper with the re-maining Parmesan cheese and turn out the roulade onto this.

Cover the roulade again with the damp tea towel.

To make the filling, put the smoked haddock in a pan with the milk, bay leaf, parsley and celery. Poach over a moderate heat for about 8 minutes. Drain the fish. Strain the milk and set aside. Flake the fish.

Melt the butter in a pan and stir in the flour. Cook, stirring, over a moderate heat for 2 minutes, then remove from the heat and gradually stir in the milk in which the fish was cooked. Return the pan to the heat and cook, stirring, for 2 minutes more, until thickened and smooth. Add the haddock, and season to taste with pepper. Salt will probably not be necessary.

Spread the haddock mixture over the roulade, then roll it up from the long side. Wrap the greaseproof paper round it firmly and store in the refrigerator until needed. Cut in slices, and garnish with lemon wedges and sprigs of watercress.

This dish is included in a menu on the opposite page.

STATELY PICNIC A cloth spread on the grass in a romantic setting can present as elegant a meal as any served indoors. Watercress roulade filled with smoked haddock, and boned, stuffed duckling are accompanied by spinach, Roquefort and pomegranate salad, and potatoes with basil. Bowls of strawberries soaked in sweet white wine — Muscat de Beaumes-de-Venise — make a summery conclusion to the picnic.

SMOKED SALMON TAGLIATELLE

Chanterelle mushrooms are the best for this dish – they stay firm when cooked and have a distinctive flavour. They, and other wild mushrooms, can sometimes be found in specialist shops and delicatessens at the end of summer and in early autumn. Otherwise, use ordinary button mushrooms. If no fresh dillweed is available, fennel or parsley may be used instead.

Pack the tagliatelle in a plastic box or a tightly covered salad bowl. If possible, carry it in an insulated coolbox. The dish should be eaten within 24 hours.

PREPARATION TIME: *10 minutes*
CHILLING TIME: *1 hour*
COOKING TIME: *10 minutes*

INGREDIENTS – *serves 4:*
6 oz (175 g) smoked salmon
1 lb (450 g) green tagliatelle
2 tablespoons olive oil
6 oz (175 g) chanterelles or button mushrooms
1 level tablespoon chopped fresh dillweed
Salt and freshly ground black pepper
¼ pint (150 ml) soured cream
GARNISH
Sprigs of fresh dillweed

Cut the smoked salmon into fine strips with a sharp knife or kitchen scissors.

Cook the tagliatelle in plenty of boiling, salted water for 8-10 minutes, or until tender, but still al dente – just firm to the bite. Drain and rinse in a colander under cold running water. Return to a cold pan or bowl and toss in 1 tablespoon of olive oil, making sure that all the pasta is evenly coated. Chill in the refrigerator.

Slice the mushrooms. Heat the remaining tablespoon of oil in a small pan, then gently fry the mushrooms for 2 minutes, until just coloured. Cool, then chill in the refrigerator.

Mix together the salmon, tagliatelle, mushrooms and dill. Season to taste with salt and pepper. Turn into the container in which it will be carried and spoon the soured cream on top. Garnish with a few small sprigs of dill. Just before serving, toss lightly with the soured cream.

Serve with a salad, using a simple oil and vinegar dressing. This dish is included in a menu on page 305.

DAPPLED SALAD Pale green tagliatelle is tossed with strips of smoked salmon, chanterelle mushrooms, soured cream and dill.

MARINATED MACKEREL

Vinegar changes the texture of the fish in this recipe so that it becomes opaque and flaky, just as though it had been 'cooked' by heat. Use the freshest fish possible. Herring can be used instead of mackerel.

The dish can be prepared 2-3 days in advance and kept in the refrigerator. Carry the mackerel and marinade in a plastic box with a leakproof lid.

PREPARATION TIME: *20 minutes*
MARINATING TIME: *at least 2 hours*

INGREDIENTS – *serves 4:*
1 lb (450 g) fresh mackerel, cleaned and filleted (page 373)
7 fl oz (200 ml) white wine vinegar
2 cloves garlic
1 small red onion
1 small lemon
3 fl oz (90 ml) olive oil
1 crisp, green dessert apple
2 oz (50 g) black olives
Salt and freshly ground black pepper
1 level tablespoon chopped parsley

Cut the mackerel into fine strips (they do not have to be skinned). Lay them in a shallow dish and pour over the wine vinegar. Cover and chill in the refrigerator for at least 2 hours.

Meanwhile, peel and crush the garlic, skin and finely slice the onion, and finely pare a strip of rind from the lemon. Cut the rind into very fine strips. Squeeze the juice from the lemon and mix with the oil. Core and thinly slice, but do not peel, the apple.

Toss the apple slices with the mackerel and vinegar and add the garlic, onion and lemon-peel strips. Spoon over the oil and lemon mixture, and scatter with black olives. Season well with salt and pepper, then garnish with chopped parsley and serve with crusty bread.

MONKFISH SATAY

A satay (*saté*) is an Indonesian dish of pieces of meat or fish, marinated and then cooked on skewers, similar to kebabs. The pieces are then dipped in a hot, spicy sauce before eating. The satay can be grilled before the picnic and taken along cold, packed in plastic boxes. Carry the sauce in a separate container. For a picnic where there is to be an open fire, take the satay along in the marinade and cook it there.

PREPARATION TIME: *15 minutes plus marinating time*
COOKING TIME: *10 minutes*

INGREDIENTS – *serves 4:*
1 lb (450 g) monkfish fillet
MARINADE
1 tablespoon dry sherry
1 tablespoon soya sauce
1 tablespoon sesame oil
Finely grated rind and juice of ½ lemon
1 level tablespoon sesame seeds

SAUCE
2 oz (50 g) creamed coconut
¼ pint (150 ml) hot water
4 oz (115 g) crunchy peanut butter
1 level teaspoon chilli powder
1 level teaspoon demerara sugar
2 teaspoons soya sauce
1 level tablespoon minced or very finely chopped onion

Cut the monkfish into 1in (25mm) cubes. Mix together all the marinade ingredients and toss the monkfish in the mixture to coat evenly. Cover the dish and chill in the refrigerator for 3-4 hours or overnight, turning occasionally.

To make the sauce, melt the creamed coconut in the hot water in a saucepan over a gentle heat. Stir in the peanut butter, chilli powder, sugar, soya sauce, and minced onion. Stir until well combined, then set on one side to cool.

Thread the monkfish onto fine wooden skewers. Heat a grill or barbecue to high and then grill the skewered fish for about 10 minutes until cooked, turning occasionally. Serve hot or cold, with the peanut sauce spooned over.

LAZY DAY COOKING Cubes of monkfish, marinated in soya sauce and sherry, are barbecued then dipped in a spicy Indonesian sauce.

MEAL IN THE DUNES Chick pea and bacon croquettes, and mushroom, tomato and chive salad will satisfy appetites sharpened by sea air and a game of cricket on the sands.

CHICK PEA AND BACON CROQUETTES

Rashers of bacon hold the shape of these croquettes. Tinned chick peas can be used instead of dried to save time. Carry the croquettes packed in plastic boxes.

PREPARATION TIME: *15 minutes*
SOAKING TIME: *overnight*
COOKING TIME: *40 minutes*

INGREDIENTS – *serves 6:*
6 oz (175 g) dried chick peas
2 oz (50 g) Cheddar cheese, coarsely grated
8 rashers streaky bacon
1 small onion
1½ oz (40 g) dried white breadcrumbs
¾ oz (20 g) sesame seeds
½ teaspoon dried sage
Salt and freshly ground black pepper
1 large egg, lightly beaten
Oil for shallow-frying

Soak the chick peas overnight in cold water.

Drain the chick peas well. Place in a pan of fresh water, bring to the boil and simmer for about 30 minutes or until tender. Drain well, then mash the chick peas roughly. Mix in the cheese.

Remove the rind from the bacon and finely chop 2 rashers. Peel and finely chop the onion. Fry the bacon in its own fat with the onion for about 2 minutes, until they are lightly browned. Add to the chick peas.

Mix together on a plate the breadcrumbs, sesame seeds, sage, a little salt and the pepper, and put to one side. Bind the chick pea mixture with about half the beaten egg. Season to taste with a little salt and pepper. Transfer the remaining egg to another plate. With your hands, mould the chick pea mixture into 6 even-sized barrel shapes, about 2½in (65mm) long.

With a knife, stretch the remaining rashers of bacon. Wrap a rasher around each croquette, spiralling to cover most of the length. If necessary, secure each one with a cocktail stick. Roll each croquette first in the beaten egg, then in the seasoned breadcrumbs, to coat evenly.

Heat the oil in a frying pan, until a piece of bread sizzles when dropped into it. Fry the croquettes, turning frequently, for 4-6 minutes. Drain well on absorbent paper.

For a picnic, let the croquettes cool. They may also be served warm. This dish is included in a menu on the opposite page.

Make the full quantity of all the recipes – the extra two croquettes, and the remainder of the cheesecake, can be kept for another meal if not eaten this time.

IN ADVANCE Start to soak the chick peas 2 days in advance. Allow about 2 hours the day before to make the croquettes and the mango cheesecake, and prepare the stuffed eggs ready to be fried the next day.

ON THE DAY Allow about 45 minutes. Deep-fry the eggs then make the salad and the dressing.

TO DRINK Chilled dry white wine or lager, soft drinks for the children.

THAI-STYLE STUFFED EGGS

The combination of pork and crabmeat is familiar in Thai cuisine. The eggs may be stuffed up to 24 hours in advance ready for frying on the day of the picnic. Carry in plastic boxes.

PREPARATION AND COOKING TIME: *40 minutes*

INGREDIENTS – *serves 4:*
4 large eggs
4 oz (115 g) minced pork
4 oz (115 g) crabmeat
1 clove garlic
1 level teaspoon caster sugar
¼ teaspoon salt
¼ teaspoon ground pepper
*1 level tablespoon chopped
  coriander leaves*
*2 level tablespoons creamed
  coconut*
Oil for deep-frying

BATTER
4 oz (115 g) plain flour
¼ pint (150 ml) cold water
2 teaspoons vegetable oil
½ teaspoon salt
COATING
*2 level tablespoons desiccated
  coconut*

Place the eggs in a pan of very hot water and bring to the boil. Simmer gently for 10 minutes to hard-boil the eggs. Drain, and crack the shells. Run the eggs under cold water to cool them quickly, then peel.

While the eggs are cooking, mix together the minced pork and crabmeat. Skin and crush the garlic and stir into the meat

EXOTIC EGGS A typically Thai mixture of pork, crabmeat and coconut, fills hard-boiled eggs coated in batter and deep-fried.

mixture with the sugar, salt, pepper, coriander and creamed coconut. Mash to a smooth paste with a fork.

Cut the eggs in half lengthways and scoop out the yolks. Mix the yolks with the pork and crab mixture. Fill the egg halves with this mixture, and mould each of the 8 filled halves back into the shape of a whole egg with your hands.

To make the batter, sieve the flour into a bowl and gradually beat in the water, vegetable oil and salt. Beat well until smooth.

To deep-fry (page 372), heat the oil to 190°C (375°F). Quickly dip the egg shapes into the batter, then drop them carefully into the hot oil using a slotted spoon. Cook, two at a time, for about 4-5 minutes, turning once. Remove with a slotted spoon onto absorbent paper to drain, then toss in desiccated coconut and allow to cool, before packing. This dish is included in a menu on this page.

CHICKEN DRUMSTICKS IN HONEY AND MUSTARD

Because they are so easy to eat with fingers, chicken drumsticks are convenient for picnics. Chicken thighs or wings may be used instead of drumsticks. Cook the drumsticks the day before the picnic, and store in plastic boxes ready for carrying.

PREPARATION TIME: *10 minutes
  plus marinating time*
COOKING TIME: *30 minutes*
OVEN TEMPERATURE: *preheat to
  200°C (400°F, gas mark 6)*

INGREDIENTS – *serves 4:*
8 chicken drumsticks
1 oz (25 g) butter
2 tablespoons Dijon mustard
2 tablespoons clear honey
2 tablespoons lemon juice
GARNISH
Coriander leaves or parsley

Wipe the chicken drumsticks with kitchen paper. Cut two or three deep slashes in the flesh of each drumstick, then place them in a deep bowl.

Heat the butter gently in a small pan until just melted. Mix together the mustard, honey, melted butter and lemon juice, and spread over the chicken. Leave to marinate in a cool place, turning occasionally, for several hours or overnight.

Place the drumsticks on a baking sheet and cover loosely with foil. Bake in the preheated oven for 20 minutes. Remove the foil and baste the chicken with the juices, then return to the oven for a further 10 minutes or until the juices run clear when the drumsticks are pierced with a skewer.

For a picnic, allow the drumsticks to cool completely, then pack. Garnish with sprigs of coriander or parsley. The drumsticks can also be served hot.

This dish is included in a menu on page 312.

CHICKEN AND HAM EN BRIOCHE

Brioche dough is used in this recipe to encase a rich chicken and ham filling. The brioches can be kept overnight in the refrigerator wrapped in kitchen foil. On the morning of the picnic refresh them by placing in a hot oven for about 10 minutes.

If you wish to use ready-cooked chicken you will need 1½lb (700g) of boneless meat.

SAVOURY BRIOCHE Yeasty brioche dough makes a light wrapping for a mixture of chicken and ham.

PREPARATION TIME: *50-60 minutes plus cooling time*
RISING TIME: *1½ hours*
COOKING TIME: *1 hour*
OVEN TEMPERATURE: *preheat to 230°C (450°F, gas mark 8)*

INGREDIENTS – *serves 8:*
FILLING
1 oven-ready chicken, about 2½ lb (1.1 kg)
1 level tablespoon whole black peppercorns
1 carrot, chopped
Parsley stalks
8 oz (225 g) cup mushrooms
1 chicken liver
2 shallots
1 oz (25 g) butter
8 oz (225 g) cooked gammon
2 level tablespoons parsley
2 tablespoons whisky or brandy
1 egg, lightly beaten
2 teaspoons Worcestershire sauce
Salt and freshly ground black pepper
BRIOCHE DOUGH
12 oz (350 g) strong plain flour
Pinch of salt
1½ level teaspoons dried yeast and ½ teaspoon caster sugar OR ⅓ of a sachet easy-blend dried yeast
5 tablespoons warm water
2 eggs
2 oz (50 g) butter
GLAZE
1 egg yolk
1 tablespoon water

Place the chicken in a deep pan and add just enough cold water to cover. Add the peppercorns, chopped carrot and parsley stalks. Bring to the boil, cover and simmer gently for about 40 minutes, or until the chicken pulls away from the bone easily. Remove from the stock and leave until cool enough to handle. The stock may be kept for use in another recipe. Remove all the meat from the chicken and set aside.

Wipe and roughly chop the mushrooms. Chop the chicken liver. Peel and chop the shallots. Melt the butter in a frying pan and sauté the mushrooms and liver over medium heat for 3-4 minutes, until beginning to brown. Add the shallots to the pan and cook for a further 1 minute. Cool.

Place the chicken, mushroom mixture, gammon and parsley in a food processor and chop very finely. Alternatively, mince it finely. Stir in the whisky, beaten egg, Worcestershire sauce and salt and pepper to taste.

To make the dough, sieve the flour and salt into a bowl. Mix the yeast and sugar with the water. Leave for 10 minutes or until frothy. If using easy-blend dried yeast, follow the instructions on the packet.

Beat the eggs and melt the butter, then add to the flour with the yeast mixture and work to a soft dough. Knead on a lightly floured surface for about 5 minutes. Put the dough in a large bowl. Cover with a damp cloth or an oiled plastic bag. Leave in a warm place for about an hour, until doubled in size.

Brush a large baking sheet with oil. Knead the dough well then divide into 8 equal pieces. Roll each piece out to a thin round and place a generous amount of the chicken mixture onto it. Pull up the sides around the filling and pinch together well to seal.

Place the filled dough parcels, joins underneath, onto the baking sheet, in a cluster so that the edges just touch. Cover with a damp cloth and leave to stand in a warm place for about 30 minutes, until well risen and springy to the touch.

Mix the egg yolk with the water and brush over the dough to glaze. Bake in the preheated oven for about 20 minutes, until firm and golden-brown. Serve hot or cold. Carry wrapped in kitchen foil or in a plastic box.

CHICKEN LIVER CROISSANTS

Golden, flaky and rich, croissants filled with sautéed chicken livers, tomato and herbs are redolent of warm, southern Europe. The croissants can be prepared the evening before the picnic and kept in the refrigerator ready for baking in the morning. Allow to cool, then pack in a plastic box. Croissant dough (page 26) can be used instead of puff pastry.

PREPARATION TIME: *30 minutes*
COOKING TIME: *25 minutes*
OVEN TEMPERATURE: *preheat to 200°C (400°F, gas mark 6)*

INGREDIENTS – *serves 4:*
8 oz (225 g) chicken livers
1 small onion
½ oz (15 g) butter
½ teaspoon herbes de Provence
  OR mixed herbs
8 oz (225 g) prepared weight
  puff pastry (page 394)
4 level teaspoons tomato purée
1 medium-sized firm tomato
Freshly ground black pepper
GLAZE
Milk
Paprika

Roughly chop the chicken livers. Peel and finely slice the onion. Melt the butter in a frying pan and sauté the livers and onion over a high heat until both are lightly browned and most of the liquid has evaporated. Add the herbs. Allow to cool slightly.

Roll out the pastry and cut into four triangles, about 9in × 9in × 6in (230mm × 230mm × 150mm). Spread each triangle with tomato purée.

Chop the tomato into small pieces and mix into the liver mixture with a little pepper.

Spoon a quarter of the mixture onto each triangle close to the short side. Roll up each triangle, starting from the short side, enclosing the filling. Moisten the tip of the triangle and stick it down. Curl the ends around to form a crescent, pinching the edges together. Glaze the pastry with milk, and sprinkle with paprika. Bake in the preheated oven for about 25 minutes, until the croissants are golden-brown. Serve warm or cold.

BONED STUFFED DUCKLING

Boning a duckling is particularly worthwhile for a picnic because the boned bird is very easy to carve. Cook it the day before the picnic and chill overnight. Carry it in a plastic box, or wrapped in greaseproof paper and kitchen foil or clingfilm.

PREPARATION TIME: *1½ hours*
COOKING TIME: *1 hour 40 minutes*
OVEN TEMPERATURE: *preheat to 200°C (400°F, gas mark 6)*

INGREDIENTS – *serves 8-10:*
1 duckling, about 5 lb (2.3 kg)
8 oz (225 g) veal shoulder
8 oz (225 g) lean belly pork
4 oz (115 g) onion
3 oz (75 g) fresh white
  breadcrumbs
2 level tablespoons fresh sage
  leaves
2 oz (50 g) ham
2 level tablespoons green
  peppercorns
¼ teaspoon celery salt
4 tablespoons brandy
1 small egg, lightly beaten
6 whole pickled walnuts
Fine cotton string and a needle
GARNISH
Fresh sage leaves

Bone the duckling as for chicken (page 378).

If the duckling comes with giblets, reserve the liver and chop roughly. Chop the veal, pork and onion then feed into a mincer or food processor to

mince or chop evenly. Mix with the chopped liver and the breadcrumbs. Roughly chop the sage leaves and add to the mixture. Dice the ham evenly and stir in, together with the peppercorns, celery salt and brandy. Bind with the beaten egg.

Lay the boned duckling, skin side down, on the work surface. Arrange half the stuffing down the centre, then place a row of walnuts down the middle. Cover

with the remaining stuffing. Wrap the duckling over, tucking in the end flaps to enclose the stuffing, and sew up firmly with fine cotton string, but not too tightly or it will burst.

Place the duckling, seam side down, on a rack over a roasting tin and roast for about 1 hour 40 minutes, basting once, halfway through cooking. When the duckling is cooked, the juices should run clear when it is

DAINTY DUCK A boned duckling is stuffed with veal, pork and ham wrapped round pickled walnuts.

pierced with a fork. Serve hot, or allow to cool then chill in the refrigerator until needed. Serve the cold duckling cut in slices, garnished with fresh sage leaves, and accompanied by crusty bread and a salad. This dish is included in a menu on page 296.

PITTA SALAD POCKETS

Middle-Eastern pitta bread is flat, oval and opens into a pocket, which makes a perfect container for a variety of fillings – in this case, salad. The Feta cheese can be replaced by another firm white cheese, and ham or salami can be used instead of anchovies. Fill the pitta pockets on the morning of the picnic. Wrap them in foil after filling.

PREPARATION TIME: *20 minutes*

INGREDIENTS – *serves 6:*
6 pitta breads
6 tomatoes
1 bunch watercress
2 oz (50 g) pitted black olives
4 oz (115 g) Feta cheese
1 small onion
1¾ oz (50 g) tin anchovy fillets
Freshly ground black pepper
2 tablespoons olive oil

Cut each pitta bread in half, and open each half into a pocket.

Cut the tomatoes into thin wedges. Wash and trim the watercress, discarding all tough stalks. Mix together the tomato wedges, watercress and olives. Dice the Feta cheese, peel and finely slice the onion and add to the mixture. Drain the anchovy fillets and chop roughly. Stir into the salad with plenty of black pepper and the olive oil. Fill the pitta pockets with the salad. This dish is included in a menu on page 312.

GREEN SUMMER VEGETABLE TERRINE

Young summer vegetables, layered and cooked in the oven, retain all their tenderness, colour and flavour. The base of the tin is lined with slices of courgette, which are revealed when the terrine is turned out for serving. If the terrine is not to be turned out, arrange the slices on top instead. Make the terrine the day before the picnic. Carry the terrine in the tin, covered with foil.

PREPARATION TIME: *45 minutes plus chilling time*
COOKING TIME: *1 hour*
OVEN TEMPERATURE: *preheat to 150°C (300°F, gas mark 2)*

INGREDIENTS – *serves 8:*
1 lb (450 g) fresh young spinach leaves
8 oz (225 g) courgettes
8 oz (225 g) french beans
4 oz (115 g) onion
1 oz (25 g) butter
3 level tablespoons chopped parsley
3 level tablespoons chopped chives
¼ pint (150 ml) double cream
2 eggs
Salt and freshly ground pepper

Grease a 2lb (900g) loaf tin, and line the base.

Wash the spinach leaves several times in cold water, then drain well. Place in a pan with a close-fitting lid. No water is needed other than the drops that cling to the leaves. Cook over a fairly high heat for about 4 minutes, shaking occasionally, until the spinach is cooked down. Drain well, pressing out any excess moisture.

Top and tail the courgettes. Slice one courgette thinly, and blanch the slices in boiling water for 1 minute. Use the courgette slices to line the base of the prepared loaf tin. Slice the remaining courgettes lengthways, into long thin sticks about ¼in (5mm) across and blanch in boiling water for 1 minute.

Top and tail the beans, and blanch for 2 minutes. Drain.

Peel and chop the onion. Melt the butter in a pan and fry the onion for 2 minutes to soften. Place in a food processor or liquidiser with the spinach, parsley, chives, cream and eggs. Blend until smooth. Season well with salt and pepper.

Pour a little of the puréed spinach mixture into the loaf tin, taking care not to disturb the courgettes on the bottom,

ALL ASHORE Spread out on a secluded stretch of river bank are green summer vegetable terrines, smoked salmon tagliatelle, carrot and orange salad, apple and redcurrant lattice, and spiced pears in wine.

then arrange a few courgette sticks and beans on top. Pour over a little more spinach mix, then more courgettes and beans, and so on until all the ingredients are used up. Finish with a layer of spinach.

Cover the tin closely with buttered kitchen foil or double-thickness greaseproof paper. Place in a roasting tin filled with about 1in (25mm) of hot water. Cook in the preheated oven for about 1 hour, or until just firm to the touch. Leave to cool in the tin, then chill in the refrigerator until needed. Serve, turned out onto a plate and cut into slices with fresh, crusty bread. This dish is included in a menu on the opposite page.

PICNIC FRIDGE *Wine bottles cool in the river, safely moored to the bank.*

M E N U

Country Picnic
for 12 to 16

**GREEN SUMMER
VEGETABLE TERRINE**
opposite page

**SMOKED SALMON
TAGLIATELLE** *page 298*

**CARROT AND ORANGE
SALAD** *page 311*

❧

**APPLE AND REDCURRANT
LATTICE** *page 314*

SPICED PEARS IN WINE
page 313

Make double the quantity given in all the recipes except the smoked salmon tagliatelle, which should be trebled or quadrupled depending on numbers.

IN ADVANCE Allow around 3½ hours the day before to make the terrines, the apple and redcurrant lattice and the spiced pears. The evening before, cook the pasta and make the dressing for the carrot and orange salad.

ON THE DAY Allow about 40 minutes to complete the smoked salmon tagliatelle and make the salad.

TO DRINK Dry white wine.

VEGETARIAN PICNIC PIE

Broccoli, in its various varieties, is available all year round. However, this pie could also be made to use up cooked vegetables such as courgettes or beans – vary the combination to suit the season. The Gouda may be replaced by another hard cheese such as Cheddar or Emmenthal, and cashew nuts can be used instead of peanuts.

To protect the pastry, carry the pie in its tin. Wrap pie and tin, when completely cold, with kitchen foil. The pie is at its best on the day it is made, but it can be made the day before the picnic and stored in the refrigerator until needed.

PREPARATION TIME: *35 minutes*
COOKING TIME: *40-50 minutes*
OVEN TEMPERATURE: *preheat to 200°C (400°F, gas mark 6)*

INGREDIENTS – *serves 6:*
PASTRY
9 oz (250 g) wholemeal flour
4½ oz (130 g) block vegetable margarine
Cold water to mix
FILLING
8 oz (225 g) broccoli
8 oz (225 g) carrots
2 oz (50 g) salted peanuts
6 oz (175 g) Gouda cheese
3 tablespoons single cream or top of the milk
Salt and freshly ground black pepper
GLAZE
Milk

WHOLEWHEAT PIE Strips of pastry cover a filling of broccoli, carrots, peanuts, cheese and cream.

To make the pastry, place the flour in a mixing bowl and rub in the margarine until the mixture resembles breadcrumbs. Stir in just enough cold water to mix to a firm dough. Roll out about two-thirds of the pastry and use it to line the base and sides of an 8in (200mm) loose-based sandwich tin, or a plain flan ring on a baking sheet.

To make the filling, trim and break the broccoli into small florets. Blanch the broccoli in boiling water for about 3 minutes, then drain well. Peel and coarsely grate the carrots.

Arrange the broccoli in the pastry-lined case and sprinkle the carrots and peanuts on top. Coarsely grate the cheese and mix with the cream and salt and pepper. Pour over the vegetables, spreading evenly.

Roll out the remaining pastry and cut into strips about ¾in (20mm) wide. Arrange these over the top of the pie, overlapping to form a lattice (page 288). Press the edges down well, and trim with a sharp knife.

Glaze with milk and bake in the preheated oven for about 40-50 minutes, or until firm and golden-brown. Serve either warm or cold with a salad, or, as a supper dish, with a vegetable accompaniment such as *Two beans in tomato* (page 357).

AUBERGINE CAVIAR

A fleeting resemblance in taste and appearance to the real thing has caused this exotic Middle-Eastern purée of aubergines and olive oil to be called 'poor man's caviar'. However, the name was probably the product of wishful thinking on someone's part and does not do justice to the subtle, distinctive flavour of the dish. Aubergine purée is found throughout the Middle East, where it can be traced back hundreds of years. It is also eaten in Russia.

Yoghurt somewhat lightens the purée – which is otherwise very rich – but it can be omitted. Aubergine caviar can be served either as a first course or as a dip, or as a main course with salad. It can be made a day ahead and kept, covered, in the refrigerator. Carry it to the picnic in plastic boxes.

PREPARATION TIME: *25 minutes*
COOKING TIME: *30 minutes*
OVEN TEMPERATURE: *preheat to 190°C (375°F, gas mark 5)*

INGREDIENTS – *serves 4:*
3 medium aubergines
6 tablespoons olive oil
2 level tablespoons finely chopped parsley
¼ teaspoon ground cumin
1 clove garlic
¼ pint (150 ml) natural yoghurt
Salt and freshly ground black pepper

Place the whole, unpeeled aubergines on a baking sheet, and bake in the preheated oven for about 30 minutes or until the flesh is tender and the skins are dry and wrinkled. Cut each aubergine in half and scoop out the flesh. Put the aubergine into a liquidiser or food processor. Blend until smooth, then very gradually add the oil, as though making mayonnaise, continuing to blend until the oil has all been incorporated. Alternatively, mash the aubergines in a bowl with a wooden spoon or pound in a pestle and mortar, then gradually beat in the oil.

Stir in the chopped parsley with the cumin. Peel and crush the garlic and stir in with the yoghurt. Season to taste with salt and pepper, and chill in the refrigerator until required.

Serve with warm pitta bread or vegetable crudités (page 320).

RADISH BUTTER ON PUMPERNICKEL

Peppery radishes make a fresh-tasting summer sandwich filling which particularly suits pumpernickel or a coarse, granary bread. Use the radish butter the same day it is made.

Wrap each slice separately in kitchen foil for carrying.

PREPARATION TIME: *25 minutes*

INGREDIENTS – *serves 4:*
1 bunch radishes
Salt
2 oz (50 g) butter
3 level tablespoons mayonnaise, homemade (page 369) or ready-made
Freshly ground black pepper
4 slices pumpernickel bread
GARNISH
Mustard and cress

Trim the roots and leaves from the radishes and wash thoroughly. Thinly slice two radishes and set aside for garnish. Grate the remaining radishes coarsely and sprinkle lightly with salt. Leave to stand for 15 minutes, then press out the excess moisture.

Beat the butter until soft, then mix with the mayonnaise and grated radishes. Season well with black pepper. Divide between the slices of pumpernickel and spread evenly. Garnish with slices of radish and a few sprigs of mustard and cress.

The radish butter is also very good on *Black rye bread (page 30)* instead of pumpernickel.

PAN BAGNA

Provence in southern France is the source of pan bagna – a classic picnic dish. Use very fresh bread, and make pan bagna several hours in advance so that the flavours can mingle.

PREPARATION TIME: *25 minutes plus standing time*

INGREDIENTS – *serves 4-6:*
1 long French stick
1 clove garlic, halved
4 fl oz (115 ml) olive oil
1¾ oz (50 g) tin anchovy fillets
1 lb (450 g) tomatoes
4 oz (115 g) stoned black olives, halved
3 tablespoons capers (optional)

With a sharp knife, split the French loaf in half, lengthways. Open out the loaf and rub each cut surface with the cut side of a half clove of garlic. Sprinkle each half of bread with olive oil.

Drain the anchovy fillets and arrange over the bread. Slice the tomatoes and lay them on top of the anchovies. Scatter over the olives and capers. Sandwich the loaf back together.

Wrap tightly in foil, sealing all edges, then place a weight on top and leave to stand at room temperature for at least 2-3 hours. Serve in thick slices.

PROVENÇAL SANDWICH With a filling of tomatoes, anchovies, olives, garlic and olive oil, pan bagna is clearly from the South of France.

CASHEW NUT ROLLS

Chopped nuts give a crunchy texture to these herb-flavoured bread rolls. To vary the recipe, try peanuts instead of cashews, or a different herb.

Do not tear the rolls apart until they are needed, they will keep fresh for longer. As a change, the dough can be formed into a plaited loaf.

PREPARATION TIME: *40 minutes*
RISING TIME: *1-1½ hours*
COOKING TIME: *20-25 minutes*
OVEN TEMPERATURE: *preheat to 220°C (425°F, gas mark 7)*

INGREDIENTS – *makes 16:*
1 lb (450 g) strong white flour
1 level teaspoon salt
1 oz (25 g) lard
*2 level teaspoons dried yeast and
 1 level teaspoon caster sugar* OR
*⅔ sachet easy-blend dried
 yeast*
¼ pint (150 ml) warm water
¼ pint (150 ml) warm milk
1 small onion
*2 level teaspoons chopped fresh
 thyme* OR *1 level teaspoon dried
 thyme*
*2 oz (50 g) salted cashew nuts,
 chopped*
GLAZE
Milk
*Grated Parmesan cheese to
 sprinkle on rolls*

Sieve the flour and salt into a bowl. Rub in the lard until the mixture resembles breadcrumbs. Place the yeast in a bowl with the sugar, warm water and milk

and leave in a warm place for about 10 minutes until frothy. If using easy-blend yeast, follow the instructions on the packet.

Peel and very finely chop the onion, and stir into the flour mixture with the thyme and half the chopped cashew nuts. Stir the frothy yeast mixture into the flour, and knead until smooth. Cover and leave in a warm place until doubled in size.

Grease a large baking sheet.

Turn out the dough onto a floured surface and knead again until smooth. Divide into 16 equal pieces and knead into smooth balls. Arrange, almost touching, on the baking sheet. Cover and leave to rise again in a warm place until doubled in size and springy to the touch.

When the dough is well-risen, brush with milk and sprinkle with a little Parmesan cheese and the remaining chopped

SIMPLE PLEASURES Fresh cashew nut rolls are the only companions needed for a piece of ripe Camembert and a crisp green apple.

cashew nuts. Bake for 20-25 minutes in the preheated oven until firm and golden-brown. Cool on a wire rack.

Serve with soup, or split in half and filled. The rolls go well with cheese or pâté.

HAM AND LYCHEE ROLLS

The distinctive scented flavour of lychees mingles well with mild blue cheese and ham. Another crumbly blue cheese such as blue Wensleydale can be used instead of Danish Blue. Carry the rolls wrapped in kitchen foil.

PREPARATION TIME: *20 minutes*

INGREDIENTS – *serves 6:*
*1 lb (450 g) cold cooked
 gammon, unsmoked*
*8 oz (225 g) fresh or well-
 drained tinned lychees*
3 oz (75 g) black grapes
*3 oz (75 g) mellow Danish Blue
 cheese*
*2 level tablespoons mayonnaise,
 homemade (page 369) or
 ready-made*
2 teaspoons lemon juice
Freshly ground black pepper
6 crusty bread rolls
Parsley sprigs

Cut the gammon into ½in (15mm) cubes. Peel, halve and stone fresh lychees. Halve tinned lychees. Halve the grapes and remove the seeds. Crumble the cheese roughly and mix with the gammon, lychees and grapes. Stir in the mayonnaise and lemon juice. Season with pepper.

Cut the top third from each of the rolls and scoop out the crumbly centre from the base. Pile the ham mixture into the rolls and top each with a parsley sprig. Replace the tops.

CALZONE

The southern Italian city of Naples is the home of calzone – a near relative of the pizza. The baggy shape may have suggested the name – *calzoni* literally means 'trousers' in Italian. For a picnic on a cold day, bake the calzone just before leaving, then wrap them in kitchen foil and several layers of newspaper and carry them in an insulated bag. They will stay hot for up to 2 hours. If they are to be eaten cold, wrap them in kitchen foil, or pack in plastic boxes.

PREPARATION TIME: *35 minutes*
RISING TIME: *45 minutes*
COOKING TIME: *15 minutes*
OVEN TEMPERATURE: *preheat to 220°C (425°F, gas mark 7)*

INGREDIENTS – *serves 4:*
1½ lb (700 g) strong plain flour
2 level teaspoons salt
1 level tablespoon dried yeast and 2 level teaspoons caster sugar OR 1 sachet easy-blend dried yeast
¾ pint (450 ml) warm water
3 fl oz (90 ml) olive oil
FILLING
1 aubergine, about 6 oz (175 g)
1¼ lb (575 g) firm tomatoes
8 oz (225 g) chèvre (goat cheese)
8 oz (225 g) Mozzarella cheese
2 level tablespoons chopped fresh basil OR 2 level teaspoons dried basil
2 level teaspoons chopped fresh thyme OR 1 level teaspoon dried thyme
Freshly ground black pepper

Sieve the flour and salt into a large bowl. Sprinkle the dried yeast and caster sugar into the water, then leave to stand for 10-15 minutes until the mixture is frothy. If using easy-blend dried yeast, follow the instructions on the packet.

Mix the yeast liquid into the flour with the olive oil. Knead thoroughly for about 5 minutes, until the dough is smooth. Cover and leave in a warm place until doubled in size and springy to the touch.

Meanwhile, cut the aubergine in half lengthways and place, cut side up, under a hot grill. Cook until tender. Scoop out the flesh and chop roughly. Chop the tomatoes and dice the cheeses. Mix together the aubergine, tomatoes, cheeses, basil, thyme and pepper.

Grease two baking sheets.

Divide the dough into four. Roll out one piece to a large circle. Place a quarter of the filling mixture on one side of the circle. Moisten round the edge of the circle then fold it in half to enclose the filling. Turn over the edges to seal, pinching together with your fingertips. Make a small slit in the top, and place on the baking sheets. Cover with a damp cloth and leave to rest for about 15 minutes at room temperature. Fill the remaining pieces of dough in the same way.

Bake in the preheated oven for about 15 minutes, until well risen, firm and golden-brown. Serve warm or cold.

SALADS

POTATOES WITH BASIL

New potatoes need little adornment, but they are enhanced by the summery flavour of basil in this light dressing. Choose small, even-sized potatoes with firm, unwrinkled skins and use them while they are still fresh. Make the salad the day before the picnic. Carry in a plastic box or in an unbreakable salad bowl covered tightly.

PREPARATION AND COOKING TIME: *30 minutes plus chilling time*

INGREDIENTS – *serves 6:*
2½ lb (1.1 kg) small new potatoes
Large handful of fresh basil leaves, about ¾ oz (20 g) OR 2 level tablespoons dried basil
¼ pint (150 ml) natural yoghurt
1 tablespoon lemon juice
1 tablespoon clear honey
Salt and freshly ground black pepper

Scrub the potatoes clean, but do not rub off the skins. Plunge them into a pan of lightly salted, boiling water and simmer for 10-15 minutes – depending on the size of the potatoes – until just tender when pierced with a knife. Drain well and leave on one side to cool.

Finely chop the basil leaves and mix with the yoghurt, lemon juice and honey. Season to taste with salt and pepper. While the potatoes are still slightly warm, stir them into the basil sauce, mixing well so that they are coated evenly. Chill well in the refrigerator. Mix the potatoes and dressing again before serving. This dish is included in a menu on page 296.

SUMMER POTATOES *The sweet fragrance of fresh basil mingles with yoghurt, lemon and honey in a dressing which brings out all the flavour of tiny new potatoes.*

Wash and dry the mangetout, and top and tail. Wipe, top and tail, and thinly slice the courgettes. Peel the grapefruit and cut out the segments, discarding all the white pith and membrane (page 398). If the segments are large, tear them in half, crossways, to make bite-sized pieces. Mix together the mangetout, courgette slices and grapefruit.

To make the dressing, mix together the mustard, lemon juice and caster sugar in a bowl. Pour in the wine vinegar, whisking with a fork, and gradually whisk in the oil. Season well with salt and pepper and stir in the coriander.

Toss the vegetables and the grapefruit in the dressing, and chill until required.

SPINACH, ROQUEFORT AND POMEGRANATE SALAD

The sweet-sour flavour of pomegranate seeds combines well with the astringency of spinach and blue cheese. The pomegranate season runs from the end of summer to Christmas, but they sometimes appear earlier in the year or the seeds can be frozen. Roquefort is the best cheese, but it is very expensive and another blue cheese such as Stilton can be used instead if you wish.

Carry the salad in a plastic box large enough to toss it in, or in a large unbreakable salad bowl covered tightly. Take the dressing separately to the picnic in a screw-top jar.

PREPARATION TIME: *30 minutes*

INGREDIENTS – *serves 4-6:*
1 lb (450 g) young fresh spinach leaves
3 oz (75 g) Roquefort cheese
1 pomegranate
DRESSING
1 teaspoon Dijon mustard
1 tablespoon white wine vinegar
3 tablespoons walnut oil or olive oil
Salt and freshly ground black pepper

Remove the stems from the spinach leaves and wash the leaves very thoroughly in cold water. Drain well. Tear the spinach into small strips. Cut the cheese into rough cubes and mix with the spinach leaves.

Cut the pomegranate in half and scoop out the juicy seeds, discarding all the white membrane and pith. Add the seeds to the spinach and cheese, and toss well. Chill in the refrigerator, until required.

To make the dressing, shake together all the ingredients in a screw-top jar until well combined. Adjust the seasoning if necessary and chill in the refrigerator until required. Toss the salad in the dressing just before serving. This dish is included in a menu on page 296.

COURGETTE, MANGETOUT AND GRAPEFRUIT SALAD

Make this salad in early summer when mangetout and courgettes are young and at their most tender. As a variation, pomelo, the largest of the citrus fruit, can be substituted for grapefruit.

Its flesh consists of small, fibrous pockets which hold masses of sweet juice.

Carry the salad in a large plastic box or an unbreakable salad bowl tightly covered.

PREPARATION TIME: *20 minutes*

INGREDIENTS – *serves 4:*
8 oz (225 g) mangetout
2 medium-sized courgettes
2 grapefruit
DRESSING
1 teaspoon Dijon mustard
1 tablespoon lemon juice
1 level tablespoon caster sugar
1 tablespoon red wine vinegar
3 tablespoons olive oil
Salt and freshly ground black pepper
1 level tablespoon finely chopped coriander leaves
GARNISH
Coriander leaves

CARROT AND ORANGE SALAD

Slice large carrots very thinly for this salad, but the thin, finger carrots of summer may simply be cut into chunks.

Eat the salad within 4 hours once it has been mixed with the dressing. Carry it in a plastic box or an unbreakable salad bowl covered tightly.

PREPARATION TIME: *25 minutes*

INGREDIENTS – *serves 6:*
1 lb (450 g) young carrots
3 medium oranges
1 in (25 mm) piece of fresh root ginger
DRESSING
1 tablespoon orange juice
3 tablespoons olive oil
Salt and freshly ground black pepper
1 level tablespoon poppy seeds

Scrub the carrots then slice very thinly, cutting diagonally to produce oval slices. Peel the oranges and cut out the segments, discarding all the white pith and membrane (page 398). Peel and finely dice the ginger. Mix the carrots, orange segments and ginger in the container in which the salad is to be carried.

To make the dressing, shake together the orange juice, olive oil, salt and pepper in a screw-top jar. Pour over the salad and toss. Scatter the poppy seeds over the salad. Chill in the refrigerator. This dish is included in a menu on page 305.

MUSHROOM, TOMATO AND CHIVE SALAD

The visual effect of this salad is greatest if it is made with cherry tomatoes and button mushrooms of similar size, but ordinary tomatoes cut into quarters can be used instead. Carry the salad in a plastic box or an unbreakable salad bowl tightly covered. Carry the dressing in a screw-top jar.

PREPARATION TIME: *15 minutes*

INGREDIENTS – *serves 4-6:*
12 oz (350 g) firm cherry tomatoes
8 oz (225 g) small white button mushrooms
4 level tablespoons roughly chopped chives
DRESSING
¼ pint (150 ml) soured cream
2 tablespoons lemon juice
2 teaspoons coarse grain mustard
½ teaspoon caster sugar
Garlic salt and freshly ground black pepper

Remove the stalks from the tomatoes, wipe with a damp cloth and leave whole. Wipe the mushrooms and leave whole. Combine the tomatoes and mushrooms in the serving dish. Mix in the chives.

To make the dressing, mix all the ingredients in a bowl. Season to taste with salt and pepper. Just before serving, spoon the dressing over the salad.

This dish is included in a menu on page 301.

PUDDINGS

STRAWBERRIES BEAUMES-DE-VENISE

The sweet and scented Muscat dessert wine from the village of Beaumes-de-Venise, in the Côtes du Rhône, complements ripe strawberries perfectly, but if it is unavailable, use another dessert wine instead.

Carry the strawberries either in a plastic box in an insulated coolbox, or in wide-mouthed vacuum flasks.

PREPARATION TIME: *10 minutes*
CHILLING TIME: *1-2 hours*

INGREDIENTS – *serves 4-6:*
1 lb (450 g) fresh strawberries
½ pint (285 ml) Muscat de Beaumes-de-Venise
DECORATION
Fresh borage flowers

Hull the strawberries and place in a bowl. Pour over the Beaumes-de-Venise and cover tightly. Chill in the refrigerator for 1-2 hours. Serve scattered with a few borage flowers. This dish is included in a menu on page 296.

FORGOTTEN FRAGRANCE The lingering scent of elderflowers, typical of Muscat wines, suffuses a bowl of strawberries steeped in Muscat de Beaumes-de-Venise and decorated with borage flowers.

Make half the amount given in the recipes for the chicken and the pitta salad. Make the full amount of the soup and the banana pecan loaf; the remainder of both can be frozen or stored for another occasion.

IN ADVANCE The day before, prepare and cook the chicken, bake the banana pecan loaf and make the soup but do not add the cream.

ON THE DAY Allow about 45 minutes. Make the salad and use it to stuff 4 pitta halves. Slice some of the banana pecan loaf. Reheat the soup with the cream, and put it into a vacuum flask.

TO DRINK Lager in cans, or water.

BANANA PECAN LOAF

Although pecan nuts are expensive, they do give this moist teabread a distinctive flavour. Walnuts can be used instead, however. Choose really ripe bananas; they will mash more easily. Packed in kitchen foil the loaf will keep moist for up to a week.

PREPARATION TIME: *25 minutes*
COOKING TIME: *1¼ hours*
OVEN TEMPERATURE: *preheat to 180°C (350°F, gas mark 4)*

INGREDIENTS – *makes one 2 lb (900 g) loaf:*
12 oz (350 g) bananas
2 oz (50 g) pecan nuts
7 oz (200 g) self-raising flour
¼ teaspoon bicarbonate of soda
½ teaspoon salt
3 oz (75 g) butter
6 oz (175 g) light soft brown sugar
2 eggs, lightly beaten
3 oz (75 g) marzipan (page 400)

POWER PACK *Energy-rich bananas and nuts make a moist loaf to stow away for a day's walking.*

Grease a 2lb (900g) loaf tin and line it with greaseproof paper.

Peel and mash the bananas. Reserve a few nuts for decoration, then roughly chop the rest. Sieve the flour with the bicarbonate of soda and salt.

Cream the butter with the sugar until light and fluffy, then gradually beat in the eggs. Beat in the bananas and pecan nuts. Fold in the flour mixture. Roughly chop the marzipan and stir in. Turn the mixture into the prepared tin and smooth level. Decorate the top with the reserved nuts.

Bake for about 1¼ hours, until well risen and golden-brown. Turn out and cool on a wire rack. Serve plain, or spread with butter. This loaf is included in a menu on this page.

MANGO CHEESECAKE

The sweet, scented flavour of mango permeates this very creamy cheesecake. If the weather is very warm, add an extra level teaspoon of gelatine to the mixture. Carry the cheesecake in its tin, wrapped in foil, in an insulated coolbox if possible.

PREPARATION TIME: *45 minutes*
SETTING TIME: *2-3 hours*

INGREDIENTS – *serves 8:*
BASE
4 oz (115 g) ginger nut biscuits
1 oz (25 g) walnut halves
2 oz (50 g) butter

TOPPING
8 oz (225 g) cottage cheese
8 oz (225 g) cream cheese
¼ pint (150 ml) double cream
3 oz (75 g) caster sugar
1 large mango
2 fl oz (50 ml) fresh orange juice
1 level tablespoon, or 1 envelope, powdered gelatine
DECORATION
Walnut halves

Line the base of an 8in (200mm) loose-based cake tin.

Crush the ginger nut biscuits. Finely chop the walnuts and stir into the biscuit crumbs. Melt the butter and stir into the crumbs. Press the mixture into the base of the tin, and leave in the refrigerator to set.

Press the cottage cheese through a fine sieve into a bowl, and mix in the cream cheese and cream. Stir in the sugar.

Peel the mango and remove the stone (page 397). Dice about a quarter of the flesh and reserve for decoration. Mash the rest and stir into the cheese mix.

Put the orange juice into a small bowl and sprinkle over the gelatine. Set the bowl over a pan of hot water. When the gelatine is completely dissolved, stir it quickly into the cheese mixture. Turn into the prepared tin and smooth the surface level. Chill for 2-3 hours or until set. Decorate with the reserved chopped mango and walnut halves. Run a knife round the inside of the tin. Remove the cheesecake and serve in wedges. This dish is included in a menu on page 301.

DRIED FRUIT COMPÔTE

As rich in flavours as any fruit salad at the height of summer, this compôte has the advantage that it can be served hot for a winter picnic or chilled, with cream, in summer. Use any dried fruits to hand. The flavours in the compôte improve if it is left to stand for several hours.

PREPARATION TIME: *10 minutes plus standing time*
COOKING TIME: *10-15 minutes*

INGREDIENTS – *serves 6:*
4 oz (115 g) dried apple rings
4 oz (115 g) dried figs
4 oz (115 g) dried apricots
2 oz (50 g) dried bananas
2 oz (50 g) sultanas
2 in (50 mm) piece of cinnamon stick
½ pint (285 ml) medium cider
2 tablespoons dark rum

Cut up the dried fruit if the pieces are very large. Place in a large pan with the cinnamon stick and cider. Heat gently until almost boiling, then cover the pan, lower the heat and cook gently, without boiling, for about 10-15 minutes, to soften the fruit. Remove the pan from the heat and leave to stand for at least an hour.

Return the pan to the heat and add the rum. Heat until almost boiling, then transfer to a wide-necked vacuum flask. Remove the cinnamon stick before serving.

SPICED PEARS IN WINE

Pears gently poached in spiced red wine turn a soft pink colour, soaking up all the different flavours.

Carry the pears in a plastic box, or an unbreakable dish covered tightly.

PREPARATION TIME: *30 minutes*
COOKING TIME: *1 hour*
CHILLING TIME: *overnight*

INGREDIENTS – *serves 6:*
6 firm dessert pears
¾ pint (450 ml) red wine
2 tablespoons lemon juice
1 cinnamon stick
7 oz (200 g) caster sugar
1 level tablespoon coriander seeds

Peel the pears and leave them whole, with their stalks on.

Pour the red wine into a large pan and add the lemon juice, cinnamon and sugar.

Tie the coriander seeds loosely in a small square of muslin

and add them to the pan. Heat gently, stirring, until the sugar has dissolved. Add the pears, spooning the wine over them, and cover the pan. Reduce the heat to very low and cook the pears gently, turning occasionally. The liquid should be just below boiling point all the time. After about an hour, the pears should be soft and translucent, but still whole, not mushy.

Remove the pears from the liquid and arrange in a large plastic box or unbreakable dish.

POACHED PEARS Whole pears soak up the flavours of cinnamon, lemon and coriander as well as red wine.

Cover and then place in the refrigerator. Strain the liquid, discarding the cinnamon stick and the bag of coriander seeds, then allow to cool. Pour over the pears and chill in the refrigerator overnight.

Serve chilled with cream. This dish is included in a menu on page 305.

REVEALING LATTICE Glimpsed beneath interwoven strips of cinnamon-flavoured pastry are juicy redcurrants and slices of apple.

APPLE AND REDCURRANT LATTICE

The best results are obtained if this tart is cooked in a loose-based metal French flan tin to get a crisp, well-cooked base to the pastry. Keep the tart in the tin to carry it. Wrap tart and tin in greaseproof paper and kitchen foil or clingfilm. The golden granulated sugar adds to the appearance and flavour of the flan, but if it is not available, use ordinary white sugar.

PREPARATION TIME: *40 minutes*
COOKING TIME: *45 minutes*
OVEN TEMPERATURE: *preheat to 200°C (400°F, gas mark 6)*

INGREDIENTS – *serves 6:*
PASTRY
10 oz (275 g) plain flour
½ teaspoon ground cinnamon
1 level teaspoon caster sugar
6 oz (175 g) butter, softened
1 egg yolk
1-2 tablespoons water
FILLING
1 lb (450 g) Bramley apples
3 oz (75 g) fresh or frozen redcurrants
1½ oz (40 g) golden granulated sugar
GLAZE
Lightly beaten egg white

Sieve the flour and cinnamon into a mixing bowl and stir in the caster sugar. Make a well in the centre and add the butter, egg yolk and a little water. Mix the flour in with your fingertips to make a soft dough, adding more water if necessary. Roll the pastry out carefully.

Grease a 9in (230mm) French flan tin and line with three-quarters of the pastry. Press the pastry into the sides of the tin, sealing any cracks. Trim away the surplus pastry.

To make the filling, peel, core and thinly slice the apples, and arrange in the pastry-lined ring. Scatter the redcurrants and sugar on top. Roll out the reserved pastry, cut it into thin strips and make a lattice across the top of the flan (page 288). Brush the lattice with egg white.

Bake in the preheated oven for 30 minutes. Lower the oven temperature to 190°C (375°F, gas mark 5) and cook for a further 15 minutes, or until golden-brown and firm. Serve either warm or cold with cream. This dish is included in a menu on page 305.

CHOCOLATE CRÈME BRULÉE

Crunchy, caramelised sugar seals these little pots of rich chocolate cream. Wrap them in kitchen foil and carry in an insulated coolbox. The chocolate cream may be prepared up to two days in advance and kept covered in the refrigerator.

PREPARATION TIME: *20 minutes plus chilling time*
COOKING TIME: *30 minutes*

INGREDIENTS – *serves 6:*
½ pint (285 ml) double cream
½ pint (285 ml) single cream
1 vanilla pod
4 oz (115 g) plain dessert chocolate
4 egg yolks
1 level tablespoon light soft brown sugar
TOPPING
6 tablespoons caster sugar

Half fill the base of a double saucepan with water, or place a mixing bowl over a pan of hot water so that it is not touching the water. Pour the creams into the double saucepan or bowl and stir, then add the vanilla pod. Place over a moderate heat until the cream reaches scalding point, 52°C (125°F). It is important not to over-heat the cream. Take the cream off the pan of hot water and remove the vanilla pod.

Melt the chocolate in a separate bowl over the hot water and stir into the cream.

Cream the egg yolks with the soft brown sugar. Pour the chocolate cream mixture onto the egg yolks, whisking. Return to the double saucepan and stir over a moderate heat with a wooden spoon, until the mixture thickens enough to coat the back of the spoon. Do not allow the mixture to boil.

Strain the mixture through a sieve into six small ramekin or flameproof dishes. Chill in the refrigerator for 2-3 hours or overnight.

Heat the grill to high. Sprinkle the caster sugar in a fairly thick layer over the chocolate creams and place the ramekins under the grill. Brown until the sugar caramelises. Watch it carefully to see that it does not burn. Chill in the refrigerator for a further 30 minutes. It is best not to add the sugar topping more than 3-4 hours in advance because the caramel gradually softens and dissolves.

Barbecues

IT COMES with something of a jolt to learn that the original barbecues were wooden frames on which the Arawak Indians of the Caribbean used to smoke and slow-cook the limbs of their unfortunate enemies before eating them. The French, it seems, had the most delicate flavour, while the Spanish were chewy and gave rise to indigestion. The name barbecue comes from the American-Spanish word for the frame – 'barbacoa'.

Cooking over charcoal has appeared in almost every culture at one time or another. It is a clean fuel, it can produce great heat from a small bulk and it is easily transportable. It was, therefore, from Roman times, the fuel of the soldier, the shepherd and the wandering herdsman who used to grill meat, fish and vegetables in much the same way as the present day barbecue enthusiast. All the same, it is surprising that, in the Western world at least, electricity and gas have not obliterated this kind of primitive cookery for ever.

Far from it, in the 20th century barbecues are held on a scale that would have astonished a Greek shepherd. At American political clambakes, to entertain loyal party workers, hundreds of lobsters, steamer clams, sweetcorns, potatoes and spare ribs are cooked on the beach over huge pits of charcoal, and under seaweed. At the Texas equivalent, a steer is roasted whole upon hot stones.

In Britain, thousands of trays of charcoal twinkle in gardens on warm summer evenings. The food cooked over them is no less adventurously flavoured, and for the housewife there is the added advantage that on these occasions at least, it is the men who usually insist on doing the cooking.

Planning & Preparation

A barbecue party combines all the pleasure of eating campfire food with the convenience of being in your own garden, near your own kitchen. The equipment need not be elaborate or expensive (see pages 339–340).

Siting the barbecue

Place the barbecue fairly close to the kitchen so that it is easy to carry things backwards and forwards, and also near a power point in case you need extension leads for lighting or music. Unless you have absolute confidence in a fine forecast, try to site it close to some sort of shelter as well, such as a barn, lean-to or covered-in patio to which you can retreat if it rains. Alternatively, try to borrow or hire a canvas or tarpaulin canopy which can be attached to the side of the house. As a last resort, cook the food on the barbecue outside the house, in the garage for example, keep it warm in the oven and serve it indoors. Never light a barbecue in a confined space, there is not sufficient ventilation. If you have to cook in the garage, keep the doors wide open.

Position the barbecue between the tables from which the food is to be served and those which hold the uncooked food and the cooking equipment. Keep the drink separate from the food – this makes it easier to serve and cuts down on the chance of accidents.

Lighting

For an evening barbecue, lighting may be needed. The lights from the house or a few spotlights may be enough to eat by. Candles or nightlights stuck in jam jars can be dotted around the garden. These can also be used to warn of possible dangers such as ponds. Also available are flares which are simply stuck into the ground and will burn for several hours. It is essential to have good lighting around the barbecue itself both for safety and so that the cook can see what she is doing.

Seating

Provide some tables and chairs. Temporary ones can easily be made by laying old doors on something firm such as trestles or milk crates, and resting planks on paint cans. Cushions on rugs on the ground will also do. If the evening is expected to stretch on, lay ground sheets or plastic sheeting to protect against the rising dew.

Planning the menu

Consider the amount of space you have and the size of your barbecue, as well as the occasion, when deciding how many guests to invite. If necessary, borrow or hire an extra barbecue, and organise help with the cooking. Appetites increase outdoors. It is wise to provide more food than you might do if cooking a conventional meal.

For a very informal party, with teenagers, for example, serve plenty of quick, simple food which can be eaten with the fingers such as burgers in baps, sausages for hot dogs or chicken drumsticks. Paper plates and napkins are perfectly adequate for this type of party. Choose paper plates with laminated surfaces; barbecue food tends to be greasy, making ordinary paper plates soggy.

For a slightly more formal party it is a good idea to provide a first course for the guests to eat while the food is cooking. For this kind of party provide china plates that will not be missed if they are broken. Not only is it easier to cut meat on a china plate with proper knives and forks, it does seem to make the food look and taste better.

Timing

Aim to have the fire at the correct temperature for cooking about half an hour after the guests arrive. The barbecue is ready for cooking when the coals have formed a grey ash all over. This usually takes 30-45 minutes. Gas barbecues take considerably less time (see also page 339). If you are not sure how long your barbecue takes to heat up, have a practice run before the party.

Prepare everything possible in advance. Once the cooking begins the cook needs to be able to concentrate on looking after the barbecue.

RECIPES FROM OTHER CHAPTERS

Many recipes from other chapters are suitable for barbecues – some dishes cooked on a grill or in the oven can also be cooked on a barbecue. The following are some suggestions:

Chicken drumsticks in honey and mustard 301
Grilled Halumi cheese with mint 195
Hot mincemeat loaf 30
Langoustines in ginger butter 206
Monkfish satay 299
Rump burgers with Mozzarella 67
Sage sausages with mustard sauce 21
Spiced butterfly prawns 295
White herb sausages 22
Yakitori 83

COOKING TIMES FOR SIMPLE BARBECUED FOOD

Even the plainest chop tastes delicious cooked on a barbecue. A marinade or sauce (see pages 332–333) adds interest. The timings below are approximate – much depends on the heat of individual barbecues.

FOOD	TEMPERATURE	COOKING TIME
SAUSAGES	Hot	About 5 minutes each side for full-sized sausages. Sausages can be part-cooked indoors first to cut down on spattering from the fat.
LAMB CHOPS	Medium	5–10 minutes each side depending on taste and size of chop. Lamb that has not previously been frozen can be served pink.
PORK CHOPS *about 1in (25mm) thick*	Medium	15–20 minutes each side. Pork must be well cooked.
HAMBURGERS	Medium	Rare: 3–4 minutes each side. Medium: 5–6 minutes each side. Well done: 7–10 minutes each side.
STEAKS *about 1in (25mm) thick*	Hot	Rare: 3–4 minutes each side. Medium: 5–6 minutes each side. Well done: 7–10 minutes each side.
	Medium	Rare: 5–6 minutes each side. Medium: 7–10 minutes each side. Well done: 10–12 minutes each side.
CHICKEN DRUMSTICKS	Medium	10–15 minutes each side. Chicken must be well cooked.

SOUPS & STARTERS

CARROT, POTATO AND CORIANDER SOUP

A soup as richly aromatic as this makes a warming start to a barbecue or a picnic. It can be frozen for up to 2 months, but do not add the milk, herbs or cream until just before serving.

PREPARATION TIME: *20 minutes*
COOKING TIME: *40 minutes*

INGREDIENTS – *serves 6:*
1 large onion
1 lb (450 g) carrots
12 oz (350 g) potatoes
8 oz (225 g) tomatoes OR 8 oz (225 g) tin peeled tomatoes (including juice)
1³⁄₄ pints (1 litre) chicken or beef stock (page 367)
1¹⁄₂ level teaspoons ground coriander
Salt and freshly ground black pepper
2-3 teaspoons lemon juice
2 level teaspoons tomato purée
¹⁄₂ pint (285 ml) milk
2-3 level tablespoons freshly chopped coriander or parsley
¹⁄₄ pint (150 ml) single cream OR 6 tablespoons soured cream, or lightly whipped double cream

Peel and chop the onion, carrots and potatoes. If you are using fresh tomatoes, skin (page 389) and slice them. Put the onion, carrots, potatoes and tomatoes, into a saucepan with the stock, coriander, salt and pepper, lemon juice and tomato purée. Bring to the boil, cover and simmer very gently for about 40 minutes or until everything is very tender. Cool a little, then rub through a sieve, or purée in a food processor or liquidiser.

Return the soup to a clean saucepan and add the milk. Adjust the seasoning. Bring back to the boil and then lower the heat and simmer for 2 minutes.

Before serving, stir in the chopped coriander or parsley and the single cream. Alternatively, swirl the cream into each portion of soup, or top each portion with a spoonful of soured cream or lightly whipped double cream.

This dish is included in a menu on page 336.

CHILLED LEMON AND ALMOND SOUP

Almonds were once a much more common thickening agent for soups than they are today. The 'white soup', for the Netherfield ball in Jane Austin's *Pride and Prejudice*, was probably an almond soup. Because of the delicate flavour of this soup, it is particularly important to use good-quality chicken stock.

PREPARATION TIME: *20 minutes plus chilling time*
COOKING TIME: *20 minutes*

INGREDIENTS – *serves 6:*
1¹⁄₂ oz (40 g) butter
1 onion, peeled and chopped
1 clove garlic, crushed (optional)
1 oz (25 g) flour
1¹⁄₂ pints (850 ml) chicken stock (page 367)
Grated rind and juice of 1 lemon
1 bay leaf
Pinch of ground mace
Salt and freshly ground black pepper
¹⁄₂ pint (285 ml) single cream
2 oz (50 g) flaked almonds, toasted
GARNISH
Thin lemon slices

Melt the butter in a saucepan and fry the chopped onion and the garlic, if used, very gently until soft but not coloured. Stir in the flour. Cook for 1-2 minutes, stirring continuously, then gradually add the chicken stock and bring to the boil.

Add the lemon rind, lemon juice, bay leaf, mace, and salt and pepper to taste. Cover the pan and simmer the soup gently for 20 minutes.

Discard the bay leaf and mace. Let the soup cool a little and then rub it through a sieve, or purée it in a liquidiser or food processor. Put the soup into a large bowl, and stir in the cream. Chop about two-thirds of the toasted almonds and stir them into the soup. Taste and add salt and pepper if necessary. Cover the bowl and leave the soup until cold, then chill thoroughly in the refrigerator until required.

When ready to serve, pour the soup into individual bowls, then garnish each portion with thin slices of lemon cut into quarters, and the remaining toasted flaked almonds.

FLAVOUR OF GREECE Almonds and lemon, key ingredients of many Greek dishes, combine to make a cool, delicate soup. Served with pitta bread warmed on the fire, it brings the flavour of the Greek islands to any barbecue.

SMOKED MACKEREL MOUSSE

The strong, rich flavour of smoked mackerel is moderated in this recipe, to produce a light, summer first course. Other fish such as smoked salmon, smoked trout or smoked haddock (cooked and flaked), can be substituted for mackerel. The mousse can be prepared a day in advance. Without the layer of aspic it can be frozen.

PREPARATION TIME: *30 minutes plus cooling time*
CHILLING TIME: *2-3 hours*

INGREDIENTS – *serves 6-8:*
12 oz (350 g) smoked mackerel, flaked
1 oz (25 g) butter
1 level tablespoon flour
¼ pint (150 ml) milk
Salt and freshly ground black pepper
Good pinch of ground mace or nutmeg
2 egg yolks
1 tablespoon water
1 tablespoon lemon juice
1½ level teaspoons powdered gelatine
¼ pint (150 ml) soured cream
1 egg white
7 fl oz (200 ml) liquid aspic jelly (made from powdered aspic)
GARNISH
Slices of hard-boiled egg
Watercress

Melt the butter in a pan over a moderate heat, stir in the flour and cook for 1 minute. Add the milk gradually and bring to the boil, stirring continuously. Simmer for 1 minute. Remove from the heat and season well with salt and pepper, and mace or nutmeg. Beat in the egg yolks, then cover and leave the mixture until cold.

Put the water and lemon juice into a small basin, sprinkle in the gelatine, then set the bowl over a pan of gently simmering water. When the gelatine has completely dissolved, beat it into the sauce, followed by the soured cream and flaked mackerel. Quickly whisk the egg white until stiff, and fold it into the mousse. Divide between six small dishes or ramekins and chill until set – about 2-3 hours.

When the mousses have set, pour a layer of liquid aspic over each one and chill again until the aspic has set. Garnish with slices of hard-boiled egg and sprigs of watercress. Serve with fingers of hot toast, hot finger rolls and butter, or Melba toast.

To make Melba toast, cut thin slices of white bread and remove the crusts. Toast the slices under a hot grill then cut them in half horizontally. Return the slices to the grill and toast the uncooked sides, or bake them in a moderately hot oven. Stale bread, cut very thinly, can also be used for making Melba toast. Bake on a tray in the bottom of the oven until the toast is crisp and curling at the edges.

TOMATO AND PRAWN RING

A ring of spicy tomato jelly filled with avocado and prawns can be served as a first course, or as an accompanying salad. An alternative filling is chopped, seeded cucumber dressed with yoghurt or soured cream, and freshly chopped mint.

The jelly should be chilled for several hours before serving. It can be prepared as much as a day ahead and kept in the refrigerator.

PREPARATION TIME: *40 minutes*
CHILLING TIME: *2-3 hours*

INGREDIENTS – *serves 8:*
1 pint (570 ml) tomato juice
3 tablespoons white wine vinegar or cider vinegar
1 teaspoon Worcestershire sauce
1 level tablespoon grated onion, or very finely chopped spring onions
4 level teaspoons powdered gelatine
12 oz (350 g) tomatoes, skinned (page 389), seeded and chopped
FILLING
2-3 ripe avocados
Juice of 1 lemon
4 tablespoons vinaigrette (page 371)
2 tablespoons soured cream or fresh cream
8 oz (225 g) cooked, peeled prawns
GARNISH
Watercress
A few whole prawns in shells

Lightly oil a 1½ pint (850ml) ring mould.

Mix the tomato juice with the vinegar, Worcestershire sauce and the onion. Put 3 tablespoons of this mixture into a small basin. Sprinkle in the gelatine, and then set the bowl over a pan of gently simmering water. When the gelatine has completely dissolved, mix it thoroughly into the rest of the tomato juice mixture. Stir in the chopped tomatoes. Leave the mixture to stand in a cool place or in the refrigerator until it is beginning to thicken – this may take from about 30 minutes to an hour. Mix it well and turn it into the prepared ring mould. Chill in the refrigerator until set.

When almost ready to serve, halve the avocados, remove the stones, scoop out the flesh and chop roughly. Put the avocado into a basin and toss in the lemon juice until evenly coated.

Mix the vinaigrette and cream together in a bowl. Add the peeled prawns and toss lightly. Drain the avocados and toss lightly with the prawns and dressing.

Carefully turn the tomato ring out onto a serving plate, and spoon the avocado mixture in the centre. Garnish with watercress and whole prawns.

This dish is included in a menu on page 329.

This dish is included in a menu on page 329.

M E N U

Sunday Lunch for Six to Eight

SPINACH NIÇOISE
opposite page

BARBECUED VENISON
page 327

BARBECUED VEGETABLES
page 331

GINGER TRIFLE
page 334

IN ADVANCE The day before, make the ginger trifle and marinate the venison.
ON THE DAY Start to cook the venison. Prepare the spinach niçoise and the dressing. Pre-cook onions and corn on the cob, and prepare any other vegetables for the barbecue. Finish decorating the trifle. Allow 1-1½ hours for the potatoes to cook.

Toss the salad with the dressing and serve. While the guests are eating the salad, cook the remaining vegetables.
TO DRINK A substantial red wine will complement the barbecued venison.

SPINACH NIÇOISE

Some inhabitants of the city of Nice in the South of France claim that a true *salade niçoise* should consist chiefly of tomatoes, with cucumber, peppers, onion, hard-boiled eggs, olives, and anchovies *or* tuna fish, but not both, and never any cooked vegetables. But today, even the Niçois mix tuna and anchovy, and lettuce and cooked french beans are ingredients frequently used in France as well as abroad.

This salad is yet a further departure from the original, with crisp cooked bacon instead of tuna, and the lettuce replaced by fresh young spinach leaves.

The French almost always serve salade niçoise as a first course, but this salad can also be served as an accompaniment to fairly plain meat.

Part of the appeal of this salad is its rustic appearance, so cut or tear the ingredients generously without too much concern over neatness.

CLASSICAL VARIATIONS Like many great ideas, salade niçoise inspires more. Here the tang of crispy bacon replaces the traditional tuna fish and fresh young spinach leaves are used instead of lettuce to make a refreshingly different barbecue salad bowl. But not too different: the black olives, anchovies and sliced hard-boiled eggs, waiting in the wings, proclaim that this salad remains authentically niçoise.

PREPARATION TIME: *20-25 minutes*

INGREDIENTS – *serves 6-8:*
8 oz (225 g) streaky bacon rashers, rind removed
8 oz (225 g) fresh young spinach leaves or spinach beet, trimmed
1 Spanish onion, peeled and very thinly sliced
1 green or red pepper, seeded and thinly sliced
4 oz (115 g) french beans, cooked and cut into 1½ in (40 mm) lengths
3 tomatoes, each cut into 6 wedges
6-8 tablespoons vinaigrette (page 371)
GARNISH
2-3 hard-boiled eggs, sliced or cut into wedges
1¾ oz (50 g) tin anchovies, drained
Black olives

Fry or grill the bacon until crisp. Set aside to cool on absorbent kitchen paper.

Wash the spinach very carefully, drain well and dry thoroughly. Tear up the spinach leaves and put them into a salad bowl. Add the onion, pepper, beans and tomatoes and mix lightly. Chop or crumble the bacon and add to the salad. Cover and leave in a cool place until ready to serve.

Sprinkle the vinaigrette over the salad and garnish with slices or wedges of egg, anchovy fillets and black olives. This dish is included in a menu on the opposite page.

CRUDITÉS WITH DIPS

While the main course sizzles happily on the barbecue, already sharpening appetites, the guests can pass round the crudités (literally 'rawnesses') with some mouth-watering dips. The vegetables for the crudités can be varied according to season.

Prepare the dips and crudités earlier in the day. Place the bowls of dips on the serving dish and cover. Arrange the crudités on the dish and cover completely. Set aside in a cool place or the refrigerator. Alternatively, store the crudités in a plastic bag in the refrigerator.

PREPARATION TIME: *45 minutes*

INGREDIENTS – *serves 8:*
EGG DIP
2 tablespoons mayonnaise, homemade (page 369), or ready-made
3 tablespoons soured cream
2 teaspoons lemon juice
½-1 level teaspoon curry powder
Salt and freshly ground black pepper
2-3 hard-boiled eggs, finely grated
½ bunch watercress leaves, chopped

CRISP CRUDITÉS Neatly trimmed crisp, raw vegetables make an appetising start to a barbecue when served with Stilton dip, egg and liver pâté dips, and – garnished with chopped nuts – pecan dip.

LIVER PÂTÉ DIP
4 oz (115 g) smooth liver pâté
1 clove garlic, crushed
1 teaspoon mushroom ketchup
1 tablespoon brandy or port
2 tablespoons soured cream
1 level teaspoon capers, finely chopped
Salt and freshly ground black pepper

STILTON DIP
4 oz (115 g) Stilton cheese
3 oz (75 g) full fat soft cream cheese
1 level tablespoon finely chopped spring onions
2 teaspoons lemon juice
2 tablespoons soured cream
Salt and freshly ground black pepper

PECAN DIP
3 oz (75 g) full fat soft cream cheese
2-3 tablespoons natural yoghurt
A few drops Worcestershire sauce
1 oz (25 g) raisins, chopped
1½ oz (40 g) shelled pecan nuts or walnuts, roughly chopped
Salt and freshly ground black pepper

CRUDITÉS
4 carrots, peeled and cut into narrow sticks
1 small cucumber, cut into narrow sticks
½ cauliflower, cut into florets
1-2 heads calabrese or broccoli, cut into florets
1 bunch radishes, trimmed
4 sticks celery, cut into narrow lengths
4 oz (115 g) button mushrooms, washed and halved or quartered
1 bunch spring onions, trimmed
1 red or yellow pepper, seeded and cut into strips
1 green pepper, seeded and cut into strips

To make the egg dip, combine the mayonnaise, soured cream and lemon juice. Add curry powder and salt and pepper to taste. Beat in the grated egg and chopped watercress.

To make the liver pâté dip, mash the pâté until smooth, then beat in the rest of the ingredients until quite smooth, adding salt and pepper to taste.

To make the Stilton dip, mash the Stilton and the cream cheese together until smooth. Add the rest of the ingredients, seasoning to taste with salt and pepper, and mix together until evenly blended.

To make the pecan dip, soften the cream cheese with a wooden spoon and then beat in the yoghurt followed by the Worcestershire sauce, raisins, nuts and salt and pepper to taste.

Serve the four dips with the prepared crudités.

MAIN COURSES

TROUT OR MACKEREL WITH FENNEL

The delicate aniseed flavour of fennel complements oily fish such as trout or mackerel, and is supposed to make such fish easier to digest.

PREPARATION TIME: *20 minutes*
MARINATING TIME: *2 hours*
COOKING TIME: *10-20 minutes*

INGREDIENTS – *serves 6:*
6 large trout or medium mackerel, about 1 lb (450 g) each
6 tablespoons oil
3 level tablespoons freshly chopped fennel OR 1 level tablespoon dried fennel
Salt and freshly ground black pepper
Several sprays of fresh fennel
ORANGE AND GARLIC DRESSING
Grated rind and juice of 1 orange
1 tablespoon lemon juice
Salt and freshly ground black pepper
2 cloves garlic, crushed
6 tablespoons olive oil
1-2 level tablespoons freshly chopped fennel OR 1-2 level teaspoons dried fennel
1 level tablespoon finely chopped or grated onion

Clean the fish (page 373) but leave on the heads, unless you really do not like the sight. Wipe inside and out, then make two or three slashes on both sides of each fish. Lay the fish in a shallow dish. Combine the oil, chopped fennel and salt and pepper, and pour over the fish. Cover and marinate for about 2 hours, turning once.

Whisk all the ingredients for the dressing together and put it into a bowl or jug ready to serve with the fish.

When ready to cook, remove the fish from the marinade, and put a large sprig of fresh fennel inside each one. Press a small piece of fennel into each of the slashes in the fish. Cook on a moderately hot barbecue for 5-8 minutes on each side, or until cooked through. Take great care when turning the fish, as they are rather fragile and tend to break easily. Just before they are cooked, lay more sprigs of fresh fennel over the fish – the fennel will burn and give extra flavour to the fish.

Serve the fish with the dressing handed separately – each person must stir it well before spooning it over the fish – and plenty of crusty bread and salad.
COOKING INDOORS Line a grill pan with kitchen foil, grease lightly, and lay the fish in it.

FEATHERY FENNEL The delicate aniseed flavour of fronds of fennel and a light orange and garlic dressing bring out the best in trout.

Cook under a moderate heat for 7-10 minutes each side. Take care not to break the fish when turning them over. Do not lay fennel over the fish as it finishes cooking – the burning may be dangerous in the kitchen.

STEAK ROLLS WITH MUSTARD SAUCE

Thin slices of steak spread with a coarse grain, herb-flavoured mustard, rolled up loosely and cooked on skewers, make a change from the usual barbecued steaks. Thin slices of rump steak, or quick-fry steak if well beaten, can be used instead of sirloin, but slices of fillet steak are not usually large enough to roll up. Use a prepared, herb-flavoured mustard.

HIDDEN TANG Herb-flavoured mustard spread inside rolls of thinly sliced meat adds piquancy to steak. The rolls are garnished with thyme and served with a salad of endive, oak leaf lettuce, lamb's lettuce and red radicchio tossed in vinaigrette.

PREPARATION TIME: *15 minutes*
MARINATING TIME: *1 hour*
COOKING TIME: *8-20 minutes*

INGREDIENTS – *serves 6:*
12 thin sirloin steaks, 4-5 oz (115-150 g) each, about ¼ in (5 mm) thick
About 3 tablespoons coarse grain mustard, flavoured with tarragon, thyme or other herbs
Coarse sea salt
Freshly ground black pepper
SAUCE
¼ pint (150 ml) mayonnaise, homemade (page 369), or ready-made
3 tablespoons thick natural yoghurt
2 teaspoons coarse grain mustard
1 teaspoon Dijon mustard
1 tablespoon wine vinegar
1 level teaspoon caster sugar
Salt and freshly ground black pepper

GARNISH
Lemon wedges
Sprigs of fresh tarragon or thyme

Lay the steaks on a board and spread the mustard on one side only. Sprinkle lightly with the sea salt and the pepper. Stand in a cool place for about an hour.

When ready to cook, roll up the steaks loosely with the mustard inside and impale on two or three long skewers, leaving a gap between each roll.

To make the sauce, blend all the ingredients together. Serve in a bowl or jug.

Cook the steak rolls, turning the skewers once, for about 8-10 minutes for rare steaks or longer according to taste. Serve, garnished with lemon wedges and fresh herbs, with the mustard sauce and salad.

COOKING INDOORS Cook under a grill, preheated to a moderate heat, turning the skewers once, for 8-10 minutes for a rare steak or longer according to taste.

This dish is included in a menu on page 336.

MIXED LAMB KEBABS

Shish kebabs – from the Turkish *sis* meaning 'skewer' and *kebap* meaning 'roast meat' – were first cooked by soldiers in the army of the Ottoman Empire in the 15th and 16th centuries. They are now eaten all over the Middle East and in Europe and North America as well.

PREPARATION TIME: *30 minutes plus marinating time*
COOKING TIME: *about 15 minutes*

INGREDIENTS – *serves 6:*
Large half leg of lamb (fillet end), about 2½ lb (1.1 kg)
8 oz (225 g) lamb's liver, thickly sliced
6 lamb's kidneys
12 rashers streaky bacon, rind removed
MARINADE
3 tablespoons Marsala or sweet sherry
1 tablespoon lemon juice
4 tablespoons oil
¼ teaspoon freshly ground coriander
1 clove garlic, crushed
Salt and freshly ground black pepper

Trim the fat from the lamb, remove the meat from the bone and cut it into 1in (25mm) cubes. Place in a dish.

To make the marinade, whisk together the Marsala, lemon juice, oil, coriander, garlic, and salt and pepper to taste. Pour the marinade over the lamb, mix well, cover and leave to marinate for at least an hour.

Cut the liver into at least 12 even-sized cubes, add them to the marinade and leave to stand for a further half hour or so.

Halve the kidneys, skin them if necessary, and cut out the cores. Wrap a rasher of bacon around each half kidney.

When ready to cook, drain the meat and liver, reserving the marinade. Divide the pieces of meat and liver, and the bacon-wrapped kidneys, between 6 long skewers, and thread them on, alternating the ingredients.

Put the skewers carefully on the barbecue rack and cook the kebabs for about 10 minutes, turning the skewers once. Brush the kebabs with the marinade, then cook for a further 4-5 minutes or until cooked through. Serve with hot crusty bread or boiled rice, and salads or baked vegetables.

COOKING INDOORS Turn on the grill to moderate heat. Place the kebabs in the grill pan so that each kebab will receive an equal amount of heat. If the grill is not large enough, cook half the kebabs then keep them warm in the oven while cooking the rest. Allow a total of 6-8 minutes each side, turning the kebabs at least twice during cooking and brushing with the marinade each time they are turned.

ASSORTED MARINATED CHOPS

A selection of three or four types of lamb chops, each marinated in a different mixture, adds variety to a barbecue. Pork chops or pieces of chicken can also be used, with or without the lamb.

PREPARATION TIME: *30 minutes*
MARINATING TIME: *at least 2 hours*
COOKING TIME: *10-20 minutes*

INGREDIENTS – *serves 6:*
*Selection of lamb chops – loin,
   butterfly (double loin), chump
   and cutlets – allowing 2 chops
   per person*
MINT MARINADE
3 level tablespoons mint jelly
2 tablespoons oil
1 tablespoon wine vinegar
*Salt and freshly ground black
   pepper*
GINGER MARINADE
3 level tablespoons ginger preserve
2 tablespoons oil
1 tablespoon lemon juice
1 tablespoon wine vinegar
Grated rind of ½ lemon
*Salt and freshly ground black
   pepper*
PORT AND MARMALADE
MARINADE
*3 level tablespoons coarse cut
   orange marmalade*
2 tablespoons port
1 tablespoon oil
1 tablespoon wine vinegar
*Salt and freshly ground black
   pepper*
GARLIC AND CORIANDER
MARINADE
4 cloves garlic, crushed
4 tablespoons oil
2 tablespoons red wine
1 level teaspoon ground coriander
*Salt and freshly ground black
   pepper*
GARNISH
Sprigs of fresh mint
Preserved stem ginger
Slices of fresh orange
Fresh coriander leaves

Wipe the chops and put each
type of chop in a separate shallow dish or container. Mix the

ingredients for each marinade
together and pour a different
marinade over each type of
chop. Turn the chops and spoon
over the marinade, then cover
the dishes and leave the chops to
marinate for at least 2 hours,
turning them once.

   Remove the chops from the
marinades and cook them on a
moderately hot barbecue, allowing 5-10 minutes each side,
depending on the heat of the
barbecue and the thickness of
the chops. Turn them over once
or twice during cooking. Once
they are ready, arrange them on
a serving dish.

   Spoon a little of the remaining
marinade over each variety of
chops before serving. Garnish

*LAMB CHOPS IN FOUR VARIATIONS
Marinades can be used to produce
richly varying flavours. Here chump
chops are marinated in mint, lamb
cutlets in ginger, butterfly chops in
garlic and coriander, and loin chops
in a mixture of port and marmalade.*

the chops marinated in mint
with sprigs of fresh mint, the
ginger chops with chopped preserved stem ginger, the marmalade chops with segments of
fresh orange cut into quarters,
and the garlic chops with fresh
coriander leaves.

   Serve with fresh, crusty bread
and a simple green salad.
COOKING INDOORS Turn on the
grill to moderate heat. Put two

types of chop onto the grill rack,
cook under the preheated grill
for 5-10 minutes each side until
they are cooked through, turning once. Keep them warm in
the oven while you are cooking
the remaining chops.

MARINATED
PORK FILLETS

Fillet of pork (tenderloin) is, as
its name suggests, very lean and
tender – perfect in that respect
for barbecuing. However, because of the lack of fat, it needs
to be well marinated and then
brushed with oil to prevent it
drying out during cooking.

PREPARATION TIME: *20 minutes*
MARINATING TIME: *2-6 hours*
COOKING TIME: *15 minutes*

INGREDIENTS – *serves 6:*
*4 pork fillets, about 12 oz
   (350 g) each*
3-4 tablespoons oil
MARINADE
3 tablespoons soya sauce
6 tablespoons medium sherry
7 fl oz (200 ml) dry white wine
1-2 cloves garlic, crushed
Freshly ground black pepper
*1 small onion, peeled and very
   finely chopped*
1 level teaspoon dried mixed herbs
Salt

First make the marinade. Put
the soya sauce, sherry, wine,
crushed garlic, black pepper,
chopped onion and herbs into a
fairly shallow dish or bowl.

   Trim the pork fillets, removing any gristle or sinews, and cut
them into 2in (50mm) slices. Put
the pork into the marinade,
cover and leave for at least 2
hours – up to 6 hours if possible
– turning occasionally.

   When almost ready to cook,
remove the meat from the
marinade and thread the pieces
onto 6 long skewers. Rest the
skewers on a plate and brush the
meat all over with the oil.

   Make a sauce by putting the
marinade (including the chopped onion) into a small saucepan
and bringing it slowly to the
boil. Simmer gently for 3-4 minutes, add salt and pepper to
taste and remove from the heat.

   Brush the pork liberally once
more with the oil, and then put
it onto the barbecue and cook
for about 5 minutes each side.
Turn over again and continue to
cook for about 2-3 minutes, or
until cooked through. Take care
not to overcook the pork, or it
will be very dry. While the pork
is cooking, stand the saucepan of
marinade sauce on the edge of
the barbecue to heat up.

   Serve the pork at once with
the sauce poured over it and
with crusty bread and salad.
COOKING INDOORS Turn on the
grill to moderate heat. Line a
grill pan with foil, grease lightly,
and place the skewers of pork in
the pan and brush with the oil.
Cook for about 10 minutes each
side, turning the pork several
times while cooking. Turn the
grill down when the pork is well
browned all over.

CORSICAN PORK CHOPS

The mountainous island of Corsica has been disputed over the years by the Italians and the French. In dishes such as this one, with sweet peppers and onion, Corsican cooking shows the influence of both her Mediterranean neighbours. The final flambé of brandy and herbs makes a splendid spectacle as well as enhancing the flavour.

PREPARATION TIME: *15 minutes plus marinating time*
COOKING TIME: *20 minutes*

INGREDIENTS – *serves 6:*
6 large pork chops
Salt and freshly ground black pepper
½ teaspoon ground coriander
6 tablespoons oil
1½ level tablespoons finely chopped fresh thyme or rosemary or 1½ level teaspoons dried thyme or rosemary
1 clove garlic, crushed
1 large onion, peeled and sliced
1 red pepper, seeded and sliced
1 green pepper, seeded and sliced
GARNISH
Sprigs of fresh thyme or rosemary
4-6 tablespoons brandy

Rub the chops first with salt and pepper, and then with the ground coriander. Brush the chops each side with 4 tablespoons of the oil and sprinkle with the thyme or rosemary. Put the chops on a plate, cover and leave in a cool place for up to 4 hours, until required.

Heat the remaining 2 tablespoons of oil in a pan, and fry the garlic and onion gently until almost soft. Add the peppers and continue frying for just a few minutes longer, then set the pan aside.

Drain off excess oil from the chops and cook them on a moderately heated barbecue for about 10 minutes each side, or until the chops are completely cooked through.

While the chops are cooking, reheat the pepper and onion mixture on the side of the barbecue. When the chops are cooked, transfer them to a flameproof serving dish and spoon the pepper and onion mixture over them. Lay the sprigs of fresh herbs on top, pour the brandy over them and, standing well back, set them alight. As soon as the flames die down, remove the burnt herbs and serve the chops and sweet pepper sauce immediately.

COOKING INDOORS The chops can be cooked under a moderately hot grill, allowing about 10 minutes each side or until they are cooked through. However, if possible, flambé the chops outdoors, for safety.

SPATCHCOCKED GROUSE Splitting the birds and flattening them with skewers ensures that they are cooked quickly and evenly. A sweet and sour barbecue sauce complements the distinctive flavour of the grouse.

SPATCHCOCKED GROUSE

Spatchcocking is an old English method of cooking birds by splitting them down the back, laying them out flat and grilling them over charcoal. The name is derived from 'dispatch-cock' – a fowl killed and cooked in a hurry. Small oven-ready chickens (poussins) can be spatchcocked as well.

PREPARATION TIME: *20 minutes*
MARINATING TIME: *2-12 hours*
COOKING TIME: *20 minutes*

INGREDIENTS – *serves 6:*
6 oven-ready young grouse
Juice of 1 lemon
2 cloves garlic, crushed
6 tablespoons oil
Salt and freshly ground black pepper
GARNISH
Watercress
Lemon wedges

Wipe the grouse with a damp cloth. Cut off the feet if you wish. Using a sharp knife, a pair of poultry shears or even strong kitchen scissors, cut carefully along one side of the backbone of each bird. Press the bird open, flat, cracking any bones as necessary. Wipe the inside of the bird, then hold it flat by inserting two skewers (metal or wooden) diagonally across it.

Rub the grouse all over, first with lemon juice and then liberally with the crushed garlic. Coat lightly with oil, then season with salt and pepper.

Put the birds into a shallow baking dish, or on a large serving dish, and cover. Leave to marinate in a cool place, for at least 2 hours or up to 12 hours.

Cook the grouse on a moderately heated barbecue. Allow 10-20 minutes each side, and take care not to overcook. Turn four times during cooking, or as necessary. Serve garnished with watercress and lemon, with chilli or sweet and sour barbecue sauce (page 333).

COOKING INDOORS Both grouse and poussin prepared in this way can be cooked under the grill. Because they are quite large, however, only two birds will usually fit under the grill so this is really a dish to make for only two people when cooking inside. Allow 10-15 minutes each side under a moderate to low grill. Take care not to burn the birds – it is best to start with lower heat and increase it towards the end of cooking.

BARBECUED VENISON

For centuries in Britain, wild deer were preserved for hunting by the king and court. William the Conqueror and his successors established savage laws to protect the deer. Today, a commoner no longer risks having his eyes put out for disturbing the animals, neither is hunting deer a royal prerogative, although they are still protected by Acts of Parliament.

Venison is increasing in popularity and becoming easier to obtain from butchers and game shops. The meat is lean and dark red, with a strong gamey flavour if it has been properly hung.

It is difficult to give an exact cooking time because the heat of every barbecue varies. As an alternative, the venison may be pre-cooked in the oven, and then put on the barbecue for the final browning. Follow the instructions given below for cooking indoors, until the last 20 minutes and then continue as for barbecuing.

PREPARATION TIME: *10 minutes*
MARINATING TIME: *at least 6 hours or overnight*
COOKING TIME: *2-3 hours*

INGREDIENTS – *serves 6:*
3¹/₂-4 lb (1.6-1.8 kg) joint of venison (use haunch, saddle, or loin, on the bone)
8 oz (225 g) streaky bacon rashers

MARINADE
6 tablespoons oil
¹/₂ pint (285 ml) red wine or medium dry sherry
1 clove garlic, crushed
2 dried bay leaves, crumbled
Salt and freshly ground black pepper
GARNISH
Watercress
Shredded white cabbage

Lay the joint of venison in a dish just large enough to hold it. Mix together the oil, wine or sherry, crushed garlic, bay leaves and salt and pepper and pour over the meat. Rub the marinade well into the flesh, then cover and marinate in a cool place or the refrigerator for at least 6 hours or overnight, basting occasionally with the marinade. Venison tends to be dry and so needs to be well marinated.

When ready to cook, remove the venison from the marinade (set aside the marinade). Wrap the rashers of bacon around the joint, then wrap everything in foil, securely, but fairly loosely. Place on a moderately heated barbecue and cook, allowing about 30 minutes per pound (450g), turning the joint several times during cooking. Unwrap the foil and remove the joint. Take care not to let any juices splash onto the charcoal in the barbecue – they might extinguish it. Put the joint directly onto the barbecue rack and cook for a further 15-20 minutes, turning once, to brown the meat well and complete the cooking.

While the joint is finishing cooking, put the meat juices from the foil into a small pan and strain in the reserved marinade. Put the pan on the side of the barbecue for the juices to warm through.

Put the joint onto a board and garnish with watercress and white cabbage. Serve, cut into fairly thick slices, with the hot meat juices, jacket potatoes, salad and chilli or sweet and sour barbecue sauce (page 333).
COOKING INDOORS Venison does not cook well under the grill. It can, however, be cooked in foil in the oven, preheated to 200°C (400°F, gas mark 6). Allow about 40 minutes per pound (450g), folding back the foil for the last 20 minutes to brown the joint.

This dish is included in a menu on page 318.

RIGHT ROYAL VENISON Once the meat of the king and his court, venison is now available to discerning commoners. Here it is cooked in a manner worthy of a royal banquet. Bowls of hot meat juices and chilli barbecue sauce are ready to pour over the venison which is served with jacket potatoes and a salad of red and white cabbage, apple, button mushrooms, grated orange rind and chopped parsley, tossed in vinaigrette.

327

INDIAN SPICED CHICKEN

The marinade for this dish is based on traditional Indian tandoori recipes. The rubbing in and marinating processes impart a unique flavour to the chicken, and yoghurt – which is the basis of the marinade – tenderises it. Food colouring, often used by Indian cooks, gives the chicken the characteristic appearance of tandoori dishes, but it can be omitted.

The dish can be prepared up to 2 days in advance – the flavour improves the longer the chicken is left in the marinade.

PREPARATION TIME: *25 minutes*
MARINATING TIME: *24-48 hours*
COOKING TIME: *30-40 minutes*

INGREDIENTS – *serves 6:*
3 oven-ready chickens, 2½ lb
(1.1 kg) each
6 tablespoons wine vinegar
¾ pint (450 ml) natural yoghurt
2 large onions, peeled and
quartered
3-4 cloves garlic, peeled
3 oz (75 g) fresh ginger, peeled
½ lemon, sliced OR finely grated
rind and juice of ½ lemon (see
method)
1½ level teaspoons garam masala
¾ teaspoon chilli powder
¾ teaspoon paprika
1-2 teaspoons yellow liquid food
colouring (optional)
1-2 teaspoons cochineal or red
food colouring (optional)
1 level teaspoon salt
About 2 tablespoons lemon juice

GARNISH
Crisp lettuce leaves
Lemon or lime wedges
Tomato slices
Onion slices

Cut the chickens in half completely, and cut off the wing tips. Remove the skin. Using a sharp knife, make three or four deep slashes in the flesh.

Place the vinegar and a little of the yoghurt in a liquidiser or food processor. Switch to the lowest setting – if it has variable speed – and gradually add the onion, garlic and ginger, blending until the mixture is thoroughly puréed. Then add the sliced lemon and continue until blended, followed by the spices and colourings, the rest of the yoghurt but not the salt. Alternatively, if you do not have a liquidiser or processor, chop the onion very finely, or mince it. Chop the garlic and ginger finely, then grind to a paste in a pestle and mortar or with the end of a rolling pin. In the pestle and mortar, or a mixing bowl, stir together the vinegar and a little of the yoghurt, then add the onion, garlic, ginger, rind and juice of the half lemon, spices and colourings and the rest of the yoghurt. Stir until thoroughly mixed.

Rub the chicken pieces all over first with the salt and then with the lemon juice, making sure both are rubbed well into the cuts.

Put the chicken into a large dish or shallow baking tray and pour the marinade over it. Cover the dish or tray very securely with kitchen foil to contain the rather pungent smell, and put it into the refrigerator for 24-48 hours. Turn the chicken over once or twice during this time, if possible.

When ready to cook, drain off excess marinade and cook the pieces of chicken on a moderately heated barbecue for 15-20 minutes each side, or until cooked through. Arrange on a bed of lettuce, and garnish with lemon or lime wedges, and slices of tomato and raw onion. Serve with a crisp salad.

COOKING INDOORS This dish can be cooked under a moderate grill, standing the pieces of chicken in the grill pan and allowing 15 minutes or so each side. Alternatively, preheat the oven to 180°C (350°F, gas mark 4). Put the chicken, still on its marinating tray (provided it is ovenproof), but without the foil, into the preheated oven for about 1½ hours until well browned and cooked through.

This dish is included in a menu on the opposite page.

INDIAN MIDSUMMER Chicken prepared with a marinade of spices and yoghurt brings a suggestion of India to a midsummer party. When cooking for large numbers it is more convenient to use chicken legs than halved chickens. The broccoli salad includes spring onions, new potatoes and cubes of smooth Edam cheese tossed in a light dressing.

MENU

Midsummer Barbecue for 25

TOMATO AND PRAWN RING
page 318

INDIAN SPICED CHICKEN
opposite page

PASTA MEDLEY *page 330*

BROCCOLI SALAD *page 330*

GREEN SALAD

HERB AND GARLIC BREADS *page 333*

CHESTNUT SOUFFLÉ *page 335*

BELGIAN TORTE *page 334*

CHEESE

For the tandoori chicken, buy 25-35 chicken legs rather than half chickens. Make 4 times the quantity of marinade. Make 3 times the quantity of the pasta and broccoli salads and the bread. Make two tomato and prawn rings, two Belgian torten and three soufflés.
IN ADVANCE 2 days before, prepare the chicken and leave to marinate until needed. Allow about 3 hours the day before, to make the torten, the prawn and tomato rings and the chestnut soufflés.
ON THE DAY Allow about 3 hours. Make the macaroni and broccoli salads. Prepare the green salad and the dressing. Make the sauce for the torten. Prepare the herb and garlic breads ready for cooking. Decorate the soufflé.

Allow plenty of time for cooking the chicken – especially if you have to do it in batches. Start to heat the herb and garlic breads 10 minutes before serving.
TO DRINK Lager or dry white wine.

SALADS & VEGETABLES

RADICCHIO SALAD

Until fairly recently it would have been necessary to take a trip to Italy to find radicchio, but it is now becoming much more readily available here. If no radicchio is available, however, the salad can be made without it, although the appearance will not be as striking.

PREPARATION TIME: *20 minutes*

INGREDIENTS – *serves 8:*
1 medium head radicchio
1 small head endive OR ½ large head endive
½ cabbage lettuce OR ¼ Webb's lettuce OR 1 Little Gem or Density lettuce
15 oz (425 g) tin artichoke hearts, drained and sliced (optional)
6 oz (175 g) french beans, cooked and cut into 1 in (25 mm) lengths
4 sticks celery, thinly sliced
2 in (50 mm) piece cucumber, diced or sliced
4 oz (115 g) green grapes
1 punnet mustard and cress
About ¼ pint (150 ml) vinaigrette (page 371)

Trim the radicchio and tear up the leaves if they are too large, otherwise leave them whole. Put the leaves into a salad bowl. Wash and thoroughly dry the endive and cabbage lettuce. Tear the leaves into pieces and add them to the radicchio with the sliced artichoke hearts, if used, french beans, celery and cucumber. Halve the grapes and remove the pips. Cut the mustard and cress from the punnet. Add the grapes and cress to the salad, and toss together until well mixed.

Serve the salad accompanied by the vinaigrette in a separate bowl, so that each person can help himself. Alternatively, add the vinaigrette to the salad and toss lightly just before serving.

RICH RED RADICCHIO A dash of Italian flair and colour is brought to a salad when red and white radicchio is mixed with artichoke hearts.

PASTA MEDLEY

Any type of pasta – plain, wholewheat or spinach-flavoured – can be used in this colourful salad of pasta, nuts, vegetables and dried fruit. The shape of pasta can also be varied, and any of the many pasta shapes, noodles, or even spaghetti cut into short lengths, are possible alternatives to the varieties of pasta suggested here.

The salad, without the dressing, can be prepared earlier in the day, and kept covered in a cool place. Add the dressing up to 2 hours before serving.

PREPARATION AND COOKING
TIME: *30 minutes*

INGREDIENTS – *serves 8:*
4 oz (115 g) wholewheat, ridged macaroni
4 oz (115 g) plain pasta shells
4 oz (115 g) green eliche
3 tablespoons oil
Salt
¼ cucumber, diced
3-4 carrots, peeled and cut into narrow sticks or diced
1 green pepper, seeded and finely chopped
8 spring onions, trimmed and sliced
4 oz (115 g) salted peanuts
2 oz (50 g) raisins or stoned, chopped ready-to-eat prunes
2 tablespoons single cream
2 tablespoons vinaigrette (page 371)
2 level teaspoons French coarse grain mustard
Freshly ground black pepper

Bring three saucepans of water to a fast boil. Add 1 tablespoon of oil and 1 level teaspoon of salt to each one. Cook the three pastas separately for about 10 minutes, or according to the instructions on the packets, until just tender. Do not overcook. The pasta should be *al dente* – still with a slight bite to it. Drain, rinse under cold running water and drain again very thoroughly.

Mix the three pastas in a large bowl. Add the cucumber, carrots, pepper, spring onions, peanuts, and raisins or prunes. Leave to cool.

Mix the cream with the vinaigrette, mustard, and salt and pepper to taste. Pour over the salad, and toss well.

This dish is included in a menu on page 329.

HARLEQUIN SALAD Ridged wholewheat macaroni, pasta shells, and green eliche (shaped like screw propellers) are combined with vegetables and dried fruit to make a multicoloured salad.

BROCCOLI SALAD

Fresh broccoli or calabrese give the best texture for this salad, but frozen broccoli can also be used as long as it is cooked only briefly. If you prefer a more crumbly cheese than Edam or Svenbo, substitute Cheshire or Lancashire.

PREPARATION AND COOKING
TIME: *40 minutes*

INGREDIENTS – *serves 6-8:*
1½-2 lb (700-900 g) tiny new potatoes, well scrubbed
¼ pint (150 ml) vinaigrette (page 371)
2-3 tablespoons single cream or natural yoghurt
1 lb (450 g) broccoli or calabrese
1 bunch spring onions, trimmed and thinly sliced
8 oz (225 g) Edam or Danish Svenbo cheese
Salt and freshly ground black pepper

Cook the new potatoes in their skins in boiling salted water for about 10 minutes, or until just tender.

Drain the potatoes and put them into a bowl. Halve or quarter any large ones.

Shake the vinaigrette well, and mix it with the cream or yoghurt. Pour the dressing over the hot potatoes. Mix well, cover and leave until cold.

While the potatoes are cooling, cut the broccoli or calabrese into smallish pieces, and cook them in boiling salted water for

a few minutes until tender but still crisp. Drain, rinse under cold running water and drain again very thoroughly. Add to the potatoes with the sliced spring onions and mix lightly.

Cut the cheese into ½in (15mm) cubes and add it to the salad. Mix well, and season to taste with salt and pepper. Turn the salad into a bowl and cover. Keep in a cool place until needed. This dish is included in a menu on page 329.

SUMMER POTATO SALAD

If very tiny potatoes are unavailable for this salad, use larger ones, peeled and cooked whole. Cut the potatoes into smaller pieces before tossing them with the vinaigrette.

PREPARATION AND COOKING
TIME: *45 minutes*

INGREDIENTS – *serves 8:*
1½-2 lb (700-900 g) tiny new potatoes, well scrubbed
3 tablespoons vinaigrette (page 371)
2-3 eggs
8 oz (225 g) streaky bacon rashers, rind removed
½ bunch spring onions, trimmed and thinly sliced OR 3 level tablespoons snipped chives
2 bunches watercress, washed, dried and trimmed
2 level tablespoons freshly chopped mixed herbs or chopped parsley

SAUCE
¼ pint (150 ml) soured cream
1 level tablespoon mild French
    mustard
1 level teaspoon caster sugar
1 tablespoon wine vinegar or
    lemon juice
Salt and freshly ground black
    pepper

Cook the potatoes in boiling salted water until they are just tender – do not overcook. Drain them well and put them into a bowl. Add the vinaigrette, toss well and leave until cold.

While the potatoes are cooling, hard-boil the eggs. Run them under cold running water, then shell and chop them.

Cook the bacon rashers under a moderate grill until well browned and crisp, turning once. Drain on absorbent paper. When cold, crumble the bacon and mix with the spring onions or chives and the chopped eggs. Add to the potatoes, tossing until all the ingredients are evenly mixed. Turn the salad into a serving bowl and arrange sprigs of watercress around the edge of the bowl.

To make the sauce, combine all the ingredients, whisking well together. Season to taste with salt and pepper.

Spoon the sauce over the salad so it trickles down﹑between the potatoes. Sprinkle with the chopped fresh herbs or parsley and keep covered until needed.

This dish is included in a menu on page 323.

BARBECUED VEGETABLES

Vegetables can be cooked on the barbecue, either impaled on skewers or wrapped in foil. Some are best partly pre-cooked, which can be done earlier in the day. Select the vegetables so that all those on one skewer will take about the same cooking time.

Small vegetables tend to pick up the flavour of the barbecue better than large ones, and they also cook more quickly. All barbecued vegetables are improved if chopped fresh herbs are added to the oil with which the vegetables are brushed.

CORN ON THE COB Strip the husks off the corn and remove the silky threads (page 386). Put the cobs into boiling salted water and boil for 10-20 minutes, until they just give when pierced with a knife. Drain and wrap in buttered foil. If they are very large, cut each cob in half or even smaller.

Place the foil-wrapped corn on the barbecue rack for 15-20 minutes, turning several times. Unwrap the cobs and eat them as they are, or impale them on skewers and return them to the barbecue for about 5 minutes to brown and pick up a more smoky flavour. Serve with melted butter.

GREEN OR RED PEPPERS Cut the peppers into quarters or smaller pieces. Remove the seeds, then brush the peppers with oil and impale them on skewers. The pieces of pepper need only a few minutes on the barbecue (turned once). Alternatively, wrap them in buttered foil and cook them for about 20 minutes on the barbecue. Small squares of pepper can also be threaded on skewers with pieces of meat.

ONIONS Put them into boiling, salted water and boil for about 10-15 minutes, depending on their size, to half cook them. Pierce with a sharp knife to make sure that they are still

PIPING HOT VEGETABLES *Chopped herbs in oil, brushed over onions, courgettes, peppers, potatoes and sweetcorn, enhances the taste of vegetables which are given even more flavour by the barbecue.*

slightly firm. If they are too soft they will fall off the skewers. Brush with oil and impale on skewers. Cook for about 10 minutes more on the barbecue.

COURGETTES Top and tail the courgettes. Cut them into thick slices, or simply in half lengthways. If you like courgettes crisp, do not pre-cook them. If you prefer them to be more tender, blanch the slices in boiling water for 1 minute or the halves for 2 minutes. Brush them with oil, impale them on skewers and cook for 5-8 minutes on the barbecue, turning once or twice.

POTATOES Use only medium potatoes or, better still, quite small ones. It is preferable to serve two or three small potatoes each than wait hours for large ones to cook. Scrub the potatoes well and dry them thoroughly with kitchen paper. Prick each with a fork and rub with oil or butter before wrapping in foil. Cook for about 1½ hours on the barbecue, turning several times. The foil can be removed for the last few minutes to crisp the skin.

This dish is included in a menu on page 318.

SAUCES & SUNDRIES

TOMATO MUSHROOM SAUCE

A little sauce helps enormously in barbecue cookery, particularly with fish, which can sometimes be dry. This mild tomato-based sauce brings out the flavour of the fish without dominating it.

PREPARATION AND COOKING
    TIME: *15 minutes*

INGREDIENTS – *serves 6:*
¼ pint (150 ml) tomato ketchup
¼ pint (150 ml) white wine
1-2 cloves garlic, crushed
4 oz (115 g) button mushrooms, chopped
Salt and freshly ground black pepper

Put the ketchup, wine and crushed garlic into a saucepan and bring slowly to the boil. Simmer uncovered for 10 minutes, stirring occasionally. Add the mushrooms and continue simmering for a few minutes longer until the sauce has thickened and darkened in colour. Add salt and pepper to taste, and serve hot or cold.

CITRUS BARBECUE SAUCE

A combination of orange and lemon with soya sauce and ginger gives a sharper flavour to fish, and is especially good with oily fish such as mackerel.

PREPARATION AND COOKING
    TIME: *15 minutes*

INGREDIENTS – *serves 6-8:*
¼ pint (150 ml) dry white wine
Grated rind of 1 orange
Juice of 2 oranges
1 tablespoon soya sauce
¼ teaspoon ground ginger
Grated rind and juice of 1 lemon
2 tablespoons oil
2 level tablespoons brown sugar
Salt and freshly ground black pepper
1½ level teaspoons cornflour (optional)

Put all the ingredients except the cornflour into a saucepan and bring slowly to the boil. Simmer, uncovered, for about 3-4 minutes. Taste and add more salt and pepper if necessary.

   If you want to thicken the sauce, blend the cornflour with a little cold water and then stir it into the sauce. Bring back to the boil, and simmer until clear. Serve hot or cold.

A TOUCH OF SAUCE Two subtle combinations, tomato and mushroom and orange and lemon, stand ready to bring out the best in sea bass and mackerel cooked on the beach.

CHILLI BARBECUE SAUCE

The strength of this sauce can be varied according to the amount of chilli powder that you add. It is better to err on the side of caution initially, more can be added later if the sauce is too mild. The sauce can be served hot if the pan is placed at the side of the barbecue, or allowed to cool and served in a bowl.

PREPARATION AND COOKING
TIME: *15 minutes*

INGREDIENTS – *serves 6:*
2 tablespoons oil
1 onion, peeled and very finely chopped
¼ pint (150 ml) tomato ketchup
3 tablespoons Worcestershire sauce
1 level teaspoon chilli powder
¼ pint (150 ml) wine vinegar, red or white
2 tablespoons clear honey
1 level teaspoon dry mustard powder
2-3 tablespoons water
Salt and freshly ground black pepper

Heat the oil in a saucepan and fry the chopped onion gently until soft. Add the ketchup, Worcestershire sauce, chilli powder, vinegar and honey and bring to the boil. Blend the mustard powder with the water and then stir it into the sauce. Simmer gently, uncovered, for 5 minutes, then add salt and pepper to taste.

SWEET AND SOUR BARBECUE SAUCE

Simple pieces of barbecued meat and poultry taste more interesting with a sauce. This can be served hot or cold.

PREPARATION AND COOKING
TIME: *20 minutes*

INGREDIENTS – *serves 6:*
2 tablespoons oil
1 clove garlic, crushed
1 onion, peeled and very finely chopped
5 level tablespoons tomato purée
3 tablespoons lemon juice
3 level tablespoons brown sugar
3 tablespoons brown sauce (optional)
1 level teaspoon prepared English mustard
¼ pint (150 ml) red wine vinegar
Grated rind of 1 small orange
2 tablespoons orange juice
Salt and freshly ground black pepper

Put all the ingredients into a saucepan and bring to the boil, stirring occasionally. Simmer gently for 15 minutes and add salt and pepper to taste.

BARBECUE BAKEHOUSE Fresh bread tastes especially good outdoors, but even this can be improved. Here a wholemeal French stick has been spiced with melting herb butter and a plain one with curry butter. White rolls have been transformed into tomato bread with tomato butter.

HERB AND GARLIC BREADS

Although garlic is the most familiar flavouring for hot bread, others are just as good.

PREPARATION TIME: *25 minutes*
COOKING TIME: *10 minutes*

INGREDIENTS – *serves 6:*
2 long French sticks OR 4 Vienna loaves OR 12 muffins OR 6-12 pitta breads OR 12 rolls (brown or white)
8 oz (225 g) butter
3 cloves garlic, crushed
4 level tablespoons freshly chopped mixed herbs OR 2 level tablespoons dried mixed herbs
Kitchen foil

Cut French sticks or Vienna loaves to within about ½in (15mm) of the bottom crust, in slanting slices 1in (25mm) thick. Cut muffins or rolls almost in half, leaving a hinge at one side. Split pitta breads down one side and open carefully.

To make the savoury butter, soften the butter in a bowl and then beat in the crushed garlic and herbs until they are evenly distributed. Spread the butter over each slice of the French sticks or Vienna loaves, re-assembling the loaf as you go; or spread one side of the muffins, rolls or pitta breads and then close up.

Wrap the loaves or other bread in suitable sized packages of kitchen foil: about half a French stick per package, or one Vienna loaf, or 4-6 muffins, rolls or pittas.

When ready to cook, put the packages onto the barbecue for about 5 minutes on each side until they are piping hot. Open the package and fold back the foil. Put the bread into a basket and serve straight from the foil while still hot.

ANCHOVY BREAD Drain a 1¾oz (50g) tin of anchovies. Finely chop the anchovies and then beat them into the butter with plenty of black pepper, but no salt (the anchovies are salty). Omit all the other ingredients.

CURRY BREAD Beat into the butter about 1 level tablespoon of curry powder (adjust the amount according to taste) or a mixture of curry powder and curry paste. Omit all the other ingredients.

CHIVE BREAD Beat into the butter 8 level tablespoons of finely chopped chives. Omit all the other ingredients.

TOMATO BREAD Beat into the butter 2 level tablespoons of tomato purée. Omit all the other ingredients.

MUSTARD BREAD Beat into the butter 3-4 level tablespoons of coarse grain mustard. Omit all the other ingredients.

COOKING INDOORS Preheat the oven to 180-200°C (350-400°F, gas mark 4-6). Heat the foil-wrapped bread in the oven for 10-15 minutes.

This dish is included in a menu on page 329.

PUDDINGS & DESSERTS

GINGER TRIFLE

A trifle is one of those dishes which invites experiment. Almost any jam can be used, raspberry or apricot jam are more familiar alternatives to ginger preserve. Vary the fruit and the jam to complement each other; strawberries with strawberry jam, for example, peaches or apricots with apricot or ginger jam, and guavas or kiwi fruit with a jam such as gooseberry or greengage. The sponge can be soaked in sherry or white wine instead of ginger wine, and the decoration made of fresh or crystallised fruit, or glacé cherries and angelica.

PREPARATION TIME: *30 minutes plus chilling time*

INGREDIENTS – *serves 8:*
8 trifle sponge cakes OR *a Victoria sponge (page 149) made with twice the basic mixture and baked in two 7 in (180 mm) round sandwich tins*
6 oz (175 g) ginger preserve
¼ pint (150 ml) ginger wine
8 oz (225 g) raspberries, fresh, or frozen and thawed

CUSTARD
¾ pint (450 ml) milk
3 egg yolks
1 egg
A few drops vanilla essence
Caster sugar to taste
1 level teaspoon cornflour
DECORATION
½ pint (285 ml) whipping cream
1-1½ oz (25-40 g) blanched almonds, cut into slivers and toasted
A few pieces preserved stem or crystallised ginger
Gold or silver dragees

Split the trifle sponge cakes in half, spread each half with the ginger preserve, and sandwich them back together. If you are using a Victoria sponge, sandwich the whole cakes together with the ginger preserve. Cut the cakes into cubes and lay them in a glass or china serving dish, keeping the top fairly even. Pour the ginger wine over the cake, then sprinkle with the raspberries (as well as any juice if the fruit was frozen).

To make the custard, blend 2 tablespoons of milk with the egg yolks, whole egg, vanilla essence, 1-2 level tablespoons caster sugar and the cornflour in a heatproof bowl or basin. Heat the remaining milk in a saucepan until just below boiling point.

Pour the hot milk onto the egg mixture and mix thoroughly. Stand the bowl over a pan of gently simmering water and cook, stirring frequently, until the custard thickens. Do not let it boil, or the custard will curdle. Remove from the heat, allow to cool a little and add extra sugar if necessary, to taste. Pour the custard over the trifle, cover and leave until cold. Then chill in the refrigerator. It can be left overnight.

Just before serving, whip the cream until stiff, then spread it roughly over the custard. Sprinkle with toasted almonds and decorate with pieces of ginger and dragees.

This dish is included in a menu on page 318.

GLITTERING TRIFLE Gold and silver dragees, almonds and stem ginger add a theatrical touch to a trifle made with ginger wine and raspberries.

BELGIAN TORTE

Many continental torten are rich confections of cake and cream, but this one is an example of another kind – where the layers are pastry and jam or fruit – which is more practical for outdoor eating. The torte can be made 1-2 days in advance.

PREPARATION TIME: *1¼ hours*
COOKING TIME: *1½ hours*
OVEN TEMPERATURE: *150°C (300°F, gas mark 2)*

INGREDIENTS – *serves 8-10:*
3 oz (75 g) dried apricots, finely chopped
3 tablespoons brandy
8 oz (225 g) slightly salted butter
3 oz (75 g) caster sugar or light soft brown sugar
2 tablespoons vegetable oil
¼ teaspoon vanilla essence
1 large egg, beaten
1 lb (450 g) plain flour
2 level teaspoons baking powder
8 oz (225 g) apricot jam
SAUCE
15 oz (425 g) tin apricot halves
2 tablespoons brandy
1 level teaspoon arrowroot
GARNISH
Icing sugar

Soak the apricots in the brandy for about an hour, until the liquid has been absorbed.

To make the dough, cream the butter until soft, beat in the sugar and continue beating until smooth and creamy. Beat in the oil then the vanilla essence and beaten egg. Sieve the flour with the baking powder and gradually work it into the creamed mixture. Knead the mixture until smooth.

Grease an 8in (200mm) loose-based cake tin.

Divide the dough in half and coarsely grate one half into the tin, so that it covers the base evenly. Beat the jam with a wooden spoon until it is smooth, then beat in the apricot brandy mixture. Spoon the mixture evenly over the grated dough. Grate the remaining dough over the apricot filling.

Bake in the preheated oven for 1½ hours until lightly browned. Remove the torte from the oven and leave to cool. Run a sharp knife round the inside of the tin. When it is cold, remove the torte from the tin and wrap it in kitchen foil.

To make the sauce, drain the tinned apricots, reserving half the juice. Purée the apricots and the reserved juice in a liquidiser or food processor, or push them through a sieve. Turn the purée into a saucepan. Blend the brandy and arrowroot, add it to the puréed apricots and bring the sauce slowly to the boil, stirring frequently, until it has thickened slightly. Leave to cool.

Place the torte on a serving plate and dredge the top fairly heavily with sieved icing sugar. Serve with the apricot sauce and whipped cream. This dish is included in a menu on page 329.

CHESTNUT SOUFFLÉ

Instead of imitating the characteristic raised appearance of the baked variety, this soufflé can be set in a glass bowl. As a variation it can be made with very strong cold coffee instead of water. It can be made a day in advance or frozen, but do not decorate until just before serving.

PREPARATION TIME: *30 minutes*
CHILLING TIME: *2-3 hours*

INGREDIENTS – *serves 8:*
4 eggs, separated
6 oz (175 g) caster sugar
4 tablespoons cold water
8 oz (225 g) tin sweetened
  chestnut purée
2 tablespoons rum or brandy
4 level teaspoons powdered
  gelatine
8 fl oz (225 ml) whipping cream
Non-stick baking paper
DECORATION
1-2 oz (25-50 g) coarsely grated
  plain chocolate
A little whipped cream
2-3 marrons glacés

Prepare a soufflé dish, about 7in (180mm) in diameter, by tying a collar of double thickness non-stick baking paper around the outside of the dish, so that the top of the paper stands 2in (50mm) above the rim.

Whisk the egg yolks, sugar and 3 tablespoons of water together, using an electric beater, or in a mixing bowl set over gently simmering water, until very thick and pale in colour,

and the whisk leaves a trail when lifted. Beat the chestnut purée until smooth, then fold it evenly into the egg mixture.

Put the remaining 1 tablespoon of water and the rum or brandy in a small bowl. Sprinkle in the gelatine and set the bowl over a pan of hot water. When the gelatine has dissolved, leave it to cool a little, then stir it into

the chestnut mixture evenly.

Whip the cream and fold it into the chestnut mixture. Finally, whisk the egg whites until very stiff, and fold them into the mixture. Pour it into the soufflé dish and chill until set.

Before serving, remove the paper collar from around the dish and press the grated chocolate around the edge of the

PARTY PIECES Marrons glacés and whirls of whipped cream crown this chestnut soufflé. Less exotic, but no less delicious, is the Belgian torte with apricot sauce.

soufflé. Decorate the top with whipped cream and pieces of marron glacé. This dish is included in a menu on page 329.

WALNUT PIE

Give each guest a small portion of this flan, unless he is known to have a sweet tooth. Maple syrup makes it very sweet and sticky. The walnuts can be replaced by pecan nuts for an authentic American flavour. The pie can be made 1-2 days in advance. Wrap in kitchen foil or store in an airtight tin.

PREPARATION TIME: *20 minutes plus chilling time*
COOKING TIME: *50-55 minutes*
OVEN TEMPERATURE: *preheat to 200°C (400°F, gas mark 6)*

INGREDIENTS – *serves 6-8:*
PASTRY
6 oz (175 g) plain flour
Pinch of salt
3 oz (75 g) butter or block margarine
1½ oz (40 g) lard or white fat
1 level teaspoon caster sugar
1 egg, beaten
About 2 tablespoons milk or water
FILLING
1 oz (25 g) butter or margarine
6 oz (175 g) soft brown sugar, light or dark
3 large eggs, well beaten
6 fl oz (175 ml) maple syrup
1 teaspoon vanilla essence
Good pinch of salt
4 oz (115 g) walnut halves

To make the pastry, sieve the flour and salt into a bowl. Add the fats and rub them in until the mixture resembles fine breadcrumbs. Mix in the sugar, then add the beaten egg and enough milk or water to mix to a pliable dough. Knead it lightly, then wrap it in polythene or kitchen foil and chill in the refrigerator for 30 minutes.

Roll out the pastry and line an 8in (200mm) fluted flan ring, tin or dish. Line with greaseproof paper and baking beans and bake blind (page 393) in the preheated oven for 10 minutes. Remove the paper and beans and return to the oven for 5 minutes. (The pastry will not be completely cooked at this stage.) Remove the pastry case, then lower the oven temperature to 190°C (375°F, gas mark 5).

To make the filling, combine the butter and sugar then gradually beat in the eggs, followed by the maple syrup, vanilla essence and salt. Arrange the walnuts in the pastry case, flat side downwards, then carefully pour the filling over the nuts. Return to the oven for 35-40 minutes. The filling rises quickly, but will fall again on cooling. Serve with cream or ice cream. This dish is included in a menu on this page.

BONFIRE NIGHT PIE On a chilly November 5th, walnut pie, sweet with maple syrup, and chewy stick-jaw toffee will keep out the cold. Brightly coloured autumn leaves can be used to decorate the pie.

M E N U

Bonfire Night Barbecue for Eight

CARROT, POTATO AND CORIANDER SOUP
page 317

STEAK ROLLS WITH MUSTARD SAUCE
page 324

FRENCH BREAD, ROLLS
or PITTA BREAD

WALNUT PIE *this page*

FROSTED GINGERBREAD *page 122*

STICK-JAW TOFFEE *page 153*

Make 1½ times the quantity of soup and steak sauce (increase the quantity of steak slices to 16 and the quantity of mustard to 4 tablespoons).

Potatoes can be baked in a bonfire, if you wish. Prepare them as for *Barbecued vegetables* (page 331). Once the bonfire is burning steadily, push them into the embers at the edge with a long stick. They will take 1½-2 hours to cook.

IN ADVANCE Up to 3-4 days before, make the gingerbread but do not ice. The day before, allow about 1½ hours to make the walnut pie and the stick-jaw toffee.
ON THE DAY Allow about 1½ hours. Ice the gingerbread. Prepare the steaks and leave them to marinate while you cook the soup, and make the mustard sauce.

About 1½ hours before serving the main course, light the barbecue. While it is heating, reheat the soup and serve, then skewer the steak rolls, and cook them. The gingerbread and toffee can be eaten informally while standing round the bonfire.
TO DRINK On a cold evening, *Mulled wine* (page 180).

EMERALD AND JADE SALAD WITH ORANGE SHORTBREAD FINGERS

Any green-fleshed or green-skinned fruits can be used to make this glowing bowl of fruits steeped in a syrup of lime juice and white wine.

The fingers will keep for up to 10 days in an airtight tin.

EMERALD AND JADE SALAD

PREPARATION TIME: *40 minutes plus chilling time*

INGREDIENTS – *serves 8:*
2 limes
½ pint (285 ml) water
6 oz (175 g) caster sugar
¼ pint (150 ml) dry white wine
1 green-fleshed melon (such as Ogen or Honeydew)
8 oz (225 g) green grapes, washed
3-4 kiwi fruit
2 grapefruit
1-2 ripe avocados (but not too soft)
3 green-skinned dessert apples

Pare the rind thinly from the limes with a potato peeler, remove any white pith and cut the rind into thin strips. Set aside the peeled limes. Simmer the strips of rind in the water for 5 minutes and then strain the cooking liquor, reserving the strips of rind. Make the liquor up to ½ pint (285ml) again with more water, and put into a saucepan with the sugar. Heat gently until the sugar has dissolved, then boil for 2-3 minutes. Leave to cool, then pour into a serving dish with the wine.

Cut the melon in half, scoop out the seeds, and cut the flesh into cubes of about ¾in (20mm). Alternatively, use a melon baller and scoop out balls of the flesh – this looks more attractive, but is wasteful of the melon. Add the melon flesh to the syrup.

Halve the grapes and remove the pips. Add the grapes to the salad. Peel and slice the kiwi fruit and add to the salad. Cut the peel and white pith from the grapefruit with a sharp knife and ease out the segments from between the membranes (page 398). Add the segments to the salad together with any juice. Cover the bowl and chill.

About 2-3 hours before serving, squeeze the juice from the peeled limes into a bowl. Halve the avocado and remove the stone. Peel the avocado carefully, dice the flesh, and toss immediately in the lime juice, then drain and add to the salad. Wipe and quarter the apples and remove the cores. Slice thinly and toss in the lime juice (adding a little lemon juice if there is not enough lime juice). Add to the salad together with the remaining lime or lemon juice from the bowl and mix gently. Sprinkle the reserved strips of lime peel over the salad and chill until needed. Serve with the shortbread fingers.

ORANGE SHORTBREAD FINGERS

PREPARATION TIME: *15 minutes*
COOKING TIME: *15-20 minutes*
OVEN TEMPERATURE: *preheat to 180°F (350°C, gas mark 4)*

INGREDIENTS – *makes 25-30:*
5 oz (150 g) plain flour
1 oz (25 g) custard powder
4 oz (115 g) butter
2 oz (50 g) demerara or light, soft brown sugar
Finely grated rind of 1 small orange

Lightly grease two or three baking sheets.

Sieve the flour and custard powder into a bowl. Add the butter and sugar, and work together into a smooth dough with your hands (or blend in a food processor), then knead in the orange rind.

Roll the dough out to about ¼in (5mm) thick on a floured surface. Cut it into fingers about 3in × 1in (80mm × 25mm). Place on the baking sheets, leaving a little space between each biscuit, and prick each one several times with a fork.

Bake in the preheated oven for 15-20 minutes, until a light golden-brown. Cool on the baking sheets until firm enough to move, then carefully lift onto a wire rack to cool.

This dish is included in a menu on page 323.

COOLING DESSERT A salad of jewel-bright green fruits is served with orange-flavoured shortbread.

HAZELNUT CRISPS

PREPARATION TIME: *30 minutes*
COOKING TIME: *10-12 minutes*
OVEN TEMPERATURE: *preheat to 180°C (350°F, gas mark 4)*

INGREDIENTS — *makes 20-25:*
4 oz (115 g) shelled hazelnuts
4 oz (115 g) demerara sugar
About ½ egg, beaten
Non-stick baking paper

Line one or two baking sheets with non-stick baking paper. Toast the hazelnuts under a moderate grill until the skins split and the nuts brown. Cool, then rub off the skins and grind the nuts finely or chop them very finely.

Put the nuts and sugar into a bowl and mix well. Add enough beaten egg (a little at a time) to produce a pliable dough. Turn the dough onto a sheet of non-stick baking paper and cover with a second piece of paper. Roll the dough out until it is about ⅛in (3mm) thick.

Cut into 1½in (40mm) plain rounds using an oiled cutter, or into hearts or half moons. Transfer the biscuits very carefully to the lined baking sheets using an oiled, broad-bladed knife. If this proves very difficult, simply remove the trimmings from around the circles and transfer the paper and biscuits to a baking sheet.

Bake in the preheated oven for 10-12 minutes until golden-brown. Leave the biscuits to cool slightly on the tin and when just firm transfer them to a wire rack to finish cooling.

RUM AND PEACH SYLLABUBS WITH HAZELNUT CRISPS

The syllabub was a favourite Elizabethan dessert. Sometimes, cows were milked directly into the bowl of wine or ale to produce the frothy effect. More often cream or milk was just poured from a height. One theory about the name is that it was slang for bubbling wine.

The hazelnut crisps can be made 3-4 days in advance and stored in an airtight container.

RUM AND PEACH SYLLABUBS

PREPARATION TIME: *40 minutes*
STANDING AND CHILLING TIME: *at least 2-3 hours*

INGREDIENTS – *serves 6:*
3-4 fresh peaches
6 tablespoons rum
6 level teaspoons demerara sugar
SYLLABUB
7 fl oz (200 ml) medium white wine
Finely grated rind of 1 orange
4 level tablespoons caster sugar
1 pint (570 ml) double cream
GARNISH
Thin slices of unpeeled peach
Fresh mint leaves

At least 1-2 hours in advance, prepare the peaches. Either wipe them over with a clean damp cloth, or skin them by covering them with boiling water for 1-2 minutes and then plunging them into icy water so the skins can be peeled off easily. Halve and stone the peaches, then cut them into slices and divide them between six large glasses. Add a tablespoon of rum and a teaspoon of demerara sugar to each glass, and leave to stand.

Put the wine, orange rind and sugar for the syllabub into a large bowl, mix well and leave to stand for at least 1-2 hours.

FOAMING SYLLABUB A cloud of whipped cream and wine floats over peach slices soaked in rum. Delicate, heart-shaped hazelnut crisps provide a contrast in texture.

To complete the syllabub, add the cream to the wine mixture and mix lightly, then whisk until the mixture thickens enough to stand in soft peaks. Either pour or spoon the syllabub over the peaches in the glasses. Chill in the refrigerator for up to an hour. Garnish with peach slices and fresh mint. Serve with long spoons and the hazelnut crisps.

BARBECUE EQUIPMENT

In essence, a barbecue is just an open fire with a grill set over it to support the food, but many of the wide variety of barbecues that can be bought are highly sophisticated. If you find that you use the barbecue frequently, it may eventually be worth building a permanent one.

Types of barbecue

PORTABLE BARBECUES The most popular portable barbecue is the kind known as a *hibachi* – meaning in Japanese 'firebowl'. It consists of a rectangular or round metal firebowl (fuel tray). A grate holds the fuel – usually charcoal – just above the bottom of the firebowl, and air vents allow air to circulate underneath. The food is cooked on a grill, or grills, which are suspended over the firebowl. On the largest type enough food can be cooked for 10-12 people.

Other portable barbecues range from simple picnic barbecues which consist only of a grill supported by legs that fold under it, to elaborate ones with rotisserie spits.

BRAZIER BARBECUES Also known as party barbecues, brazier barbecues are like large round hibachis – 20in (510mm) or more across – which rest on long legs. All have windshields and on most it is possible to raise and lower the grills. Many have rotisseries for spit-roasting. On a large one it is possible to cook for 20 people.

UNIVERSAL BARBECUES The combination of two or three separate firebowls makes the universal barbecue very flexible. The firebowls can be used together or independently.

COVERED BARBECUES The lid which completely encloses the top of a covered barbecue, and reflects heat onto the food from above, makes it the most efficient kind. Whole joints can be cooked almost unattended on one. Air vents in both the lid and firebowl make it possible to control the heat inside the barbecue very precisely. If the lid is left off it can be used like an open barbecue.

WAGON BARBECUES If you give many parties, a large barbecue on a wagon or trolley may be the best type to buy.

GAS AND ELECTRIC BARBECUES With most barbecues food is cooked over charcoal. With a gas or electric barbecue, however, volcanic lava rock is heated by a gas flame or electric element until it glows – when it is hot enough to cook the food. The special flavour of barbecued food comes not from charcoal, which is odourless, but from the aromatic smoke produced when juices and fats in the food spit onto the coals – whether they are charcoal or lava rock.

Although expensive, this kind of barbecue takes only 10 minutes to get hot enough for cooking (compared to 45-60 minutes with a charcoal barbecue), and is easy to control.

Preparing the barbecue

If your barbecue does not have a charcoal grate, you must make a firebed. Line the bottom of the firebowl with heavy-duty foil, shiny side up. Pour vermiculite – sold in garden centres and barbecue shops – over the foil until you have a layer about 1½in (40mm) deep. The vermiculite will allow air to pass underneath the charcoal. A firebed should last four to six fires.

CHARCOAL Two forms of charcoal are available: lumpwood

COVERED BARBECUE
(GAS-FUELLED)

BRAZIER BARBECUE

PORTABLE BARBECUE
(HIBACHI)

PORTABLE
BARBECUE

WAGON BARBECUE

charcoal (loose pieces) and briquettes (charcoal compressed into small squares or ovals). Briquettes burn for about twice as long as lumpwood charcoal yet cost about the same.

Lighting the fire

Use only non-toxic barbecue firelighters – never flammable liquids such as petrol.

1 Build a pyramid-shaped pile of charcoal on top of the charcoal grate or firebed. The base of the pyramid should be just a little larger than the area taken up by the food to be cooked.

2 Insert pieces of a solid firelighter halfway up the pyramid, or squirt liquid firelighter onto the cold charcoal and leave for a few minutes. Light with a long taper or spill.

3 Let the fire burn for about 15 minutes until it is well established. Then spread out the coals evenly so that they are still touching each other.

4 Leave for 30-45 minutes until the coals are glowing, with a film of grey ash covering them. Hold your hand at about the height at which the food will be. If you cannot hold it there for more than 2-3 seconds, the fire is ready for cooking.

Preparing for cooking

To grill food directly over the glowing coals, it is only necessary first to spread the coals so that there is about 1in (25mm) between each coal.

When spit-roasting fatty foods, such as joints of beef or lamb, however, fats and juices in the food may spit onto the coals and flare up dangerously. To avoid such flare-ups with an open barbecue, clear a space in the centre of the firebowl and put in a large foil drip pan. Push back the coals so that they are piled two layers deep against the sides of the drip pan. Cook the food over the pan so that it catches any juices and fats.

With a covered barbecue, pile the coals only one layer deep against the sides of the drip pan if you want the food to cook slowly, or two layers deep if you want the food to cook fast.

If the fire does flare up, damp down the flames immediately with a water spray.

Controlling the fire

There are three ways to control the heat of the fire and the rate at which the food cooks.

● To increase the heat of the fire bring the coals closer together. To cool it, spread the coals farther apart.

● Adjust the height of the grill. Lower it to seal the surface of the food and for quick cooking. Raise it for slow cooking.

● Adjust the air vents. Open them to raise the temperature. Half close them to lower the temperature.

Putting out the fire

● With an open barbecue, transfer the burning coals to a metal-lidded coal bucket and close the lid. Alternatively, tip the coals into a metal bucket filled with water, then drain and leave them to dry.

● With a covered barbecue, simply close the air vents in the lid and firebowl.

Never pour water onto a hot barbecue. The sudden change in the temperature may warp the barbecue badly.

Cooking equipment

In addition to the barbecue, this equipment is essential.

BARBECUE TOOLS Long, wood or plastic-handled tools including tongs, a fork and a slice.

SKEWERS Flat-backed skewers for cooking kebabs.

BASTING BRUSH Long-handled brush made with real bristles, not synthetic ones which burn or melt in the heat.

OVEN GLOVES Well-padded cloth gloves, not plastic-coated.

KNIVES For paring and carving.

CHOPPING BOARD Solid, heavy wooden board.

MEAT THERMOMETER For cooking whole poultry or joints of meat.

WATER SPRAY A small spray of the kind used to spray house plants – to cool the fire if it gets too hot or flares up.

Also useful are steak and fish holders and a rotisserie set.

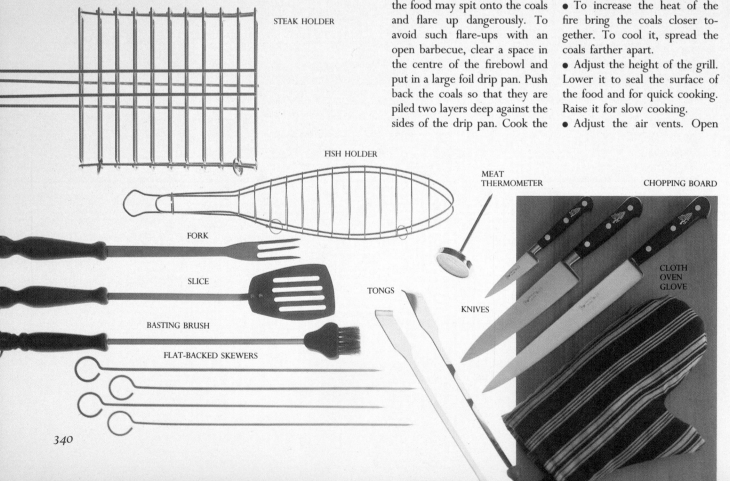

STEAK HOLDER

FISH HOLDER

MEAT THERMOMETER

CHOPPING BOARD

FORK

SLICE

BASTING BRUSH

FLAT-BACKED SKEWERS

TONGS

KNIVES

CLOTH OVEN GLOVE

Emergency Entertaining

SHOULD THE CAR of somebody royal break down outside your home on a rainy night when you have nothing in the larder but a few eggs, some herbs from the garden and a tin of beans, draw comfort from the case of Mrs MacDonald, of Monkstadt House in Skye. On an evening in 1746 she was kissed on her own doorstep by a strange, tall woman with a rasping growth of beard. Recoiling, Mrs MacDonald demanded of her husband who the strange creature might be. 'My dear,' he answered, 'it is your Prince' — as indeed it was, the fugitive Bonnie Prince Charlie. Disguised as the maid of the MacDonalds' young kinswoman, Flora, he had made the perilous crossing from Benbecula 'over the sea to Skye' and landed on the beach below the house.

Mrs MacDonald's reactions were, under the circumstances, a model. Beginning with a wail of 'We are a' ruined and undone! We will a' be hanged now' (for sheltering a fugitive), she proceeded to a panic-stricken review of her cupboard, which contained little more than eggs, cheese and butter, and concluded with a cry that she 'knew not how to behave before Majesty'. The hungry Prince reassured her on all counts, eggs were roasted with collops and plenty of bread and butter, and the meal was rounded off with bottles of small beer. 'God do him good of it', said Mrs MacDonald later. 'For well I wat, he had my blessing to go down with it.'

The moral of this and similar occasions is pointed out in a 19th-century cookery book. 'Perhaps there are few incidents in which the respectability of a man is more immediately felt, than in the style of dinner to which he accidentally may bring home a visitor.'

Planning & Preparation

When guests are unexpected the problems are: to produce a meal when nothing has been planned; to turn a family supper into a dinner party; or to stretch an existing meal to accommodate extra guests.

A well-stocked freezer, especially if you also have a microwave oven, is one solution to the problem of providing food on the spur of the moment. However, the recipes in this chapter can all be made quickly and easily from the contents of a reasonably well-stocked store cupboard (see pages 364-365). Many of them can be adapted to different ingredients. Do not reject very simple dishes such as an omelette with fresh herbs, scrambled eggs with anchovies, or spaghetti tossed in butter and Parmesan cheese, and a simple salad. Such an impromptu dish might very well taste better than something that has been planned weeks in advance.

The simplest way to stretch a meal is to add extra courses – first course, salad, pudding or cheese, for example – or extra side dishes, usually vegetables.

When turning a family meal into a dinner party, the quickest solution of all is a change in presentation. A meal intended to be eaten off family plates with glasses of water will look much more special served on the best china with pretty cloths and glassware and a bottle of wine. Add extra ingredients such as wine or cream to the food, and be thoughtful with garnishes (pages 285-290) and you have a dinner party.

First courses

- If your guests have to wait while you cook the meal, the time will pass more quickly if you give them something to eat. Provide nuts, olives and crisps, or make up some simple cocktail snacks (see pages 169-171) instead of a first course.
- The addition of a first course will stretch a meal – pâté and bread, for example, a tomato salad, grilled grapefruit, or lightly cooked or tinned vegetables tossed in vinaigrette.

Soups

- Add extra liquid – milk or stock – to a soup to make it go further. Remember to add extra flavouring as well. Thinned, chunky soups may have a better texture if they are liquidised. Alternatively, re-thicken the soup with cornflour.
- Croutons (page 286), chunks of warm bread or garlic bread (page 333), or small dumplings, will both stretch a soup and make it more special.
- Wine, port, sherry or cream can be added to a family soup –

give wine time for the flavour to be absorbed or it will taste raw.
- Swirls of cream, spoonfuls of whipped cream, liberal sprinklings of chopped nuts, fresh herbs, toasted almonds, paprika, finely diced tomato or cucumber or julienne vegetables (page 286) will all improve the appearance of a soup.
- The flavour of tinned soups is improved by the addition of herbs, alcohol or cream.

Main courses

- To stretch a casserole, add extra vegetables, a topping of mashed potato, pastry or circles of scone dough, or dumplings.
- Serve extra vegetables with a joint of meat or whole piece of fish, or include something filling like Yorkshire pudding, stuffing or forcemeat balls.
- If you have only a certain number of chops or chicken pieces, remove the meat from the bone and casserole it, or cut it into very thin slices and sauté it. Poach or bake fish, fillet or flake them, and serve with a sauce or as a fish pie.
- Serve a special sauce with a piece of meat or fish, or add wine or cream to a casserole. An accompanying sauce always makes a course appear more substantial.

Vegetables

- If you only have small quantities of each kind of vegetable, mix them together tossed in butter, purée them together (see *Carrot and potato purée*, page 356),

or turn them into a soufflé (see *Asparagus soufflé*, page 352).
- Fill out salads with extra ingredients (see page 389).
- Toss vegetables for a dinner party in butter and herbs, or add toasted almonds or walnuts to brussels sprouts. Serve Hollandaise sauce with warm vegetables, and mayonnaise or plain yoghurt with cold.

Puddings

- Fresh fruit makes the simplest pudding. Almost as good is cheese – a plain piece of Cheddar looks even better if it is presented on a cheese board with biscuits or bread.
- Fresh or tinned fruit is also the basis for many of the quickest puddings – fruit salad (with liqueur for a special occasion), peaches in wine, hot or chilled stewed fruit, fruit pies or casseroles. Some preserved fruit – bottled plums and exotic fruit such as lychees or guavas, for example – are good enough to be served on their own.
- Sauces can be used to add interest to ice cream (see *Butterscotch sauce*, page 361) and fruit.
- Pancakes (page 390) served with cream, ice cream or fruit make impressive puddings.

Wine

- To make a little wine go a long way, serve it as spritzers, poured into tall glasses and topped up with sparkling mineral water or soda water; or mix white wine with orange juice and mineral water.

SOUPS & STARTERS

CURRIED ALMOND SOUP

In winter, this unusual soup is a warming start to a meal. The curry adds a touch of spice and the almonds give body. In summer, it can be chilled and served with a swirl of natural yoghurt. Liquidising the soup makes it creamier, but this is not essential. For the best flavour use homemade stock or a good quality stock cube.

PREPARATION AND COOKING TIME: *20 minutes*

INGREDIENTS – *serves 4:*
1 oz (25 g) butter
1 large onion, finely chopped
2 level tablespoons mild curry powder
4 oz (115 g) ground almonds
1½ pints (850 ml) chicken stock (page 367)
Salt and freshly ground black pepper
1–2 teaspoons lemon juice (optional)
GARNISH
Coriander leaves, chopped chives or parsley, or a few toasted almonds

Melt the butter in a large saucepan over a low heat and cook the onion until it is transparent. Stir in the curry powder and cook, stirring, for 1-2 minutes, then add the ground almonds and the chicken stock.

Bring to the boil and simmer for about 10 minutes. Remove the soup from the heat and liquidise. Return to the heat. Add salt and pepper to taste, and lemon juice if used. Warm the soup through before serving. Garnish with coriander leaves, chopped chives or parsley, or toasted almonds.

This dish is included in a menu on page 357.

LENTIL AND TOMATO SOUP

Lentils are one of man's oldest foods. The Biblical 'red pottage' for which, according to the Book of Genesis, Esau sold his birthright to Jacob, was probably a pot of red lentils. Dried lentils will keep for several months, if they are stored in a dry place in an airtight container. They should be washed before cooking to remove any bits of grit. Unlike most other pulses – all dried beans, peas and lentils – they do not need to soak for long before cooking.

This recipe makes a thick, creamy, deep orange soup. For a thinner soup, dilute it with extra stock. To save time, use a tin of ready-chopped tomatoes.

PREPARATION TIME: *15 minutes*
COOKING TIME: *15 minutes*

INGREDIENTS – *serves 4:*
14 oz (400 g) tin tomatoes
2 level tablespoons margarine or oil
1 large onion, thinly sliced
2 slices smoked bacon, finely chopped
4 oz (115 g) red lentils
1 pint (570 ml) chicken stock or ham stock (page 367)
Salt and freshly ground black pepper
GARNISH
About 2 tablespoons double cream

Drain the tomatoes, reserving the juice from the tin, and roughly chop them.

Melt the margarine or oil in a large pan, and cook the onion and bacon together over a low heat until the onion is soft and just beginning to brown.

Stir in the lentils, then add the stock, chopped tomatoes and reserved juice, and stir well. Bring to the boil, then reduce the heat and simmer, covered, for about 15 minutes, until the lentils are tender.

Liquidise or sieve the soup, and add salt and pepper to taste.

Garnish each bowl of soup with a swirl of cream. Serve with fresh, crusty bread or toast.

30 MINUTE SOUP Lentils do not need lengthy soaking and simmering, unlike other pulses. Combined with tomatoes and smoked bacon they make a quick, sustaining soup.

POTATO AND ONION SOUP

Potatoes and onions on their own may seem ordinary, but this soup is not. A quickly made variation on the traditional French onion soup, it makes a hearty dish which can be served almost on its own for a light lunch or supper. The onion must be cooked very carefully without allowing it to catch and burn on the bottom of the pan, in order to achieve a good, rich brown colour. Use a well-flavoured stock to ensure that the soup itself has flavour.

PREPARATION TIME: *20 minutes*
COOKING TIME: *10-15 minutes*

INGREDIENTS – *serves 4:*
1 oz (25 g) butter or margarine
1 large onion, finely sliced
12 oz (350 g) potatoes, peeled and finely diced
1 1/2 pints (850 ml) beef stock (page 367)
1 bay leaf
Salt and freshly ground black pepper
GARNISH
Grated Cheddar or Swiss cheese

Melt the butter in a heavy-based pan. Slowly cook the onion until it is evenly browned.

FRENCH SIMPLICITY Onions, potatoes and cheese are all that is needed to create a warming variation on a classic French soup.

Add the diced potatoes, and stir until they have absorbed the fat and are beginning to brown. Pour in the stock, add the bay leaf, and bring to the boil. Reduce the heat and simmer for 10-15 minutes until the potatoes are cooked through. Add salt and pepper to taste.

Remove the bay leaf before serving very hot with grated cheese sprinkled on top, and with fresh brown bread.

SMOKED HADDOCK SOUP

The boil-in-the-bag variety of fish fillets is particularly convenient because it can be cooked straight from the freezer without defrosting. Dried parsley or tarragon can be used in this recipe if dillweed is not available.

PREPARATION AND COOKING TIME: *25 minutes*

INGREDIENTS – *serves 4:*
6 oz (175 g) boil-in-the-bag smoked haddock fillets
1 oz (25 g) butter
1 small onion, finely chopped
1 level tablespoon plain flour
3/4 pint (450 ml) fish stock or light chicken stock (page 367)
1 level teaspoon dried dillweed
Salt and freshly ground black pepper
1/2 pint (285 ml) milk
1 egg yolk
GARNISH
Croutons (page 286)

Cook the fish for 5 minutes less than the time stated on the packet. Drain, reserving the juices from the bag.

While the fish is cooking, melt the butter in a large pan over a low heat and gently cook the chopped onion until soft but not brown. Stir in the flour and cook for 1 minute. Stir in the juices from the fish bag. Add the stock, stirring, and bring to the boil. Turn down the heat and leave to simmer gently.

Remove the skin and any bones from the fish. Flake the fish and stir it into the soup with the dillweed, and salt and pepper to taste (no salt may be needed because of the saltiness of the fish).

Bring the soup to the boil. Remove from the heat. Mix together the milk and egg yolk and stir into the soup. Check the seasoning. Reheat before serving, but do not boil again. Serve garnished with croutons.

JELLIED CONSOMMÉ

Consommé is a useful item to keep for soups, and for dishes such as this. The brands of tinned consommé vary widely in quality, so it is worth trying several before deciding which one to store.

The curry-flavoured cream in this dish can be omitted, if you wish. The consommé can be served just with lumpfish roe or a little watercress or chopped parsley for garnish.

PREPARATION TIME: *15 minutes*
SETTING TIME: *15-20 minutes*

INGREDIENTS – *serves 4:*
14 oz (400 g) tin beef consommé
1 level teaspoon gelatine powder
4 tablespoons dry sherry
8 tablespoons double cream
1/2 tablespoon mild curry paste OR 1/2 tablespoon mild curry powder mixed with 1/2 tablespoon boiling water
4 level tablespoons lumpfish roe

Put the consommé in a pan, sprinkle the gelatine on top and heat gently until the gelatine is dissolved. Remove from the heat, cool slightly, and stir in the sherry. Place the base of the pan in a bowl of ice to cool.

Pour the consommé into four ramekin dishes, and put into the refrigerator or freezer to set. If the consommé is to be turned out, small tea cups or coffee cups can be used instead of ramekins.

Stir the curry paste or curry powder into the cream and whisk until thick but pourable. If serving the jellied consommé in the ramekins, spoon the cream over the top and decorate with the lumpfish roe.

To unmould the consommé, dip the base of the ramekins into very hot water for a second then invert onto a plate. Spoon the curry cream over the top so that it begins to trickle down the sides. Decorate with lumpfish roe and serve at once.

CHEESE PUFFS

Crisp puffs of deep-fried, cheese-flavoured choux pastry are a good first course when there is time to give them the necessary last-minute attention. They can also be served for a light lunch with salad. Instead of being deep-fried, the puffs can be cooked in a hot oven – 220°C (425°F, gas mark 7) – for about 15 minutes until puffed and browned, but they will not have the same crispness as the deep-fried version. The choux paste can be prepared up to 24 hours in advance and kept in the refrigerator until you are ready to deep-fry the cheese puffs (see also page 395).

PREPARATION TIME: *20 minutes*
COOKING TIME: *8-10 minutes*

INGREDIENTS – *serves 4:*
2½ oz (65 g) plain flour
¼ pint (150 ml) water
2 oz (50 g) butter
2 eggs
1½ oz (40 g) strong Cheddar or
  Parmesan cheese, grated
1 tablespoon prepared English
  mustard
¼ teaspoon paprika
Salt and freshly ground black
  pepper
Oil for deep-frying
GARNISH
Grated Parmesan cheese
Paprika

Sieve the flour and set aside on a piece of greaseproof paper.

Put the water and butter together in a large pan and heat gently until the butter has melted. Raise the heat and, when the liquid is boiling, tip in the sieved flour. Beat the mixture with a wooden spoon until it is smooth and leaves the sides of the pan. Allow the mixture to cool until you can comfortably hold your hand against the side of the pan, then one by one beat in the eggs and continue beating until the mixture is glossy. Stir in the grated cheese, mustard and paprika. Season to taste with salt and pepper.

To deep-fry (page 372), heat the oil to 190°C (375°F). Put teaspoons of the mixture, one at a time, into the hot oil, in several batches. (The mixture makes 12-16 puffs.) Fry for 4-6 minutes until puffed up and browned. Remove with a slotted spoon and drain on kitchen paper. Keep the cooked puffs warm in a low oven while frying the remainder.

Pile the hot cheese puffs onto a plate and sprinkle with Parmesan cheese and paprika. The puffs can be dipped into a sauce made with ¼ pint (150ml) of soured cream seasoned with 2 level tablespoons of chopped chives and a pinch of paprika.

LIGHT AND CRISP Cheese puffs, deep-fried for crispness, are flavoured with Parmesan cheese and paprika.

ON THE DAY Allow about 1½ hours. Prepare the ham loaf, then while it is cooking, prepare the eggs and place in the refrigerator, prepare the apricots and cook the artichokes.

Complete and grill the apricots while you are clearing away the main course from the table.

TO DRINK Dry white wine such as Soave or Muscadet.

CHILLED CAVIAR EGGS

An ordinary meal can be quickly turned into something special with this colourful, easily prepared, first course. If no lumpfish roe – 'mock caviar' – is available, use chopped anchovy fillets instead.

PREPARATION AND COOKING
 TIME: *25 minutes plus cooling time*

INGREDIENTS – *serves 4:*
4 large eggs
Salt and freshly ground black pepper
1 oz (25 g) butter
2 tablespoons single cream or top of the milk
1 small jar of black lumpfish roe

Whisk the eggs well with salt and pepper. Only a very small pinch of salt is needed, because the lumpfish roe is salty.

Melt the butter in a saucepan. Pour in the whisked eggs and cook over a low heat, stirring constantly until the eggs are lightly scrambled but still soft and creamy. Remove from the heat and stir in the cream to stop the eggs cooking further.

Leave until cool, stirring occasionally. To speed cooling, spread the eggs on a plate.

Have ready four ramekin dishes or small plates. Using about half of the egg mixture, spoon a layer of egg into each dish. Cover with a layer of roe, reserving 3 teaspoons of the roe to use as a garnish. Then cover with the remaining egg mixture. Heap half a teaspoon of roe in the middle of each dish. Chill in the refrigerator before serving with hot buttered toast.

This dish is included in a menu on this page.

SARDINE PÂTÉ

A light seasoning of paprika gives this easy pâté a slightly pink colour and a mildly spicy taste. It can be served as a first course with hot buttered toast, or as a canapé spread on cheese biscuits or small rounds of fried bread (see *Canapés*, page 172).

The pâté will keep in the refrigerator, covered, for 2-3 days. The preparation time is greatly reduced if a food processor is used.

PREPARATION TIME: *20 minutes*

INGREDIENTS – *serves 4:*
4 oz (115 g) tin sardines in oil, drained
2 hard-boiled eggs
2 oz (50 g) butter
1 oz (25 g) fresh brown breadcrumbs
½ teaspoon paprika
Salt and freshly ground black pepper
2-3 tablespoons lemon juice
GARNISH
Lemon slices
Paprika

Mash the sardines in a bowl with a wooden spoon or the end of a rolling pin. Finely chop the egg whites, then mash the yolks and whites together.

Cream the butter well and add the breadcrumbs, mashed sardines, mashed eggs, paprika, salt, pepper and lemon juice to taste. Mix everything together well. Alternatively, blend all ingredients in a food processor until smooth.

Serve in small individual bowls, garnished with lemon slices and a sprinkling of paprika. This dish is included in a menu on page 352.

SPICY SARDINE Tinned sardines make an excellent pâté, especially when spiced with paprika. A garnish of lemon slices, a sprinkling of paprika, and its humble origins are quite forgotten.

PRAWN VOL-AU-VENTS

Vol-au-vent cases can be cooked straight from the freezer for this dish, and the prawn filling made while they are in the oven. The quantities here are for a first course, but by using larger cases and more filling, the recipe will do for a main course.

Vol-au-vent cases may alternatively be filled with Béchamel sauce (page 368) mixed with ingredients such as tinned salmon or tuna, ham, smoked haddock, cooked chicken or sautéed mushrooms; or with any of the fillings for the *Tartlets or barquettes* (page 162).

PREPARATION AND COOKING TIME: *25 minutes*

OVEN TEMPERATURE: *preheat to 200°C (400°F, gas mark 6) or according to the instructions on the vol-au-vent packet*

INGREDIENTS – *serves 4:*
8 small uncooked vol-au-vent cases
8 oz (225 g) frozen peeled prawns
½ oz (15 g) butter
1 tablespoon oil
1 small onion, very finely chopped
Pinch of cayenne pepper
1 level tablespoon plain flour
1 level tablespoon tomato purée
1 level tablespoon mango chutney
1 tablespoon Worcestershire sauce
¼ pint (150 ml) fish stock (page 367) or water
Salt and freshly ground black pepper

Cook the vol-au-vent cases according to the instructions on the packet – they usually take about 15 minutes.

Put the prawns in a sieve and run them under the cold tap to defrost.

Melt the butter and oil in a saucepan over low heat, and cook the onion until soft and beginning to brown. Stir in the cayenne pepper and the flour, and stir over the heat for a few seconds. Add the tomato purée, chutney and Worcestershire sauce and stir in the stock or water. Season to taste with salt and pepper. Bring to the boil, simmer for 1 minute and stir in the prawns. Heat the prawns through, but do not boil again.

Remove the tops from the vol-au-vent cases and fill with the prawn mixture. Replace the tops and return to the oven for 5-10 minutes to heat through before serving.

LITTLE HAM MOUSSES

Veiled in pale green asparagus sauce and garnished with asparagus tips, these pale pink mousses make an elegant hot first course for a dinner party. A food processor greatly speeds up the preparation.

PREPARATION TIME: *30 minutes*
COOKING TIME: *30 minutes*
OVEN TEMPERATURE: *preheat to 180°C (350°F, gas mark 4)*

INGREDIENTS – *serves 4:*
½ oz (15 g) butter
1 small onion, finely chopped
8 oz (225 g) cooked ham
Salt and freshly ground black pepper
2 egg whites (reserve the yolks for the sauce)
¼ pint (150 ml) double cream
SAUCE
12 oz (350 g) tin asparagus spears
¼ pint (150 ml) single cream
2 egg yolks
½ oz (15 g) butter
1 tablespoon lemon juice

Butter four ramekin dishes (or individual moulds) generously.

Melt the ½oz (15g) butter in a small saucepan over a low heat. Add the chopped onion and cook until just soft, then leave to cool.

Process or finely mince the ham together with the onion. Add salt and pepper to taste. Gradually mix the ham and onion with the egg whites and then the cream.

Divide the mixture between the prepared ramekin dishes. Cover each dish with a sheet of greaseproof paper or foil and put them in a roasting tin. Fill the tin with hot water to come halfway up the sides of the ramekins. Bake in the preheated oven for about 30 minutes or until firm to the touch.

While the mousses are cooking, drain the asparagus and chop off the tips.

Make the sauce by processing or liquidising the stems of the asparagus with the cream and the egg yolks. Alternatively sieve the asparagus stems, and mix the purée with the cream and egg yolks.

Stir the sauce over a gentle heat until it is slightly thickened, but do not let it boil.

Melt the butter in a pan over a low heat, add the lemon juice then the asparagus tips and warm through gently.

To serve, turn the mousses

ELEGANT MOUSSE Asparagus sauce adds sophistication to a simple ham mousse – and careful presentation enhances it. Pouring the warm sauce over only half the mousse reveals a delicate colour combination of pink and pale green.

out of the ramekins onto plates and pour the sauce on top. Decorate with the asparagus tips and serve immediately.

347

MAIN COURSES

TUNA FISH KEDGEREE

Brown rice is the base for this variation on the Victorian breakfast dish but white rice can be used instead, cooked for about 12 minutes. The tuna can be replaced by tinned salmon, frozen kipper fillets or smoked haddock (cooked, skinned and flaked), prawns, or a combination of several different types of fish, depending on what is available. For a spicy flavour, substitute 1 level tablespoon of mild curry paste or curry powder for the garlic.

PREPARATION TIME: *15 minutes*
COOKING TIME: *25 minutes*

INGREDIENTS – *serves 4:*
8 oz (225 g) brown rice
2 oz (50 g) butter
1 clove garlic, crushed
4 hard-boiled eggs, chopped
8 oz (225 g) tin tuna fish, flaked
*Salt and freshly ground black
  pepper*
*¼ pint (150 ml) soured cream or
  natural yoghurt or double
  cream soured by stirring in
  1 teaspoon lemon juice*
GARNISH
Chopped parsley

Simmer the rice in plenty of lightly salted water for about 25 minutes, until soft but still slightly crunchy.

Melt the butter in a large saucepan over a low heat and stir in the crushed garlic. Stir in the cooked rice, chopped hard-boiled eggs, flaked tuna fish and salt and pepper to taste. Heat through, then stir in the soured cream or natural yoghurt and serve very hot, garnished with chopped parsley.

This dish is included in a menu on page 362.

GNOCCHI DI SEMOLINA ALLA ROMANA

In Italy, these baked dumplings – golden-brown and topped with melted butter and cheese – are traditionally served as a first course. They can also be served as a main course for a light lunch or supper, or as an alternative to potatoes or rice. The quantities here are sufficient for a main course for four.

These gnocchi are made with semolina – there are other members of the gnocchi family made with potatoes or flour. Some

*BUBBLING GOLDEN GNOCCHI Baked
dumplings Italian style, sizzling
straight from the oven, are equally
irresistible as a first course, light
lunch or supper.*

gnocchi are also flavoured with chopped spinach.

The gnocchi can be shaped well in advance: cover the cut gnocchi with foil and keep them in the refrigerator, for up to 48 hours, until needed. The mixture can also be frozen, but once baked the gnocchi should be eaten hot and bubbling, straight from the oven.

PREPARATION TIME: *25 minutes
  plus cooling time*
COOKING TIME: *15 minutes*
OVEN TEMPERATURE: *preheat to
  230°C (450°F, gas mark 8)*

INGREDIENTS – *serves 4:*
1½ pints (850 ml) milk
8 oz (225 g) semolina
*4 oz (115 g) Parmesan or strong
  Cheddar cheese, grated*
3 oz (75 g) butter
2 egg yolks
*Salt and freshly ground black
  pepper*

In a large pan, bring the milk almost to the boil. Stir well while slowly trickling in the semolina, and continue stirring until the mixture is thick enough to stand a spoon in. Remove from the heat and stir

in half the grated cheese, half the butter and the egg yolks. Season to taste with salt and pepper.

Dampen a baking sheet and spoon the mixture onto it, spreading and flattening it to about ½in (15mm) thick with a wet spatula. Leave for about 15-20 minutes, until the mixture is cool and firm.

With a dampened biscuit cutter or an upturned jam jar, cut circles from the gnocchi mixture. Butter a shallow oven-proof dish and cover the base of the dish with the offcuts from

between the circles. Sprinkle with half the remaining cheese and cover with the circles of gnocchi, overlapping like roof tiles. Sprinkle with the last of the cheese and dot with butter.

Bake in the top of the pre-heated oven for about 15 minutes until the gnocchi are puffed up, and brown and crisp on top.

Serve at once with a green salad or a vegetable such as grilled tomatoes or *Sautéed artichoke hearts* (page 357).

SPAGHETTI ALLA CARBONARA

One of the classic Italian pasta dishes, spaghetti alla carbonara is also one of the most simple to make. However, it is important not to overcook the eggs. The heat from the spaghetti cooks the eggs just enough to make a light, creamy sauce. But if the pan is left on the heat too long the eggs will scramble.

The bacon is grilled to make it crisp and not too fatty but it can, if you prefer, be chopped and fried gently in the butter before adding the cooked and drained spaghetti. Milk can be used instead of cream, but the sauce will not be quite as rich. If possible use freshly grated Parmesan. Ready-grated Parmesan is too often dry and flavourless. A piece of Parmesan will keep for several months in the refrigerator, wrapped in grease-proof paper and kitchen foil.

PREPARATION AND COOKING
  TIME: *25 minutes*

INGREDIENTS – *serves 4:*
1 lb (450 g) spaghetti
8 oz (225 g) lean bacon rashers
½ oz (15 g) butter
3 large eggs
¼ pint (150 ml) single cream
*Salt and freshly ground black
  pepper*
GARNISH
Grated Parmesan cheese

Bring a large pan of lightly salted water to the boil. Add the spaghetti and cook, uncovered, for 10-12 minutes until the spaghetti is tender but still firm to the bite – *al dente.*

While the spaghetti is cooking, grill the bacon until crisp, drain on kitchen paper then chop into small pieces.

Whisk the eggs together with the cream, a pinch of salt and pepper. Melt the butter in a large saucepan, add the bacon and heat through.

Drain the spaghetti, rinse it under the hot tap, drain thoroughly, and add to the bacon in the pan. When piping hot, pour on the egg mixture, stir it in, then remove immediately from the heat. Sprinkle with Parmesan cheese and serve.

SPAGHETTI ALLA CARBONARA The Italian answer to bacon and eggs is one of the quickest pasta dishes to make. Spaghetti is tossed with cream, eggs and crisp-fried bacon and sprinkled with Parmesan cheese.

CHEESE PUDDING

Brown or white bread can be used in this savoury version of the familiar bread and butter pudding. Brown bread gives a nutty taste, while white bread allows the cheese flavour to dominate.

PREPARATION TIME: *35 minutes*
COOKING TIME: *40 minutes*
OVEN TEMPERATURE: *preheat to 180°C (350°F, gas mark 4)*

INGREDIENTS – *serves 4:*
4 eggs
¾ pint (450 ml) milk
1 level teaspoon dry mustard
1 level teaspoon paprika
Salt
8 slices bread, buttered
*6 oz (175 g) strong Cheddar
   cheese, grated*
Freshly ground black pepper

Whisk together the eggs, milk, mustard, paprika and salt to taste. Remove the crusts from the bread and cut each slice into quarters.

Grease a soufflé dish or deep baking dish, about 2 pints (1.1 litres) in capacity, and put a layer of bread on the bottom. Do not overlap the slices. If necessary, cut the slices to fit the dish. Cover it generously with grated cheese, then some freshly ground black pepper and another layer of bread, continuing in this way until the dish has been filled.

Carefully pour over the egg mixture and leave it for 15 minutes to allow the bread to swell and absorb the liquid.

Bake in the preheated oven for about 40 minutes, or until firm to the touch, puffed up and browned on top.

Serve cheese pudding by itself, or with a vegetable such as peas or grilled tomatoes.

MACARONI CHEESE AND TOMATO

The sauce for macaroni cheese should be abundant and flavoured with a good, strong Cheddar. This is a basic macaroni cheese with a layer of tomato in the middle. It can be made into a more substantial dish by adding ingredients such as chopped ham, frankfurters, peas or peeled broad beans. These should be stirred into the sauce with the macaroni.

PREPARATION TIME: *30 minutes*
COOKING TIME: *30 minutes*
OVEN TEMPERATURE: *preheat to 200°C (400°F, gas mark 6)*

INGREDIENTS – *serves 4:*
10 oz (275 g) macaroni
*8 oz (225 g) tin tomatoes OR
   4-6 fresh tomatoes*
2 oz (50 g) butter or margarine
1½ oz (40 g) plain flour
1 pint (570 ml) milk
*1 tablespoon prepared English
   mustard*
*4 oz (115 g) strong Cheddar
   cheese, grated*
*Salt and freshly ground black
   pepper*

Cook the macaroni according to the instructions on the packet, until it is *al dente* – just firm to the bite. Drain it well. While the macaroni is cooking, drain the tinned tomatoes and chop roughly, or slice the fresh tomatoes, if they are used.

To make the sauce, melt the butter over a low heat in a large pan. Stir in the flour with a wooden spoon. Add the milk gradually, and stir or whisk over low heat until smooth. Bring to the boil and simmer for 1 minute.

Add the mustard and 3oz (75g) of the cheese, stirring until the cheese has just melted. Do not overcook. Add salt and pepper to taste.

Mix the macaroni into the sauce. Grease an ovenproof dish, and pour in half the mixture. Cover with tomatoes and then add the remaining macaroni mixture. Sprinkle the rest of the cheese on top.

Bake in the preheated oven for about 30 minutes until golden-brown on top and heated right through.

Macaroni cheese needs no accompaniment, but it is very good served with *Buttered peas and beansprouts* (page 356) or a green vegetable or salad.

This dish is included in a menu on the opposite page.

ENDURING FAVOURITE Good strong Cheddar cheese and a layer of tomatoes in the centre give simple macaroni cheese plenty of flavour.

Family Lunch for Four

**MACARONI CHEESE
AND TOMATO**
opposite page

**BUTTERED PEAS
AND BEANSPROUTS**
page 356 or
GRILLED TOMATOES

VANILLA ICE CREAM
with
BUTTERSCOTCH SAUCE
page 361

If the ice cream is the hard kind, take it out of the freezer when you start cooking and put it in the refrigerator to soften.

ON THE DAY Allow about an hour. While the macaroni cheese is cooking, make the butterscotch sauce. Set it aside, ready to be reheated just before serving. Prepare the peas and beansprouts or the tomatoes so that they will be ready to serve when the macaroni cheese comes out of the oven.

TO DRINK Fresh fruit juice mixed with some sparkling mineral water.

ANCHOVY EGGS

Add only a tablespoon of the anchovy essence at first when making the sauce for this dish of eggs, tomatoes and anchovies – food essences can vary in strength. As an extra decoration, remove the dish from the oven about 5 minutes before the end of cooking time, arrange halved and stoned black olives on the top, then return to the oven to complete cooking.

PREPARATION TIME: *40 minutes*
COOKING TIME: *25 minutes*
OVEN TEMPERATURE: *preheat to 180°C (350°F, gas mark 4)*

INGREDIENTS – *serves 4:*
4 tomatoes, sliced OR *8 oz (225 g) tin of tomatoes, chopped and drained*
8 hard-boiled eggs, sliced
1¾ oz (50 g) tin anchovy fillets
2-3 tablespoons milk for soaking the anchovies
1 oz (25 g) butter
¾ oz (20 g) flour
½ pint (285 ml) chicken stock (page 367)
¼ pint (150 ml) milk
1 tablespoon anchovy essence or purée
Salt and freshly ground black pepper

Lay the sliced or chopped tomatoes in the base of a shallow ovenproof dish. Arrange the egg slices on top.

Drain the anchovies, spread them out in a small dish, cover with the milk and leave to soak while you prepare the sauce.

Melt the butter in a pan over a low heat. Blend in the flour. Gradually stir in the stock and then simmer for about 5 minutes, stirring, until the sauce is thickened and smooth. Stir in the ¼ pint (150ml) milk, and the anchovy essence. Taste for strength, adding more essence if necessary. Season to taste with salt and pepper. You may find no salt is needed because of the saltiness of the anchovies.

Pour the sauce over the eggs and tomatoes. Drain the anchovies, slice them in half lengthways and arrange them in a lattice fashion over the sauce.

Bake in the preheated oven for about 25 minutes until sizzling. Serve with crusty bread and a green vegetable or salad.

PIPÉRADE

In the Basque region of southwest France, where pipérade originates, it is often served with a slice of grilled or fried ham, particularly ham from the town of Bayonne – *jambon de Bayonne*. Pipérade is like a cross between scrambled eggs and an omelette. Traditionally the recipe is kept very simple, but according to what is available the basic recipe may be varied and made more substantial by adding extra ingredients: strips of green pepper, chopped bacon, mushrooms, diced cooked ham or potatoes, prawns, or black olives and anchovies. Cook the bacon, mushrooms or green pepper with the onions, add the other ingredients with the tomatoes. Pipérade may be served as a lunch or supper dish for two, or a first course for four.

PREPARATION AND COOKING TIME: *25 minutes*

INGREDIENTS – *serves 2-4:*
8 oz (225 g) tin tomatoes, drained
½ oz (15 g) butter
2 tablespoons olive oil
1 large onion, finely sliced
1 level teaspoon dried oregano
6 eggs
Salt and freshly ground black pepper

Chop the tomatoes roughly and leave them in a sieve to drain thoroughly.

Melt the butter and oil in a frying pan and cook the onion slowly, until soft and just beginning to brown. Add the tomatoes and the oregano and cook over a low heat, stirring occasionally, until heated through.

Whisk the eggs with the salt and pepper. Pour them into the pan and stir gently over low heat until the eggs are just set. It is important that the eggs do not become too dry, otherwise the whole character of the dish, which is light and creamy, is spoilt.

Serve at once with chunks of fresh, crusty bread or triangles of fried bread. A simple green salad tossed in vinaigrette (page 371) can also be served.

ASPARAGUS SOUFFLÉ

Contrary to myth, soufflés are not difficult to make. The secret is to whisk the egg whites until they just stand in peaks – but no more – and to fold the beaten egg whites very carefully into the sauce with a metal spoon, trying to lose as little of the air as possible. A soufflé should be served straight from the oven – it sinks as it cools – but the sauce can be made in advance leaving only the egg whites to whisk and fold in, so the soufflé's arrival at the table can be timed fairly accurately.

The flavour of this soufflé can be varied by the addition of 2oz (50g) of finely grated Gruyère cheese, or the asparagus may be replaced by puréed spinach with a pinch of grated nutmeg.

PREPARATION TIME: *20 minutes*
COOKING TIME: *35-40 minutes*
OVEN TEMPERATURE: *preheat to 180°C (350°F, gas mark 4)*

INGREDIENTS – *serves 3-4:*
12 oz (350 g) tin asparagus tips
1½ oz (40 g) butter
1 oz (25 g) plain flour
6 fl oz (175 ml) milk
3 egg yolks
Salt and freshly ground black pepper
4 egg whites

Grease a 7in (180mm) diameter soufflé dish.

Drain the tinned asparagus and process, liquidise or sieve it to a fine purée.

Melt the butter in a large pan over a low heat. Stir in the flour, then remove from the heat. Gradually pour on the milk, stirring continuously. Return to the heat and stir or whisk while bringing to the boil. Simmer for 1 minute. Remove from the heat, and leave to cool for 5 minutes.

Stir in the egg yolks, one by one, and then the asparagus. Add salt and pepper to taste.

Whisk the egg whites and gently fold them into the mixture with a metal spoon. Pour into the prepared soufflé dish and bake in the preheated oven for 35-40 minutes, until the soufflé is well risen and browned on top. Serve immediately. A simple green salad is a good accompaniment.

SPINACH AND CHEESE EN CROÛTE

Many cheeses work well in this recipe – Mozzarella or a blue cheese, for example. Hard cheeses, such as Cheddar, must be very thinly sliced to ensure that they cook right through. Softer cheeses can be used in thicker slices. As another variation, thin slices of cooked meat, such as ham or salami, can be added to the filling.

PREPARATION TIME: *30 minutes plus cooling time*
COOKING TIME: *25 minutes*
OVEN TEMPERATURE: *preheat to 220°C (425°F, gas mark 7)*

INGREDIENTS – *serves 4:*
12 oz (350 g) frozen chopped spinach
Salt and freshly ground black pepper
6 oz (175 g) Cheddar or other cheese
7½ oz (215 g) packet puff pastry
GLAZE
1 egg white mixed with a pinch of turmeric powder

Cook the spinach gently until it has completely thawed and all the water has evaporated. Season to taste with salt and pepper. Leave to cool.

Cut the cheese into slices (see introduction).

Roll out the pastry thinly and cut it into four squares, about 6in × 6in (150mm × 150mm). Place a slice of cheese in the middle of each pastry square, spread with spinach and continue adding layers of cheese and spinach until they have been used up.

Brush the pastry edges with egg white and draw the four corners of each square into the middle, sticking the edges together and crimping them with the fingers.

Put the parcels onto a greased baking sheet and brush them all over with the egg glaze.

Bake in the preheated oven for about 25 minutes until puffed and golden-brown. Serve hot with tomato sauce (see the recipe included in *Spiced turkey meatballs in tomato sauce*, page 261) on the side of the plate.

M E N U

Family Lunch for Four

SARDINE PÂTÉ
page 346

TARTE NIÇOISE
this page

GREEN SALAD
or a CRISP
GREEN VEGETABLE

PEAR MERINGUES
page 361

ON THE DAY Allow about 1½ hours. Make the pastry for the tart. While it is chilling make the pâté. Complete the tart. While it is cooking do the initial preparation for the pears, make the chocolate sauce and prepare the salad or cook the green vegetable.

Just before the meal, complete the pear meringues and put them in the oven. Once cooked they can be left to stand in a warm place until needed.

TO DRINK A well-chilled dry white wine.

TARTE NIÇOISE

The combination of tomatoes, oregano and garlic appears in many dishes from the area around the city of Nice in the South of France. This flan is best eaten hot from the oven, but it can also be served cold. It can be made more substantial and varied by adding flaked tuna, chopped anchovy fillets and black olives. These should be added at the same time as the tomato slices.

PREPARATION TIME: *20 minutes plus chilling time*
COOKING TIME: *30-35 minutes*
OVEN TEMPERATURE: *preheat to 200°C (400°F, gas mark 6)*

INGREDIENTS – *serves 4:*
Shortcrust pastry (page 392) made with 4 oz (115 g) flour
FILLING
8 oz (225 g) tin tomatoes
2 tablespoons olive oil
1 small clove garlic, peeled and roughly chopped
1 medium onion, finely chopped
1 level teaspoon dried oregano
1 oz (25 g) Cheddar cheese, grated
2 large eggs
¼ pint (150 ml) single cream or top of the milk
Salt and freshly ground black pepper

Line an 8in (200mm) flan dish with the pastry. Chill in the refrigerator for about 30 minutes. If you are short of time, put it in the freezer for 10 minutes.

Prick the base and line with kitchen foil and baking beans. Bake the flan blind (page 393) in the preheated oven for 10 minutes. Remove the foil and baking beans and cook for a further 5 minutes.

While the pastry is cooking, prepare the filling. Drain the tomatoes, saving the juice, and slice or chop. Heat the oil in a small pan over low heat then add the chopped garlic. Stir the garlic around in the oil for 1 minute, then remove it with a slotted spoon.

Cook the chopped onion gently in the flavoured oil until nearly soft. Stir in the oregano and tomato juice, and continue to cook until virtually all the juice is absorbed. Spread this mixture into the pastry case and cover with the tomatoes and grated cheese. Whisk the eggs with the cream, and pour over the top. Bake in the oven until set and browned on top (about 15-20 minutes).

Serve with a green salad or a vegetable such as french beans. This dish is included in a menu on the opposite page.

TASTE OF THE MIDI A golden tart is proof of the expertise of Niçois cooks. They take simple, everyday ingredients such as eggs, tomatoes and onions, add a few herbs and a hint of garlic, and produce a dish as delicious as many a more elaborate concoction. All that is needed to go with it is a simple green salad and a glass of white wine.

BACON AND EGG BAKE

An American-style 'hash' of onions, potatoes and bacon baked with eggs makes a quick, substantial supper dish. Ham or other cooked meat can be used instead of bacon. Add it to the softened potatoes and onions when the heat is turned up to brown them.

PREPARATION TIME: *40 minutes*
COOKING TIME: *10-15 minutes*
OVEN TEMPERATURE: *preheat to 200°C (400°F, gas mark 6)*

INGREDIENTS – *serves 4:*
2 level tablespoons dripping, butter, oil or margarine
1½ lb (700 g) potatoes, peeled and finely diced
1 large onion, finely chopped
10 rashers streaky bacon, chopped
4 large eggs

Melt the dripping in a large frying pan. Add the potatoes and chopped onion and cook together over a low heat, stirring occasionally, for about 5 minutes. Add the chopped bacon and continue cooking until the potatoes are cooked through. Raise the heat and then cook, stirring, until everything is brown and crisp. Add salt and pepper to taste.

Put the mixture into a buttered, shallow ovenproof dish. Make four hollows in the surface and carefully break an egg into each. Bake in the preheated oven for about 10-15 minutes, until the eggs are set. Serve at once with a simple green vegetable. This dish is also included in a menu on page 360.

BAKED EGGS Sautéed potatoes, bacon and onions make a tasty 'nest' for a perfect dish of baked eggs.

HAM LOAF WITH GREEN PEPPERCORNS

Crushed green peppercorns add a subtle, spicy flavour to this simple meat loaf.

Tinned hams vary greatly in quality, but the more expensive brands tend to contain less water. A food processor will greatly speed up the preparation time, but a mincer will do.

PREPARATION TIME: *20 minutes*
COOKING TIME: *50-60 minutes*
OVEN TEMPERATURE: *preheat to 190°C (375°F, gas mark 5)*

INGREDIENTS – *serves 4:*
1 lb (450 g) tin cooked ham, jelly removed
1 small onion
2 eggs
4 oz (115 g) fine, fresh white breadcrumbs
¼ pint (150 ml) milk
1 level tablespoon green peppercorns, crushed
Salt

Grease a 1lb (450g) loaf tin.

Finely mince the ham and onion, and lightly whisk the eggs. Mix all the ingredients together. Add salt to taste.

If using a food processor, put all the ingredients in together and process until smooth.

Put the mixture into the prepared tin and bake in the preheated oven for 50-60 minutes, or until firm to the touch.

Turn the loaf out of the tin and serve either hot or cold with new potatoes, peas or french beans, or a green salad. The ham loaf goes well with *Sautéed artichoke hearts* (page 357) or *Buttered peas and beansprouts* (page 356).

This dish is included in a menu on page 346.

SPICED MINCE AND POTATO PIE

A variety of different spices are combined in this pie. It consists of layers of potato and mince, and the mince can be used straight from the freezer. Alternatively, this pie is a very good way of using up leftover roast beef, lamb or pork. The dish can be made without root ginger if none is available.

PREPARATION TIME: *35 minutes*
COOKING TIME: *40 minutes*
OVEN TEMPERATURE: *preheat to 200°C (400°F, gas mark 6)*

INGREDIENTS – *serves 4:*
1½ lb (700 g) small waxy potatoes
2 tablespoons oil or margarine
1 large onion, finely chopped
1 small clove garlic, crushed
1 level tablespoon finely chopped root ginger
1 lb (450 g) mince
1 tablespoon horseradish sauce
1 level tablespoon dry mustard
1 level tablespoon crushed allspice
1 tablespoon Worcestershire sauce
¼ pint (150 ml) beef stock (page 367)
Salt and freshly ground black pepper
½ oz (15 g) butter

Peel the potatoes and boil in salted water until almost cooked – about 15 minutes. Drain and run the potatoes under the cold tap for about a minute.

While the potatoes are cooking, melt the oil or margarine in a large saucepan, add the onion and cook slowly until it begins to brown. Stir in the crushed garlic and the chopped ginger, then add the mince, breaking it up if frozen. Stir in the remaining ingredients, adding salt and pepper to taste. Simmer for 5 minutes.

Slice the potatoes very thinly. Grease an ovenproof dish and put a layer of potatoes in the bottom. Cover with a layer of the mince then another layer of potatoes, continuing in this way until the dish is full. Finish with a layer of potatoes.

Cover the dish with kitchen foil and bake in the preheated oven for about 20 minutes. Remove the foil and dot the potatoes with the butter. Cook for a further 15-20 minutes until sizzling and browned on top. Serve with a green vegetable or salad. This dish is included in a menu on page 357.

TONGUE WITH NUT AND RAISIN SAUCE

A sauce of tomato, walnuts and raisins transforms tongue into a dish suitable for any dinner party. Other cooked meat such as pork or ham can be used. If you have fresh herbs available, they can add flavour and colour to the dish as a garnish.

PREPARATION AND COOKING
   TIME: *30 minutes*

INGREDIENTS – *serves 4:*
*1 lb (450 g) tinned ox or lamb's
   tongue*
1 oz (25 g) butter
1 tablespoon sunflower oil
1 medium onion, finely chopped
2 sticks celery, finely chopped
*1 oz (25 g) walnuts, finely
   chopped*
1 oz (25 g) raisins
*2 level tablespoons wholewheat or
   plain flour*
2 level tablespoons tomato purée
*1/2 pint (285 ml) chicken stock
   (page 367)*
*Salt and freshly ground black
   pepper*
GARNISH
Chopped fresh herbs (optional)

Cut the tongue into cubes.

Melt the butter and oil in a large pan over a low heat. Add the chopped onion and celery, and cook gently until soft. Add the walnuts and raisins.

Stir in the flour and cook for 2-3 minutes, then add the tomato purée and stock. Bring the sauce to the boil, stirring all the time, then simmer for 1 minute. Add the tongue. Stir gently for about 5 minutes until the tongue is heated through. Add salt and pepper to taste. Transfer to a serving dish, and sprinkle with fresh herbs. Serve with mashed potatoes or tagliatelle, and a green salad.

VEGETABLES

STIR-FRIED CARROTS

The Chinese stir-fry their vegetables in a wok – a wide, bowl-shaped metal pan which makes it possible to keep the ingredients moving over a high heat. If you do not have a wok, a large, deep frying pan will do almost as well for this dish. Stir the ingredients constantly so that they all cook through evenly. The orange juice in this recipe brings out the sweetness of the carrots. The finished dish has quite a strong ginger taste – the amount of ginger may be reduced according to preference.

Eat stir-fried food as soon as it is cooked – it loses its crispness if allowed to stand – but the ingredients can be prepared in advance. See also page 372.

PREPARATION AND COOKING
   TIME: *20 minutes*

INGREDIENTS – *serves 4:*
1 lb (450 g) carrots
2 tablespoons sunflower oil
1 small onion, finely chopped
*1 level tablespoon finely chopped
   root ginger*
Juice of 2 oranges
*Salt and freshly ground black
   pepper*

Cut the carrots into 2in (50mm) lengths, and cut them lengthways into matchstick pieces.

Heat the oil in the wok or frying pan and cook the chopped onion over moderate heat until it is just beginning to brown. Stir in the chopped root ginger, then the carrots, and fry over a high heat, stirring constantly for about 3 minutes.

CRISP CARROTS Fresh orange juice and root ginger enliven the flavour of carrots cut into matchstick lengths. Quick stir-frying ensures that the carrots stay crisp.

Add the orange juice, cook for 1 minute, season to taste with salt and pepper and serve at once.

CARROT AND POTATO PURÉE

Puréeing is a particularly successful way of serving those frozen or tinned vegetables that tend to lose their crispness in the preserving process. The addition of cream and plenty of spices gives richness and flavour.

A sieve, food mill, liquidiser or processor can all usually be used to make a purée, but do not liquidise or process potatoes because they tend to become starchy and sticky.

PREPARATION AND COOKING
    TIME: *15 minutes*

INGREDIENTS – *serves 4:*
14 oz (400 g) tin new potatoes
14 oz (400 g) tin carrots
1½ oz (40 g) butter
4 tablespoons cream or top of milk
Salt and freshly ground black pepper
Pinch of ground nutmeg, paprika or coriander
GARNISH
Chopped chives or parsley

Drain the tinned potatoes and carrots and push through a sieve. Put the puréed vegetables into a bowl set over a pan of simmering water.

Add the butter and stir over the heat until melted. Stir in the cream, and salt, pepper and nutmeg, or other spice, to taste.

Heat through until the purée is very hot. Serve sprinkled with chopped chives or parsley.

BUTTERED PEAS AND BEANSPROUTS

Beansprouts stay crisp when tinned, and are a good standby vegetable. They can also be sprouted at home. Buy mung beans, cover them with luke-warm water, soak overnight, then drain. Place a piece of kitchen paper or damp blotting paper in a large jam jar. Put in the beans and cover. Leave in a dark place for about three days, sprinkling twice a day with luke-warm water.

PREPARATION AND COOKING
    TIME: *15 minutes*

INGREDIENTS – *serves 4:*
1½ oz (40 g) butter
1 lb (450 g) frozen petit pois
1 level tablespoon dried mint
  OR *2 level tablespoons chopped fresh mint*
10 oz (275 g) tin beansprouts OR *8 oz (225 g) fresh beansprouts*

Melt the butter in a large frying pan over a low heat. Add the peas and cook slowly until the peas are defrosted. Stir in the mint, and continue cooking until any moisture has evaporated and the peas are cooked.

Rinse the beansprouts well with cold water. Drain them and add to the peas. Raise the heat and cook briskly for a minute or two, stirring all the time and mixing everything well together. Serve at once. This dish is included in a menu on page 351.

SWEETCORN FRITTERS

Sweetcorn is one of the most versatile tinned vegetables to keep in the store cupboard. It can be used in many dishes, including fritters, one of the specialities of the southern United States.

PREPARATION AND COOKING
    TIME: *25 minutes*

INGREDIENTS – *serves 4:*
11 oz (300 g) tin sweetcorn kernels
2 eggs, separated
Salt and freshly ground black pepper
1 level teaspoon baking powder
3-4 oz (75-115 g) fresh breadcrumbs
1 oz (25 g) butter
2 tablespoons oil

Drain the corn and rinse under the cold tap. Drain again.

Beat the egg yolks and stir in the corn with salt and pepper to taste. Beat the egg whites until stiff, and fold them into the corn mixture.

Mix in the baking powder, then add enough breadcrumbs to make the mixture stick together. Using your hands, form the mixture into 16 flat cakes.

Heat the butter and oil together in a frying pan over a medium heat. Cook the fritters until golden-brown – about 4 minutes on each side. Serve hot, with grilled or fried meat such as chicken or gammon.

GLAZED ONIONS

If they are in season, use whole button onions for this recipe. If not, small or medium-sized ordinary onions may be used instead. Peel them and cut in half. Cut out some of the solid core, but not all of it, or the onions will fall apart during cooking.

PREPARATION AND COOKING
    TIME: *20 minutes*

INGREDIENTS – *serves 4:*
1 lb (450 g) button onions
2 oz (50 g) butter
2 level tablespoons granulated sugar
Salt and freshly ground black pepper

Peel the onions and cook in boiling, salted water for 7 minutes. Drain well.

Melt the butter with the sugar in a large saucepan. Add the onions, sprinkle with salt and pepper and cook uncovered over a low heat until the onions are cooked through and well glazed. Shake the pan from time to time to prevent the onions sticking to the bottom.

The onions go well with fairly plain dishes, particularly roast meat. This dish is included in a menu on the opposite page.

IMPRESSIVE PAIR Neither artichoke hearts sautéed with tomatoes, onion and thyme, nor shiny glazed onions are difficult to make, but either one will transform a meal.

M E N U

*Dinner
for Four*

CURRIED
ALMOND
SOUP
page 343

❧

SPICED MINCE AND
POTATO PIE
page 354

GLAZED ONIONS
opposite page

❧

FRUIT MACAROON
BRULÉE
page 358

ON THE DAY Allow about 1½ hours. Prepare the brulée and leave to chill. Make the pie. While it is cooking, make the soup and prepare the glazed onions.

Grill the brulée while you are clearing away the main course.

TO DRINK Dry cider or a dry white wine.

❧

SAUTÉED ARTICHOKE HEARTS

An impressive but easily made vegetable dish with the flavour of Italy, this also makes a good sauce for pasta if the artichokes are cut into smaller pieces.

PREPARATION AND COOKING
TIME: *25 minutes*

INGREDIENTS – *serves 4:*
½ oz (15 g) butter
1 tablespoon sunflower oil
1 medium onion, chopped
½ clove garlic, crushed
*2 × 14 oz (400 g) tins
  artichoke hearts*
8 oz (225 g) tin tomatoes
½ tablespoon sugar
*1½ level teaspoons chopped fresh
  thyme OR ½ teaspoon dried
  thyme*
*Salt and freshly ground black
  pepper*

Drain the artichokes, rinse under a cold tap and halve.

Melt the butter and oil together in a frying pan over a gentle heat, and cook the onion until soft but not browned. Stir in the crushed garlic and cook for a further minute.

Add the halved artichokes and sauté for 1-2 minutes. Add the tomatoes, chopping them roughly with a spoon. Stir in the sugar, the thyme, and salt and pepper to taste. Simmer for 10 minutes to thicken the sauce.

This dish goes well with grilled meat. It is included in a menu on page 346.

TWO BEANS IN TOMATO

A combination of broad beans and sliced runner beans cooked in a tomato sauce can be served as a side dish or as a light sauce for pasta such as tagliatelle. Frozen broad beans sometimes have tough skins, but these are easily removed after softening in boiling water.

PREPARATION AND COOKING
TIME: *30 minutes*

INGREDIENTS – *serves 4:*
1 lb (450 g) frozen broad beans
14 oz (400 g) tin tomatoes
*1 level teaspoon dried thyme or
  oregano*
1 level dessertspoon sugar
*Salt and freshly ground black
  pepper*
*8 oz (225 g) frozen sliced runner
  beans*

Cook the broad beans in boiling salted water for 2 minutes. Drain, run the beans under the cold tap and pop them out of their skins.

Put the tomatoes and their juice, the thyme or oregano and the sugar in a pan. Season to taste with salt and pepper. Bring to the boil, squashing the tomatoes with a spoon. Add the runner beans and boil for about 5 minutes, until the beans are tender. Stir in the broad beans and simmer for a further minute before serving.

This dish goes well with roast or grilled meat.

PUDDINGS & DESSERTS

CHERRY AND CINNAMON PUFF FLAN

The base of this simple puff pastry flan is spread with whipped cream, but if you have no cream to hand, arrange the cherries directly in the pastry case and then glaze. Any sieved red jam can replace the jelly.

If the puff pastry is frozen, leave it to thaw for an hour in a warm place before use.

PREPARATION TIME: *35 minutes*
COOKING TIME: *15–20 minutes*
OVEN TEMPERATURE: *preheat to 220°C (425°F, gas mark 7)*

INGREDIENTS – *serves 4:*
13 oz (375 g) prepared weight puff pastry (page 394)
A little milk
2 level teaspoons ground cinnamon
1 level tablespoon caster sugar
14 oz (400 g) tin pitted black cherries
2 level tablespoons redcurrant jelly
1 level tablespoon arrowroot
¼ pint (150 ml) double cream

To make the flan case, roll out the pastry thinly into a rectangle, about 12in × 8in (300mm × 200mm). Cut a strip 1in (25mm) wide from each edge to use as borders. Transfer the pastry rectangle onto a dampened baking tray. Brush the edges with milk, then position the border strips round the edges, trimming them to fit. Press lightly in place. Prick the pastry base all over with a fork.

Mix together the cinnamon and sugar. Brush the pastry base with milk and then sprinkle with the cinnamon and sugar mixture.

Bake the flan case in the preheated oven for 15–20 minutes, until well risen around the edges. Transfer the flan case to a wire rack, and leave to cool.

While the pastry is cooking, drain the cherries well, reserving 6fl oz (175ml) of the juice.

When the pastry has cooked, melt the redcurrant jelly in a small pan over low heat. Mix the arrowroot with the reserved cherry juice and stir into the melted jelly. A whisk may help to break up the lumps in the jelly. Stir over the heat until it thickens.

Whip the cream, and spread over the pastry base. Arrange the cherries on top and brush with the glaze. Do not leave too long before serving, because the pastry will lose its crispness.

FRUIT MACAROON BRULÉE

Pears and apricots go particularly well with the macaroons in this dessert, but almost any tinned, frozen or fresh fruit can be used. Sponge fingers or ratafia biscuits may be substituted for the macaroons.

The fruit, cream and biscuit base may be prepared in advance. A few minutes under the grill, just before serving, to produce the caramel topping is the only cooking required. The finished dish can either be served hot or, if there is time, chilled. The caramel topping becomes hard and crunchy, creating a satisfying contrast of textures.

PREPARATION AND COOKING TIME: *25 minutes plus chilling time*

INGREDIENTS – *serves 4:*
2 oz (50 g) small macaroons
2 tablespoons sherry
2 × 8 oz (225 g) tins fruit
8 fl oz (225 ml) double cream
Caster sugar

Turn on the grill to full heat.

Lay the macaroons so that they cover the base of an ovenproof dish – such as a 2 pint (1.1 litre) soufflé dish. Sprinkle the sherry over them.

Drain the tinned fruit and chop it roughly. Whip the cream until stiff, then fold the fruit into the cream. Spread the cream and chopped fruit mix-

SHARP CONTRAST A crunchy sheet of hot, 'burnt' sugar seals in a soft, cool mixture of macaroons, fruit salad, sherry and cream.

ture over the layer of macaroons and smooth with a spatula. Chill, if there is time.

Cover the surface with a good, even layer of caster sugar about ⅛in (3mm) thick and put the dish immediately under the very hot grill. Watch it carefully and remove as soon as the sugar has melted and caramelised. Turn the dish, if necessary, so that the topping browns evenly and does not burn.

Serve at once or refrigerate for a few hours. This dish is included in a menu on page 357.

OATY FRUIT CRUMBLE

Many varieties of fresh or tinned fruit can form the basis of a crumble. Apples are the traditional filling, but rhubarb, apricots, peaches, pears, plums or gooseberries also work well. This is a good winter pudding. The crumble is made with oat flakes which give it a coarser, more crunchy texture than the usual all-flour topping. Use a shallow dish if possible, to give layers of fruit and crumble topping that are of equal thickness.

PREPARATION TIME: *30 minutes*
COOKING TIME: *35-40 minutes*
OVEN TEMPERATURE: *preheat to 180°C (350°F, gas mark 4)*

INGREDIENTS – *serves 4:*
1½ lb (700 g) apples (Cox's if available)
2 oz (50 g) raisins or sultanas
Grated rind of 1 orange
4 oz (115 g) demerara sugar
3 oz (75 g) butter
4 oz (115 g) plain flour
3 oz (75 g) oat flakes

Grease a large, shallow ovenproof dish.

Peel, core and quarter the apples. Slice them very thinly. Mix with the raisins, grated orange rind and 1oz (25g) of the sugar. Turn into the dish.

To make the crumble, rub the butter into the flour until the mixture resembles fine breadcrumbs, then stir in the remaining 3oz (75g) of the demerara sugar and the oat flakes. Spread the crumble over the fruit and press it down.

Bake in the preheated oven for 35-40 minutes. Serve the crumble hot, with whipped cream or custard.

DANISH APPLE PUDDING

Crisp, toffee-coated breadcrumbs alternating with creamy apple purée create a contrast of textures and flavours. The breadcrumbs can be made in a food processor or liquidiser, or simply by rubbing the bread between your fingers. The effect is best, however, if the crumbs are not too fine.

For a special occasion, the dessert can be made in individual glass bowls and decorated with whipped cream and strips of apple peel added at the last moment.

PREPARATION AND COOKING TIME: *35 minutes*

INGREDIENTS – *serves 4:*
1½ lb (700 g) dessert apples
1½ oz (40 g) butter
5 oz (150 g) fresh brown breadcrumbs
2 oz (50 g) dark, soft brown sugar
¼ pint (150 ml) natural yoghurt or cream

Peel, core, quarter and slice the apples. Put them into a heavy-based pan with 3 tablespoons of water and cook, covered, over a low heat stirring from time to time until the apples are soft (5-10 minutes). Mash them roughly and turn them into a shallow bowl to cool.

While the apples are cooking, melt the butter in a large frying pan and cook the breadcrumbs, stirring and turning them over medium heat for 2-3 minutes. Add the sugar, raise the heat and continue cooking for 5-10 minutes until the breadcrumbs are crisp and toffee-like. Leave to cool on absorbent kitchen paper for about 5 minutes.

Stir the yoghurt or cream into the puréed apples and spread a layer of the mixture over the bottom of a glass dish. Crush and separate the breadcrumbs if they have stuck together, and sprinkle a layer over the apple. Repeat the process, finishing with a layer of breadcrumbs.

Do not leave the pudding too long before serving, because the breadcrumbs will begin to lose their crispness. Serve with extra cream or yoghurt if you wish.

DANISH DELIGHT A slender curl of green apple gives a clue to what lies below – apple purée mixed with natural yoghurt or cream, forming a layered confection with crisp, sweet caramelised breadcrumbs.

DRIED FRUIT FOOL

The name 'fool' for desserts made with puréed fruit and custard or cream, probably stems from the 16th century, as does the name of another light and frivolous concoction – trifle.

Prunes simmered in tea to enhance their flavour are used in this recipe, but dried apricots, peaches, pears or even a mixture of dried fruits can be substituted. Simmer fruit other than prunes in water or fruit juice rather than tea. The purée can be made by sieving the fruit, but this takes much longer than using a food processor or liquidiser. Either natural yoghurt or cream can be used, depending on what is available.

PREPARATION AND COOKING TIME: *35 minutes plus cooling time*

INGREDIENTS – *serves 4:*
8 oz (225 g) pitted prunes (no-soak variety)
½-1 pint (285-570 ml) black tea
3 level tablespoons custard powder
2 level tablespoons caster sugar
1 pint (570 ml) milk
4 tablespoons bottled lemon juice OR *juice of 1½ fresh lemons*
¾ pint (450 ml) thick natural yoghurt or vanilla yoghurt or lightly whipped double cream
DECORATION
Chopped nuts OR *prunes, halved and rolled in caster sugar*

Put the prunes into a pan and cover them with the tea. Bring to the boil, then simmer until the prunes are tender and the tea has almost evaporated.

Make a thick custard using the quantities of custard powder, sugar and milk given above. This will make a thicker custard than usual.

Purée the prunes in a food processor or liquidiser. Mix the purée with the custard while both are still warm. Stir in the lemon juice. Let the mixture cool slightly, then refrigerate it.

Once the mixture is cooled, add the yoghurt or cream. Mix it in lightly, so that the fool is marbled. Turn the mixture into a large bowl or individual glass dishes. Decorate with chopped nuts or prunes rolled in caster sugar. This dish is included in a menu on this page.

M E N U

Family Supper for Four

BACON
AND EGG
BAKE
page 354

GREEN SALAD
or PEAS

DRIED FRUIT
FOOL
this page

ON THE DAY Allow about 1½ hours. Prepare the fool and set it aside to cool, then make the bacon and egg bake. While it is cooking make the salad, or cook the peas, and fold the cream or yoghurt into the fool ready for serving.

GRILLED APRICOTS

Golden crystals of demerara sugar sprinkled over apricots turn to bubbling caramel under the grill. Other brown sugars may be used instead, but real demerara – named after the Demerara district of Guyana in the West Indies – has the finest flavour. The apricots may be replaced by other fruit such as peaches or pears.

PREPARATION TIME: *10 minutes*
COOKING TIME: *5-10 minutes*

INGREDIENTS – *serves 4:*
2 oz (50 g) butter
2 × 14 oz (400 g) tins apricot halves
3-4 oz (75-115 g) demerara sugar

Turn on the grill to full heat.

Cover the base of a shallow ovenproof dish with half the butter.

Drain the apricots and lay them, hollow side upwards, in the dish. Sprinkle enough sugar over the top to cover them. Dot over the remaining butter and immediately put the dish under the grill.

Grill for 5-10 minutes, until the sugar has caramelised and the dish is sizzling.

Serve hot, with cream, vanilla ice cream or thick, creamy Greek yoghurt, depending on what is available. This dish is included in a menu on page 346.

MARBLED FOOL A dessert that adds a touch of luxury to a meal is quickly made by lightly mixing a purée of dried fruit with custard, and cream or yoghurt. Prunes make a rich, dark fool: apricots make a lighter dessert. The fools are decorated with small bay leaves and sugared fruit.

BUTTERSCOTCH SAUCE

Ice cream, kept in the freezer, is an instantly available simple pudding. When served with a well-chosen sauce, it becomes a special dessert. This hot butterscotch sauce takes only about 10 minutes to make, and becomes like deliciously chewy toffee when poured over cold ice cream. It can be made in advance and reheated. If it is kept warm for any length of time it becomes very sticky.

Other quick sauces for serving with ice cream include the chocolate sauce served with *Pear meringues* (this page); tinned or bottled fruit heated in their own juices that have been thickened slightly with arrowroot or cornflour; fresh or frozen raspberries, puréed and sweetened to taste with caster sugar; or Mars bars gently melted with a little brandy.

PREPARATION AND COOKING
TIME: *10 minutes*

INGREDIENTS – *serves 4:*
3 tablespoons golden syrup
6 level tablespoons demerara
  sugar
1½ oz (40 g) butter
4 tablespoons water

Put the golden syrup, sugar and butter in a non-stick saucepan, and cook over a low heat until the sugar has dissolved. Bring to the boil, stirring constantly. Then simmer until the syrup is a good dark brown – this should take 1-2 minutes.

Stir in the water and boil fiercely for about 2 minutes, until the sauce is like toffee. Serve hot. This sauce is included in a menu on page 351.

PEAR MERINGUES

Baked pears crowned with meringue and surrounded by a rich chocolate sauce make a pudding that is elaborate in appearance and suitable for a dinner party. It is also very easy to make. The meringue can, if you wish, be piped onto the pear halves. Although the meringue needs to be made at the last minute, the pears and chocolate sauce can be prepared in advance. Peach halves may be used instead of pears, and the dried apricots replaced by sultanas.

PREPARATION TIME: *25 minutes*
COOKING TIME: *15 minutes*
OVEN TEMPERATURE: *preheat to*
  180°C (350°F, gas mark 4)

INGREDIENTS – *serves 4:*
8 small pear halves, approximately
  2 × 14 oz (400 g) tins
4 tablespoons apricot jam
2 oz (50 g) macaroon biscuits or
  ginger biscuits
1 oz (25 g) dried apricots
2 egg whites
4 oz (115 g) caster sugar
3 oz (75 g) plain chocolate
¼ pint (150 ml) single cream or
  top of the milk
½ oz (15 g) butter

Arrange the pears in a shallow ovenproof dish, hollow side upwards. Melt the jam and spread some over each pear.

Crush the biscuits, finely chop the dried apricots and mix together. Spoon some of the mixture over each pear.

To make the meringue, whisk the egg whites until stiff, then fold in the caster sugar. Cover each pear with meringue.

Put the dish into the preheated oven for 15 minutes, or until the meringue is lightly browned and crisp on top.

While the pears are cooking, make the sauce. Melt the chocolate in a bowl over a pan of simmering water. Gently heat the cream and butter in a nonstick saucepan until the butter has melted. Pour the cream onto the melted chocolate and mix well. Return the sauce to the pan and bring it to the boil, stirring well. Lower the heat and keep the sauce warm, adding more cream if it gets too thick. If the sauce has to be kept warm for some time, transfer it to a bowl set over hot water.

Remove the pears from the oven and transfer to hot plates. Pour the sauce around the pears on each plate and serve at once. This dish is included in a menu on page 352.

SILHOUETTE PEARS Pale against pools of hot, dark chocolate sauce, are pear halves, swathed in meringue which conceals apricot jam, crushed macaroons and chopped apricots.

M E N U

*Informal
Supper
for Eight*

TUNA FISH
KEDGEREE
page 348

CHOCOLATE
AND GINGER
FRIDGE CAKE
this page

Make twice the quantity given in each of the recipes. A green or mixed salad can also be served with the kedgeree if you have the ingredients. The cake can be made in advance.

ON THE DAY Allow about an hour. Make the chocolate and ginger fridge cake and while it is chilling in the refrigerator, make the tuna fish kedgeree.

TO DRINK A medium dry white wine.

CAKE WITHOUT COOKING An hour in the refrigerator is all the 'cooking' needed for this luxurious chocolate and ginger cake. For a special occasion, decorate it with grated chocolate and chocolate chips as well as icing sugar.

CHOCOLATE AND GINGER FRIDGE CAKE

Instead of being cooked, this rich cake is set in the refrigerator. The recipe can be varied, using glacé cherries or raisins, for example, instead of ginger.

PREPARATION TIME: *15 minutes*
CHILLING TIME: *1 hour*

INGREDIENTS – *serves 4:*
4 oz (115 g) plain chocolate
2 oz (50 g) butter
1 egg
3 oz (75 g) ginger nut biscuits
*2 oz (50 g) crystallised ginger,
    roughly chopped*
*1 tablespoon brandy or orange
    juice*
Icing sugar

Melt the chocolate gently in a bowl over a pan of hot water. Melt the butter in a small pan over low heat.

Whisk the egg until frothy, then whisk in the melted chocolate and the melted butter.

Put the biscuits into a plastic bag and crush them with a rolling pin. Stir the pieces into the chocolate mixture with the crystallised ginger and the brandy or orange juice.

Press the mixture into a small flan dish and put it into the coldest part of the refrigerator for about an hour to set.

Serve in small wedges, dusted with icing sugar. This dish is included in a menu on this page.

BREAD AND BUTTER PUDDING

This pudding is too good to be left merely as a memory of childhood. Raisins and mixed peel, or currants, can be used instead of sultanas. Finely grated lemon or orange rind added to the custard, or cinnamon or nutmeg sprinkled on top before baking, will vary the flavour.

PREPARATION TIME: *30 minutes*
COOKING TIME: *30 minutes*
OVEN TEMPERATURE: *preheat to 180°C (350°F, gas mark 4)*

INGREDIENTS – *serves 4:*
About 2 oz (50 g) butter
4 oz (115 g) thinly sliced white bread
2 oz (50 g) sultanas
2 large eggs
1 oz (25 g) vanilla sugar or caster sugar
¾ pint (450 ml) milk

Butter a 2 pint (1.1 litre) oven-proof dish.

Butter the slices of bread and cut them into quarters. Arrange the slices in the dish in alternate layers with the sultanas. Do not overlap the slices of bread: cut them to fit the dish if necessary. Finish with a layer of bread – butter side up.

Beat the eggs with all but a teaspoon of sugar. Bring the milk almost to the boil, then pour it onto the beaten eggs. Strain through a sieve onto the bread. Sprinkle the remaining sugar on top.

Leave to stand for 15 minutes, to allow the bread to absorb the custard. Bake in the preheated oven for about 30 minutes, until the pudding is set and lightly browned on top.

QUEEN OF PUDDINGS

Queen Charlotte, wife of George III, was responsible for the rise in popularity of this pudding. It is rich, and extremely sweet. The Queen considered that it was particularly nutritious, and an economical dish to serve to patients in her hospital – Queen Charlotte's Maternity Hospital in west London.

PREPARATION TIME: *30 minutes*
COOKING TIME: *40 minutes*
OVEN TEMPERATURE: *preheat to 180°C (350°F, gas mark 4)*

INGREDIENTS – *serves 4:*
Grated rind of 1 small lemon
½ pint (285 ml milk)
½ oz (15 g) butter
1 oz (25 g) vanilla sugar or caster sugar
2 oz (50 g) fresh white breadcrumbs
2 large eggs, separated
About 4 oz (115 g) strawberry or raspberry jam
3 oz (75 g) caster sugar

Grease an ovenproof dish such as a 2 pint (1.1 litre) pie dish.

Put the grated lemon rind and the milk in a pan and bring to the boil. Add the butter and sugar, and stir until the sugar

has dissolved. Remove from the heat and stir in the breadcrumbs, then the egg yolks. Put the mixture in the dish and leave to stand for 15 minutes.

Bake in the preheated oven for about 20 minutes until set. Remove from the oven and leave to cool for 5 minutes.

Warm the jam in a small pan, and spread it gently over the top of the pudding.

To make the meringue topping, whisk the egg whites until stiff, then gently fold in the caster sugar. Pile the meringue on top of the jam. Return to the oven for about 15 minutes until the top is golden-brown.

ORANGE SOUFFLÉ

Using sugar lumps to extract the oil from the zest of oranges is an old-fashioned method that captures the full flavour of the oranges for this hot soufflé.

PREPARATION TIME: *30 minutes*
COOKING TIME: *35-40 minutes*
OVEN TEMPERATURE: *preheat to 180°C (350°F, gas mark 4)*

INGREDIENTS – *serves 4:*
2 large oranges
2 oz (50 g) lump sugar
½ pint (285 ml) milk
2 oz (50 g) butter
1 oz (25 g) cornflour
3 egg yolks
4 egg whites
1 tablespoon orange liqueur such as Grand Marnier, Curaçao or Cointreau OR orange juice

Grease a 2 pint (1.1 litre) soufflé dish with butter.

Wash and dry the oranges, then rub the sugar lumps all over the skins to extract the oil. Put the sugar lumps into a saucepan with all but 4 tablespoons of the milk. Dissolve the sugar over low heat. Bring to the boil, then remove from the heat.

Melt the butter in a large saucepan over low heat. Mix the cornflour with the remaining milk, pour onto the butter and stir until thick. Gradually add the milk and sugar, the egg yolks, and then the liqueur. Remove from the heat.

HEADY ORANGE A light orange soufflé, fortified with liqueur, is served with segments of fresh orange.

Whisk the egg whites until stiff, and gently fold them in with a metal spoon.

Turn the mixture into the prepared soufflé dish and bake in the preheated oven for 35-40 minutes, until well risen.

While the soufflé is cooking, cut away all the peel and pith from the oranges with a sharp knife. Cut out the orange segments (page 398).

Serve the soufflé as soon as it is cooked, with the orange.

THE STORE CUPBOARD

As supermarkets and corner shops vie with each other to see who can stay open longer hours, the idea of a store cupboard might seem very old-fashioned. But keeping a well-stocked cupboard makes good sense. It ensures that you never run out of basic cooking ingredients and that if you need to produce a meal unexpectedly you will have the ingredients to hand.

BUYING

Food bought for the store cupboard must always be in perfect condition. Dented tins, or food that has reached its 'sell-by' date, are often a very good bargain but should only be bought for immediate consumption.

● Check fruit and vegetables that are to be kept for more than a day or two carefully for blemishes. Avoid anything that is overripe or mouldy.

● Check the date-stamping on all dairy products, supermarket meat and vacuum-packed food, and the 'best before' dates on packets of dried food.

● Do not buy any packets or cartons that look swollen; any tins that are dented, rusty, swollen or showing signs of leakage; or torn packets of dried food.

● Buy eggs that are less than a week old. Boxes of eggs are stamped either with an actual packing date, or a code number.

The first week in January is 1, 52 is the last week in December. If you are not sure how long you have kept an egg that is not packed in a date-stamped carton, put it on its side into cold water. A very fresh egg will remain horizontal on the bottom of the bowl. A slightly stale egg will tilt and rise a little – it should not be poached or boiled but is fine for other cooking. A very stale egg will float and should be discarded.

● Avoid any frozen food with broken packaging or signs of freezer burn – white spots on the surface.

STORAGE

Once you have bought food for the store cupboard, there are certain principles to follow to ensure that it will keep well.

Keep food used every day readily accessible – in jars near the work surface, for example. Refill jars from larger packets kept in the store cupboard. Rotate food in the store cupboard, putting new tins and packets to the back as you buy them and bringing the older ones to the front.

There are three basic types of storage area: cupboards for dry and tinned goods; a cool larder for fresh goods and vegetables; and the refrigerator for perishable goods. In addition to these,

if you have a freezer you will be able to store frozen food (see page 406), and if you have a cool, dark cellar or garden shed you will be able to store larger quantities of potatoes, onions, carrots and apples than can be kept in a larder.

● A food cupboard should be as cool and dry as possible, well away from any source of heat.

● A larder should be well-ventilated and cool – about 12°C (54°F) on average. If you have no larder use the refrigerator instead.

● The coldest part of a refrigerator is on the middle and top shelves. The least cold part is the door. Store highly perishable foods, fish for example, in the coldest part. Store cooked meats above uncooked meats.

Fresh food

● Do not store strong-smelling food (raw onions, garlic, cheese, fish, melons) next to eggs, opened milk or other absorbent ingredients.

● Supermarket packs of meat should be unwrapped, then loosely rewrapped in plastic food bags, greaseproof paper or waxed paper, or put into plastic boxes, and refrigerated.

● Vacuum packs – of bacon, for example – should be put in the refrigerator still sealed, then treated as fresh once opened.

● Check the condition of fruit and vegetables regularly as mould spreads quickly. Store soft fruit spread out – on a baking tray, for example – not in a bowl, and uncovered.

Dry food and tins

● If you do not use the entire contents of a tin after opening it, place the remainder in a non-metallic container, cover, and store in the refrigerator. Use it within 1-2 days of opening.

● Once packeted foods, such as cereals, have been opened, they should be used quickly.

SUBSTITUTES

It is often not necessary to dismiss a recipe just because you lack one ingredient. Experiment and substitute something you do have or try some of the following ideas.

● Yoghurt, soured cream and cream are interchangeable for many dishes. Yoghurt can be stabilised so that it does not curdle when added to hot food. Whisk one small carton with ½ teaspoon of cornflour. Simmer for 5 minutes before using.

● Soured cream can be made by stirring 1 teaspoon of lemon juice into 5fl oz (150ml) of double cream. Left at room temperature, it will thicken and sour in about 30 minutes.

● Cream can easily be made from unsalted butter and milk, either with a special cream maker or by the following method. Put 4oz (115g) of unsalted butter into a pan with

4fl oz (115ml) of milk and heat gently until the butter melts. Blend the mixture thoroughly in a liquidiser. Chill in the refrigerator for several hours or overnight to thicken. To make a thicker, whipping cream use 5oz (150g) of butter.

● Plain chocolate can be replaced by cocoa powder. Mix 3 level tablespoons of cocoa powder with 1 level tablespoon of unsalted butter and 2 level tablespoons of caster sugar for each 1oz (25g) of chocolate required for the recipe.

STOCKING THE STORE CUPBOARD
The contents of your store cupboard should be planned around your own cooking habits. This chart is made up of dry and tinned goods that can be stored for several months or longer; fresh goods – such as eggs and cheese – which will keep for several days or weeks; and a small amount of frozen food. It is divided into two categories: basic necessities and optional items that will add variety. Make up your own list, drawing from the items suggested and adding any others that you use regularly.

All the recipes in Emergency entertaining (pages 341-363) can be prepared using the basic or optional items suggested.

STORAGE

	Cool, dark, dry cupboard
	Larder or refrigerator
	Refrigerator
	Freezer

TYPE OF FOOD	SHELF LIFE	COMMENTS
DAIRY PRODUCTS *basic*		
Butter and margarine	2 weeks	
Cheese – *Cheddar*	4-6 weeks	Wrap in foil or store in a covered plastic box.
Cheese – *Parmesan*	1 year	Wrap in foil.
Eggs	3-4 weeks	
Milk (fresh)	2-3 days	
Milk (long-life)	as dated	
Yoghurt	as dated	
optional		
Cream (long-life)	as dated	
Ice cream	4 months	
Milk (dried)	6 months	Airtight jar or tin.
MEAT *basic*		
Bacon – *green*	5 days	Vacuum packs as dated, as
– *smoked*	1 week	fresh after opening.
optional		
Ham (tinned)	1½-2 years	
Mince	3-4 months	
Suet (packeted)	6 months	After opening, 4 months.
Tongue (tinned)	1½-2 years	
FISH *basic*		
Sardines (tinned)	1 year	Sardines in olive oil or brine are the most useful.
optional		
Anchovies (tinned)	1 year	
'Boil in the bag' fish fillets	as dated	
Lumpfish roe	6 months	Refrigerate after opening and use within 1 week.
Peeled prawns	3-4 months	
Salmon (tinned)	1 year	
Tuna (tinned)	1 year	
FRUIT *basic*		
Apples/pears	3-4 weeks	
Lemons	3-4 weeks	
Oranges	3-4 weeks	
Peaches/pears/ apricots (tinned)	18 months	
optional		
Soft fruit	2-3 months	Raspberries, currants.

TYPE OF FOOD	SHELF LIFE	COMMENTS
VEGETABLES *basic*		
Carrots	2 months	Do not wash.
Garlic	2 months	
Onions	2 months	
Potatoes	2 months	Do not wash.
Tomatoes (tinned)	2 years	
optional		
Artichoke hearts (tinned)	2 years	
Asparagus (tinned)	2 years	
Bean sprouts (tinned)	2 years	
Broad beans/brussels sprouts/ french beans/runner beans/ peas/spinach	1 year	
Sweetcorn (tinned)	2 years	
PASTA, RICE, PULSES, CEREALS *basic*		
Lentils (dried)	2 years	Sealed packet or airtight jar.
Pasta	2 years	Spaghetti, macaroni.
Porridge oats	1 year	Sealed packet or airtight jar.
Rice – *long grain/short grain*	2 years	Sealed packet or airtight jar.
optional		
Cornmeal	9 months	Sealed packet or airtight jar.
Red kidney beans (tinned)	2 years	
Semolina	9 months	Sealed packet or airtight jar.
Pulses	18 months	Haricot beans, chick peas, split peas.
BAKING INGREDIENTS *basic*		
Baking powder	6 months	Airtight container.
Bicarbonate of soda	6 months	Airtight container.
Chocolate – *plain*	6 months	
Cocoa powder	1 year	Sealed packet or airtight jar.
Cornflour	6 months	Sealed packet or airtight jar.
Cream of tartar	6 months	Airtight container.
Flour – *plain*	6-8 months	Airtight container. After
– *wholemeal*	2 months	opening, 1-3 months.
Gelatine	1 year	
Golden syrup	2 years	
Sugar – *granulated/caster/ soft brown/icing*	3 years	Airtight container.
Sultanas/raisins	2 years	Sealed packet or airtight jar.

TYPE OF FOOD	SHELF LIFE	COMMENTS
BAKING INGREDIENTS *optional*		
Almonds/walnuts	6 months	Sealed packet or airtight jar.
Candied fruit	8 months	Mixed peel, cherries.
Dried apricots/prunes	2 years	'Ready-to-eat' varieties are the most useful.
Macaroons/ratafias	6 months	Sealed packet or airtight tin.
Sugar – *demerara/ muscovado*	1-2 years	Airtight container.
Vanilla essence	3 years	
SUNDRIES *basic*		
Biscuits	6 months	Sealed packet or airtight tin.
Bread	1 week	Plastic bag.
Chutney	2 years	
Coffee – *instant*	1 year	
Coffee – *beans*	indefinitely	Vacuum-packed. See also *Coffee* page 50.
Herbs (dried)	6 months	See also *Herbs* page 382.
Honey	1 year	
Jam/marmalade	1 year	
Ketchups, sauces	6-12 months	Refrigerate after opening.
Mustard	1 year	Powder and French mustard.
Oil	1 year	Olive oil for salads. Corn oil, sunflower oil or vegetable oil.
Peppercorns – *black*	5 years	
Salt	5 years	
Spices	3-12 months	See also *Spices* page 384.
Stock cubes	1 year	
Tea	8 months	See also *Tea* page 140.
Tomato purée	6 months	Refrigerate after opening.
Vinegar – *wine*	5 years	
optional		
Consommé (tinned)	18 months	
Fruit juices (concentrated)	as dated	
Olives (bottled)	18 months	Refrigerate after opening.
Peppercorns – *green* (tinned)	18 months	Refrigerate after opening.
Puff pastry	3 months	
Vol-au-vent cases	3 months	
Yeast (dried)	6 months	

BASIC TECHNIQUES AND RECIPES

The cooking techniques and basic recipes that will ensure success with all the recipes in this book

STOCKS

Stock is liquid flavoured by meat, fish or vegetables. It generally is used to add flavour and the quality of the stock can often be crucial to the success of the dish.

The most commonly used stocks are brown stock (made from browned beef and veal bones), white stock (made from chicken or veal bones), fish stock and vegetable stock. When 'beef stock' is needed in a recipe, use brown stock. When 'chicken stock' is called for, use white stock made with chicken.

All stocks should be clear and have a good colour; impurities in the stock spoil the flavour and the texture of the dish for which it is intended. For ordinary purposes – vegetable soups for example, or casseroles – it is enough to strain the stock through muslin or a fine sieve. For dishes needing a really clear stock – aspic, a fine sauce or consommé, for example – it is necessary to clear (clarify) the stock. Mix a lightly beaten egg white with crushed ice, then stir the mixture into the stock while it is still warm. Bring to the boil, stirring constantly. Any sediment is trapped by the congealed egg white and becomes heavy and clogs together. Strain through muslin or a fine sieve.

Brown and white stocks can be kept in the refrigerator for up to 4 days. To keep them fresh, boil them up every other day.

Fish and vegetable stocks should be used within 24 hours. All stocks can be kept frozen for up to 3 months.

When making stock with stock cubes, remember that the cubes are highly concentrated. It is generally best to add half the suggested amount of stock cube to the water. Stock cubes also tend to be heavily seasoned; so be careful when adding any seasoning to the dish.

BROWN STOCK

Beef and veal bones for making brown stock can be bought from any butcher. A cheap, gristly cut of meat or meat scraps can also be added.

Use brown stock in soup or casseroles made with red meat or vegetables, and in well-flavoured sauces.

INGREDIENTS – *makes about 3 pints (1.7 litres):*
1½ lb (700 g) beef bones
1½ lb (700 g) veal bones
8 oz (225 g) onions, peeled and roughly sliced
8 oz (225 g) carrots, peeled and roughly sliced
1 bouquet garni
1 level teaspoon black peppercorns
½ teaspoon salt
7 pints (4 litres) hot water

1 Wipe the bones with a clean damp cloth. If they are large, chop them up.

2 Spread out the bones, onions and carrots in a large roasting tin. Roast for 30-35 minutes in an oven preheated to 200°C (400°F, gas mark 6) until well browned. Turn the bones and vegetables once during roasting.

3 Put the bones and vegetables into a large, deep, heavy-based pan with the bouquet garni, peppercorns, salt and hot water. Bring the mixture slowly to the boil.

4 With a large spoon, skim off the scum that forms on the surface of the stock.

5 Cover the pan, with the lid tilted at a slight angle, and simmer over a very gentle heat for 3½-4 hours until the stock has been reduced by about a half. Skim off the surface scum regularly during simmering.

6 Strain the stock through muslin or a fine sieve into a china or glass bowl (metal bowls give a metallic flavour).

7 If the stock is needed immediately, leave it for a few minutes to allow the fat to rise to the surface, then remove the fat by drawing absorbent kitchen paper over the stock.

8 If the stock is not needed immediately, leave it to cool completely.

9 When cold, scrape the congealed fat off the surface of the jellied stock with a large spoon. The last traces of fat can be removed with kitchen paper. Cover the stock and store in the refrigerator.

WHITE STOCK

Instead of using boiling fowl, you can make white stock with a chicken carcass and scraps of skin or bone, or veal bones.

Use white stock in chicken, veal and rabbit dishes, in pale cream soups and for aspic.

INGREDIENTS – *makes about 2 pints (1.1 litres):*
1 boiling fowl, ready for cooking
3½ pints (2 litres) water
1 bouquet garni
1 small onion, peeled and stuck with 4 cloves
Salt and freshly ground black pepper

1 Put the fowl and water into a large pan and bring to the boil slowly.

2 With a large spoon, skim off the scum that forms on the surface. Add the bouquet garni, onion stuck with cloves, and salt and pepper to taste.

3 Cover, with the lid tilted at a slight angle, and simmer over a very gentle heat for 1½ hours, skimming regularly.

4 Remove the fowl, then strain the stock and remove the fat as for brown stock.

FISH STOCK

Fish stock should not be cooked for more than 30 minutes. Otherwise the bones soften and give the stock a bitter taste.

INGREDIENTS – *makes 1½-2 pints (850 ml-1.1 litres):*
2¼ lb (1 kg) fish trimmings
1 small onion, finely chopped
2 medium leeks, split, cleaned and chopped
2 sprigs fresh fennel
1 oz (25 g) white mushroom skins and stalks (optional)
2 pints (1.1 litres) water
7 fl oz (200 ml) dry white wine
Salt and freshly ground black pepper

1 Wash the fish trimmings and put into a large pan with the onion, leeks, fennel, mushroom skins and stalks, and water. Bring to the boil slowly.

2 With a large spoon, remove the surface scum. Add the white wine and salt and pepper to taste. ▶

3 Simmer very gently for 30 minutes, skimming off the scum once or twice. Do not boil fish stock or it will be cloudy.

4 Strain through muslin or a fine sieve.

VEGETABLE STOCK

Almost any leftover pieces of vegetable can be used in vegetable stock. This recipe merely gives the basic ingredients. Use a balanced mixture, and avoid starchy root vegetables such as potatoes, parsnips or turnips; they will make the stock cloudy.

Vegetable stock is essential for vegetarian dishes.

INGREDIENTS – *makes about*
1½ pints (850 ml):
1 leek, split, cleaned and roughly chopped
2 sticks celery, roughly chopped
2 large carrots, roughly chopped
1 large onion with the skins, roughly chopped
2 cloves garlic with the skins, roughly chopped
1 bouquet garni (optional)
3 pints (1.7 litres) water
Salt and freshly ground black pepper

1 Put all the ingredients, including the water, into a large pan. Season lightly with salt and pepper.

2 Bring to the boil. Cover, then simmer over a very gentle heat for 2 hours.

3 Strain through muslin or a fine sieve.

SAUCES

Sauces provide one of the main opportunities for creativity in cooking. Many classic dishes are meat, fish or vegetables, simply cooked but accompanied by an interesting sauce.

There are six basic sauces which fall into two categories – roux-based sauces and emulsion sauces. There are also variations on these basic sauces. Some are given here, but the basic sauces should be starting points for your own experiments.

Simple sauces can also be made by diluting the juices remaining in the pan after cooking food or by thickening the cooking liquid with flour or with eggs and cream.

There are also many sauces included in the recipes in this book. See *Index*.

ROUX-BASED SAUCES

In roux-based sauces, liquid is thickened with a 'roux' – a mixture of flour and fat. The basic types of roux-based sauce are the white sauces – Béchamel and velouté – and brown sauce.

White sauce

Most savoury white sauces are based on a lightly cooked butter and flour roux. White wine, milk or chicken stock (or combinations of them) are added to the roux, with flavourings, to make the different sauces.

Béchamel sauce

The simplest of the white roux-based sauces is Béchamel, thought to be named after Louis de Béchamel, Marquis de Nointel, and Lord Steward at the French court of Louis XIV.

This recipe gives a moderately thick sauce of coating consistency which is suitable for pasta, for example. To serve Béchamel as an accompanying sauce, thin it with a little chicken stock or dry white wine.

Béchamel has lengthy simmering to give it a concentrated flavour. For a more simple white sauce – for pouring over vegetables for example – just simmer the sauce for 3-5 minutes to cook the flour.

INGREDIENTS – *makes about*
⅓ pint (190 ml):
½ pint (285 ml) milk
1 small onion, peeled and stuck with 4 cloves
6 white peppercorns
Piece of blade mace
1 bay leaf
¾ oz (20 g) butter
¾ oz (20 g) plain flour
Salt and freshly ground white pepper

1 Put the milk, the onion stuck with cloves, peppercorns, mace and bay leaf in a pan. Simmer over a very gentle heat for 5 minutes, without letting the milk boil.

2 Remove from the heat and pour into a jug. Leave for 30 minutes to let the flavourings infuse into the milk.

3 To make the roux, melt the butter in a pan. Stir in the flour to make a smooth paste and cook for 30 seconds, stirring constantly. Remove the pan from the heat.

4 Strain the milk and gradually stir it into the roux. Make sure to stir in all the roux from the edges of the pan.

5 Return the pan to the heat. Stir the sauce continuously over a moderate heat until it comes gently to the boil so that it thickens evenly. Then simmer the sauce gently for a further 20 minutes.

6 Add salt and pepper to taste. If necessary, you can at this stage pass the sauce through a fine sieve to make it absolutely smooth. Alternatively, you can use an electric beater or liquidiser to blend in any lumps that remain.

Béchamel variations

SAUCE MORNAY Add 3oz (75g) of finely grated cheese to the basic sauce. A mixture of Parmesan and Gruyère is traditional but other cheeses, such as Cheddar and Lancashire or a blue cheese such as Stilton, can be used. With stronger cheese you will need to add less. Heat the sauce just enough to melt the cheese, but no more. Serve with fish, eggs and vegetables.

ONION SAUCE Boil 2 medium-sized onions until tender. Drain them and chop finely. Add them to the basic sauce with a pinch of nutmeg.

ANCHOVY SAUCE Add 2 teaspoons of anchovy essence to the basic sauce. Serve with fish, veal, pork chops or chicken.

Velouté sauce

Translated literally from French, velouté sauce is 'velvety sauce'. It is similar to Béchamel but the roux is cooked a little longer and diluted with a mixture of chicken or fish stock and white wine, instead of milk. Velouté sauce can be enriched by the addition of egg yolk and cream.

Serve velouté sauce with poached fish or white meat. The liquid in which the fish was poached can be used instead of or with the chicken stock to make the sauce.

INGREDIENTS – *makes about*
½ pint (285 ml):
¾ oz (20 g) butter
¾ oz (20 g) plain flour
¼ pint (150 ml) chicken stock (page 367)
¼ pint (150 ml) dry white wine
Salt and freshly ground white pepper
A few drops of lemon juice
1 egg yolk (optional)
3 tablespoons double cream (optional)

1 Melt the butter in a pan. Add the flour and cook for 1 minute, stirring constantly. Remove from the heat.

2 Gradually stir in the chicken stock and the white wine to make a smooth sauce. Be sure to stir in all the roux from the edges of the pan.

3 Return the pan to the heat. Stir the sauce continuously over a moderate heat until it comes gently to the boil so that it thickens evenly.

4 Add salt and pepper to taste and the lemon juice. Simmer gently for 10 minutes.

5 You can at this stage sieve the sauce to make it absolutely smooth, or use an electric beater or liquidiser to blend in any lumps.

6 Beat the egg yolk with the cream and then add to the sauce. Stir over a gentle heat for 1 to 2 minutes, without letting the sauce boil.

Velouté variations

PARSLEY SAUCE Add 4 tablespoons of chopped fresh parsley to the basic velouté sauce. Reheat gently. Serve with gammon, fish and vegetables.

SAUCE AURORE Add 4 large tomatoes, skinned (page 389), seeded and finely chopped, to the basic velouté sauce. Reheat gently. Serve with eggs, poultry, fish and vegetables.

Brown sauce

The base for a wide variety of sauces is brown sauce. Unlike Béchamel or velouté it is rarely served in its basic form. It is made from a roux of flour and oil or dripping. The roux is cooked until it is deep brown, then diluted with brown stock.

In this recipe for brown sauce, chopped vegetables are added to the fat before the flour – they are later sieved out. The vegetables give the sauce an extra depth of flavour.

INGREDIENTS – *makes about ½ pint (285 ml):*
3 tablespoons oil
1 small carrot, peeled and finely chopped
1 small onion, peeled and finely chopped
2 sticks celery, finely chopped
1 level tablespoon plain flour
¾ pint (450 ml) brown stock (page 367)
1 bouquet garni
1 teaspoon tomato purée
Salt and freshly ground black pepper

1 Heat the oil in a large saucepan. Add the chopped vegetables and cook them, stirring constantly, over a low heat for about 10 minutes – until they just start to turn a light brown colour.

2 Stir in the flour and cook over a moderate heat, stirring from time to time, until a russet-coloured roux is formed. Remove the pan from the heat.

3 Gradually stir the brown stock into the roux.

4 Return the pan to the heat and bring to the boil, stirring constantly.

5 Add the bouquet garni, tomato purée, salt and pepper to taste. Simmer gently for 20 minutes.

6 Pass the sauce through a fine sieve.

● To make the sauce extra smooth, bring it just to the boil in a clean pan. Holding the pan at a slight angle over the heat, add 4 tablespoons of cold brown stock. Skim off the fat that rises to the surface.

Brown sauce variations

SAUCE CHASSEUR Fry some chopped shallots and sliced mushrooms. Add to the basic brown sauce with a little extra tomato purée and salt and pepper to taste. Reheat gently. Serve with grilled and roast meat, chicken and game.

SAUCE BIGARADE Add a little red wine or port, redcurrant jelly and orange juice and rind to the basic brown sauce. Reheat gently. Serve with duck.

MADEIRA SAUCE Add a large glass of Madeira to the basic brown sauce. Reheat gently. Serve with veal and tongue.

SAUCE PIQUANTE Add some tarragon vinegar, capers, chopped fresh herbs and extra tomato purée to the basic sauce. Reheat gently. Serve with beef, lamb and mixed grills.

EMULSION SAUCES

In emulsion sauces, tiny droplets of fat are held suspended in a liquid. The main types are mayonnaise, Hollandaise and vinaigrette.

Mayonnaise

In spite of the mystique that surrounds it, mayonnaise is not difficult to make. The quality of the mayonnaise depends on the quality of the oil used to make it. Use a relatively mild olive oil: one that is too fruity will make the mayonnaise overpowering. A lighter sauce can be made with a mixture of equal quantities of olive oil and any good vegetable oil, such as corn, groundnut or sunflower oil.

The mayonnaise is flavoured with wine vinegar, lemon juice – or a flavoured vinegar such as tarragon vinegar. Malt vinegar is much too strong.

All the ingredients must be at room temperature. Take the eggs out of the refrigerator at least an hour in advance.

Mayonnaise will keep in the refrigerator for 2-3 days, covered. Beat it before serving.

INGREDIENTS – *makes about ½ pint (285 ml):*
½ pint (285 ml) olive oil
2 egg yolks
About 1 tablespoon wine vinegar or lemon juice
½ teaspoon French mustard
Salt and freshly ground black pepper
1-2 tablespoons hot water

1 Measure the oil into a jug or a bottle with a lip.

2 Put the egg yolks into a bowl with the vinegar or lemon juice. Beat with a balloon whisk, or an electric whisk, until well blended.

3 Beat in the mustard. Add the mustard after the vinegar or lemon juice – or it will make the yolks flake.

4 Start adding the olive oil drop by drop, whisking constantly. Continue until about a quarter of the oil has been added and the mayonnaise no longer looks thin and watery but has developed the consistency of thin cream – this means that an emulsion has started to form.

5 Now add the oil in a fine but steady stream, still whisking constantly.

6 Once the mayonnaise has really thickened – after about half the oil has been added – you can start adding the oil more quickly, but do not add it any faster than you can beat it in. If it seems to be getting too thick too quickly, thin the mixture with a little vinegar or lemon juice. When all the oil has been added, the mayonnaise will hold its shape.

7 Season to taste with salt and pepper. Adjust the flavour with more vinegar or lemon juice if you wish.

8 Beat in 1-2 tablespoons of hot water to lighten the texture of the mayonnaise.

Blender mayonnaise

A lighter mayonnaise can be made in a liquidiser or food processor. Use 2 whole eggs instead of just egg yolks.

1 Beat the eggs and vinegar or lemon juice in the liquidiser or processor. Beat in the mustard.

2 With the motor running slowly, add the oil in a fine trickle until the mayonnaise begins to thicken.

3 Increase the speed of the motor slightly, then add the rest of the oil in a steady stream.

4 Blend in salt and pepper to taste and the hot water.

If mayonnaise separates

If the ingredients are too cold, or if the oil is added too quickly, the sauce may separate.

1 Break a new egg yolk into a clean bowl.

2 Use a tablespoon to add the curdled mixture, drop by drop, to the egg yolk, beating

constantly until all the curdled mixture has been incorporated.

3 Continue to add any remaining oil – drop by drop – as before.

Mayonnaise variations

Mayonnaise can be mixed with equal quantities of yoghurt to make it less rich; or it can be flavoured with crushed garlic, anchovy essence, chopped cucumber or tomato purée and basil, for example. Here, in addition are a few more complex mayonnaise-based sauces:

AIOLI See page 64. Serve with raw and cooked vegetables, snails, fish dishes and fish soups.

SAUCE RÉMOULADE Combine 2 tablespoons each of French mustard, chopped capers, chervil, gherkins, parsley and tarragon and add anchovy essence to taste. Blend the mixture into ½ pint (285ml) of mayonnaise. Serve with salads and cold shellfish and egg dishes.

SAUCE TARTARE Mix 4 tablespoons of chopped capers with 6 chopped cocktail gherkins, 2 tablespoons of chopped parsley and 2 tablespoons of double cream. Blend into ½ pint (285ml) of mayonnaise. Serve with fried or grilled fish.

SAUCE VERTE Blanch 10 sprigs of watercress, 4 sprigs each of tarragon and parsley and 10 spinach leaves, in boiling water for about 3 minutes. Strain, dry and press them through a fine sieve or chop very finely. Blend into ½ pint (285ml) of mayonnaise. Serve with salmon, trout and cold egg dishes.

Hollandaise sauce

Like mayonnaise, the emulsion in Hollandaise sauce is based on egg yolks and fat, but whereas mayonnaise is made with oil and served cold, Hollandaise is made with butter and served warm. It is excellent with asparagus, artichokes and fish, for example.

The sauce is best made in a heavy-based pan set over very gentle heat. If the heat from your ring is too fierce, you can cook it in a bowl set over a pan of hot, but not boiling, water or in the top of a double boiler, but the heat is usually more difficult to control.

White wine or lemon juice can be used instead of vinegar.

INGREDIENTS – *makes about*
   ⅓ pint (190 ml):
3 tablespoons white wine vinegar
8 white peppercorns
Piece of blade mace
Small bay leaf
2 egg yolks
3½ oz (90 g) butter, cut into
   small cubes and chilled
Salt and freshly ground white
   pepper

1 Put the white wine vinegar, peppercorns, mace and bay leaf into a heavy-based pan. Bring to the boil and leave to simmer over a moderate heat until reduced to about 1 dessertspoon. Keep an eye on it – it reduces surprisingly quickly.

2 Remove from the heat and lift out the peppercorns, bay leaf and mace with a slotted spoon. Leave until lukewarm. If

the vinegar is too hot the eggs will start to scramble.

3 Gradually beat in the egg yolks and continue beating until they have the consistency of thin cream.

4 Place the pan over very gentle heat. Add the cubes of butter a few at a time, beating continuously with a balloon whisk. Make sure that each addition of butter has been thoroughly beaten in before adding the next, otherwise the emulsion will not form.

5 Continue beating until the sauce is light and smooth with the consistency of mayonnaise but still pourable.

6 Season to taste with salt and pepper. The sauce can be kept warm for a short while in a covered warmed jug, set in a pan of warm water.

If Hollandaise begins
to separate

If the sauce begins to look slightly granular, it is becoming too hot and about to separate. If

the sauce is left on the heat when it starts to separate, it will form into separate flakes like scrambled eggs and the sauce will be impossible to save.

1 Remove the pan from the heat immediately.

2 Beat in 1 tablespoon of cold water or add an ice cube and beat it in as it melts.
● It is also a good idea to have a bowl of iced water by you when you make Hollandaise. If the sauce begins to separate you can plunge the base of the pan in the water as well as adding the cold water or ice cube.

Blender Hollandaise

Hollandaise sauce made in a liquidiser or food processor is not quite as smooth as when made in a pan, but it is very good nonetheless. Because the eggs are not cooked over heat, it is important that the melted butter should be very hot.

1 Pour the reduced vinegar into the liquidiser or food processor and add the egg yolks and salt and pepper to taste.

2 Blend vinegar and eggs together with the machine at its highest speed.

3 Melt the butter in a small pan and bring it just to boiling point.

4 With the machine at high speed, pour the melted butter onto the eggs in a thin, steady stream.

5 Continue blending for a few seconds until the sauce is light and smooth.

Béarnaise sauce

Béarnaise sauce is made the same way as Hollandaise but it is strongly flavoured with tarragon. Traditionally, it is served with grilled steak but can also be served with fish, chicken and egg dishes.

INGREDIENTS – *makes about*
⅓ pint (190 ml):
2 tablespoons tarragon vinegar
2 tablespoons white wine vinegar
½ small onion, finely chopped
A few leaves fresh tarragon,
*   roughly chopped*
Freshly ground black pepper
2 egg yolks
3½ oz (90 g) butter, cut into
*   small cubes and chilled*
Salt

1 Put the vinegars, onion, tarragon and a little pepper into a heavy-based pan and simmer over moderate heat until reduced to 1 dessertspoon.

2 Continue as for Hollandaise sauce.

Vinaigrette (French dressing)

Vinaigrette is the simplest salad dressing – vinegar, olive oil and seasonings, beaten into a temporary emulsion.

Use good quality olive oil. Garlic or tarragon vinegar can be used to give extra flavour. The proportion of olive oil to vinegar is usually 1 part vinegar to 4 parts of olive oil, but this can be varied according to taste.

Vinaigrette can be kept for up to a week in a screw-top or stoppered bottle in a cool place.

INGREDIENTS – *makes about*
⅓ pint (190 ml):
2 tablespoons white wine vinegar
8 tablespoons green olive oil
1 clove garlic, finely crushed
1 teaspoon French mustard
Salt and freshly ground black
*   pepper*

● Put all the ingredients into a screw-top jar and shake well until they are evenly mixed and form a thick dressing.
● Alternatively, mix the vinaigrette in a jug with a fork or small whisk.

Variations on vinaigrette

● Add a pinch of sugar to give the vinaigrette a round, less sharp flavour.
● Add about 1 level tablespoon of finely chopped fresh herbs.
● Add the finely chopped white and sieved egg yolk of a hard-boiled egg to give the vinaigrette a thicker, smoother texture.
● Use fruit juice, such as freshly squeezed orange juice or lemon juice, instead of vinegar. This is particularly good for a chicken, duck or game salad.
● Use dry sherry or vermouth instead of the vinegar to make a good dressing for raw mushroom salad.
● For a dressing for a spinach or raw cabbage salad, add about 2 level teaspoons of freshly grated Parmesan cheese.

INTEGRAL SAUCES

Sauces such as mayonnaise or Béchamel are made separately from the food they are to accompany. However, many very simple sauces can be made after the food has been cooked, either with the juices and sediments produced while it was cooking, or by thickening the liquid in which it was cooked.

Gravies

Gravies are made by adding liquid – and, for thick gravy, flour – to the juices and sediment left in the pan after meat or poultry has been roasted or sautéed. The liquid used can be, for example, water, stock, wine, sherry, port, beer or cider.

Thin gravy

1 Spoon off all the fat in the pan, leaving only the dark meat juices and sediment.

2 Place the pan over heat so that the sediment dries out, but do not let it burn.

3 Gradually stir in the liquid to dissolve the sediment.

4 Allow to bubble briskly for a minute or two. Season to taste with salt and freshly ground black pepper.

Thick gravy

1 Spoon off the fat until only about 2 tablespoons are left in the pan with the meat juices and sediment.

2 Gradually stir in enough flour (about 1 tablespoon) to absorb the fat. Place the pan over heat and make a brown roux (see page 369).

3 Gradually stir in the liquid until you have a gravy of the thickness you want.

4 Simmer for 1-2 minutes, then season to taste with salt and pepper.

Thickening cooking liquids

Sauces can also be made by thickening the liquid in which food has been cooked. Thickening agents are *beurre manié* (a paste of flour and butter kneaded together) and a 'liaison' of egg yolks and cream.

Beurre manié

Use beurre manié to thicken the liquid from braised meat, also thin soups and gravy.

1 To thicken ½ pint (285ml) of cooking liquid, mix ½oz (15g) of softened butter and ½oz (15g) of plain flour to a smooth paste.

2 Bring the liquid to the boil. Lower the heat, then add the beurre manié in small knobs a few at a time. Stir the sauce continuously with a balloon whisk or wooden spoon until it has thickened and is smooth.

3 Continue stirring over a very low heat for 5-10 minutes to cook the flour and get rid of the raw taste. Do not allow the liquid to boil

Egg yolk and cream liaison

For making creamy-textured sauces or soups, use an egg yolk and cream liaison.

1 To thicken ¾ pint (450ml) of cooking liquid, beat 2 egg yolks with ¼ pint (150ml) of double cream in a small bowl.

2 Beat in 5 or 6 tablespoons of the hot cooking liquid.

3 Pour the mixture into the rest of the cooking liquid. Stir continuously over the heat until the liquid thickens. Do not let it boil. A few knobs of butter beaten into the sauce will make it more glossy and rich.

STIR-FRYING

Stir-frying is a Chinese cooking technique in which food cut into small pieces is fried in a small amount of very hot oil in a very hot pan. During frying the food is constantly stirred and tossed around the pan to expose each piece evenly to the heat and to prevent the pieces from being scorched. In this way the food is cooked exceptionally quickly and so retains its fresh flavours, colours and texture.

Woks

A round metal casserole or deep frying pan can be used for stir-frying, but it is best to use a Chinese wok. Woks are round-bottomed pans, usually made of thin carbon steel which allows the heat to spread rapidly and evenly. The shape of the pan means that food can be tossed inside it without spilling.

Woks perform best on gas hobs because the heat can be controlled more quickly. They can be used on an electric hob with a wok stand, but take longer to heat. Special woks with flattened bottoms can be bought for use on an electric hob, but the heat is not distributed as efficiently as it is with the traditional wok.

Oils and seasonings

The best oils to use in stir-frying are groundnut and corn oil because they can be heated to a high temperature. When stir-frying, the Chinese often flavour the oil – to 'arouse the wok' – by first stir-frying some finely chopped garlic, root ginger or spring onions, or all three, before adding the main ingredients. Soya sauce and sugar are also used for seasoning.

Most vegetables will benefit from being blanched – cooked very briefly in boiling water, then plunged into cold water – before stir-frying. Hard vegetables such as carrots need to be cooked until almost tender.

If you are stir-frying more than one ingredient, add the ingredients that take longest to cook first – carrots, for example. More delicate food, such as Chinese leaf or bean sprouts, should only be added near the end of the stir-frying.

1 Wash the ingredients and cut them into fine strips, slices or small cubes. All the pieces must be roughly the same size to cook at the same rate. Dry them thoroughly.

2 Measure out the seasonings so that they can be added quickly during stir-frying. If using salt, sugar and soya sauce, mix them in a small bowl.

3 Turn the heat up full under the wok and leave it for a few seconds until a little water dropped onto it sizzles and evaporates immediately.

4 Add the oil and swirl it over the inside of the wok. Leave it to heat for about a minute, but do not let the oil overheat. If it starts to smoke, remove it from the heat and let it cool slightly. If the oil discolours, discard it and start again, adding new oil.

5 If using garlic, ginger or spring onions to flavour the oil, add them to the wok. Using a metal wok spatula or long-handled spoon toss them around the wok for a few seconds.

6 Add the main ingredients. Slide the spatula under the food to the bottom of the wok, then twist and turn the spatula to toss the food from the centre of the wok to one side. Repeat, tossing the food to the other side of the wok. Continue in this way, keeping the food moving fast over the surface of the wok until it is cooked through, but is still crisp with bright colour.

7 Quickly add any seasonings and continue stirring and tossing for a minute until the food and the seasonings are thoroughly mixed together.

DEEP-FRYING

When food is deep-fried it is totally immersed in very hot fat so that the outside seals very quickly, becoming crisp. All the moisture is sealed inside. Most foods are given a coating of batter or breadcrumbs which prevents the fat from leaking into the food. Foods without a coating must be thoroughly dried, or the moisture will cause the fat to spit. The best fats to use are colourless, odourless oils, such as groundnut, corn or sunflower oil.

A deep-frying thermometer is best for showing the temperature of the fat. If you do not have a thermometer, drop a cube of bread into the oil. If the bread goes brown in 60 seconds, the temperature of the fat is about 182°C (360°F). If it takes 40 seconds, the temperature is about 190°C (375°F); and if it takes 20 seconds, the temperature is about 195°C (385°F). If it takes less than 20 seconds, the fat is dangerously hot: remove it from the heat at once.

Most food is deep-fried at 190°C (375°F), although occasionally a recipe will specify a different temperature.

The time taken to cook a piece of food will depend on its nature and size. As an approximate guide: croquettes take 2-3 minutes; fritters 3-5 minutes; potato chips 4-6 minutes; pieces of fish in batter 5-10 minutes; and chicken joints 15 minutes.

1 Lay out some absorbent kitchen paper. If you have more than one batch of food to deep-fry, preheat the oven to 120°C (250°F, gas mark ½) to keep the food warm while other batches are being fried.

2 Half fill the pan with fat and drop in the frying basket, if you are using one. Heat the oil (see above).

3 Add the food in small batches. Stand back quickly to avoid being spattered by hot fat. Small pieces, such as vegetables, can be dropped into the fat. Lower in larger or more delicate pieces, such as croquettes, with a slotted spoon. Batter-coated food is best lowered in with tongs.

4 Fry the food for the correct time (see above).

5 Lift the food out in the basket or with a slotted spoon or tongs.

6 Spread the food out on the kitchen paper to drain, or if there is more food to fry, put it in the oven to keep warm. Leave the food uncovered and the oven door open – otherwise the crust will become soggy.

7 Allow the fat to return to the right temperature and repeat the process.

FISH

Fresh fish should have a firm body. The skin colours should be bright and the eyes should be full and bright. It should smell of the sea, not fishy.

ROUND FISH

There are two kinds of round fish – oily fish (such as herring and mackerel) and white fish (such as haddock and cod). In oily fish, the oil content is distributed throughout the body; in white fish it is concentrated in the liver. Round fish are cooked whole, boned or filleted.

Cleaning the outside

1 Cut off the fins with scissors.

2 If the fish has loose, hard scales, hold it firmly at the tail end and scrape the scales off with the back of a knife blade, working towards the head.

3 Wash the fish under cold running water.

Gutting through the belly

1 Slit open the fish's belly from just in front of the tail to just behind the gills with the tip of a sharp knife. The head can be cut off the fish at this stage if you wish.

2 Scrape out and discard the entrails.

3 Remove and discard the gills; they may need to be snipped away, top and bottom, with scissors.

4 Scrape out the black blood vessel running along the backbone. It may be necessary to rub the flesh with salt to help to remove any traces of black on the flesh.

5 Clean the inside of the fish thoroughly under cold running water.

Gutting through the gills

You can gut the fish without slitting the belly open.

1 Insert a finger through the gill openings just behind the head. Hook it round the gills and loosen them, snipping them free with scissors at top and bottom if necessary.

2 Inserting your finger through the gill opening again, loosen the intestines inside the belly.

3 Carefully pull the gills and entrails out through the opening; they should come out in one piece.

4 With your finger remove any remaining pieces of entrail in the belly. Wash the inside of the fish thoroughly with cold running water.

Boning delicate fish

Fish with delicate flesh, such as trout, salmon trout or char, need careful boning.

1 Slit open the belly and gut the fish.

2 Lay the fish on its side and hold the belly open. With a small paring knife, gently prise away the ribs and the backbone on the lower side of the fish.

3 Turn the fish over and prise away the ribs and backbone on the other side.

4 Snip the backbone free at the head end. Lift the skeleton and snip the backbone free at the tail end.

Boning firm fish

Herring and mackerel have firm flesh and can be boned in a quicker, less delicate way.

1 Slit open the belly, gut the fish and cut off the head.

2 Spread the fish out with the exposed flesh down.

3 Push down firmly along the spine until it lies flat.

4 Turn the fish over. Starting at the head end, run your thumb between the ribs and flesh on one side, loosening the bones. Repeat on the other side.

5 Lift up the backbone and snip it free at the tail end.

373

Filleting

1 Clean and gut the fish. It is not necessary to cut off the head before filleting.

2 Lay the fish on its side. With a sharp, flexible knife, slit along the back and through the flesh to the backbone.

3 Lift up the loosened flesh, and pull it gently away from the ribs prising it off with the knife, using gentle slicing movements.

4 Turn the fish over and remove the other fillet.

FLATFISH

Flatfish range in size from the North Atlantic halibut, which can be up to 7ft (2.1m) long, to much smaller sole, plaice and dabs. The larger flatfish are generally sold cut into steaks or fillets. The smaller flatfish are generally sold whole. The fish can be cooked whole or as fillets. The coarse dark upper skins (which are camouflaged to make the fish blend with the surrounding seabed) are generally removed before cooking, but the delicate white skins on the undersides can be left.

Gutting

Most flatfish have their entrails removed at sea, but sometimes a fish which needs to be gutted will come your way. Even if the fish has already been gutted, there may still be some pieces of entrail left in the small pocket behind the head which should be scraped out.

1 Lay the fish, dark side down, on the work surface.

2 Make a semicircular slit just behind the head, opening up the small pocket containing the entrails, then scrape them out with the tip of a knife.

Skinning

1 Lay the fish with the white side on the work surface. Slit the dark upper skin across the point at which the tail joins the body.

2 Insert your thumb between the skin and the flesh and run it up along the edge of the fish as far as the head. Repeat along the other edge.

3 Hold the fish firmly by the tail and pull off the skin.

4 If removing the white skin, turn the fish over and repeat the process.

5 Trim the fish by cutting off the bony fins on either side of the body and removing the skin from the tail.

6 Cut off the head and stomach cavity.

Filleting

1 Lay the fish on the work surface with the dark side uppermost.

2 With a sharp, flexible knife, cut lengthways down the centre of the fish through to the backbone.

3 Insert the knife between the flesh and the rib bones on one side. With short strokes, keeping the blade close to the bones, prise off the fillet.

4 Repeat with the other fillet on the dark side.

5 Remove the two fillets on the white side.

6 To skin each fillet, lay it with the skin side down. Insert the knife between the flesh and skin at one end of the fillet. Hold the skin tightly at the end and push the knife along between the skin and flesh in a sawing movement, holding the knife at a slight angle with the blade towards the skin. Keep the knife blade as close to the skin as possible. The white side fillets do not need to be skinned.

7 Remove any black membrane from the flesh by rubbing it with salt.

SQUID

Another name for squid is calamary – from the Latin *calamus* meaning 'pen'. It owes this name to the thin transparent bone, called the pen, that runs along the inside of its body and looks like an old-fashioned quill. Squid used also to be known as 'sea clerke' and 'inkhorn fish'.

There are about 350 species of squid ranging from giant 60ft (18m) squid to tiny ones no more than a few inches long. The ones eaten in Europe usually have bodies between 3in (80mm) and 9in (230mm) long.

Preparing squid

A squid's body is pouch-like with a wing or fin on either side. Hidden inside the body pouch are the pen, entrails and, attached to the entrails, a sac containing a dark brown liquid, or 'ink', which the squid squirts at its predators to distract them. The head and the tentacles are also attached to the entrails and stick out of the body pouch.

To prepare squid for cooking, the pen, entrails and head are discarded, leaving the tentacles and body pouch. The body pouch is then skinned and the wings separated from it. For some recipes the ink sac is kept.

Small squid can be poached or grilled. Alternatively, the body pouch can be cut into rounds. The rounds and tentacles are then battered and fried. Larger squid need longer cooking to tenderise the flesh, and so are usually stewed or braised.

1 Remove the pen by lifting up the edge of the body pouch and pulling the pen out firmly but with care.

2 Hold the body pouch in one hand and the tentacles in the other and pull them apart to separate the body from the soft entrails, head and tentacles. Set aside the body pouch.

3 Lay out the entrails, head and tentacles. With a sharp knife, cut between the tentacles and head, leaving just a thin rim of flesh at the top of the tentacles to hold them together. If using the ink in cooking, carefully cut out the long, narrow ink sac from the entrails and set it aside, before discarding the head and entrails.

4 Pull the loose purple-mottled skin off the body pouch. If you have any difficulty removing the skin, rub your fingers in salt and the skin will come off more easily.

5 Pull off the wings and then skin them too.

6 Wash the wings and body pouch thoroughly under cold running water.

7 Poke out and discard the hard beak-like mouth inside the rim where the tentacles meet. If necessary, cut the membrane attaching the beak to the rim.

8 Wash the tentacles under cold running water.

SHELLFISH

Most shellfish on sale in Britain is quite safe. To avoid the danger of contamination from polluted water, many shellfish are specially farmed in clean sea water. Others spend a period of time in tanks of clean water before being sold.

Eat shellfish bought fresh (live, raw or cooked) on the day you buy it. Frozen shellfish should not be stored for longer than a month in the freezer. Eat it as soon as it has thawed.

CRAB

Crabs are almost always sold ready-cooked. The best crabs for eating are medium-sized – weighing 2-3lb (900g-1.4kg) – but heavy for their size. When cooked crabs are shaken, there should be no sound of water inside them. A good medium-sized crab should yield about 1lb (450g) of crab meat, enough for three or four people.

Meat can be extracted from most parts of the crab. The brown meat from the hard upper shell is rich and oily and has the fullest flavour. The white meat comes from the body, legs and claws and is more flaky.

To prepare a cooked crab so that it can be eaten whole or so that meat can be used in a recipe, the gills (known as the dead men's fingers), and the stomach sac which is inedible, must be carefully removed.

1 Twist off the claws and legs. Set them aside.

2 Pull off and discard the pointed flap (tail).

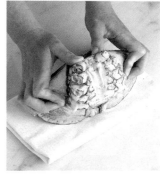

3 Hold the crab upright with the brown upper shell towards you and the tail end uppermost. Hold the upper shell with both hands and push the body free with your thumbs.

4 Pull the two sections carefully apart. The body section consists of a mass of thin bone, white crab meat and the dead men's fingers. ▶

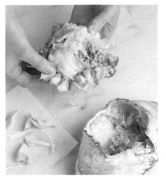

5 Pull off the greyish-white bulbous dead men's fingers and the feathery wisps attached to them. Most are attached to the edge of the body, but some may have fallen into the shell. Make sure to remove them all and discard them.

6 Spoon out the brown meat from the shell. Scrape off any of this meat sticking to the body. Set aside.

7 Clean out the inside of the shell, discarding the stomach sac and the transparent membrane lining the shell. Thoroughly scrub both the inside and outside of the shell. If you wish to give the shell an extra gloss, brush it lightly with vegetable oil.

8 Break the irregular inner edge of the shell back to the dark line that runs round the shell near the outer edge.

9 With the tip of a skewer poke out the white flaky meat from the leg and claw sockets in the body and from all the body's other crevices. It may be necessary to cut the body in half to get all the meat out. Set the meat aside.

10 With a kitchen weight, hammer or pair of nutcrackers, crack open all the joints in the claws and legs. Do not hit them too hard or bits of shell will get into the meat. Prise the pieces of flaky white meat from the shells with the tip of a skewer and set aside.

11 To dress the crab, arrange the meat in the cleaned shell with the brown meat in the middle and the white meat on either side. Two lines of chopped parsley can be used to separate the brown and white meats.

LOBSTER

Lobsters are available throughout the year. Alive they are dark blue – they only turn bright pink when they are cooked. Freshly cooked lobsters from the fishmonger should smell clean, not 'fishy', and the tail should spring back when opened out. A medium-sized lobster – about 1½-2lb (700-900g) – provides enough meat for two people. Choose one that feels heavy for its size.

To prepare a lobster so that it can be eaten whole or so that the meat can be used for cooking, the inedible stomach sac, gills and intestinal vein are removed. The red roe, 'coral', lodged in the tails of female lobsters can be used in any accompanying sauce. The greenish liver is a delicacy and can be served as a garnish. The meat must also be extracted from the claws and legs. However, some people prefer to do this for themselves at the table and special crackers and picks can be bought for the purpose.

1 Twist off the claws and legs and set them aside. If the lobster is female, open out the tail and scrape out the roe from the underside.

2 Lay the lobster, back uppermost, on a board. With a large sharp knife, split the tail in half, starting where the tail meets the head and cutting down along the back. If necessary, hit the back of the knife with, for example, a kitchen weight to help the blade to penetrate the shell.

3 Split the head down the centre in the same way, starting where it meets the tail. Pull the two halves of the lobster apart.

4 Remove the transparent stomach sac and gills which lie in the head near the tip. There may be part of the stomach and gills in both halves of the lobster.

5 With the tip of the knife, remove the beige or grey-coloured intestinal vein running down the tail. There may be bits of the intestinal vein in both halves of the lobster.

6 Take the claws and crack them open with a kitchen weight, hammer or nutcrackers. Do not crush the claws completely – otherwise bits of shell will get into the meat. If possible, try to extract the claw meat whole.

7 Crack open the legs and extract the meat.

8 To serve the lobster, slice the claw and leg meat and arrange neatly on top of the meat in the shell.

MUSSELS

Live mussels are available from September to March. They are generally sold in pints. A pint (570ml) of mussels is roughly equivalent to 1lb (450g) in weight. Allow 1½ pints per person. Mussels are always eaten cooked. If you are cooking the mussels later in the day, keep them alive in cold water.

Mussels can be bought cooked and shelled: 3-4oz (75-115g) of shelled mussels is equivalent to 1 pint of live mussels.

Preparing live mussels for cooking

1 Discard any mussels with cracked or broken shells and any that are not closed or do not close when tapped.

2 Scrape any barnacles off the shells and pull out the thread-like 'beards' coming out of the shells. Scrub the shells clean under the cold tap.

3 Rinse the mussels several times in cold water, changing the water between each rinse.

Cooking

If you have a lot of mussels, they may have to be cooked in batches. The pan must not be more than half filled otherwise you will not be able to see when all the mussels have opened.

1 Put the prepared mussels in a large heavy-based pan. Add ½in (15mm) of water or white wine, with sliced onion or shallots, chopped parsley, celery, a bay leaf, some thyme, crushed garlic and salt.

2 Cover the pan and leave over a low heat for about 5 minutes until the shells begin to open. Shake the pan from time to time so that the mussels are evenly cooked.

3 Drain the mussels in a colander, catching the juices in a bowl. Discard any that have not opened.

4 Strain the juices through muslin and pour them over the cooked mussels.

PRAWNS

Prawns are available throughout the year. Fresh prawns are generally sold cooked, but they may need to be shelled and the intestinal vein running down the centre should be removed.

1 Twist off the head, then hold the body with the legs upwards and break the shell open with your thumbs. Peel away the shell and legs.

2 Cut along the back of the prawn to expose the black intestinal vein.

3 Lift the vein out with the tip of the knife.

OYSTERS

Portuguese oysters are available all year. The more highly prized English oysters are in season from September to April.

Oysters should already be closed or should close when tapped. They are usually eaten raw, but they are occasionally cooked (see *Baked oysters*, page 158). Do not open them until just before using. Allow six oysters per person.

Opening

1 Scrub the shell with a stiff brush to remove any grit.

2 Hold the oyster firmly, flat side uppermost, in a folded tea towel. The towel will protect your hand if the knife slips.

3 Insert the tip of an oyster knife (or any short, strong knife) into the small cavity at the sharp end of the shell. Twist the knife to prise the two halves of the shell slightly apart.

4 Push the blade right into the shell and raise the tip. Keeping the blade inside the shell with the tip raised, slide the knife along one side of the shell to loosen the oyster from the upper half of the shell. Be careful not to spill the juices while doing this.

5 Pull off the upper half of the shell. If it does not come off easily, insert the knife into the shell from the other side and loosen the oyster on that side.

6 Loosen the oyster from the lower half of the shell.

Serving

Oysters to be eaten raw are served with their juices in their lower shells. Arrange them on a bed of cracked ice. Serve with brown bread and butter, lemon wedges and black pepper.

Some people swallow oysters whole out of their shells; others prefer to chew them.

SCALLOPS

Fresh scallops are available from September to March. They can sometimes be bought in their shells, open or closed. They are also available frozen, without their shells, all year round.

Scallops are usually cooked, but some small species are occasionally eaten raw like oysters.

Opening and cleaning

1 Hold the scallop with the flat shell uppermost. Insert a thin, sharp knife between the shells opposite the hinge, and carefully cut the flat shell free from the scallop in the curved shell. Remove the flat shell.

2 Wash out any grit with cold water.

3 Slide the knife under the membrane that attaches the scallop to the curved shell. Cut the scallop free.

4 Trim off the membranes, black stomach sac and black intestinal vein, leaving only the white flesh and orange 'coral', or roe.

CHICKEN

JOINTING A CHICKEN

Pieces of chicken on the bone – joints – are chiefly used for casseroles. Chickens are often quartered, but jointing into eight results in pieces of a more convenient size.

To joint a chicken, you need a 'cook's knife' – a strong knife with a broad blade about 8in (200mm) long – or poultry shears. Alternatively, use two knives, a large strong one for cutting through the bones and a small sharp one for finer work.

1 Cut off the wing tips at the last joint.

2 Lay the chicken on its back on a chopping board. Pull one of the legs away from the body. With short slicing strokes, cut through the skin and flesh to the ball and socket joint where the thigh joins the body. Twist the thigh free from the body, cutting any white ligaments that connect the ball and socket

joint. Break the joint. Cut through the skin still attaching the leg to the body. Repeat with the other leg.

3 Hold the chicken upright with the neck end down. Holding the blade of the knife across the raised end of the chicken, cut down through the ribs to separate the breast and wings from the lower carcass. When you have cut a little over halfway through the chicken, put down the knife and pull the breast and lower carcass completely apart. Cut the skin at the neck.

4 Place the breast on the board, skin side up. Cut it

in half by cutting just to one side of the ridge bone. If necessary, hit the back of the knife with, for example, a kitchen weight to help get the knife blade through the breastbone.

5 Divide each breast half in half again, cutting it just behind the wing.

6 Spread out each leg, then cut it in half, separating the drumstick from the thighbone at the joint.

BONING A CHICKEN

Some dishes require a chicken – or turkey, goose or duck – to be boned whole. A boned, stuffed bird has only to be sliced at the table, avoiding carving.

Chicken, turkey, goose and duck are all boned in the same way. It is not difficult, but does require patience, allow 45-60 minutes the first time you try. Use a knife with a very sharp blade about 5in (130mm) long. Aim to leave the skin in one piece so that when the bird is cooked it will not split. By making short cuts and keeping the knife blade as close to the bone as possible, you will reduce the risks of cutting the skin.

Ideally the flesh should also be as whole as possible, but any pieces of meat left on the carcass can be cut off and placed in the boned bird later. The bones and other discarded pieces of the bird can be used to make stock.

1 Cut off the parson's nose and cut off the wing tips at the last joint.

2 Lay the chicken on its breast. Working from the

neck, cut along the ridge of the back to expose the backbone.

3 Starting at the tail end, carefully scrape the meat down off the rib cage on one side. As you free the meat, carefully pull it away from the rib cage.

4 When you reach the joint where the thighbone joins the body, carefully scrape away the meat that surrounds the joint. Then cut through all the tough white ligaments that hold the ball and socket together. Twist the ball free from the socket.

5 Scrape the meat off the lower part of the rib cage and the shoulder bone. (The

shoulder bone is the bone that lies against the rib cage at the neck end and is joined at the base to the wing.)

6 When you reach the wing joint, scrape away the meat that surrounds the joint. Then cut through the white ligaments and twist the wing free from its socket.

7 Scrape the meat off the breastbone. Scrape down as far as the ridge of the breastbone but do not attempt to free it yet.

8 Repeat the process on the other side of the chicken, carefully scraping away the meat from the rib cage.

bone, pulling the leg inside out like a sleeve as you go, until you reach the end joint. Cut the bone free.

9 Lift the rib cage and, with great care because there is very little meat at this point to protect the skin, cut along the ridge of the breastbone to free it. The carcass of the chicken can now be removed completely.

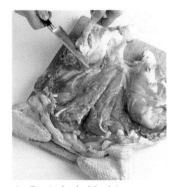

10 Take hold of the exposed end of one of the thighbones and scrape the meat down and away from the bone until the next joint is reached. Clear the flesh from round the joint and cut the sinews that hold it together – but do not break the joint.

11 Continue to scrape the flesh away from the

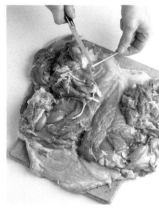

12 In the same way scrape the meat from the wing bone on the same side, and repeat with the leg and wing bones on the other side.

13 Cut out the white sinews attached to the meat of the legs and wings.

14 Lay out the chicken ready for stuffing. Keep the legs and wings turned inside out so that the bird forms a neat rugby football shape when it is sewn up.

ROASTING MEAT

Only tender cuts of meat should be roasted. During roasting, the fibres and tissues in the meat become taut, and meat that is already tough will only get tougher. Of the beef cuts, the best for roasting are sirloin, fillet and rib of beef. Of lamb cuts, the best for roasting are loin, leg, best end of neck and shoulder. The best veal cuts for roasting are fillet, loin, leg, breast, shoulder and best end of neck. Almost all pork cuts can be roasted and so can all birds. (Old chicken suitable only for boiling are rarely seen nowadays.) Joints on the bone cook quicker than rolled, off-the-bone joints.

Because no two joints or birds roast at exactly the same rate, a useful aid is a meat thermometer (see page 380).

Preparation before roasting

Before preparing meat for roasting, weigh the joint or bird and calculate the roasting time (see chart). The preparation suggested below is for oven-ready pieces of meat and birds.

BEEF With the exception of fillet of beef (see below), joints of beef require little preparation. Simply rub the joint all over with freshly ground black pepper or mustard.

LAMB For a piece of lamb, no preparation is necessary.

PORK If the butcher has not already done so, score the rind by making a series of deep, even cuts in it with the tip of a sharp knife. Rub oil into the rind and sprinkle plenty of coarse salt over it. The salt will make the rind crackly when roasted. See also *Roast loin of pork with cheese and fig stuffing* (page 74).

VEAL AND FILLET OF BEEF Both meats are very lean and have to be threaded – or 'larded' – with strips of fat before roasting.

To lard a piece of meat, cut some pork fat into slices ¼in (5mm) thick. Cut the slices into strips, also ¼in (5mm) thick. Thread a strip of fat into a larding needle.

Fat is threaded through the meat.

Use the needle to pull lengths of fat through the meat, leaving some sticking out at each end. Continue until the joint is evenly threaded with fat.

CHICKEN AND TURKEY Stuffing (forcemeat) keeps the flesh

moist and its flavour permeates the flesh. Chickens are usually stuffed in the body cavity. Turkeys are usually stuffed at both ends. Allow about 4oz (115g) of stuffing to every 1lb (450g) that the bird weighs.

A simple stuffing for chicken consists of 4oz (115g) of breadcrumbs mixed with 1oz (25g) of melted butter, a small, finely chopped onion, some chopped fresh herbs, such as sage or marjoram, an egg, and enough water to give the stuffing a firm but moist consistency.

Alternatively, simply put a lump of butter in the bird's body cavity together with some sprigs of fresh herbs.

The breast meat of chicken and turkey is lean, so smear the breast with plenty of soft butter and cover it with fat, streaky bacon rashers.

DUCK AND GOOSE With a skewer, prick the bird all over, penetrating deep into the flesh, to allow the fat to escape during cooking. Rub the duck or goose all over with salt and freshly ground pepper.

Duck and goose are both stuffed in the body cavity. A simple bread stuffing is often used to absorb some of the fat from the goose — it is discarded rather than being eaten.

GAME BIRDS Check over the birds to see whether there is any lead shot and remove it.

Because game birds are very lean they must be protected against drying out with rashers of fat, streaky bacon laid over the breast and legs. Place a knob of butter inside the body cavity.

Roasting

1 Put the prepared meat on a wire rack in a roasting tin. Lay joints on the bone with the fat side uppermost. Lay birds with the breast uppermost.

2 Place the tin in the centre of an oven preheated to the temperature indicated on the chart. While the meat is roasting, baste it from time to time by spooning up the juices in the bottom of the tin and pouring them over the meat. (Do not baste goose or duck which are both very fatty.)

3 When the roasting time is up, test the meat to see whether it is done. Stick a skewer into the centre — near a bone if the joint is on the bone, the thickest part of the thigh, in the case of birds. For pork, veal and poultry — all of which need to be well cooked — the juices that emerge should be a clear, golden colour with no trace of pinkness. For beef and lamb, the juices should be pink, if you like the meat rare. If you like it well done, they should be clear and golden. Alternatively, use a meat thermometer. Stick it into the meat towards the end of the cooking time. If the thermometer indicates that the meat has reached the correct temperature, it is cooked. Otherwise remove the thermometer and try again a few minutes later.

4 Before carving the meat, leave it to rest in a warm place out of the oven, covered in a tent of kitchen foil, for 15 to 30 minutes. This allows the fibres in the meat to contract and so makes it easier to carve.

● Meat can also be roasted in kitchen foil. This prevents the fat spitting over the inside of the oven, eliminates the need for basting, and retains all the juices. However, it does take longer to cook meat in foil — allow an extra 5-10 minutes per pound (450g). Wrap the joint or bird loosely in kitchen foil, sealing the edges. Roast on a wire rack in a roasting tin. For the last 30 minutes pull back the foil to brown the outside.

Creative ideas for roasting

USING HERBS Before roasting large joints make small cuts in the meat with the tip of a knife and insert sprigs of herbs — rosemary for lamb, marjoram or tarragon for beef.

Alternatively, remove the joint of meat, or the bird, from the oven 30 minutes before it finishes roasting. Sprinkle over it chopped fresh herbs, then return to the oven. The herbs will form a crusty coating.

Butter mixed with chopped herbs can be inserted between the flesh and the skin of a chicken. See *Herbs* (page 382).

USING SPICES Rub spices into the outer surface of a joint before roasting, making little cuts in the fat to let the spices seep right in.

With chicken, try rubbing celery salt and ground coriander into the skin. Finely crushed peppercorns can be rubbed sparingly into the skin of duck or goose. See *Spices* (page 384).

STUDDING WITH GARLIC Lamb and beef, in particular, are good studded with garlic. Peel some garlic cloves and cut them into slivers. With the tip of a knife, make cuts all over the joint and tuck a sliver of garlic into each.

MARINATING See *Wine in cooking* (page 385).

ROASTING TIMES

BEEF	*On the bone — rare*		20 mins at 220°C (425°F, gas mark 7) + 15 mins per lb at 190°C (375°F, gas mark 5)
		medium	20 mins at 220°C (425°F, gas mark 7) + 20 mins per lb at 190°C (375°F, gas mark 5)
	Off the bone		20 mins at 220°C (425°F, gas mark 7) + 25 mins per lb at 190°C (375°F, gas mark 5)
LAMB	*On the bone*		20 mins per lb + 20 mins extra at 180°C (350°F, gas mark 4)
	Off the bone		25 mins per lb + 25 mins extra at 180°C (350°F, gas mark 4)
PORK AND VEAL	*On the bone*		25 mins per lb + 25 mins extra at 220°C (425°F, gas mark 7)
	Off the bone		35 mins per lb + 35 mins extra at 190°C (375°F, gas mark 5)
CHICKEN			20 mins per lb at 190°C (375°F, gas mark 5)
TURKEY *Quick roast*	*8-10lb (3.6-4.5kg)*		30 mins at 220°C (425°F, gas mark 7) + 3-3½ hrs at 180°C (350°F, gas mark 4)
	10-14lb (4.5-6.4kg)		30 mins at 220°C (425°F, gas mark 7) + 3½-4 hrs at 180°C (350°F, gas mark 4)
	14-18lb (6.4-8.2kg)		30 mins at 220°C (425°F, gas mark 7) + 4-4½ hrs at 160°C (325°F, gas mark 3)
	18-20lb (8.2-9.1kg)		30 mins at 220°C (425°F, gas mark 7) + 4½-5 hrs at 160°C (325°F, gas mark 3)
Slow roast	*up to 12lb (5.4kg)*		25 mins per lb at 160°C (325°F, gas mark 3)
	over 12lb (5.4kg)		20 mins per lb at 160°C (325°F, gas mark 3)
DUCK			30 mins per lb at 180°C (350°F, gas mark 4)
GOOSE			20 mins at 220°C (425°F, gas mark 7) + 15 mins per lb at 180°C (350°F, gas mark 4)

CARVING

A carving knife should be very sharp, slightly flexible and between 8in (200mm) and 14in (355mm) long. It should have a pointed tip to get all the meat off the bone. A carving fork should be strong to keep the joint steady. The board or dish should be flat and resting on a mat to prevent it slipping.

Leave a joint or bird for about 15 minutes after roasting, covered in foil in a warm place. The meat sinews will contract and be easier to carve.

RIB OF BEEF

Ask the butcher to cut through the chine bone (the thick bone at right angles to the ribs) just above the point where it joins the ribs. It is too thick to be dealt with at home.

1 Stand the joint with the ribs on the bottom. Cut down between the chine bone and the meat to separate them. Discard the bone.

2 Holding the knife horizontally, cut between the meat and the end rib to free the meat from the rib.

3 Carve the meat that has been freed from the rib vertically into slices.

4 Repeat the process until enough meat has been carved.

LEG OF LAMB OR PORK

1 Place the roasted leg on a board with the rounded side on top. Make a vertical cut in the meat across the width of the leg near the knuckle. Make another cut slightly farther from the knuckle and at about 45 degrees to the first cut. Set aside the resulting small wedge-shaped slice of meat.

2 Carve a slice of meat parallel to the second cut.

3 Continue carving similar parallel slices of meat along the length of the joint until you reach the H-bone at the broad end. Near the end of the leg, it may be necessary to pivot the knife around the central bone in order to carve complete slices.

4 When all the meat has been carved from the top of the leg, take it by the knuckle and hold it firmly so that one side of the leg is raised slightly. Holding the knife roughly horizontally, slice the meat on the raised side of the leg.

5 Turn the leg over and slice the meat on the other side.

HAM JOINT

A proper ham stand is the best thing to support a ham when carving; it enables you to get at the joint from all angles. It is also possible to improvise one from an upturned cake stand or to use a spiked carving board instead.

Use a tea towel or a paper frill to hold the knuckle of the joint when carving.

1 Take the joint firmly by the knuckle and hold it on its side so that the exposed meat – or 'slipper' – opposite the knuckle is uppermost. Cutting away from you, carve a slice of meat off the slipper.

2 Continue carving slices parallel to the first slice until you reach the bone – known as the pin bone – about halfway along the top.

3 When you reach the pin bone, turn the knife slightly and carve slices off the remaining meat on either side of the bone.

4 Still holding the joint firmly by the knuckle, turn it over so that it is now resting on the slipper.

5 Carve a vertical slice off the far end of the joint.

6 Working back towards your body, continue carving off vertical slices. As you work back you will have to pivot the knife round the central bone to carve complete slices. It is usually best to discard the gristly meat close to the knuckle – or save it for stock.

CHICKEN AND TURKEY

Carving the breast meat of a chicken or turkey is easier if you have removed the wishbone before roasting the bird. To remove the bone, pull back the neck flap to expose the breast flesh. Use a small sharp knife to dig out the V-shaped wishbone which lies just below the surface of the flesh.

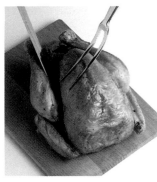

1 Place the roasted bird breast uppermost on the carving board. Cutting down through the joint where the thigh joins the body, cut off the leg on one side of the bird.

2 Cut the leg to separate thigh and drumstick.

3 Cut down through the corner of the breast near where the wing joins the body, to separate the wing from the body on one side.

4 Slice the breast meat, starting at the wing end and working back.

5 Repeat the process on the other side of the bird.

DUCK AND GOOSE

As with chicken and turkey, it is much easier to carve the breast meat of a duck or goose if the wishbone has been removed before the bird is roasted. Remove the wishbone in the same way as for a chicken or turkey (see above).

1 Place the roasted bird breast uppermost on the board. Cutting down through the joint where the thigh joins the body, cut the leg on one side of the bird free from the body. The leg is not usually large enough to be halved.

2 Cut down through the corner of the breast near the wing to separate the wing from the body.

3 Cutting vertically along the length of the body, carve the breast meat into long narrow slices.

4 Repeat the process on the other side of the bird.

HERBS

Herbs add variety to cooking, bringing subtle changes of flavour to every type of dish. Roast lamb, for example, can appear in at least four separate guises depending on whether you flavour it with rosemary, garlic, mint or marjoram; and that is before you start experimenting with other herbs.

Herbs are the leaves, stems or – in the case of garlic – bulbs of aromatic plants. Often the seeds are also used (dill and fennel, for example), but these are usually counted as spices.

Fresh herbs

Use fresh herbs whenever possible. Much of the subtlety of flavour is lost when they are dried. Fresh herbs can also be used as garnishes (see page 285). Most herbs can be grown in the garden or indoors in pots. Some of the more common herbs can be bought loose from a greengrocer. They can be kept in the refrigerator, loosely packed in a plastic bag, for up to three days.

Fresh herbs can be frozen for up to three months. Chop the herbs and pack them into small freezer bags, excluding as much air as possible.

Dried herbs

Dried herbs are invaluable in winter, or where there is no source of fresh herbs. When you use them, remember that their flavour is more concentrated than the flavour of fresh herbs. As a rough guide you should only use a third of the quantity recommended for fresh herbs.

Keep dried herbs in airtight jars in a dry but not hot place and away from direct natural light which will bleach them. Dried herbs will not keep for more than about six months – after that they lose their pungency. Only keep in stock those herbs that you use regularly. Buy others in small quantities when you need them.

Bouquets garnis

When making soups, stocks and casseroles, a small bundle of herbs whose flavours combine well are often added to the dish. This is known as a *bouquet garni*. A basic bouquet garni consists of a bay leaf, a sprig of thyme and three sprigs of parsley – but other herbs, such as sage, rosemary or tarragon, can be added as well, depending on the dish (see chart). Tie the herbs into a bundle inside a celery stick and leek leaves, or put them in a small muslin bag. Dried bouquets garnis can be bought.

COOKING WITH HERBS This chart is a guide to the most readily available herbs. A ● in one of the columns means that a herb goes well with a particular type of food or dish – bay with fish, for example. In some cases a herb goes especially well with certain foods within one of the categories – tarragon with shellfish, for example – and this is indicated. It is worth experimenting to find new combinations of food and herbs.

COOKING WITH HERBS

	STOCKS	SOUPS	MEAT	POULTRY AND GAME	FISH	EGG DISHES	SAUCES	VEGETABLES	SALADS	FRUIT	OTHERS
ANGELICA									●	Stewed fruit	
BASIL		●	Stews			Omelettes	Milk-based sauces	Mushrooms	Tomatoes		Pasta
BAY	●	●	Stews	●	●		Milk-based sauces	Cauliflower			Milk-based puddings and marinades
BORAGE									●		Wine cups
BURNET		●			●		Mayonnaise and milk-based sauces		●		
CHERVIL		●			●	●	Egg and cream sauces	Potatoes and carrots	●		
CHIVES		●			●	●		Potatoes	●		Cream cheese
CORIANDER		●	Curries and stews	Curries		●	Tomato sauces	Rice	Avocados		Milk-based puddings
DILL		●	Stews	●	●	Scrambled eggs ●		Potatoes	Cucumber and salad dressings		
FENNEL		Fish soups	Pork, veal and stews	Chicken	Mackerel and red mullet			Young vegetables	●		
GARLIC	●	●	●	●	●		●		●	●	Pasta, pizzas
HYSSOP		Vegetable soups	Stews	Use in stuffing				●	●	Fruit salads and grapefruit	
LEMON BALM				Use in stuffing	●		Mayonnaise and milk-based sauces		Salad dressings	Fruit salads and stewed fruit	Wine cups and lemonade
LOVAGE	●	Vegetable soups	Stews			Omelettes	Cream sauces	●	●		
MARJORAM		●	●	Use in stuffing	●	Omelettes			Tomatoes and salad dressings		Milk-based puddings
MINT			Mutton, lamb and veal		●	Scrambled eggs ●		Potatoes and peas	●	Fruit salads	Fruit and wine cups
OREGANO		Vegetable soups	Steak			Omelettes			Salad dressings	Stewed fruit	Pizzas
PARSLEY	●	●	Lamb and stews	Use in stuffing	●	Omelettes	Mayonnaise and cream sauces ●		Salad dressings		
ROSEMARY		●	Pork and lamb	Chicken							
SAGE		Vegetable soups	Pork and sausages	Goose and duck	Oily fish	Omelettes		Tomatoes			Cream cheese
SAVORY			●	Use in stuffing	Trout		●	Peas and beans			
SORREL		●	Veal		●				●		
SWEET CICELY									●	Stewed fruit	
TARRAGON		●	Veal	●	Shellfish	●	Egg and cream sauces		●	Tomatoes and salad dressings	
THYME	●	●	Stews	Use in stuffing	●		Cream and tomato sauces	●	●		Marinades

SPICES

Spices are the source of a wealth of different flavours. They can be bark, roots, fruit, flowers or aromatic seeds. Most are dried and then used whole, lightly crushed, or finely ground. If possible, buy whole spices and crush or grind them as needed. They have the crispest flavour.

Spices will not keep for ever. Use ready-ground spices within two to three months. The pungency of the peppery spices, such as cayenne and paprika, fades particularly quickly. Keep spices in airtight containers, away from direct light and heat, which robs them of their flavour.

Seasoning with spices is very much a matter of personal taste, and suggested quantities can only serve as a guide. With all but the very hot spices, try ¼ teaspoon of spice for every pound (450g) of meat, fish or vegetables, or for every pint (570ml) of sauce or soup. With very hot spices, such as cayenne, start with even less. Add spices cautiously; too much can easily kill other flavours.

The following are some of the most common spices.

ALLSPICE

Flavour reminiscent of nutmeg, cinnamon and cloves.
WHOLE Use in pickling.
GROUND Use on baked fruits, in root vegetable purées, in chocolate puddings and cakes.

ANISEED

Flavour reminiscent of liquorice.
WHOLE Use in sweet tea breads; fruit compôtes and pie fillings.
GROUND Use in biscuits, savoury stuffings for fish, and milk puddings.

CARAWAY SEED

WHOLE Use in cheese dips and fillings, sauerkraut and cabbage salads, sprinkled over pork before roasting.

CARDAMOM

Flavour reminiscent of eucalyptus.
PODS Crush whole pods. Use in curries and other Indian dishes.
SEEDS Use in custards, baked fruits and Danish pastries.

CAYENNE

Very hot – from the same family as chilli – use sparingly.
GROUND Sprinkle over egg and cheese dishes; use in fish sauces.

CELERY SEED

WHOLE Use in meat loaves, cabbage dishes and stuffings.
GROUND Use in soups, stews, fish dishes and salad dressings.

CHILLI POWDER

Varies – according to the brand – from pure ground chilli pepper, which is very hot, to a milder mix of ground chilli with other spices, usually cumin. The seeds are the fiercest part of whole dried chillis.

Use in meat loaves, hamburgers and spicy meat dishes, such as chilli con carne; sparingly in fish casseroles, soups, and scrambled eggs.

CINNAMON

It is almost impossible to grind the sticks of dried bark at home. Buy it ready ground if needed.
STICKS Use when pickling, stewing and baking fruit; in mulled wine.
GROUND Use in coffee and chocolate cakes, biscuits, milk puddings, fruit pies; for spicing drinks such as hot chocolate.

CLOVES

Very pungent – use sparingly.
WHOLE Use with baked fruits, fruit pies, and cooked gammon, pork and salt beef joints.
GROUND Use in cooked bean dishes and milk puddings.

CORIANDER

Flavour reminiscent of orange peel, particularly used in southern-Mediterranean and Indian cooking.
GROUND Use in meat and vegetable dishes; in marmalade and in syrup for fruit salad.

CUMIN SEED

Pungent, essential to curry.
WHOLE Use in sauerkraut, cabbage and pork dishes.
GROUND Use in cheese and egg dishes, and curries.

CURRY POWDER

A mixture of ground spices. Varies in strength. Garam masala is a similar mixture.

To make about 10oz (275g) standard curry powder, grind together 2oz (50g) whole cardamom pods, 1½oz (40g) cloves, 1½oz (40g) cumin seeds, 1oz (25g) coriander seeds, 2oz (50g) black peppercorns and 1oz (25g) turmeric. Mix with ¾oz (20g) ground cinnamon.

Use in curries and other highly spiced dishes; sparingly in fish soups, baked tomatoes, cooked shellfish dishes and sauces for vegetables.

CURRY PASTE

A mixture of spices in oil. Use in curries and marinades.

DILL SEED

Can be used as a milder substitute for caraway.
WHOLE Use in cabbage dishes, potato salad, and lamb stews.
GROUND Use in salad dressings and cheese dips.

FENNEL SEED

Delicate aniseed flavour.
WHOLE Use with fish, roast pork and in coffee cakes.

GINGER

ROOT Lightly crush or bruise a piece of root ginger. Use when poaching fruits, in mulled wine.
GROUND Use in cakes such as gingerbread, biscuits, apple sauce, and fruit puddings.

JUNIPER

The basic flavouring in gin.
WHOLE Use with cooked vegetables; lightly crushed in game and pork dishes.

MACE

The husk of a nutmeg; with a similar but stronger taste.
WHOLE Use when stewing meat, and cooking fruit.
GROUND Use in biscuits, milk puddings, soups, fish dishes, sweet pastries; with vegetables.

MUSTARD SEED

WHOLE Use when pickling onions and other vegetables.
GROUND Use in hot sauces; sparingly with vegetables (particularly cabbage) and salads.

NUTMEG

GROUND Use in sweet egg dishes such as custards, in spicy cakes and biscuits, with cooked vegetables (particularly spinach).

PAPRIKA

Relatively mild, sweet pepper.
GROUND Use in spicy meat dishes such as goulash, cheese dishes and cream soups.

PEPPER

Comes in the form of white, black or green peppercorns. White consist of the fiery kernel only. Black also have the aromatic outer husk. Green are immature berries.
WHOLE Use in pickling and preserving; marinades; when boiling whole pieces of meat.
GROUND Use in most savoury dishes.

SAFFRON

Vivid yellow colour.
GROUND To colour and flavour rice; to colour fish sauces.

Instead of grinding, steep a few strands in a little hot water for 30 minutes, then strain the liquid and add to the dish.

TURMERIC

Pungent, slightly bitter taste. Vivid yellow colour.
GROUND Use in pickles, in rice dishes instead of saffron, sparingly in egg and fish dishes.

WINE
IN COOKING

Added to savoury or sweet dishes, wine brings out and enhances the natural tastes of the food and also imparts its own depth of flavour. It is principally used either to marinate food or is added to the dish during cooking. When cooked, wine loses its alcohol content.

Use reasonably cheap, full-bodied wines for cooking. Red wine is generally used in cooking dark meats, such as beef and game. With white meats use white wine. Use sweet white wine for marinating fruits, adding to whisked desserts, such as syllabub, and for giving extra body to sweet sauces.

MARINADES To make a savoury marinade for meat, mix wine with sliced onion, crushed garlic, fresh or dried herbs (see page 382), and seasonings. The herbs and seasonings should be carefully matched to the meat.

The amount of marinade used depends on the size and shape of the meat. As a general guide, however, ½ pint (285ml) of marinade is enough for a 3lb (1.4kg) piece of meat.

To make a sweet marinade – for fruit, for example – the grated rind of citrus fruit and spices such as cinnamon can be added to sweet white wine.

Turn the food from time to time while it is marinating so that the flavour of the marinade penetrates it evenly.

CASSEROLES AND MEAT DISHES If the meat in a dish is not marinated before cooking, wine can be added as part of the cooking liquid. The wine should make up at least half the liquid – otherwise its flavour is drowned.

SAUCES If you are using wine in a roux-based sauce, the liquid should have equal quantities of wine and stock.

Very simple sauces can be made after frying or sautéeing meat: put a few tablespoons of wine into the hot frying pan; let it bubble while you scrape all the sediment off the sides and base of the pan, then pour the sauce over the meat.

Other alcoholic drinks in cooking

Fruit liqueurs, sherry, vermouth, beer, and spirits such as brandy and whisky, can also be used in cooking. Vermouth, diluted, makes a good substitute for wine. Sherry, vermouth or spirits are often added, for example, to dishes of sautéed meat or poultry at the beginning of cooking. Liqueurs, spirits and vermouth are also sometimes added to sweet sauces.

Spirits are used to flame (*flambé*) dishes. The spirit is spooned over food simmering in a shallow pan and, once it is really hot, set alight. Let the flames die down before serving.

To flame a Christmas pudding, warm the spirit (usually brandy or whisky) in a metal ladle or deep spoon, then carefully set it alight and pour the burning spirit over the pudding.

RICE

There are many varieties of rice – between 300 and 400 in general cultivation in India alone. They are distinguished by the shape and the starch content (this affects the stickiness of the cooked rice), but the main difference is between brown and white rice. Unpolished or brown rice has had only the husks removed, leaving the brown skin round each grain. It has a stronger, nuttier flavour than polished, white rice which has had the brown skin removed. It is also richer in essential nutrients, particularly vitamin B1, and has more fibre. White rice, on the other hand, has a much more delicate flavour and takes less time to cook.

There are three principal grains – long, medium and short. In general, long-grain rice is less sticky than short-grain rice, but there are exceptions; for example, some Indian rice, used for pilaus, and not sticky, is short-grained. Each type of rice is best suited to a particular type of cooking and they cannot be substituted with success.

LONG-GRAIN When cooked, the grains of long-grain rice are fluffy and separate. It is the best rice for paellas, pilaus, rice salads and with curries.

MEDIUM-GRAIN Slightly stickier than long-grain when cooked, medium-grain rice is suitable for making croquettes and fritters.

It is not as commonly available in Britain as either long- or short-grain rice.

SHORT-GRAIN The fat, almost round grains of short-grain rice become creamy when cooked. Short-grain rice is the traditional rice for sweet milk puddings. Italian short-grain rice, such as Arborio, is the best variety for making risottos.

Cooking rice

The most reliable way to cook rice is by absorption. Once the rice has absorbed a measured amount of liquid it is ready. Rice and liquid are measured by volume. You can use cups (2 cups of water for every cup of rice), but the simplest way to measure the rice is in a measuring jug. Allow 2-3fl oz (50-90ml) per person.

1 For each ¼ pint (150ml) of rice, allow ½ pint (285ml) of water or chicken stock and ½ teaspoon of salt.

2 Bring the water or stock to the boil in a large pan. Add the rice and salt. Bring back to the boil and stir once.

3 Cover the pan with a tightly fitting lid. Turn the heat down very low and cook very gently, without lifting the lid, for 15 minutes.

4 Look to see whether all the liquid has been absorbed. If not, replace the lid and cook for 2-3 minutes more until the rice is dry, tender but firm.

5 Stir with a fork to separate the grains, and season with salt and pepper to taste.

● Rice can also be cooked by the absorption method in the oven if you have another dish already cooking in the oven. Put the rice and salt into a casserole, then add the boiling liquid. Stir three or four times and cover tightly. Cook in an oven preheated to 180°C (350°F, gas mark 4) for 35-40 minutes.

Brown rice

Brown rice needs to be cooked twice as long as white rice. It is firmer to the bite when cooked than white rice.

Saffron rice

Serve rice flavoured and coloured by saffron with Indian dishes or Italian dishes such as *Pollo al cacciatore* (page 84).

For 8oz (225g) of rice, pour 4 tablespoons of boiling water over ½ teaspoon of saffron strands. Leave to steep for 30 minutes. Strain the liquid and then mix it into the rice cooking liquid before adding the rice.

Reheating cooked rice

Rice will keep for up to 24 hours in the refrigerator once cooked. To reheat rice, put it in a large heavy-based saucepan. Add 2 tablespoons of water. Cover the pan and heat through gently, shaking occasionally. Alternatively, heat the cold cooked rice by leaving it for a few minutes in a large metal sieve placed over a pan of gently simmering water.

VEGETABLES

Fresh, simply cooked vegetables are often the best accompaniment to a main course. Some also make good first courses. Choose vegetables in season; they usually have a better flavour than forced or imported ones.

Cooking

If in doubt always undercook vegetables; it is simple to cook them a little longer but almost impossible to retrieve a soggy mass of overcooked vegetables.

BOILING Put root vegetables in a pan with just enough cold water to cover them. Bring to the boil, then cover and cook over a moderate heat until tender.

With all other vegetables use the minimum of water or stock; a little over 1in (25mm) in the pan is usually ample. Bring the liquid to the boil, then add the vegetables. Return to the boil, then cover and cook over a moderate heat until tender.

STEAMING Most vegetables can be steamed, but large vegetables need to be broken or cut into small pieces beforehand.

Put the prepared vegetables in a steamer or metal colander over steadily simmering water. Cover with a lid and steam until the vegetables are tender.

BRAISING Blanch the vegetables in boiling water for 2-3 minutes. Drain them, then fry lightly in butter in a pan until just turning golden. Add enough chicken stock to the pan to half cover the vegetables and then season.

Cover, then either simmer, or cook in an oven preheated to 180°C (350°F, gas mark 4) until tender. Remove the vegetables. Reduce the juices or thicken them (see *Integral sauces*, page 371). Pour them over the vegetables.

First course vegetables

Vegetables such as asparagus and globe artichokes have to be eaten with the fingers, so provide finger bowls.

ASPARAGUS
SEASON Available from January to July. Best in May and June.
BUYING Allow 6-8 spears per person.
PREPARATION Trim off 1in (25mm) from each stalk. Peel the tough outer layer off the bottom half of older stalks.

Cooking upright protects the tips.

COOKING Tie the spears with string into bundles of about eight with tips together.

Stand upright in simmering salted water with the tips well above the water. Either use a double boiler with the top half inverted over the bottom half, or an ordinary pan with another pan or a heatproof bowl inverted over it. A metal vegetable steamer can be used to hold the asparagus upright. Leave for 12-15 minutes until the stalks are just tender. Alternatively, steam them for 10-15 minutes.
SERVING Hot, with melted butter or Hollandaise sauce (page 370). Cold, with vinaigrette (page 371).

To eat asparagus, hold it by the base and dip the tip in the butter or sauce. Eat the top two-thirds only, unless the spears are very young.

AVOCADO PEARS
SEASON All year.
BUYING Choose avocados that give slightly when pressed.
PREPARATION Cut in half lengthways. Carefully pull the two halves apart. Strike the stone sharply with a sharp knife so that the blade lodges firmly in the stone. Pull up the knife and the stone with it. Brush the flesh with lemon juice if it is to be left exposed for more than 5-10 minutes.
SERVING Halved, with vinaigrette; or with a filling such as seafood mixed with soured cream or mayonnaise; or add the flesh to a salad.

CORN ON THE COB
SEASON Available all year. Best from August to October.

BUYING Allow one medium cob per person.
PREPARATION Hold in both hands. With your thumbs, pull back the green husks and silky threads beneath to expose the yellow cob. Pull off the husks and silky threads.
COOKING Boil in unsalted water for about 5-10 minutes.
SERVING With plenty of butter. Special prongs for holding the cobs can be bought, but fingers and napkins will do just as well.

GLOBE ARTICHOKES
SEASON Available all year. Best late summer.
BUYING Allow one artichoke per person.
PREPARATION If the tips of the leaves are spiky and sharp, trim with scissors. Cut off the stalk as close to the base of the artichoke as possible.

The top of the globe is trimmed.

Trim a little over ½in (15mm) off the top of the artichoke to give it a flat top.
COOKING Boil in salted water for 20-30 minutes (until a leaf easily pulls away from the base); or steam for 45-50 minutes.

SERVING Stand the cooked artichoke on its base. Gently pull back the green outer leaves on top to expose the soft, purplish inner leaves.

The inedible choke is scooped out.

With a teaspoon, dig out the inner leaves to expose the fluffy choke beneath. Scrape out the choke. Beneath is the greyish, edible heart, or fond. Drain the artichoke upside down for a few minutes. Serve with melted butter or Hollandaise sauce.

To eat an artichoke, pull out each green outer leaf and dip its fleshy base into the sauce. Eat the base of the leaves only. Finally, pour some sauce over the fond and eat it with a knife and fork.

Root vegetables

It is generally best to buy root vegetables with earth still on them. Although ready-cleaned vegetables are easier to prepare, they go green more quickly and the high-pressure hoses used commercially to clean them tend to damage the skins. Some early vegetables, such as new potatoes, will be clean anyway.

BEETROOT

SEASON All year.

BUYING Often bought ready-cooked. If buying raw, choose firm, dark purple beetroots with unblemished skins. One medium-sized beetroot serves two people.

PREPARATION Trim off the leaf stalks about 1in (25mm) above the root. Carefully wash the root in cold running water. Try not to break the skin, or the colour will bleed out during cooking.

COOKING Boil in plenty of water for about an hour. When cooked, push off the skin.

SERVING Dice or slice hot cooked beetroot and sprinkle with a little white wine vinegar. Dice or slice cold cooked beetroot to serve in salads.

CARROTS

SEASON All year.

BUYING Allow a little over 4oz (115g) per person.

PREPARATION Scrub in cold water. Top and tail. Peel fully grown carrots with a potato peeler; scrape or scrub new ones. Slice full-grown carrots; leave new carrots whole.

COOKING Simmer in water or chicken stock for 10 minutes; or steam for 15-20 minutes.

SERVING Toss in butter with chopped parsley or mint. Grate raw carrots and serve with vinaigrette or mayonnaise.

CELERIAC

SEASON September to March.

BUYING Choose smooth, firm roots. Allow a little over 4oz (115g) per person.

The outer layer is pared thickly.

PREPARATION Scrub in cold water. Peel and cut into small cubes or matchstick strips.

COOKING Boil in water for about 10 minutes.

SERVING Cooked, with Béchamel sauce (page 368) or Hollandaise sauce. Raw, peeled and grated, tossed in vinaigrette.

PARSNIPS

SEASON September to April.

BUYING Allow one average-sized parsnip per person.

PREPARATION Scrub and trim off roots and tops, then peel. If fully grown, cut in half or quarters and cut out the woody core. If young, slice thickly.

COOKING Simmer in water or chicken stock for 25-30 minutes or cut into matchstick strips and steam for 15-20 minutes.

To roast, first blanch in salted water for 5 minutes. Dry, then roast with hot dripping in an oven preheated to 190°C (375°F, gas mark 5) for 45 minutes; or roast in the tin in which a joint is being roasted.

SERVING Toss boiled parsnips in butter with pepper and chopped parsley; or purée them.

POTATOES

PRINCIPAL TYPES Small new or early potatoes (especially suitable for boiling), and larger maincrop potatoes.

SEASON New potatoes: all year but best in early summer. Maincrop potatoes: all year.

BUYING Allow about 4oz (115g) of new potatoes per person or 6oz (175g) of maincrop potatoes.

BOILED AND MASHED Scrub new potatoes in cold water. Scrub maincrop potatoes then either leave the skins on, or peel them as finely as possible and cut into even-sized pieces.

Boil new potatoes (and peeled maincrop potatoes) in lightly salted water, with mint leaves, for about 15 minutes. Boil unpeeled maincrop potatoes for about 20 minutes, then peel.

To mash maincrop potatoes, drain and dry well. Mash them with a potato masher until smooth, or press them through a sieve or a food mill. For every pound (450g) of potatoes, add 1oz (25g) of butter, a little hot milk and plenty of salt and pepper. Beat with a wooden spoon until smooth and fluffy.

Toss boiled potatoes with butter and finely chopped mint. For potato salad, dice, then toss in vinaigrette or mayonnaise (page 369) while still warm.

ROAST Scrub and peel maincrop potatoes, then cut into even-sized pieces.

Blanch in boiling water for 5 minutes. Drain and dry well. Put in a roasting tin with hot dripping and roast in an oven preheated to 220°C (425°F, gas mark 7) for 1 hour, or roast in the tin with a roasting joint.

SAUTÉED Scrub and peel maincrop potatoes, then cut into slices about ¼in (5mm) thick.

Boil in salted water for about 5 minutes until almost cooked. Drain and fry in hot fat, turning frequently, for about 5 minutes until golden and crisp.

CHIPS Scrub and peel maincrop potatoes. Cut into slices a little over ¼in (5mm) thick, then cut the slices into strips a little over ¼in (5mm) wide. Rinse in cold water, then drain and dry well.

In a deep-fryer or pan (see *Deep-frying*, page 372), heat enough oil to cover the chips to 190°C (375°F), or until a chip dropped into it comes back up to the surface surrounded by bubbles. Add the chips and cook until tender and just starting to turn brown. Remove and drain well on kitchen paper. Before serving, return to the oil and fry until golden-brown. Drain well, and sprinkle with salt.

BAKED Choose large, even-sized, maincrop potatoes. Scrub, wash and dry thoroughly. Prick the skins with a fork.

Bake in an oven preheated to 220°C (425°F, gas mark 7) for 1-1½ hours until the potatoes give slightly when squeezed. To speed up cooking, stick a skewer through each potato to conduct heat into its heart.

SERVING Cut open and top with butter or soured cream.

SALSIFY

SEASON October to May.

BUYING Choose salsify with fresh green-grey leaves and regularly shaped roots. Allow 6-8oz (175-225g) per person.

The black skin is scraped away.

PREPARATION Scrub and trim off the ends. Remove the skin. Cut into 2in (50mm) lengths.

COOKING Simmer in water with a little lemon juice for about 40 minutes.

SERVING Tossed in butter. Or coarsely grate peeled, raw salsify and serve with vinaigrette.

SWEDE – see Turnip.

TURNIP

PRINCIPAL TYPES New or early turnips; maincrop turnips.

SEASON New turnips: April to June. Maincrop turnips: all year.

BUYING Allow about 6oz (175g) per person.

PREPARATION Top and tail, scrub and peel thickly. Leave new turnips whole; cut maincrop ones into even-sized pieces.

COOKING Simmer in water or chicken stock for about 20 minutes. Drain and dry in the

pan over a gentle heat.
SERVING Toss with butter and salt and pepper or mash with butter, cream and salt and pepper. Or leave raw and serve, grated, in salad.
Swede: available from September to May. Prepare and cook as maincrop turnips.

Green vegetables

Choose green vegetables with a bright green colour and no sign of yellow. Their leaves or pods should be crisp and unwrinkled.

BROAD BEANS
SEASON April to September.
BUYING Allow 8oz (225g) of beans in their pods per person.
PREPARATION Remove large beans from their pods. Leave very young beans in their pods but top and tail the pods. Skin very large, old beans.
COOKING Simmer in water or chicken stock for 10-15 minutes; or steam for 10 minutes.
SERVING Toss in butter with chopped chives. Alternatively, blanch for 2-3 minutes in boiling water, and serve in salads.

BROCCOLI – see Cauliflower.

BRUSSELS SPROUTS
SEASON August to March. Best after first frosts.
BUYING Allow 4oz (115g) per person.
PREPARATION Trim base and remove loose outer leaves. Cut a cross in the base.
COOKING Simmer in water for 8-10 minutes or steam for 12-15 minutes.

SERVING Toss with melted butter and salt and pepper.

CABBAGE
PRINCIPAL TYPES Red cabbage (actually purple); crinkly savoy and winter cabbages; densely packed white cabbage; green spring and summer cabbages.
SEASON Mainly autumn and winter, except for spring and summer cabbages.
BUYING Allow 4oz (115g) per person.
PREPARATION Remove coarse outer leaves. Cut into wedges and remove the hard centre core. Shred or leave as wedges.
COOKING Simmer in about 1in (25mm) of water or chicken stock in a covered pan. Simmer wedges for 12 minutes, shredded cabbage for 5 minutes. Turn once or twice during cooking.
SERVING Toss with butter and pepper. Serve shredded raw cabbage in salads.
Kale: available from November to May. Trim off stems and remove midribs from leaves. Shred and cook as cabbage.
Spring greens: available from November to April. Shred the leaves and cook and serve as cabbage.

CAULIFLOWER
SEASON All year.
BUYING One large head serves four people.
PREPARATION Wash thoroughly. Trim the stalk and remove the outer leaves. Leave the head whole or break into even-sized clumps of florets.
COOKING Simmer whole head

in water for 15-20 minutes or clumps of florets for about 8 minutes.
SERVING Topped with melted butter and fried breadcrumbs or with Béchamel or Mornay sauce (page 368).
Broccoli: purple, white and green-sprouting (calabrese) varieties. Cook and serve as cauliflower.

FRENCH BEANS – see Runner beans.

KALE – see Cabbage.

MANGETOUT – see Peas.

PEAS
SEASON May to October.
BUYING Allow 8oz (225g) per person.
PREPARATION Remove from the pods.
COOKING Simmer in water, with mint, for 10 minutes.
SERVING Toss in butter with chopped mint.
Mangetout: also known as sugar or snow peas. Main season is spring and early summer. Simply top and tail pods. Cook whole in a very little water for 5 minutes and serve as peas.

RUNNER BEANS
SEASON July to October.
BUYING Allow a little over 4oz (115g) per person.
PREPARATION Top and tail and trim off a thin strip on either side of each bean. Cut into oblique slices or shred.
COOKING Simmer in salted water for 5 minutes.
SERVING Toss in butter with

plenty of chopped parsley.
French beans: available all year but best from June to September. Top and tail. Simmer for 5 minutes; or steam for 10 minutes. Serve as runner beans.

SORREL – see Spinach.

SPINACH
SEASON All year.
BUYING Allow 8oz (225g) per person.
PREPARATION Wash several times in cold water.
COOKING Do not dry after washing. Lift straight into a pan, then cover and cook for 6-8 minutes over gentle heat. Drain and press out water.
SERVING Season with nutmeg and toss in butter or a little cream. Serve young spinach leaves raw in salads.
Sorrel: available spring and early summer. Prepare, cook and serve as spinach.

SPRING GREENS – see Cabbage

Other vegetables

Although tomatoes are strictly fruit, and mushrooms are fungi, they are both generally eaten as vegetables.

CELERY
SEASON All year.
BUYING One head should serve five people.
PREPARATION Trim off the roots and leafy tops. Separate the sticks and scrub clean. Cut the sticks into 4in (100mm) lengths.
COOKING Simmer in chicken stock for 10-15 minutes; or

steam for 5-10 minutes; or braise them in the oven for 30 minutes.
SERVING With Béchamel or Mornay sauce. Or leave raw and serve, sliced, in salads.

CHICORY
SEASON September to June.
BUYING Choose chicory with crisp, firmly packed heads. Allow one head per person.
PREPARATION Remove discoloured outer leaves.
COOKING Simmer in chicken stock for 12-15 minutes.
SERVING With Béchamel sauce, or raw, shredded, in salads.

COURGETTES – see Marrow.

FLORENCE FENNEL
SEASON All year.
BUYING Appearance is not necessarily a guide to flavour. Allow one head per person.

The feathery leaves are cut off.

PREPARATION Trim off the roots, shoots and feathery leaves. Scrape off any brown marks.
COOKING As for celery.
SERVING As for celery.

LEEKS

SEASON August to May.

BUYING Allow 8oz (225g) per person.

PREPARATION Trim off the roots and most of the top leaves. If the leeks are to be cooked whole, stand them, top down, in a large jug of water so that the earth soaks away. Otherwise, slit the leeks down to within about 1½in (40mm) from the base and wash thoroughly under cold running water.

COOKING Boil whole in salted water for 15 minutes; or fry strips lightly in butter for 6-8 minutes; or braise whole, leaving to simmer for 1 hour.

SERVING Boiled, with Béchamel or Mornay sauce. Fried, sprinkled with chopped herbs.

MARROW

SEASON April to October, but best in summer.

BUYING Choose smaller marrows. Allow about 4oz (115g) per person.

PREPARATION Peel old marrows; leave young ones unpeeled. Halve lengthways. Scoop out seeds, then cut into slices about ½in (15mm) thick.

COOKING Simmer in water or chicken stock for 5 minutes, or fry lightly in butter.

To bake, blanch the pieces in boiling water for 1 minute, then drain. Put in an ovenproof dish or casserole. Top with knobs of butter and bake in an oven preheated to 180°C (350°F, gas mark 4) for 30 minutes.

SERVING Toss in butter and sprinkle with chopped herbs.

Courgettes (zucchini): available all year but best in summer. Trim off ends and slice thickly. Simmer as marrow or steam for 10 minutes, or shallow-fry in butter or oil. Serve as marrow.

MUSHROOMS

PRINCIPAL TYPES Mild-flavoured button mushrooms; cup mushrooms; strong-flavoured flat mushrooms; also wild mushrooms, such as chanterelles.

SEASON All year. Wild mushrooms usually only available in the autumn.

BUYING Allow 2-3oz (50-75g) per person.

PREPARATION Wipe button or cup mushrooms clean with a damp cloth, then dry. Trim stalks. Remove stalks from flat mushrooms and peel the caps.

COOKING Fry in butter with a little lemon juice for 3-4 minutes; or grill for 3-4 minutes.

SERVING With pan juices, a dash of lemon juice, thyme or chopped parsley and salt and pepper. Or serve button mushrooms raw in salads.

TOMATOES

PRINCIPAL VARIETIES Small cherry tomatoes; salad tomatoes; large Mediterranean (beefsteak) tomatoes.

SEASON All year, but best in summer.

PREPARATION Wash and remove stalks.

COOKING Halve unpeeled tomatoes. Top with a knob of butter, a little dried basil and salt and pepper. Grill under moderate heat for 4-6 minutes.

SERVING Grilled, as a first course or as an accompanying vegetable. Raw, sliced or quartered in salads or on their own with olive oil and chopped fresh basil or chives.

Hot water loosens the skins.

SKINNING Nick the skin of each tomato with a sharp knife. Place in a heatproof bowl and cover with boiling water. When the skins start to crack, remove from the water and peel.

Salad vegetables

The best salads are often improvised from ingredients that happen to be to hand. When making a salad, bear in mind its appearance, texture and flavour. Mix soft vegetables, such as lettuce, with more crunchy ones, and offset acid-flavoured ones with, for example, sweet tomatoes. The colours should complement each other.

Use a china or glass salad bowl. Wooden ones will soak up the dressing and eventually give salads a rancid taste. The top of the bowl should be wide so that you can toss salads easily.

Many other vegetables in addition to those described below can be used in salads. See the entries under root, green and other vegetables. Vegetables with soft or crunchy flesh can be served raw. Others with tougher flesh, such as french beans, should first be blanched briefly.

Tinned vegetables – tinned sweetcorn, for example – and left-over cooked vegetables can also be mixed with fresh ones. Other ingredients can be used in salads as well as vegetables. For example: eggs; cheese; pasta; rice; fresh, dried or tinned fruit; olives; anchovies and nuts.

BEAN SPROUTS

PRINCIPAL TYPES Adzuki bean, alfalfa, fenugreek, mung bean and soya bean sprouts.

PREPARATION Rinse and serve whole.

CHINESE LEAF (Chinese cabbage)

SEASON December to April.

PREPARATION Wash and shred the leaves.

SERVING As lettuce. Can also be stir-fried or cooked as for cabbage but allowing less time.

CUCUMBER

SEASON All year.

BUYING Avoid any more than about 2in (50mm) in diameter.

PREPARATION Simply wash, or if preferred, peel, then slice thinly. Some people prefer to seed cucumbers, in which case cut in half lengthways and scoop out the seeds with a teaspoon.

SERVING In salads or with white wine vinegar, chopped fresh dill, salt and pepper; or with yoghurt, garlic and chopped fresh mint.

LAMB'S LETTUCE (corn salad, mâche)

SEASON November to March.

PREPARATION Wash the leaves very thoroughly. Pat dry or dry in salad shaker or spinner.

SERVING With vinaigrette.

LETTUCE

PRINCIPAL TYPES Cabbage or round lettuce; tall cos lettuce; crisp Webb's and Iceberg lettuce; curly endive; red oak-leaf lettuce.

SEASON All year.

PREPARATION Separate leaves and wash. Pat dry or dry in salad shaker or spinner.

SERVING With vinaigrette.

Radicchio: prepare and use as for lettuce.

MUSTARD AND CRESS

PREPARATION Cut from its bed with kitchen scissors. Rinse thoroughly in a colander. Dry.

PEPPER (or pimento)

PRINCIPAL TYPES Red, green and yellow peppers.

SEASON All year.

PREPARATION Cut off a thin slice at the stalk end. Scoop out seeds and excess white membrane. Cut into thin rings or strips.

RADICCHIO – see Lettuce.

RADISHES

SEASON All year. Best from March to May.

PREPARATION Wash. Merely trim tops, leaving about ½in (15mm) of green stalks, or slice. Leave in iced water for 30 minutes before serving.

SPRING ONIONS
SEASON All year. Best from
March to May.
PREPARATION Trim roots and
tops. Peel off outer skin, if
damaged. Leave whole or finely
chop bulbs and stems.

WATERCRESS
SEASON All year.
PREPARATION Trim the stalks
and discard any discoloured
leaves. Wash and shake dry.
Divide into sprigs.

Salad dressing

The kind of dressing used with a
salad depends on the ingredients. With a light green salad,
for example, serve a delicate oil
and vinegar or lemon juice
dressing (see page 371). The
flavours of a more substantial
winter salad of cabbage and
carrots are complemented by a
heavier mayonnaise-based dressing (see page 369). Yoghurt
seasoned with salt and pepper,
and perhaps some chopped
watercress or chives, also makes
a good dressing.

Do not add too much dressing; it should enhance the
flavours of the salad, not drown
them. It is always best to toss
the salad carefully and gently,
and to do it by hand.

Many other dressings are included in recipes in this book
and can be adapted to other
dishes (see *Index*).

PANCAKES

A pancake or crêpe pan usually
measures between 6-8in (150-
200mm) across, and has shallow,
gently sloping sides so that the
pancakes can be slipped out
easily onto a plate. An omelette
pan or a heavy-based frying pan
can be used instead, but the
process will not be quite as
easy.

When making pancakes, be
prepared for the first couple to
fail until the pan reaches just the
right degree of heat and oiliness.
At first you will have to cook the
pancakes over a high heat, but
turn the heat down as the pan
gets hotter.

When folding or rolling pancakes, remember that the side
that was cooked first looks best
and should be on the outside.
Unfilled pancakes can be stored
stacked between layers of lightly
greased greaseproof paper. They
will keep for a week in the
refrigerator and for 2 months in
the freezer, wrapped in foil or
polythene.

PREPARATION TIME *40 minutes
plus standing time*

INGREDIENTS – *makes about
twelve 6 in (150 mm)
pancakes:*
4 oz (115 g) plain flour
Pinch of salt
1 egg, beaten
½ pint (285 ml) milk
*1 tablespoon melted butter or
vegetable oil*
Vegetable oil

1 Sieve the flour and salt into a
mixing bowl.

2 Make a well in the centre
of the flour, and drop the
egg into the well. Pour in half
the milk. Add the butter or oil.

3 With a wooden spoon,
gradually draw the flour
into the egg and milk mixture,
beating well all the time.

4 When all the flour has been
incorporated and the
mixture is smooth, beat in the
remaining milk. Go on beating
with a wooden spoon or an
electric whisk until the batter is
smooth and bubbly, with the
consistency of single cream.
● As an alternative, pour all the
ingredients into a liquidiser or
food processor and blend for
about 1 minute.

5 Leave the batter to stand
for about 30 minutes
(1 hour if you have used
wholemeal flour). Stir the batter
just before using. Use a ladle or
a small jug for pouring the
batter into the pan.

6 Pour a little oil into the
pancake pan. Heat until the
oil starts to smoke slightly,
tipping and tilting the pan so
that the base and sides are
covered with a thin film. Pour
off any excess.

7 Aiming for the centre of
the pan, pour in just
enough batter (usually about a
ladleful) to cover the base of the
pan thinly.

8 As you pour in the batter,
quickly tip and tilt the pan
so that it runs and swirls evenly
over the base before it cooks.
Pour off any excess.

9 Cook until the top of the
pancake dries and changes
colour and the underside is
golden-brown. To check the
colour of the underside, lift up a
corner of the pancake with a
spatula. If the pancake still
seems sticky let it cook a little
while longer.

10 Slide the spatula under
the centre of the
pancake and flip it over. Cook
until the side of the pancake that
is now underneath is also
coloured golden-brown.

11 Slide the pancake out of
the pan onto a plate lined
with greased greaseproof paper
and lay another sheet of greased
greaseproof paper over it.
Continue making pancakes in
this way until all the batter is
used up.

PASTA

Fresh pasta enriched with eggs –
pasta all'uovo – has more flavour
than dried pasta and takes less
time to cook. The simple shapes
can be made at home with little
trouble.

It is not essential to have any
special equipment. However, a
pasta machine makes the task
much easier and quicker.

If you are making pasta by
hand, use strong breadmaking
flour. If you have a machine use
ordinary plain flour. Wholemeal
flour can also be used.

Fresh pasta can be wrapped
loosely and kept in the refrigerator for up to 24 hours.
Tagliatelle or fettucine hung up
and left to dry slightly, until no
longer floppy, will keep in the
refrigerator for up to 5 days.
Fresh pasta can also be frozen
for up to 6 months. Squares of
pasta to be made into cannelloni
must be used immediately, or
they will not roll up.

PREPARATION TIME: *20-25
minutes with a machine,
1 hour by hand plus resting
time*

INGREDIENTS – *serves 4-6:*
11 oz (300 g) plain flour
1 level teaspoon salt
3 large eggs
1 tablespoon olive oil
A little water, if necessary

1 Sieve the flour and salt into a
mixing bowl. Make a well in
the centre.

2 Beat together the eggs and olive oil, then pour into the well. With a knife, gradually draw the flour into the egg and oil mixture.

3 Go on mixing with the knife until the eggs and oil are thoroughly absorbed by the flour. The dough should neither be sticky nor too dry. Add a little more flour if the dough is too sticky, or a few drops of water if it is too dry.

SPINACH PASTA Mix 3oz (75g) finely chopped cooked spinach with the dry ingredients.
TOMATO PASTA Mix 4 tablespoons of tomato purée with the dry ingredients.
HERB PASTA Mix 2 level tablespoons finely chopped fresh herbs with the dry ingredients.

Rolling out the dough by machine

1 Knead the dough for 3-4 minutes. Divide the dough into fist-sized lumps.

2 Feed one of the lumps of dough through the rollers on a reasonably wide setting.

3 Fold the resulting sheet of dough in three; then slightly reduce the setting on the machine and roll the dough through the machine again.

4 Roll the dough through the machine four or five more times, reducing the setting each time, until the dough is paper-thin, smooth and silky. If it sticks in the rollers, sprinkle it lightly with flour.

5 Hang the rolled-out dough on a broomstick suspended between two chairs or tables or on a coathanger.

Rolling out the dough by hand

1 Knead the dough for about 15 minutes until smooth and elastic. Cover with a cloth and leave to rest for 1 hour.

2 Place a lump on a floured surface. Using a heavy wooden pin, roll it out to a smooth, paper-thin rectangle. Keep the surface underneath the dough well floured and work quickly – or the dough will become too dry to manage.

3 Hang the rolled-out dough on a broomstick or coathanger as above.

Cutting the pasta to shape

As the pasta is cut out, lay the shapes out on a teacloth sprinkled with flour and leave them to dry for an hour.

HAND-CUT TAGLIATELLE Lightly flour each sheet of dough, then roll it up like a swiss roll. Cut the rolls into strips ¼-½in (5-15mm) wide. With floured hands, shake out each strip. To make fettucine, cut the rolls into strips ⅛in (3mm) wide.

MACHINE-CUT TAGLIATELLE Adjust the pasta machine to cut strips. Feed through one of the sheets of dough.

LASAGNE Cut each sheet of dough into rectangles about 3½in × 4in (90mm × 100mm).

FARFALLE With a pastry wheel, cut each sheet of dough into small rectangles about 2in × 1¼in (50mm × 32mm). Pinch the centre of each rectangle to make a bow or butterfly shape.

Cooking pasta

About 5 pints (2.8 litres) of water is needed for cooking 1lb (450g) of pasta. With less water, the pasta will be sticky and taste of paste. Use a large pan so that the water does not boil over. Allow 3-4oz (75-115g) of pasta per person.

The cooking times of different types of pasta and even different brands of the same type of pasta vary considerably. Wholemeal pasta takes a little longer to cook than ordinary pasta, and fresh pasta always cooks much more quickly than dried pasta. To be sure of cooking pasta to the right consistency, remove a piece every now and then and bite it to test the texture. It should be *al dente*, 'firm to the bite', yet cooked through.

Approximate cooking times

LONG PASTA: *dried 8-10 minutes*
fresh 3-4 minutes
LARGE SHAPED PASTA: *6-8 minutes*
SMALL SHAPED AND FOLDED PASTA: *2-3 minutes*
FILLED PASTA: *4-6 minutes*

To cook lasagne and cannelloni, see *Seafood lasagne* (page 256) and *Tuna cannelloni* (page 94).

1 Put 5 pints (2.8 litres) of water in a large pan and add 1 level teaspoon of salt and a teaspoon of olive, vegetable or corn oil (this helps to keep the pieces of pasta separate). Bring the water to a rapid boil.

2 Add the pasta. With long, dried pasta, hold one end and lower the other into the boiling water. As the pasta in the water starts to soften, curl it round the pan and push the rest into the water.

3 Stir the pasta once and bring the water quickly back to a rolling boil. Leave to boil steadily uncovered.

4 When the pasta is cooked remove from the heat and immediately pour into a colander. Shake the colander thoroughly to drain off the water, then transfer the pasta to a serving dish and mix with the sauce. Serve it as quickly as possible. The pasta will go on cooking in its own heat and will overcook and become sticky if left too long.

PASTRY

Flour, fat and liquid – water, milk or egg – are combined into many different pastries, from simple shortcrust to puff pastry which rises into thousands of fragile layers.

In addition to the shortcrust, puff and choux pastries described here, recipes for other pastries can be found elsewhere in the book: rich, sweet shortcrust under *Fresh fruit tartlets* (page 37) and *Torte de Albicocche* (page 234), chocolate shortcrust under *Chocolate pretzels* (page 135), cheese choux under *Cheese puffs* (page 345), hot water crust under *Hare pie* (page 272), and strudel pastry under *Cherry strudel* (page 45).

Each pastry has a different proportion of ingredients and a different technique, but certain tips are common to all.

● Sieve the flour. This aerates it.
● Keep everything as cool as possible – if the fat starts to melt the pastry will be difficult to handle and end up tough. Keep the kitchen cool by opening windows if necessary. (It is often best to save pastry-making for a cool day.) If your hands are hot, rinse them under cold water or rest them for a few seconds on a sealed polythene bag filled with ice cubes.
● Use only the tips of your fingers when handling the pastry. They are cooler than palms and this also prevents you overhandling the pastry.

Rolling out pastry

1 Use a marble or wooden work surface. Both are poor conductors of heat and so the surface will stay cool.

2 Flour the board and the pin but not the pastry. Too much flour will spoil the balance in the pastry and make it tough.

3 Use a wooden rolling pin without handles so that you get a wide, even distribution of pressure on the pastry.

4 Use quick, light strokes, pressing evenly on the pin with both hands.

5 Roll in a forwards direction, lifting the pin after each stroke.

6 Do not roll the edges of the pastry or you will press out the pockets of air.

7 Turn the pastry rather than the board when you want to roll the pastry in a different direction.

SHORTCRUST PASTRY

Shortcrust pastry can be used for pies (both sweet and savoury), flans, quiches and all kinds of tarts and tartlets.

Basic shortcrust pastry consists of flour and fat – half as much fat as flour – bound together with water.

The fat can be butter, margarine (block, not soft), lard or white vegetable fat. Butter and margarine give the best flavour, but lard and white vegetable fat make 'shorter' pastry – pastry with a more crumbly, melting texture. To combine the advantages of both, use equal quantities of either butter or margarine and lard. The fat should be at room temperature.

Plain flour is the best type for shortcrust pastry. Self-raising flour can be used but tends to make the pastry overcrumbly. Wholemeal flour is best mixed with an equal quantity of self-raising flour.

Shortcrust pastry can be varied. To make sweet shortcrust for sweet flans and tarts to be served cold, add 1oz (25g) of caster sugar to the basic mixture and use cold milk instead of water. A rich, sweet shortcrust (pâte sucrée) is made with eggs, sugar and extra butter (see *Fresh fruit tartlets*, page 37). To make cheese shortcrust add a pinch of cayenne pepper and up to 4oz (115g) of grated, strongly flavoured hard cheese, such as Cheddar. Use butter or margarine only and a mixture of water and lightly beaten egg instead of water on its own.

Uncooked shortcrust pastry will keep for 3 days wrapped in the refrigerator. It can be kept frozen for 3 months.

Quantities of shortcrust pastry needed for recipes are usually indicated by the amount of flour used – '4oz (115g) shortcrust pastry', for example, means pastry made with 4oz (115g) of flour. The weight of the made pastry is roughly the weight of the flour and fat combined: 6oz (175g) of ready-made shortcrust, for example, has been made with only 4oz (115g) of flour.

PREPARATION TIME: *20 minutes plus resting time*

INGREDIENTS – *makes enough to line a 9 in (230 mm) flan ring or cover a 2 pint (1.1 litre) pie dish:*

8 oz (225 g) plain flour
½ teaspoon salt
2 oz (50 g) butter
2 oz (50 g) lard
2–3 tablespoons cold water

1 Sieve the flour and salt into a large mixing bowl.

2 With a round-bladed knife, cut the butter and lard together on a plate. Add the butter and lard mixture in pieces to the flour in the bowl, distributing the pieces evenly over the flour.

3 Rub the fat into the flour with the tips of your fingers, lifting the mixture up and letting it fall back into the bowl to keep it cool and aerated. Continue until all the fat has been rubbed in and the mixture resembles fine breadcrumbs.

4 Sprinkle the water, a little at a time, evenly over the mixture. Stir the water into the mixture with the round-bladed knife, gradually binding the dough together. Add just enough water to produce a soft but not sticky dough which comes away cleanly from the sides of the mixing bowl.

5 Turn the dough out onto a floured surface. Knead it gently one or two times, but no more, to remove any cracks. Cover the ball of dough with the upturned bowl and leave to rest for 20-30 minutes.

6 Roll the dough out on a floured surface.

Lining a flan tin

Flans, quiches and tarts are best made in loose-based metal flan tins or flan rings – large rings, either plain or fluted, which are placed on a baking tray. Porcelain dishes look attractive, but porcelain is a poor conductor of heat and flans cooked in such dishes tend to have soggy bases.

1 Roll out the pastry in a circle that is large enough to cover both the base and sides of the flan tin and leave a little to spare all round.

2 Roll the pastry loosely around the rolling pin.

3 Lift the rolling pin and pastry over the tin. Unroll the pastry to cover the tin.

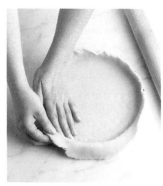

4 Ease the pastry gently into the base of the tin and, using your fingertips, press from the centre out to expel any air bubbles trapped beneath it. Press the pastry into the flutes and corners and up the sides.

5 Roll the pin across the top of the tin so that the sharp edges trim off the pastry edges. Lift away the trimmings.

Baking blind

If the filling for a flan, quiche or tart needs little or no baking then the pastry case is baked blind, that is before the filling is added. Baking beans hold the pastry down and ensure that the case holds its shape. Baking beans can be pulses, rice or pasta shapes kept specially for the purpose and used repeatedly – or you can buy specially made ceramic or aluminium beans.

1 Prick the base of the pastry lining. This lets the air out.

2 Take a piece of greaseproof paper – or kitchen foil – large enough to cover the flan tin. Crumple the paper, then use it to line the pastry case, tucking it into the sides.

3 Cover the paper with a layer of baking beans.

4 Bake for about 15 minutes in the centre of an oven preheated to 190°C (375°F, gas mark 5), then lift out the beans and paper.
● If the pastry case is to be cooked further with a filling, simply return the empty case to the oven for 2-3 minutes to dry out and crisp the pastry.
● If the pastry case is not to be cooked with a filling, return the empty case to the oven for a further 15 minutes to dry out and cook completely.

Covering a pie dish

A rim of pastry holds the pastry lid of a pie to the rim of the pie dish and prevents juices leaking during cooking.

1 Roll out the pastry to an oval 2-3in (50-80mm) larger than the top of the dish all round.

2 Invert the dish onto the pastry and trim the pastry so that it is about ¾in (20mm) larger than the top of the dish all round. Set aside both the inner oval of pastry (the lid) and the remaining outer rim.

3 Wet the rim of the dish. Lay on the outer rim of pastry and press it in place.

4 Fill the pie dish. If there is not enough filling to make a pile in the centre of the dish, put an egg cup or pie funnel in the centre of the pastry to hold up the lid.

5 Brush the pastry rim of the dish with water and lift the lid over the dish. Press the lid onto the rim.

6 Lift up the pie dish in one hand. With a knife held at a slight angle in the other hand, trim off the excess pastry from beneath so that the pastry on top of the edge slightly overhangs the pastry below.

7 Put the dish down to 'knock up' the edges. With the back of your forefinger, press down lightly just behind the edge of the pastry lid. At the same time make a series of shallow horizontal cuts in the edge beneath with the back of the knife. Continue in this way all round the dish.

8 The edge can be decorated by fluting. Pinch the top edge of the pastry between finger and thumb. Make a vertical cut into the side of the pastry held between finger and thumb. Repeat all round the pie.

9 Make two slits in the centre of the pastry lid (over the pie funnel if there is one) to allow steam to escape.

PUFF PASTRY

Since it combines equal quantities of fat and flour, puff pastry is very rich. The fat is not rubbed into the flour but incorporated into the pastry, with air, as the dough is repeatedly rolled, folded, then rolled again.

Puff pastry is best made with strong (breadmaking) white flour. Wholemeal flour is too heavy. The best flavour comes from butter, which should be cold but not absolutely hard.

The pastry requires careful, even rolling. If it is stretched or is not level or square it will rise unevenly when baked. If the top of the pastry is glazed with beaten egg or milk, be careful not to let the glaze run down the edge; it will seal the layers together and cause the pastry to rise unevenly. Any decorative marking on the pastry – scoring or a crisscross design, for example – should be done after it has been glazed.

Uncooked puff pastry can be kept in the refrigerator for 2-3 days ready to be rolled out when needed. It will keep in the freezer for 3-4 months, wrapped very securely. Allow frozen pastry to thaw completely – about 1-1½ hours – before trying to roll it out. Bought puff pastry should be rolled out thinner than homemade pastry because it rises higher.

The quantities given in the recipes in this book are for 'prepared weight' of pastry. To make the pastry, use half the given weight of flour and half the given weight of butter.

PREPARATION TIME: *3½ hours including chilling time*

INGREDIENTS – *makes about 1¼ lb (575 g) prepared weight puff pastry:*
8 oz (225 g) plain flour
About ¼ pint (150 ml) iced water
1 teaspoon lemon juice
8 oz (225 g) unsalted butter, in a block

1 Sieve the flour into a mixing bowl. Add the iced water and lemon juice. Mix with a round-bladed knife to a firm but not hard dough.

2 Turn the dough onto a lightly floured surface and knead it until it is smooth and silky – usually 5-10 minutes. Wrap the dough in a polythene bag and chill for 15-20 minutes in the refrigerator.

3 Put the block of butter between two layers of greaseproof paper or polythene. Flatten the block by beating it with a rolling pin to make a neat rectangle about ¾in (20mm) thick. Roll the top of the butter to make it smooth.

4 On a floured surface and with a floured rolling pin, roll out the dough to a rectangle about 1in (25mm) wider than the butter is long and about three times as long as the butter is wide.

5 Position the dough with one short side facing you, then lay the butter across the centre. Fold the bottom third of the dough up over the butter. Fold the top third down over the bottom third. Press down on the open edges with the rolling pin to seal them.

6 Give the dough a quarter turn clockwise so that one of the short sides is facing you. Brush off any excess flour and roll the dough out to its original

size, taking care that the butter does not break through the surface of the dough.

7 Repeat the folding process and seal the edges, then wrap the dough and chill for 30 minutes.

8 Repeat the rolling, folding, sealing and chilling process five more times. To keep track of the number of times the dough has been rolled out, make small depressions in it with your fingers every time it is chilled.

9 Roll out the pastry to the right thickness and shape.

10 Leave it in a cool place for 10 minutes to relax before putting it into the oven. This will reduce the shrinkage.

Vol-au-vent cases

Vol-au-vent cases can be made in many different sizes. Cut them out with biscuit cutters or a sharp knife. Unbaked cases can be cooked from frozen.

1 Roll out the pastry to ½in (15mm) thick.

2 Cut out rounds using a floured 3in (80mm) fluted biscuit cutter.

3 Transfer the rounds carefully to a wetted baking sheet using a palette knife.

4 Brush the top of each pastry round lightly with beaten egg.

5 With a 2in (50mm) fluted biscuit cutter, cut halfway through the depth of each round. This central section will form the lid.

6 When cooked, ease off the lid with the point of a knife. Scoop any soft pastry out of the centre of the vol-au-vent case and discard it.

CHOUX PASTRY

Unlike other pastries, choux pastry is made in a saucepan and rather than being rolled, the soft, glossy dough is piped or spooned into shape. The best flour to use is strong white plain (breadmaking) flour. Use butter for the best flavour.

The pastry can be made up to 14 hours in advance and kept wrapped in polythene in the refrigerator. Baked, unfilled puffs or eclairs will keep crisp for a day in an airtight tin.

PREPARATION TIME: *20 minutes*

INGREDIENTS – *makes 15 eclairs or 30 puffs:*
2½ oz (65 g) plain flour
Pinch of salt
2 oz (50 g) butter
¼ pint (150 ml) water
2 eggs, beaten

1 Fold a large piece of greaseproof paper in half. Unfold it again and lay it out flat. Sieve the flour and salt together onto the paper.

2 Put the butter and water into a heavy-based pan. Heat gently, stirring all the time, until the butter has melted. Turn up the heat and bring to a full, rolling boil.

3 Turn off the heat. Form the folded greaseproof paper into a chute, and tip the flour and salt very quickly into the pan. At once start beating the mixture vigorously with a wooden spoon. Continue until the flour has been absorbed.

4 Return the pan to a gentle heat and continue beating the mixture for about a minute until it forms a smooth dough which comes away from the sides. Remove from the heat.

5 Let the dough cool for a few minutes until you can comfortably hold your hand against the sides of the pan.

6 Add the beaten eggs, a little at a time, beating thoroughly with a wooden spoon after each addition.

7 Continue beating until the dough is smooth and glossy.
● The eggs can be beaten into the dough with an electric whisk, in which case first tip the dough into a large mixing bowl.

8 Cover the pan or mixing bowl and leave it in the refrigerator until ready to use.

9 Once the eclairs or puffs have been piped out (see below), bake in an oven preheated to 220°C (425°F, gas mark 7) unless the recipe states otherwise. Do not open the oven door during baking.

10 Bake until perfectly crisp and dry – usually 15-20 minutes.

11 Remove from the oven and make a small slit in the side of the puffs or eclairs to let the steam out. Return to the oven for 5 minutes to dry out.

Piping eclairs

1 Fit a piping bag with a ½in (15mm) plain nozzle.

2 Hold the bag in one hand a little over halfway up. Fold the top of the bag down over your hand and spread out your fingers to open up the bag.

3 Fill the piping bag tightly with choux pastry.

4 Fold the top of the bag back up, then twist it, forcing the pastry down until it is just about to come out of the end of the nozzle.

5 Grasping the bag so that it is pinched closed just above the pastry, squeeze it until the required length of choux pastry has been forced out onto a baking tray – greased or lined with greaseproof or non-stick baking paper.

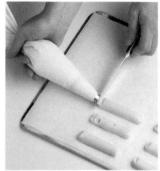

6 With a wet knife held against the nozzle, cut off the length of pastry, lifting the nozzle as you cut.

7 Give the bag a twist to maintain the pressure on the pastry. Leaving a 2in (50mm) space between the eclairs to allow for expansion during cooking, pipe out another length of pastry.

Shaping choux puffs

● Drop spoonfuls of pastry onto a baking tray. Use a teaspoon for puffs intended to be 1-1½in (25-40mm) in diameter. Use a dessertspoon for larger buns.

● Puffs can also be piped onto the baking tray. Fill a piping bag fitted with a ½in (15mm) plain nozzle. Holding the bag vertically over the tray, squeeze out a mound of pastry then cut it off with a wet knife. To make small puffs, each mound should be the size of a walnut; to make large puffs, each should be the size of a plum.

Filling choux puffs

1 Fit a forcing bag with a ¼in (5mm) nozzle. Fill the bag with the filling for the puffs.

2 Take one of the baked puffs and squeeze in the filling through the hole made in the puff to let out the steam.

3 Shake the puff gently to get the filling into all its corners inside. Then top up the puff with more filling.
● Alternatively, cut the baked puffs almost in half horizontally. Open them up and fill them from the forcing bag or with a teaspoon.
● Fill eclairs by piping or spooning filling through the slit in the side.

FRUIT

Regardless of how simple or grand a meal may be, fruit is always an appropriate dessert. As long as the fruit is perfectly ripe and unblemished, a bowl of strawberries or a luscious peach will compete with the most elaborate cream confection.

Many types of fruit need little or no preparation for serving as a dessert: provide small knives and forks with which to eat the fruit and, ideally, finger bowls. Fruit salads and poached fruit are simple, yet provide scope for imaginative combinations.

Fruit salads

Choose the best fruit in season for a fruit salad. There is the greatest selection in summer and autumn, but in the winter citrus fruit, pears and apples are at their best and fresh dates and lychees are available.

Most fruit can be used in fruit salad. Fresh dates, fresh figs, some dried fruit (such as dried apricots), chopped preserved stem ginger or even avocados (see *Emerald and jade salad*, page 337) can also be added. Generally, 2lb (900g) of fruit makes a salad for six people.

1 Make the syrup. For 2lb (900g) of fruit, mix 4oz (115g) of caster sugar and ¼ pint (150ml) of water in a small pan. Stir over low heat until the sugar has dissolved.

2 Bring to the boil, then simmer for 2 minutes. Leave to cool.

3 Add 2 tablespoons lemon juice and, if you wish, a tablespoon or more of kirsch, brandy, sherry, ginger wine or liqueur (orange-flavoured liqueurs are very good). Pour the syrup into a serving bowl.

4 Prepare the fruit (see the following list of fruits).

5 Add the fruit to the syrup in the bowl and mix thoroughly. Cover and leave in a cool place or the refrigerator for a few hours, to let the flavours blend and develop.

Poaching fruit

The syrup in which fruit is poached can be flavoured with, for example, the juice and grated rind of an orange, lemon or lime, a vanilla pod, cloves, cinnamon or ginger. Brandy, port, sherry, kirsch or liqueur can be sprinkled over when the fruit has been poached. The amount of sugar used in the syrup may have to be altered slightly, depending on the sweetness or acidity of the fruit.

1 Prepare the fruit (see the following list of fruits).

2 Make the syrup. For 1lb (450g) of fruit, mix in a large pan 4oz (115g) of sugar, ½ pint (285ml) of water and any flavourings. Stir over low heat until the sugar has dissolved.

3 Cover the pan and bring the syrup to the boil. Lower the heat and simmer for 2 minutes.

4 Add the fruit and poach in the gently simmering syrup until the fruit is tender but still holding its shape – usually 10-15 minutes. Turn the fruit with a slotted spoon once or twice during poaching.

APPLES
PRINCIPAL TYPES Sweet dessert apples (such as Cox's Orange Pippin and Golden Delicious); acid-flavoured cooking apples (such as Bramley's Seedling). Firm dessert apples can be cooked and keep their shape better than cooking apples. Use dessert apples for topping apple flans, for example.
SEASON Dessert and cooking apples are available all year.
SERVING AS A DESSERT
● Whole.
● Peeled, cored and sliced in fruit salad.
● Poached: peel, core and slice the apples; add the grated rind and juice of a lemon, a stick of cinnamon and some Calvados to ½ pint (285ml) of syrup.
● Baked: core the apples and make a cut in the skin round the middle. Fill the centre with brown sugar, a little butter and dried fruit such as sultanas, chopped dates, figs or apricots. Bake with a few tablespoons of water for about 30 minutes in an oven preheated to 180°C (350°F, gas mark 4), basting occasionally with the juices. Serve with cream or custard.

APRICOTS
SEASON May to August, and December to February.
BUYING Choose firm apricots with brightly coloured, unbruised skins.
SERVING AS A DESSERT
● Whole: serve whole only if perfectly ripe – if they smell very sweet like honey and give readily to gentle pressure. Usually, the more brightly coloured apricots are the sweetest. Keep pale apricots for cooking.
● Halved and stoned, in fruit salad.
● Poached: blanch and skin the apricots; add a vanilla pod or a cinnamon stick to ½ pint (285ml) syrup.

AVOCADOS – see Vegetables.

BANANAS
SEASON All year.
BUYING Choose bananas with unbruised, yellow skins flecked with brown; they generally have a better flavour. Buy bunches rather than individual bananas; the bananas are less likely to be bruised beneath the skin than individual bananas.
SERVING AS A DESSERT
● Whole.
● Sliced, with cream, or in a fruit salad, added at the last moment.
● Sautéed: split whole bananas lengthways; sauté in butter with grated orange rind and a little rum. Serve warm with cream.
● Baked: bake or grill in skins until skins are charred (this can be done on a barbecue); peel and serve warm with cream.

BLACKBERRIES – see Raspberries.

CHERIMOYAS – see Custard apples.

CHERRIES
PRINCIPAL TYPES Sweet dessert cherries, further divided into black cherries (in fact, a rich purple) and white cherries (light red or pink); and acid Morello cherries, only used for cooking.
SEASON Dessert cherries: June and July. Morello cherries: April to August.
SERVING AS A DESSERT Dessert cherries:
● Whole.
● Stoned in a fruit salad.
Dessert or Morello cherries:
● Poached: stone the cherries; use ½ pint (285ml) of red wine in the syrup instead of water. Serve chilled.

STONING A CHERRY If a special cherry stoner is used the cherries stay whole. The cherry is inserted in the cup of the stoner and the prong forces out the stone.

The cherries can instead be halved to remove the stones. This is fine for fruit salad, but the cherries will not hold their shape when cooked.

CURRANTS

PRINCIPAL TYPES Redcurrants, blackcurrants and white currants.

SEASON July and August.

SERVING AS A DESSERT Strip currants from their stalks (see below); rinse and drain.

● Stirred into lightly sweetened cream and *fromage blanc*, with a little brandy or sherry.

● In fruit salad.

STRIPPING CURRANTS Hold a bunch of currants over a bowl. Hook the stalks between the prongs of a fork and pull the currants away from the stalks.

CUSTARD APPLES

SEASON September to February.

SERVING AS A DESSERT

● Halved, with cream. To eat, scoop out the flesh with a teaspoon. Do not eat the seeds. *Sweet-sops, cherimoyas:* serve and eat as custard apples.

DAMSONS – see Plums.

DATES (fresh)

SEASON September to March.

SERVING AS A DESSERT

● Whole. Pinch off the stalk, then squeeze the opposite end.

The skin will slip off.

● Stoned, sliced in fruit salad.

● Stoned and stuffed with cream cheese.

FIGS (fresh)

SEASON August to December.

SERVING AS A DESSERT Wipe first with a damp cloth.

● Quartered (see below), with cream. The skins can be eaten as well as the flesh.

● Sliced and soaked in a little medium dry sherry or Marsala.

PRESENTING A FRESH FIG Cut the fig almost into quarters so that only the skin at the bottom holds the segments together.

GOOSEBERRIES

PRINCIPAL TYPES Small green cooking berries; green, red, white and yellow dessert berries.

SERVING AS A DESSERT Top and tail before serving.

● Dessert berries: whole, sprinkled with sugar.

● Cooking berries: poached. Add a few heads of elderflower in a muslin bag to the syrup.

GRAPES (dessert)

PRINCIPAL TYPES Black grapes and white grapes.

SEASON Available all year, but cheaper in late summer and autumn.

SERVING AS A DESSERT Rinse and drain grapes before serving.

● Whole – provide a small pair of scissors for snipping off small bunches.

● In fruit salad: remove the pips and, if you prefer, peel the grapes (see below).

REMOVING PIPS FROM GRAPES

● Halve the grapes and flick out the pips with the tip of a knife.

● Alternatively, to keep the grapes whole, dig the pips out of each grape with the rounded end of a hair grip or a small paper clip inserted through the hole where the stem was.

PEELING GRAPES Peel with your fingers. If the skins do not come away easily, put in a heatproof bowl and cover with boiling water. Leave for 30 seconds. Transfer to a bowl of cold water, then peel with your fingers.

GRAPEFRUIT

PRINCIPAL TYPES Ordinary grapefruit (suitable for breakfast and first courses); sweeter pink grapefruit (suitable for dessert as well).

SEASON All year.

SERVING

● Halved. For a first course, sprinkle each half with brown sugar and some sherry or vermouth. Place under a hot grill until the sugar caramelises.

● Peeled and sliced or segmented (as for oranges); in fruit salad.

Ugli Fruit: available from October to February. Serve and eat as grapefruit.

GREENGAGES – see Plums.

KIWI FRUIT (Chinese gooseberries)

SEASON June to March.

SERVING AS A DESSERT

● Halved. To eat, scoop out the flesh with a teaspoon.

● Peeled and sliced in fruit salad.

KUMQUATS

SEASON All year.

SERVING AS A DESSERT

● Sliced in fruit salad.

● Poached.

LOGANBERRIES – see Raspberries.

LYCHEES

SEASON December to February.

SERVING AS A DESSERT

● Whole, chilled.

● Peeled (see below) and stoned, in a fruit salad.

● Poached in a ginger-flavoured syrup. Serve poached lychees well chilled.

PEELING A LYCHEE Crack the brittle skin with your fingernail, then carefully peel the skin off with your fingers.

MANDARIN ORANGES – see Satsumas.

MANGOES

SEASON Available all year but cheapest from January to September.

BUYING Choose mangoes that give slightly when pressed.

SERVING AS A DESSERT

● Whole. To eat, first prod the mango with a sharp knife to find out which way the large, flattish stone is lying. Cut the flesh as cleanly as possible off one side of the stone, and then repeat with the other side. Scoop the flesh out with a teaspoon.

● Sliced, in a fruit salad.

Peeling and slicing a mango

1 Score the skin of the mango, cutting right round the fruit lengthways. Make another cut perpendicular to the first, so that the skin is cut into quarters.

2 Hold the mango with a fork. With a knife, peel back each quarter of skin. With some varieties, the skin may not come off easily, in which case, use a potato peeler.

3 Cut the flesh lengthways into wedge-shaped slices.

MELON

PRINCIPAL TYPES Cantaloupe (with perfumed orange flesh); Charentais (small with a more delicate flavour); Honeydew (oval, with green flesh); Ogen (with yellow-green flesh).
SEASON All year.
BUYING Choose melons that give slightly at the stalk end.
SERVING
● Chilled and cut lengthways into segments with the seeds removed. Serve with ginger or cured meat, such as Parma ham. Serve at breakfast or as a starter.
● Halved across the middle, seeded and filled with port or ginger wine.
● In a fruit salad: halve and remove the seeds, then use a melon baller or spoon to scoop out the flesh into the salad.
Watermelons: available from March to December. Cut lengthways into segments or scoop the flesh into a fruit salad.

NECTARINES – see Peaches.

ORANGES

PRINCIPAL TYPES Sweet oranges (such as Jaffa and navel oranges); bitter Seville oranges.
SEASON Sweet oranges are available all year but generally best in winter and spring. Seville oranges are available in January and February.
SERVING AS A DESSERT
● Whole.
● Peeled and sliced or segmented (see below), soaked in an orange-flavoured liqueur and sprinkled with cinnamon.
● Peeled and sliced or segmented in fruit salad.

Removing peel and pith

1 Cut off a thin slice of skin at the top of the orange to expose the flesh. Cut off a similar slice at the bottom.

2 Rest the orange on its base. Cutting downwards, remove a thin vertical strip of skin and pith to expose the flesh. Continue to cut off the pith all round the orange.

3 Trim off any remaining bits of pith.

Segmenting an orange

1 Remove the peel and pith from the orange.

2 Hold the orange over a bowl. With a very sharp knife, cut out each segment by slicing down between the segment and the membrane on one side of it, cutting as close to the membrane as possible. In the same way, slice down between the segment and membrane on the other side.

3 When all the segments have been cut out, squeeze the membranes tightly in your fist to extract the remaining orange juice.

PASSION FRUIT (granadillas)

SEASON All year.
BUYING Choose fruit with brittle, deeply wrinkled skins.
SERVING AS A DESSERT
● Halved across the middle, with cream. Eat with a teaspoon.
● In a fruit salad: scoop the flesh into the salad.

PREPARING A PASSION FRUIT Halve the fruit across the middle. Scoop out the soft, pulpy flesh with a teaspoon.

PAPAYAS (papaws)

SEASON All year.
BUYING Choose papayas that give slightly when pressed.

SERVING
● Chilled and cut lengthways into segments, with the seeds removed. Serve with lime at breakfast or as a dessert. As a starter, serve with smoked ham such as Parma ham.
● In a fruit salad: halve and remove the seeds, then chop the flesh and add to the salad.

PEACHES

SEASON Available from March to December but best in summer.
BUYING Choose fruit that is firm but not hard.
SERVING AS A DESSERT
● Whole.
● Peeled, pierced with a skewer and marinated for an hour in a liqueur, such as Cointreau or Grand Marnier.
● Chopped and peeled (as for grapes) in fruit salad.
● Poached: peel, halve and stone the peaches; add a vanilla pod to ½ pint (285ml) of syrup. Serve chilled.
Nectarines: available from July to September. Serve and eat as peaches.

PEARS

PRINCIPAL TYPES Dessert pears (such as Conference pears); cooking pears (such as Pitmaston Duchess pears). Firm dessert pears can also be cooked.
SEASON Pears are available all year but are usually best during autumn and winter.
SERVING AS A DESSERT
● Whole.
● Peeled, halved, cored and brushed well with lemon juice. Sprinkle with liqueur or brandy.

● Chopped in fruit salad.
● Poached: peel, halve and core the pears; add the grated rind and juice of a lemon and either a vanilla pod or ½ teaspoon of ground ginger to ½ pint (285ml) of syrup.

PERSIMMONS

PRINCIPAL TYPES In this country, the most common variety is the Sharon from Israel (also known as Sharon fruit).
SEASON October to January.
BUYING Choose firm, fleshy, Sharon persimmons that are a pale orange colour. Other persimmons must be completely soft and almost rotten.
SERVING AS A DESSERT Sharon persimmons:
● Whole, with sugar and cream. Eat the skin as well as the flesh.
● In fruit salad: sliced crossways or halved and the flesh scooped into the salad.
Other persimmons:
● Cut in half. To eat, scoop out the flesh with a teaspoon.
● In fruit salad: scoop the flesh into the salad.

PREPARING THE FLESH OF A PERSIMMON The skin of the Sharon persimmon, although edible, is quite tough and in some cases it is better to halve the fruit across the middle and scoop out the flesh with a teaspoon.

PINEAPPLES
SEASON All year.
SERVING AS A DESSERT
● Sliced (see below), sprinkled with kirsch or a fruit-flavoured liqueur, with cream.
● Sliced in fruit salad.

Slicing a pineapple

1 Lay the pineapple on its side. Slice off the top and bottom ends, then cut the pineapple through its centre into slices ½in (15mm) thick.

2 With a sharp knife, cut the coarse skin off each slice. Prise the woody 'eyes' out with the tip of the knife.

3 With an apple corer or small pastry cutter, cut out the centre core of each slice.

PLUMS
PRINCIPAL TYPES Dessert plums (such as Victoria and Czar plums); cooking plums (most other purple plums). Dessert plums can also be cooked.
SEASON Late summer and autumn.
SERVING AS A DESSERT
● Whole.
● Halved and stoned in fruit salad.
● Poached: halve and stone the plums; add a stick of cinnamon, 3 cloves and the grated rind and juice of a lemon to ½ pint (285ml) of syrup.

Damsons: serve poached in a red wine syrup.
Greengages: serve whole or in fruit salad as plums.

POMEGRANATES
SEASON September to January.
BUYING Choose pomegranates with a firm bright red, yellow or pink skin.
SERVING AS A DESSERT
● Halved. Only the seeds, enclosed in pink jelly, are eaten.
● Scoop out the seeds and serve them very well chilled.
● In a fruit salad: scoop the seeds into the salad.

REMOVING THE SEEDS FROM A POMEGRANATE Halve the fruit across the middle. Scoop out the shiny red or pink seeds – not the bitter white or yellow membrane – with a teaspoon.

RASPBERRIES
SEASON June to August.
SERVING AS A DESSERT Rinse and drain before serving.
● Hulled, with cream and sugar.
● Hulled, in a fruit salad.
Blackberries: available July to October. Serve as raspberries.
Loganberries: available July and August. Serve as raspberries.

RHUBARB
PRINCIPAL TYPES Early or forced rhubarb; maincrop rhubarb.
SEASON Forced rhubarb: December to March. Maincrop rhubarb: March to June.
SERVING AS A DESSERT
● Poached: cut off the base of the stalks and the poisonous leaves. Cut out any bruised or damaged parts. Peel maincrop rhubarb. Wash and dry. Cut into 1in (25mm) pieces. Add the grated rind and juice of an orange and either a ground stick of cinnamon or ½ teaspoon of ground ginger to ½ pint (285ml) of syrup. Serve hot or chilled.

SATSUMAS
SEASON October to February.
SERVING AS A DESSERT
● Whole.
● In a fruit salad: segmented.
Mandarin oranges: serve as satsumas.
Tangerines: serve as satsumas.

STRAWBERRIES
SEASON Available all year but best from May to July.
SERVING AS A DESSERT
● Hulled and left whole with cream and sugar. Spoon over a little wine, orange or lemon juice, or orange-flavoured liqueur.
● Whole with *Fromage à la crème* (page 235).
● Hulled in a fruit salad.

SWEET-SOPS – *see Custard apples.*

TANGERINES – *see Satsumas.*

UGLI FRUIT – *see Grapefruit.*

JAMS AND JELLIES

To make jams and jellies, fruit is first simmered in water to release pectin, a substance found in the fruit which causes the preserve to set. Sugar is then added and dissolved. It is best to warm the sugar for 15-20 minutes beforehand in a warm oven.

Testing for setting point

Jam sets when the pectin gels – at about 105°C (220°F). The saucer (or wrinkle) test is the most reliable method of testing for a set.

1 Chill two or three saucers in the refrigerator.

2 Remove the pan of preserve from the heat. Put a teaspoon of preserve onto one of the chilled saucers. Leave in the refrigerator for a minute.

3 Push the preserve with your finger. If the surface wrinkles, and the preserve stays apart, setting point has been reached. Otherwise, return the pan to the heat for 5 minutes, then test again.

Potting and sealing

1 Thoroughly clean and dry the jars. Warm them in an oven preheated to 110°C (225°F, gas mark ¼) for a few minutes.

2 Fill the jars to the brim, holding them at an angle to prevent air bubbles forming.

3 If using screw-top lids, put them on immediately. If using Cellophane or plastic covers, put a waxed paper disc, waxed side down, on top of the preserve in each jar. Press the disc to force out air bubbles.

4 While the preserve is still very hot or when it is completely cold, cap the jars with the covers. Dampen one side and lay them, damp side up, on the jars. Hold them in place with rubber bands.

CAKE DECORATING

The basic skills of icing and decorating a cake are quickly mastered and can be used to turn a plain cake into the focal point of a celebration.

Recipes for glacé icing and buttercream (soft and suitable for icing soft sponges), royal and fondant icings (harder and suitable for firm fruit cakes), and marzipan are given below. Several other icings and fillings are included in recipes in this book. See *Index*.

Useful pieces of equipment are a palette knife for applying and spreading the icing, a plastic cake scraper, an icing ruler and a piping bag and nozzles for piping decorations.

GLACÉ ICING

Glacé icing is usually used to coat sponge cakes or buns – it is rarely used for piping.

PREPARATION TIME: *10 minutes*

INGREDIENTS – *makes enough to ice the top and sides of a 7 in (180 mm) round cake or 15 buns:*
6 oz (175 g) icing sugar
2-3 tablespoons hot water
A few drops food colouring (optional)

Sieve the icing sugar into a bowl and mix in the water a little at a time. If you want to ice the top and sides of a cake, make the icing thick enough to coat the back of a spoon but thin enough to flow easily. If you just want to ice the top of a cake use less water. Add the food colouring, if being used.

Use the icing at once because it sets quickly.
VANILLA GLACÉ ICING Beat in ¼ teaspoon of vanilla essence.
LEMON GLACÉ ICING Beat in 1 tablespoon of lemon juice and make up the liquid with 2-3 tablespoons of hot water.
ORANGE GLACÉ ICING Use fresh orange juice instead of water.
COFFEE GLACÉ ICING Beat in 1½ teaspoons of coffee essence.
CHOCOLATE GLACÉ ICING Sieve 3 level teaspoons of cocoa into the bowl with the icing sugar. Beat in a few drops of vanilla essence.

Applying glacé icing

1 Set the cake on a wire rack and pour the icing onto it. Using a warmed palette knife spread the icing over the top of the cake only, or let it run evenly down the sides.

2 Arrange any decorations after the icing has stopped flowing, but before it sets.

3 Do not move the iced cake for at least an hour – or the icing will crack.

● To 'feather' glacé icing on a cake, spread icing smoothly over the top of the cake. Pipe thin lines of icing in a contrasting colour about 1in (25mm) apart, using a piping bag with a writing nozzle. Quickly, before the icing has set, use the tip of a knife to score lines across the top of the cake perpendicular to the lines of coloured icing. Turn the cake round and score lines, between the first set, in the opposite direction (see page 290).

BUTTERCREAM

Buttercream can be used as a filling and as an icing. It is also easy to pipe and is particularly suitable for decorating children's birthday cakes.

PREPARATION TIME: *15 minutes*

INGREDIENTS – *makes enough to fill and ice the top and sides of an 8 in (200 mm) round cake:*
5 oz (150 g) unsalted butter, softened
10 oz (275 g) icing sugar, sieved
Flavouring (see below)
1-2 tablespoons milk (optional)

Cream the butter with a wooden spoon or an electric beater until soft and fluffy. Gradually beat in the icing sugar and any flavouring. For a lighter texture, beat in some milk, a little at a time, until the consistency is right.
ORANGE BUTTERCREAM Beat in the finely grated zest of ½ orange and 1 tablespoon of orange juice.
LEMON BUTTERCREAM Beat in the finely grated zest of ½ lemon and 1 tablespoon of lemon juice.
CHOCOLATE BUTTERCREAM Melt 1½oz (40g) of chocolate in a bowl over simmering water. Beat the chocolate into the icing.
COFFEE BUTTERCREAM Dissolve 1 level tablespoon of instant coffee in 1 tablespoon of boiling water. Allow to cool a little, then beat into the icing.
MINT BUTTERCREAM Beat in a few drops of oil of peppermint or peppermint essence and a few drops of green food colouring.
VANILLA BUTTERCREAM Beat in ½ teaspoon of vanilla essence.

Applying buttercream

1 Spread the buttercream evenly over the cake with a palette knife.

2 Swirl the icing with a knife or rough it up.

MARZIPAN

This rich mixture of ground almonds, sugar and egg is also known as 'almond paste' or 'almond icing'. Marzipan can be used on its own as a decoration for cakes – see *Simnel cake* (page 127) and *Gold and silver marble cake* (page 128) – but its most common use is as a base covering for rich fruit cakes, which are then iced with royal or fondant icing. It provides a smooth foundation and a surface to which the icing will stick.

Two egg yolks or two egg whites can be used instead of the whole egg. The yolks make a yellower, richer marzipan than the whites.

The marzipan will keep, wrapped, for up to 2 weeks in the refrigerator. Ready-made marzipan can be bought. The 'white' variety is generally better quality than the yellow.

PREPARATION TIME: *10 minutes*

INGREDIENTS – *makes 1½ lb (700 g), enough to cover the top and sides of an 8 in (200 mm) square cake or a 9 in (230 mm) round cake:*
6 oz (175 g) icing sugar
6 oz (175 g) caster sugar
12 oz (350 g) ground almonds
1 egg
2 teaspoons lemon juice
2 teaspoons brandy (optional)

Sieve the icing sugar into a bowl. Add the caster sugar, ground almonds, egg, lemon juice and brandy, if used. Mix together to a smooth dough. Briefly knead the mixture in the bowl, then shape it into a ball. Do not handle the marzipan more than necessary otherwise it will become oily. Wrap the marzipan in greaseproof paper or a plastic bag and store in a cool place until needed.

Applying marzipan

To help the marzipan to stick to the cake, and to hold down any loose cake crumbs, the surface of the cake is first brushed with apricot glaze. To make enough glaze to cover an 8in (200mm) square cake or 9in (230mm) round cake, melt 2 heaped tablespoons of apricot jam with 2 teaspoons of water or lemon juice. Sieve out any lumps in the glaze, if necessary. Lightly beaten egg white can be used instead of apricot glaze.

A cake covered with marzipan should be covered with a tea

towel or greaseproof paper and left to dry for at least 24 hours before being iced. If the cake is going to be kept for a long time, leave it to dry for a week before icing over the marzipan.

1 If the top of the cake is domed, slice off most of the dome. Put the cake upside down on a cake board so that the flat bottom is now on top. Fill any gaps round the base with thin strips of marzipan.

2 Divide the marzipan in half. Set one half on one side, divide the other half into half again.

3 Sprinkle the work surface with sieved icing sugar. Roll out each of the smaller portions of marzipan to a strip a little wider than the depth of the cake and about half the circumference of the cake in length (measure the cake with a tape measure or some string).

4 Trim one long edge of each strip straight with a knife, using a clean ruler as a straight edge. Trim the ends so that each strip of marzipan is a little less than half the circumference of the cake in length.

5 Using a pastry brush, brush the sides of the cake with apricot glaze. Press the flat strips of marzipan against the sides. At one join, the two strips should butt up against each other. On the other side there will be a small gap to allow the marzipan to expand when rolled.

6 With a straight-edged glass or a jam jar, roll the marzipan so that it fits smoothly onto the sides of the cake and closes the gap. Alternatively, tip the cake up on its side and roll it gently like a wheel.

7 Trim off the top edges of the marzipan with a sharp knife laid flat on top of the cake.

8 Roll out the remaining portion of marzipan and use the cake tin as a guide to cut out a circle of marzipan to go on top of the cake. Brush the top of the cake with apricot glaze and carefully lift the marzipan onto it.

9 Gently roll the marzipan so that it fits the top exactly.

10 Seal the gap between the marzipan on the top and sides of the cake with a palette knife (warmed in hot water, then dried).

ROYAL ICING

Firm, white royal icing is the traditional covering for rich fruit cakes. Omit the glycerine if the icing has to be hard enough to support the upper tiers of a wedding cake. The icing will keep in an airtight container for up to 2 days. Stir it before use.

PREPARATION TIME: *15 minutes plus standing time*

INGREDIENTS — *makes enough to give two thin coats to the top and sides of an 8 in (200 mm) square cake or a 9 in (230 mm) round cake:*
2 lb (900 g) icing sugar
4 egg whites
2 teaspoons lemon juice
2 teaspoons glycerine

Sieve the icing sugar onto a plate. Beat the egg whites until frothy. Add the icing sugar a tablespoon at a time, beating well after each addition, until half the sugar has been used. Beat well for 5-10 minutes until the mixture grows in bulk and becomes fluffy.

Gradually add the lemon juice, glycerine and the remaining sugar, beating the mixture well after each addition. Go on beating until the icing stands in peaks and loses its shine.

Cover with a damp cloth and leave to stand for a few hours to let the air bubbles disperse.

Applying royal icing – Christmas cake

Royal icing can be used to make a very simple but effective decoration for a Christmas cake (see page 121). A smooth layer of icing serves as the foundation for a golden piped 'Merry Christmas', a shell border, and a top layer of rough icing. Ribbons and gold dragees add some glitter to the cake.

Allow 2-3 days for icing.

If you wish to use royal icing for a wedding cake, simply smooth ice the cake, but apply three or four coats.

Preparations

1 Make a 9in (230mm) round *Rich fruit cake* (page 120).

2 Cover the cake with marzipan (see opposite page), and let it dry for 1-2 days.

3 Make royal icing with 3lb (1.4kg) icing sugar – enough for all the decoration.

Smooth icing

The first layer of smooth icing usually has a number of air bubbles and is never completely smooth. Other coats have to be added before the icing is really smooth. Two thin coats should be enough for this cake, which will then be rough iced.

1 Spoon some icing onto the top of the cake. Work the air bubbles out of the icing by spreading it vigorously to and fro across the top of the cake with a long palette knife.

2 Take a long ruler in both hands and, holding it at an angle of about 30 degrees to the top of the cake, draw it towards you over the top of the cake to level off the icing. Hold the ruler upright and run it round the side of the cake to scrape off any excess icing that has spread over the edges.

3 Rest the cake and cake board on top of a turntable or cake tin and, using the palette knife, cover the sides with icing. Scrape the icing smooth with a cake scraper (or palette knife held upright), revolving the cake as you work round it. It is not necessary to neaten the top edge at this stage. That can be done later, once the icing has dried completely. ▶

4 Leave the cake for at least 4 hours in a warm place to let the icing dry. Apply a second thin layer of icing to give a smooth surface.

5 Leave the icing to dry for 24 hours. Using a sharp knife, gently scrape away the hardened rim of excess icing sticking up round the top edge of the cake.

Lettering and rough icing

It is safest to design the lettering on a piece of tracing paper – rather than piping it directly onto the cake. The design can then be pricked out onto the top of the cake.

If you feel uncertain of your skills in piping out lettering, practise on a piece of grease-proof paper. If you do make a mistake while piping out the lettering on the cake itself, you can usually simply scrape it off and start again.

The large gold dragees and edible gold lustre powder colour used to decorate the cake can be bought in specialist grocers, confectioners and kitchen shops.

1 Rest the cake and its board on a cake tin. Cut out a long piece of greaseproof paper about ¼in (5mm) wider than the ribbons you will be using to tie round the cake. Wrap the greaseproof paper round the base of the cake, holding it in place with dots of icing.

2 Take a piece of tracing paper, about 8in × 6in (200mm × 150mm), and write

'Merry Christmas' on it. Use detached letters and make them large with open loops to allow for the thick piping. Draw a border line round the lettering.

3 Place the tracing paper on top of the cake, fixing it in place with some pins. Use a pin to prick the design of the lettering and border onto the icing. Remove the tracing paper.

4 Fill a piping bag fitted with a thick writing nozzle with royal icing. If the icing is stiff, it may be necessary to thin it with a little lemon juice so that it is easy to pipe and does not break off. Pipe out the lettering, applying steady pressure on the bag and following the lines of pinpricks on the cake.

5 Cover the top of the cake outside the border round the lettering, and the sides of the cake above the band of greaseproof paper, with rough icing. Simply dab a blob of icing onto the cake with a palette knife, then sharply lift the knife again to bring the icing up into a spiky peak. Leave it and dab on another blob of icing next to it. Continue in this way until the whole area to be rough iced is covered.

6 Using an eight-point star nozzle, pipe out the shell border round the lettering. Starting at the top of the border, squeeze out a series of small shell-like blobs of icing. Continue down one side until you reach the bottom, then start again at the top and work down to the bottom on the other side. Where the two sides of the shell border meet, make two longer blobs that trail slightly over the edge of the cake.

7 Before the icing dries, decorate the top of the cake with the dragees, pressing them down gently into the icing so that they stick.

8 On a plate, mix together some gold lustre colour and water, then use a fine paintbrush to paint the lettering.

9 Remove the band of greaseproof paper round the base and leave the cake in a warm place for 24 hours to dry.

Final decorations

For the final decorations, you will need some broad, brightly coloured ribbons and three or four small gold doilies.

1 Cut off the frilly outer edges of the doilies, discarding the centres. Attach the frills to the cake board all round the cake.

2 Wrap the ribbons round the base of the cake, tying the ends together in a large decorative bow.

FONDANT ICING

Fondant icing – also called 'moulding icing' – is one of the easiest icings to apply. It is simply rolled out like pastry and placed over the cake.

The icing can be kept for up to 3 days in an airtight container

in the refrigerator. Liquid glucose can be bought from a chemist. Fondant icing can also be bought ready-made from grocers and confectioners. It can be coloured and used for modelling cake decorations.

PREPARATION TIME: *15 minutes*

INGREDIENTS – *makes enough to ice the top and sides of an 8 in (200 mm) round cake:*
1 lb (450 g) icing sugar
1 egg white
2 oz (50 g) liquid glucose
A few drops food colouring (optional)

Sieve the icing sugar into a large bowl. Make a well in the centre of the icing sugar and add the egg white and glucose. Beat with a wooden spoon, gradually drawing in the sugar from the sides. Continue beating until the icing becomes stiff and firm. If the icing is too soft, knead in more icing sugar.

If using colouring, add a few drops and knead it in.

Applying fondant icing – Rose wedding cake

Fondant icing can be used to create an impressive and suitably romantic two-tier wedding cake. The cake is simply covered with icing then decorated with large fondant-icing roses, ribbons and lace. It could be made over a weekend, 2-3 weeks in advance.

The fondant roses and ribbons used to decorate the cake can be white (see pages 270-271) or pink (see pages 178-179).

Preparations

1 Make two round *Rich fruit cakes* (page 120). One should be 9in (230mm) and one 7in (180mm) in diameter.

2 Cover the cakes with marzipan (see page 400). You will need about 2½lb (1.1kg) of marzipan altogether.

Icing the cakes

To cover both the cakes that make up the wedding cake, you will need fondant icing made with 3lb (1.4kg) of icing sugar.

1 Sprinkle a work surface with icing sugar. Roll out about one-third of the icing to a circle large enough to cover easily both the top and sides of the smaller cake.

2 Roll the circle of icing onto the rolling pin, then unroll it over the top of the cake.

3 Press the icing firmly and evenly onto the cake on the top and round the sides. Shape the icing gently over the cake with your hands until the surface is completely smooth.

4 With a sharp knife, trim away the excess icing.

5 Repeat the process with the larger cake. Let the icing dry for at least 24 hours.

Making fondant roses

Use a real rose as a model for making the fondant roses. Make about 15 roses with fondant icing made with about 1½–2lb (700–900g) icing sugar. Work with several roses at a time.

1 Flatten four or five small knobs of icing on a work surface lightly dusted with icing sugar. Press out the edges so that they are very thin.

2 Roll one of the discs up on itself, then wrap three or

four more discs round it to make the central bud of the rose. Pinch off the bottom.

3 Break off a slightly larger knob of icing. Flatten it and press out the edges. Pinch together one end of the disc and curl the opposite edges so that the disc is like one of the looser outer petals of the rose. Press it onto the bud. Let the rose dry briefly in a bun tin.

4 Continue building up the fondant rose, making the petals larger and looser as you go, and allowing the rose to dry a little after adding every one or two petals. In the end the rose should be about 3in (80mm) across. Keep pinching off the excess icing around the base.

5 Leave the finished roses to dry for at least 24 hours in the bun tin until quite firm.

6 To make pink roses for the pink cake, you will need blossom blusher powder colouring, available from specialist grocers and confectioners. Mix the blossom blusher with a little icing sugar. When the roses are dry, dab the blusher mixture onto the petals with a soft brush.

Assembling the cake

Paper lace, satin ribbons and real roses complete the decorations. You will need about 2yds (1.8m) of paper lace or *broderie anglaise*, at least 3½yds (3.2m) of ribbon 1–1¼in (25–32mm) wide (to tie round the cake bases) and 7yds (6.4m) of narrow ribbon (to tie to the pillars). Use three pillars to support the top tier.

1 Wrap the paper lace round the base of each of the cakes. Secure it with dots of glacé icing. Wrap the thick ribbon round the lace on each cake. Tie it with a bow, leaving plenty of ribbon hanging loose from the ends of the bow.

2 Position the three pillars in the centre of the larger cake to support the smaller cake. Tie a bow of narrow ribbon to the top of each pillar.

3 Arrange the fondant roses round the edge of the lower cake, sticking them onto the cake with dots of glacé icing.

4 Position the smaller cake on the pillars. Put a small vase of real roses in the middle, then arrange fondant roses round it. Drape some narrow ribbon over it all.

USING KITCHEN EQUIPMENT

Modern kitchen equipment has revolutionised cooking. A meal that would have taken Mrs Beeton's cook many laborious hours to prepare can today be produced in a fraction of the time using machines such as food processors. Other dishes that she could have made only as limited seasonal treats, you can put on the table any time thanks to the freezer, or store for months and then serve piping hot after only minutes in a microwave oven.

PREPARING

One of the most important groups of mechanical aids in cooking are those for processing and mixing food.

Food mill (mouli)

A food mill is the most basic form of food processor. It purées food by forcing it through a metal sieving plate. The mill is supplied with several plates, each with holes of different sizes, which allow you to vary the texture of the purée.

A food mill can purée soups, vegetables or fruit. Because it sieves as well as purées, it removes seeds or skins from fruit or vegetables such as tomatoes.

Food mills make less watery purées than liquidisers or food processors because the food is sieved rather than pulped, so if you need texture – as in a potato purée, for example – it is best to use a food mill.

Liquidiser (blender)

A liquidiser consists of a jug or goblet with a set of cutting blades in the base that is driven by an electric motor. The blades will blend mixtures of liquids and solids (as in a soup) to an even texture.

For the liquidiser to work efficiently, the contents must be fairly liquid, otherwise they will not circulate properly. The blades must be covered, but the goblet should not be more than two-thirds full. Liquidise large quantities in batches.

Use the liquidiser for making soups, fruit purées and batters. Salad dressings can be made in a liquidiser; so too can *Mayonnaise* (page 369) and *Hollandaise sauce* (page 370).

Some liquidisers can be used for grinding nuts or making breadcrumbs. Sometimes they come with a coffee grinder, interchangeable with the goblet, which can also be used for those tasks. A liquidiser cannot mince meat, or shred, slice or chop vegetables.

Food processor

The food processor consists of a straight-sided bowl which fits over an electric motor. A central spindle spins a blade inside the bowl. A processor is supplied with a set of standard blades, usually one for shredding, one for slicing, and a plastic one for mixing dough. Additional blades can also be bought. Some food processors have juice extractors.

Food processors can be used for most of the basic tasks in preparing food, from mixing and blending to puréeing, grating and chopping. They also make excellent pastry, provided that the ingredients are not processed too quickly or too long, in which case the pastry will shrink and turn out tough.

Food processors are not so good, however, at mincing meat – especially raw meat – because they tend to pulp it. If fruit and vegetables are overworked in a processor, the result can be watery. Processors do not usually whisk egg whites well because they do not incorporate enough air. Special attachments for whisking eggs can be bought for some processors.

Mixer

A mixer has an electrically driven beater or pair of beaters. There are hand-held mixers, and much larger table mixers with their own bowls and the beaters held in a fixed arm.

As well as standard beaters, a number of mixers also have special hooks for kneading dough, and lighter wire beaters for whisking eggs.

Several other attachments, such as a liquidiser, slicer and shredder, mincer, juice extractor and coffee grinder can often be bought for table mixers, giving them much the same capacity as a food processor.

A mixer is invaluable for making anything that requires lengthy beating – for example

PREPARATION MADE EASY A food mill (bottom) is one of the simplest mechanical aids for preparing food. The sieving plates produce purées of varying texture. A liquidiser (right) purées food and blends liquids and solids with the help of an electric motor. The food processor (left) is the most sophisticated piece of equipment. It will shred, slice, chop, mix or blend in a matter of seconds.

whisked sponges or royal icing, or large quantities of food. Mixers usually whisk egg whites successfully as well.

COOKING

The oven is still the main means of cooking food in most kitchens, but it has been joined by increasingly sophisticated pieces of equipment including slow cookers, pressure cookers and the microwave oven.

Oven

Most ovens are heated either by gas or electricity, and the heat circulates by convection – the natural process of warm air rising and cool air falling.

GAS OVEN The burners are generally at the bottom and back of gas ovens. The ovens have distinct temperature zones. The centre usually corresponds to the temperature of the oven setting. The top shelf is just under 14°C (25°F or one gas mark) hotter, and the bottom shelf is cooler by the same amount. This variation can be put to use. Several dishes can be cooked at different temperatures at the same time on different shelves.

ELECTRIC OVENS The elements are usually in the sides of an electric oven. The temperature variation between shelves is less than in gas ovens, although it is still often necessary to swop or rotate food in the oven to ensure that it cooks evenly.

FAN OVEN The only ovens which have a more or less even temperature throughout are fan ovens (also called 'controlled airflow' ovens). A fan at the back distributes the heat evenly round the oven. This makes the transfer of heat to the food more efficient, so it is effectively cooking at a higher temperature than in a conventional oven. The difference can be as much as 10-20°C (18-36°F). On some ovens the scale on the temperature control has been altered to compensate for this. With others the oven has to be set at a lower temperature than that suggested for a conventional oven. The instruction booklet will explain what system is used with your type of oven.

All the temperatures in this book are for conventional convection ovens.

OTHER OVENS Solid-fuel cookers and cookers such as the Aga work on the principle of stored heat. They are permanently alight and usually have two or four permanently heated ovens, each at a different temperature. They are often more economical than gas or electric cookers and heat is permanently available for cooking. By varying cooking times most dishes can be cooked just as successfully as on a gas or electric cooker.

TEMPERATURE CHECK It is a good idea to check the temperature of your oven from time to time. With older ovens the temperature can often be out by as much as 20-30°C (50°F or two gas marks). You can test it with an oven thermometer.

GETTING THE BEST OUT OF YOUR OVEN

If you are heating your oven to cook one dish, it is often sensible to take advantage of the available space in the oven to cook more.

● Double or treble the quantities of the dish and freeze the excess amount.

● Use the oven to cook other dishes in the meal. Choose a baked pudding, for example, and baked vegetable dishes such as *Spiced red cabbage with juniper* (page 221). Cook jacket potatoes rather than boiling them on the hob. Wrap simple vegetables in foil parcels, adding a little liquid (water, stock or wine) and butter to each parcel.

● If your oven has an automatic timing device, you can cook a whole meal in the oven while you are out – so long as the different dishes require roughly the same temperature and cooking time. Do not do this in hot weather, however; there is a danger that meat or fish will go off.

● If you are batch baking for the freezer and filling all three shelves in the oven, put the top two shelves in the top two positions and the bottom shelf in the bottom position. This keeps the whole of the oven at a more even temperature.

Microwave oven

In a microwave oven, electricity is converted into high-frequency electromagnetic waves (similar to radio waves). Bounced off the oven walls into the food, the microwaves are absorbed by the water molecules in the food and converted into heat. The food is cooked by this heat within it, unlike in a conventional oven where the food is cooked from the outside by hot air circulating inside the oven. Because plates and dishes do not contain water molecules they remain cool (except for any transferred heat from the food).

The principal advantage of microwave ovens is that they save time – substantial amounts of time, not just minutes. A potato, for example, can be baked in its jacket in a microwave in under 10 minutes. Dishes need to be timed very accurately in a microwave to avoid over-cooking them.

Practice is needed to be able to use a microwave to its best advantage. Most foods can be cooked in a microwave oven, but it does not always produce perfect results. It is generally at its best as a companion to a conventional oven (some cookers are now produced that combine the two). As such it is useful when entertaining.

● Dishes can be cooked conventionally in advance and then reheated (from frozen if necessary) just before serving (see *Buffet parties*, page 250).

● Soups and sauces can be made in advance and heated through.

● Vegetables can either be cooked entirely in a microwave (if it is large enough), or cooked in advance and then, rather than drying out or overcooking as they are kept warm, be allowed to cool and then reheated at the last moment. (Roast vegetables, however, cannot be reheated successfully.)

USING THE MICROWAVE Certain types of dish are cooked particularly successfully in a microwave – often better than in a conventional oven. They include vegetables, fish, fruit and anything else that would ordinarily be boiled or poached. The vegetables lose less flavour and keep more texture and nutrients when cooked in a microwave.

The microwave is also particularly useful for defrosting and reheating. Because it reheats quickly and thoroughly it is actually safer for reheating than a conventional oven.

Certain other foods, however, are best cooked conventionally. They include:

● Eggs in their shells or anything else in a skin. Potatoes, for example, must be pricked all over before cooking. The rapid expansion inside will cause the egg, or whatever, to explode.

● Anything requiring hot air around it to rise; pastry, Yorkshire pudding or soufflés, for example. Ready-cooked pastry can be reheated in a microwave, however.

● Roast meat (and vegetables).

A microwave does not actually 'roast' meat because there is no hot air circulating round the meat to brown and crisp the surface – this affects taste as well as the appearance. Browning dishes which are used to sear the meat or a built-in conventional heating element solve this problem to a certain degree.

● Tougher cuts of meat. The microwave does not have the tenderising effect of long, slow cooking.

● Fruit cakes.

● Meringues.

● Egg custards that require long, undisturbed cooking.

Pressure cooker

A pressure cooker is a large pan with a closely fitting lid. A certain amount of liquid is boiled in the sealed pan with the food, and the build-up of steam under pressure inside the pan means that some foods can be cooked in less than half the time usually taken. It is also possible to cook more than one food at a time in a pressure cooker.

Pressure cookers can be used to cook any food or dish that is normally boiled, steamed or stewed. They are especially good for cooking the following foods:

● Soups and stocks.

● Poultry and some large meat joints, such as gammon joints. Cooked quickly in a pressure cooker, these meats shrink less and stay moist. This is a useful way to cook meat needed cold for another dish.

● Pulse vegetables, such as dried beans and chick peas, which can be cooked in a pressure cooker in 15-20 minutes, as opposed to an hour or two, and do not need to be soaked overnight.

● Steamed puddings, such as Christmas puddings. A 1lb (450g) Christmas pudding will take just 1¾ hours to cook in a pressure cooker, instead of 6 hours or so.

A pressure cooker, however, is not good for cooking delicate foods such as fish.

Slow cooker

A slow cooker is like a ceramic casserole with an electric element in it. It cooks food very gently and slowly so that the natural flavours are concentrated and preserved without the food burning and drying out. Very often a dish can be left to cook in a slow cooker all day, and an extra hour or so will not cause it to spoil.

Most foods and dishes that require long, slow cooking are suitable for cooking in a slow cooker. They include:

● Stocks and soups.

● Cheese fondues.

● Meat terrines and patés.

● Casseroles.

● Tougher cuts of meat. These cuts are often the richest in flavour and nutritive value. Slow cooking tenderises them, and there is no loss of flavour or moisture because of spitting or evaporation.

● Egg custards.

● Lemon curd, and the oranges for marmalade.

PRESERVING

For the last 20 years or so, the principal method of preserving food in the home has been by deepfreezing.

Freezer

In a freezer, food is stored at temperatures of around – 20°C (– 4°F). The microorganisms and enzymes that cause food to spoil are made temporarily inactive at these temperatures.

There are many different ways of putting a freezer to use. For some it is a convenient home for a packet of frozen peas; for others a vast store for garden produce, sides of raw meat and an inexhaustible supply of prepared dishes. It is an invaluable tool for anyone cooking for the family (see *Lunch, dinner and supper*, page 52).

It can also relieve some of the pressures of entertaining. One or more of the dishes for a party (the pudding, for example) can be cooked in advance and frozen. The freezer must be used thoughtfully, however, to ensure both that the food does not deteriorate with freezing, and that none of the pleasure of cooking for a party is diminished – a meal drawn entirely from the freezer gives very little satisfaction to the cook.

In addition to ready-cooked dishes and raw foods (see *The store cupboard*, pages 364-365) the freezer is also a convenient store for some items that are useful for emergencies: sauces, to transform a simple piece of meat or a pudding; flavoured butters, for topping steaks or grilled fish; chopped fresh herbs; fruit purées for turning into mousses; lemon and orange slices for garnishing drinks.

WHAT NOT TO FREEZE There are some foods that do not freeze well. They include:

● Eggs in their shells – they will burst.

● Cream, yoghurt and emulsions, such as mayonnaise, which separate when thawed. (Whipped double cream, however, does freeze well.)

● Jellies and aspics.

● Dishes that include egg yolks or unwhipped cream. Freeze such dishes without the cream or egg yolks.

● Cooked meat without a sauce.

● Watery vegetables, such as lettuce and tomatoes which lose their crispness and become mushy when thawed.

● Soft fruits such as strawberries and bananas.

● Soft cheeses.

GETTING THE BEST RESULTS FROM THE FREEZER

Foods need to be prepared and packed carefully before being frozen – otherwise they will lose much of their flavour and texture.

● Leave out most of the seasoning before freezing. Add it when the dish is reheated.

● Blanch vegetables in boiling water for 2-4 minutes before being frozen. This increases their storage time.

● Divide food into small parcels so that it freezes and defrosts as fast as possible. This also saves having to divide larger packs of food.

● Packaging should be moisture and vapour-proof, greaseproof and durable. Special freezer packaging has been tested to ensure that it withstands low temperatures.

● Separate slices of meat, chops or fish fillets with waxed paper so that they are easy to divide before thawing.

● Exclude as much air as possible when packing solid foods. Leave space at the top of liquid containers to allow for expansion – allow about 1in (25mm) of space for every pint (570ml) of liquid.

● Use a wax crayon or freezer-proof pen to label and date food, so that it is not kept too long in the freezer. The *Menu planner* (pages 407-416) gives freezing times for recipes that are included in this book.

● Do not refreeze food after thawing. The only exceptions to this rule are bread and plain, undecorated cakes, which can usually be safely refrozen once.

THE COOK'S MENU PLANNER

Every cook knows the importance of planning before a meal. How do you get more variety into meals? Is the menu properly balanced, so that guests will rise from the table with appetites satisfied – or will they feel unpleasantly full because too many courses have been very rich? How much time is needed to prepare and cook the dishes? And how does the cost of the meal fit into your budget?

This chart brings together all of the more than 500 recipes contained in this book. It will help you to plan an endless variety of meals.

The chart is divided into six sections: FIRST COURSES, MAIN COURSES, VEGETABLES AND SALADS, PUDDINGS AND DESSERTS, SNACKS AND SANDWICHES and SUNDRIES. If you are planning a formal dinner party you may use all six sections. If you are arranging an informal meal at home or a picnic you may want to use only one or two.

Type of dish

All the recipes in the first five sections of this chart are colour coded to show how rich or substantial a dish is. Rich recipes are the darkest colour and light recipes are the palest colour. By taking note of the colours when choosing recipes you can be sure that your meal will be as rich or as light as you wish, without having to read each recipe first. Balance the dishes so that if, for example, you have a very rich main course, the first course and pudding are quite light.

Practical points

Nine column headings point you towards those recipes that will fulfil any practical requirements. If you are looking for a recipe that is quick to prepare or inexpensive, for example, follow down from each column heading and you will find a symbol which indicates how long the dish will take to prepare or an asterisk against those recipes that are inexpensive.

TYPE OF DISH

- Rich or filling
- Moderately rich or filling
- Light

SEASON

This indicates when any fresh ingredients are at their best. The recipe can often be made out of season by using tinned or frozen substitutes
W Winter
Sp Spring
S Summer
A Autumn

PREPARATION AND COOKING TIMES

Preparation time includes time for processes such as marinating and setting when relevant

- O Under 30 minutes
- ◐ 30 minutes – 2 hours
- ● More than 2 hours

FIRST COURSES
Starters and savouries

	Season	Can be prepared in advance	Preparation time	Cooking time	Easy	Inexpensive	Low fat	Can be frozen (months)	Vegetarian
Aubergine caviar 306		*	O	◐	*		*		*
Baked oysters 158			O	O	*				
Basil and Mozzarella pancakes 194	Sp, S		◐	O	*				
Broccoli mousse 253		*	●	O		*			
Carpaccio with fresh fig purée 201	A		◐				*		
Cheese éclairs stuffed with avocado and bacon 254			◐	◐		*			
Cheese puffs 345			O	O		*			*
Chilled caviar eggs 346		*	O	O	*	*	*		
Crudités with dips 320		*	◐		*				
Devils 164		*	◐	O	*	*			
Eggs tonnato 252		*	O	O	*	*			
Escabeche de pescado frito 252		*	●	O	*		*		
Feuilletés d'asperges 196	Sp, S	*	◐	O					*
Garlic and pine kernel tartlets 193	Sp, S	*	◐	◐					*
Grilled Halumi cheese with mint 195	Sp, S, A		◐	O	*	*			*
Hot coriander mushrooms 58			O	O	*	*			*
Jellied consommé 344		*	◐		*	*			
Little ham mousses 347			◐	◐					
Lobster pâté with rosé sauce 198		*	●						
Mangetout and Brie mousse 194	Sp, S	*	●	O		*			*
Marinated halibut with watercress mousseline 199		*	●		*				
Minted fruit salad 255	Sp, S, A	*	◐		*	*	*		*
Potted trout 20		*	O		*	*		3	
Prawn mousse with avocado sauce 200		*	●	◐					

407

Starters and savouries (continued)	Season	Can be prepared in advance	Preparation time	Cooking time	Easy	Inexpensive	Low fat	Can be frozen (months)	Vegetarian
Prawn vol-au-vents 347			○	○	*				
Quail eggs in sherry jelly 191		*	●						
Sardine pâté 346		*	○		*	*			
Sesame prawn toasts 58		*	◐	○	*			1	
Smoked mackerel mousse 318		*	●						
Soft cheese galette 195		*	◐	○					*
Sole ceviche 157		*	●		*		*		
Spiedini di taleggio e frutti di mare 196	A, W		●	○					
Spinach Niçoise 319	Sp, S	*	○		*				
Stilton and grape pastries 254		*	◐	○		*			*
Stuffed mushrooms 165		*	○	○	*	*			
Sweet and sour fish balls 198		*	●	○	*	*	*		
Sweetbread terrine with cream chive sauce 200	Sp, S, A	*	●	◐					
Tomato and prawn ring 318		*	●		*				

Cold soups

	Season	Can be prepared in advance	Preparation time	Cooking time	Easy	Inexpensive	Low fat	Can be frozen (months)	Vegetarian
Artichoke and martini soup 192		*	●	○	*				*
Chilled cherry soup 11	S	*	●	○	*		*		*
Chilled lemon and almond soup 317		*	◐	○	*	*		1	*
Iced apple soup 251		*	●	○	*	*			*
Iced fennel soup 251		*	●	◐	*	*		3	*

Hot soups

	Season	Can be prepared in advance	Preparation time	Cooking time	Easy	Inexpensive	Low fat	Can be frozen (months)	Vegetarian
Carrot, potato and coriander soup 317		*	○	◐	*	*		2	*
Chestnut soup 192	A, W	*	◐	○				3	*
Courgette soup with garlic and blue cheese 54	S, A	*	◐	◐	*			2	*
Creamy beetroot soup 293		*	○	◐	*	*		3	*
Curried almond soup 343		*	○	○	*	*			*
Jamaican pumpkin soup 293	A	*	○	◐	*			3	*
Lentil and tomato soup 343		*	○	○	*	*		3	

	Season	Can be prepared in advance	Preparation time	Cooking time	Easy	Inexpensive	Low fat	Can be frozen (months)	Vegetarian
Potato and onion soup 344		*	○	○	*	*	*		*
Smoked haddock soup 344		*	○	○	*				
Tomato and sorrel soup 294	Sp, S	*	○	◐	*	*	*	3	*

MAIN COURSES

Soups

	Season	Can be prepared in advance	Preparation time	Cooking time	Easy	Inexpensive	Low fat	Can be frozen (months)	Vegetarian
Belgian waterzootje 57		*	◐	◐	*		*		
Chilli bean soup 294		*	●	◐	*	*		1	*
Chunky chowder 56		*	◐	◐					
Meaty minestrone 56		*	◐	◐	*				
Prawn gumbo 54		*	○	○	*		*		
Singapore laksa 53		*	◐	◐	*				
Split pea and sausage soup 55		*	◐	◐	*	*		3	

Fish and shellfish

	Season	Can be prepared in advance	Preparation time	Cooking time	Easy	Inexpensive	Low fat	Can be frozen (months)	Vegetarian
Buckwheat blinis with creamed kipper 19			●	○		*			
Burgundy fish casserole 204	W, A		◐	◐					
Butterfly salmon 202			◐	○					
Cappon magro 264		*	●	●					
Champagne shrimp risotto 206			◐	◐	*		*		
Chinese steamed fish 63			◐	○	*		*		
Crab and asparagus flan 264	Sp, S	*	◐	◐	*			1	
Crespellini 62		*	◐	○				1	
Fish and prawn terrine 262		*	●	◐				1	
Fish cakes with egg sauce 17		*	◐	○	*	*		3	
Fish kebabs 322		*	●	○	*				
Langoustines in ginger butter 206			○	○	*				
Marinated mackerel 298		*	●	○	*	*			
Mediterranean fish salad 64	Sp, A, W	*	◐	◐					
Mini stargazy pies 296		*	◐	○	*	*			
Monkfish in sorrel sauce 264	Sp, S	*	◐	○	*		*		
Monkfish satay 299		*	●	○	*				
Oriental fish curry 64		*	◐	◐	*			3	

	Season	Can be prepared in advance	Preparation time	Cooking time	Easy	Inexpensive	Low fat	Can be frozen (months)	Vegetarian
Rouget à la Provençal 203		*	●	○	*				
Salmon en croûte with dill sauce 257	S	*	◐	◐				2	
Salmon in raspberry vinegar and pink peppercorn sauce 203	S		◐	○			*		
Salmon with cucumber and green peppercorns 202			○	○	*				
Scallops in pastry shells 205	Sp, A, W	*	◐	○				1	
Seafood lasagne 256	A, W	*	◐	◐				3	
Smoked salmon tagliatelle 298		*	◐	○	*				
Spanish fish casserole 60			◐	◐	*				
Spiced butterfly prawns 295		*	◐	○	*				
Trout in aspic with smoked cod's roe 263		*	◐	◐					
Trout or mackerel with fennel 321	Sp, S, A	*	●	○	*	*			
Watercress and smoked haddock roulade 296		*	◐	○			*	3	
Watercress stuffed trout with lemon butter sauce 62			◐	○					

Beef and veal

	Season	Can be prepared in advance	Preparation time	Cooking time	Easy	Inexpensive	Low fat	Can be frozen (months)	Vegetarian
Barbecued beef stew 66		*	●	◐	*			3	
Beef studded with smoked oysters 208			◐	●					
Bobotie 144		*	○	◐	*	*		1	
Burgers 323		*	○	○	*	*		3	
Calf's liver with lime and sage butter 70			◐	○					
Cashew spiced beef 68		*	◐	◐	*			3	
Chilli beef cabbage rolls 68			◐	◐		*			
Creamed chipped beef 24			○	○	*				
Fegato alla frutta secco 210			◐	○	*				
Irish tavern pie 258		*	◐	●		*		3	
Mexican pancake stack 259		*	◐	◐	*	*		3	

	Season	Can be prepared in advance	Preparation time	Cooking time	Easy	Inexpensive	Low fat	Can be frozen (months)	Vegetarian
Rendang 65		*	○	◐	*			3	
Roast beef with mustard sauce 266		*	●	◐					
Rump burgers with Mozzarella 67		*	◐	○				3	
Sautéed veal with redcurrants and cream 211	S		○	○	*				
Somerset cider and steak pie 70		*	●	●				3	
Spiced mince and potato pie 354			◐	◐	*	*			
Steak and prawn kebabs 322		*	◐	○	*				
Steak in horseradish pancakes 210			●	○					
Steak rolls with mustard sauce 324		*	◐	○	*				
Stir-fried beef and broccoli 207			◐	○	*				
Stufato di manzo 66		*	○	◐					
Stuffed breast of veal with red pepper sauce 267		*	◐	●			*		
Tongue with nut and raisin sauce 355			○	○	*				
Veal paprikash 72		*	◐	◐	*			3	

Pork and ham

	Season	Can be prepared in advance	Preparation time	Cooking time	Easy	Inexpensive	Low fat	Can be frozen (months)	Vegetarian
Bean and bacon mess pot 144		*	●	◐	*	*			
Beaune ham 267		*	●	●	*	*			
Black pudding with apple sauce 24		*	○	○	*	*			
Chinese pork slices with garlic sauce 269		*	●	●	*				
Corsican pork chops 326			●	○	*	*			
Escalopes tagine 76			●	○			*		
Ham and lychee rolls 308		*	○		*				
Ham loaf with green peppercorns 354		*	○	◐	*			3	
Honey-glazed pork chops 72			○	◐	*				

Pork and ham (continued)

	Season	Can be prepared in advance	Preparation time	Cooking time	Easy	Inexpensive	Low fat	Can be frozen (months)	Vegetarian
Marinated pork fillets 325		*	●	○	*				
Noisettes of pork with prunes and calvados 207			○	◐		*			
Pork stuffed with prunes 268		*	●	●		*			
Pork with watercress sauce 260			◐	○	*	*			
Red hot ribs 73			○	◐	*	*			
Roast loin of pork with cheese and fig stuffing 74			◐	●					
Sage sausages with mustard sauce 21		*	●	○				3	
Spicy pork and sausage ragoût 75		*	◐	◐	*	*		3	
Stir-fried pork with red pepper and cucumber 76			◐	○	*				

Lamb

	Season	Can be prepared in advance	Preparation time	Cooking time	Easy	Inexpensive	Low fat	Can be frozen (months)	Vegetarian
Assorted marinated chops 324		*	●	○	*				
Lamb chops with tarragon and cucumber 79			○	○					
Lamb curry with coconut and okra 82		*	◐	◐				3	
Lamb cutlets with greengage sauce 212			○	○	*	*			
Lamb in wine and anchovy sauce 260		*	◐	●	*	*		3	
Lamb with lime and Pernod 81			◐	○	*				
Minted meatballs with yoghurt sauce 78	Sp, S, A	*	●	◐		*		3	
Mixed lamb kebabs 324			●	○	*				
Olive-studded lamb with olive and pepper purées and garlic creams 212		*	●	◐					
Pot roast leg of lamb 81		*	●	◐	*				
Sautéed kidneys with croutons 22			○	○	*	*			
Spiced lamb pilau 77		*	◐	◐	*				

Poultry

	Season	Can be prepared in advance	Preparation time	Cooking time	Easy	Inexpensive	Low fat	Can be frozen (months)	Vegetarian
Boned chicken with pistachio stuffing 84		*	◐	◐			*	2	
Boned stuffed duckling 303		*	◐	◐				1	
Chicken and ham en brioche 302		*	●	◐				3	
Chicken drumsticks in honey and mustard 301		*	●	◐	*	*	*	3	
Chicken hymettus 85		*	●	◐	*		*	3	
Chicken liver croissants 302		*	◐	○	*	*		3	
Chicken salad Veronica 86		*	●	◐					
Chicken with walnut and tarragon sauce 213	S	*	●	◐			*		
Duck breasts with blackberry and apricot sauce 214	A		●	◐	*				
Duck with plum and ginger glaze 88		*	○	◐	*				
Gamekeeper's casserole 89		*	◐	◐	*			3	
Indian spiced chicken 328		*	●	◐			*		
Kotopoulo kapama 82		*	◐	◐	*		*	3	
Pintade aux quarante gousses d'ail 220			◐	◐					
Pollo al cacciatore 84		*	◐	◐	*		*	3	
Rabbit and sage fricassée 218			○	◐	*				
Smoked chicken and mango salad 269		*	◐		*		*		
Spiced turkey meatballs in tomato sauce 261		*	◐	◐		*	*	3	
Stir-fried turkey with celery, walnuts and orange 87			○	○	*	*	*		
Turkey galantine 270		*	●	●				3	
Turkey groundnut stew 86		*	○	◐	*	*		3	
Turkey in crab sauce 272		*	◐	●	*				
White herb sausages 22		*	●	◐		*		3	
Yakitori 83		*	●	○	*		*		

Game

	Season	Can be prepared in advance	Preparation time	Cooking time	Easy	Inexpensive	Low fat	Can be frozen (months)	Vegetarian
Barbecued venison 327	S, A, W		●	●					
Bstilla 218	Sp, S	*	◐	◐				3	
Hare pie 272	A, W	*	●	●		*		3	
Pot roast pheasant with claret and orange sauce 214	A, W		◐	◐					
Spatchcocked grouse 326	A	*	●	○			*		
Wild duck with kumquats 216	A, W		◐	◐					

Eggs and cheese

	Season	Can be prepared in advance	Preparation time	Cooking time	Easy	Inexpensive	Low fat	Can be frozen (months)	Vegetarian
Anchovy eggs 351			◐	○	*	*			
Asparagus soufflé 352			○	◐		*			*
Bacon and egg bake 354			◐	○	*	*			
Calzone 309		*	◐	○					*
Cauliflower blue cheese soufflé with sage 90			◐	◐		*			*
Cheese nutburgers 100		*	○	○	*	*		3	*
Cheese pudding 350			◐	◐	*	*			*
Creamy tomato and coriander omelette 14			○	○		*			*
Crispy baked potato skins with avocado and blue cheese dip 60		*	◐	◐	*				
Cucumber and watercress mousse 91		*	●			*			*
Curried eggs in cream sauce 256		*	○	○	*	*			*
Devilled eggs 17			○	◐		*			*
Egg and herring danwich 15			○	○	*	*			
Egg and salmon cocottes 16			○	○	*				
Eggs soubise 16			○	○					
Mexican eggs 92		*	○	◐	*	*			*
Mushroom, sausage and bacon fondue 25			○	○					
Persian eggah 90			◐	○		*			*
Pipérade 351			○	○	*	*			*
Pizza alla casalinga 59		*	●	◐	*			3	

	Season	Can be prepared in advance	Preparation time	Cooking time	Easy	Inexpensive	Low fat	Can be frozen (months)	Vegetarian
Smoked halibut and lumpfish roe scramble 19			○	○	*				
Spinach and cheese en croûte 352		*	◐	○	*	*			*
Tarte Niçoise 352		*	○	◐	*	*		3	*
Thai-style stuffed eggs 301		*	○	○		*			
Torta pasqualina 92		*	◐	○		*		3	*
Watercress and Ricotta quiche 89		*	◐	◐	*	*		1	*

Pasta, rice and pulses

	Season	Can be prepared in advance	Preparation time	Cooking time	Easy	Inexpensive	Low fat	Can be frozen (months)	Vegetarian
Bacon and avocado kedgeree 20			○	○	*	*			
Chick pea and bacon croquettes 300		*	●	◐		*		1	
Chilli bean and wholewheat pie 104			●	◐	*	*			*
Dal croquettes with yoghurt and mint sauce 98		*	◐	○	*	*		3	*
Gnocchi di semolina alla Romana 348		*	◐	○		*		3	*
Khichri 96			◐	○	*	*			*
Macaroni cheese and tomato 350			◐	◐	*	*			
Monkfish and mussel paella 95	A, W		◐	○			*		
Pasta Mexicana 93			○	◐	*	*	*		*
Risotto ai quattro formaggi 97			○	○	*	*			*
Spaghetti alla carbonara 349			○	○	*	*			
Tuna cannelloni 94		*	◐	◐		*		3	
Tuna fish kedgeree 348			○	○	*	*			

Vegetables and salads

	Season	Can be prepared in advance	Preparation time	Cooking time	Easy	Inexpensive	Low fat	Can be frozen (months)	Vegetarian
Chinese vegetable stir-fry 104			◐	○					*
Gado-gado 102			◐		*				*
Green summer vegetable terrine 304	Sp, S	*	◐	◐			*		*

Vegetables and salads (continued)

	Season	Can be prepared in advance	Preparation time	Cooking time	Easy	Inexpensive	Low fat	Can be frozen (months)	Vegetarian
High-fibre salad 100			●		*	*			*
Mediterranean terrine with hummus sauce 273		*	●	◑		*	*		*
Pitta salad pockets 304		*	○		*	*			
Spanish hot potato salad 98			◑	○	*				
Spinach and Boursin roulade 228			◑	○		*			*
Vegetable moussaka 102		*	●	◑				3	*
Vegetable samosas 101		*	◑	○		*		3	*
Vegetarian picnic pie 306		*	◑	◑	*	*			*
West coast salad 274		*	◑		*	*			

VEGETABLES AND SALADS
Vegetables

	Season	Can be prepared in advance	Preparation time	Cooking time	Easy	Inexpensive	Low fat	Can be frozen (months)	Vegetarian
Almondine potatoes 220		*	●	◑	*	*		6	*
Barbecued vegetables 331			○	○	*	*	*		*
Bemuelos 228		*	●	○				6	*
Brussels sprout, orange and cinnamon purée 223	A, W	*	○	○	*	*		3	*
Buttered peas and beansprouts 356			○	○	*	*			*
Carrot and ginger soufflé 222			◑	◑	*	*			*
Carrot and potato purée 356		*	○	○	*	*			*
Glazed onions 356	A		○	○	*	*			*
Gratin of parsnips and potatoes 222	A, W	*	◑	◑	*	*		3	*
Haricots verts au gratin 226	S	*	◑	○	*				*
Hash browns 25			○	◑	*	*			
Lotus-wrapped rice 224		*	◑	◑			*		
Mung bean dal 228			●	○	*	*	*		*
Mushrooms in oyster sauce 225			◑	○	*	*	*		
Polenta 229		*	◑	◑	*	*		3	*
Potato and chive galette 226	Sp, S, A	*	◑	◑	*	*		6	*
Sautéed artichoke hearts 357			○	○	*		*		*
Sorrel and lemon purée 226	Sp, S		○	○	*		*		*

	Season	Can be prepared in advance	Preparation time	Cooking time	Easy	Inexpensive	Low fat	Can be frozen (months)	Vegetarian
Spiced red cabbage with juniper 221	A, W	*	○	●	*	*		3	
Steamed vegetable julienne in vine leaves 223		*	◑	○					*
Stir-fried carrots 355			○	○	*	*	*		*
Sweetcorn fritters 356			○	○	*	*			
Tian de légumes 227	S, A	*	○	◑	*			3	*
Two beans in tomato 357			○	○		*	*		*

Salads

	Season	Can be prepared in advance	Preparation time	Cooking time	Easy	Inexpensive	Low fat	Can be frozen (months)	Vegetarian
Broccoli salad 330	Sp, S	*	○	○	*	*			*
Carrot and orange salad 311		*	○		*	*	*		*
Chicory, orange and almond salad 275	A, W, Sp		○			*	*		*
Chinese salad 275	W, Sp	*	○		*	*	*		*
Cos lettuce with tomato and tarragon vinaigrette 232		*	○		*		*		*
Courgette, mangetout and grapefruit salad 310	Sp, S	*	○				*		*
Flageolet bean salad 277		*	●	◑	*	*	*		*
Lettuce hearts with cream dressing 274		*	○		*	*			*
Mixed green salad 274	Sp, S		○		*	*	*		*
Mushroom, tomato and chive salad 311		*	○		*	*			*
Orange, avocado and coriander salad 232			●						*
Pasta medley 330		*	○	○	*				*
Pasta salad with broad beans 276	Sp, S	*	◑	○	*	*	*		*
Port and Stilton salad 230		*	○		*				*
Potatoes with basil 309	Sp, S	*	◑	○	*	*	*		*
Potato salad with green dressing 275	Sp, S	*	◑		*	*			*
Radicchio salad 329			○		*		*		*

	Season	Can be prepared in advance	Preparation time	Cooking time	Easy	Inexpensive	Low fat	Can be frozen (months)	Vegetarian
Salade aux crottins de chèvres 229		*	◐		*				*
Salade de mâche tiède 231	Sp, S		○	○					
Spicy brown rice salad 276		*	○	◐	*	*	*		*
Spinach, Roquefort and pomegranate salad 310	S, A	*	○		*				*
Summer potato salad 330	Sp, S	*	○	○	*	*			*
Tabbouleh with lime and marinated red peppers 233		*	●						*
Tomato and onion salad with avocado dressing 277		*	○		*	*			*
Winter slaw 276	A, W	*	◐	-		*	*		*

PUDDINGS AND DESSERTS
Cold puddings

	Season	Can be prepared in advance	Preparation time	Cooking time	Easy	Inexpensive	Low fat	Can be frozen (months)	Vegetarian
Alsace chocolate gateau 280		*	●	◐				1	*
Amaretti and ice cream loaf 280		*	●	◐				1	*
American butterscotch pie 108		*	●	○		*			*
Apple and redcurrant lattice 314	S	*	◐	◐	*	*		2	*
Belgian torte 334		*	◐	◐				1	*
Big ugly green monster cake 146		*	◐	◐		*		3	*
Butterscotch frozen yoghurt 146		*	●		*	*		3	*
Charlotte malakoff 281		*	●					1	*
Cherry and almond cheesecake 236	S	*	●	◐				3	*
Chestnut soufflé 335		*	●			*			*
Chilled banana soufflé with burnt orange sauce 240		*	●	○					*
Chocolate crème brulée 314		*	●	◐					*
Cider sorbet 278		*	●	○	*	*	*	6	*
Coconut and ginger jelly with lychees 242	W	*	●		*		*		*
Croquembouche 278		*	◐	○		*			*
Danish apple pudding 359		*	◐		*	*			*

	Season	Can be prepared in advance	Preparation time	Cooking time	Easy	Inexpensive	Low fat	Can be frozen (months)	Vegetarian
Dried fruit fool 360		*	◐		*	*			*
Emerald and jade salad with orange shortbread fingers 337	S, A, W	*	●		*	*	*		*
Fresh fruit pavlovas 106	Sp, S	*	◐	◐	*		*		*
Fresh raspberry porridge 12	S	*	◐	○	*				*
Fromage à la crème with charentais melon 235	Sp, S	*	●						*
Geranium cream 243	Sp, S	*	●		*	*			*
Ginger and kiwi ice cream 110	S, A, W	*	●		*			1	*
Ginger trifle 334	S	*	●		*	*			*
Hazelnut and banana muesli 13		*	○		*	*	*		*
Lime and mint cheesecake 282	Sp, S	*	●	◐	*			2	*
Lime and pineapple icebox pudding 105		*	●		*			3	*
Mango cheesecake 312		*	●		*			1	*
Minted apple snow 106	Sp, S	*	●	○	*	*	*		*
Minted raspberry and yoghurt ice 108	S	*	●		*	*		1	*
Mocha chocolate cheesecake 106		*	●	◐				3	*
Orange and apple boodle 283		*	●		*	*			*
Orange and cranberry brunch bowl 11	W	*	●	○	*	*	*		*
Orange crowns 145		*	●		*	*		3	*
Pêches à la Belle Sandrine 238	Sp, S	*	◐						*
Plum tart 282	A, W	*	◐	◐	*	*			*
Raspberry and ratafia terrine 238	S	*	●					2	*
Red fruit salad 284	Sp, S	*	●	○	*		*		*
Rhubarb, fig and grapefruit compôte 14	Sp	*	◐	○	*	*	*		*
Rum and peach syllabubs with hazelnut crisps 338	Sp, S	*	●	○					*
St Clement's mousse 111		*	●					3	*
Spiced pears in wine 313		*	●	◐	*	*	*		*
Strawberries Beaumes-de-Venise 311	Sp, S	*	●		*		*		*

Cold puddings (continued)

Cold puddings (continued)	Season	Can be prepared in advance	Preparation time	Cooking time	Easy	Inexpensive	Low fat	Can be frozen (months)	Vegetarian
Strawberry and cassis sorbet 239	Sp, S	*	●		*		*	6	*
Strawberry galette 284	Sp, S	*	◐	○					*
Sunshine ring 146		*	●		*	*	*		*
Symphonie de trois couleurs 240	Sp, S	*	●						*
Torta di albicocche con zabaglione all'Amaretto 234	S	*	◐	◐				3	*
Vacherin aux fraises 241	Sp, S	*	●	◐		*			*
Walnut pie 336		*	◐	◐	*	*		1	*
Whisked jelly 148		*	●		*	*			*
Yoghurt 12		*	●	○	*	*			*

Hot puddings

Hot puddings	Season	Can be prepared in advance	Preparation time	Cooking time	Easy	Inexpensive	Low fat	Can be frozen (months)	Vegetarian
Ataïf 242		*	◐	○					*
Bread and butter pudding 363			◐	◐	*	*			*
Cherry and cinnamon puff flan 358			◐	○	*				*
Christmas pudding with foaming Cointreau sauce 244		*	◐	●					*
Dried fruit compôte 313		*	◐	○	*	*	*	3	*
Fruit macaroon brulée 358		*	◐	○	*	*			*
Grilled apricots 360			○	○	*	*	*		*
Individual pear puffs 109	A, W		◐	○		*			*
Marmalade and fig sponge 110			◐	◐		*			*
Oaty fruit crumble 359			◐	◐	*	*			*
Orange soufflé 363			◐	◐		*			*
Pear meringues 361			○	○					*
Queen of puddings 363			◐	◐		*			*
Steamed coffee soufflés with hot chocolate sauce 237			◐	○					*
Sweet coconut rice 107			○	◐	*	*			*
Tarte au sucre 243			●	◐	*	*	*		*
Tarte clafoutis 112	S		◐	◐				3	*
Torta di mele 108			◐	◐		*			*

	Season	Can be prepared in advance	Preparation time	Cooking time	Easy	Inexpensive	Low fat	Can be frozen (months)	Vegetarian
Tortillas with cheese and raisin filling 13			◐	○	*				*

SNACKS AND SANDWICHES

SNACKS AND SANDWICHES	Season	Can be prepared in advance	Preparation time	Cooking time	Easy	Inexpensive	Low fat	Can be frozen (months)	Vegetarian
Almond olives 168		*	◐		*				*
Canapés 172		*	◐						
Cat's whiskers 143		*	◐			*			*
Cherry tomatoes with three fillings 167		*	◐		*				
Craft at sea 143		*	○		*	*	*		*
Cucumber filled with tapénade 166		*	◐		*				
Epicurean butter sandwiches 137		*	○		*	*			
Glazed frankfurters 164			○	○	*	*			
Gorgonzola bites 159		*	◐	○	*	*		3	*
Greek spinach rolls 162		*	◐	○		*		3	*
Lemon dip 168		*	◐		*	*			*
Mangetout and cucumber mélange 166	Sp, S	*	●						
Mini choux with savoury fillings 160		*	◐	○		*		3	
Mini quiches with three fillings 160		*	◐	○				2	
Pan bagna 307		*	●		*	*			
Prawn and ginger dip 168		*	○		*				
Quick cocktail snacks 169		*	○	○	*				
Rabbit faces 143			○		*	*	*		*
Radish butter on pumpernickel 307		*	○		*	*			*
Rolled smoked salmon sandwiches 138		*	○					3	
Savoury stuffed prunes and dates 159		*	◐		*	*			
Spicy almonds 157		*	○	○	*	*			*
Tartlets or barquettes 162		*	◐	○				3	

SUNDRIES
Cakes and biscuits

	Season	Can be prepared in advance	Preparation time	Cooking time	Easy	Inexpensive	Low fat	Can be frozen (months)	Vegetarian
Almond meringues 130		*	◐	●					*
Apple sauce cake 41		*	○	◐	*			3	*
Baklava 46		*	○	○	*				*
Brandy snaps filled with ginger cream 120		*	○	○					*
Bûche de Noël 123		*	◐	○				3	*
Butterscotch cookies with date filling 47		*	●	○	*				*
Cherry strudel 45	S	*	◐	◐					*
Chocolate and ginger fridge cake 362		*	◐		*	*			*
Chocolate-coated gingernuts 40		*	○	○	*	*			*
Chocolate cream torte 42		*	●	●					*
Chocolate crunch 40		*	○	◐	*	*			*
Chocolate dominoes 152		*	◐	○	*	*		3	*
Chocolate hedgehogs 152		*	○		*	*			*
Chocolate pretzels 135		*	◐	○		*		3	*
Chocolate strawberry gateau 132	Sp, S		◐	◐					*
Coffee sponge roll with marsala cream 39		*	◐	○		*			*
Florentines 40		*	◐	○		*			*
Fresh fruit tartlets 37	S	*	◐	○					*
Frosted gingerbread 122		*	◐	◐	*	*		3	*
Gold and silver marble cake 128		*	◐	◐				3	*
Happy men biscuits 151		*	◐	○	*	*		3	*
Hungarian raisin cheesecake 42		*	◐	◐				3	*
Iced petits fours 38		*	●	○		*			*
Irish tea brack 124		*	●	◐	*	*	*	3	*
Kugelhopf 44		*	●	◐		*		3	*
Lebkuchen 46		*	◐	○		*	*	3	*
Lemon curd cup cakes 126		*	◐	○		*		3	*
Mince pies and mince tarts 122		*	◐	○	*	*		3	*
Mocha eclairs 125		*	◐	◐				3	*
Orange flower sponge cake 133		*	○	○	*	*		3	*
Palmiers 41		*	◐	○	*				*

	Season	Can be prepared in advance	Preparation time	Cooking time	Easy	Inexpensive	Low fat	Can be frozen (months)	Vegetarian
Panforte di Siena 49		*	◐	◐					*
Passion cake 48		*	◐	◐	*				*
Polish honey cake 126		*	◐	◐	*			3	*
Rich fruit cake 120		*	◐	●	*			3	*
Rocket cake 148		*	◐		*				*
Rum and raisin cake 124		*	◐	◐	*	*		3	*
Sherry gateau 119		*	●	○					*
Simnel cake 127		*	◐	●				3	*
Swedish cardamom cake 131		*	○	◐	*	*		3	*
Treasure chest birthday cake 150		*	◐	◐					*
Victoria sponge 149		*	○	◐	*	*		3	*
Viennese biscuits 44		*	◐	○	*	*		3	*
Walnut layer cake with seven-minute frosting 136		*	●	○		*		3	*
Wholewheat sponge cake with mango filling 134		*	◐	◐	*			3	*

Breads

	Season	Can be prepared in advance	Preparation time	Cooking time	Easy	Inexpensive	Low fat	Can be frozen (months)	Vegetarian
Apricot and orange tea-bread with orange honey butter 134		*	●	◐	*	*		3	*
Banana pecan loaf 312		*	○	◐	*	*		2	*
Black rye bread 30		*	◐	◐		*		3	*
Cashew nut rolls 308		*	●	○	*	*	*	6	*
Cheese and herb shortbread 29		*	○	◐	*	*			*
Chocolate muffins 27		*	○	○	*			3	*
Croissants 26		*	●	○				3	*
Date and walnut loaf 28		*	○	◐	*			3	*
Fruit muffins 27		*	○	○	*	*			*
Herb and garlic breads 333		*	○	○	*	*		1	*
Hot cinnamon ring 48			●	○					*
Hot cross buns 128	Sp	*	●	○		*	*	3	*
Hot mincemeat loaf 30		*	○	◐	*				*
Molasses oatcakes 29		*	○	○	*	*	*	3	*
Pear and lemon bread 28		*	○	◐	*			3	*
Pecan waffles 31			○	○					*

Breads (continued)

	Season	Can be prepared in advance	Preparation time	Cooking time	Easy	Inexpensive	Low fat	Can be frozen (months)	Vegetarian
Sally Lunn tea cakes 132		*	●	○		*		3	*
Snipdoodle 30			○	◐	*	*			*
Wholewheat raisin scones 136		*	○	○	*	*		3	*

Sauces

	Season	Can be prepared in advance	Preparation time	Cooking time	Easy	Inexpensive	Low fat	Can be frozen (months)	Vegetarian
Bearnaise sauce 371			○	○					*
Béchamel sauce 368		*	○	○	*	*	*		*
Butterscotch sauce 361			○	○	*	*	*		*
Chilli barbecue sauce 333		*	○	○	*	*	*	3	*
Citrus barbecue sauce 332		*	○	○	*	*	*	3	*
Hollandaise sauce 370			○	○					*
Mayonnaise 369		*	○						*
Sweet and sour barbecue sauce 333		*	○	○	*	*	*	3	*
Tomato mushroom sauce 332		*	○	○	*	*	*	3	*
Velouté sauce 368		*	○	○	*				*
Vinaigrette (French dressing) 371		*	○		*	*			*

Sweets

	Season	Can be prepared in advance	Preparation time	Cooking time	Easy	Inexpensive	Low fat	Can be frozen (months)	Vegetarian
Candied dates 236	A, W	*	●		*	*			*
Chocolate marzipan fingers 244		*	●						*
Fudge 153		*	○	○	*				*
Stick-jaw toffee 153		*	◐		*				*
Toffee apples 154		*	◐	○					*

Jams and preserves

	Season	Can be prepared in advance	Preparation time	Cooking time	Easy	Inexpensive	Low fat	Can be frozen (months)	Vegetarian
Dark Seville orange marmalade 32	A, W	*	◐	●		*	*		*
Dried apricot jam 32		*	●	◐			*		*
Fresh coconut chutney 294		*	○		*	*			*
Greengage jelly 32	S	*	●	●	*	*			*
Lime curd 138		*	○	○	*	*			*
Orange, lime and ginger marmalade 33		*	◐	◐			*		*

	Season	Can be prepared in advance	Preparation time	Cooking time	Easy	Inexpensive	Low fat	Can be frozen (months)	Vegetarian
Peach conserve 139	S	*	◐	◐			*		*
Strawberry jam 138	Sp, S	*	◐	◐			*		*
Walnut and orange mincemeat 138		*	●	○	*				*

Drinks

	Season	Can be prepared in advance	Preparation time	Cooking time	Easy	Inexpensive	Low fat	Can be frozen (months)	Vegetarian
Apple and ginger fizz 154		*	○		*	*	*		*
Bloody Mary 178		*	○		*		*		*
Brandy Alexander 176			○		*				*
Buck's fizz 176			○		*		*		*
Champagne punch 33			○		*		*		*
Dry martini 177		*	○		*		*		*
Gin sling 176		*	○		*		*		*
Glögg 180		*	●		*		*		*
Harvey wallbanger 178			○		*		*		*
Kir 176			○		*	*	*		*
Lemonade 154		*	○	○	*	*	*		*
Margarita 177			○		*		*		*
Mint julep 175	Sp, S, A		○		*		*		*
Mulled wine 180		*	○		*		*		*
Pink gin 177			○		*		*		*
Planters' punch 180			○		*		*		*
Pussyfoot 176			○		*	*	*		*
Strawberry bowle 178	S	*	●		*		*		*
Strawberry shrub 34	S	*	◐	◐			*		*
Whisky sour 175			○		*		*		*
White lady 177			○		*		*		*

INDEX

A

AUSTRIAN, GERMAN
AND EASTERN
EUROPEAN RECIPES

*Buckwheat blinis with creamed
  kipper 19*
Cherry strudel 45
Chocolate cream torte 42
Chocolate pretzels 135
Florentines 40
Hungarian raisin cheesecake 42
Kugelhopf 44
Lebkuchen 46
Polish honey cake 126
Veal paprikash 72
Viennese biscuits 44

B

TYPESETTING Tradespools Limited, Frome SEPARATIONS Grafascan Limited, Dublin PAPER Townsend Hook and Company Limited, Snodland; Pollock and Searby Limited, Alton
PRINTING AND BINDING Fabrieken Brepols N.V., Belgium